Supervision

QUALITY AND DIVERSITY THROUGH LEADERSHIP

Supervision

QUALITY AND DIVERSITY THROUGH LEADERSHIP

Samuel C. Certo
Crummer Graduate School of Business at Rollins College

APPLICATION EXERCISES

Corinne Livesay
Liberty University

AUSTEN
PRESS

IRWIN

Burr Ridge, Illinois
Boston, Massachussetts
Sydney, Australia

Publisher: William H. Schoof
Acquisitions Editor: Mary Fischer
Production Manager: Bob Lange

Development, production, and composition provided by
Elm Street Publishing Services, Inc.
Text and Cover Design: Jeanne Calabrese Design

Typeface: 10/12 Janson
Printer: Von Hoffmann Press, Inc.

Library of Congress Cataloging-in-Publication Data

Certo, Samuel C.
    Supervision : quality and diversity through leadership / Samuel C. Certo.
        p.   cm.
    Includes bibliographical references and index.
    ISBN 0-256-11982-1
    1. Supervision of employees.   I. Title.
    HF5549.12.C42   1993
    658.3'02—dc20   93–15518

Printed in the United States of America
  2 3 4 5 6 7 8 9 0 VH 9 8 7 6 5

Address editorial correspondence:
Austen Press
18141 Dixie Highway
Suite 111
Homewood, IL 60430

Address orders:
Richard D. Irwin, Inc.
1333 Burr Ridge Parkway
Burr Ridge, IL 60521

Austen Press
Richard D. Irwin, Inc.

Cover art: Kroeber Series # 17, © 1980 Jay Dunitz

To Mimi, Trevis, Matthew, Sarah, and Brian
—My reason for being and doing

Preface

This book prepares students to be supervisors. Today's students of supervision are entering the work force at an exciting time. Changes in the way companies are organized, the way supervisors must manage, and the nature of the workplace are pervasive. With this dynamic environment in mind, *Supervision: Quality and Diversity through Leadership* has been developed to meet the needs of students attempting to learn how to supervise in the modern world.

Overview of Text Development

Designing a book and learning package for supervision students of today was a challenging task indeed. To accomplish my vision of providing the most complete and up-to-date learning materials available in this area, in cooperation with the Austen Press, I designed and implemented an extensive project plan.

In the fall of 1991, a survey was mailed to instructors of the course and supervisors around the country to gather information about what would be needed to develop the best supervision learning package for the course. A response rate of 20 percent from this questionnaire provided information and ideas that were then presented for evaluation and feedback to focus groups around the country in the form of a preliminary book and package plan.

The results of the research indicated that in addition to more traditional topics supervision instructors were faced with focusing on such key contemporary issues as quality, diversity, and team building. The research also showed that, in terms of support materials for instructors, this course has been sorely neglected. In other words, materials available to support instructors in the classroom were very limited.

The overall publishing objective generated from the research became clear: to create a book and complete teaching package for the supervision course that would provide the necessary coverage of relevant topics in a real-life format.

Teamwork

Trends in supervision research and reports by professional supervisors regarding the challenges they face both indicated the importance of teams in the workplace. As you will see, teams are an important part of this book!

Skilled professionals were used at every step of project development to help create a book and package of the highest quality. My standards for presenting theoretical material clearly and concisely, for developing learning materials that reflect an empathy for and enhancement of the student learning process, and for providing instructional support materials that facilitate the design and conduct of only the best courses were emphasized. Insight, hard work, and enthusiasm provided by these professionals have elevated this book to the highest possible quality. Figure A depicts relationships among this team of professionals.

Overview of the Text

Supervision: Quality and Diversity through Leadership is divided into four parts: "The Role of the Supervisor," "Skills of the Supervisor," "Supervision and Human Resources," and "Special Challenges of the Supervisor." The following sections describe the parts and chapters and present comments offered by text reviewers that highlight key text characteristics.

Part One, "The Role of the Supervisor," lays the necessary groundwork for the study of supervision:

Chapter 1, "The Supervisor and Diversity," explains the role of the supervisor and focuses on the current challenge of supervising workers with varying cultural backgrounds.

Reviewer highlight: A unique feature of this chapter, according to reviewer Carl Sonntag of Pikes Peak Community College, is the detailed coverage of diversity and the use of interviews with real managers.

Chapter 2, "The Supervisor as Planner," and Chapter 3, "The Supervisor as Organizer and Delegator," respectively highlight how managers must take steps to reach objectives and allocate resources.

Reviewer highlight: In Chapter 2, reviewer Barbara Whitney of St. Petersburg Junior College applauds the exercises on Gantt and Pert charts, while Kim McDonald of Indiana's Purdue University at Fort Wayne finds Chapter 3's explanation of the factors influencing span of control a particular strength (see page 59).

Chapter 4, "The Supervisor as Leader," discusses current theories on how to guide workers in appropriate directions.

Reviewer highlight: James Day of Grambling State University finds the coverage of traits, styles, teamwork, and diversity excellent in this chapter.

Chapter 5, "The Supervisor as Controller," emphasizes that supervisors must take action to make sure that events occur as they were planned.

Reviewer highlight: Vincent Kafka of Effective Learning Systems finds the exhibits particularly helpful in this chapter, especially Table 5.1, "Sample Performance Record" (see page 104).

FIGURE A
Supervision: **The Professional Team**

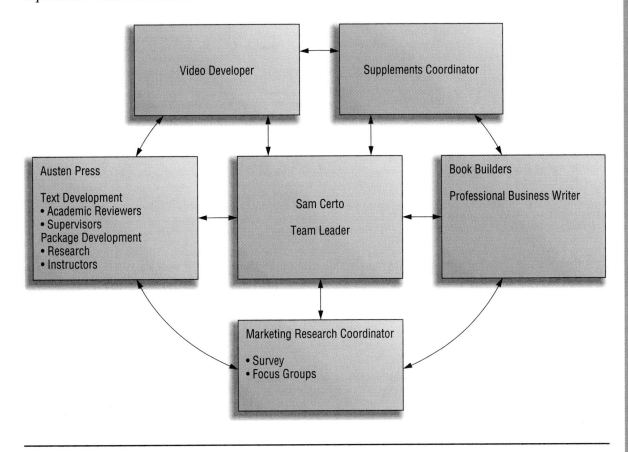

The last chapter in this section, Chapter 6, "Maintaining and Improving Quality," focuses on the supervisor's critical role in the organizational quest of building quality into all phases of operations.

Reviewer highlight: Jim Mulvihill of Mankato Technical Institute especially likes the exercise on constructing a house in this succinctly written chapter.

Part Two, "Skills of the Supervisor," focuses on critical abilities that supervisors need to be successful:

Chapter 7, "Communicating," describes how supervisors share information with other people throughout the organization and in different situations.

Reviewer highlight: Sylvia Ong of Scottsdale Community College finds the cultural difference section (see pages 163–165) excellent given the current emphasis on international trade.

Chapter 8, "Problem Solving and Decision Making," illustrates that supervisors must solve problems and describes the decision-making process as a tool to be used in solving those problems.

Reviewer highlight: Linda Massa of Santa Barbara Business College cites the "Guidelines for Decision Making" as good use of practical, real-life examples (see page 191).

Chapter 9, "Motivating Employees," presents various practical ways that supervisors can motivate workers.

Reviewer highlight: Medhat Farooque of Central Arizona College points out the strength of the coverage of money as a motivator in this chapter.

Chapter 10, "Improving Productivity," explains what productivity is and suggests steps that can be taken to raise productivity in organizations.

Reviewer highlight: Smita Jain Oxford of Commonwealth College finds this chapter very practical and applications oriented, especially the "Tips from the Firing Line" box (see page 256).

Chapter 11, "Managing Time and Stress," and Chapter 12, "Managing Conflict and Change," combine to help students understand the importance of these skills on supervision.

Reviewer highlight: Chapter 11's coverage of time wasters is praised by several reviewers, as is Chapter 12's section on responding to conflict.

Part Three, "Supervision and Human Resources," focuses on how supervisors can help provide the "right" people for organizations:

Chapter 13, "Selecting Employees," focuses on the process of choosing the right person to fill an open position—the sources, methods, and legal issues that must be considered.

Reviewer highlight: All reviewers like the separate chapter on selection rather than having the material incorporated with orientation and training. Deb Jansky of Milwaukee Area Tech praises the "Dealing with Diversity" box on disability myths (see page 349).

Chapter 14, "Training Employees," emphasizes the process of orienting new employees, developing skills in workers, and evaluating training methods.

Reviewer highlight: Corinne Livesay of Liberty University points out the strength of the orientation section and its importance to new employees (see page 358).

Chapter 15, "Appraising Performance," discusses the importance of a systematic performance appraisal and provides several examples of appraisal methods.

Reviewer highlight: Reviewers like the thorough discussion of appraisal techniques and coverage of bias in the appraisal.

Chapter 16, "Supervising 'Problem' Employees," discusses workers who require unusual attention from the supervisor and offers ways to deal with the various problems they present.

Reviewer highlight: Reviewers cite the section on handling substance abuse as a key strength.

Part Four, "Special Challenges of the Supervisor," discusses three important areas on which the supervisor must focus to have a productive unit:

Chapter 17, "Groups and Teamwork," defines characteristics and types of groups and teams to help students acquire an understanding of their importance in supervision.

Reviewer highlight: Including teamwork in this chapter is a strong point for all reviewers.

Chapter 18, "Safety and Health in the Workplace," provides students with an understanding of the regulations and issues supervisors encounter and describes ways of keeping workers free from harm.

Reviewer highlight: The role of OSHA in the workplace and dealing with shift work are two highlights.

Chapter 19, "Ethics and Organization Politics," presents the issues supervisors need to consider and understand because of the influence they have on the overall organization.

Reviewer highlight: Coverage of power is unique.

The book concludes with two features. "Reference Guide: Building a Career" is a practical resource that individuals can use to develop their careers as supervisors. Network development, résumé preparation, and goal evaluation are a few of the topics covered in the Reference Guide. The "Résumé Workbook" section, written by Denise Colby, gives useful tips on writing résumés and cover letters. This practical feature not only guides students through the steps in writing résumés and job-application letters but provides examples and "hands-on" exercises.

A special "Application Exercises" section at the end of each part of the text, developed by Corinne Livesay of Liberty University, is based on the philosophy that students learn better when they can apply the material to personal experience. These applications are in addition to the Self-Quizzes and Exercises in each chapter and are designed to help students to develop useful supervisory skills. The applications reinforce the three major themes of the text—teams, quality, and diversity—and focus on employing these skills for leadership.

Overview of Text Learning System

The pedagogy for each chapter of this text has been designed to make the study of supervision interesting, enjoyable, effective, and efficient.

Chapter Quotations   The quotes that begin each chapter are drawn from business experts, historical figures, and company policies and are designed to help frame the topics presented in the chapters. For instance, here is the quote that opens Chapter 4 on leadership:

Leadership is not a spectator sport. Leaders don't sit in the stands and watch. But hero myths aside, neither do leaders join in the game to substitute for players. Leaders coach....
—James M. Kouzes and Barry Z. Posner

Chapter Outlines   The chapter outlines are provided at the beginning of each chapter and are tools that students can use to preview the chapter and review the material prior to testing (see page 2 in Chapter 1 as an example).

Learning Objectives   The key points of the chapter's content form the basis for the learning objectives. This list (see page 2 for an example) serves as a guide for studying the material and as a means of organizing the material in the chapter Summary and in the *Instructor's Manual.*

Opening Vignettes   The chapter openers are primarily interviews with actual supervisors on the job. For instance, in Chapter 8, "Problem Solving and Decision

Making," the chapter opens with Marilyn Bowie, a nurse manager for obstetrical care at St. Joseph's Hospital and Medical Center in Phoenix, Arizona, who moved from being a nurse to managing nurses. The vignette discusses how she had to switch to solving different kinds of problems when she became a supervisor.

Margin Definitions   Key terms are defined in the margin and are highlighted in color. Students can use these definitions to test their understanding of the terms and to find the places where important concepts are discussed (see page 4 for one example).

Figures and Tables   Illustrations and tables are used extensively to clarify and reinforce text concepts. (See, for example, Figure 17.5 on page 462 that illustrates guidelines for conducting a meeting.)

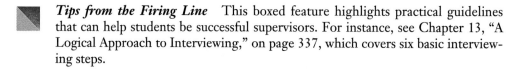

Tips from the Firing Line   This boxed feature highlights practical guidelines that can help students be successful supervisors. For instance, see Chapter 13, "A Logical Approach to Interviewing," on page 337, which covers six basic interviewing steps.

Dealing with Diversity   This boxed feature prepares students for the work force of today and tomorrow. Overall, this feature emphasizes common pitfalls in supervising employees with widely varying backgrounds and demonstrates how supervisors and companies are capitalizing on the advantages diversity brings. For instance, see Chapter 7, "Communicating across Cultures," on page 165, where the issue of supervisors directing employees to serve customers from other cultures necessitates being aware of and learning different communication styles.

Self-Quizzes   Most chapters contain short, engaging self-assessment quizzes, which help students see the kinds of supervisors they can be. For instance, in Chapter 6, on page 134, "Your Level of Quality Awareness," is a short 10-question quiz that asks students to look at their own views of quality.

Summary   Learning objectives are recapped at the end of each chapter with quick summaries of the chapter concepts for each learning objective. For example, on page 114 in Chapter 5, learning objective 5.4 is repeated with a paragraph highlighting the main concepts.

Key Terms   Each chapter includes a list of key terms at the end of the chapter. Reading this list can help students review by testing their comprehension of the terms. The page number where the term is first defined is included in the glossary at the end of the book.

Review and Discussion Questions   These questions test understanding of the chapter concepts and ask students to apply this knowledge to mini cases. These questions can be used independently by students or by instructors as a method of reviewing the chapters. A special feature of the questions is "**A Second Look**." The question in this section returns to the scenario presented in the chapter opener and asks students to respond to questions by applying the chapter's concepts to the scenario. For instance, the Chapter 8 opener about nursing manager Marilyn Bowie asks the student to describe how Bowie applied the principles of group decision making to solving the two key problems she faced.

Class Exercise   Class exercises at the end of each chapter help students apply the concepts they have just studied. By using these new concepts immediately, students can build the supervisory skills that can be applied in their careers. For instance, in Chapter 13 the exercise simulates an abbreviated version of the selection process for hiring a new server at a Denny's restaurant (see page 353).

Cases   The concluding pages of each chapter contain a short case that further applies the chapter's concepts to various supervision situations. Questions following each case provoke students' thinking and help them synthesize ideas. This feature can also be used independently by students or instructors for course assignments or classroom discussion. For instance, in Chapter 12 the case, "A Conflict over Job Discrimination," describes a real-life situation in which a woman police officer dealt with sexual bias and the ensuing conflict on the job (see page 316).

Photo Essays   Full-color photo essays throughout the text depict real supervisors and the varied environments in which they work. The photos capture the reader's interest and help bridge the gap between supervision theory and actual supervisory situations.

Color   A quick look at this text reveals that it is in full color. Color has been used not simply for the sake of color but to highlight important concepts and reinforce them visually. For example, the marginal glossaries and main text headings are highlighted in color so that they stand out on the text pages.

End-of-Book Glossary   Terms and definitions are gathered from each chapter and provided at the end of the book. This provides ready reference for students and instructors. To encourage student review, the text pages where the terms are first defined and discussed are included.

The Supervision *Video Series: A Special Learning Feature*

A series of videos has been developed especially for *Supervision* to help engage students in the learning process and show actual supervisors at work. These tapes have been carefully planned and scripted to illustrate five key areas in the text and course: Role of the Supervisor, Quality, Motivation, Training, and Work Groups.

Video 1: The Role of the Supervisor   Joanne Wilson is a supervisor for Handy Andy Home Improvement Centers. The program follows Joanne through a typical day. In this predominantly male industry, Joanne demonstrates her exceptional ability to plan, organize, and lead her employees. The students viewing the video are asked to perform an evaluation of Joanne's abilities, utilizing the concepts presented in the textbook as the evaluation criteria.

Video 2: Quality   Not only is Aleta Holub in charge of quality at the First National Bank of Chicago, she is one of the nine members of the Malcolm Baldrige Award Committee. Quality at First Chicago starts with the chairman and is the primary responsibility of every employee at the bank. The video demonstrates how the department supervisors implement, maintain, and control quality.

Video 3: Motivation   Motivation is the key to being competitive in the new global marketplace. In this program, J.C. Penney demonstrates how it uses nonfinancial incentives to motivate its retail sales associates, and Nucor Steel, the nation's fastest-growing and most profitable steel company, explains how its unique financial incentive system has motivated its employees to be the most productive in the world.

Video 4: Training   Classroom and on-the-job training are two of the most common methods of training. Karen Lohss, professional trainer at LaMarsch & Associates, demonstrates how she applies both techniques when training visually impaired supervisors. The University of Michigan Hospital recently became the first medical institution to adopt the concepts of Total Quality Management. The secret to this successful venture was the extensive training program that every individual in the hospital underwent.

Video 5: Groups and Teamwork   Southwest Airlines is the only company ever to win the coveted Triple Crown from the Department of Transportation: for best on-time performance, best baggage handling record, and fewest customer complaints. Southwest demonstrates how their use of teamwork has won them the distinction of being one of the ten best companies to work for in America.

Video Instructor's Manual   A *Video Instructor's Manual* accompanies the video series. Each segment includes a synopsis of the video, teaching notes on how to integrate the video with the chapters and other package components, a list of the chapter concepts covered in the video, and in-class exercises to use with each video, with accompanying handouts.

All of the videotapes are available *free* to each school using *Supervision: Quality and Diversity through Leadership.*

Ancillaries

As I mentioned earlier, one of our objectives was to provide the best teaching package available. We hope you have seen evidence of this in the description of the text and video series. But there is more: Additional instructional materials are available to further enrich the supervision learning experience. Each ancillary and its highlights follow.

Test Bank and Computerized Test Bank   We all know the importance of a high-quality *Test Bank* in teaching. The development of such a *Test Bank* to accompany *Supervision* was of the utmost importance. The *Test Bank* includes more than 2,000 questions and is available in printed form, in computerized format, and through the Teletest (phone-in) service. Each chapter includes multiple-choice questions with mini cases to allow application of the principles, true/false questions, short essay questions, matching, and crossword puzzles. Additionally, a prepared quiz is provided for each chapter; the quiz is ready for duplication or for use as a transparency. Each question includes the answer, the corresponding text page where the answer can be found, and the rationale for the answer. All questions are graded by level of difficulty and are organized according to the text learning objectives for consistency with the entire teaching package. Sylvia Ong of Scottsdale Community College is the author of the *Test Bank*.

Instructor's Manual   Each chapter of the *Instructor's Manual*, which is really much more like an arsenal of teaching materials, is organized according to the text learning objectives. Part I provides a quick summary for each chapter. Part II, "Teaching the Concepts by Learning Objectives," includes the following for each learning objective:

1. Key terms and their definitions from the text.
2. Teaching notes. These notes describe the focus of the text section where the learning objective is discussed and point out areas where the student might become confused. Suggestions for clarifying the material are provided.
3. Fresh examples not used in the text are provided and are frequently supported by supplementary transparencies or handouts.
4. A new exercise is also provided, and details on using the exercise and the anticipated results are included.

Part III, "Notes on the Boxed Features," provides a synopsis of the "Dealing with Diversity," "Tips from the Firing Line," and "Self-Quiz" features in each chapter, along with teaching tips on how to utilize these in your lectures.

Part IV, "Answers to Review and Discussion Questions," provides the answers or suggested answers for each question.

Parts V and VI provide answers and solutions to the end-of-chapter exercises and case.

Throughout the *Instructor's Manual*, each transparency is referenced in the chapter next to the area of possible use and highlighted in the margin.

Ruby Ivens of Lansing Community College is the author of the *Instructor's Manual*.

Transparency Masters   We are all familiar with the need for supplemental overheads of exhibits not in the text that are clear, legible, and useful even in large classrooms. As a result, we designed a transparency package to meet those criteria. The package is divided in two parts:

1. All figures and tables from the text adjusted for use as transparencies to maximize readability.
2. Supplemental transparencies—Ten to twelve *new* transparencies for each chapter.

All the transparencies include teaching notes that describe the transparency and outline the key points for the student to notice. Corinne Livesay of Liberty University developed the transparency package and organized it for efficient use with the *Instructor's Manual*.

Lecture Supplements   A special feature of the *Supervision* package is the additional five complete lectures on key topics. Authored by Corinne Livesay of Liberty University, this supplement includes lecture outlines, transparencies, and application materials for the following areas:

1. Personal Organizing Skills
2. Team Leadership
3. Improving Listening Skills
4. Interviewing Strategies
5. Meeting Management

Experience indicates that the highest quality supervision courses expose students to appropriate concepts, give students an opportunity to apply these concepts to solve problems, and provide an opportunity for students to learn from their experiences. The *Supervision* learning package has been designed to allow flexibility in emphasizing any or all of these components in your supervision course. I sincerely wish you well in building your course around *Supervision: Quality and Diversity through Leadership*. Have a great class!

Acknowledgments

I extend my sincere thanks to all the members of the *Supervision* team who helped craft this fine teaching package. A special thank you to Karen Schenkenfelder for contributions and support throughout the project.

Reviewers

James Day
Grambling State University

Medhat Farooque
Central Arizona College

Debbie Jansky
Milwaukee Area Technical College

Bonnie Johnson
Fashion Institute of New York

Vincent Kafka
Effective Learning Systems

Corinne Livesay
Liberty University

Kim McDonald
IPFW

Lynda Massa
Santa Barbara Business College

James Mulvihill
Mankato Technical Institute

Sylvia Ong
Scottsdale Community College

Smita Jain Oxford
Commonwealth College

Carl Sonntag
Pikes Peak Community College

Barbara Whitney
St. Petersburg Junior College

Focus Group Participants

Dick Brigham
Brookhaven College

Arnold Brown
Purdue University North Central

Randy Busch
Lee College

Gloria Couch
Texas State Technical Institute

Richard Gordon
Detroit College of Business

Ruby Ivens
Lansing Community College

James Kennedy
Angelina College

Russell Kunz
*Collin County Community College
—Spring Creek*

Sue Kyriazopoulous
DeVry Institute

Allen Levy
Macomb Community College Center

John Maloney
College of DuPage

Kim McDonald
IPFW

Steven Pliseth
University of Wisconsin, Platteville

Charles Riley
Tarrant County Community College

Ralph Schmitt
Macomb Community College South

David Way
Galveston College

Dan Yovich
Purdue University North Central

Survey Respondents

Raymond Ackerman
Amber University

Rex Adams
*Southside Virginia Community
College, Daniels*

Musa Agil
Cape Fear Community College

Linda Alexander
Southeast Community College, Lincoln

Gemmy Allen
Mountain View College

Scott Ames
North Lake College

E. Walter Amundsen
Indiana University Southeast

Paul Andrews
Southern Illinois University

Solimon Appel
College for Human Services

Bob Ash
Rancho Santiago College

Glenda Aslin
Weatherford College

Bob Baker
Caldwell Community College

James Bakersfield
North Hennepin Community College

Robert Barefield
Drury College, Springfield

Laurence Barry
Cuyamaca College

Perry Barton
Gwinnett Area Technical

Becky Bechtel
Cincinnati Technical College

Kenneth Beckerink
Agricultural and Technical College

Gina Beckles
Bethune-Cookman College

Jim Beeler
*Indiana Vocational and Technical
College, Indianapolis*

Robert Bendotti
Paradise Valley Community College

Jim Blackwell
Park College

David Bodkin
Cumberland University

Arthur Boisselle
Pikes Peak Community College

Robert Braaten
Tidewater Community College

James Brademas
University of Illinois, Urbana

Suzanne Bradford
Angelina College

Richard Braley
Eastern Oklahoma State College

Janis Brandt
Southern Illinois University

Stanley Braverman
Chestnut Hill College

Duane Brickner
South Mountain Community College

Eugene Buccini
West Connecticut State University

Gary Bumbarner
Mountain Empire Community College

Kick Bundons
Johnson County Community College

Bill Burmeister
New Mexico State University

Randy Busch
Lee College

Oscar S. Campbell
Athens State College

Marjorie Carte
D.S. Lancaster Community College

Joseph Castelli
College of San Mateo

James Chester
Cameron University

William Chester
University of the Virgin Islands

Jack Clarcq
Rochester Institute of Technology

Charles Clark
Oklahoma City Community College

Sharon Clark
Lebanon Valley College

Virgil Clark
Sierra College

Jerry Coddington
*Indiana Vocational and Technical
College, Indianapolis*

Bruce Conners
Kaskaskia College

Ronald Cornelius
University of Rio Grande

Gloria Couch
Texas State College Institute

Darrell Croft
Imperial Valley College

Joe Czajka
University of South Carolina

Beatrice Davis
Santa Fe Community College

Irmagard Davis
*University of Hawaii, Kapiolani
Community College*

Richard De Luca
Bloomfield College

Edwin Deshautelle, Jr.
Louisiana State University at Eunice

Richard Deus
Sacramento City College

Ruth Dixon
Diablo Valley College

Leroy Drew
Central Maine Technical College

Janet Duncan
City College of San Francisco

Ron Eads
Labette Community College

Patrick Ellsberg
Lower Columbia College

Earl Emery
Baker College, Flint

Roland Eyears
Central Ohio Technical College

Tom Falcone
Indiana University

Jim Fatina
Triton College

Jack Fleming
Moorpark College

Lee Fleming
El Centro College

Charles Flint
San Jacinto College Central

Toni Forcioni
Montgomery College, Germantown

Laurie Francis
Mid State Technical College

Cheryl Frank
Inver Hills Community College

Connie French
Los Angeles City College

Larry Fudella
Erie Community College South

William Fulmer
Clarion University of Pennsylvania

Autrey Gardner
*Industrial Technology Department,
Warren Air Force Base*

Jon Gartman
TS JC at Waco

David Gennrich
Waukesha County Technical College

Sally Gillespie
Broome Community College

Catherine Glod
Mohawk Valley Community College

Tim Gocke
Terra Technical College

Richard Gordon
Detroit College of Business, Dearborn

Greg Gorniak
Pennsylvania State University, Behrend

Valerie Greer
University of Maryland

James Grunzweig
Lakeland Community College

James Gulli
Citrus College

Bill Hamlin
Pellissippi State Technical College

Willard Hanson
Southwestern College

James Harbin
East Texas State University

Carnella Hardin
Glendale Community College

Scott Harding
Normandale Community College

Louis Harmin
Sullivan County Community College

Lartee Harris
West Los Angeles College

Edward L. Harrison
University of South Alabama

Paul Hedlund
Barton County Community College

Kathryn Hegar
Mountain View College

Gene Hilton
Brookhaven College

Jean Hiten
Owensboro Community College

Roger Holland
Cerritos College

Larry Hollar
Catawba Valley Community College

Russ Holloman
Augusta College

Tonya Hynds
Indiana University at Kokomo

Robert Ironside
North Lake College

Ellen Jacobs
College of St. Mary

Bonnie Jayne
Bryant & Stratton

Sarkis Kavookjian
*Delaware Technical and
Community College*

Bernard Keller
Pikes Peak Community College

Robert Kemp
Peralta Laney College

James Kerrigan
Stonehill College

Scott King
Sinclair Community College

Edward Kingston
Piedmont Virginia Community College

Ronald Kiziah
Caldwell Community College

Mary Lou Kline
Reading Area Community College

Jay Knippen
University of South Florida

Howard Korchin
Fashion Institute of Technology

Thomas Lloyd
*Westmoreland County
Community College*

Barbara Logan
*Albuquerque Technical-
Vocational Institute*

Rosendo Lomas
Lawrence Technical University

Frances Lowery
Brewer State Junior College

Henie Lustgarten
University of Maryland

Alvin Mack
Everett Community College

Jon Magoon
Santa Rosa Junior College

Marvin Mai
Empire College

Joseph Manno
Montgomery College

Edward Mautz
El Camino College

Ron Maxwell
*Indiana Vocational and Technical,
Terre Haute*

Joseph McShane
Gateway Technical Institute, Kenosha

Robert McDonald
Central Wesleyan College

William McKinney
University of Illinois, Urbana

Raymond Medeiros
Southern Illinois University

Unny Menon
California State Polytechnic University

Dorothy Metcalfe
*Fashion Institute of Design and
Merchandising, Los Angeles*

Eugene Meyers
Western Kentucky University

Charles Miller
Los Angeles Southwest College

Dominick Montileone
Delaware Valley College

Wayne Moorhead
Brown Mackie College

Peter Moran
Wisconsin Indianhead Technical College

Ed Mosher
Laramie County Community College

Donald Mossman
Concordia College

John Mudge
*Community College of
Vermont, Rutland*

Hershel Nelson
Polk Community College

John Nugent
Montana Technical College

Cruz Ortolaza
Catholic University of Puerto Rico

Joseph Papenfuss
Westminster College, Salt Lake City

John Parker
Manchester Community College

James Peele
Carl Sandburg College, Galesburg

Joe Petta
Regis College

Bonnie Phillips
Casper College

Martha Pickett
University of Arkansas at Little Rock

Barbara Pratt
Community College of Vermont

Robert Priester
Madison Area Technical College

Barbara Prince
Cambridge Community College Center

John Pryor
Northern Nevada Community College

Marcia Ann Pulich
University of Wisconsin-Whitewater

Peter Repcogle
Orange County Community College

Margaret Rdzak
Cardinal Stritch College

William Redmon
Western Michigan University

Arnon Reichers
Ohio State University

Charles Reott
Western Wisconsin Technical Institute

Richard Rettig
University of Central Oklahoma

Harriett Rice
Los Angeles City College

Robert Richardson
Iona College

Charles Riley
Tarrant County Junior College

Richard Riley
National College

Michael Rogers
Albany State College

Robert Roth
City University, Bellvue

Larry Runions
North Carolina Vocational Textile

Henry Ryder
Gloucester County College

Larry Ryland
Lurleen B. Wallace Junior College

Duane Schecter
Muskegon Community College

S. Schmidt
Diablo Valley College

Irving Schnayer
Peralta Laney College

Greg Schneider
Waukesha County Technical College

Arthur Shanley
Milwaukee School of Engineering

Margie Shaw
Lake City Community College

Allen Shub
Northeastern Illinois University

Pravin Shukla
Nash Community College

Clay Sink
University of Rhode Island

Ron Smith
DeKalb Institute of Technology

Steve Smith
Mid State Technical College

Wanda Smith
Ferris State University

Carl Sonntag
Pikes Peak Community College

Marti Sopher
Cardinal Stritch College

Jerry Sparks
Cannon International Business College

David Spitler
Central Michigan University

Richard Squire
Northwest Technical College

Dick Stanish
Tulsa Junior College

Gene Stewart
Brookhaven College

John Stout
University of Scranton

Art Swenney
Troy State University

Sally Terman
Scottsdale Community College

Sherman Timmons
University of Toledo

Dan Tomal
Purdue University

Donna Treadwell
Johnson County Community College

Ron Tremmel
Rend Lake College

Guy Trepanier
Iona College

John Tucker
Purdue University

Bill Tyer
Tarrant County Junior College

Robert Ulbrich
Parkland College

Diann Valentini
Fashion Institute of Technology

Steven Vekich
Washington State Community College

Michael Vijuk
William Rainey Harper College

Charles Wall
Bakersfield College

Kathy Walton
Salt Lake City Community College

Robert Way
Milwaukee Area Technical College

Rick Webb
Johnson County Community College

Ronald Webb
Messiah College Grantham

Alan Weinstein
Canisius College

Bill Weisgerber
Saddleback College

Julia Welch
University of Arkansas Medical School

Floyd Wente
St. Louis Community College at Florissant Valley

Ron Weston
Contra Costa College

Charles Wetmore
California State University, Fresno

Jerry Wheaton
North Arkansas Community College

Luther White
Central Carolina Community College

Michael White
University of Northern Iowa

Sara White
University of Kansas Medical Center

Barbara Whitney
St. Petersburg Junior College

Tim Wiedman
Thomas Nelson Community College

Stephen Winter
Orange County Community College

Arthur Wolf
Chestnut Hill College

Barry Woodcock
Tennessee Technological University

Michael Wukitsch
American Marketing Association

Catalina Yang
Normandale Community College

Charles Yauger
Arkansas State University

Morrie Yohai
New York Institute of Technology

Teresa Yohon
Hutchinson Community College

James Yoshida
University of Hawaii, Hawaii Community College

Allan Young
Bessemer State Technical College

Marilyn Young
Waukesha County Technical College

Richard Young
Pennsylvania State University

Fred Ziolhowski
Purdue University

Karen Zwissler
Milwaukee Area Technical College

Application Exercises Contributors

E. Walter Amundsen
Indiana University Southeast

Stanley A. Braverman
Chestnut Hill College

Bruce L. Conners
Kaskaskia College

James E. Fatina
Triton College

Peter J. Gummere
Community College of Vermont

Bernard Keller
Pikes Peak Community College

Edward A. Kingston
Piedmont Virginia Community College

Joseph R. Manno
Montgomery College

Arnon E. Reichers
Ohio State University

John P. Wanous
Ohio State University

Charles Wetmore
California State University

Michael R. White
University of Northern Iowa

Timothy G. Wiedman
Thomas Nelson Community College

Stephen I. Winter
Orange County Community College

Fred J. Ziolkowski
Purdue University

Samuel C. Certo
August 1993

Dr. Samuel C. Certo is Professor of Management and former Dean at the Roy E. Crummer Graduate School of Business at Rollins College. He has been a professor of management for more than fifteen years and has received prestigious awards, including the Award for Innovative Teaching from the Southern Business Association, the Instructional Innovation Award granted by the Decision Sciences Institute, and the Charles A. Welsh Memorial Award for outstanding teaching at the Crummer School. Dr. Certo's numerous publications include articles in such journals as *Academy of Management Review, The Journal of Experiential Learning and Simulation,* and *Training.* He has also written several successful textbooks, including *Modern Management: Quality, Ethics, and the Global Environment, Strategic Management: Concepts and Applications,* and *Supervision: Quality and Diversity through Leadership.* A past chairman of the Management Education and Development Division of the Academy of Management, he has been honored by that group's Excellence of Leadership Award. Dr. Certo has also served as president of the Association for Business Simulation and Experiential Learning, as associate editor for *Simulation & Games,* and as a review board member of the *Academy of Management Review.* His consulting experience has been extensive, with notable experience on boards of directors.

NOTE TO THE INSTRUCTOR

Austen Press texts are marketed and distributed by Richard D. Irwin, Inc. For assistance in obtaining supplementary material for this and other Austen Press titles, please contact your Irwin sales representative or the customer service division of Richard D. Irwin at (800) 323-4560.

BRIEF CONTENTS

CONTENTS

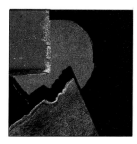

PART FOUR
Special Challenges of the Supervisor 437

PART ONE

The Role of the Supervisor

1

The front-line supervisor is probably the strongest motivating or demotivating element of all.

—Harvey L. Miller

The Supervisor and Diversity

LEARNING OBJECTIVES

1.1 Define what a supervisor is.

1.2 Describe the basic types of supervisory skills.

1.3 Describe how the growing diversity of the work force affects the supervisor's role.

1.4 Identify the general functions of a supervisor.

1.5 Explain how supervisors are responsible to higher management, employees, and co-workers.

1.6 Describe the typical background of someone who is promoted to supervisor.

1.7 Identify characteristics of a successful supervisor.

TWO SUPERVISORS' TALES

Joyce Gurtatowski and John David are both supervisors, but their jobs look quite different on the surface. Gurtatowski is an assistant vice-president with La Salle Bank Matteson in Calumet City, Illinois. She supervises six personal bankers. David is a senior property manager for Standard Parking, a job that involves supervising the 30 employees of several parking garages in Chicago.

On a typical day, Gurtatowski arrives at the bank at about 7:30 A.M. and does paperwork such as auditing department accounts. When the bank is open for business, she spends much of her time answering questions from personal bankers and tellers about nonroutine customer problems and questions. According to Gurtatowski, "Every customer is a new situation," and that variety is what poses challenges to her employees—and what makes her own job interesting. From the time when the bank lobby closes (most days at 3:00 P.M.) until she leaves at about 5:30, Gurtatowski returns phone calls from customers and prepares her department schedule for the next day. In addition, she trains staff members at weekly meetings and conducts performance appraisals.

David reports that he spends about 60 percent of his day with people, both customers and employees. His time with employees is devoted primarily to following up to see that they are carrying out instructions. Most of the remainder of David's day is taken up with paperwork, including monthly parking accounts, market analyses, and efforts related to marketing the garage. Working with employees is particularly interesting and challenging because they come from many countries, including Ethiopia, Kuwait, Ghana, Pakistan, and Nigeria, as well as the United States. Sometimes, because of cultural differences, the employees need special training for serving American customers. For example, an employee from Ethiopia would speak in a monotone because this tone of voice shows respect in his culture. David had to train this employee to speak more enthusiastically to American customers.

supervisor
A manager at the first level of management.

Like Joyce Gurtatowski and John David, the following people are all supervisors: a foreman in a Rollerblade skate factory, the head teller at a branch of Wells Fargo Bank, the principal of your neighborhood elementary school, the patient care coordinator (head nurse) in the orthopedics unit of a hospital, the manager of a Burger King restaurant, and a sergeant on a police force or in the army. A **supervisor** is a manager at the first level of management. "First-level management" means that the employees reporting to the supervisor are not managers. From this definition and the examples opening this chapter, you can see that many different kinds of organizations need supervisors. Figure 1.1 reprints actual want ads for a variety of supervisory jobs.

In general, the job of managers is to see that the organization is meeting its goals. For the top executives of the organization, this means making sure that the organization as a whole is heading in a direction that will allow it to meet its goals through the years ahead. At the level of the supervisor, managing means seeing that the employees in a particular department are doing what they need to for the department to make its contribution to the organization's goals. Usually supervisors focus on day-to-day problems and on goals to be achieved in one year or less. This chapter introduces what supervisors do and what skills and characteristics they need to be effective.

Types of Supervisory Skills

Although a supervisor in a Pizza Hut restaurant and one in a Bethlehem Steel factory work in very different environments, the skills they need fall into the same basic categories. In fact, these are the categories of skills used by all levels of managers in all kinds of organizations. Thus, if you develop them for your first supervisory job, they will be useful in every job you hold throughout your management career. The types of skills are technical, human relations, conceptual, and decision-making skills.

Categorizing the Skills

technical skills
The specialized knowledge and expertise used to carry out particular techniques or procedures.

Technical skills are the specialized knowledge and expertise used to carry out particular techniques or procedures. A United Way fund-raiser who knows how to persuade executives to write big checks has technical skills in that area. A Goodyear mechanic who seems able to bring any automobile's engine back to life also has excellent technical skills. An insurance salesperson who earns big commissions has technical skills related to selling. As you can see from these examples, skills do not have to be mechanical or scientific in order to be "technical"; they can involve any work-related technique or procedure.

human relations skills
The ability to work effectively with other people.

Supervisors also have to be able to work effectively with other people. This ability is known as **human relations skills**. Human relations skills include the ability to communicate with, motivate, and understand other people. Supervisors use their human relations skills to impress their boss and other superiors, to inspire employees to work efficiently, to defuse conflicts, to get along with co-workers in other departments, and in many other ways.

FIGURE 1.1

A Sampling of Supervisory Positions to Be Filled

Advertising
PRODUCTION MANAGER
Electronic desktop production agency seeks self-starting, problem-solving Production Manager to supervise catalogue/retail page construction in Mac platform. Minimum 5-7 yrs. experience in managing production and personnel required. Service bureau background a plus. Send resume and salary requirements to:
Dept. A-7
P.O. Box 200
Ski Springs, CO 80300

AUTOMATIC SCREW MACHINE SECOND SHIFT SUPERVISOR
Established growing suburban manufacturer looking for qualified individual to supervise second shift of manufacturing operations. Must have knowledge and experience on multiple/single spindle machines. Enjoy excellent working conditions in a new plant. Very good salary and full benefit package. Submit resume to:
P.O. Box 1234
Industrious, IN 46000

Health Care
CHIEF PHYSICAL THERAPIST
Rural health care consortium has an immediate opening for a licensed physical therapist to develop a progressive, sophisticated therapy delivery system. The ideal candidate should understand sound management principles and possess strong assessment and clinical skills. Candidate must also be willing to assume department leadership. Competitive salary and benefit package. Send resume to:
Director of Human Resources
Quality Care Health Services
Minuscule, NM 87000

SECRETARIAL SUPERVISOR
Large law firm seeks Secretarial Supervisor to join our secretarial management team. Responsibilities include orienting, coordinating, and evaluating a secretarial staff of approximately 200. Previous law firm experience (supervisory or secretarial) preferred. Ideal candidate will be able to work well with a variety of personalities in a demanding, fast-paced environment. We offer state-of-the-art technology, an excellent benefits package and salary commensurate with experience. For immediate, confidential consideration send resume and salary history to:
Personnel
P.O. Box 987
City Center, TN 38000

SALES MANAGEMENT
Our growing organization is seeking an experienced Sales Management candidate to lead our expanding Color Copier Department. The successful candidate will have 3-5 years sales management experience in planning, organizing, hiring, and motivating a team of sales professionals. Previous sales experience, account development techniques, and vertical market success are required. Familiarity with printing, graphic arts, office equipment or other related industry experience helpful. To be considered for this exceptional career opportunity, please send your resume with salary requirements to:
Dept. 001
Suburbanite, NJ 07000

ASSISTANT DIRECTOR OF HOUSEKEEPING
Large luxury hotel is accepting resumes for an Assistant Director of Housekeeping. College degree and 4-5 years of Housekeeping Management experience required. Preferred applicants will have experience as a Director of Housekeeping for a small to medium size hotel or Assistant Director at a large hotel. Must have excellent administrative and supervisory skills. Interested candidates should send resume in confidence to:
Luxurious Suites
1000 Upscale Blvd.
Villa Grande, CA 90000

---

conceptual skills
The ability to see the relation of the parts to the whole and to one another.

In addition, supervisors need **conceptual skills**, or the ability to see the relation of the parts to the whole and to one another. For a supervisor, conceptual skills include recognizing how the department's work helps the entire organization achieve its goals and how the work of the various employees affects the performance of the department as a whole. The supervisor of a manufacturing department at, say, General Motors should be able to see that the company's reputation depends on the department's making high-quality products. He or she should also realize that for the company's salespeople to be able to keep their promises, it is important for the manufacturing department to meet its production quotas.

decision-making skills
The ability to analyze information and reach good decisions.

Finally, supervisors must have **decision-making skills**, or the ability to analyze information and reach good decisions. For example, a supervisor might have to decide which of three candidates for a job will work out best or which of two conflicting deadlines has a higher priority. Someone who has strong decision-making skills can think objectively and creatively. (Chapter 8 provides a more detailed look at how to make decisions effectively.)

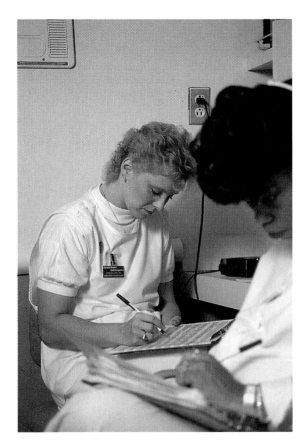 

Supervisors must possess technical, human relations, conceptual, and decision-making skills. All four skills are used daily: Jenean Lord (left), administrative supervisor at Humana Hospital, reviews the morning report with an LPN. Mark Fricke ("Ron" at right), at Shop 'n Save's meat department, supervises high-quality meat preparation.

Source: Photos courtesy of Humana Inc., and Wetterau Inc.

In general, the relative importance of each type of skill depends on the level of management. As shown in Figure 1.2, human relations skills are important at every level of management. However, supervisors rely more on technical skills than do higher-level managers. That is because when employees have a problem doing their job, they go to the supervisor and expect help.

What is the purpose of learning that management skills can be categorized in this way? Supervisors can use this information to recognize the different kinds of skills needed. For example, a person in sales can see that being able to sell successfully does not in itself make him or her a good sales manager. This person will also have to develop skills in working with others and making decisions. One way to develop the variety of skills needed for supervising is to learn and practice applying the concepts discussed in this book. It is also important to get to know good supervisors and managers and to observe how they handle situations. Supervisors who continually develop their skills in each area are the ones most likely to be promoted to higher levels of management.

FIGURE 1.2

Relative Importance of Types of Skills for Different Levels of Managers

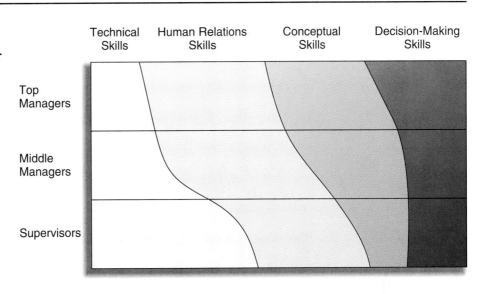

Supervisory Skills for a Diverse Work Force

Good human relations skills are especially important in today's environment because of the increasing diversity of the U.S. work force. Whereas almost half (49 percent) of the work force in 1976 consisted of white males, this category is expected to make up only 12 percent of net new hires (total hired minus total leaving the work force) by the year 2000.[1] Therefore, white males' share of the work force is expected to fall to 39 percent by the year 2000.[2] While the share of white males in the labor force declines, the share of black, Hispanic, and Asian workers is expected to rise.[3] Women are entering the labor force at about the same rate as men, but men are retiring at a faster rate; therefore, women, like racial and ethnic minorities, will have a greater role.[4] In addition, the over-65 segment of the U.S. population is growing faster than younger age groups.[5] Together, these changes mean that the supervisor of tomorrow can expect to have more employees who are female, are of a race other than white, and have more experience—perhaps even holding a job following retirement. As described in later chapters, these trends mean that supervisors will be able to draw on a greater variety of talent and gain insights from a greater variety of perspectives than ever before.

Diversity is not an entirely new issue, of course. Management professor William P. Anthony describes how his grandfather, Alberto Spina, addressed similar needs during his career with American Manganese Steel Company in Chicago Heights, Illinois, from 1907 to 1944.[6] Most of the immigrant workers Spina supervised were white males, but they came from different cultural backgrounds and

Good human relations skills are especially important in today's environment because of the increasing diversity of the U.S. work force.

Source: © Douglas E. Walker/Masterfile.

spoke the various languages of their countries of origin—England, Germany, Italy, Ireland, and the Slavic nations. Sometimes he had to use a translator to communicate with his employees.

Although diversity is not a new issue, the even greater diversity expected in the U.S. work force of the future—coupled with laws and policies intended to ensure that the various groups are treated fairly—means that supervisors will have to be able to work successfully with a wider variety of people than ever before. The "Dealing with Diversity" box addresses some of the subtle but widespread concerns that supervisors face in this regard. Also, throughout this book, you will find ideas for meeting the diversity challenge as it relates to the chapter topics.

General Functions of the Supervisor

Jennifer Plotnick is a supervisor at her city's board of education. Her responsibilities include ensuring that the employees in her department are doing a good job, preparing a budget for her department, making sure not to spend more than the budgeted amounts, explaining to employees what they are expected to do, and justifying to her boss why she needs to add people to her department next year. In contrast, supervisors in different settings may spend most of their time enabling employees to do their jobs, rather than handling the diversity of responsibilities that Jennifer has.

Although the settings and degrees of responsibility may differ, supervisors and other managers carry out the same types of functions. To describe these common

DEALING WITH DIVERSITY

Subtle Discrimination

Nowadays hardly anyone would say that it is OK to discriminate or that a manager should be allowed to give preference to employees of the manager's race or sex. However, according to management professor Mary Rowe, subtle forms of discrimination persist in every workplace. Rowe says that everyone has some stereotypes and that these consciously or unconsciously influence how we behave. The subtle discrimination that results may include such behavior as ignoring the input from the only woman at the meeting or mistaking an African-American professional for someone with a less prestigious job such as receptionist or janitor.

If subtle discrimination is so prevalent, is there anything the supervisor can do about it? Rowe says that there is and that the solution starts with addressing people's attitudes. She recommends several tactics:

- Supervisors and other managers should have their employees work with someone who is different. This gives the employees a chance to educate themselves about others.
- Supervisors should use the kind of behavior they expect their employees to exhibit. They should demonstrate respect for others.

- Supervisors should pay attention to negative stereotypes and question them. When an employee makes an offensive comment, the supervisor can point out the damage it does and ask the employee to avoid such remarks in the future.

One consequence of subtle discrimination is that many supervisors still work for organizations that fail to see the advantages of hiring and developing a diverse work force. What can a supervisor do if he or she works for an organization where management is not committed to these goals? One tactic is to provide advice and coaching to female and nonwhite employees, helping them get along in the organization. The supervisor also can make a point of learning about the various employees in the department, such as what motivates them and what their career goals are.

Sources: Adapted from Audrey Edwards, "The Sting of the Subtle Snub," *Working Woman*, January 1991, pp. 53, 55; and Abby Livingston, "What YOUR Department Can Do," *Working Woman*, January 1991, pp. 59, 61.

activities, management experts categorize them as planning, organizing, staffing, leading, and controlling. The management functions are illustrated in Figure 1.3. As the figure shows, all of the activities should be directed toward enabling employees to deliver a high quality of goods and services—whether to customers of the organization or to colleagues in another department.

Planning

planning
Setting goals and determining how to meet them.

Common sense tells us that we do our best work when we know what we are trying to accomplish. Thus, the supervisor's job includes deciding on the department's goals and the ways to meet them. This is the function of **planning**. In some cases, the supervisor has a substantial say in determining the goals themselves; other supervisors must focus their efforts on how to achieve goals that higher-level managers have set.

As mentioned earlier, the supervisor's job is to help the organization meet its goals. Organizational goals result from planning by top managers. The purpose of planning by supervisors, then, is to determine how the department can contribute

FIGURE 1.3

**Functions of
Supervisors and
Other Managers**

to achieving the organization's goals. This includes planning how much money to spend (and, for a retailer or sales department, how much money to bring in), what level of output to achieve, and how many employees will be needed. (Chapter 2 discusses planning in greater detail.)

Organizing

organizing
Setting up the group, allocating resources, and assigning work to achieve goals.

Once the supervisor figures out what needs to get done, the next step is to determine how to set up the group, allocate resources, and assign work to achieve the goals efficiently. This is the function of **organizing**.

Somebody has to decide how to set up the overall organization, creating departments and levels of management. Of course, not many supervisors get much of a say in those kinds of decisions. At the supervisory level, organizing usually involves such activities as scheduling projects or assigning duties to employees. In addition, modern supervisors are increasingly often responsible for setting up and leading teams of workers to handle special projects or day-to-day operations. (Chapter 3 discusses organizing in greater detail. Chapter 17 addresses leading a team, and the case at the end of Chapter 1 is an example of how teamwork affects the supervisor's job.)

Staffing

staffing
Identifying, hiring, and developing the necessary number and quality of employees.

The supervisor needs qualified employees to carry out the tasks that he or she has planned and organized for. The activities involved in identifying, hiring, and developing the necessary number and quality of employees are known as the function of **staffing**. While an operative employee's performance is judged usually on the basis of the results that that employee has achieved as an individual, a supervisor's performance depends on the quality of results that the supervisor achieves through his or her employees. Therefore, staffing is crucial to the supervisor's success. (The various activities of the staffing function are addressed in Part Three [Chapters 13 through 16].)

Leading

No matter how clear and inspired is the supervisor's vision of how the department and its employees should work, this vision will not become a reality unless employees know and want to do their part. The supervisor is responsible for letting employees know what is expected of them and for inspiring employees to do good work. Influencing employees to act (or not act) in a certain way is the function of **leading**.

leading
Influencing people to act (or not act) in a certain way.

Whereas organizing draws heavily on the supervisor's conceptual skills, leading requires good human relations skills. The supervisor needs to be aware of and use the kinds of behavior that employees respond to as desired. (Chapter 4 includes a more detailed discussion of leading. Other chapters discuss some of the ways in which supervisors influence employees to act, such as by communicating [Chapter 7], motivating [Chapter 9], and disciplining [Chapter 16].)

Controlling

The supervisor needs to know what is happening in the department. When something is going wrong, the supervisor must find a way to fix the problem. Monitoring performance and making needed corrections is the management function of **controlling**. (Chapter 5 discusses controlling in more detail.)

controlling
Monitoring performance and making needed corrections.

Relationships among the Functions

Notice that Figure 1.3 shows the management functions as a process in which planning comes first, followed by organizing, then staffing, then leading, and, finally, controlling. That is because each function depends on the preceding function(s). Once the supervisor has planned what the department will do, he or she can figure out the best way to organize work and people to accomplish those objectives. Then the supervisor needs to get the people in place and doing their jobs. At that point, the supervisor can direct their work and inspire their efforts, then evaluate results to make sure work is getting done properly. When controlling, the supervisor may find that some goals should be revised, at which point the whole process begins again.

Of course, real-life supervisors do not spend one week planning, then one week organizing, and so on. Rather, they often carry out all of the management functions during the course of a day. For example, a patient care coordinator in a hospital might start the day by checking to see how nurses are doing (controlling), then attend a meeting to discuss the needs of the patients on the floor (planning), then resolve a dispute between a nurse and a physical therapist (leading). Thus, Figure 1.3 is a very general model of managing that shows how the functions depend on each other, not how the supervisor structures his or her work.

Typically, supervisors spend most of their time leading and controlling. That is because supervisors work directly with the employees who are producing or selling or providing support services. Planning, staffing, and organizing take up less of a supervisor's time. In contrast, because higher-level managers are responsible for setting the overall direction for the organization, they spend more time on planning and organizing.

Responsibilities of the Supervisor

"I wish I were the manager," grumbled Hal O'Donnell, a cook at a pizza chain. "Then I'd be in charge and wouldn't get bossed around all the time." Perhaps Hal has not thought about it, but getting a promotion to supervisor (or any level of management) does not lessen a person's burdens. In fact, when an employee becomes a supervisor, he or she gives up all the "rights" listed in Table 1.1. In other words, supervisors have more power than nonmanagers but also many responsibilities—to higher management, to employees, and to co-workers.

Types of Responsibilities

Supervisors are responsible for carrying out the duties assigned to them by higher-level managers. This includes giving managers timely and accurate information for planning. They also must keep their boss informed about the department's performance. Supervisors are expected to serve as a kind of "linking pin" connecting their employees and the organization's management. Thus, their responsibilities include building employee morale and carrying employee concerns to the relevant managers.

Some supervisors may question the notion that they have a responsibility to their employees. After all, the employees are responsible for doing what the supervisors say. Nevertheless, because supervisors link management to the employees, the way they treat employees is crucial. Supervisors are responsible for giving their employees clear instructions and making sure they understand their jobs. They must look for problems and try to correct them before employees' performance deteriorates further. They also need to treat their employees fairly and to speak up for their interests to top management. Here is advice from William Bottom, a supervisory carpenter at the Lazarus department store in Lexington, Kentucky:

> You shouldn't give your crew an assignment that you'd hesitate to take on yourself. Don't allow top bosses to push more work on your crew than they can reasonably be expected to do. Employees will work smarter and harder for a supervisor who puts their welfare first.[7]

Finally, supervisors are responsible for cooperating with their co-workers in other departments. They should respond promptly when a co-worker in another department requests information. They should share ideas that will help the organization's departments work together to accomplish goals they hold in common. And supervisors should listen with an open mind when co-workers in other departments make suggestions about how to improve the way things are done. When

TABLE 1.1

"Rights" That Employees Lose When They Become Supervisors

The right to lose their temper

The right to hobnob and be "one of the crowd"

The right to shut the door

The right to bring personal problems to work

The right to speak freely

The right to be against change

The right to pass the buck

The right to get even

The right to choose favorites

The right to think of themselves first

The right to ask an employee to do something they would not do

The right to expect immediate reward for their work

supervisors learn from each other's ideas, the whole organization benefits, and the supervisors have the satisfaction of working together as members of a team.

Responsibilities Following Restructuring

In recent years, many organizations have attempted to cut costs by reducing the number of levels of management. The managers eliminated in this process are typically middle managers, those ranking between supervisors and the top executives. For example, the Diner's Club unit of Citicorp went from eight layers of management between the president and first-line supervisors to four layers. Other companies that have cut out layers of management include Corning, Inc., and Eastman Kodak Company.[8] As a result, today's supervisors often have more responsibilities than supervisors of even a decade ago. While continuing to work closely with employees, they must also handle much of the planning and organizing done by middle managers.

Responsibilities and Accountability

accountability
The practice of imposing penalties for failing to adequately carry out responsibilities and of providing rewards for meeting responsibilities.

Whatever the responsibilities of a particular supervisor, the organization holds the supervisor accountable for carrying them out. **Accountability** refers to the practice of imposing penalties for failing to adequately carry out responsibilities, and it usually includes giving rewards for meeting responsibilities. Thus, if customer service supervisor Lydia Papadopoulos effectively teaches the telephone representatives on her staff to listen carefully to customers, the company might reward her with a raise. In contrast, a boss who gets frustrated with a supervisor who never keeps him informed about what is happening in the department might eventually fire the supervisor for failing to carry out this responsibility.

At Walgreen's Colorado Springs store, store manager Dick Enders (right) supervises employees such as camera clerk Bob Parker (left), and he must also handle much of the planning and organizing for the store.

Source: Courtesy of Walgreen Co., 1992 Annual Report.

Becoming a Supervisor

Joyce Gurtatowski, whose job at La Salle Bank Matteson was described at the beginning of this chapter, started as a teller with the bank and worked in several areas, including more than five years in personal banking. Like Gurtatowski, most supervisors started out working in the department they now supervise. Because technical skills are especially important for first-level managers, the person selected to be supervisor is often an employee with a superior grasp of the technical skills needed to perform well in the department. Perhaps the person also has more seniority than many of the other employees in the department. Another reason for selecting an employee to be a supervisor is that he or she has good work habits and leadership skills. Sometimes a company will hire a recent college graduate to be a supervisor, perhaps because the person has demonstrated leadership potential or a specialized skill that will help in the position.

Unfortunately, none of these bases for promotion or hiring guarantee that a person knows how to supervise. When salesperson Rick Horn was promoted to inside sales manager, he was unprepared for some aspects of supervising a sales force.[9] Instead of receiving formal training in supervision, says Horn, "I was just kind of dropped off the end of the pier." He was especially challenged by the task of figuring out how to lead his former colleagues. Recalling an early effort at handling a salesperson's poor performance, Horn says, "She screwed up, and I yelled at her. She started crying, I didn't know what to do, and my boss just looked at me and shook his head." Fortunately, Horn learned to refine his human relations skills, and he now heads Iowa Mold Tool Corporation of Garner, Iowa.

As Horn discovered, becoming a supervisor is a big change in a person's work life. The new supervisor suddenly must use more human relations and conceptual skills. He or she must devote more time to planning ahead and keeping an eye on the department's activities. Also, there is a change in the supervisor's relationships with the employees in the department. Instead of being one of the crowd, the supervisor becomes a part of management—even the target of blame or anger when employees resent company policies. All these changes are bound to lead to at least a little anxiety. It is natural to wonder whether you are qualified or how you will handle the problems that are sure to arise.

Preparing for the Job

One way to combat the anxiety is to prepare for the job. The new supervisor can learn about management and supervision through books and observation. He or she can think about ways to carry out the role of supervisor. More important than friendliness are traits such as fairness and a focus on achieving goals. The supervisor can also make an effort to learn as much as possible about the organization, the department, and the job.

Once on the job, the supervisor needs to continue the learning process. More important than understanding the layout of the workplace is knowing about the employees in the department or work group.[10] Who are the quiet but productive workers, for example, and who are the unofficial leaders? To get to know employees, the supervisor can talk to his or her boss and read performance appraisals, but the most reliable sources of information are the employees themselves. Especially in the early days on the job, the supervisor should take time to discuss goals with employees and observe their work habits.

The supervisor may learn that one or more employees had been a candidate for the supervisor's job and therefore may be jealous. One constructive approach to this problem is to acknowledge to the other person that he or she may feel uncomfortable, to ask for the employee's support, and to discuss his or her long-term goals. Marie Davis of IDS Financial Services did this with a staff member who had applied for the same job that Davis was chosen for. The staff member said that her goal was to "break into management." Says Davis, "I told her, without making false promises, that I would do what I could to help her." Until this employee moved into a management job six months later, she was one of the top performers among Davis's employees.[11] An important aspect of this approach is that the supervisor is helping the employees meet or exceed their own goals. For example, a sales supervisor can help a potentially jealous salesperson increase sales. Says Hugh Allen, a sales executive with Lawson Products, Inc., "You'd be surprised how much better a manager [employees] think you are when you make more money for them."[12]

Obtaining and Using Power and Authority

To carry out his or her job, a supervisor needs not only knowledge but also power (the ability to do certain things) and authority (the right to do certain things). With regard to acquiring power when one assumes the job of supervisor, it may help for the new supervisor's boss to make an official announcement of the promotion.[13] When accepting the job, the supervisor can ask his or her boss to announce the promotion at a meeting of the employees. Then the supervisor can take the opportunity to state his or her expectations, desire to work as a team, and interest in hearing about work-related problems.

A new supervisor should not rush too fast to make changes in the department. Instead, he or she should first understand how the department works and what employees expect. Making changes quickly and without seeking input from employees can alienate them and put them on the defensive. The supervisor can build support for change by introducing it gradually after inviting suggestions where appropriate.

(Chapter 3 discusses the delegation of authority, and Chapter 19 covers sources and types of power. Chapter 12 provides more information about managing change.)

Characteristics of a Successful Supervisor

Unfortunately, many of us have at some time worked for someone who seemed to stifle our best efforts or to anger us with unfair decisions. Many of us have also worked for a supervisor who taught us new skills, inspired us to do better than we thought we could, or made us look forward to going to work each day. What is behind the success of this second category of supervisors? Figure 1.4 illustrates some characteristics of successful supervisors. Take the self-quiz on page 18 to see whether supervising is a good fit with your current traits and interests.

A successful supervisor has a *positive attitude*. Employees tend to reflect the attitudes of the people in charge. When the supervisor's attitude toward work and the organization is positive, employees are more likely to be satisfied with and interested in their work. Furthermore, managers and co-workers prefer working with someone who has a positive attitude.

Successful supervisors are *loyal*. As a part of the management team, they must take actions that are best for the organization. This may include making decisions that are unpopular with employees. In such situations, supervisors must recognize that taking on a supervisory job means they cannot always be "one of the gang."

Successful supervisors are *fair*. Supervisors who play favorites or behave inconsistently will lose the support and respect of their employees. Therefore, they will not be able to lead effectively. Furthermore, when supervisors make assignments and decisions based on whom they like best, they will not necessarily make the assignments and decisions that are best for the organization. Another aspect of being fair is to follow the rules yourself. The supervisor can set a good example by, for example, being on time and refraining from doing personal work on the job or taking supplies home.

FIGURE 1.4

Characteristics of a Successful Supervisor

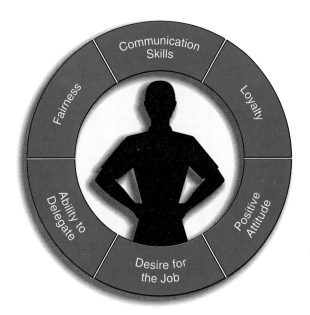

Supervisors also need to be *good communicators.*[14] Employees and bosses alike depend on the supervisor to keep them informed of what is going on. Employees who receive clear guidance on what is expected of them will not only perform better but will be more satisfied with their jobs. Good communication also includes making contact with employees each day and listening to what they have to say. (Chapter 7 takes a more in-depth look at the communications skills that supervisors need to develop and use.)

To be successful, a supervisor must be *able to delegate*—that is, to give their employees authority and responsibility to carry out activities. As supervisors tend to have excellent technical skills, delegating may be a challenge. The supervisor may resist giving an assignment to someone who may not carry it out as easily or as well. Nevertheless, a supervisor cannot do the work of the whole department. Therefore, he or she must assign work to employees. Equally important, the supervisor should give them credit for their accomplishments. This, in turn, makes the supervisor look good; the employees' successes show that the supervisor is able to select and motivate employees as well as delegate effectively. The "Tips from the Firing Line" on page 19 provide some ideas for making employees look good. (Chapter 3 discusses delegation in greater detail.)

Finally, a successful supervisor must *want the job.* Some people are happier carrying out the technical skills of their field, whether carpentry, respiratory therapy, or financial management. People who prefer this type of work to the functions of managing will probably be happier if they turn down an opportunity to become a supervisor. In contrast, people who enjoy the challenge of making plans and inspiring others to achieve goals are more likely to be effective supervisors.

S E L F - Q U I Z   *Is Supervising Right for You?*
Answer each of the following questions Yes or No.

		Yes	No
1.	Do you consider yourself a highly ambitious person?	☐	☐
2.	Do you sincerely like and have patience with people?	☐	☐
3.	Could you assume the responsibility of decision making?	☐	☐
4.	Is making more money very important to you?	☐	☐
5.	Would recognition from others be more important to you than taking pride in doing a detailed job well?	☐	☐
6.	Would you enjoy learning about psychology and human behavior?	☐	☐
7.	Would you be happier with more responsibility?	☐	☐
8.	Would you rather work with problems involving human relationships than with mechanical, computational, creative, clerical, or similar problems?	☐	☐
9.	Do you desire an opportunity to demonstrate your leadership ability?	☐	☐
10.	Do you desire the freedom to do your own planning rather than being told what to do?	☐	☐

Give yourself one point for each Yes answer. If your score is 6 or more, you might be happy as a supervisor. If your score was 5 or less, you should think hard about your preferences and strengths before jumping into a supervisory job.

Source: Reprinted with the permission of Macmillan Publishing Company from SUPERVISOR'S SURVIVAL KIT: Your First Step Into Management, Sixth Edition, by Elwood N. Chapman. Copyright © 1993 by Macmillan Publishing Company.

About This Book

This book introduces the many kinds of activities supervisors must carry out to accomplish their overall objective of seeing that employees contribute to achieving the organization's goals. The book begins by devoting Part One to a broad view of the supervisor's role. The chapters in this part examine four basic functions of the supervisor—planning, organizing, leading, and controlling. All of these functions, when done well, lead to high-quality products and services. Thus, the final chapter in Part One addresses the role of the supervisor in maintaining and improving quality.

Part Two describes skills needed by supervisors in all kinds of organizations. Individual chapters cover ways supervisors can communicate, solve problems and make decisions, motivate their employees, improve productivity, manage time and stress, and manage conflict and change. These skills are important at all levels of management, as well as in all types of organizations.

Making Employees Look Good

A smart tactic for both the new and the experienced supervisor is to make sure that his or her employees get recognized for their accomplishments. It is the fair thing to do, and it also makes the supervisor look good. It shows higher-level management that you know how to lead your employees in getting results. Bonnie Jones, the manager of employee communications for GTE Telephone Operations in Irving, Texas, recommends putting employees' accomplishments in writing. Jones suggests the following approach:

- To get the news out fast, use a memo or an article in the company newsletter. If your company does not publish an employee newsletter, you might publish one for your department.
- Keep the language simple. Often a department uses special jargon that others in the company will not easily understand. Use plain English instead.
- Tell how the accomplishment contributes to meeting the organization's goals. For example, tell how your employees saved money, boosted earnings, or made a customer very happy.

Source: Adapted from Jonathan Schmidt, "How to Put Your Staff in the Spotlight," *Working Woman*, August 1990, p. 18.

Next, Part Three addresses activities related to managing the organization's human resources—its employees. Chapter 13 covers the supervisor's role in selecting new employees. Chapter 14 discusses the process of training new and existing employees. Chapter 15 describes how supervisors appraise their employees' performance, and Chapter 16 discusses approaches to supervising employees whose behavior poses problems in the workplace.

The last part of the book describes some special challenges faced by modern supervisors. First, Chapter 17 covers groups and teamwork, reflecting the increasingly common role of the supervisor as a team leader. Government regulations and advancing technology make it more and more complex to keep the workplace safe— the topic of Chapter 18. Finally, supervisors and managers need to consider the ethical implications of their decisions and the ways their actions influence their position in the organization. Thus, Chapter 19 discusses ethics and organization politics.

In each part, the chapters include some special features designed to help you apply the principles to the practice of supervising real people in a real organization. These features include boxed items discussing issues related to diversity in the work force and offering practical tips on effective supervision. Self-quizzes can help you appreciate your own strengths and interests with regard to the chapter topics. Chapter-opening stories and end-of-chapter cases show how real supervisors and organizations have approached issues covered in each chapter.

Following the chapters, a reference guide discusses issues related to building and managing your career. The reference guide describes some basics of planning a career and includes exercises to help you plan your own career and write a résumé.

An end-of-book glossary provides quick reference for all key terms. For review, text page numbers where the terms are defined are listed at the end of the definitions.

The Leadership Skills portion of the text contains self-assessments, skill-building exercises, role-playing exercises, information applications, and mini case studies. These allow you to use text concepts and develop leadership abilities.

Summary

1.1   Define what a supervisor is.
A supervisor is a manager at the first level of management. That is, the employees reporting to the supervisor are not themselves managers.

1.2   Describe the basic types of supervisory skills.
The basic supervisory skills are technical, human relations, conceptual, and decision-making skills. Technical skills are the specialized knowledge and experience used to carry out particular techniques or procedures. Human relations skills are skills that enable the supervisor to work effectively with other people. Conceptual skills enable the supervisor to see the relation of the parts to the whole and to one another. Decision-making skills are those needed to analyze information and reach good decisions.

1.3   Describe how the growing diversity of the work force affects the supervisor's role.
Compared with the current makeup of the U.S. work force, an increasingly large share of employees will be female, nonwhite, and relatively old. As a result, supervisors in the future will typically have a more diverse group of employees to manage. This means that supervisors can benefit from a greater variety of talents and viewpoints. It also requires supervisors to draw on more sophisticated human relations skills than in the past.

1.4   Identify the general functions of a supervisor.
The general functions of a supervisor are planning, organizing, staffing, leading, and controlling. Planning involves setting goals and determining how to meet them. Organizing is determining how to set up the group, allocate resources, and assign work to achieve goals. Staffing consists of identifying, hiring, and developing the necessary number and quality of employees. Leading is the function of getting employees to do what is expected of them. Controlling consists of monitoring performance and making needed corrections.

1.5   Explain how supervisors are responsible to higher management, employees, and co-workers.
Supervisors are responsible for doing the work assigned to them by higher management and for keeping management informed of the department's progress. They link higher management to the employees. Supervisors are responsible for treating employees fairly, making instructions clear, and bringing employee concerns to higher management. Supervisors are responsible for cooperating with co-workers in other departments. Organizations hold supervisors accountable for meeting these various responsibilities.

1.6   Describe the typical background of someone who is promoted to supervisor.
Most supervisors started out as employees in the department they now supervise. They usually have superior technical skills and may have seniority or demonstrate leadership potential.

1.7   Identify characteristics of a successful supervisor.
A successful supervisor is usually someone who has a positive attitude, is loyal, is fair, communicates well, can delegate, and wants the job.

Key Terms

supervisor	decision-making skills	leading
technical skills	planning	controlling
human relations skills	organizing	accountability
conceptual skills	staffing	

Review and Discussion Questions

1. What are some ways a supervisor's job is the same as that of managers at other levels? How does the supervisor's job differ from that of other managers?
2. Identify whether each of the following skills is a technical skill, a human relations skill, a conceptual skill, or a decision-making skill.
   a. The ability to communicate well with one's boss.
   b. The ability to create advertisements that grab people's attention.
   c. The ability to select the most appropriate safety training program for the housekeeping staff.
   d. The ability to see the big picture in order to understand a situation fully.
   e. Knowledge of how to machine a part without unnecessary changes in the setup of equipment.
3. Which category of skills do supervisors rely on most often? Why?
4. Population trends suggest that the work force will become increasingly diverse. What are some advantages of greater diversity? What challenges does it pose to the supervisor?
5. What are the basic functions of a supervisor? Which functions do supervisors spend most of their time on?
6. Explain how the basic functions of a supervisor are related.
7. What responsibilities do supervisors have to each of these groups?
   a. Higher management
   b. The employees they supervise
   c. Co-workers in other departments
8. Carlos Suarez is the supervisor of customer service at the headquarters of a large retailer such as J. C. Penney. The company has just announced that it will be restructuring, a move that involves a number of changes, including layoffs of many middle managers. One of the managers who will go is Carlos's boss; Carlos will now report to a more senior manager. In general, how do you think this change will affect Carlos's responsibilities?
9. Why does becoming a supervisor often make a person feel anxious? What are some ways the new supervisor can combat this anxiety?
10. List the characteristics of a good supervisor. Besides the characteristics mentioned in the chapter, add any others you believe are important. Draw on your own experiences as an employee and/or a supervisor.

A SECOND LOOK

According to the description of the two supervisors at the beginning of this chapter, what management functions do each of these supervisors carry out? What skills do you think are important in each job?

Class Exercise

Create a customized panel discussion for your class. Use one of these options:

1. List the different kinds of organizations and departments in which class members work. Pick a few, and have students volunteer to ask their supervisor to visit the class to participate.
2. If some class members are themselves supervisors, they may volunteer to be on the panel. If possible, use class members from a variety of types of organizations or departments.
3. The instructor may select and invite people to be on a panel.

Have the members of the panel sit in the front of the classroom, and invite each panel member to give a brief description of his or her job. Then students may ask the panel members questions. Here are some ideas for questions:

- What do you do in the course of a typical day?
- How much of your time is spent working with people?

- What is the hardest part of your job?
- What is the most satisfying part of your job?

- Do you participate in each of the management functions (planning, organizing, staffing, leading, controlling)?

CASE

Supervisors' Changing Role at Kodak

Kodak's Eastman Chemicals Division, located in Kingsport, Tennessee, has been attempting to get employees more involved in decisions related to running the company. One of the company's programs is called the New Work System. According to Charles A. Gibson, the division's director of industrial relations, the New Work System is intended to encourage employees "to learn skills that will enable them to be a self-regulating team."

To operate under this arrangement, employees must be trained in one another's jobs and in the various tasks related to producing the division's products. Ideally, the employees themselves will be responsible for handling maintenance, ordering supplies, and planning production.

Where does this leave the supervisors of the Eastman Chemicals Division? Clearly they are giving up much of the control that traditionally went with the position. Gibson describes their resulting responsibilities:

> Supervisors at Eastman are becoming trainers, coaches, and facilitators to help teams work out problems. They are the liaison between employees and management, and between work units that need to cooperate with one another. They are also responsible for helping teams to anticipate their own needs and the needs of teams with which they interact. They are responsible for ensuring that team members' work hours are scheduled—an important factor in a facility that runs 24 hours a day, as ours does. And each team leader [supervisor]

is charged with empowering, training, and enabling his or her team to manage itself and to operate and manage the business.

Not surprisingly, many of the division's supervisors were nervous when the changes were introduced, and many of them resisted the changes. Many were afraid they would lose status but have to work harder. The company tried to make sure that supervisors would be able to have jobs of equal or higher value. Many supervisors have found that they have benefited from greater variety in their jobs and a more direct contribution to the company's success. Overall, the division reports that morale and output are better than before the changes were made.

1. How did the changes at Kodak's Eastman Chemicals Division affect the kinds of skills the supervisors need?
2. What kind of person do you think is most likely to succeed as a supervisor in the division as it is currently set up?
3. Would you prefer the old-fashioned kind of supervisory job, in which supervisors decide what needs to be done and who will do it, or the kind of positions that have been created in the Eastman Chemicals Division? Why?

Source: "First-Line Supervisors, First-Line Responsibilities," *Employee Relations and Human Resources Bulletin*, November 7, 1991, pp. 6–8.

2

Management has no choice but to anticipate the future, to attempt to mold it, and to balance short-range and long-range goals. It is not given to mortals to do well any of these things. But lacking divine guidance, management must make sure that these difficult responsibilities are not overlooked or neglected, but taken care of as well as is humanly possible.

—Peter Drucker, *Management*

The Supervisor as Planner

LEARNING OBJECTIVES

2.1 Identify advantages of planning in organizations.

2.2 Differentiate the types of planning that go on at different levels of the organization.

2.3 Define *policies, procedures,* and *rules*.

2.4 Describe the supervisor's role in the planning process.

2.5 List the characteristics of effective objectives.

2.6 Explain why supervisors should involve employees in setting objectives and how they can do this.

2.7 Describe the role of action plans.

2.8 Explain why and how supervisors develop contingency plans.

2.9 Describe the use of management by objectives.

PLANNING FOR EFFICIENCY

When crew members from Stamford, Connecticut-based One Call Does It All Maintenance Company went to someone's home or business to make repairs, they often had to interrupt their work to make trips back to the shop. It occurred to the company's operating manager, Tom Kipphut, that the company would run more efficiently if crew members did not have to do all that traveling. When he began to keep track of why workers were coming back to the shop, he found that it was almost always because they did not have all the tools and supplies they needed.

Kipphut decided that the solution was to plan for what crew members would need. With some thought, he determined that most repair jobs required just a few basic tools: a couple of sizes of Phillips and flat-head screwdrivers, a crescent wrench, duct tape and electrical tape, and a tape measure.

Next Kipphut thought about the kinds of tools that were needed for specific kinds of jobs. He added these tools to the basic ones to create job-specific tool kits. For example, to answer a call about a blocked or overflowing toilet, the crew member would take a kit containing a plumber's snake, a plunger, and a wax seal (in case the worker had to reinstall the toilet). The toilet repair kit also contained the parts for the flush assembly, so if the worker found another common problem with the toilet, he or she could offer to repair that on the spot.

Kipphut assembled each set of tools in a plastic carrying case. He cut a block of Styrofoam to fit inside and carved out compartments to hold each piece of equipment. That made it easy to replace any parts used on a job. Besides the plumbing kits, the company now has kits for general-appliance repair and general electronics.

The cost of providing workers with parts in advance is less than what the company would spend by having workers go to the nearest store and pay full retail price. The company also avoids the time and cost of the extra traveling that crew members had done. Furthermore, employees find their work less frustrating when they are prepared for an assignment and know where the tools are. Perhaps most important, customers are so pleased by the fast service that referrals have caused the business to grow substantially.

Source: "Planning: Job-Specific Tool Kits," *Maintenance Supervisor's Bulletin* (Bureau of Business Practice), January 25, 1992, pp. 1–3. Photo courtesy of Comstock © 1992.

By seeing the need for and preparing tool kits, Tom Kipphut was thinking ahead. He considered the future needs of his employees and customers, and he devised an efficient way to meet those needs. He determined how his crew members could meet his objective of providing fast service.

planning
The management function of setting goals and determining how to meet them.

Through planning, supervisors and other managers handle what Drucker terms their responsibilities of anticipating and attempting to mold the future. As you learned in Chapter 1, **planning** is the management function of setting goals and determining how to meet them. For supervisors, this includes figuring out what tasks the department needs to carry out to achieve its goals and how and when to perform those tasks. This chapter describes how the planning process works.

The Need for Planning

For action-oriented people, planning can seem time-consuming and tedious. But the need for planning is obvious, especially if you consider what would happen in an organization where no one plans. For example, if a store did not implement planning, customers would not know when the store would be open, and employees would not know what inventory to order or when to order it. The location of the store would be an accident, not based on where business would be good enough to generate a profit. The managers would not know how many employees to hire, because they would have no idea how many customers they would be serving. You can elaborate on this example to see the endless problems that would arise. Clearly, this business would fail in the task of providing its customers with high-quality service and merchandise.

Supervisors and other managers plan for several reasons. Knowing what the organization is trying to accomplish helps them set priorities and make decisions aimed at accomplishing their goals. Planning forces managers to spend some time focusing on the future and establishes a fair way for evaluating performance. It helps managers use resources efficiently, minimizing wasted time and money. For example, Japanese managers spend more of their time planning than U.S. managers do, but they spend less time correcting problems.[1] Time spent in planning a project can reduce the time required to carry it out. As shown in Figure 2.1, the total time for planning and execution can actually be shorter for a thoroughly planned project than for one started in haste.

Finally, the other functions that managers perform—organizing, staffing, leading, and controlling—all depend on good planning. Thus, before supervisors and other managers can allocate resources and inspire employees to achieve their objectives, or before they can determine whether employees are meeting those objectives, they need to know what they are trying to accomplish.

How the Organization Plans

Supervisors rarely have much input into the way an organization does its planning. Rather, they participate in whatever process already exists. To participate constructively, supervisors should understand the process.

FIGURE 2.1
Planning Time Pays Off

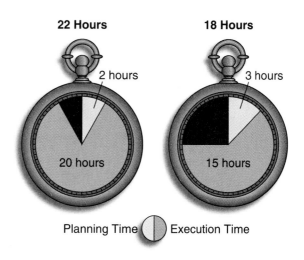

Source: Corinne Livesay, Liberty University, Lynchburg, Va.

objectives
The desired accomplishments of the organization as a whole or of part of the organization.

goals
Objectives, often those with a broad focus.

Planning centers on the setting of goals and objectives. **Objectives** specify the desired accomplishments of the organization as a whole or of a part of the organization. According to one school of thought, **goals** are objectives with a broad focus. For example, an organization seeks to be the number-one supplier of nursing home care by the end of next year. That would be considered a goal. In contrast, the accounting department seeks to have all invoices mailed within two weeks of a patient's departure; this is more specific and is therefore an objective. This text uses the term *objectives* in most cases and treats the two terms as being synonymous.

Objectives serve as the basis for action plans and contingency plans, which are discussed near the end of the chapter. Figure 2.2 shows the relationships among these areas of planning.

Levels of Objectives

strategic planning
The creation of long-term goals for the organization as a whole.

operational planning
The development of objectives that specify how divisions, departments, and work groups will support organizational goals.

Planning should begin at the top, with a plan for the organization as a whole. **Strategic planning** is the creation of long-term goals for the organization. These typically include the type and quality of products or services the organization is to provide and, for a business, the level of profits it is to earn. Usually the people who engage in strategic planning are the top managers; in other cases, a planning department prepares objectives for approval by top management. Either way, the managers at the top are the ones who decide where the organization should be going.

The objectives for divisions, departments, and work groups support the goals developed in strategic planning. These objectives, developed through **operational planning**, specify how the group will help the organization achieve its goals. Operational planning is done by middle managers and supervisors. Table 2.1 summarizes the characteristics of strategic and operational planning.

FIGURE 2.2

Areas of Planning

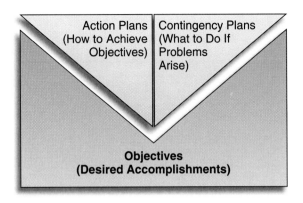

TABLE 2.1

Characteristics of Strategic and Operational Planning

	Strategic Planning	Operational Planning
Planners	Top managers, possibly with a planning department	Middle managers and supervisors
Scope	Objectives for the organization as a whole	Objectives for a division, department, or work group
Time Frame	Long range (more than one year)	Short range (one year or less)

Middle managers set objectives that will enable their division or department to contribute to the goals set for the organization. Supervisors set objectives that will enable their department or work group to contribute to divisional or departmental goals. For example, if the organizational objective for a bank is to increase profits by 8 percent next year, the goal of a branch located in a high-growth area might be to increase its own profits by 9 percent. At this branch, the vice-president (supervisor) in charge of lending operations might have the objective to increase loans to businesses by 15 percent. The head teller might have the objective to keep customer waits to five minutes or less. (The good service is designed to support organizational objectives by attracting new customers to the bank.)

Notice that in the example, the objectives become more specific at lower levels of the organization. This is the usual pattern for planning in an organization. Planning at lower levels also tends to focus more on shorter time spans. Thus, top managers spend a lot of their time thinking ahead over several years, whereas much of the supervisor's planning may involve what to do in the current week or month.

Besides planning for the department as a whole, each supervisor should apply good planning practices to his or her individual efforts. This includes determining what to do to help the department meet its objectives, as well as how to meet the supervisor's own career objectives. Also, an important application of planning is in

Goals are objectives with a broad focus. In its 1992 Annual Report, Weyerhaeuser Company stated that its vision was to be "The Best Forest Products Company in the World:" a goal with a very broad focus.

Source: Courtesy of © Sherman Hines/Masterfile.

managing your own use of time. (Chapter 11 discusses time management, and the Reference Guide to this book presents ideas for career management.)

Policies, Procedures, and Rules

To meet his objective of staffing his information systems department with top-quality employees, Bruce Frazzoli hired some people he used to work with at his former job. He was later embarrassed to be called on the carpet for violating his employer's policy that managers must work with the personnel department in making all hiring decisions. As Bruce learned, in setting objectives, supervisors and other managers must consider the organization's policies, procedures, and rules. The content of the objectives and the way they are carried out must be consistent with all three.

policies
Broad guidelines for how to act.

Policies are broad guidelines for how to act; they do not spell out the details of how to handle a specific situation. A real estate developer may have a policy of assigning at least 10 percent of its construction jobs to minority contractors. This policy does not specify which contractors will be asked to bid on particular jobs or which jobs will be awarded to minority contractors. Those details are up to the person awarding those contracts. Another policy addressing the diversity of the work force is the policy of Monsanto Company described in the "Dealing with Diversity" box on page 30.

procedures
The steps that must be completed to achieve a specific purpose.

Procedures are the steps that must be completed to achieve a specific purpose. An organization might specify procedures for hiring employees, purchasing equipment, filing paperwork, or many other activities. For example, publishing company Richard D. Irwin's management guidelines include suggested procedures

DEALING WITH DIVERSITY

Monsanto's Policy to Build a Diverse Work Force

Monsanto Company, a chemical and drug maker based in St. Louis, has a policy of increasing the number of women and minorities in its work force. This policy is designed to meet federal requirements, as well as what management sees as its moral duty. Between 1988 and 1990, the percentage of nonunion new-hires who are minorities rose from 15 to 17 percent. During the same time period, the percentage of women rose from 21 to 29 percent.

Does this mean Monsanto's managers have been carrying out the company's policy? In the sense of who has been hired, yes. However, the policy was designed ultimately to build a diverse work force, and the women and minorities who had been hired were also leaving the company in large numbers. By 1990 the percentages of minorities and women leaving the company were 26 and 20 percent, respectively.

Interviews with the employees who were leaving revealed that they felt they had been treated unfairly at Monsanto and that they could find greater job opportunities elsewhere. These results were not altogether surprising to the company's supervisors. Nora Castaneda, a Hispanic project engineering supervisor, recounts her own experience: "I wasn't fitting in, so I started trying to act like a white male. I started dressing like a man, I always made sure I had a comb sticking out of my back pocket, and I cussed up a storm—all of it just trying to be accepted."

Gregg Goodnight, technical services superintendent, describes the status quo: "There was a lot of pressure to keep the numbers up to meet our [hiring] targets, so very poor performers were carried. That kind of coddling erects a barrier with other workers.... They were always a separate group that didn't get the feedback or the occasional kick in the tail they needed to develop, and eventually a lot of them got tired of that treatment and quit."

These supervisors' experiences suggest that many managers at Monsanto had followed the company's policy only in the limited sense of seeing that they hired enough people from diverse groups. However, they hadn't adhered to the spirit of the policy. To change the atmosphere at the company, the company began holding workshops on cultural diversity, where participants identify and discuss their biases and stereotypes.

In addition, the company set up a program called "Consulting Pairs." This program trains employees to serve as in-house consultants, working in pairs matched by race or sex, advising their co-workers on how to participate in a diverse work force. One of the pairs' major jobs is to hold sessions with newly hired employees and their immediate supervisors. At these sessions, the discussion centers on the manager's and employee's expectations about the job. If the manager and employee don't bring up race, sex, or age differences, the pairs do. Says Nancy L. Gheen, Monsanto's manager of work-force diversity, "Once people begin to talk about these things, they're not as afraid of them and can learn to handle them."

Source: Adapted from James E. Ellis, "Monsanto's New Challenge: Keeping Minority Workers," *Business Week*, July 8, 1991, pp. 60–61.

---

for how to conduct performance appraisals and employment interviews. With regard to activities carried out in his or her own department, a supervisor may be responsible for developing the procedures. For example, a restaurant manager might spell out a cleanup procedure, or a maintenance supervisor might detail the shutdown procedure for a piece of machinery. Procedures free managers and employees from making decisions about activities they carry out repeatedly.

rules
Statements of specifically what to do or not do in a given situation.

Rules are statements of specifically what to do or not do in a given situation. Unlike policies, they are not flexible nor open to interpretation. For example, one rule at Joslyn Power Products Corporation states that safety glasses and safety shoes (shoes with steel toes or leather uppers) must be worn in the factory. Restaurants have rules stating that employees must wash their hands before working. Note that rules such as these are often imposed on the organization by law.

The Supervisor's Role

In most organizations, supervisors participate in the planning process in several ways. These include providing information to higher management and making plans that affect the supervisor's own department. In general, these plans contain four kinds of information:[2]

1. *Goals*—The objectives the department and supervisor need to meet.
2. *Tasks*—The jobs that each person needs to do to achieve an objective.
3. *Resources*—The number of people and the amount of time and materials needed to achieve an objective.
4. *Responsibilities*—The individuals who will perform each task.

As you can imagine, planning sometimes involves quite a bit of paperwork. Although supervisors often resist spending time on paperwork, well-conceived planning activities are certainly worth the investment of time and effort.

Providing Information and Estimates   As the manager closest to day-to-day operations, the supervisor is in the best position to keep higher-level managers informed about the needs, abilities, and progress of his or her department or work group. For that reason, higher management relies on supervisors to provide estimates of the personnel and other resources they will need in order to accomplish their work.

Allocating Resources   The department for which the supervisor is responsible has a limited number of resources. These take the form of people, equipment, and money. The supervisor's job includes deciding how to allocate resources to the jobs that will need to be done.

The process of allocating human resources includes determining how many and what kind of employees the department will need to meet its objectives. If the department's work load is expanding, the supervisor may need to plan for hiring new employees. He or she also must plan for employee vacations and other time off, as well as for turnover of employees.

The process of allocating equipment resources includes determining how much equipment is needed to get the job done. For example, does every bookkeeper need a personal computer, or will adding machines be enough? The supervisor may find that the department needs to acquire more equipment. In that case, the supervisor must justify the request to buy or rent it by showing how it will benefit the organization.

The process of allocating money resources is called budgeting, discussed next.

budget
A plan for spending money.

Developing a Budget   A **budget** is a plan for spending money. Many households use budgets for deciding how much of each paycheck should go for housing, car payments, food, savings, and so on. Likewise, businesses and other organizations

TABLE 2.2

Sample Budget for a Manufacturing Project

BUDGET MONITORING REPORT

Organizational unit	Machine shop	Job number	1763	Period	January–June	
Total parts needed	6,000	Parts produced to date	2,700	Remaining work	3,300	
Parts per month projection	1,000	Current production per month	900	Difference	(–100)	

Line item	Budgeted amount	Actual expenditures					
		January	February	March	April	May	June
Direct labor	$60,000	$10,000	$10,000	$10,000			
Indirect labor	5,400	900	900	900			
Material	13,200	2,195	3,156	1,032			
Operating supplies	3,000	1,200	0	296			
Equipment repair	5,400	0	0	3,600			
Total	$87,000	$14,295	$14,056	$15,828			

Source: Reprinted with the permission of Merrill, an imprint of Macmillan Publishing Company from INDUSTRIAL SUPERVISION IN THE AGE OF HIGH TECHNOLOGY by David L. Goetsch. Copyright © 1992 by Merrill Publishing Company.

use budgets to break down how much to spend on such items as wages and salaries, rent, supplies, insurance, and so on. These items would be part of an *operating budget*; big-ticket items such as purchases of machinery or a new building would more likely be accounted for separately as part of a *capital budget*.

Some organizations expect their supervisors to prepare a budget showing what they think they will need to spend in the next year to meet departmental goals or carry out a specific project. Table 2.2 illustrates a sample budget for a manufacturing project. The line items show different categories of expenses. The first column of figures contains the amounts budgeted to be spent in each category. To the right are columns where the supervisor records how much was actually spent each month in each category. These actual amounts are used by the supervisor in controlling, which is described in Chapter 5.

In preparing a budget, the supervisor typically has rules and guidelines to follow. For example, one company may say that pay increases for the department as a whole must be no more than 5 percent of the previous year's budget for salaries. Another organization may specify a total amount that the department may spend, or it may give the supervisor a formula for computing the department's overhead expenses. Based on these guidelines, the supervisor then recommends how much to spend in each area. In most cases, the supervisor and his or her boss review the budget. The supervisor must be willing to modify it when higher-level managers require a change.

scheduling
Setting a precise timetable for the work to be done.

Scheduling The supervisor needs to continually think about how much work the department needs to accomplish in a given time period and how it can meet its deadlines. Setting a precise timetable for the work to be done is known as **scheduling**. This includes deciding which activities will take priority over others, as well as deciding who will do what tasks and when.

Many organizations expect supervisors to use one or more of the techniques and tools that have been developed to help with scheduling. Two of the most widely used techniques are Gantt charts and PERT networks. A **Gantt chart** is a scheduling tool that lists the activities to be completed and uses horizontal bars to graph how long each activity will take, including its starting and ending dates. Figure 2.3 is an example of a Gantt chart.

Gantt chart
Scheduling tool that lists the activities to be completed and uses horizontal bars to graph how long each activity will take, including its starting and ending dates.

The **program evaluation and review technique (PERT)** is a scheduling tool that identifies the relationships among tasks as well as the amount of time each task will take. To use this tool, the planner creates a PERT network such as the one in Figure 2.4. In this figure, the circles represent the tasks that must be completed in order to change a tire. The arrows between the circles represent the activities needed to carry out each task. The numbers in the circles represent the order of tasks, and the numbers above the arrows represent the time required to complete each task. An important piece of information in a PERT network is the *critical path*—the sequence of tasks that will require the greatest amount of time. A delay that occurs in the critical path will cause the entire project to fall behind.

program evaluation and review technique (PERT)
Scheduling tool that identifies the relationships among tasks as well as the amount of time each task will take.

Besides these tools, supervisors may use a computer to help with scheduling. Many project management software packages have been developed for this application. Programs such as *Superproject for Windows*, *Project Scheduler 5*, and *Time Line* make it easier for a planner to create and update Gantt charts, look at graphs of cost along with time, and even schedule multiple projects, specifying the priorities of each.[3]

Setting Objectives

A part of the planning process that goes on, formally or informally, at every level of management is setting objectives. For the supervisor, objectives can range from the tasks he or she intends to accomplish on a certain day to the level of production the department is to achieve for the year. To be an effective planner, the supervisor should be familiar with how to set good objectives.

Characteristics of Effective Objectives

To be effective—that is, to do their job of telling people how to focus their efforts—objectives should have certain characteristics. They should be written, measurable, clear, specific, and challenging but achievable (Figure 2.5).

Sometimes it might seem like a nuisance to write down objectives. But putting them *in writing* gives them importance; employees can see they are something to which managers have devoted time and thought. When objectives are in writing, the people who are to carry them out can look them up for a reminder of what they are supposed to be accomplishing, and they can take time to make sure they under-

FIGURE 2.3

Sample Gantt Chart for Building a Church

Activities	Mar '91					Apr '91					May '91				Jun '91				Jul '91				
	25	4	11	18	25	1	8	15	22	29	6	13	20	27	3	10	17	24	1	8	15	22	29
1. Elev. shaft wall system		▀																					
2. Interior framing		▀▀▀																					
3. Rough fire protection		▀▀▀																					
4. Rough plumbing		▀▀▀▀																					
5. Rough HVAC		▀▀▀▀▀▀																					
6. Hydraulic elevator		▀▀▀▀▀▀▀																					
7. Rough electrical		▀▀▀▀▀▀▀▀																					
8. Gypsum drywall			▀▀▀																				
9. Slate roofing											▀▀												
10. Misc. metals			▀	▀	▀	▀		▀		▀	▀	▀	▀	▀	▀								
11. Waterproofing				▀																			
12. Stair following lift				▀																			
13. Exterior masonry (West elev.)						▀▀▀																	
14. Interior taping & painting						▀▀▀▀▀▀▀▀▀▀▀▀▀▀▀																
15. Exterior stucco (West elev.)								▀															
16. Exterior masonry (South elev.)								▀▀▀▀															
17. Exterior stucco (Northeast elev.)								▀▀▀▀▀▀															
18. Exterior stucco (South elev.)										▀▀													
19. Exterior masonry (Northeast elev.)										▀▀													
20. Exterior alum windows								▀	▀	▀	▀	▀	▀	▀	▀								
21. Joint Sealers																							

Source: "How to Plan Any Project: A Self-Teaching Guide." Belanger, Thomas C., DMSI, Nashua, NH 03060, 1991. p. 98.

stand the objectives. Finally, writing down objectives forces the supervisor to think through what the objectives say.

Making objectives *measurable* provides the supervisor with a way to tell whether people are actually accomplishing them. Measurable objectives might specify a dollar amount, a time frame, or a quantity to be produced (e.g., number of sales calls made, parts manufactured, VCRs repaired, customers served). The words *maximize* and *minimize* are tip-offs that the objectives are *not* measurable. If the objective is "maximize quality," how will anyone be able to know whether maximum quality has been obtained? Rather, the objective might call for a defect rate of no more than 2 percent or for no customer complaints during the month. Other objectives that are difficult to measure are ones that simply call for something to "improve" or get "better." Again, the person writing the objective should specify a way to measure the improvement.

Making objectives *specific* means spelling out who is to do what, and by when, in order to accomplish the objective. Specific objectives describe the actions people

FIGURE 2.4

PERT Network for Changing a Flat Tire

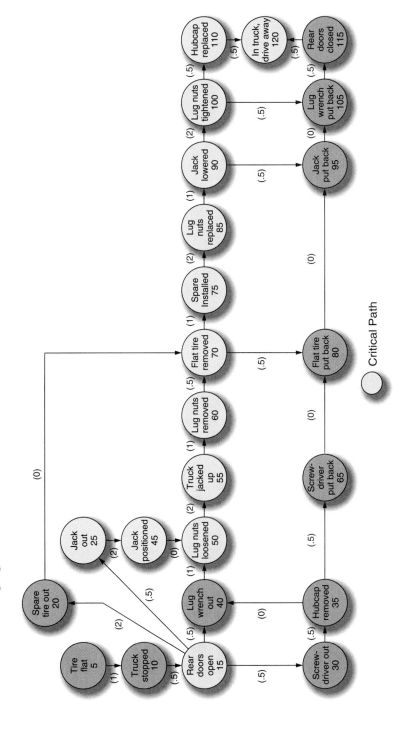

Source: Samuel C. Certo and Lee A. Graf, *Experiencing Modern Management*, 5th ed. (Boston: Allyn and Bacon, 1992), p. 133. Reprinted with permission of Allyn and Bacon.

FIGURE 2.5
Characteristics of Effective Objectives

are to take and what is supposed to result from those actions. For example, instead of saying, "Computer files will be backed up regularly," a specific objective might say, "Each word-processing operator will back up his or her files at the end of each workday." Being specific simplifies the job of ensuring that the objectives are being accomplished; the supervisor knows just what to look for. Also, objectives that are specific help the employees understand what they are supposed to be doing.

When the supervisor needs other people to play a part in accomplishing objectives, those people must understand the objectives. Thus, it is easy to see why objectives should be *clear*. How does the supervisor make sure they are clear? He or she can spell them out in simple language and ask employees whether they understand the objectives. Also, measurable and specific objectives are more apt to be clear than broadly stated guidelines.

Objectives that are *challenging* are most likely to stimulate employees to do their best. Easy objectives are less stimulating. However, the employees have to believe they are *capable of achieving* the objectives. Otherwise, they will just get frustrated or angry at what seem to be unreasonable expectations. Most of us have had the experience of tackling a challenging job, then enjoying the sense of pride and accomplishment that comes with finishing it. In setting goals, the supervisor should remember how stimulating and confidence-building such experiences can be.

Involvement of Employees

To make sure that employees understand objectives and consider them achievable, it helps to involve them in the goal-setting process. When employees are involved, they tend to feel more committed to the objectives, and they may be able to introduce ideas that the supervisor has not thought of. In many cases, employees who help set objectives agree to take on greater challenges than the supervisor might have guessed.

One way to get employees involved in setting objectives is to have them write down what they think would be good objectives for them to accomplish in the coming year (or month or whatever time period). Then the supervisor discusses the ideas with each employee, modifying the objectives to meet the department's overall needs. Another approach is to hold a meeting of the entire work group at which the employees and supervisor develop objectives as a group. (Chapter 17 provides ideas for holding successful meetings.)

Updating Objectives

Once the supervisor has set objectives, he or she should monitor performance and compare it with the objectives. (Chapter 5 discusses this process in detail.) Sometimes the supervisor determines that objectives need to be modified.

When should supervisors update the objectives for their department or work group? They will need to do so whenever top management updates organizational objectives. Also, organizations with a regular procedure for planning will specify regular intervals at which supervisors must review and update their objectives.

Action Plans

action plan
The plan for how to achieve an objective.

When the supervisor has finished setting objectives, he or she must determine how the department will achieve them. The plan for how to achieve an objective is known as an **action plan**. If you think of objectives as being statements of where you want to go, then an action plan is a map that tells you how to get there. For a successful trip, you need to have both kinds of information.

The supervisor creates an action plan by answering the questions *what, who, when, where,* and *how:*

- *What* actions need to be taken? Do sales calls need to be made, customers served in a certain way, goods produced? The supervisor should outline the specific steps involved.
- *Who* will take the necessary steps? The supervisor may do some things him- or herself, but many activities will be assigned to specific employees or groups of employees.
- *When* must each step be completed? With many types of processes, certain steps (those along the critical path) will determine when the whole project is completed. The supervisor should be particularly careful in scheduling those activities.
- *Where* will the work take place? Sometimes this question is easy to answer, but a growing operation may require that the supervisor plan for new space requirements. Some activities may require that the supervisor consider the arrangement of work on the shop floor or the arrangement of items in a warehouse or supply room.

The plan for how to achieve an objective is known as the action plan. At the Springfield, Virginia station for Federal Express, an action plan was designed to reduce the number of packages delivered late. Thanks to better techniques for sorting packages, couriers were on the road 12 minutes earlier, and late packages dropped from 39 to 17 per day. (Federal Express Corporation 1990 Annual Report, p. 10).

Source: © 1992 Comstock, Inc.

- *How* will the work be done? Are the usual procedures and equipment adequate, or does the supervisor need to innovate? Thinking about how the work will be done may alert the supervisor to a need for more training.

Contingency Planning

A lot of people believe in Murphy's law, which says, "If anything can go wrong, it will." Even those who are less pessimistic recognize that things don't always go as planned. A delivery may be delayed by a strike or a blizzard, a key employee may take another job, a "foolproof" computer system may crash. The sign of a good supervisor is, not so much that he or she never has these nasty surprises, but rather that he or she is prepared with ideas on how to respond.

contingency planning
Planning what to do if the original plans don't work out.

Planning what to do if the original plans don't work out is known as **contingency planning**. The wise supervisor has contingency plans to go with every original plan. One useful technique for contingency planning is to review all objectives, looking for areas where something might go wrong. Then the supervisor determines how to respond if those problems do arise.

Contingency planning is not always formal. It would be too time-consuming to create a written contingency plan for every detail of operations. Instead, for

Contingency plans help in times of disaster, but it would have been difficult to write a plan for all the details of operation necessary to conduct business during and after the effects of Hurricane Andrew, which struck Florida in September 1992.

Source: Courtesy of Dan Helms/Compix.

some details, the supervisor simply has in mind how to respond if activities do not go as planned.

Management by Objectives

management by objectives (MBO)
A formal system for planning in which managers and employees at all levels set objectives for what they are to accomplish, after which their performance is measured against those objectives.

Many organizations use a formal system for planning known as **management by objectives (MBO)**. This is a process in which managers and employees at all levels set objectives for what they are to accomplish, after which their performance is measured against those objectives. Basically, MBO involves three steps:

1. All individuals in the organization work with their managers to set objectives, specifying what they are to do in the next operating period (such as a year).
2. Each individual's manager periodically reviews the individual's performance to see whether he or she is meeting the objectives. Typically, these reviews take place two to four times a year. The results of the reviews help the individual and his or her manager decide what corrective actions they need to take, and they provide information for setting future objectives.
3. The organization rewards the individuals based on how close they come to fulfilling the objectives.

FIGURE 2.6

The MBO Process

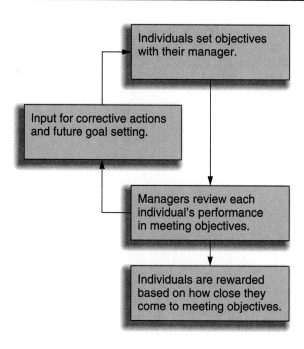

Figure 2.6 summarizes the MBO process, and the case at the end of this chapter describes an actual company's experience with MBO.

For an organization to use MBO effectively, the managers at all levels (especially top management) must be committed to the system. Also, the objectives they set must meet the criteria for effective objectives, described earlier. For example, a salesperson would not merely be expected to "sell more." Rather, he or she would help to develop specific objectives, such as "make forty sales calls a month" and "sell fifty copiers by December 31, 1996." Finally, managers and employees must be able to cooperate in the objective-setting process.

Some people dislike MBO because setting and monitoring the achievement of objectives can be time-consuming and requires a lot of paperwork. However, the organization can benefit from involving employees in setting goals, which may lead to greater commitment in achieving them. Furthermore, the employees can benefit from a system of rewards that is rational and based on performance rather than personality. In light of these advantages, a supervisor may want to use the principles of MBO with the employees in his or her own department even if the organization as a whole does not use a formal MBO system.

Summary

2.1   Identify advantages of planning in organizations.

Planning helps supervisors and other managers set priorities, make decisions, and use resources efficiently. It encourages them to focus on the future and provides a fair way for evaluating performance. It lays the foundation for carrying out the other management functions.

2.2   Differentiate the types of planning that go on at different levels of the organization.

At the top level, managers develop a strategic plan, which spells out the long-term goals of the organization. The plans for divisions, departments, and work groups are known as operational plans and are set by middle managers and supervisors. Operational plans support the strategic plan; they are more specific and focus on a shorter time frame.

2.3   Define *policies*, *procedures*, and *rules*.

Policies are broad guidelines for how to act. Procedures are the steps that must be completed to achieve a specific purpose. Rules are statements of specifically what to do or not to do in a given situation.

2.4   Describe the supervisor's role in the planning process.

Supervisors provide information and estimates to higher-level managers to help them plan. They allocate resources within their department or work group. They often develop a budget proposal. They schedule the work that takes place within their department, using a variety of scheduling tools such as Gantt charts, PERT networks, and project management software.

2.5   List the characteristics of effective objectives.

To be effective, objectives should be written, measurable, clear, specific, and challenging but achievable.

2.6   Explain why supervisors should involve employees in setting objectives and how they can do this.

Involving employees makes it more likely that they will understand objectives and consider them achievable. Employees who help set objectives tend to be more committed to achieving them and may take on greater challenges. They also may contribute ideas the supervisor would not have thought of. To get employees involved, the supervisor can have them write down what they think would be good objectives, then discuss the employees' ideas, modifying them if necessary. The supervisor can also set objectives with the employees during a meeting.

2.7   Describe the role of action plans.

Besides knowing where they want to go, supervisors must know how to get there. Action plans meet this need by detailing how to achieve objectives. The supervisor develops an action plan by deciding what actions need to be taken, who will carry them out, when each step must be completed, where the work will take place, and how the work will be done.

2.8   Explain why and how supervisors develop contingency plans.

Supervisors develop contingency plans because problems arise that interfere with the accomplishment of the original plans. Contingency plans prepare supervisors to handle such problems. Supervisors can develop contingency plans by reviewing their objectives, looking for areas where something might go wrong, and then determining how to respond.

2.9   Describe the use of management by objectives.

Management by objectives is a process in which managers and employees at all levels set objectives for what they are to accomplish; then their performance is measured against those objectives. Employees work with their supervisor in setting the objectives they are to achieve; then the supervisor reviews their performance regularly, comparing it with the objectives. Individuals are rewarded according to how close they come to meeting their objectives.

Key Terms

planning

objectives

goals

strategic planning

operational planning

policies

procedures

rules

budget

scheduling

Gantt chart

program evaluation and review technique (PERT)

action plan

contingency planning

management by objectives (MBO)

Review and Discussion Questions

1. Many supervisors complain that they are too busy "putting out fires" to spend time planning. What is wrong with this view?

2. Do supervisors have a greater role in strategic planning or in operational planning? In carrying out this planning, how far ahead do supervisors generally need to think?

3. What are policies, procedures, and rules? In what ways are they important to the planning process?

4. How do supervisors typically participate in the planning process? What activities do they carry out?

5. Assume you are the supervisor of the machine shop whose budget appears in Table 2.2.
   a. Modify the budgeted amounts to create a budget for a new project of the same size and type. Use the following assumptions and guidelines:
      • The organization says that direct labor costs may increase by no more than 6 percent.
      • You have been instructed to cut expenses for equipment repair by 10 percent.
      • You expect that materials costs will increase about 5 percent.
   b. What additional assumptions did you make in order to create the budget?

6. What is wrong with each of the following objectives? Rewrite each so that it has the characteristics of an effective objective.
   a. Improve the procedure for responding to customer complaints.
   b. Meet or exceed last year's sales quotas.
   c. Minimize the number of parts that are defective.
   d. Communicate clearly with patients.

7. What are some advantages of involving employees in the process of developing objectives? How can supervisors do this?

8. When should supervisors update objectives?

9. Jill Donahue is the supervisor of the telephone operators who handle emergency calls from citizens and dispatch police, fire fighters, and ambulances as needed. For the coming year, she has the objective of reducing the average time it takes for calls to be answered from one minute to half that amount (thirty seconds). How can she go about creating an action plan to achieve this objective? What questions must she answer? Suggest a possible answer or two for each question.

10. As warehouse supervisor, Patrick Johnson is responsible for overseeing the unloading of household appliances delivered from factories, storing them so that they are safe and accessible, and getting them loaded onto the trucks delivering them to stores. Patrick thinks that contingency planning is only for people who don't know how to create good plans in the first place. In his view, a good plan will avoid errors and surprises.

    What do you think of this viewpoint? Should contingency planning be part of Patrick's job? Defend your position.

11. Describe the steps involved in using management by objectives. What are some benefits of using MBO?

A SECOND LOOK

In the story of One Call Does It All Maintenance Company at the beginning of this chapter, how might Tom Kipphut have involved his employees in the planning task described? Do you think involving the employees would have resulted in better planning? Why or why not?

Class Exercise

Assume that the following numbers represent the average daily orders for a variety of products at a fast-food restaurant.

Item	Mon.	Tues.	Wed.	Thurs.	Fri.	Sat.	Sun.
Hamburgers	73	70	72	69	79	82	66
Cheeseburgers	106	100	99	103	114	120	115
Fish sandwiches	56	47	48	50	69	53	51
French fries	171	159	161	156	188	211	202
Soft drinks	212	188	172	170	205	237	245

Imagine that you are a manager of the restaurant and must use such numbers when planning how much food to order. Next month, the chain will be running a promotion featuring hamburgers at half price. Based on this information, discuss the following questions:

1. To plan your food needs for next month, what additional information would you like to have?
2. How do you think the price promotion for hamburgers will affect the daily consumption of each item shown in the table? Try to agree on new numbers to use during the promotion.
3. Based on your new figures, what will you need to order more of during the promotion? What will you need to order less of? About the same? (Keep in mind that you would not order fully prepared hamburgers for your restaurant, you would order buns, meat, and other ingredients.)

CASE

Management by Objectives at Cunningham Communication

When Andrea Cunningham started a public relations agency in Santa Clara, California, she wanted it to be something special. She wanted her firm, Cunningham Communication, Inc. (CCI), to deliver high-quality services by building long-term relationships between its employees and clients. This strategic goal depended on attracting excellent employees and retaining them over the years. In contrast, the normal career path in the PR industry involves hopping from one firm to another.

One of the ways Cunningham seeks to keep her 20-plus employees happy and challenged is with a compensation and goal-setting plan that includes management by objectives (MBO). CCI has job descriptions for each of nine levels of associates. The descriptions include objectives for performing tasks, such as the number of hours per week they will bill clients, as well as types of skills they will need, such as "ability to construct strategic memos to clients." Different salary ranges are tied to each level. Employees determine the level of responsibilities they plan to work toward over the next year, and that selection determines their salary range.

Once a month, each CCI associate meets with his or her boss, or "adviser," to review the associate's work for the previous month. At this meeting, the associate also submits a list of objectives for the coming month. The associate's salary reflects the extent to which he or she meets the objectives and skill levels planned for.

Employees like to know where they stand. Says associate Toni Giusti, "Every month I pretty much knew I was on track." At one point, she was receiving somewhat less than the salary she was working toward because her writing and counseling skills needed improvement. That seemed reasonable to Giusti because of the feedback she was getting from her boss. Giusti said, "Every month your manager would tell you, 'This is the kind of thing that was great this month, and this is what you need to think about next time.' So it wasn't a surprise."

Associate Lisa Goldman likes the control MBO gives her over her work and her career.

"Before [the MBO system]," says Goldman, "goals were less clearly defined, and there wasn't a clear ladder. Now you can get to where you want to be, with more control on *your* part."

1. What is the strategic plan described for CCI? How does the agency attempt to carry out this plan?

2. Does the MBO system described in this case fit the text description of how MBO works? Explain.

3. What benefits does CCI receive from involving employees (associates) in setting objectives?

Source: Adapted from Leslie Brokaw, "Playing for Keeps," *Inc.*, May 1992, pp. 30–32ff.

3

The best executive is the one who has sense *enough to pick good men to do what he wants done, and* self-restraint *enough to keep from meddling with them while they do it.*
—Theodore Roosevelt

The Supervisor as Organizer and Delegator

LEARNING OBJECTIVES

3.1 Describe organization charts.

3.2 Identify basic ways in which organizations are structured.

3.3 Define *authority*.

3.4 Distinguish between line and staff authority and between centralized and decentralized authority.

3.5 Explain how power and responsibility differ from authority.

3.6 Identify the steps in the process of organizing.

3.7 Describe four principles of organizing.

3.8 Discuss why and how supervisors delegate.

3.9 Identify causes of reluctance to delegate.

WHOSE RESPONSIBILITY IS IT?

On April 13, 1992, in a disaster that came to be called the Great Chicago Flood, water from the Chicago River poured into a freight tunnel under downtown Chicago streets, flooding basements and shutting businesses and government offices. According to one estimate, 350 million gallons of water had to be pumped out. How could the tunnel walls have been so neglected as to permit a leak that caused millions of dollars' worth of damage?

One view came from the city's general services commissioner, Benjamin Reyes. In an interview with the *Chicago Tribune*, department head Reyes blamed his subordinates for not taking quick action when they learned of structural problems with the aging tunnel. Said Reyes of his own role, "I didn't do anything wrong. I didn't know anything about it."

A cable television company working in the tunnel had informed Reyes's staff of the leak in February 1992, but the department didn't inspect it until March 16. The cable company told an inspector named James McTigue the tunnel was cracked. In the department's chain of command, McTigue should have informed the department's chief construction engineer, who should have notified a deputy commissioner.

McTigue's version was that the day he learned of the damage from the cable company, he reported it to his supervisor. He researched the company's report, found the leak, and again reported to his supervisors. McTigue added that he told another superior about the problem on March 17, and that manager said he told Reyes.

McTigue and other critics attributed management's inaction in part to a recent reorganization in city departments. In an attempt to make the Public Works department more efficient, it was split in two: Transportation and General Services. Due to layoffs accompanying the reorganization, there were no city employees who could repair the tunnel. Also, several commissioners complained that the reorganization had led to "mass confusion" in early 1992.

Reyes's reasoning that he was not responsible for the crisis was his newness to the department. With 350 other employees, he had been transferred to General Services on January 1, 1992. Said Reyes, "The first contact I had with Jim McTigue was when the water started rushing through the tunnels."

Chicago mayor Richard Daley fired acting transportation commissioner John LaPlante, who had failed to act in spite of receiving an April 2 memo warning of possible disaster. Daley absolved Reyes of responsibility. The mayor reasoned that employees in Reyes's department had informed Transportation, which should have repaired the damage. Although Reyes was in charge of tunnel inspections, the job of freight tunnel inspector had been cut in 1987. Daley sought to fire McTigue, who appealed, claiming he was a scapegoat.

Source: John Kass, "Daley Aide Reyes Denies Tunnel Responsibility," *Chicago Tribune*, April 17, 1992, sec. 2, pp. 1, 8; *Chicago Tribune*, April 20, 1992, sec. 1, pp. 1, 12; John Kass, "City Worker Hits Back at Daley Flood Bashing," *Chicago Tribune*, May 7, 1992, sec. 2, pp. 1, 6. Photo courtesy of *Chicago Tribune*, 1992, world rights reserved.

organizing
The management function of setting up the group, allocating resources, and assigning work to achieve goals.

In the opening story, the organization and reorganization of city departments played a role in the failure to repair damage leading to the Great Chicago Flood. As you read in Chapter 1, **organizing** is the management function of setting up the group, allocating resources, and assigning work to achieve goals. By organizing, supervisors and other managers put their plans into action. When done well, organizing also helps to ensure that the organization is using its resources—especially human resources—efficiently. For this reason, a business that is well organized is in a better position to be profitable.

Managers in even the simplest organizations need to organize. If you were to set up a softball team, you would have to collect equipment, arrange for a place to play, find players, decide what position each is to play, and create a batting lineup. If you were operating a one-person business, you would have to decide where you would work, what activities you would need to accomplish, and whether you should contract with vendors to provide some services.

This chapter describes the ways organizations are structured and the way supervisors organize. The process of organizing includes sharing authority and responsibility. The chapter explains how supervisors share both of these with the people who report to them.

The Structure of the Organization

Some of the most fundamental and far-reaching organizational decisions involve the structure of the organization as a whole. For example, top management could assign managers authority for a particular product, a particular geographic region served by the organization, or a particular specialty such as sales or finance. Supervisors have little, if any, input into such decisions. However, supervisors need to understand how they and their department fit into the big picture, and that includes understanding the structure of the organization.

Organization Charts

Businesspeople have come up with a standard way to draw the structure of an organization: the organization chart. Such charts use boxes to represent the various positions or departments in an organization (usually just at management levels). Lines connecting the boxes indicate who reports to whom. Figure 3.1 is an organization chart showing the structure of an international company. Note, for example, that someone is in charge of all North American operations, and someone is in charge of all international operations; these two managers report to the person who serves as president and chief operating officer of the entire company.

The positions at the top of an organization chart are those with the most authority and responsibility. Logically enough, the people in these positions are referred to as the top managers. By following the lines from the top managers down the chart to the lower levels, you can see which middle managers report to these top managers. In other words, the top managers have authority to direct the work of the middle managers who report to them, and the top managers are

FIGURE 3.1

Organization Chart: An International Company

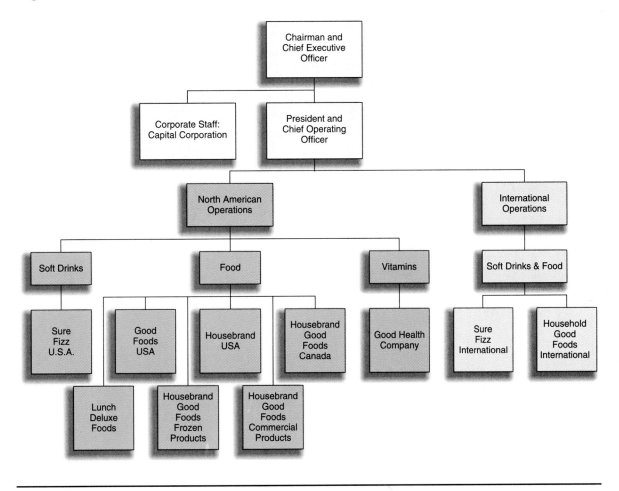

responsible for the performance of those middle managers. The bottom of the chart may show the first-level managers (or sometimes the operative employees). Supervisors are not shown on the chart in Figure 3.1.

Note that organization charts sometimes show only a portion of an organization. Like Figure 3.1, a chart may show just the top levels of management, or it may show a single division in a large company. Reading the titles of the people associated with each box gives an indication of the scope of a particular organization chart.

Being able to understand organization charts enables supervisors to figure out where they fit in the organization and where there might be opportunities for future promotions. Supervisors can see the variety of responsibilities held by others at their level in the organization. Knowing where they fit in helps supervisors see how their department or group contributes to achieving the goals of the organization.

Types of Structures

An organization with more than a handful of people works most efficiently when it is grouped into departments. A **department** is a unique group of resources that management has assigned to carry out a particular task, such as selling the company's products to customers in the Midwest, treating patients with cancer, or teaching mathematics. The way management sets up the departments—an activity called **departmentalization**—determines the type of structure the organization has.

Over the years, organizations have been structured in a limited number of ways. When you look at organization charts, you will probably find that they fall into these categories: functional structure, product structure, geographic structure, and customer structure.

Functional Structure   A functional structure groups personnel and other resources according to the types of work they carry out. For example, a business might have vice-presidents of finance, production, sales, and human resources. Assigned to each vice-president would be the staff needed to carry out these activities. Figure 3.2 is an example of a company with a functional structure. At this company—Wiss, Janney, Elstner Associates, an architectural firm—one vice-president is responsible for operations (that is, the work of all the architects and engineers who provide services to customers), and the other is responsible for administration (that is, support services). Under the vice-president of administration, the organization is divided into such functions as marketing and personnel.

Product Structure   In an organization with a product structure, work and resources are assigned to departments responsible for all the activities related to producing and delivering a particular product or service. In an automobile business, there might be one department for each make of automobile. Colleges and universities are often departmentalized according to subject matter being taught and studied. At the company shown in Figure 3.1, North American operations are departmentalized according to three product categories: soft drinks, food, and vitamins. Figure 3.3 illustrates a product structure at a division of the Evangelical Lutheran Church in America (ELCA). For example, one director is concerned with disaster relief, while another is responsible for health care programs.

Geographic Structure   A geographic structure results when an organization is departmentalized according to the location of the customers being served or the goods or services being produced. A manufacturing company might have a department for each of its factories scattered around the world. An insurance company might have a department for each of its 12 sales territories. The manager of each department would be responsible for producing and/or selling all the company's products or services in that geographic region. At the architectural firm in Figure 3.2, operations are departmentalized on the basis of the cities where the offices are located, including Dallas, Denver, Seattle, and Washington, D.C.

Customer Structure   A customer structure departmentalizes the organization according to the type of customer being served. For example, an aerospace company might have different departments serving business, the military, and the space program. Digital Equipment Corporation recently reorganized its sales force so

department
A unique group of resources that management has assigned to carry out a particular task.

departmentalization
Setting up departments in an organization.

FIGURE 3.2

Functional Structure

Partial organization chart for Wiss, Janney, Elstner Associates

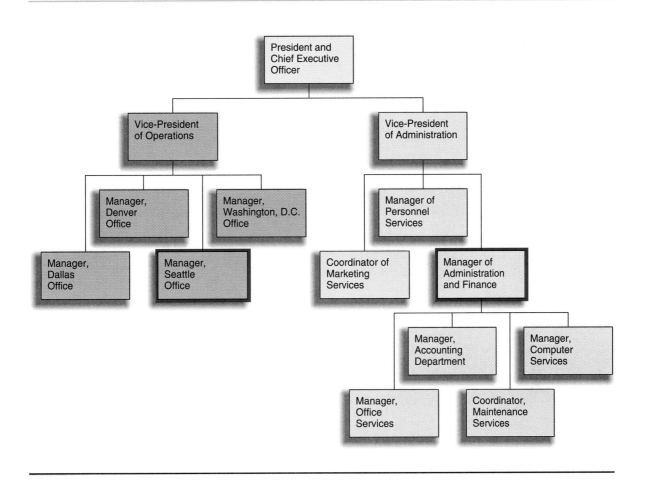

that each account manager is responsible for all locations of each of his or her accounts (for example, all factories or branch offices of a single business) rather than for a single geographic location.[1]

As you can see from the figures, organizations often combine these types of structures. Thus, Figure 3.1 combines geographic and product structures, while Figure 3.2 combines functional and geographic structures. A typical arrangement would be a large corporation with divisions for each of its product lines. Within each division, managers are assigned responsibility for carrying out a particular function, including production and sales. Each sales department in turn is structured geographically.

FIGURE 3.3

Product Structure

Partial organization chart for ELCA Division for Social Ministry

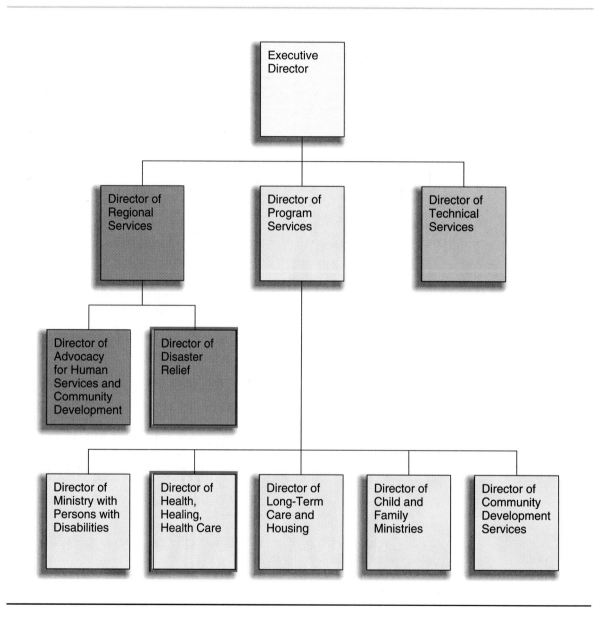

Various combinations of structures occur when the organization forms teams of employees to meet objectives such as improving quality, developing products, or applying new technology. These teams may require diverse kinds of expertise, so the organization brings together people who perform different functions or work

Cindy Munoz is a pipeline foreman for UP Liquid Pipeline, Inc. in Corpus Christi, Texas. The Union Pacific subsidiary ships feedstocks into five refineries in the area, and its pipeline department is an example of departmentalization according to functional structure.

Source: Courtesy of Union Pacific Corporation.

in different geographical areas. Often these teams of employees are grouped according to product or customer. For example, a team formed to develop a new kind of stereo speakers might combine people from sales, engineering, and production functions, under the umbrella of that new product. For a more in-depth discussion of forming and leading teams, see Chapter 17.

In deciding which types of structure to use and how to combine them, managers look for the organizational arrangement that will best achieve the company's goals. As top managers learn from their experiences or as the company and its environment change, it may be necessary to adjust the structure. Thus, the "restructuring" that has occurred at many organizations in recent years consists of adjustments in the structure designed to respond to stiffer competition, tougher economic conditions, or the desire to benefit from new practices such as decision making by teams of employees. The story at the beginning of this chapter illustrates an occasion when such restructuring seems not to have been working smoothly, and the case at the end of the chapter describes restructuring designed to make a hospital a more appealing place to work.

Authority

authority
The right to perform a task or give orders to someone else.

When a supervisor assigns duties, he or she gives employees authority to carry them out. **Authority** is the right to perform a task or give orders to someone else. The supervisor, in turn, has authority in certain areas, and his or her boss has even broader authority.

Dave Tierney (right) is a district sales manager for DeKalb Plant Genetics. Dividing the salesforce departments by districts is an example of departmentalization according to geographic structure.

Source: Courtesy of DeKalb Plant Genetics.

Line, Staff, and Functional Authority

line authority
The right to carry out tasks and give orders related to the organization's primary purpose.

The basic type of authority in organizations is **line authority**, which is the right to carry out tasks and give orders related to the organization's primary purpose. Line authority gives a production supervisor at Deere & Co. the right to direct a worker to operate a machine; it gives the head chef in a restaurant the right to direct the salad chef to prepare a spinach salad using certain ingredients. At the architectural firm represented in Figure 3.2, the manager of the Seattle office has line authority.

staff authority
The right to advise or assist those with line authority.

In contrast, **staff authority** is the right to advise or assist those with line authority. For example, the employees in the human resources department help the other departments by ensuring that they have qualified workers. The quality-control manager at a manufacturing company helps the production manager see that the goods produced are of acceptable quality. In Figure 3.2, the manager of administration and finance has staff authority.

One way to appreciate the difference between line authority and staff authority is to think of a lawyer's job. In a law firm, the lawyer has line authority (he or she delivers the services the firm is selling). But in the legal department of a manufacturing company, the lawyer has staff authority (supporting the firm in producing and selling goods).

Conflicts often arise between line and staff personnel. Line personnel may feel that staff workers are meddling and don't understand their work or how important it is. Staff personnel may conclude that line personnel are resisting new ideas and don't appreciate the valuable assistance they are getting. Whether the supervisor has line or staff authority, it helps to be aware that these kinds of conflicts are common and to try to appreciate the other person's point of view.

functional authority
The right given by higher management to specific staff personnel to give orders concerning an area in which the staff personnel have expertise.

Supervisors and other personnel with staff authority may also have **functional authority**. This is the right given by higher management to specific staff personnel

A supervisor and employee at Cooper's Gardner-Denver Industrial Machinery Division's Sedalia, Missouri, plant perform a final check on industrial blowers before shipment to the customer is made. The supervisor has the line authority to direct employees to perform tasks and to operate equipment to efficiently manufacture and distribute Cooper's products. Their human resources department has the staff authority to assist supervisors with personnel decisions.

Source: Courtesy of Cooper Industries, Inc. Photography, Keith Wood Photography, Dallas, Texas.

to give orders concerning an area in which the staff personnel have expertise. For example, members of the accounting department might have authority to request the information they need to prepare reports. Or the human resources manager might have authority to ensure that all departments are complying with the laws pertaining to fair employment practices.

Centralized and Decentralized Authority

In some organizations, the managers at the top retain a great deal of authority; in others, management grants much authority to middle managers, supervisors, and operative employees. Organizations that share relatively little authority are said to be centralized; in other words, a great deal of authority is centered in a few people. Organizations that share a lot of authority are said to be decentralized.

These terms are relative. In other words, no organization is completely centralized or decentralized, but organizations fall along a range of possibilities from one extreme to another. An example of a decentralized organization is steelmaker Nucor Corporation, which has only four levels of management. Supervisors (foremen) report to department heads (such as a manager of rolling or melting and casting). They in turn report to a general manager of the facility, who reports to top management. With 22 factories, Nucor has only 17 employees at its headquarters, including secretaries and the company's chairman—the smallest headquarters of any *Fortune* 500 company. This structure gives each general manager relatively great independence and control in operating a particular facility.[2] In contrast, a reporter recently determined that General Motors (admittedly a larger company) had 36 vice presidents and more than 20 layers of management.[3] In a more centralized organization such as this, supervisors can expect to have much less decision-making authority.

If supervisors know whether their employer has a centralized or decentralized structure, they have a clue about how much authority they can expect to take on. Consider a supervisor who is comfortable with his or her current job and who wants to take on more authority in order to make improvements in the department. This ambition will probably be viewed less favorably in a centralized organization than in a decentralized one.

Power and Responsibility

power
The ability to get others to act in a certain way.

It is easy to confuse authority with power or responsibility, but when we use the terms precisely, they do not mean the same thing. **Power** is the ability (as opposed to the right) to get others to act in a certain way. The supervisor's authority usually gives him or her a degree of power; employees generally do what their boss asks them to. However, some people have power that comes from sources other than their position in the organization. Also, some people with authority have trouble getting others to act in the desired way. (Chapter 19 discusses power in greater detail.)

responsibility
The obligation to perform assigned activities.

Responsibility is the obligation to perform assigned activities. People who accept responsibility commit themselves to completing an assignment to the best of their ability. Of course, it is easier to do a good job when you have authority to control the necessary resources, including personnel. Also, recall from Chapter 1 that organizations use accountability to see that employees at all levels accept responsibility. In other words, employees who accept responsibility may be rewarded for doing a good job, and those who do not may be punished.

The Process of Organizing

For a supervisor, organizing efforts are generally focused on allocating responsibilities and resources in a way that makes the department or work group operate effectively. In addition, supervisors may want or need to set up teams—that is, groups of employees who work together to meet common goals. (Chapter 17 describes the use of teams in modern organizations and discusses how supervisors can set up and lead teams.)

Whether the organizing job involves setting up a whole new company, restructuring an existing one, or deciding how to organize a department or team, the process should be basically the same. The supervisor or other manager should define the objective, determine what resources are needed, and then group activities and assign duties. This three-step approach, illustrated in Figure 3.4, leads to a structure that supports the goals of the organization.

Define the Objective

As Chapter 1 explained, the management process begins with planning. The manager's other activities should support the objectives developed during the planning process. In the case of organizing, the supervisor or other manager should begin by

FIGURE 3.4
**The Process of
Organizing**

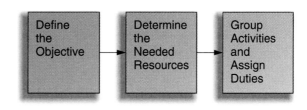

defining what objective the department or work group is supposed to be achieving. If the supervisor does not know, then he or she has not finished planning and should complete that job before trying to organize work.

Determine the Needed Resources

Also as a result of the planning process, the supervisor should have an idea of what resources are needed to achieve goals. Resources include personnel, equipment, and money. The supervisor should review the plans and identify which resources are needed for the particular areas being organized.

Group Activities and Assign Duties

The final step in the process is what most people think of when they think of organizing. The supervisor groups the necessary activities and assigns work to the appropriate employees. The remainder of this chapter discusses how to carry out this step of the organizing process.

Principles of Organizing

Supervisors, especially those who are new to the job, may not be sure how to group activities and assign duties. The task sounds so abstract. Fortunately, management experts have developed some principles that can guide the supervisor. These are the parity principle, unity of command, chain of command, and span of control.

Parity Principle

parity principle
The principle that personnel who are given responsibility must also be given enough authority to carry out that responsibility.

Parity is the quality of being equal or equivalent. Thus, according to the **parity principle**, personnel must have equal amounts of authority and responsibility. In other words, when someone accepts a responsibility, he or she also needs enough authority to be able to carry out that responsibility. If a head teller at a Citicorp branch is responsible for providing high-quality customer service but does not have the authority to fire a surly teller, the head teller will find it difficult or impossible to carry out this responsibility well.

Unity of Command

Meredith Buckle handled the maintenance jobs for a small office building. When building occupants experienced a problem, whether a leaky faucet or a cold office, they would call Meredith. Often, to get a faster response, they would call her repeatedly, complaining about how the problem was interfering with work. As a result, Meredith felt she could never keep everyone satisfied, and she had trouble deciding what jobs to do first.

unity of command
The principle that each employee should have only one supervisor.

According to the principle of **unity of command**, each employee should have only one supervisor. Employees who are receiving orders from several people tend to get confused and aggravated. As a result, they tend to do poor work. The example of Meredith is a case in point. It would have helped her if the building manager had collected messages through his secretary and assigned Meredith the jobs, along with a schedule for completing them.

Sometimes a supervisor finds that his or her boss violates this principle by directing the employees who report to the supervisor. This puts the employees in the awkward position of receiving directions from two people (the supervisor and his or her boss), and it puts the supervisor in the awkward position of needing to correct the behavior of his or her boss. Norma Jean Schmieding, a professor who advises nurses on management issues, recommends that a supervisor tell his or her boss, "I find my staff gets confused when both you and I give them directions. I'd prefer that you discuss with me what you want, and I'll relate it to the staff. Do you have any objections to doing it this way?"[4] Of course, the supervisor should also refrain from directing employees who report to someone else.

Chain of Command

In a chain, each link is connected to no more than two links, one on either side. In an organization, authority progresses like the links on a chain. Along this **chain of command**, authority flows from one level of management to the next, from the top of the organization to the bottom. The story at the beginning of this chapter describes the chain of command that James McTigue was to follow in reporting damage to the freight tunnel.

chain of command
The flow of authority in an organization from one level of management to the next.

When someone skips a level, the principle of chain of command is violated. For example, imagine that Fred Paretsky wants to take Friday off, but he suspects that the division manager will be more sympathetic to his request than his supervisor will. So Fred goes directly to the division manager, who grants permission. Unfortunately, the division manager does not know it, but now Fred's group will be understaffed on Friday because two other workers also will be absent. By violating the chain of command, Fred and the division manager have created a staffing problem that the supervisor might have been able to avoid with some planning. Similarly, in the earlier example of a supervisor's boss directing the supervisor's employees, the boss is violating the chain of command as well as unity of command.

Of course, taking every decision through every level of the organization can sometimes be overly time-consuming and difficult, especially in an organization with many layers of management. The solution is to use common sense. For example, a request for information probably does not have to travel through every layer of management. In contrast, a decision that will affect the group's operations should probably pass through the chain of command.

Span of Control

It is clearly easier to keep track of one employee than to keep track of 100 employees, but it would be tremendously expensive for the organization to hire a supervisor for every employee. The number of people a manager supervises is known as the manager's **span of control**. The more people the manager supervises, the greater his or her span of control.

span of control
The number of people a manager supervises.

In organizing, managers must be aware of how many people they can supervise effectively. Ideally, managers supervise as many people as they can effectively guide toward meeting their goals. That number depends in part on several factors that describe the work situation:[5]

- *Similarity of functions*—The more similar the functions performed by employees, the greater the span of control can be.
- *Geographic closeness*—The closer subordinates are physically, the greater the span of control can be.
- *Complexity of functions*—The simpler the functions performed by subordinates, the greater the span of control can be.
- *Coordination*—This refers to how much time managers must spend coordinating their subordinates' work with that of other employees. The less time they need to spend on coordination, the greater the span of control can be.
- *Planning*—The less time a manager needs to spend on planning, the greater the span of control can be.
- *Availability of staff support*—If staff specialists are available to provide support in a variety of areas, the span of control can be larger.
- *Performance standards*—If there are clear, objective standards for performance, and if employees are familiar with them, the span of control can be larger than in a situation where the supervisor must keep clarifying what is expected of employees.

Characteristics of the managers and employees also are important. Managers may find that as their experience grows, so does the number of people they can supervise effectively. Managers with strong skills in areas such as time management and decision making also are likely to be able to supervise more employees. With regard to employees, the more able they are to work independently, the greater the span of control can be.

Delegating Authority and Responsibility

The concept of organizing implies that one person cannot do all the work of an organization. Even a sole proprietorship (one-person business) usually contracts with outside people to provide some services. For example, a hairdresser who sets up shop might arrange for experts to prepare tax returns, design and print stationery, and provide legal advice. Giving someone else the authority and

delegating
Giving another person the authority and responsibility to carry out a task.

responsibility to carry out a task is known as **delegating**. You can test your awareness of delegation principles by taking the Self-Quiz.

Benefits of Delegating

Whereas the performance of most nonmanagement employees is evaluated in terms of their individual accomplishments, a supervisor's performance is evaluated according to what the department as a whole achieves. Thus, the department's output is of the highest quality and the supervisor looks best when he or she draws on the expertise of employees. In the words of consultant DeAnne Rosenberg, supervisors who delegate are not "limited by what they can do but, rather, by what they can assign."[6] For example, a production supervisor might establish a team of employees to devise ways to make the workplace safer. Those employees are likely to come up with more ideas than the supervisor could identify alone. Some employees might have backgrounds or areas of expertise that lead them to notice needs for improvement that the supervisor might never have thought of.

A supervisor who delegates also has more time available for the jobs only a supervisor can do, such as planning and counseling. Kelly Hancock, who supervises the employees who take orders for classified ads at the *Toronto Sun*, says, "Delegating gives me more opportunity to do tasks of a more pressing, creative nature. I can work on special projects…such as sales contests for the staff." One way to think of this benefit of delegating is that it is an important tool for time management (discussed in Chapter 11). In the example of the production supervisor, if he or she handled all aspects of safety, it could take weeks just to identify and describe safety problems and solutions. That time might be better spent in other activities such as scheduling work and arranging for employees to receive various types of training.

Another benefit of delegating is the effect it has on employees. Delegation of work to employees gives them a chance to develop their skills and their value to the organization. Depending on the kinds of tasks delegated, this can enhance their career and their earning potential. It can also make employees' work more interesting. As will be discussed in Chapter 9, it is reasonable to expect that employees who are more interested in their work and more involved in meeting the organization's objectives are likely to do higher-quality work and remain with the organization longer. Thus, in the example, the production employees who serve on the safety team might find that this added responsibility leads them to care more about the quality of their day-to-day work.

These benefits of delegating are the reason that many organizations use employee involvement to improve the quality of their goods and services (see Chapter 6). In other words, they delegate to employees decision-making authority and responsibility in a variety of areas. The hope is that employees will provide more insight and expertise than managers can provide alone, and that this participation will make employees more committed to doing their best.

The Process of Delegating

When delegating effectively, the supervisor is not just handing out jobs at random. Instead, he or she should be following a logical process: deciding what work

SELF-QUIZ   *Test Your Understanding of Delegation*

Put a check (✓) next to the correct answer.

1. There are some tasks a supervisor should never delegate.

_____ True   _____ False

2. If you want something done right, it is best to do it yourself.

_____ True   _____ False

3. Delegation is an important motivational tool.

_____ True   _____ False

4. Effective delegation involves transferring responsibility to another person.

_____ True   _____ False

5. The degree to which a supervisor can delegate is defined by the competence of his or her subordinates.

_____ True   _____ False

6. The biggest problem with delegating is the increased possibility of mistakes.

_____ True   _____ False

7. Controls and feedback are necessary parts of every delegated task.

_____ True   _____ False

8. In delegating, supervisors have a choice of a range of degrees of responsibility and authority that they can give an employee.

_____ True   _____ False

9. Not every supervisor has a need to delegate.

_____ True   _____ False

10. There are some tasks that should not be delegated because it takes more time to delegate them than to do them.

_____ True   _____ False

Answer Key

1.	True	6.	False
2.	False	7.	True
3.	True	8.	True
4.	False	9.	False
5.	True	10.	True

Source: Adapted from David Engler, *Delegating Effectively* (Vital Learning Corp., 1986), pp. 5–7.

to delegate, assigning the work, creating an obligation, granting authority, and following up. Figure 3.5 illustrates this process, and the "Tips from the Firing Line" box on page 63 suggests how to delegate effectively.

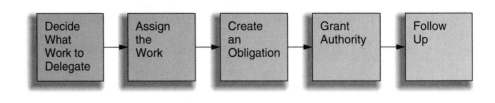

FIGURE 3.5

The Process of Delegating

Decide What Work to Delegate   There are several ways to select which tasks to delegate. When an employee knows how to do a particular task better than the supervisor, it certainly makes sense to delegate that task. Another approach is to select simple tasks that employees clearly can handle. For example, Kelly Hancock of the *Toronto Sun* has her employees handle administrative duties such as counting the lines for birth and death notices. The supervisor also can delegate the tasks that he or she finds most boring. This approach can backfire, however, if employees perceive they are always being picked to do the dirty work. Tasks performed routinely are good candidates for delegation because it may be worth the effort to train employees to do them.

Of course, there are some tasks the supervisor should *not* delegate. These include activities that involve personnel matters and activities assigned specifically to the supervisor. Thus, the supervisor should not assign duties such as appraising performance and resolving conflicts. Likewise, if a sales supervisor's boss has asked her to fly to Vancouver in order to resolve a customer complaint, it would be inappropriate for the supervisor to hand over this assignment to someone else.

Assign the Work   The supervisor begins the delegation process by telling employees what they are supposed to do. In delegating a particular task, the supervisor considers who is available, asking questions such as the following:[7]

- Who can do the job best?
- Who can do it least expensively?
- Who can save the most time?
- Who would gain the most growth from the assignment?

The supervisor also weighs the personalities involved, safety considerations, and any company policies or union rules that may apply. Notice that supervisors can be most effective in carrying out this step when they know their employees well.

When two jobs must be done at the same time and the same person is best qualified to do both, the process of selecting an employee to do the work becomes quite complex. In such cases, the supervisor must set priorities. The supervisor must consider how important the particular task is to achieving the department's goals and serving customers. If it is not clear which jobs should have greater priority, the supervisor should check with his or her boss.

When assigning work, the supervisor must be sure that the employees understand what they are supposed to be doing and have the knowledge and skills needed to do it. (Employees should be able to exercise some freedom in deciding

Effective Delegation

To succeed in delegating, supervisors can follow these suggestions:

- Give employees freedom to carry out activities in their own way.
- Discuss and agree on desired results and performance standards for delegated tasks.
- Encourage employees to take an active role in defining tasks, implementing them, and communicating progress.
- When possible, make employees responsible for carrying out an entire project or task.
- Explain how delegated tasks are relevant to larger projects or to the goals of the department or organization.

- Give employees the authority they need to complete tasks.
- Give employees access to any additional information, people, or other resources they need to carry out tasks.
- Make sure employees have the training and guidance they need to succeed at the delegated tasks.
- When possible, delegate tasks according to employees' interests and abilities.

Source: Samuel C. Certo, *Principles of Modern Management*, 5th ed. (Boston: Allyn and Bacon, 1992), p. 298.

exactly how to carry out the assignment, however.) Employees also need to know which jobs have the greatest priority. To communicate this information clearly, it helps to be specific and to ask employees to restate the assignment in their own words. (Chapter 7 provides more information on how to communicate clearly.)

Create an Obligation When the supervisor makes an assignment, he or she needs to be sure that the employee accepts responsibility for carrying it out. Since a sense of responsibility comes from within a person, supervisors cannot force employees to feel responsible. Fortunately, many employees willingly take on responsibility as a matter of course. In addition, by making employees accountable for their actions, supervisors lead them to accept responsibility. The supervisor can encourage employees to accept responsibility by involving them in making decisions and by listening to their ideas. Workers who feel involved are more apt to feel responsible.

Although the employee should accept responsibility for carrying out a task, this does not mean that the supervisor gives up the responsibility for its proper completion. Rather, the organization will still hold the supervisor accountable. Therefore, following delegation, both parties have responsibility for the work. The supervisor's job becomes one of seeing that the task is completed and meets quality standards. The supervisor does so through the management function of controlling, described in Chapter 5.

Failure to understand this principle of delegation can cause major problems. According to professor and consultant Peter F. Drucker, one of the reasons the Reagan administration's "Irangate" policies became a scandal was that the administration confused delegation of authority with abdication of responsibility. Therefore, it failed to exercise tight control over those who carried out the policy, allowing them to "protect" the president by keeping secrets from him.[8]

As manager of implementation for Walgreen Drug Stores, Dan Manning (right) completed scanning installation chainwide for Walgreens in 1991. "Scanning Manning" accomplished the massive effort by granting the authority for training to employees such as Lisa Avella (left), Chicago North Suburban District trainer, who is pictured with Assistant Store Manager Paul Arends (center).

Source: © 1991 Walgreen Annual Report.

Grant Authority   Along with responsibility, supervisors must give employees the authority they need to carry out their jobs. This is how supervisors follow the parity principle, discussed earlier in the chapter. Thus, if a supervisor at Abbott Laboratories gives a researcher responsibility to carry out a particular procedure, the researcher must also be given the authority to obtain the materials and equipment he or she needs to do the job.

Follow Up   After assigning duties and authority to carry them out, the supervisor needs to give the employees some freedom to act independently and creatively. However, this does not mean that the supervisor should abandon employees to succeed or fail on their own; after all, the supervisor, too, is responsible for the success of the work. Therefore, the supervisor should make sure that employees know he or she is available for guidance and should set forth a plan for periodically checking on the progress of the work. Perhaps the supervisor will find that employees need additional information in order to complete a task, or perhaps they simply need praise for the work they have done so far.

If employees' performance of an unfamiliar task is less than perfect, the supervisor should not be discouraged from delegating in the future. Everyone needs time to learn, and disappointing performances may offer a chance for the supervisor to learn what is needed to strengthen employees' skills. In addition, poor performance may have resulted from the way the work was delegated, not from a problem with the employees. The supervisor can check whether he or she has observed the dos and don'ts of delegation listed in Table 3.1.

TABLE 3.1	Do	Don't
Some Dos and Don'ts of Delegating	Establish goals and performance standards for the tasks.	Delegate responsibilities without the necessary authority and training.
	Tell employees what to do, not how to do it.	Sit back and wait for employees to sink or swim.
	Be familiar with employees' strengths and interests.	Delegate personnel problems, most planning activities, and tasks specifically assigned to the supervisor, such as taking a trip, attending a meeting or seminar, and serving on a committee.
	Delegate on the basis of employee interests when possible.	
	Delegate authority as well as responsibility.	Be afraid of delegating too much.
	Assign entire projects when possible, rather than portions of a project.	Expect perfection the first time.
	Practice and encourage good communication.	
	Give employees time to try before offering assistance.	

Reluctance to Delegate

Ruby Singh works late every night, reviewing all her employees' work and preparing detailed instructions for them for the next day. Her own boss has suggested that she give the workers more freedom, which would save her a lot of time and would probably make them more satisfied with their work. However, Ruby is afraid that if she does not keep close tabs on them, the department's performance will suffer.

Ruby is hardly alone in her reluctance to delegate authority and responsibility to employees. In a recent study, economics professor Peter Sassone found that managers spent only 30 percent of their time doing work that could not be delegated to lower-level employees.[9] Assuming that this means organizations are paying too much to get the rest of the work done, Sassone estimates that the failure to delegate costs the average corporation an extra 15 percent in payroll costs.

Many supervisors are convinced that they are able to do a better job than their employees can. They might even say, "If you want something done right, you have to do it yourself." Often they may be correct, but the overall, long-term performance of the department requires that the supervisor let employees work up to their potential. This means that the supervisor must overcome reluctance, delegate work, and let employees learn from their experiences. If employees really seem unable to carry out the jobs that need to be done, the supervisor should see whether the department's hiring and training practices need improvement.

As mentioned earlier, delegating frees supervisors to concentrate on the tasks they do best or that only a supervisor can do. Sometimes a supervisor is more comfortable being an expert at employees' work than struggling with such supervisory responsibilities as motivating employees and resolving conflicts. However, he or she must overcome that discomfort or fear, because the organization needs supervisors who supervise.

Summary

3.1 Describe organization charts.
Organization charts are a standard way to draw the structure of an organization. Boxes represent the departments or positions, and connecting lines indicate reporting relationships. The positions at the top of the organization chart have the most authority and responsibility.

3.2 Identify basic ways in which organizations are structured.
Unless they are very small, organizations are grouped into departments. An organization with a functional structure groups personnel and other resources according to the types of work they carry out. A product structure groups work and resources according to the product being produced and delivered. In a geographic structure, the departments are set up according to the location of the customers being served or the goods or services being produced. A customer structure departmentalizes the organization according to the category of customer being served.

3.3 Define *authority*.
Authority is the right to perform a task or give orders to someone else.

3.4 Distinguish between line and staff authority and between centralized and decentralized authority.
Line authority is the right to carry out tasks and give orders related to the organization's primary purpose. Staff authority is the right to assist those with line authority. Personnel with staff authority may also be given functional authority, or the right to give orders related to some aspect of their area of expertise. Authority is centralized when much of it is retained by top management. When top management shares a relatively large amount of authority, the organization's authority is decentralized.

3.5 Explain how power and responsibility differ from authority.
Power is the ability, as opposed to the right, to get others to act in a certain way. Authority may enhance a person's power. Responsibility is the obligation to perform assigned activities. A person who has responsibility also needs enough authority to do a good job.

3.6 Identify the steps in the process of organizing.
To organize a department or work group, the supervisor should first define the goal of the organization, then determine what resources are needed. Finally, the supervisor groups activities and assigns duties.

3.7 Describe four principles of organizing.
According to the parity principle, personnel who are given responsibility must also be given enough authority to carry out that responsibility. The principle of unity of command states that each employee should have only one supervisor. A chain of command is the flow of authority from one level of the organization to the next; most decisions and information should flow along the chain of command. Finally, supervisors and other managers should have an appropriate span of control; the best number for a specific situation depends on a variety of factors.

3.8 Discuss why and how supervisors delegate.
Supervisors delegate to enhance the quality of the department's and supervisor's performance by drawing on the expertise of employees. Delegation also frees time for supervisory tasks. It may improve employee morale and performance by allowing employees to develop their skills and by making their work more interesting. To delegate,

supervisors follow a five-step process: decide what work to delegate, assign the work, create an obligation, grant authority, and follow up. When delegating, supervisors must make sure employees understand and are able to do the work, and they retain the responsibility to see that the work is done properly.

3.9   Identify causes of reluctance to delegate. Many supervisors are reluctant to delegate because they believe no one else can do the job as well. They may not want to give up activities they enjoy. Some supervisors are more comfortable doing what their employees should be doing than in carrying out supervisory responsibilities.

Key Terms

organizing	staff authority	unity of command
department	functional authority	chain of command
departmentalization	power	span of control
authority	responsibility	delegating
line authority	parity principle	

Review and Discussion Questions

1. What is organizing? Which of the following organizing activities is a supervisor likely to carry out?
   a. determining the structure of the organization
   b. delegating work to employees
   c. scheduling activities in the department
2. As shown in Figure 3.6 (page 68), operations at Joslyn Power Products Corporation include manufacturing engineering (planning how to make products and maintaining the machinery), production, materials planning, and purchasing. Based on the information in this organization chart, answer the following questions.
   a. Which person(s) is(are) middle managers?
   b. Which are supervisors?
   c. What type of structure is this? How can you tell?
3. As shown in Figure 3.7 (page 69), the management of Rosary College includes deans with responsibility for three graduate schools plus the undergraduate faculty. Based on this information, what type of organizational structure does the school have? Explain.
4. Which of the following supervisors have primarily line authority? Which have staff authority?

   a. the production supervisor at a publishing company, who is responsible for getting books typeset and printed
   b. the housekeeping supervisor at a hospital
   c. the word-processing supervisor at a law firm
   d. the payroll department supervisor for a fire department
5. In recent years, many organizations have become more decentralized. Typically this change involves eliminating middle-management jobs and sharing more control with those at lower levels of the organization. How do you think this affects the role of supervisors in those organizations?
6. Does someone with authority always have power? Does a person who accepts responsibility necessarily have authority? Explain.
7. What are the steps in the process of organizing? How would they apply to the manager of an Olive Garden restaurant who needs to schedule employees? Explain in general how this supervisor could follow each step.
8. Describe each of the following principles of organizing.
   a. parity principle

FIGURE 3.6

Partial Organization Chart for Joslyn Power Products Corporation

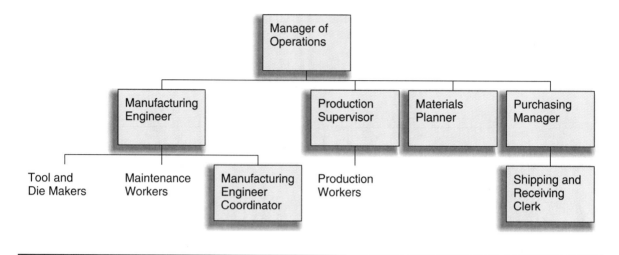

b.   unity of command
c.   chain of command
d.   span of control

9.   A production supervisor at a company that makes furniture learns about the factors that should influence the span of control. The supervisor believes that his own span of control is too large for him to supervise effectively. Is there anything a person in his position can do? If not, explain why. If so, suggest what he can try.

10.   Harry Jamison, CPA, is planning to set up a business to prepare tax returns. Harry is the only person in the business, at least for now. Can he delegate any work? Should he? Explain.

11.   Some supervisors find it difficult to delegate authority and responsibility. What are some causes of this problem?

> **A SECOND LOOK**
>
> The story at the beginning of this chapter describes some events leading up to the Great Chicago Flood. Based on the information given, which of the people named do you think were responsible for the disaster? To what extent do you think the organization of the city departments was to blame? Explain.

Class Exercise

Divide the class into groups of five or six students. Each group is to prepare a one- to three-minute presentation on any of the following topics:

*   A summary of the material in Chapter 3.
*   An example of how an actual company is organized.

*   A real or fictional anecdote about delegating, such as a summary of a real supervisor's experience or a skit showing how not to delegate.

The instructor will decide whether the presentations are to take place after a designated preparation time during class or during another class session.

FIGURE 3.7
Partial Organization Chart for Rosary College

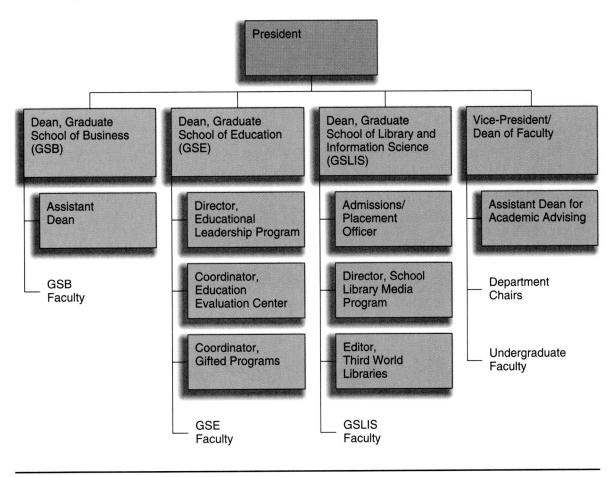

1. Decide what you are trying to accomplish. Which topic will you cover? How do you want to present it? Will you need to do research?
2. Determine the needed resources. Will you have audiovisual aids? Costumes or props? What activities will need to be done?
3. Group activities and assign duties. Who will do the various activities? What is your basis for delegating these tasks? How will you get your presentation ready on time and keep it within the required time limit?

After each group has made its presentation, the class should discuss the process of organizing the presentations. Which presentations were most interesting? What made them work? Were responsibilities shared fairly within your group? Why or why not? What different skills did you see in group members? Did this affect which tasks each group member took on? How would you have handled this project differently if you had been the supervisor of the group, rather than a member of the group?

CASE

Restructuring to Attract Employees

During the late 1980s, the Robert Wood Johnson University Hospital, located in New Brunswick, New Jersey, found that demand for its services was growing but that the pool of nurses and other workers was shrinking. The need to create a work environment that would attract and retain employees provided an impetus to revise the hospital's structure.

Rather than structuring jobs based on the workers' specializations, the new organization has a team of employees serving the needs of a group of patients. Thus, the Support Services Division no longer has departments for housekeeping, dietary needs, supplies, and so on. Instead, employees in the division now hold the position of support service host or hostess, which combines aspects of the previous jobs of housekeeper, dietary aide, supply clerk, and nurse aide. These employees are no longer clustered together according to function but are located on the patient care units, where they can be near the patients they are supposed to be serving.

In their new role as part of a patient care team, the primary nurses have more time to devote to direct patient care. The nurses' supervisor, the head nurse, is no longer primarily concerned with personnel issues but acts as head of a department providing a variety of services. Instead of focusing his or her efforts on telling nurses what to do, the head nurse now focuses on coordinating the efforts of the team members and making it possible for them to work effectively. This requires time in developing staff members' skills and in planning for the future of the patient care unit.

1. Based on the information in the case, how was Robert Wood Johnson University Hospital departmentalized before the changes in its organization? (In other words, what type of structure did it have?) How was it departmentalized afterward?
2. How did changing the structure of the organization affect the job of the head nurse?
3. Do you think these changes are likely to succeed in meeting the hospital's objectives to attract and keep nurses and other staff members? Explain.

Source: Mary Crabtree Tonges, "Work Designs: Sociotechnical Systems for Patient Care Delivery," *Nursing Management*, January 1992, pp. 27–31.

4

Leadership is not a spectator sport. Leaders don't sit in the stands and watch. But hero myths aside, neither do leaders join in the game to substitute for the players. Leaders coach. They show others how to behave, on and off the field. They demonstrate what is important by how they spend their time, by the priorities on their agenda, by the questions they ask and the people they see.

—James M. Kouzes and Barry Z. Posner, "The Credibility Factor: What Followers Expect from Their Leaders"

The Supervisor as Leader

LEARNING OBJECTIVES

4.1 Discuss the possible link between personal traits and leadership ability.

4.2 Describe leadership styles that a supervisor might adopt.

4.3 Explain contingency theories of leadership.

4.4 Identify criteria for choosing a leadership style.

4.5 Describe guidelines for giving directions to employees.

4.6 Tell why supervisors need to understand and improve their views of themselves.

4.7 Explain how supervisors can develop and maintain good relations with their employees, boss, and peers.

LEADERSHIP WITH STYLE

After years as a pro-football coach and a commentator for NBC, Bill Walsh accepted a position as head coach at Stanford University. The move surprised many observers because going from professional to college football looked like a step down (and involved a pay cut). The change came despite Walsh's notable track record as coach of the San Francisco 49ers, including three Super Bowl victories. Walsh has a reputation as being an excellent mentor of quarterbacks and developer of offensive tactics.

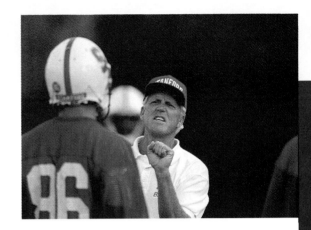

Walsh explains his desire to coach at Stanford as being an opportunity to return to the kind of work he loves. In fact, Walsh accepted Stanford's initial offer and did not seek a lot of extras. Says Ted Leland, Stanford's athletic director, "I said, 'Take six cars.' He said, 'No, no, I only need one.'" Walsh is drawn to opportunities for teaching others the game. At Stanford, he develops not only the players but also the assistant coaches, some of whom are former 49ers with coaching experience.

Walsh's style is informal. He asks players to use his first name. Walsh's sense of humor can surprise those who do not yet know him well. In his early days on the job, he baffled players by disguising himself as a bellhop and trying to get tips from players exiting the team bus at the hotel. Observes junior quarterback Steve Stenstrom, "In the beginning he would say something funny, but we weren't sure we should laugh. Now we laugh at his jokes every day. He keeps us loose."

At the same time, Walsh insists on high quality. For example, he did not hesitate to teach the Stanford players the offense he used as coach of the 49ers. "The whole network of terms had to be learned and applied," he explains, "with really no room for mistakes."

Some people have interpreted certain of Walsh's actions as evidence that he is unfeeling. For example, when he left the 49ers, he never called the players together to announce his retirement. However, Walsh says of himself, "You want to get up and make an emotional speech, and you can't because you know your nerve endings are exposed. You know you'll never be able to finish." He has also found it difficult—but necessary—to take actions that individual players will not like but that are necessary for the team's overall performance.

One person who gives high marks to Walsh's leadership style is James Stockdale, who was Ross Perot's running mate in the 1992 presidential election. Says Stockdale, "He is absolutely straight with his men. No matter what pressure he was under, he never lashed out at anybody.... No one can top Bill for compassionate, clean effectiveness."

Sources: Kenny Moore, "Back to School," *Sports Illustrated*, November 2, 1992, pp. 42–44ff; and Paul Witteman, "The Second Coming," *Time*, November 2, 1992, pp. 62–64. Photo courtesy of Peter Read Miller/*Sports Illustrated*.

leading
The management function of influencing people to act or not act in a certain way.

When the supervisor knows what the department should be doing and who should be doing it, the job becomes one of getting people to do what is required of them. As you learned in Chapter 1, the management function of influencing people to act or not act in a certain way is known as **leading**. In other words, supervisors must be leaders. The opening quote for the chapter provides one view of what this entails.

This chapter takes a look at what makes leadership work. It describes a variety of leadership styles and discusses how to give directions. The chapter concludes by discussing how supervisors can effectively relate with the various people in an organization.

Characteristics of a Successful Leader

According to business professor Paul B. Malone III, an important distinction between managers and leaders is that whereas a manager focuses just on getting a task done, a leader focuses on getting it done in a way that gives employees a feeling of accomplishment and willingness to follow the leader again.[1] Are some people better equipped to do this than others? Figure 4.1 shows the results of a survey that asked over 5,200 top-level managers to identify the traits they most admire and look for in a leader.[2] As you can see from the graph, most managers seek leaders who are honest, competent, forward-looking, and inspiring.

To find out whether some people are natural leaders, social scientists have studied the personalities of effective leaders, looking for traits they hold in common. Presumably, such traits would be predictors of good leadership. Here are some traits that might be considered significant:

- *Sense of responsibility*—A person who is promoted to a supervisory position is given responsibility for the work of others as well as for his or her own performance. Supervisors must be willing to take this responsibility seriously.
- *Self-confidence*—A supervisor who believes in his or her ability to get the job done will convey confidence to employees.
- *High energy level*—Many organizations expect supervisors to willingly put in long hours to handle the variety of duties that come with the job. Some supervisory positions are also physically challenging, requiring that the supervisor actively observe and participate in what is happening in the workplace.
- *Empathy*—In settling disputes, answering questions, and understanding needs, supervisors need to be sensitive to the feelings of employees and higher management. Supervisors who have difficulty understanding what makes people tick will be at a disadvantage.

internal locus of control
The belief that you are the primary cause of what happens to yourself.

- *Internal locus of control*—An **internal locus of control** is the belief that you are the primary cause of what happens to yourself. In contrast, people with an *external locus of control* tend to blame others or events beyond their control when something goes wrong. People with an internal locus of control are thought to be better leaders because they try harder to take charge of events.
- *Sense of humor*—People with a good sense of humor are more fun to work with and to work for. (Of course, this means appropriate humor, not racist or sexist anecdotes and usually not rehearsed jokes that are unrelated to work.) Communications consultant Roger Ailes reports that among people who lose

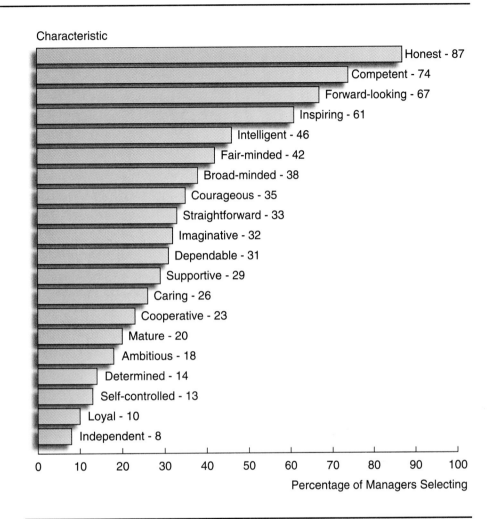

FIGURE 4.1

What Managers Admire and Look for in a Leader

Characteristic

- Honest - 87
- Competent - 74
- Forward-looking - 67
- Inspiring - 61
- Intelligent - 46
- Fair-minded - 42
- Broad-minded - 38
- Courageous - 35
- Straightforward - 33
- Imaginative - 32
- Dependable - 31
- Supportive - 29
- Caring - 26
- Cooperative - 23
- Mature - 20
- Ambitious - 18
- Determined - 14
- Self-controlled - 13
- Loyal - 10
- Independent - 8

Percentage of Managers Selecting

Source: Data from James M. Kouzes and Barry Z. Posner, "The Credibility Factor: What Followers Expect from Their Leaders," *Management Review*, January 1990, p. 33.

their jobs, the most common cause is personality conflicts, and the most common reason for disliking someone is that the person takes him- or herself too seriously—the person lacks a sense of humor. Observes Ailes, "It's important to take your *job* seriously. But people who take *themselves* too seriously tend to believe that their title or their intelligence makes them more important than others."[3]

Using a focus on traits such as these, ask yourself whether you have leadership qualities.

While these traits do sound plausible as characteristics of a successful leader, results of the various studies of leadership traits have been inconsistent. Some studies have found one set of traits to be significant, and others have identified a completely different set of traits. As a result, research has not established a clear link between personality traits and leadership success. So, if you have most of the traits

The U.S. Air Force claims to know the traits necessary for good leadership and recognizes one such leader in this ad, hoping to attract others with similar qualities.

Source: Painted by SSGT. Ruben Armenta, U.S. Air Force.

described here, you may be a successful leader, but your success is not guaranteed. Also, if you do not have many of these traits, you need not be discouraged; you can still develop the skills that effective leaders use.

Leadership Styles

Anita O'Donnell runs a tight ship; she lays down the rules and tolerates no deviation from them. Greg Petersen focuses on what he perceives to be the needs of his employees; they, in turn, do good work out of loyalty to him. George Liang is an easygoing supervisor when the work is routine, but when a big order comes in, he turns tough.

If you have worked for more than one boss, chances are that you have experienced more than one leadership style. Anita, Greg, and George illustrate only some of the possibilities. Some supervisors instinctively lead in a way they are comfortable with, while others adopt their style of leadership consciously. However, a supervisor who is aware of basic types of leadership styles is probably in the best position to use the style (or styles) that will get the desired results.

Degree of Authority Retained

One way to describe leadership styles is in terms of how much authority the leader retains. Do employees get to make choices and control their own work? Or does the supervisor make all the decisions? To describe the possibilities, management theorists refer to authoritarian, democratic, and laissez-faire leadership.

Authoritarian leadership is a leadership style in which the leader retains a great deal of authority. Such a leader makes decisions and dictates instructions to employees. An example would be a military commander who expects unquestioning obedience.

Some supervisors share more authority than do authoritarian supervisors. With **democratic leadership**, the supervisor allows employees to participate in decision making and problem solving. A social work supervisor whose style of leadership is democratic might have the staff meet weekly to discuss how to improve client relations. When a conflict arises, this supervisor asks the group to discuss possible solutions and to select one.

At the opposite extreme from authoritarian leadership is **laissez-faire leadership**. A laissez-faire manager is uninvolved. He or she lets employees do what they want. Supervisors are rarely, if ever, able to practice this style of leadership, because the nature of the supervisor's job requires close involvement with and monitoring of employees.

Nor are many supervisors totally autocratic or totally democratic. Most supervisors give employees some degree of freedom to do their jobs but also make some of the decisions for the department. Years ago, Robert Tannenbaum and Warren H. Schmidt drew a graph showing the continuum, or range of possibilities, for the degree of authority a manager can retain. This continuum, shown in Figure 4.2, is still popular today as a way to picture the possibilities.

authoritarian leadership
A leadership style in which the leader retains a great deal of authority.

democratic leadership
A leadership style in which the leader allows subordinates to participate in decision making and problem solving.

laissez-faire leadership
A leadership style in which the leader is uninvolved and lets subordinates direct themselves.

Task Oriented versus People Oriented

Another way to look at differences in leadership styles is to consider what supervisors focus on in making decisions and evaluating accomplishments. In general terms, leaders may be task oriented or people oriented. A task-oriented leader is one who focuses on the jobs to be done and the goals to be accomplished. When the work gets done correctly and on time, such a leader is satisfied. On the other hand, a people-oriented leader is concerned primarily about the well-being of the people he or she manages. This type of leader emphasizes such issues as morale, job satisfaction, and relationships among employees. To see whether you are inclined to be task-oriented or people-oriented, take the Self-Quiz on pages 79–80.

Of course, the organization expects that its supervisors and other managers will care about meeting organizational objectives. However, it seems reasonable to assume that satisfied, healthy, cooperative workers will perform the best over the long run. In that regard, consultant Peter L. Thigpen has concluded that one source of the high level of commitment in the marine corps lies with some unwrit-

FIGURE 4.2

Possibilities for Retaining Authority

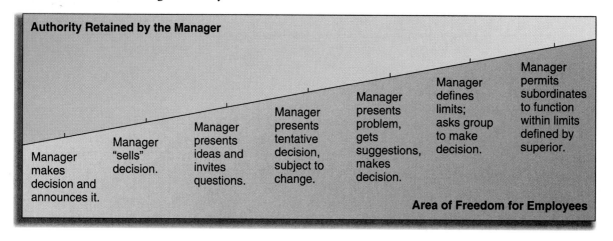

Source: Adapted from Robert Tannenbaum and Warren H. Schmidt, "How to Choose a Leadership Pattern," *Harvard Business Review*, May–June 1973.

ten rules of behavior for the officers. The four rules that Thigpen recalls reflect deep concern for the troops:[4]

- Never eat before your troops eat.
- Never bed down until your guards are posted and your troops are bedded down.
- Your job, up to and including the commandant of the marine corps, is to support the private rifleman on the front line.
- Never ask your troops to do something you wouldn't do.

These rules incorporate a people-oriented view of leadership in an organization where leaders are also committed to getting the job done.

Most organizations expect that their supervisors can combine some degree of task orientation with some degree of people orientation. A supervisor who tends to focus on getting out the work needs to remember to check sometimes on how employees are feeling and getting along. A supervisor who regularly sticks up for employees' welfare should make sure that he or she also remembers to promote the organization's goals.

In fact, researchers Robert R. Blake and Jane S. Mouton recommend that supervisors and other managers be strong in both leadership orientations. They developed a "Managerial Grid®" (Figure 4.3, on page 81) that identifies five of the eight types of leadership by managers. Along one axis is the manager's concern for people, and along the other is the manager's concern for production. Blake and Mouton's research led them to conclude that productivity, job satisfaction, and creativity are highest with a (9,9), or team management, style of leadership, which is high in both concern for people and concern for production. To apply this model of leadership, supervisors identify where their current style of leadership falls on the managerial grid, then determine the kinds of changes they need to make to adopt a (9,9) style.

◢ SELF-QUIZ   *Assessing Your Leadership Style*

This is the T–P (task-oriented–people-oriented) Leadership Questionnaire. The following items describe aspects of leadership behavior. Respond to each item according to the way you would most likely act if you were the leader of a work group. Circle whether you would most likely behave in the described way: always (A), frequently (F), occasionally (O), seldom (S), or never (N).

A F O S N   1. I would most likely act as the spokesperson of the group.

A F O S N   2. I would encourage overtime work.

A F O S N   3. I would allow members complete freedom in their work.

A F O S N   4. I would encourage the use of uniform procedures.

A F O S N   5. I would permit members to use their own judgment in solving problems.

A F O S N   6. I would stress being ahead of competing groups.

A F O S N   7. I would speak as a representative of the group.

A F O S N   8. I would needle members for greater effort.

A F O S N   9. I would try out my ideas in the group.

A F O S N   10. I would let members do their work the way they think best.

A F O S N   11. I would be working hard for a promotion.

A F O S N   12. I would tolerate postponement and uncertainty.

A F O S N   13. I would speak for the group if there were visitors present.

A F O S N   14. I would keep the work moving at a rapid pace.

A F O S N   15. I would turn the members loose on a job and let them go to it.

A F O S N   16. I would settle conflicts when they occur in the group.

A F O S N   17. I would get swamped by details.

A F O S N   18. I would represent the group at outside meetings.

A F O S N   19. I would be reluctant to allow the members any freedom of action.

A F O S N   20. I would decide what should be done and how it should be done.

A F O S N   21. I would push for increased production.

A F O S N   22. I would let some members have authority which I could keep.

A F O S N   23. Things would usually turn out as I had predicted.

A F O S N   24. I would allow the group a high degree of initiative.

A F O S N   25. I would assign group members to particular tasks.

A F O S N   26. I would be willing to make changes.

A F O S N   27. I would ask the members to work harder.

A F O S N   28. I would trust the group members to exercise good judgment.

A F O S N   29. I would schedule the work to be done.

A F O S N   30. I would refuse to explain my actions.

A F O S N   31. I would persuade others that my ideas are to their advantage.

A F O S N   32. I would permit the group to set its own pace.

A F O S N   33. I would urge the group to beat its previous record.

A F O S N   34. I would act without consulting the group.

A F O S N   35. I would ask that group members follow standard rules and regulations.

T_____   P_____

The T–P Leadership Questionnaire is scored as follows:

a. Circle the item number for items 8, 12, 17, 18, 19, 30, 34, and 35.

b. Write the number 1 in front of a *circled item number* if you responded S (seldom) or N (never) to that item.

c. Also write a number 1 in front of *item numbers not circled* if you responded A (always) or F (frequently).

d. Circle the number 1s that you have written in front of the following items: 3, 5, 8, 10, 15, 18, 19, 22, 24, 26, 28, 30, 32, 34, and 35.

e. *Count the circled number 1s.* This is your score for concern for people. Record the score in the blank following the letter P at the end of the questionnaire.

f. *Count uncircled number 1s.* This is your score for concern for task. Record this number in the blank following the letter T.

Source: The T–P Leadership Questionnaire was adapted by J. B. Ritchie and P. Thompson in *Organization and People* (New York: West, 1984). Copyright 1969 by the American Educational Research Association. Adapted by permission of the publisher.

Leader Attitudes

Theory X
A set of management attitudes based on the view that people dislike work and must be coerced to perform.

Theory Y
A set of management attitudes based on the view that work is a natural activity and that people will work hard and creatively to achieve objectives they are committed to.

In observing the behavior of managers, Douglas McGregor noted that many of them tended to have a group of attitudes that reflected their beliefs about workers and the workplace. He termed this set of attitudes **Theory X**. To summarize, a Theory X manager assumes that people dislike work and try to avoid it, that they therefore must be coerced to perform, that they wish to avoid responsibility and would prefer to be directed, and that their primary need is for security. Not surprisingly, these beliefs influence how supervisors and other managers behave. A Theory X supervisor would adopt an autocratic role. He or she would tend to keep a close eye on employees, looking for occasions when they need to be disciplined to keep them performing adequately.

McGregor advises that managers could benefit by adopting a much different set of beliefs, which he terms **Theory Y**. According to Theory Y, working is as natural an activity as resting or playing, and people will work hard to achieve objectives they are committed to, they can learn to seek responsibility, and they can be creative in solving organizational problems. Supervisors and other managers who adhere to Theory Y focus on developing the potential of their employees. Their style of leadership tends to be democratic. Today a common view among

FIGURE 4.3

The Managerial Grid

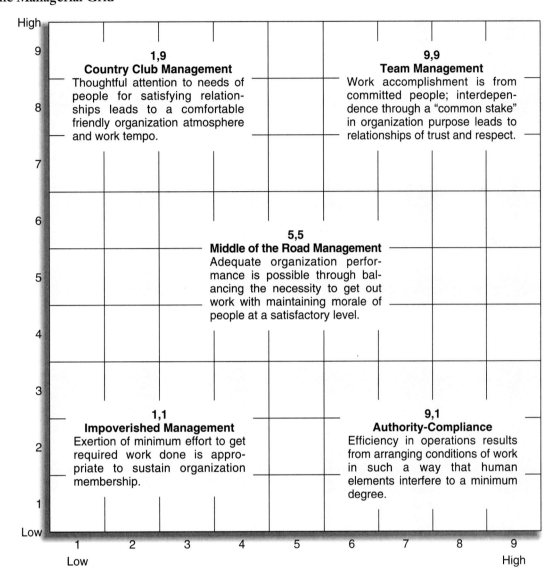

Source: The Leadership Grid® Figure for Leadership Dilemmas—Grid Solutions, by Robert R. Blake and Ann Adams McCanse. (Houston Gulf Publishing Company), page 29. Copyright 1991 by Scientific Methods, Inc. Reproduced by permission of the owners.

Theory Z
A set of management attitudes that emphasize employee participation in all aspects of decision making.

people studying management is that Theory Y is appropriate for many (but not necessarily all) situations. Table 4.1 summarizes these two sets of assumptions.

In the last decade, management experts extended their view of managing and leading to include **Theory Z**. Theory Z supervisors seek to involve employees in

TABLE 4.1	*Theory X*	*Theory Y*
Contrasting Leader Attitudes	People dislike work and try to avoid it.	Working is as natural an activity as resting or playing.
	People must be coerced to perform.	People will work hard to achieve objectives they are committed to.
	People wish to avoid responsibility and prefer to be directed.	People can learn to seek responsibility.
	People's primary need is for security.	Many people are able to be creative in solving organizational problems.

making decisions, consider long-term goals when making plans, and give employees relatively great freedom in carrying out their duties. This theory is based on comparisons of management styles in the United States and Japan, and it assumes that where Japanese workers are more productive than their U.S. counterparts, the difference stems in part from different management styles. Thus, Theory Z was developed in an attempt to adapt some Japanese management practices to the U.S. workplace. The Japanese practices include employee involvement and lifetime employment.

Contingency Theories of Leadership

With all of these possibilities, is there one best approach to leading employees? Should the supervisor consciously cultivate one leadership style? A common view is that the best style of leadership depends on the circumstances.

Fiedler's Contingency Model   One of the first researchers to develop such a theory—called a contingency theory—was Fred Fiedler. As shown in Figure 4.4, Fiedler held that whether relationship-oriented (people-oriented) or task-oriented leaders perform better depends on leader-member relations, task structure, and the position power of the leader. Leader-member relations refers to the extent to which the leader has group members' support and loyalty. Task structure refers to whether there is a specified procedure to follow in carrying out the task. Position power refers to the leader's formal authority, granted by the organization.

Fiedler recommends that a leader determine whether his or her preferred leadership style fits the situation. If it does not, Fiedler says, the leader should try to change the characteristics of the situation.

Hersey-Blanchard Theory   Fiedler's work led others to develop their own contingency theories of leadership. For example, Paul Hersey and Ken Blanchard developed a model called the life cycle theory. This model, like Fiedler's, considers degrees to which managers focus on relationships and tasks. However, unlike Fiedler's model, the Hersey-Blanchard theory assumes that the leader's behavior should adapt to the situation. More specifically, their theory says that the leadership

FIGURE 4.4

Fiedler's Contingency Model of Leadership

Leader-Member Relations	Good	Good	Good	Good	Poor	Poor	Poor	Poor
Task Structure	Structured	Structured	Unstructured	Unstructured	Structured	Structured	Unstructured	Unstructured
Leader Position Power	Strong	Weak	Strong	Weak	Strong	Weak	Strong	Weak
Which Leader Performs Better?	Task-Oriented Leader	Task-Oriented Leader	Task-Oriented Leader	Relationship-Oriented Leader	Relationship-Oriented Leader	Relationship-Oriented Leader	Task- or Relationship-Oriented Leader	Task-Oriented Leader

Source: Adapted from Fred E. Fiedler, "Engineer the Job to Fit the Manager," *Harvard Business Review*, September–October 1965.

style should reflect the maturity of the followers as measured by such traits as ability to work independently.

According to the Hersey-Blanchard life cycle theory, leaders should adjust the degree of task and relationship behavior in response to the growing maturity of their followers. As followers mature, leaders should move through the following combinations of task and relationship behavior:

1. High task and low relationship behavior
2. High task and high relationship behavior
3. Low task and high relationship behavior
4. Low task and low relationship behavior

Under special conditions, such as short-term deadlines, the leader may have to adjust the leadership style temporarily. However, according to Hersey and Blanchard, this pattern of choosing a leadership style leads to the most effective long-term working relationship between leader and followers.

Choosing a Leadership Style

Viewing contingency theories as a whole leads to some general guidelines for choosing a leadership style. To identify the most effective style, the supervisor should consider the characteristics of the leader, of the subordinates, and of the situation itself. Figure 4.5 shows some key characteristics to weigh.

FIGURE 4.5
Characteristics Affecting Choice of Leadership Style

Leadership Style		
Leader Characteristics	**Subordinate Characteristics**	**Situation Characteristics**
• Values • Confidence in employees • Leadership strengths • Tolerance for ambiguity	• Need for independence • Readiness to take responsibility • Tolerance for ambiguity • Interest in problem • Understanding of and identification with goals • Knowledge and experience • Expectations	• Type of organization • Effectiveness of group • Problem or task • Time available

Characteristics of the Leader   Since no single type of personality is associated with good leadership, it is not surprising that different leaders prefer different styles of leading. Whereas one supervisor feels most comfortable when backed up by a clear system of rules, regulations, and schedules, another prefers to come up with creative approaches on the spur of the moment. One supervisor likes the results of involving employees in decision making, whereas another one cannot quite get used to the time and effort this requires.

To some extent at least, the supervisor gets the best results when using a leadership style that feels comfortable to him or her. Here are some characteristics that influence how supervisors feel about various approaches to leading:

- *The manager's values*—What is most important to the supervisor in carrying out his or her job? Is it the department's contribution to company profits? The employees' or the manager's own growth and development? A manager concerned about developing employees is most likely to involve them in making decisions.
- *Level of confidence in employees*—The more confident in employees the supervisor is, the more he or she will involve them in planning and decision making.
- *Personal leadership strengths*—Some supervisors have a talent for leading group discussions; others are better at quietly analyzing information and reaching a decision. Some are good at detecting employee wants and needs; others excel at keeping their focus on the numbers. Effective leaders capitalize on their strengths.
- *Tolerance for ambiguity*—When the supervisor involves employees in solving problems or making decisions, he or she cannot always be sure of the outcomes.

Some supervisors are more comfortable with this ambiguity (i.e., uncertainty) than others.

With greater diversity in the workplace, we can expect to see greater diversity in some of these characteristics, such as values and leadership strengths. The "Dealing with Diversity" box on the next page takes a look at some implications of women taking more leadership roles.

Characteristics of the Subordinates In selecting a leadership style, the smart supervisor considers the employees as well as him- or herself. Employees who are at their most creative and productive when they have a lot of freedom will dig in their heels if their supervisor is autocratic with them, even if that is the most natural leadership style for the supervisor. At the other extreme, employees who expect and rely on structure and direction will tend to drift and even become paralyzed if their leader has a laissez-faire or even democratic style.

What should the supervisor look for in deciding on the kind of supervision employees want? Here are some characteristics that should influence the choice:

- *Need for independence*—People who want a lot of direction will welcome autocratic leadership.
- *Readiness to assume responsibility*—Employees who are eager to assume responsibility will appreciate a democratic or laissez-faire style of leadership.
- *Tolerance for ambiguity*—Employees who are tolerant of ambiguity will accept a leadership style that gives them more say in solving problems.
- *Interest in the problem to be solved*—Employees who are interested in a problem and think it is important will want to help solve it.
- *Understanding of and identification with goals*—Employees who understand and identify with the organization's or department's goals will want to play an active role in deciding how to meet those goals. Furthermore, the supervisor will find that such employees are reliable in carrying out their responsibilities. Employees who don't identify with goals may need more active direction and control from the supervisor.
- *Knowledge and experience*—Employees with the knowledge necessary to solve a problem are more apt to want to help find a solution. Furthermore, their input will be more valuable to the supervisor. Thus, someone who is new on the job will probably need a supervisor who engages in both task-oriented and relationship-oriented behavior, but the supervisor can become less involved as the employee gains experience.
- *Expectations*—Some employees expect to participate in making decisions and solving problems. Others think that a boss who does not tell them what to do is not doing a good job. Cultural standards can also influence employees' expectations. For example, Arthur Edwards supervises Vietnamese immigrants at a computer company in California's Silicon Valley. To build more friendly relations with his employees, he took such actions as working alongside them and joining them for lunch in the employees' cafeteria. However, the Vietnamese culture expects managers to be more formal, and the employees distanced themselves from Edwards.[5]

DEALING WITH DIVERSITY

Women in Leadership Roles

In the United States, the model for effective leadership has long been based on experiences in sports and the military. Such a model focuses on competition and winning at all costs. An assumption is that you must be on top or be a loser—kill or be killed.

In a culturally diverse workplace, it is no longer realistic to assume that the people in leadership roles can draw on these common experiences. Asks consultant Anne P. Hyde, "How are you going to get everyone to 'play by the rules' when tomorrow's corporation will have managers who have been socialized in eight different countries, all with different values and rules?"

Particularly noteworthy is the different set of values and experiences that most women bring to the workplace. For example, UCLA professor Helen Astin, who conducted a study of well-known women leaders, believes that there is a "feminine way of leadership." She claims that women tend to focus on interpersonal issues and that this focus is precisely what leaders will need in the workplace of the future.

The most significant characteristic of "feminine" leadership that Astin identified in her study was an emphasis on collective leadership, on empowering one's followers. The women leaders she studied tended to emphasize accomplishments as being the accomplishments of the whole group, not just the leader. Similar results came from a study by Alice H. Eagly, a social psychology professor at Purdue University. In a review of more than 360 studies on gender and leadership, Eagly found that the only significant difference was that women tend to be more democratic in their leadership style.

In many cases, this leadership style is supported by a view that the people in an organization are interdependent, not independent of one another. A leader who believes in interdependence is more likely to respond to a problem by saying to employees, "Let's work out a solution."

Of course, women are not the only leaders who adopt a democratic, interdependent leadership style. In the words of Anne Hyde, "Women value humanistic qualities and place an emphasis on the individual, not just the goal, because they have been rewarded in society for doing so. That is not to say men don't share humanistic values, or that men never use this new management paradigm. It is just that society has not encouraged men to manage in this way." Some people think that the current emphasis on working in teams is helping to lead more men to adopt aspects of the leadership style that now characterizes women.

Source: Charlotte Taylor, "Taking the Lead," *Entrepreneurial Woman*, April 1992, pp. 42–47.

Characteristics of the Situation   Besides the personalities and preferences of supervisor and subordinates, the situation itself helps to determine what leadership style will be most effective. Several characteristics are important:

- *Type of organization*—Organizations often lend themselves to one leadership style or another. If the organization expects supervisors to manage large numbers of employees, a democratic leadership style may be time-consuming and relatively challenging to use. If higher-level managers clearly value one style of leadership, the supervisor may find it difficult to use a different style and still be considered effective.

- *Effectiveness of the group*—Regardless of the characteristics of individual employees, some groups are more successful in handling decisions than others. If a department or work group has little experience in making its own decisions, the

The job situation itself often helps determine what leadership style will be most effective. Even within a single company, styles vary. The diverse departments led by Financial Accounting and Reporting Manager Donna Walter and Production Plant Manager Thelma Holmbeck in Pioneer Hi-Bred International require varied leadership styles.

Source: Courtesy of Pioneer Hi-Bred International, Inc.

supervisor may find that an authoritarian approach is easier to use. Supervisors should delegate decisions to groups that can handle the responsibility.

- *The problem or task*—For some problems, the work group or the individual employees involved can easily reach a solution. When problems are more complex or difficult, the supervisor should retain more control. This is the case for leading in crisis situations, says consultant Hap Klopp, citing the example of a Himalayan mountain-climbing expedition that fell apart because the leader asked the group to choose a route to the top and the group members could not agree. "Democracy doesn't work at 20,000 feet," says Klopp.[6] Besides difficulty, the supervisor should consider how structured a task is. A structured task—that is, one with a set procedure to follow—is easiest for an autocratic leader to manage. However, some tasks, such as generating ideas to improve customer service or planning the department picnic, are relatively unstructured. Such tasks benefit from the employee involvement sought by a democratic, people-oriented leader.
- *Time available*—An autocratic leader is in a position to make decisions quickly. Group decision making usually requires more time for discussion and the sharing of ideas. Thus, the manager should use a relatively democratic leadership style only when time allows for it.

More and more organizations today are promoting the idea of teamwork (see Chapter 17). When employees and managers work in teams, the appropriate leadership style is a democratic one based on Theory Y, and it emphasizes people.

Some management experts think that a good analogy for this leadership style is that of a coach.[7] Coaches delegate responsibility to carry out operations, and they are willing to share authority. They focus on picking qualified people, helping them learn to do their jobs well, and inspiring peak performance. Joseph Lipsey, who manages training and development for a major insurance company, credits this leadership style with transforming his department from one with little impact to one that works effectively: "By driving out fear, hiring top-notch people…, implementing a team structure, making decisions by consensus, and unleashing the tremendous creativity and desire to contribute and to find meaning in work that is innate to everyone, we have created a real 'force' within this organization."[8]

Giving Directions

An important way supervisors practice leadership is by giving directions. Even the most democratic leaders must occasionally tell their employees what to do. Of course, the way the supervisor gives directions can influence how willingly and well employees respond.

The supervisor should make sure that the employee understands the directions. If the supervisor says, "I need those figures today," can the employee leave a note on the supervisor's desk at 6:00 P.M., half an hour after the supervisor has left? Or does the supervisor need time to review the numbers, so that he actually needs them by a specific time, say, 3:00 P.M.? Thus, the supervisor should state directions in specific, clear terms. Other ways to make sure employees understand are to ask them to restate what they are supposed to do and to check on their progress before they are finished. (Chapter 7 provides further guidelines for effective communication.)

The supervisor should make sure that employees also see the reason for the directions. In a crisis, people are willing to pitch in; they can easily see a need. Thus, if a hospital patient has a cardiac arrest, the staff members do not object to someone barking orders in an effort to revive the patient. But sometimes the supervisor has to identify the crisis or explain the need. The supervisor on a loading dock could say, "This order is for our biggest customer, and they're getting fed up with late shipments. If we don't get the order on the truck today, we'll be in deep trouble." That approach is more likely to get results than is giving no reason and shouting, "Get moving!"

The most effective way to give instructions is to do so confidently and politely, but without being apologetic. If a supervisor says, "I'm sorry—I know you're busy, but I'd appreciate seeing those lab results by noon," the employee may think that he or she has been given an option, not instructions. The employee also may be unclear on who is in charge of the department. Rather, the supervisor can say, "Please have those lab results ready by noon." Of course, it is never appropriate to be rude.

When a supervisor finds that employees are not complying with his or her directions, the supervisor can examine whether the directions follow these guidelines. Perhaps employees do not understand what is expected of them, or perhaps they do not realize that the supervisor is giving them an order, not a suggestion.

Human Relations

Leading is clearly an application of human relations skills, introduced in Chapter 1. It is perhaps the most important measure of whether the supervisor excels at human relations with his or her employees. Of course, supervisors need good human relations skills for other relationships as well. They also need to work effectively with their boss and peers, as well as to be positive about themselves. In his book *Your Attitude Is Showing*, Elwood Chapman describes the skilled use of human relations as doing "everything you can to build strong, friendly, and honest working relationships with *all* the people you work with."[9]

Most books about business focus on the technical skills of managing. How can a supervisor develop human relations skills? Ways to get along with almost anyone include projecting a positive attitude, taking an interest in other people, and helping out. In addition, the supervisor can take some steps to work on each of the categories of relationships that are important to his or her success.

Supervisors' Views of Themselves

Order-processing supervisor Eleanor Chakonas thinks of herself as a risk taker and a person who makes things happen. When she was asked to plan the expansion of her department, she attacked the job with a gusto that inspired her employees to contribute to the effort. The result was a plan that called for extra efforts by employees but would result in the department's performing beyond management's expectations. A supervisor who considers him- or herself more cautious or prone to error than Eleanor would have approached the planning job differently.

self-concept
The image a person has of him- or herself.

The image a supervisor has of him- or herself—that is, the supervisor's **self-concept**—influences how the supervisor behaves. Someone who believes that he has power will act powerful; someone who thinks of herself as intelligent is apt to make careful decisions. It is worthwhile for supervisors to be aware of the thoughts they have of themselves.

Doing this can also help supervisors cultivate positive thoughts, which will help them act in positive ways. When you find yourself thinking something such as, "I'm so stupid," or, "I wouldn't lose my cool the way he just did," notice what you are thinking, and consider what it says about your self-concept. Take time to consider what your strengths and goals are. When you do something well, give yourself credit for your success. When someone compliments you, smile and say thank you. When you make the effort to behave this way, you will find that you not only understand yourself better, you will probably also find that your beliefs about yourself are getting more positive.

Relations with Employees

A supervisor who is liked and respected by employees will inspire them to work harder and better. This does not mean that the supervisor should be friends with employees. Rather, the supervisor should consistently treat them in a way that reflects his or her role as a part of management.

Supervisors as Role Models For employees, the supervisor is the person who most directly represents management and the organization. Thus, when employees evaluate the organization, they look at the supervisor's behavior. They also use the supervisor's behavior as a guide for how they should act. Thus, if a supervisor takes long lunch breaks, employees either will think that the use of their time is unimportant or will believe that the company unfairly lets managers get away with violating rules.

To set a good example for employees, the supervisor should follow the rules and regulations that cover employees. The supervisor should be fair in his or her treatment of employees—for example, assigning unpopular tasks to everyone, not just to certain employees. Supervisors also should be ethical—that is, honest and fair. (Chapter 19 discusses ethics in greater detail.)

Developing Trust Pat Carrigan, the first female plant manager at General Motors Corporation, says her job is to "create a climate of trust," and she evidently meets that objective. United Auto Workers official Jack Whyte says, "Pat Carrigan ain't got a phony bone in her body." Not surprisingly, Carrigan was able to obtain the union's support in making important quality improvements at GM.[10] As in this example, employees will work most cooperatively with a supervisor they trust.

Building trust takes time and effort, yet the supervisor can lose it with a single act that is unreasonable. The most important way to build trust is to engage in fair, predictable behavior. The supervisor should fulfill promises and give employees credit when they do something well. Keeping the lines of communication open (discussed in Chapter 7) also builds trust. When the supervisor listens carefully and shares information, employees will not think that he or she is hiding something from them. Training and education consultant Jim Kouzes keeps his firm's computer printer next to his desk. He considers the resulting interruptions worthwhile because of what he learns from his employees when they stop by to pick up their documents.[11]

Relations with Your Boss

No matter how good you are at planning, organizing, and leading, your ability to get along with your boss can determine the course of your career at a particular organization. That may not always seem fair, but your boss is the one who most often decides whether you will be promoted, get a juicy assignment or a raise, or even have a job next week. A boss who likes to work with you is more likely to take a favorable (or at least tolerant) view of your performance.

Expectations While every boss is different, most expect certain kinds of behavior from the people they manage. As summarized in Figure 4.6, a supervisor can reasonably assume that his or her boss expects loyalty, cooperation, communication, and results.

- *Loyalty* means that the supervisor says only positive things about company policies and about his or her boss. If the supervisor cannot think of anything positive to say, silence is better than criticism.
- *Cooperation* means that the supervisor works with others in the organization to achieve organizational goals. If the boss offers criticism, the supervisor should

FIGURE 4.6

What Bosses Expect of Supervisors

listen and try to make improvements. If the criticism seems unreasonable, the supervisor should first make sure that he or she did not misunderstand, and then try to find aspects of the criticism that are constructive.

- *Communication* means that the boss expects the supervisor to keep him or her informed about the department's performance. (Chapter 7 provides more information about communicating with one's boss.)
- *Results* means that the supervisor should see that the department meets or exceeds its objectives. The best way to look good to the boss is to have a high-performing department.

Learning about Your Boss   You can better meet your boss's expectations if you understand him or her as an individual. Observe how your boss handles various situations, and try to determine his or her leadership style. Notice what issues are most important to your boss. As much as you can, when you are with your boss, adapt your own style to match his or hers. Also ask your boss what his or her expectations are for you and how he or she will measure your performance.

If You Are Dissatisfied   Despite your best efforts, you may find that you are dissatisfied with your boss. It happens to many people at some point in their career. If you are unhappy, begin by considering what the source of the problem is. Most interpersonal problems arise from the behavior and attitudes of two people, so are there changes you can make to improve the situation?

If you cannot improve the situation enough by changing your own behavior, talk to your boss. State the types of actions you are dissatisfied with and say how those actions are affecting you. If you cannot resolve the problem with your boss,

When Your Boss Is Driving You Crazy

When your boss makes it difficult for you to do a good job or get the recognition you deserve, how should you react? First, do not leave it up to the organization to take care of you. According to Chris Malburg, a California-based consultant, "You have to remember, there is no one who will save your career other than you."

In Malburg's experience, the most common type of problem boss is one he calls the "Locomotive." This type of boss tries to get the job done through "brute force," without considering subordinates' feelings or needs. To get along with a Locomotive boss, advises Malburg, the supervisor should get close to the boss and win his or her confidence while being careful not to seem to threaten his or her authority.

Similarly, Janelle Brittain, director of the Dynamic Performance Institute in Evanston, Illinois, says most employees she works with complain about a boss who is "dominant." This type of boss is moody, likes to talk but does not listen, delegates responsibility, and demands fast answers. To work with this type of boss, Brittain advises that the supervisor model the boss's language style, using his or her pet phrases. When presenting a proposal, supervisors should make all the decisions except one; if the boss can make a decision about the proposal, he or she is not as likely to be critical later on.

In addition, here are some further tips for coping with a difficult boss:

- Discuss your goals and expectations with your boss in specific terms, then confirm in writing what you have agreed on.
- Be a good source of technical expertise and feedback so that your boss will rely on you for these.
- Get to know the boss, and consider situations from his or her point of view.
- If you are in a no-win situation—including reporting to a boss who seems to be addicted to alcohol or other substances—consider leaving the department or the organization.

Source: Gail Schmoller, "Working Smart: What to Do When the Boss Is a Pain in the Career," *Chicago Tribune*, January 5, 1992, sec. 6, p. 7.

your best bet is probably to hunt for another job. But try to keep your present job while you look for a new one. Most prospective employers look more favorably on job candidates who are already employed. The "Tips from the Firing Line" box provides more ideas for coping with a difficult boss.

Relations with Peers

If you get along well with your peers in the same and other departments, they will help you look good and get your job done. But if they resent or dislike you, the poor relations can cause an endless stream of problems. Therefore, supervisors need to cultivate good relations with their peers.

Competition Sometimes your peers will be competing with you for raises, bonuses, or promotions. Remember that the more you can cooperate, the better you will all look. This means that your competition should be fair and as friendly as possible. If you try to sabotage a co-worker, the one who ultimately ends up looking bad will probably be you.

If you get along well with your peers in the same and other departments, they will help you get your job done.

Source: © 1992 Comstock, Inc.

Criticism Because you are trying to maintain a positive attitude, you will not go looking for things to criticize in your peers or anyone else. However, if you know that a co-worker has done something that works against the organization's best interests, you should go directly to that person and point out the problem. It usually helps to be polite and diplomatic and to assume that the problem was unintended—an error or an oversight.

If the co-worker resists listening to your criticism and the problem is one that will harm the company, its employees or customers, then you should go to your boss to discuss the problem. Focus on the problem and its consequences to the organization, not on the personalities involved.

Summary

4.1 Discuss the possible link between personal traits and leadership ability.
In an effort to find which people will succeed as leaders, researchers have looked for traits that successful leaders hold in common. Traits that may be significant include a sense of responsibility, self-confidence, high energy level, empathy, an internal locus of control, and a sense of humor.

However, research results have been inconsistent, leading to the conclusion that traits alone do not predict success as a leader.

4.2 Describe leadership styles that a supervisor might adopt.

Depending on how much authority they retain, supervisors can be authoritarian (retaining much authority), democratic (sharing authority), or laissez-faire (giving up most authority). Supervisors may also be task oriented, people oriented, or both. They may build their leadership style on Theory X assumptions that employees must be coerced to work, on Theory Y assumptions that employees can be motivated to seek responsibility and achieve objectives creatively, or on Theory Z values such as employee involvement and focus on long-term goals.

4.3 Explain contingency theories of leadership.

Contingency theories of leadership hold that leaders can be most effective by matching different leadership styles to varying circumstances. For example, Fiedler's contingency model says that whether people- or task-oriented leaders perform better depends on leader-member relations, task structure, and the leader's position power. Fiedler recommends that, if the leader's preferred leadership style does not fit the situation, the characteristics of the situation should be changed. In contrast, Hersey and Blanchard's life cycle theory maintains that the leader should modify his or her behavior to fit the situation. As followers mature, leaders should use varying levels of task and relationship behavior.

4.4 Identify criteria for choosing a leadership style.

The supervisor should select a leadership style that suits the characteristics of the leader, of the employees, and of the situation. Criteria for evaluating the characteristics of the leader are his or her values, level of confidence in employees, leadership strengths, and tolerance for ambiguity. Criteria for evaluating the characteristics of employees include their need for independence, readiness to assume responsibility, tolerance for ambiguity, interest in the problem, understanding of and identification with goals, knowledge and experience, and expectations. Criteria for evaluating the characteristics of the situation include the type of organization, effectiveness of the group, the nature of the problem or task, and the time available.

4.5 Describe guidelines for giving directions to employees.

The supervisor should make sure that employees understand the directions and the reason for them. The supervisor should give the instructions confidently and politely, but without being apologetic.

4.6 Tell why supervisors need to understand and improve their views of themselves.

The image a supervisor has of him- or herself influences how the supervisor behaves. People who believe they are capable tend to act capably. The supervisor needs to cultivate a view of him- or herself as having the attributes of an effective leader.

4.7 Explain how supervisors can develop and maintain good relations with their employees, boss, and peers.

The supervisor should project a positive attitude, take an interest in others, and help out as needed. With employees, the supervisor should set a good example, be ethical, and develop trust. The supervisor should give his or her boss loyalty, cooperation, information, and results and should be aware of and respond to the boss's style. The supervisor should keep competition with peers as fair and friendly as possible and should offer criticism in a constructive way.

Key Terms

leading	democratic leadership	Theory Y
internal locus of control	laissez-faire leadership	Theory Z
authoritarian leadership	Theory X	self-concept

Review and Discussion Questions

1. According to the chapter, what traits might be associated with successful leadership? What other characteristics do you think might be important?
2. A production supervisor has been told his department must reduce its rate of defective merchandise. How would the supervisor respond, using each of the following leadership styles?
   a. authoritarian leadership
   b. democratic leadership
   c. laissez-faire leadership
3. Ann Wong is the accounts payable supervisor at an insurance company. During a time of layoffs, she decides that she should adopt a leadership style that is more people oriented than the style she normally uses. What does this change mean?
4. What are the beliefs associated with Theory X leadership? What beliefs are associated with Theory Y? What set of beliefs do you think is more correct?
5. Do you think it is more realistic to expect supervisors to adjust the situation to meet their preferred leadership style, as suggested by Fiedler's contingency model of leadership, or to adjust their leadership style to fit the situation, as suggested by Hersey and Blanchard? Explain your reasoning.
6. In which of the following situations would you recommend the supervisor use an authoritarian style of leadership? In which situation would you recommend a democratic style? Explain your choices.
   a. The supervisor's boss says, "Top management wants us to start getting employees to suggest ways to improve quality in all areas of operations." Each department has wide latitude in how to do this.
   b. A supervisor is uncomfortable in meetings and likes to be left alone to figure out solutions to problems. The supervisor's employees believe that a good supervisor is able to tell them exactly what to do.
   c. A shipment of hazardous materials is on its way to a warehouse. The supervisor is responsible for instructing employees in how to handle the materials when they arrive later that day.
7. Prakash Singh prefers a very democratic style of leadership and is uncomfortable when he has to tell someone what to do. His solution is to make his instructions as general as possible so that employees will feel they have more control. At such times, he also tends to apologize for being authoritarian. Do you think this method of giving directions will be effective? Why or why not?
8. Why should supervisors have a positive view of themselves? What are some ways a supervisor can be aware of and improve his or her self-concept?
9. Identify the human relations error in each of the following situations. Suggest a better way to handle each.
   a. Carole Fields's boss compliments her on the report she submitted yesterday. She says, "Aw, it was no big deal."
   b. When Rich Peaslee was promoted to supervisor, he told the other employees, "Now, remember, I was one of the gang before this promotion, and I'll still be one of the gang."
   c. The second-shift supervisor observes that the first-shift employees have not left their work areas clean for the last three days. He complains to his boss about the lax supervision on first shift.
10. You believe that your boss is unfair and arbitrary in her treatment of you. How can you handle this problem?

A SECOND LOOK

Based on the story of Bill Walsh at the beginning of this chapter, what kind of leadership style(s) would you say Walsh uses? Is this an effective style? Explain.

Class Exercise*

The class divides into groups of four or five students each. Each group is assigned one of the four sections in Figure 4.7, which is a checklist of ways in which employees, including supervisors, can demonstrate competence in human relations. In other words, someone who is competent in human relations follows the principles on this checklist.

Each group discusses the principles in its section of the checklist. Based on jobs they have held or situations they have observed, group members describe good or bad human relations practices. In particular, consider how you have seen supervisors practice or fail to practice these principles.

After the groups have had time to discuss these principles, the groups take turns making presentations. Each group selects one principle to present to the class. One representative (or more) from the group gives a brief illustration of that principle.

CASE

A Difficult Boss

Management consultant Nancy K. Austin tells about the first boss her stepson Jeff had upon graduating from college with a journalism degree. The job looked as though it would be excellent: a weekend sports anchor on a television station. Unfortunately, Jeff's boss—let's call her Jill—made the job more challenging than perhaps it ought to have been.

Jill watched Jeff and her other employees suspiciously. She assumed that her job as supervisor involved catching and criticizing their mistakes. Unfortunately, she was not thorough about gathering information or conveying it to her employees.

To gather information about Jeff's performance on the air, she relied on several informants who watched the newscasts (Jill did not) and discussed them with her over the phone. Their reports were sometimes contradictory and vague. For example, one of the anonymous sources said of Jeff, "Tell him to do something about his hair."

With a formal performance appraisal, Jeff might have been able to get more constructive input. Unfortunately, he had to wait a long time for his first appraisal. Jill repeatedly postponed and rescheduled his 90-day review (and any accompanying pay increase) because something "more important" kept coming up. For Jeff, a raise would have been a sign that he was improving.

1. Based on the information given, what kind of a leadership style do you think Jeff's supervisor has? Explain. (You may use more than one category to identify the type of leadership.)
2. In what ways does this supervisor fail to develop good human relations with Jeff and the other reporters?
3. How would you recommend that Jeff handle this situation?

Source: Nancy K. Austin, "How to Supervise (without) Spying," *Working Woman*, January 1991, pp. 27–28ff.

*This exercise was suggested by Corinne R. Livesay, Liberty University, Lynchburg, Virginia.

FIGURE 4.7

Human Relations Competencies Checklist

1. **Consistently communicate the following attitudes to co-workers, superiors, customers, or patients:**

☐ Send out positive verbal and nonverbal signals in all contacts, including telephone.
☐ Remain positive while working with those who are negative.
☐ Be positive and sensitive when those you are dealing with are not.
☐ Deal with all people in an honest, ethical, and moral way.
☐ Avoid ethnic or sexual remarks that could be misinterpreted.
☐ Maintain a sense of humor.
☐ Recognize when you begin to become negative, and start an attitude renewal project.
☐ Develop and maintain a good service attitude.

2. **Demonstrate the following human-relations skills in dealing with co-workers:**

☐ Build and maintain equally effective horizontal working relationships with everyone in your department. Refuse to play favorites.
☐ Build a productive, no-conflict relationship with those who may have a different set of personal values.
☐ Build relationships based on mutual rewards.
☐ Develop productive, healthy relationships with those who may be substantially older or younger.
☐ Maintain a productive relationship even with individuals who irritate you at times.
☐ Treat everyone, regardless of ethnic or socioeconomic differences, with respect.
☐ Work effectively with others regardless of their sexual orientation.
☐ Do not take human-relations slights or mistakes from others personally; do not become defensive or attempt to retaliate in kind.
☐ Repair an injured relationship as soon as possible.
☐ Even if you are not responsible for the damage to a working relationship, protect your career by taking the initiative to restore it.
☐ Permit others to restore a relationship with you.
☐ Release your frustrations harmlessly without damaging relationships.
☐ Handle teasing and testing without becoming upset.

3. **Demonstrate the following human-relations skills in dealing with your superiors:**

☐ Build a strong vertical relationship with your supervisor without alienating co-workers.
☐ Be a high producer yourself and contribute to the productivity of co-workers.
☐ Survive, with a positive attitude, under a difficult supervisor until changes occur.
☐ Establish relationships that are mutually rewarding.
☐ Show you can live up to your productivity potential without alienating co-workers who do not live up to theirs.
☐ Live close to your productivity potential without extreme highs or lows regardlesss of difficult changes in the work environment.
☐ Do not underestimate or overestimate a superior.
☐ Report mistakes or misjudgments rather than trying to hide them.
☐ Show that you can turn any change into an opportunity, including accepting a new supervisor with a different style.
☐ Refuse to nurse small gripes into major upsets.

4. **Demonstrate the following professional attitudes and human-relations skills:**

☐ Be an excellent listener.
☐ Establish a good attendance record.
☐ Keep a good balance between home and career so neither suffers.
☐ Demonstrate that you are self-motivated.
☐ Communicate freely and thoroughly.
☐ Prepare yourself for a promotion in such a manner that others will be happy when you succeed.
☐ Share only positive, nonconfidential data about your organization with outsiders.
☐ Pass only reliable data on to others.
☐ Keep your business and personal relationships sufficiently separated.
☐ Concentrate on the positive aspects of your job while trying to improve the negative.
☐ Make only positive comments about a third party not present.
☐ Leave a job or company in a positive manner; train your replacement so that productivity is not disturbed.
☐ If you prefer to be a stabilizer, develop patience; if you prefer to be a zig zagger, don't stomp on other people's feet, hands, or heads while climbing the success ladder.
☐ Always have a Plan B (a contingency plan for your career).
☐ Avoid self-victimization.

Source: Reprinted with the permission of Macmillan Publishing Company from YOUR ATTITUDE IS SHOWING: A Primer of Human Relations, Sixth Edition by Elwood N. Chapman. Copyright © 1991 by Macmillan Publishing Company.

5

Achieving good performance is a journey, not a destination.
—Kenneth H. Blanchard

The Supervisor as Controller

LEARNING OBJECTIVES

5.1 Describe the purpose of using controls.

5.2 Identify the steps in the control process.

5.3 Explain how supervisors should focus their efforts when monitoring performance.

5.4 Identify types of control.

5.5 Tell how budgets, reports, and personal observation help supervisors control.

5.6 Describe characteristics of effective controls.

CONTROLLING COSTLY MISTAKES

Lifeline Systems, Inc., of Watertown, Massachusetts, makes personal response systems—emergency-help buttons—for use in health care settings. As of 1989 the company was selling $24 million worth of merchandise a year, but every month it was issuing credit memos totaling $120,000. In other words, customers were returning about 6 percent of the systems being sold.

What was the problem? Were the products that poor? Managers investigated the records and found that almost half the units returned operated properly. This indicated that the manufacturing process could be improved but also that other problems were causing the high number of returns.

To find out the other causes of the returns, John Gugliotta, Lifeline's vice-president of operations, instructed order-entry clerks and managers to begin collecting better information from customers. When customers would call to say they wanted to return an item, the employees who took the calls would now keep a tally of the reasons.

By reviewing this information, Gugliotta learned that the leading errors were caused by salespeople who were making mistakes in the addresses, phone numbers, and subscriber numbers. Also, the six order clerks were giving out incorrect information because they did

not know enough about the products, and customers were being overcharged because of mistakes in the company's data base.

Based on this knowledge, Gugliotta was able to correct the problems. He had order forms created to help the salespeople record information more accurately. Order clerks were taught about the product. The data base was improved and updated. Finally, Gugliotta had employees continue to maintain records of customer problems. This gave employees information about what was happening and why. Now, two clerks and one supervisor process $40 million a year in orders, and the company issues credits of only $20,000 to $40,000 a month.

Source: Teri Lammers, "The Troubleshooter's Guide," *Inc.*, January 1992, pp. 65–67. Photo courtesy of Lifeline Systems, Inc.

Lifeline Systems cut its expenses and improved its customer services through the process of controlling. Supervisors carry out this process in many ways. Consider the following fictional examples:

- Bud Cavanaugh told his crew, "I expect the work area to be clean when you leave each day. That means the floors are swept and all the tools are put away."
- Once or twice each day, Maria Lopez took time to check the documents produced by the word-processing operators she supervised. Maria would look over a few pages each employee had produced that day. If one of the employees seemed to be having trouble with some task—say, deciphering someone's handwriting or preparing neat tables—Maria would discuss the problem with that employee.
- Sonja Friedman learned that citizens calling her housing department were complaining that they spent an excessive amount of time waiting on hold. She scheduled a meeting at which the employees discussed ways they could handle calls faster.

controlling
The management function of making sure that work goes according to plan.

As you learned in Chapter 1, **controlling** is the management function of making sure that work goes according to plan. This chapter takes a closer look at how supervisors control. It describes the process supervisors follow and some of the tools they use in controlling, as well as characteristics of effective controls.

The Purpose of Control

Quite simply, supervisors need to know what is going on in the area they supervise. Do employees understand what they are supposed to do, and can they do it? Is all machinery and equipment (whether a computer-operated milling machine or a touch-tone telephone) operating properly? Is work getting out correctly and on time?

To answer such questions, a supervisor could theoretically sit back and wait for disaster to strike. No disaster, no need for correction. But more realistically, the supervisor has a responsibility to correct problems as soon as possible, which means that he or she needs a way to *detect* problems quickly. And detection of problems is at the heart of the control function.

By controlling, the supervisor can take steps to ensure quality and manage costs. Visiting the work area and checking up on performance, as Maria Lopez did in the example listed, allows the supervisor to make sure that employees are producing satisfactory work. By setting standards for a clean workplace, Bud Cavanaugh reduced costs related to spending time looking for tools, or slipping on a messy floor. In many such ways, supervisors can benefit the organization through the process of control.

The Process of Controlling

While the specific ways in which supervisors control vary according to the type of organization and the employees being supervised, the basic process involves three

standards
Measures of what is
expected.

steps. First, the supervisor establishes performance standards. **Standards** are measures of what is expected. Then the supervisor monitors actual performance and compares it with the standards. Finally, the supervisor responds, either by reinforcing success or by making some adjustment to bring performance and the standards into line. Figure 5.1 illustrates this process.

Establish Performance Standards

Performance standards are a natural outgrowth of the planning process. Once the supervisor has in mind the objectives employees are to achieve, he or she can determine what employees have to do to meet those objectives. For example, assume that the objective of an eight-person telephone sales (i.e., telemarketing) office is to make 320 calls an evening, resulting in 64 sales. To achieve this objective, each salesperson should be averaging 10 calls an hour, with 2 in 10 calls resulting in a sale. Those numbers could be used as two of the office's performance standards.

As in the example, supervisors set standards for the quantity and quality of work done by employees. (The measure of quantity in the example is the number of phone calls made; the number of sales is a measure of the quality of selling—that is, the salesperson's ability to turn a phone call into a sale.) Other standards can spell out expectations for the level of service customers want to receive, the amount of money being spent, the amount of inventory on hand, the level of pollution in the workplace, and other concerns of running a business or other organization. Ultimately, all these standards measure how well the department contributes to meeting the organization's objectives for serving its customers or clients and—for a business—earning a profit.

The way supervisors set standards depends on the experience of the supervisor, the expectations of the employer, and the nature of the work being monitored. Often, supervisors use their technical expertise to estimate reasonable standards. Past performance also is a useful guide for what can be expected. However, the supervisor must take care to avoid being a slave to the past. In creating a budget, some supervisors assume that just because they have spent a given sum in a given category in the past, that expense will be appropriate in the future. Of course, the supervisor may see better alternatives if he or she is open to change. Sometimes supervisors have other sources of information in setting performance standards. Equipment manufacturers and systems designers can provide information about how fast a machine or computer system will perform. Some companies arrange for time-and-motion studies to analyze how quickly and efficiently employees can reasonably work.

To be effective, performance standards should meet the criteria of effective objectives, described in Chapter 2. That is, they should be written, measurable, clear, specific, and challenging but achievable. The "Tips from the Firing Line" box on page 103 offers some additional ideas for making standards effective.

Of course, it is not enough for the supervisor to have standards in mind. The employees should be aware of and understand those standards. In communicating performance standards, the supervisor should put them in writing, so that employees can remember and refer to them as necessary. (Chapter 7 provides more detailed suggestions for communicating effectively.)

FIGURE 5.1

The Control Process

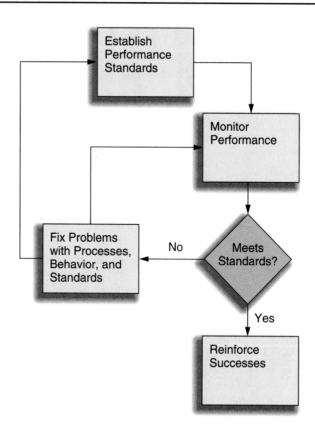

The supervisor should also be sure that the employees understand the rationale for the standards. It is human nature to resist when someone lays down rules restricting us, but the rules seem less of a burden when they serve a purpose we can understand. Thus, if a law office's word-processing department is to produce error-free documents, the department's supervisor can explain that it is part of the firm's plan to build a prestigious clientele by delivering excellent work product. With such an explanation, the word processors are less likely to feel overwhelmed by the stringent quality standard and more likely to feel proud that they are part of an excellent law firm.

Monitor Performance and Compare with Standards

Once performance standards are in place, the supervisor can begin the core of the control process: monitoring performance. In the example of the telephone sales force, the supervisor would want to keep track of how many calls each salesperson was making and how many of those calls were resulting in sales.

One way to monitor performance is simply to record information on paper or enter it into a computer. This can be done by the supervisor, the employees, or

Making Performance Standards Effective

Besides making sure performance standards have the characteristics of effective objectives, supervisors can benefit from following a few other practical guidelines:

- Make sure you are clear on what you want employees to do. Set performance standards that measure the results you want to see. Ruth N. Bramson, an executive with Employee Communications Services of Natick, Massachusetts, cites the example of a restaurant manager who hires a young man "to wash dishes." Seeing that some plates are dirty, the supervisor confronts the employee, who responds, "I washed the dishes, just like I was told to." The standard the supervisor should have expressed is that the employee is responsible for providing customers with clean dishes.

- Delegate authority and responsibility for meeting the standards. Jack Stack, president of Springfield Remanufacturing Corporation, found that overhead costs were rising too fast, so he made each supervisor and higher-level manager responsible for one of the items that made up the total overhead cost. Thus, a manager named Don Wood became responsible for the toilet paper expense for the whole company. Wood took on that responsibility with enthusiasm, tracking the company's toilet paper

expenses from week to week and from month to month. He learned that usage of toilet paper increased during the company's slow periods; he also came in under budget for his first year of monitoring that account. Thanks to the delegation, the company's total overhead expenses fell from $39 for every hour of production work to $26.32 per hour.

- Set and communicate priorities. Sometimes employees are not sure where to focus their efforts. One manager formally sets priorities at monthly staff meetings. Everyone is asked to give his or her opinion of the most important problems the department faces. The manager then weighs the employees' opinions against his own. This process reveals to the manager situations in which employees are misplacing their energy. In this way, the manager has an early warning about projects that could come in late because employees are not giving the projects enough priority.

Sources: Ruth N. Bramson, "The Secret Weapon in the War for Customers," *HRMagazine*, January 1991, pp. 65, 67ff; "Flushed with Pride," excerpt from Jack Stack, *The Great Game of Business* (Doubleday/Currency, 1992), in *Inc.*, June 1992, p. 12; and Ted Pollock, "Have You Checked Your Priorities Lately?" *Production*, July 1992, p. 10.

both. For example, the telephone salespeople might provide the supervisor with information to enter into a log such as the one shown in Table 5.1. Some types of machinery and equipment have electronic or mechanical counting systems that provide an unbiased way to measure performance. For example, the electronic scanners at store checkout stations can keep track of how fast cashiers are ringing up merchandise.

When monitoring performance, the supervisor should focus on how actual performance compares with the standards he or she has set. Are employees meeting standards, exceeding them, or falling short? Two concepts useful for maintaining this focus are variance and the exception principle.

variance
The size of the difference between actual performance and a performance standard.

Variance In a control system, **variance** refers to the size of the difference between actual performance and the standard to be met. When setting standards, the supervisor should decide how much variance is meaningful for control purposes. It can be

TABLE 5.1

Sample Performance Record

Week of _____

Performance Standard: _40_ calls,   _8_ sales

Name	Number of Calls Completed	Number of Sales Made	Action
Forrest	32	6	Discuss slow pace of work.
French	41	8	Praise performance.
Johnson	39	7	None.
Munoz	47	9	Praise performance.
Peterson	38	8	Praise performance.
Spagnoli	50	7	Praise hard work; discuss how to turn more calls into sales.
Steinmetz	29	5	Discuss poor performance; discipline if necessary.
Wang	43	9	Praise performance.
Total	319	59	None.

Bottlenecks in producing rubber parts were lowering the performance standards set by supervisors at the Tralee Park, Delaware site of E.I. duPont de Nemours and Company. This employee team increased the performance standards by solving the bottlenecks and reduced the average cycle time from 70 to 16 days, resulting in a 100 percent on-time delivery record to customers.

Source: Courtesy of DuPont, Inc.

At Frank's Nursery and Crafts retail stores, this hardware gives price verification and performs order entry, thus providing an unbiased form of employee performance monitoring.

Source: Courtesy of © 1992 Ted Kawalerski Photography, Inc.

helpful to think in terms of percentages. For example, if a hospital's performance standard is to register outpatients for lab tests in 10 minutes or less, the supervisor might decide to allow for a variance of 50 percent (5 minutes). (In a manufacturing setting, a variance of 5 to 10 percent might be more appropriate for most standards.) As described in the next chapter, some organizations strive for a standard of accepting zero defects.

exception principle
The control principle stating that a supervisor should take action only when a variance is meaningful.

The Exception Principle   According to the **exception principle**, the supervisor should take action only when a variance is meaningful. Thus, when monitoring performance in the previous example, the supervisor would need to take action only if outpatients spent more than 15 or fewer than 5 minutes registering for lab tests.

The exception principle is beneficial when it helps the supervisor to manage his or her time wisely and to motivate employees. A supervisor who did not tolerate reasonable variances might try to solve the "problem" every time an employee made one component too few or went over the budget for office supplies by the cost of a box of paper clips. In such a case, employees might become frustrated by the control system, and morale would deteriorate. At the same time, the supervisor would be too busy to focus on more significant issues.

Reinforce Successes and Fix Problems

The information gained from the control process is beneficial only if the supervisor uses it as the basis for reinforcing or changing behavior. If performance is satisfactory or better, the supervisor needs to see that this continues. If performance is

When performance exceeds standards by a significant amount, the supervisor may reward the employee with a monetary or other reward. In 1991, Senior Sales Engineer Monica Maia from Brazil, was one of 59 employees of E. I. duPont de Nemours and Company to receive the company's Marketing Excellence Award.

Source: Courtesy of DuPont, Inc.

unacceptable, the supervisor needs to make changes to correct the problem. Sometimes the problem is with the performance standard itself, in which case the supervisor's response should be to change the standard. The right-hand column in Table 5.1 describes some ways the telemarketing supervisor plans to respond to performance data.

Reinforce Successes   Employees doing excellent work, costs staying under budget—these are conditions to make any supervisor smile. The supervisor needs to make sure that such a happy situation continues. One way to do this is to reinforce successes.

reinforcement
Encouragement of a behavior by associating it with a reward.

   Reinforcement means encouraging the behavior by associating it with a reward. For performance that meets standards, an appropriate reward is praise from the supervisor for the good performance. This not only gives the employee a good feeling, it also clarifies what is expected. When performance exceeds standards by a significant amount, the supervisor may reward the employee with a monetary bonus as well as with praise. The supervisor's actions will depend on any company and union rules regarding superior performance.

problem
A factor in the organization that is a barrier to improvement.

Fix Problems   When performance significantly falls short of standards, the supervisor should investigate. Below-standard performance is often a sign that there is a **problem**—that is, a factor in the organization that is a barrier to improvement. The supervisor's task is to identify the underlying problem.

For example, the supervisor in the telephone sales company may notice that the group is not meeting its sales objectives. The supervisor could look to see who is falling short of the sales goals, either everyone or just one or two employees. If everyone is performing below standard, the problem may be that the sales force needs better training or motivation. Or the problem may lie outside the supervisor's direct control; the product may be defective, or customers may be uninterested for some other reason, such as poor economic conditions or lack of desire to buy the product at that time. If only one employee is failing to make sales, the supervisor would need to search for the problem underlying that employee's poor performance. Does the employee understand how to close a sale? Is the employee having personal problems that affect performance?

symptom
An indication of an underlying problem.

As the example suggests, the poor performance itself is not the problem in most cases. Rather, it is a **symptom**—an indication of an underlying problem. This distinction applies to a business that had trouble paying its bills on time and therefore set up a hotline, a phone number its vendors could call to find out when they would be paid. This company was treating the *symptom* of late payments by setting up a system to handle mistakes (the late payments). The company should have addressed the *problem* by figuring out how it could make payments on time in the first place.[1]

Thus, to make effective use of information gained through controlling, the supervisor needs to distinguish symptoms from problems. One way to do this is to respond to poor performance by getting a clear picture of the problem, then asking, "Why is this happening?" Figure 5.2 shows how this thinking process works.

If the control system is working properly, the supervisor should be uncovering problems before customers and management discover them. This gives the supervisor the best opportunity to fix the problem in time to minimize damage.

Fixing the problem may entail adjusting a process or the behavior of an individual employee. To bring performance into line with standards, supervisors can choose from among a number of possible actions, such as these:

- Ask employees for suggestions.
- Develop new rewards for good performance.
- Train employees.
- Improve communications with employees.
- Counsel and/or discipline poor performers.
- Fix machinery and equipment that is working improperly.

In some instances, the supervisor will find that these measures can improve performance bit by bit, rather than all at once. (Other chapters in this book elaborate on most of these ways to improve performance.)

Whatever actions the supervisor selects, it is important for him or her to give employees feedback soon after observing a deviation (performance that varies from the standard). This enables the employees to make changes before performance deteriorates further. A problem that has been allowed to continue is often harder to correct. For example, an employee may get into the habit of doing a task the wrong way or may fall so far behind that it is impossible to catch up.

Change Standards When performance does not meet standards, sometimes the problem is with the standard. This is often the case when all employees are performing significantly above or below a standard. For example, if no employees on

Identifying a Problem

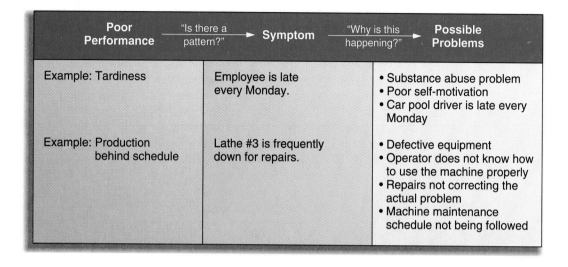

Poor Performance	"Is there a pattern?" → Symptom	"Why is this happening?" → Possible Problems
Example: Tardiness	Employee is late every Monday.	• Substance abuse problem • Poor self-motivation • Car pool driver is late every Monday
Example: Production behind schedule	Lathe #3 is frequently down for repairs.	• Defective equipment • Operator does not know how to use the machine properly • Repairs not correcting the actual problem • Machine maintenance schedule not being followed

the telephone sales force are making the number of sales they should be, the standards may be too high, given current economic or market conditions.

In such a case, the best response is to make the performance standard more appropriate. If performance is below the standard, the supervisor would make the standard less stringent. If performance is above the standard, raising the standard might be appropriate.

Modifying standards brings the control process full circle. With new standards in place, the supervisor is again ready to monitor performance.

Types of Control

From the description of the control process, it might sound as though controlling begins when employees' work is complete. The employees finish their job, then the supervisor checks to see whether it was done well. However, this is only one type of controlling. In terms of when controlling takes place, there are actually three types: feedback control, concurrent control, and precontrol.

feedback control
Control that focuses on past performance.

Feedback control is the type just described—that is, control that focuses on past performance. A supervisor reviewing customer comments about service is practicing feedback control. The customers provide information about the quality of service, and the supervisor reacts by reinforcing or trying to change employees' behavior.

concurrent control
Control that occurs while the work takes place.

The word *concurrent* describes things that are happening at the same time. Thus, **concurrent control** refers to controlling work while that work is taking place. A restaurant manager who greets customers at their tables and visits the kitchen to see how work is progressing is practicing concurrent control. This supervisor is gathering information about what is going smoothly and what problems may be developing. The supervisor can act on any problems before customers or employees become upset. Another technique for concurrent control is statistical process control, described in the next chapter.

precontrol
Efforts aimed at preventing behavior that may lead to undesirable results.

Precontrol refers to efforts aimed at preventing behavior that may lead to undesirable results. Such efforts may include setting rules, policies, and procedures. A production supervisor might provide employees with guidelines on when to detect that their machinery is not working properly. The employees can then request repairs before they waste time and materials on a machine that is not working properly. Precontrol is one of the functions of the management philosophy known as total quality management (see Chapter 6).

Tools for Control

When considering how to monitor performance, the supervisor can start with some of the basic tools used by most managers. Budgets and reports are common in most organizations. In addition, supervisors can benefit from personally observing the work taking place.

Budgets

As you learned in Chapter 2, a budget is a plan for spending money. Creating a budget is part of the planning process. In controlling, a budget is useful as a kind of performance standard. The supervisor compares actual expenses with the amounts in the budget.

Table 5.2 is a sample budget report based on the budget example that appeared as Table 2.2 in Chapter 2. The left-hand column shows each category of expenses for the manufacturing project, which was scheduled to last for six months—from January through June. Thus, the six-month budget represents the total the supervisor expected to spend in each category for the project. This report was prepared on March 31 (halfway through the project), so the next column shows what would be budgeted for half of the project. Next the actual amounts show what actually was spent during the first three months. In the right-hand column appears the variance between the actual and budgeted amounts. A positive variance is favorable in this case because it means the machine shop spent less than the budgeted amount. A negative variance is unfavorable because it means expenses went over budget. (In contrast, if the report showed earnings rather than expenses, a positive variance would be unfavorable, because it would mean the department earned less than the budgeted amount.) The negative total variance in the table shows that the project is $679 over budget for the first three months.

When using such a budget report for controlling purposes, the supervisor focuses on the variance column, looking for meaningful variances. In Table 5.2, the supervisor would note that the total unfavorable variance is due entirely to a large expense for equipment repair. The machine shop is otherwise under budget or exactly meeting the budget standards. Following the exception principle, the

TABLE 5.2
Budget Report for a Manufacturing Project

	Organizational Unit Machine Shop	Job Number 1763	Date March 31, 19xx	
Line Item	**Six-Month Budget**	**Budgeted Year to Date (Jan.–Mar.)**	**Actual Year to Date (Jan.–Mar.)**	**Variance**
Direct Labor	$60,000	$30,000	$30,000	$0
Indirect Labor	5,400	2,700	2,700	0
Material	13,200	6,600	6,383	217
Operating supplies	3,000	1,500	1,496	4
Equipment repair	5,400	2,700	3,600	−900
Total	$87,000	$43,500	$44,179	−$679

Source: Reprinted with the permission of Merrill, an imprint of Macmillan Publishing from INDUS-TRIAL SUPERVISION IN THE AGE OF HIGH TECHNOLOGY by David L. Goetsch. Copyright © 1992 by Merrill Publishing.

supervisor takes action when a meaningful variance occurs. Typically, this involves looking for ways to cut costs when the department goes over budget. The supervisor in the example will want to focus on avoiding further equipment breakdowns. Sometimes the supervisor can change the budget when a variance indicates that the budgeted figures were unrealistic.

Performance Reports

performance report
A summary of performance and comparison with performance standards.

A well-structured report can be an important source of information. **Performance reports** summarize performance and compare it with performance standards. They can simply summarize facts, such as the number of calls made by sales representatives or the number of deliveries completed by delivery personnel. The reports may also be analytical; that is, they may interpret the facts.

Most supervisors prepare as well as request performance reports. Typically, the organization requires that the supervisor do a particular type of reporting of the department's performance. The supervisor's role is to prepare the type of report requested. Supervisors also may request that employees prepare reports for them. In that case, the supervisor can influence the type of reporting.

As much as possible, supervisors should see to it that reports are simple and to the point. A table or log may be more useful than an essay-style report. Graphs can sometimes uncover a trend better than numbers in columns can. Figure 5.3 shows how the data from Table 5.1 can be converted into a graph. In this case, variances were first computed by finding the difference between each employee's performance and the performance standards. Notice how easy it is to tell from the graph that there is a wide variation in how many calls each employee made. (Does this mean some employees are working harder than others? Maybe, but remember the process of searching for a problem. It is also possible that some employees are better at keeping calls short and to the point.)

FIGURE 5.3

Graph of Variances Determined from Table 5.1

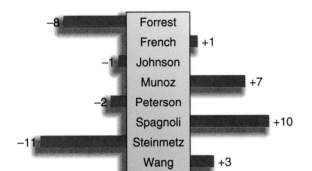

Calls Completed—Variances from a Standard of 40

−8	Forrest	
	French	+1
−1	Johnson	
	Munoz	+7
−2	Peterson	
	Spagnoli	+10
−11	Steinmetz	
	Wang	+3

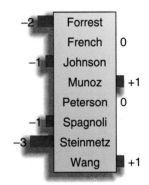

Sales Made—Variances from a Standard of 8

−2	Forrest	
	French	0
−1	Johnson	
	Munoz	+1
	Peterson	0
−1	Spagnoli	
−3	Steinmetz	
	Wang	+1

Graphs can sometimes uncover trends better than numbers in columns can. The Nielsen Workstation's powerful software and clear graphics provide a platform for integrating and analyzing complex information.

Source: Courtesy of Nielsen Marketing Research.

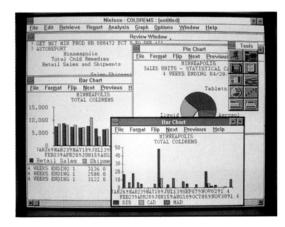

The supervisor should also determine whether every report he or she is receiving is still useful. Many reports continue to be generated long after they have lost their usefulness. In deciding whether to continue using a report, the supervisor can consider whether it has the characteristics of effective controls, described at the end of this chapter.

Personal Observation

A supervisor who spends the entire day behind a desk, reading budgets and reports, is a supervisor who is out of touch. An important part of controlling involves spending time with employees and observing what is going on. Management consultant

Tom Peters has popularized this approach, using the term "management by walking around" (MBWA). While engaged in MBWA, the supervisor can listen to employees, help them discover better ways of doing their jobs, and make the changes necessary to help employees work better. For example, a nursing supervisor might observe that the nurses frequently spend time debating which demands to respond to first. The supervisor could discuss this with the nurses and help them develop criteria for setting priorities. The inability to control through personal observation is one of the greatest challenges of supervising employees who work at home, as discussed in the "Dealing with Diversity" box.

Personal observation can help the supervisor understand the activities behind the numbers in reports. However, the supervisor must be careful in interpreting what he or she sees. Often the presence of a supervisor causes workers to alter their behavior. Also, the supervisor must visit work areas often enough to be sure of witnessing routine situations, not just an unusual crisis or break in the action. At the same time, the supervisor must take care not to spend so much time among employees that they feel the visits interfere with their work. How much time is the right amount to spend in MBWA? The supervisor probably will have to rely on trial and error, weighing employee reactions and the amount of information obtained.

Characteristics of Effective Controls

It is impossible to keep track of every detail of every employee's work. An effective control system is one that helps the supervisor direct his or her efforts toward spotting significant problems. Normally, a supervisor has to use whatever control system higher-level managers have established. However, when making recommendations about controls or when setting up controls to use within the department, the supervisor can strive for the following characteristics of effective controls.

Timeliness   The controls should be *timely*. They should enable the supervisor to correct problems in time to improve results. For example, an annual budget report does not let the supervisor adjust spending in time to meet the budget's goals. In contrast, monthly budget reports give the supervisor time to identify spending patterns that will pose a problem. If the supervisor's annual budget includes $500 to spend on overnight couriers but the department has already spent $200 by the end of February, the supervisor knows it will be necessary to plan work so that there is time to send materials by some other, less expensive means.

Cost-Effectiveness   The controls should be *economical*. In general, this means that the cost of using the controls should be less than the benefit derived from using them. In a supermarket, for example, an elaborate system designed to make sure that not a single item of inventory, not even a can of peaches, gets lost or stolen may not save the store enough money to justify the cost of the system.

Acceptability   The controls should be *acceptable to supervisor and employee*. Supervisors want controls that give them enough information about performance so that they can understand what is going on in the workplace. Employees want controls that do not unduly infringe on their privacy. One area of controversy has

Controlling Workers at Home

Single parents, parents in two-income households, and people with disabilities are among those who may find it easier to work at home than to commute every day. An estimated 5.5 million Americans worked at home for at least part of the workweek in 1991, up from 4 million the year before. This number is expected to grow steadily, fueled by employee demand and government efforts to meet air-quality standards by decreasing the number of people driving cars to work. One consequence of this trend is that supervisors must consider how they can control work being done in home offices.

The responsibility might seem daunting. How can a supervisor make sure employees are not devoting their time to raiding the refrigerator and catching up on the latest soap operas? In fact, it appears that employees who choose to work at home tend to be self-motivated. If anything, they have trouble taking a break. One worker reportedly became so wrapped up in the computer programming he was doing at home that he gave himself headaches by working for hours without interruption. He eventually had to set a clock radio to go off every two hours, reminding him to take a break.

For self-motivated workers, being at home is a way to escape the distractions of the workplace.

Claudia Cohl, editor in chief of *Home Office Computing* magazine, manages several home workers. Of one worker who lives 400 miles from the magazine offices, Cohl observes, "He's the most productive person working for me. Projects that need concentrated effort I can give to him, and they'll be great." Similarly, Chuck Hanson, a market planner for GTE Northwest in Seattle, says, "I can get done at home in a few hours what it takes a whole day to do at the office."

Of course, supervisors do face challenges in controlling work done at home. Supervisors and employees alike can benefit from special training in handling the long-distance relationship. According to Jack Nilles, a consultant on the subject, "We tell the managers they have to change from being administrators to being leaders. We tell them your job isn't to act as a cop but as a goal setter and motivator." The process works best when supervisors and employees can agree on clearly defined goals, tasks, and schedules.

Sources: Cynthia Crossen, "No Place Like Home," *The Wall Street Journal*, June 4, 1990, pp. R6–R8ff; and David Foster, "Workers Stay Home, Keep Jobs," *Chicago Tribune*, April 19, 1992, sec. 7, p. 9A.

been electronic monitoring of employee performance. For example, computers can keep track of how many phone calls operators handle and how much time they spend on each call. This gives the supervisor a lot of information—including how much time operators spend going to the bathroom. Does this close scrutiny enhance performance by encouraging employees to work hard, or does it merely lower morale and remove the incentive to take time to greet customers in a friendly way? The answer lies in part in the way supervisors use this information.

Employees also appreciate controls that focus on areas over which they themselves have some control. For example, a control that measures the number of units produced by an employee would be acceptable only if the employee always has the parts needed to produce those units. An employee whose performance looks poor because of an inventory shortage would feel frustrated by the control.

Flexibility   Finally, the controls should be *flexible*. This means the supervisor should be able to ignore a variance if doing so is in the best interests of the

At Hershey Chocolate U.S.A.'s H.B. Reese plant, Supervisor Sandra Wolfersberger (left) uses "management by walking around" (MBWA) while discussing operational improvements with employees Mary Cope (center) and Veronica Purdy (right).

Source: Courtesy of Hershey Foods Corp.

organization. For example, in comparing expenditures to a budget, a supervisor should be aware of occasions when spending a little more than was budgeted will actually benefit the company. That might be the case when employees have to put in overtime to fill an order from an important customer. In the future, better planning might make it possible to avoid the overtime, but the immediate goal is to satisfy the customer.

One reason that flexibility is important is that performance measures can be somewhat incompatible. For example, employees may find it impossible to cut costs and improve quality at the same time. In such a case, it may be up to the supervisor to set priorities or to adjust the control measures.

Summary

5.1   Describe the purpose of using controls.
By identifying problems in time for them to be corrected, controlling enables supervisors to ensure high-quality work and to keep costs under control.

5.2   Identify the steps in the control process.
The control process begins when the supervisor sets and communicates performance standards. The supervisor then monitors performance and compares it with the standards. Depending on whether performance is above, at, or below the standards, the supervisor reinforces successes or fixes problems. If the results reveal that a performance standard itself is a problem, the supervisor may change the standard.

5.3   Explain how supervisors should focus their efforts when monitoring performance.
In monitoring performance, the supervisor should look for variances, or differences between actual

performance and standards for performance. According to the exception principle, the supervisor should determine how much of a variance is significant, then concentrate on reacting only to significant variances.

5.4   Identify types of control.
Feedback control focuses on past performance. Concurrent control occurs while the work is taking place. Precontrol consists of efforts aimed at preventing behavior that may lead to undesirable results.

5.5   Tell how budgets, reports, and personal observation help supervisors control.
Budgets give supervisors information that helps them control spending. By periodically comparing actual expenses with budgeted amounts, the supervisor can determine whether the department is spending too much in some area. Performance reports provide supervisors with a written summary of performance, comparing it with standards. The supervisor can review reports to look for significant variances. Personal observation, or management by walking around, provides direct evidence of the department's activities, as well as a chance to discuss problems directly with employees and help them find solutions.

5.6   Describe characteristics of effective controls.
To be effective, controls should be timely, economical, acceptable to both supervisor and employee, and flexible.

Key Terms

controlling	reinforcement	concurrent control
standards	problem	precontrol
variance	symptom	performance report
exception principle	feedback control	

Review and Discussion Questions

1. Your best friend just got promoted to a position as a supervisor and feels uncomfortable about "checking up on people." How can you explain to your friend why controlling plays an important role in helping the organization meet its goals?
2. What are the steps in the process of controlling?
3. How is the control process related to the management function of planning?
4. At a meeting of all the company's managers, Ralph Reko, a production supervisor, has learned that his company will be positioning itself as the top-quality producer of cellular phones. Ralph decides that to support this strategy, he must devise a control system that detects every error, malfunction, and defect in his department. What are some potential shortcomings of Ralph's approach?
5. Bonnie Goode supervises telephone operators in the customer service department of a software company. The operators are expected to handle 50 phone calls per day (250 in a five-day workweek). Each Monday, Bonnie receives a report of each operator's weekly performance relative to this standard. Her most recent report contained the following information:

Operator	Mon.	Tues.	Wed.	Thurs.	Fri.	Total	Variance
Brown	10	28	39	42	16	135	−115
Lee	48	51	58	43	49	249	−1
Mendoza	65	72	56	83	61	337	87
Smith	53	48	47	40	45	233	−17

   a. As supervisor, how should Bonnie respond to each operator's performance?
   b. Is this control system an effective one for ensuring quality performance? Explain.
6. If failure to meet a performance standard indicates some type of underlying problem, how

might the supervisor attempt to solve the problem?

7. When should a supervisor respond to a variance by changing a performance standard? Give an example.

8. How can budgets help supervisors carry out the control function?

9. Mildred Pirelli supervises salespeople in a department store. One day she walked around her department to observe the salespeople in action. She saw one of them approve a charge card purchase without following the company's policy of verifying the signature on the charge card.

   a. How should Mildred respond to this variance from company policy?

   b. Should the way Mildred obtained the information (personal observation) influence her decision on how to act? Explain.

10. Why do controls need to be timely and economical?

A SECOND LOOK

In the story of Lifeline Systems at the beginning of this chapter, what symptom indicated that something was wrong? What were the underlying problems that John Gugliotta uncovered?

Class Exercise*

Divide the class into groups of five or six members. One member of each group will act as the supervisor; the rest are employees. Since few work groups actually get to choose their own supervisor, the instructor might arbitrarily designate the supervisor in each group. The instructor provides each group with square sheets of paper; $5\frac{7}{8}$" × $5\frac{7}{8}$" is a good size.

1. Each person reviews instructions for making origami yachts (see Figure 5.4).

2. The supervisor in each group sets performance standards for making the yachts in 10 minutes. These should include quality as well as quantity standards. In setting the standards, the supervisor may use whatever information he or she can obtain; it is up to the supervisor whether to seek input from the group.

   At the same time, each employee estimates how many yachts he or she can make correctly in 10 minutes. The employee writes down this estimate but does not reveal it to the supervisor at this time.

3. For 10 minutes, the employees make as many yachts as they can according to the instructions.

During that time, the supervisor tries to monitor their performance in whatever way seems helpful. If employees seem to be falling short of the performance standard, the supervisor should try to find ways to improve performance. (This may include simply waiting patiently for skills to improve, if that seems most beneficial.)

4. After the 10 minutes have ended, determine how many yachts each group made and assess the quality of the work. As a class, discuss the groups' performance. Did each group meet its supervisor's performance standards? If not, was the variance significant? Based on their own estimates of how much they could do, do employees think their supervisor's standards were reasonable?

5. The class should also consider supervisors' efforts to take corrective action. Did supervisors intervene too much, or not enough? How did supervisors' attempts help or hurt employees' efforts? What does this experience reveal about the way supervisors should behave in the workplace?

---

*Corinne Livesay of Liberty University, Lynchburg, Virginia, located the origami instructions.

FIGURE 5.4

Instructions for Origami Yachts

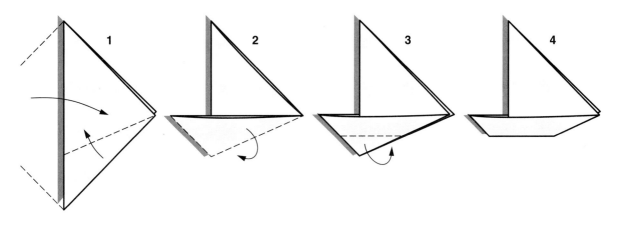

CASE

Controlling Fuel Expenses

The Pharmaseal Division of Baxter Healthcare Corporation operates a fleet of about 500 trucks, which travel a total of 30 to 40 million miles a year. Considering that the trucks' mileage is only four or five miles to the gallon, they are burning a tremendous amount of gasoline. Not surprisingly, controlling fuel expenses is an important task for Baxter.

Besides the number of miles driven, fuel consumption is influenced by drivers' practices. For example, if a driver takes a longer rest break than is allowed, then tries to make up the time by speeding, the truck will burn gas less efficiently. Some drivers have let engines idle unnecessarily, even for an hour or more.

To improve fuel efficiency, the company installed an on-board terminal (OBT) on each truck. These electronic devices continually monitor the vehicle's operation. They record vehicle operating statistics such as fuel consumption, brake usage, and wheel RPMs (measuring speed). The driver inputs additional information, including the time he or she is on duty; location; and length of breaks.

The drivers turn in the OBT cartridges when they are at the end of their shift. A Baxter employee then uses a computer to read each driver's performance. The company has a system for scoring the performance, with a perfect score being 100. When Baxter first tried using OBTs, a passing grade was considered 60 points. However, use of the OBTs has made the drivers more conscientious, and the company has gradually increased the passing score to 90.

1. What performance standard does Baxter set for its truck drivers? How does the company measure performance relative to that standard?
2. Based on the information given, does this control system seem to meet the criteria for effective controls, as described in the chapter? Explain.
3. If you supervised Baxter's truck drivers, what additional information would you want for controlling performance?

Source: "OBTs Prevent 'Fuelishness,'" *Maintenance Supervisor's Bulletin* (National Foreman's Institute), September 10, 1991, p. 2.

6

Quality is never an accident; it is always the result of intelligent effort.
—John Ruskin

Maintaining and Improving Quality

LEARNING OBJECTIVES

6.1 **Describe consequences suffered by organizations as a result of poor-quality work.**

6.2 **Compare product quality control and process control.**

6.3 **Identify techniques for quality control.**

6.4 **Explain how employee involvement teams work and what makes them successful.**

6.5 **Describe principles for successfully using total quality management.**

6.6 **Identify ways organizations measure their success in continuous quality improvement.**

6.7 **Describe guidelines for quality control.**

QUALITY FIRST

Several years ago, managers at First National Bank of Chicago learned of a problem faced by customers for the bank's letters of credit. (Letters of credit are documents that are issued by a bank and used for financing exports.) When customers called the bank about letters of credit, they often were transferred from one employee to another before finding the person who could help them. Neither the bank nor the customers considered this an acceptable quality of service.

First Chicago turned over the problem to one of its dozens of quality teams, each composed of a supervisor and several employees. The team investigated the problem and found that its source was the bank's practice of having nine different employees handle each request for a letter of credit. This assembly-line process took four days.

Next, the quality team devised a solution. Employees who issued letters of credit were trained to handle all steps in the process. Thus, one employee handled each request alone. Every time a customer requested a letter of credit, that customer was assigned to the same employee. With the new process, issuing letters of credit takes only a single day.

First Chicago has benefited in several ways from the effort to improve the quality of service. First, in five years the bank more than doubled the number of letters of credit it issued annually. In addition, it operates more efficiently, handling the higher volume with fewer employees. And the bank has developed a reputation for high quality in this area. Robert J. Haider, an international credit manager for Motorola, says, "When a customer needs a letter of credit to place an order with us, we tell them to use First Chicago if they can."

Sources: Aaron Bernstein, "Quality Is Becoming Job One in the Office, Too," *Business Week*, April 29, 1991, pp. 52–53, 56. Photo courtesy of Frank Herholdt/Tony Stone Images.

At First Chicago, the employee team sought to improve the quality of the department's work. What made the revised process of higher quality? A logical way to understand high quality is to think of it as work that meets or exceeds customers' expectations. Table 6.1 describes eight dimensions that can be used to measure the quality of goods or services.

Many of the supervisor's activities, including planning, leading, and controlling, are directed toward improving the quality of the organization's goods and services. This chapter takes a more specific look at the supervisor's role in maintaining and improving quality. The chapter also describes consequences of poor quality. It then introduces types of quality-control efforts and several techniques for quality control. Finally, the chapter discusses some general guidelines for maintaining and improving quality.

Consequences of Poor Quality

When the quality of an organization's goods or services is poor, the whole organization suffers. As word spreads about problems with the product, customers look for alternatives. The organization develops a negative image, which not only drives away customers and clients but also makes it harder to recruit superior employees or to borrow money at favorable terms. The organization loses business and, therefore, revenues.

Poor-quality work can also lead to higher costs. Ensuring that things are done right the first time might seem expensive to some managers. But the reality is that businesses spend billions of dollars each year on inspections, errors, rework, repairs, customer refunds, and other costs to find and correct mistakes.[1] And attracting new customers costs several times more per customer than keeping customers satisfied, so marketing costs are higher, too. Thus, poor quality often results in much wasted time and materials, besides requiring that unacceptable items be fixed or discarded. If the problems go undetected until after goods have been sold, the manufacturer may have to recall its products for repair or replacement. In addition, poor goods and services may result in lawsuits by disgruntled or injured customers.

A pair of examples illustrate the high costs of poor quality.[2] First, a recent Harper's Index (published in *Harper's* magazine) reported that among patients admitted to a hospital, 1 in 25 will leave with a disabling injury that directly results from treatment. Second, according to congressional investigators, the Pentagon stores hospital supplies and perishable items for such a long time that many must be discarded. At the Pentagon's hospitals and clinics, $18 million a year is wasted on drugs alone.

These kinds of issues extend to the services that one department in the organization provides to the other departments. For example, if the maintenance crew or the payroll department does a poor job, the overall work of the organization suffers. Morale may decline. Employees may find that they spend a lot of time making up for the lapses of others.

TABLE 6.1	**Dimension**	**Explanation**
Dimensions of Quality	Performance	The product's primary operating characteristic, such as an automobile's acceleration or the picture clarity of a television
	Features	Supplements to the product's basic operating characteristics—for example, power windows on a car or the ceremony with which a bottle of wine is opened in a restaurant
	Reliability	The probability that the product will function properly and not break down during a specified period—a manufacturer's warranty is often seen as an indicator of this
	Conformance	The degree to which the product's design and operating characteristics meet established standards, such as safety standards for a crib
	Durability	The length of the product's life—for example, whether a stereo lasts for 5 years or 25 years
	Serviceability	The speed and ease of repairing the product—for example, whether a computer store will send out a repairperson, service the computer in the store, or provide no maintenance service at all
	Aesthetics	The way the product looks, feels, tastes, and smells, such as the styling and smell of a new car
	Perceived quality	The customer's impression of the product's quality, such as a buyer's belief that an Audi is a safe and reliable car

Source: Adapted from David A. Garvin, "Competing on the Eight Dimensions of Quality," *Harvard Business Review*, November–December 1987.

Types of Quality Control

Because of the negative consequences of poor quality, organizations try to prevent and correct such problems through various approaches to quality control. Thus, broadly speaking, **quality control** refers to an organization's efforts to prevent or correct defects in its goods or services or to improve them in some way. Some organizations use the term *quality control* to refer only to error detection, with *quality assurance* referring to both the prevention and the detection of quality problems. However, this chapter will use *quality control* in the broader sense, as it is the simpler, more common term.

quality control
An organization's efforts to prevent or correct defects in its goods or services or to improve them in some way.

Whichever term is used, many organizations—especially large ones—have a department or employee devoted to identifying defects and promoting high quality. In these cases, the supervisor can benefit from the expertise of the quality-control personnel. Ultimately, however, the organization expects its supervisors to take responsibility for the quality of work in their department. The "Tips from the Firing Line" box offers some suggestions for fulfilling that responsibility. In

TIPS FROM THE FIRING LINE

Improving Quality: What Supervisors Can Do

Many of the ways that organizations improve quality start with the top managers. But there are practical steps that supervisors can take. Here are some suggestions:

- Emphasize quality to your employees. Make sure they know it is your top priority.
- Demonstrate a commitment to quality by using visual reminders such as posters. Before the posters get so familiar that employees stop noticing them, update them with new ones.
- Make sure employees understand the quality standards that have been set. Encourage them to exceed the standards.
- Even if the organization has quality-control personnel to conduct inspections, periodically examine employees' work yourself.

- When you see something wrong, act on it immediately.
- If your employees' work involves producing a batch of parts or products, inspect the first item in the batch so that you can spot any problems before further work takes place.
- Make sure all your employees are aware of their role in improving quality. Work with them to develop their commitment to that role.

Source: David L. Goetsch, *Industrial Supervision in the Age of High Technology* (New York: Merrill, 1992), p. 461.

Quality problems can sometimes reach crisis proportions. Business at Jack in the Box restaurants in California slid more than 20 percent in less than a month in early 1993 after meat tainted with bacteria caused two deaths and at least 300 illnesses in Idaho, Nevada, and Washington.

Source: © 1991 Comstock, Inc.

FIGURE 6.1

Types of Quality Control

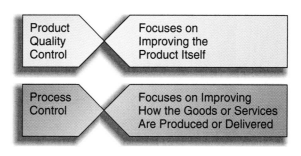

general, when supervisors look for high-quality performance to reinforce or improvements to make, they can focus on two areas: the product itself or the process of making and delivering the product. These two orientations are illustrated in Figure 6.1.

Product Quality Control

product quality control
Quality control that focuses on ways in which the product itself can be improved.

An organization that focuses on ways in which the product itself can be improved is using **product quality control**. For example, employees in a print shop might examine a sample of newsletters or envelopes to look for smudges and other defects. A city's park district might consider ways to upgrade its playground equipment or to improve the programs it offers senior citizens.

Process Control

process control
Quality control that emphasizes how to do things in a way that leads to better quality.

An organization might also consider how to do things in a way that leads to better quality. This focus is called **process control**. The print shop in the previous example might conduct periodic checks to make sure its employees understand good techniques for setting up the presses. The park district might ask the maintenance crew to suggest ways to keep the parks cleaner and more attractive. In this way, the park district can improve the process by which the crew members do their job.

A broad approach to process control involves creating an organizational climate that encourages quality. Employees at all levels, from the day they are hired, should understand that quality is important and that they have a role in delivering high quality. At the city park district in the previous example, managers and employees might consider ways to be more responsive to citizens' input. The greater responsiveness, in turn, could enable park district employees to recognize ways to better serve the community.

FIGURE 6.2
Quality-Control Techniques

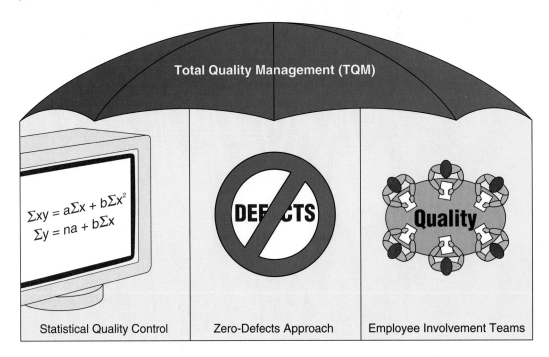

Techniques for Quality Control

Within this broad framework, managers, researchers, and consultants have identified several quality-control techniques. These include statistical quality control, the zero-defects approach, employee involvement teams, and total quality management. Figure 6.2 summarizes these techniques.

In choosing a technique—or, more commonly, applying the techniques selected by higher-level management—supervisors need to remember that a technique alone does not guarantee high quality. Rather, these techniques work when the people who use them are well motivated, understand how to use them, and exercise creativity in using them to solve problems. In the words of Boston Consulting Group's Jeanie Duck, "These [techniques] are all tools, like a computer. But a computer is not the answer, it is the tool we use to create the answer."[3]

Statistical Quality Control

In most cases, it does not make economic sense to examine every part, finished good, or service to make sure it meets quality standards. For one thing, that approach to quality control is expensive. Furthermore, examining some products, such as packages of cheese or boxes of tissues, can destroy them. Thus, unless the costs of poor

Ford Motor Company's goal, as stated in its 1991 annual report, is to be a low-cost producer of the highest quality products. It is a company that uses product quality control to achieve this goal. James Spencer examines a newly-produced windshield at the quality inspection station at the Rouge Glass plant.

Source: Courtesy of Ford Motor Company.

statistical quality control
Looking for defects in parts or finished goods selected through a sampling technique.

statistical process control
A statistical quality-control technique in which the operator of a process uses statistics to monitor production quality on an ongoing basis, making corrections whenever the results show the process is out of control.

quality are so great that every product must be examined, most organizations inspect only a sample. Looking for defects in parts or finished goods selected through a sampling technique is known as **statistical quality control**.

The most accurate way to apply statistical quality control is to use a random sample. This means selecting parts or goods in a way that each part or good has an equal chance of being selected. The assumption is that the quality of the sample describes the quality of the entire lot. Thus, if 2 percent of the salad dressing bottles in a sample have leaks, presumably 2 percent of all the bottles coming off the assembly line have leaks. The employees' and supervisor's challenge is to find out why and to correct that problem.

Rather than wait until a process is complete to take a random sample, the operators of a process can use statistics to monitor production quality on an ongoing basis—the quality-control technique known as **statistical process control (SPC)**. The operator periodically measures some aspect of what he or she is producing—say, the diameter of a hole drilled or the correctness of an account number entered onto a computer—then plots the results on a control chart such as the simplified one shown in Figure 6.3. The middle line in the chart shows the value that represents the standard—statistically speaking, the mean in this case. Above

FIGURE 6.3

Chart Used for Statistical Process Control

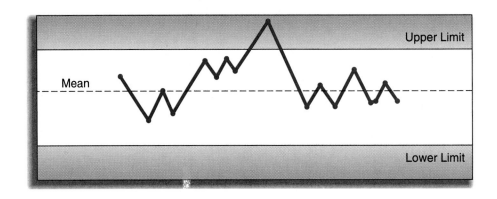

Source: Reprinted with the permission of Macmillan Publishing Company from INDUSTRIAL SUPERVISION: In the Age of High Technology by David L. Goetsch. Copyright © 1992 by Macmillan Publishing Company.

and below the mean value are lines representing the upper and lower limits that are acceptable. When a measured value falls between these limits, the operator may assume the process is working normally. When a value falls outside these limits, the operator is supposed to correct the process.

Thus, if a machine operator is supposed to machine a part to make it 0.0375 inch in diameter (the mean value in this case), the lower and upper limits might be 0.0370 inch and 0.0380 inch, respectively. If the operator measures a part and finds that its diameter is 0.0383 inch, the operator would adjust the machine or modify his or her actions to keep such errors from recurring. Judging from the measurements in Figure 6.3, for example, it appears that the operator made some needed adjustments after one measurement exceeded the upper limit. After that point, the measurements are clustered much closer to the mean; the process is again under control. As you can see from this example, SPC gives the operator a great deal of control in maintaining quality, rather than assigning that duty to specialized personnel. That is one reason SPC is increasingly popular today, especially in manufacturing firms.

The idea of using SPC or other statistical methods makes some supervisors nervous. They worry that they or their employees will be unable to handle the statistics. However, using the process requires only a basic knowledge of statistics, coupled with an understanding of what level of quality is desirable and achievable. The supervisor should see that employees who use SPC get the training they need in using the technique and in adjusting the processes they are responsible for. (Chapter 14 describes the supervisor's role in employee training.)

Zero-Defects Approach

A broad view of process quality control is that everyone in the organization should work toward the goal of delivering such high quality that all aspects of the organization's products and services are free of problems. The quality-control technique

DeKalb Plant Genetics Corporation demonstrates statistical process control by working closely with dealers and customers to evaluate hybrid performance in the field. DeKalb Agronomist Herb Brown (top) and Sales Manager Buddy Knepley are checking yield levels and moisture content.

Source: Courtesy of DeKalb Plant Genetics.

zero-defects approach
A quality-control technique based on the view that everyone in the organization should work toward the goal of delivering such high quality that all aspects of the organization's products and services are free of problems.

based on this view is known as the **zero-defects approach**. In a manufacturing organization using the zero-defects approach, the goods produced would be of excellent quality not only because production workers and management are seeking ways to avoid defects, but also because the purchasing department is ensuring a timely supply of well-crafted parts, the accounting department is seeing that bills get paid on time, the human resources department helps to find and train highly qualified personnel, and so on.

Thus, in implementing a zero-defects approach, managers and employees at all levels seek to build quality into every aspect of their work. To do so, employees work with supervisors and other managers in setting goals for quality and in identifying areas where improvement is needed. Management is responsible for communicating the importance of quality to the whole organization and for rewarding high-quality performance.

Employee Involvement Teams

employee involvement teams
Teams of employees who plan ways to improve quality in their area of the organization.

Teams of employees who plan ways to improve quality in their area of the organization became popular in the United States during the 1970s. These **employee involvement teams** may take slightly different forms, depending on their specific functions: quality circles, problem-solving teams, process improvement teams, or self-managed work groups. The concept of employee involvement teams was created in the 1920s by Walter Shewhart of Bell Laboratories and later expanded by American statistician W. Edwards Deming, whose ideas are described later in this chapter.[4]

The typical employee involvement team consists of up to 10 employees and their supervisor. The supervisor serves as the team leader. In this role, he or she schedules meetings, prepares agendas, and promotes the participation and cooperation of team members. (Chapter 17 describes general principles of teams, including the role of the team leader.)

How Employee Involvement Teams Work   Each employee involvement team in an organization holds periodic meetings. These generally take place at least once or twice a month for an hour or two during the workday. At these meetings, participants examine areas where quality needs improvement, and they develop solutions. The problems discussed may be identified by management or by operative employees. In either case, the problems should be related to the employees' everyday work, as this is where they have the greatest expertise.

In a typical process, the members of the team take steps such as the following (summarized in Figure 6.4):

1. Identify quality problems related to the employees' areas of responsibility.
2. Select the problems to focus on first. For a newly formed group, it may be helpful to focus on rather simple problems, so that the group can build on its successes.
3. Analyze the problem to identify its causes.
4. Identify possible solutions and select one to recommend to management.

Depending on the organization's policies, one or more managers generally must approve the recommendations of the employee involvement team. Once a recommendation is approved, the appropriate people in the organization must implement it. The team should follow up to make sure that the implementation actually solved the problem.

University Microfilms used this approach to respond to customer complaints that orders were not getting filled on time. The Ann Arbor, Michigan, publisher of doctoral dissertations set up quality teams to investigate. The teams learned that while it took 150 days to publish an average dissertation, only about two hours were spent working on the manuscript. The rest of the time, the manuscript sat waiting, not moving to the next stage until some action took place, such as a written response from the author. The teams developed more flexible editing standards and arranged for manuscripts to move to the next stage of the process even when awaiting corrections. The time required to process the manuscripts fell by half within six months, and eventually to 60 days.[5]

Characteristics of Successful Employee Involvement Teams   The principles of problem solving described in Chapter 8 and the guidelines for supervising groups discussed in Chapter 17 can help the supervisor make employee involvement teams a success. In addition, these teams are most likely to achieve improvements in quality when they have certain characteristics. These are summarized in Figure 6.5.

First, employee involvement teams must have support from supervisors and higher-level managers. In fact, these teams are most likely to succeed when the

FIGURE 6.4

Typical Procedure for an Employee Involvement Team

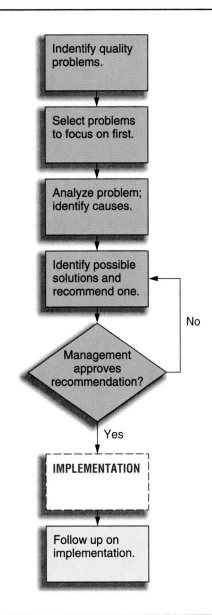

organization's top management supports them. (Of course, supervisors have little control over top managers' attitudes, but they can at least be enthusiastic themselves.) Ways that managers can demonstrate support for employee involvement teams include acting on and rewarding the ideas that these groups produce.

In addition, employee involvement teams work best when participants have the skills necessary to contribute. To get the group off to a good start, the organization can provide training at the first meeting(s). Areas in which participants may need training include problem-solving techniques and approaches to quality

FIGURE 6.5
**Characteristics of
Successful Employee
Involvement Teams**

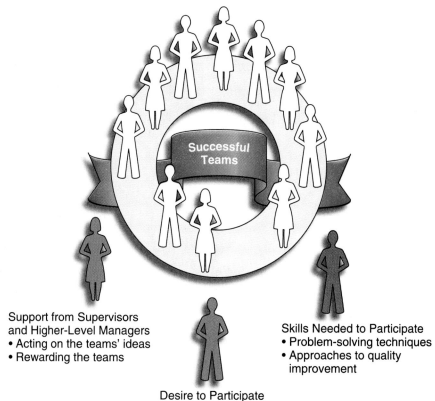

Support from Supervisors
and Higher-Level Managers
• Acting on the teams' ideas
• Rewarding the teams

Skills Needed to Participate
• Problem-solving techniques
• Approaches to quality
  improvement

Desire to Participate

improvement. The group's leader may need help in learning to lead a group discussion and to encourage participation.

Employee involvement teams are most likely to succeed when all group members want to participate. For that reason, it is a good idea to make membership in the team voluntary. Employees who are interested will make the most valuable contributions.

Total Quality Management

**total quality
management (TQM)**
An organizationwide
focus on satisfying
customers by
continuously improving
every business process
involved in delivering
goods or services.

Bringing together aspects of other quality-control techniques, some organizations today are embracing the process of **total quality management (TQM)**. This is an organizationwide focus on satisfying customers by continuously improving every business process involved in delivering goods or services.[6] Some of the leading users of TQM are Federal Express, Hewlett-Packard, Motorola, 3M, Westinghouse, and Xerox Business Products and Systems. During the Persian Gulf war, the U.S. Navy taught TQM to 1,200 leaders, including every admiral and general.[7] The Joint Commission on Accreditation of Healthcare Organizations, which

The ultimate goal at Armstrong, a manufacturer and marketer of interior furnishings, is total customer satisfaction. At Thomasville Furniture, a subsidiary of Armstrong, this process improvement team used quality-control techniques and reduced the cycle time for the production of chair seats from 48 to less than seven hours. The reduction of production time is a major contributor to increased levels of customer satisfaction.

Source: Courtesy of Armstrong World Industries.

accredits over 80 percent of U.S. hospitals, is revising its standards to include some TQM-style criteria.[8]

While TQM has as its objective meeting or exceeding customer expectations, TQM is not a final outcome but, in the words of Alan T. Lougee, president of Chicago Faucet Company, a "business philosophy."[9] As a result, organizations fully implement it only gradually. For example, at Chicago Faucet, management expects that getting started with TQM will take 5 years and getting the process fully in place will require 10 years.[10] Mike Weaver, president of Van Buren, Indiana–based Weaver Popcorn Company, puts it simply: "Quality only happens when people start caring. And they don't start caring all at once."[11]

The evidence to date seems to support the benefits of a TQM approach. In a study conducted in part to measure the impact of TQM on performance, the U.S. General Accounting Office found that at organizations using TQM, errors and defects fell by 10.3 percent, sales per employee increased 8.6 percent, and customer satisfaction increased at all companies.[12] Hewlett-Packard has seen its manufacturing productivity improve 15 percent per year over a five-year period. Ford and Xerox have credited TQM with saving their companies. At many companies using TQM, the cost of poor quality, as determined by such measures as scrap and rework, has fallen by half or even more.[13]

Advocates for Quality The popularity of TQM in recent years is due largely to the compelling case that management experts have made for an organizationwide focus on quality. Three of the experts most often associated with the TQM philosophy are Philip B. Crosby, W. Edwards Deming, and Joseph M. Juran.

Crosby is known worldwide as a quality expert; he pioneered the quality movement in the United States. To achieve product quality, Crosby maintains, the organization must be "injected" with certain ingredients, much as the injection of a vaccination serum is intended to keep a person healthy. The ingredients that an organization needs to add are of five types, as summarized here:

1. *Integrity*—Managers and employees at all levels must be dedicated to their role in providing quality to customers.
2. *Systems*—The organization needs various kinds of systems to indicate whether quality is acceptable and customers are satisfied.
3. *Communications*—Employees must be aware of their progress, and the organization must recognize their achievements.
4. *Operations*—The organization must educate suppliers, train employees, and examine and improve its procedures, all in support of high quality.
5. *Policies*—The organization needs clear policies on quality.

Deming, who was originally trained as a statistician, taught statistical quality control in Japan shortly after World War II. In that role, he became an important contributor to quality improvement efforts in Japan. In fact, Deming so impressed the Japanese with his lectures on quality that they named a prize after him. The Deming Prize is Japan's prestigious international quality award. It was not until decades later that Deming and the emphasis on total quality became widely discussed in the United States. Deming's approach is this: to achieve product quality, the organization must continually improve the product's design as well as the process of producing it.

Juran also taught quality concepts to the Japanese. He emphasizes the view that management should seek to maintain and improve quality through efforts on two levels: (1) the mission of the organization as a whole to achieve and maintain high quality and (2) the mission of individual departments in the organization to achieve and maintain high quality. In pursuing these missions, says Juran, managers must be involved in studying symptoms of quality problems, identifying the underlying problems, and carrying out solutions.

Successfully Using TQM   An organization that wants to use total quality management begins by deciding what strategies to use, then decides who will do what in order to carry out the strategies and when these steps will take place. Some basic strategies for implementing TQM include the following:

- Using groups such as employee involvement teams to identify and solve problems.
- Reviewing criteria for improving quality, such as the categories for the Baldrige Award (described later), then seeking to meet those criteria.
- Focusing on improving the processes used for delivering goods and services, rather than on the products themselves.
- Forming self-managing work teams (see Chapter 17)—groups of employees with broad responsibility for producing particular goods, services, or parts.

Some of these strategies were used at LaGrange Memorial Hospital, where a group of employees from various departments met to discuss their work. The employees discovered that when patients visited more than one of the hospital's outpatient centers, they had to answer the same questions about their medical history at each center. To improve services to these customers (the patients), the hospital now has an employee enter the information once on a computer, where it is available to all departments.[14]

Because these strategies call for the involvement of employees at all levels, the organization needs to educate employees about why quality improvement is needed and how the TQM process will work. The Self-Quiz on the next page consists of questions that identify whether a person has the kind of quality awareness that can make TQM work. Try taking it yourself to see where you stand.

According to a study by the General Accounting Office, the organizations that have used TQM most successfully have six characteristics in common:[15]

1. The company's attention is focused on meeting customers' requirements for quality.
2. Management leads in spreading TQM values throughout the organization.
3. Management asks and empowers employees to continuously improve all key business processes.
4. Management fosters a corporate culture that is flexible and responsive.
5. The organization's management systems support decision making based on facts.
6. The organization uses partnerships with suppliers to improve the delivery of the goods or services it buys.

In addition, the Quality and Productivity Management Association has identified four principles held in common by successful TQM users. These organizations believe it is important to focus on customer satisfaction, emphasize quality, continuously improve, and involve and empower employees. Furthermore, the executives and managers at these organizations spend 25 to 50 percent of their time on activities related to quality improvement.[16] The types of activities involved are listed in Table 6.2 (page 135).

One way supervisors and other managers can build an organization with these characteristics is to behave as if quality is important. Among TQM users, this is commonly called "walking the talk." For example, if everyone is to receive training in quality improvement, supervisors who walk the talk will not look for ways to get out of the training sessions, even if they do have a lot of urgent matters to attend to.

Customer Satisfaction One of the key values of total quality management is that employees at all levels should focus on meeting or exceeding the expectations of their customers. This principle assumes that everyone has a customer to serve. In the case of a salesclerk or a nurse, it is easy to say whom the employee serves. But even the back-office personnel at a manufacturer are delivering services to someone. So part of satisfying customers is knowing who they are. They may be the people who buy the company's products, the taxpayers who support the government agency, or the other employees in the organization who use the reports, advice, or other support prepared in a given department.

Knowing the customer was the approach taken by Chuck Wise, the head of Corning's tax department. The 19 people who report to Wise spend about half their time preparing federal tax returns, so Wise identified his department's major client as the Internal Revenue Service (IRS). Wise asked the IRS to evaluate Corning's returns, which included a summary of thousands of accounts itemizing each department's expenses. The IRS replied that it did not want the summary, yet found it necessary to spend hundreds of hours interpreting it. Wise's department stopped doing the summary and saved over 400 work hours a year.[17]

If Wise had not made the effort to identify and learn about his department's biggest customer, his attempts to improve quality might have been much less

SELF-QUIZ *Your Level of Quality Awareness*
Answer each question by checking Yes or No.

	Yes	No
1. Do you trust your co-workers? Is there a feeling of cooperation rather than competition?	_____	_____
2. Are you truly interested in the welfare of those with whom you work?	_____	_____
3. Can you communicate openly and honestly with the people in your department?	_____	_____
4. Do you understand your department's quality performance goals?	_____	_____
5. Are you committed to the attainment of those goals?	_____	_____
6. When you need special help, do you try to tap the resources of others?	_____	_____
7. Can you resolve conflict successfully?	_____	_____
8. When your department has a meeting, do you participate by preparing and providing your own input?	_____	_____
9. Whether you agree or not, do you respect individual differences?	_____	_____
10. Do you really like your job and your fellow workers?	_____	_____
Total number of Yes answers	_____	

Score yourself: If you had 8 to 10 Yes answers, you're a quality-oriented person and well suited for being part of a work effort aimed at quality awareness. A lower score, however, indicates that you may have good reason for self-doubt. But don't give up. We are not born with an appreciation for quality performance or even with a grasp of what constitutes a quality life-style. Those, like many of the other characteristics that shape us, are learned personality traits. Seek help from the members of your department. If a commitment to quality is your mutual goal, they will support you. And everyone will benefit equally.

Source: Reprinted with the permission of Dartnell, 4660 N. Ravenswood Ave., Chicago, Ill. 60640, (800) 621–5463.

effective. He likely would have tried to find ways to do the account summary faster, rather than finding out it was unnecessary altogether. This principle applies to any supervisor and work group looking for ways to improve quality. Identifying customers and their needs can lead to the improvements that are most meaningful.

One way a supervisor can help employees focus on customers is to have the employees ask themselves whether they would buy the goods or services themselves. Would they be satisfied with the work? If they can put themselves in their

TABLE 6.2	**Category of Activities**	**Specific Activities**
Management Activities Related to Quality Improvement	Infusing values	Valuing customer focus Valuing quality Valuing continuous improvement Valuing employee involvement and empowerment
	Institutionalizing total quality management (TQM)	Developing a mission and vision Following guiding principles Organizing and planning for quality Aligning policies and practices
	Keeping everyone informed about TQM	Assessing quality and gathering facts Providing quality education and training Communicating quality Partnering with suppliers
	Managing improvement	Removing problems and barriers Improving processes Leading teams Recognizing and rewarding

Source: Adapted from "The 'Heart' of TQM," *Commitment Plus* (Quality & Productivity Management Association), October 1991, pp. 1, 4.

customers' shoes and honestly say they would be satisfied, it is a good indicator that their work is up to quality standards.[18]

Measurement of Quality Improvement

Quality-control techniques such as statistical process control provide information about when defects occur in processes and products. But when an organization is engaged in a long-term process such as TQM, how can supervisors and others in the organization know whether they are making progress? How can they tell whether they are using practices likely to foster high quality? Three sets of guidelines for answering such questions come from the Baldrige Award, the standards known as ISO 9000, and a practice called benchmarking.

Malcolm Baldrige National Quality Award
An annual award administered by the U.S. Department of Commerce and given to the company that shows the highest-quality performance in seven categories.

The Baldrige Award

Organizations using a TQM approach often measure their progress in terms of the criteria used to judge applicants for the **Malcolm Baldrige National Quality Award**. This is an annual award administered by the U.S. Department of Commerce and given to the company that shows the highest-quality performance as measured by seven categories:

1. Leadership
2. Information and analysis
3. Strategic quality planning

In 1992 the Ritz-Carlton Hotel became the first hotel company to win the Malcolm Baldrige National Quality Award by going to great lengths to keep employees as well as customers happy.

Source: Courtesy of The Ritz-Carlton Hotel Company.

4. Human resource development and management
5. Management of process quality
6. Quality and operational results
7. Customer focus and satisfaction

Besides the approximately 100 organizations that apply for the award each year, many others use the evaluation categories as a basis for assessing their own performance. In effect, organizations use the guidelines for the award as a kind of textbook for what needs to be done to improve quality. For example, Baxter International, the world's largest supplier of health care products and services, has established a quality program called Quality Leadership Process. This program includes competition among the company's business units for the Baxter Quality Award. Winners receive trophies, plaques, and other recognition based on the same quality criteria used for the Baldrige Award.[19]

The risk of focusing on award criteria is that an organization or department can get caught up in winning an award or meeting certain criteria instead of focusing on the intended goal of delivering quality to the customer. Competing for a challenging award such as the Baldrige can be costly in terms of dollars and managers' time.[20] Many organizations find that the key is to proceed with moderation. For example, at the insurance unit of Cigna Corporation, the Baldrige award is simply an inspiration. In the words of senior vice-president David Williams, "The attention it takes to go for the award over and above the effort of creating a total quality-management process would take us off track."[21]

ISO 9000

ISO 9000
A series of standards
adopted by the
International
Organization of
Standardization to spell
out acceptable criteria
for quality systems.

Another measure of success in quality management is ISO 9000 certification.[22] **ISO 9000** is a series of standards adopted in 1987 by the International Organization of Standardization to spell out acceptable criteria for quality systems. To be certified, an organization is visited by independent audit teams; if the auditors determine that the key elements of the standard are in place, they issue certification of compliance. (Note that they are evaluating quality *processes*, not product quality.) An organization may seek ISO 9000 certification because, for example, a customer requires it as a condition of doing business or because a nation's government requires it of organizations selling in that nation. As more businesses seek certification, those that want to remain competitive will have to be certified as well.

Benchmarking

benchmarking
Identifying the top
performer of a process,
then learning and
carrying out the top
performer's practices.

Managers at all levels can evaluate their success in improving quality by comparing their processes and results with those at other departments and organizations. This practice is popularly known as **benchmarking**—identifying, learning, and carrying out the practices of top performers. In this sense, the term first referred to the practice of comparing the products and processes at one's own company with those that are the best in the world. For example, Xerox has benchmarked the highly successful distribution system of L. L. Bean.[23] While this might seem to be an activity for higher-level managers, supervisors can certainly apply the technique to their own department's operations or even to their own career and management style. For those who want to use benchmarking, one source of information is the business-supported International Benchmarking Clearinghouse of the American Productivity and Quality Center, based in Houston, Texas.[24]

Guidelines for Quality Control

As with the other responsibilities of supervisors, there is more to success than just picking the right technique. The supervisor needs a general approach that leads everyone involved to support the effort at improving quality. To develop such an approach, the supervisor can start by following the guidelines summarized in Figure 6.6. In addition, the supervisor can consider ways to build on the benefits of employee diversity, as described in the "Dealing with Diversity" box.

Prevention versus Detection

It is almost always cheaper to prevent problems from occurring than it is to solve them after they happen. In other words, designing and building quality into a product is more efficient than trying to improve the product later. Therefore, quality-

DEALING WITH DIVERSITY

The Impact of Diversity on Quality

A diverse work force, if effectively managed, can bring various benefits to an organization. Organizations that effectively draw on the variety of talents available in the work force are in the best position to deliver high-quality goods and services.

The supervisor who values diversity is in a position to help all his or her employees develop their full potential. This supervisor appreciates the various strengths of different kinds of people, which boosts employees' morale. Also, in such a climate, working relationships among people are positive.

The supervisor who values diversity also helps to make the organization a desirable place to work. This means the organization has the largest possible pool of available talent to recruit from. In addition, employee turnover in such an organization is likely to be low.

An organization that recruits employees who represent the various kinds of people in its markets will be most attractive to customers. Thus, an insurance agency that serves women as well as men benefits from having women among its staff members at all levels. Likewise, a business that sells to people of various races will appeal to more customers if its sales force also consists of people of those races. Customers and clients of various national and ethnic backgrounds appreciate a company where employees speak their language and know their customs. Not only is this kind of diverse organization more attractive to current and prospective customers, it is in a better position to understand and identify needs, giving the organization an edge in developing new products and services.

Finally, many of the quality-control techniques described in this chapter rely on the creativity of managers and employees. An organization that attracts and draws on the talents of a diverse group of employees will have the widest pool of creative thinking that it can hire. In such an organization, thinking and problem solving tend to be more flexible.

Source: Anne London and Richard L. Daft, *Managing Employee Diversity Supplement* (Fort Worth, Tex.: The Dryden Press), pp. 22–23 (supplementing Richard L. Daft, *Management*, 2nd ed.).

FIGURE 6.6

Guidelines for Quality Control

control programs should not be limited to the detection of defects. Quality control should also include a prevention program to keep defects from occurring.

One way to prevent problems is to pay special attention to the production of new goods and services. In a manufacturing setting, the supervisor should see that the first piece of a new product is tested with special care, rather than wait for problems to occur down the line. In the delivery of services, the supervisor would spend extra time evaluating the work done by new employees or employees performing a new procedure. Particularly in these situations, the supervisor might seek out feedback on customer satisfaction, rather than wait for complaints to come in. Furthermore, when prevention efforts show that employees are doing good work, the supervisor should praise their performance. Employees who are confident and satisfied are less likely to allow defects in goods or services.

Standard Setting and Enforcement

If employees and others are to support the quality-control effort, they must know exactly what is expected of them. This calls for quality standards. For example, at Corning, the chief executive officer decided that every employee would spend 5 percent of his or her time in job-related training, that errors would be cut by 90 percent, and that all new goods and services would meet customer requirements and equal the quality produced by competitors.[25]

In many cases, the supervisor is responsible for setting quality standards as well as for communicating and enforcing them. These standards should have the characteristics of effective objectives, described in Chapter 2.

In communicating standards, the supervisor should make sure that employees know why quality is important. The supervisor needs to provide specific information about the costs of poor quality and the benefits of excellent quality. For example, if employees know how much it costs to make a component, they can understand the costs of remaking one that is defective.[26] Similarly, a Taco Bell manager could tell employees that a typical repeat customer accounts for about $11,000 worth of lifetime total sales.[27] Therefore, providing the quality of food and service that makes a customer want to come back is more valuable than the price of a single meal might suggest.

In addition, employees must understand the difference between poor quality and excellent quality. One way to do this is through the use of examples. In teaching a new employee how to manufacture a part, the supervisor could show a sample of a part that meets specifications and one that does not.

To enforce the standards, the supervisor must participate in inspecting the quality of goods and services that employees produce. This may entail examining a random sample of parts, accompanying a salesperson on sales calls, or visiting the workplace where employees interact with customers. The timing of these inspections should be unpredictable enough that employees cannot adjust their performance in the expectation that the supervisor will be checking up on them that day.

When an inspection uncovers a quality problem, the supervisor should inform the responsible employees immediately. Then they should get to work on solving the problem. The appropriate response may include apologizing to customers as well as fixing a problem within the organization. Requiring a quick response demonstrates the importance of quality to the organization.

For enforcement of standards to be effective, the employees must know that management is serious about quality. A catchy slogan posted on bulletin boards, inscribed on buttons, or taped to cash registers is meaningless unless supervisors and higher-level managers pay attention to these principles, reward employees for following them, and live up to them themselves.

The Role of Suppliers

Organizations depend on suppliers in a variety of ways. An automaker relies on manufacturers of many types of components, and a law office relies on a printer to provide elegant stationery. Many businesses depend on outside suppliers of advice in areas such as accounting, investments, and the law.

The organization's performance is only as good as the inputs it gets from its suppliers. Digital Equipment Corporation, for example, limited the success of its total quality management program in the way it conducted its relationships with some vendors. Employees complained that the company did not send defective parts back to the vendors but simply scrapped the parts. Because the company was not involving the vendors in solving the problem, employees found it harder to produce quality goods.[28] At Weaver Popcorn Company, located in Van Buren, Indiana, employees became frustrated when the company continued accepting corn with a moisture level of up to 23 percent, even though specifications called for a maximum 17 percent moisture level. Production worker Marty Hall complained, "It makes my job three times harder."[29]

To avoid such problems, the quality-control effort should include setting and enforcing standards for acceptable work from suppliers. For example, the supervisor should make sure that employees have tools, materials, and supplies of acceptable quality. When choosing suppliers, the organization needs to stick to those that will be able to live up to the standards. At Weaver Popcorn, a team from the processing plant developed what it called the Preferred Supplier Program. The program gives farmers generous bonuses for meeting strict standards.[30]

Rewards for Quality

As with any area of performance that the supervisor wants to encourage, employees need valued rewards. Thus, the supervisor's job includes making sure that employees receive rewards for high-quality work. Performance measures must include an evaluation of the quality of the goods or services produced by the employees. Teams that meet or exceed the quality standards would then receive appropriate rewards (see Chapter 9). Dennis Sowards, supervisor of quality and productivity consulting for the Salt River Project, cautions that these rewards should be for doing the job right the first time, not for doing a good job of fixing a mistake. Says Sowards, "Quality is not rework with a smile."[31] (Of course, when employees make improvements, the supervisor should praise and reward their accomplishments.)

If the organization's strategy for maintaining and improving quality is total quality management or some other approach that emphasizes process control, then the rewards should reflect that emphasis. In other words, supervisors should look at improvements in the process as well as the final results achieved. For example, at Yaskawa Electric America, performance appraisals and promotions are based in part on participation in the improvement process.[32]

Motorola annually holds what it calls the Total Customer Satisfaction Team Competition. In 1992 over 3,000 teams participated worldwide. Then, 22 finalist teams met in Chicago to give 15-minute presentations on how they achieved the goal of total customer satisfaction. Presenters, often in costume, used a blend of comedy, statistics, graphs, and maps. Eight of the finalist teams won Gold Medals, but, emphasized Motorola's Gene Simpson, "There are no losers in this kind of competition."[33]

Summary

6.1 Describe consequences suffered by organizations as a result of poor-quality work.
Poor-quality work gives the organization a negative image, which drives away customers and makes it harder to recruit superior employees and borrow money. Poor-quality work can also lead to higher costs to attract customers, inspect for and correct defects, replace defective products, and defend against lawsuits.

6.2 Compare product quality control and process control.
Both types of quality control involve preventing and detecting quality-related problems. Product quality control focuses on ways in which the product can be improved. Process control focuses on how to do things in a way that results in higher quality.

6.3 Identify techniques for quality control.
Statistical quality control involves looking for defects in parts or finished goods selected through a sampling technique. In one form of this technique, called statistical process control, the operator takes samples during the process, plots the results on a chart, and makes corrections when the chart indicates the process is out of control. The zero-defects approach is quality control based on the view that everyone in the organization should work toward the goal of delivering such high quality that all aspects of the organization's products and services are free of problems. Employee involvement teams are teams of employees who plan ways to improve quality in their area of the organization. Total quality management is an organizationwide focus on satisfying customers by continuously improving every business process involved in delivering goods or services.

6.4 Explain how employee involvement teams work and what makes them successful.
Each employee involvement team in the organization holds periodic meetings at which participants examine needs for improvement and develop solutions. When management has approved suggested solutions, the team follows up to make sure that the problem is solved. These teams are most likely to achieve improvements in quality when they have support from management, when participants have the skills necessary to contribute, and when all group members want to participate.

6.5 Describe principles for successfully using total quality management.
TQM must be seen as a continuous process that unfolds gradually as employees find more and more ways to improve quality. The organization should start by deciding what strategies to use and how to carry them out. Employees must play an active role in carrying out TQM, so they must be educated about the need for quality improvement and the way the TQM process will work. The organization must focus on satisfying customers and must operate in a flexible, responsive manner.

6.6   Identify ways organizations measure their success in continuous quality improvement.

Organizations compare their practices and performance with various sets of guidelines. They may compete for the Malcolm Baldrige National Quality Award or assess their performance using its evaluation categories. They may seek certification for meeting the international standards of ISO 9000. Also, they may compare their performance with that of organizations that excel in particular areas—a practice known as benchmarking.

6.7   Describe guidelines for quality control.

The organization should focus on preventing quality problems, which is cheaper than detecting them. Supervisors and other managers should set, communicate, and enforce standards for quality control. The organization should insist upon high quality from its suppliers inside and outside the organization. Supervisors and higher-level managers should provide valued rewards for high-quality work.

Key Terms

quality control	statistical process control (SPC)	Malcolm Baldrige National Quality Award
product quality control	zero-defects approach	ISO 9000
process control	employee involvement teams	benchmarking
statistical quality control	total quality management (TQM)	

Review and Discussion Questions

1. Brand X Corporation seeks to be the lowest-cost maker of lawn chairs and toboggans. To keep costs down, management tells the production department, "Just keep that assembly line moving. We have an inspector on staff to catch the mistakes later." What are the consequences Brand X Corporation is likely to experience as a result of this approach to manufacturing?

2. What is the difference between product quality control and process control? Is balancing a checkbook a type of product quality control or process control? Explain.

3. The manager of a restaurant wants to make sure that her staff is delivering good service to customers, but she does not have time to investigate the service given to every customer. So every evening at 5:30, the manager stops at customers' tables to ask if they are satisfied with their service. In effect, this is a form of statistical quality control because she is talking to a sample of the customers.

    How can the manager improve the accuracy of the information she gets from this quality-control technique?

4. What is the zero-defects approach to quality control?

5. Winston McKenna supervises a staff of eight claims processors at an insurance company. Winston's boss has asked him to set up an employee involvement team with his staff members.
    a. What activities can Winston expect that he and his employees will perform as members of the team?
    b. What kinds of training should Winston consider for himself and his employees so that the team can work effectively?

6. What is total quality management (TQM)?

7. One of the key values of TQM is a focus on meeting or exceeding customers' expectations. Who would be the customers served by each of the following employees or groups of employees?
    a. a hairdresser in a beauty salon
    b. a maintenance crew in a factory
    c. a telephone operator at city hall
    d. the human resources department of a nursing home

8. Describe how organizations can use the Malcolm Baldrige National Quality Award as a tool for measuring their success at continuous quality improvement.

9. Imagine that you are the supervisor responsible for a pharmacy. You have received a few complaints about mistakes in customers' prescriptions. In trying to improve the quality of service delivered by the pharmacists, you can concentrate on doing a better job of catching errors in the future or on doing a better job of avoiding errors. Which approach would you choose? Explain.

10. Explain how supervisors can improve quality through the way they set and enforce standards.

11. Again imagine that you are the supervisor mentioned in question 9. To motivate employees to improve the quality of their performance, what kinds of behavior and accomplishments would you reward? Give some examples.

A SECOND LOOK

Does the story about First National Bank of Chicago at the beginning of this chapter describe an example of product quality control or process control? Explain.

Class Exercise

The class divides into groups of four to six people each. Each group receives the following materials: 20 index cards, a roll of tape, a pair of scissors, and a felt-tipped pen. To complete the exercise, the groups may use these supplies and no others.

The instructor specifies how much time the groups will have to complete the project (10 or 15 minutes is probably adequate). When the instructor gives the signal to begin, each group is to use the materials provided to construct a house. The teams may use the materials in any way they see fit, but they may not use additional materials of their own.

When time is up, someone from each group brings the group's house to a table or other designated location in the classroom. The instructor appoints five class members to serve on a panel of judges. They rate each house on a scale of 1 to 5 (with 5 representing the highest quality). The judges'

scores are totaled, and the house with the highest score is deemed the winner of this quality contest.

Finally, the class discusses the following questions:

- On what basis did the judges rate the quality of the houses? How many of the criteria in Table 6.1 did they use?
- How did your group decide on a way to make its house? How well did your group work together in producing the house?
- Given your group's experience and the information about how the judges arrived at their scores, how would you want to improve the quality of your house if you could repeat the exercise? Are your changes process improvements or product improvements?

CASE

Quality Service at a Truck Stop

David M. Armstrong heads Armstrong International, a manufacturing company with 15 divisions worldwide. He tells the following story about the quality of service he once received while on a business trip:

It was a hot day in July. A salesperson and I had just finished making a sales call, and while driving to our next appointment we decided to stop and get a cold drink. We pulled into a truck-stop restaurant. I ordered an iced tea.

"Could you bring me some Sweet n' Low with that, please?" I asked.

"The sugar is on the table," the waitress replied.

"Yes, but it doesn't dissolve in iced tea as well as Sweet n' Low does," I told her.

"I'm sorry, that's all we have."

When the waitress came back with our drinks, she placed a small metal cup down next to my iced tea.

"I'm sorry we don't have any Sweet n' Low," she said. "But I took hot water and poured it over some sugar to help dissolve it. I hope that's okay."

Now that's service!

On the way out, I went up to the waitress and gave her a $2.00 tip for my 60-cent iced tea, and I thanked her for the best service I'd had in a long time. You should have seen her co-workers' expressions.

There is no such thing as a commodity. Everything—even a glass of iced tea—can be differentiated on service. The moral of the story:

- Good service will generate future business. Will I eat at that truck stop the next time I'm in the area? You bet. Will I tell everyone I know about the service I received? I already have. I've told this story 50 times.
- Good service should exist everywhere. Remember, I got this service at a truck stop, not a five-star restaurant. At Armstrong, good service should be found in every department, not just sales.
- Good service should be rewarded. If we see a colleague providing good service, we should praise her [or him]. If we receive good service, we should do everything possible to encourage it. I made a point of making a big deal out of the service I received, in front of the waitress's co-workers. I also gave her a 333 percent tip.

1. What does high quality consist of at a truck stop? In other words, if you were a customer, what would satisfy or please you?
2. Of the principles for ensuring high quality described in the chapter, which were practiced in this case?
3. If you were the supervisor of this waitress, how (if at all) would you reward her for delivering high-quality service?

Source: Excerpted from David M. Armstrong, "Management by Storytelling," *Executive Female*, May–June 1992, pp. 38–41ff, reprinted from David M. Armstrong, *Managing by Storying Around* (Doubleday, 1992).

Part One
Application Exercises

Exercise 1. Performing Supervisory Functions

In Chapter 1 ("The Supervisor and Diversity"), you learned the general functions supervisors perform. Here you will broaden your perspective of how these functions relate to one another and often overlap.

Instructions

1. Imagine you are the supervisor in each scenario described here and you have to decide which supervisory function(s) you would use in each.
2. Many of the scenarios require more than one function. The "Answer" column lists the number of functions your answer should include. Mark your answers using the following codes:

Code	Supervisory Function	Brief Definition
P	Planning	Setting goals and determining how to meet them
O	Organizing	Determining how to set up the group, allocate resources, and assign work to achieve goals
S	Staffing	Identifying, hiring, and developing the quality of employees
L	Leading	Getting employees to do what is expected from them
C	Controlling	Monitoring performance and making needed corrections

Application Exercises were prepared by Corinne Livesay, Liberty University, Lynchburg, Virginia.

3. As a class, compare and discuss your answers and the reasoning you used in determining them.

Scenario	Answer(s)

Scenario | **Answer(s)**

Your group's work is centered on a project that is due in two months. Although everyone is working on the project, you have observed your subordinates involved in what you believe is excessive socializing and other time-consuming behaviors. You decide to meet with the group to have the members help you break down the project into smaller subprojects with mini deadlines. You believe this will help keep the group members focused on the project and the quality of the finished project will then reflect the true capabilities of your group.

(four functions)

1. _____

Your first impression of the new group you will be supervising is not too great. You tell your friend at dinner after your first day on the job: "Looks like I got a babysitting job instead of a supervisory job."

(three functions)

2. _____

Your boss asks your opinion on the promotability to a supervisory position of Andy, one of your most competent and efficient workers. Knowing Andy lacks leadership skills in many key areas, you decide not to recommend him at this time. You instead tell your boss you will work with Andy to help him develop his leadership skills so the next time there is a promotion opportunity Andy will be prepared to consider it.

(one function)

3. _____

You call a meeting of your work group and begin by letting the members know that a major procedure the group has been using for the past two years is being significantly revamped, and your department will have to phase in the change during the next six weeks. You proceed by explaining the reasoning management gave you for this change. You then say, "Take the next five to ten minutes to voice your reactions to this change." After ten minutes elapse with the majority of comments being critical of the change, you say, "I appreciate each of you sharing your reactions; and I, too, recognize that *all* change creates problems. The way I see it, however, is that we can spend the remaining forty-five minutes of our meeting focusing on why we don't want the change and why we don't think it's necessary; or we can work together to come up with viable solutions to solve the problems that implementing this change will most likely create." After about five more minutes of comments being exchanged, the consensus of the group is that the remainder of the meeting should focus on how to deal with the potential problems the group anticipates having to deal with as the new procedure is implemented.

(three functions)

4. _____

You are preparing for the annual budget allocation meetings to be held in the plant manager's office next week. You decide to present a strong case to support your department's getting money for some high-tech equipment that will help your employees do their jobs better. You will stand firm against any suggestions of budget cuts in your area.

(one function)

5. _____

Early in your career you learned an important lesson about employee selection. One of the nurses on your floor unexpectedly quit. The other nurses were putting pressure on you to quickly fill the position because they were overworked even before the nurse left. After a hasty recruitment effort, you made a decision based on insufficient information. You regretted your quick decision during the three months of problems that followed, until you finally had to discharge the new-hire. Since then, you have never let anybody pressure you into making a quick hiring decision.

(two functions)

6. _____

Exercise 2. Practicing Personal Goal Setting

This exercise provides you with an opportunity to practice what you learned in Chapter 2 ("The Supervisor as Planner"). You will practice setting personal goals (objectives) that are written, measurable, specific, clear, and challenging.

Instructions

1. In the space provided, write four goals that are important for you to achieve during the remainder of this semester.
2. Some of the goals should be short term (maybe something you need to finish by the end of this week); others should have a longer time frame (maybe by the end of the semester).
3. Write your goal statement so you can check all four boxes (measurable, specific, clear, and challenging) as being represented. Provided here is a brief summary of each term; you may also wish to review the section in Chapter 2 entitled "Characteristics of Effective Objectives" to get a more thorough explanation of each criterion.
   - *Measurable:* Provide a tangible way (dollar amount, time frame, or quantity) to determine if you have reached your goal—avoid *maximize, improve,* and other terms that cannot be measured.
   - *Specific:* Describe the actions you will need to take to achieve your goal.
   - *Clear:* Use simple language.
   - *Challenging* (yet realistic and obtainable): Choose motivating and stimulating goals that when achieved will give you a sense of pride and build your confidence.
4. Your four goals should represent several different areas (for example, academic, job, career, spiritual, family, financial, social, or physical goals). An example of a financial goal that meets all four criteria is "I will save 20 percent of every paycheck starting this Friday so I'll have enough to pay for my auto insurance when it comes due the last week of the semester." If you are having trouble meeting any of the four criteria in your personal goals, discuss your goal with a classmate or your professor to see if one of them can help you define your goal more clearly.
5. After successfully achieving each goal, write the date in the "Follow-up" column next to the goal.

Goal:

Follow-up

(When you've achieved this goal, write the date here.)

✓ if statement is: Measurable ☐   Specific ☐   Clear ☐   Challenging ☐

Goal:

Follow-up

(When you've achieved this goal, write the date here.)

✓ if statement is: Measurable ☐   Specific ☐   Clear ☐   Challenging ☐

Goal:

Follow-up

(When you've achieved this goal, write the date here.)

✓ if statement is: Measurable ☐   Specific ☐   Clear ☐   Challenging ☐

Goal:

Follow-up

(When you've achieved this goal, write the date here.)

✓ if statement is: Measurable ☐   Specific ☐   Clear ☐   Challenging ☐

It is better to lay one brick today than to propose to build a castle tomorrow.

Exercise 3. Applying Control/Quality Principles to Customer Service

Because nearly eight out of every ten jobs in this country are in the service sector, it is important to understand the significance of providing quality customer service. This exercise is designed to help you apply what you learned in Chapter 5 ("The Supervisor as Controller") and Chapter 6 ("Maintaining and Improving Quality") to a service-sector job.

Instructions

1. Form into groups of 2 or 3 people. Identify a work setting where customer service is critical. The place should be one that all of you are familiar with. It might be a workplace where one of you has worked or at least has been a customer (some examples: retail store, post office, bank, hospital, university, resort, restaurant).
2. Identify a specific job title for the work setting (e.g., waiter/waitress, nurse, clerk at the university bookstore, shoe salesperson at a store).
3. Review some of the principles covered in Chapters 5 and 6 (see Figure A). Select those that are appropriate to the job you have identified, and develop specific customer service guidelines for the employees.
4. Now select principles appropriate for a supervisor of employees in the job you have identified, and develop some supervisory guidelines that focus on customer service. For example, how should the supervisor monitor performance to determine that employees are practicing the quality service standards you have established?
5. Share your group's efforts with the class by presenting a written statement that includes: work setting, job title, principles from Figure A and how your group applied them to the job, and principles from Figure A and how your group applied them to the supervisor.

FIGURE A

Control/Quality Principles from Chapters 5 and 6

- The process of controlling:
    - Establish performance standards (written, measurable, clear, specific, and challenging but achievable).
    - Monitor performance and compare with standards.
    - Reinforce successes and fix problems.
- Types of control (feedback control, concurrent control, and precontrol)
- Process control
- Zero-defects approach
- Employee involvement teams
- Philip Crosby's five ingredients for quality (integrity, systems, communications, operations, and policies)
- Benchmarking
- Prevention versus detection
- Standard setting and enforcement
- The role of suppliers
- Rewards for quality
- Dimensions of quality (performance, features, reliability, conformance, durability, serviceability, aesthetics, perceived quality [Table 6.1])

PART TWO

Skills of the Supervisor

7

The reason why we have two ears and only one mouth is that we may listen the more and talk the less.

— Zeno of Citium

Communicating

LEARNING OBJECTIVES

7.1 Describe the process of communication.

7.2 Distinguish between hearing and listening.

7.3 Describe techniques for communicating effectively.

7.4 Identify barriers to communication, and suggest ways to avoid them.

7.5 Distinguish between verbal and nonverbal messages, and name types of verbal messages.

7.6 Identify the directions in which communication can flow in an organization.

7.7 Distinguish between formal and informal communication in an organization.

7.8 Discuss the role of the grapevine in organizations.

GETTING THE MESSAGE ACROSS

Loretta M. Flanagan is executive director of West Side Future, a community organization sponsored by the YMCA. The organization's objectives are to reduce infant mortality and address related problems in the local community. Thus, most of West Side Future's clients are pregnant women and mothers of children under the age of one. Flanagan supervises 22 employees.

Most of Flanagan's workday is devoted to writing to or talking with people. She must communicate with employees, clients, and representatives of other community organizations, the government, and key funding agencies. These communications include policy statements and strategies, as well as meetings and discussions with employees.

While Flanagan particularly enjoys the challenges and rewards of talking with others face-to-face, she finds that written words are important in some situations. For example, her staff once had 35 days in which to computerize

their client data, a deadline that put employees under a great deal of pressure. Compounding the problem, employees were also involved in the important but time-consuming process of having West Side Future recertified. In Flanagan's experience, such pressure makes it hard for employees to set priorities, and clear, brief, written directions can help them. So Flanagan worked with staff members to develop and write a brief procedure for handling client data, freeing some employees to move on to other tasks.

communication
The process by which people send and receive information.

Whether employees are in a community-based nonprofit organization such as West Side Future or an international corporation such as IBM, to do high-quality work they must be able to communicate with one another. **Communication** is the process by which people send and receive information. The information may be about opinions, facts, or feelings. Even hard-nosed businesspeople need information about feelings; for example, the supervisor should know when his or her boss is angry or when employees are discouraged.

Communication is at the heart of the supervisor's job. To work with their boss, their employees, and supervisors in other departments, supervisors send and receive ideas, instructions, progress reports, and many other kinds of information. Thus, supervisors need to know how to communicate and how to do so effectively. This chapter describes basic communication skills and the types of communication that commonly occur in organizations.

How Communication Works

As she talked to her boss, sales supervisor Mary Yu rolled her eyes. "I've told those engineers at least a half dozen times that the customers keep complaining they want the off switch located more prominently on the machines. But they haven't made a single change. I guess we just aren't communicating."

At times all of us, like Mary, have found that simply talking or writing does not guarantee that communication will occur. Rather, our intended audience should be receiving and understanding the message.

The Communication Process

Social scientists have attempted to diagram the communication process to be able to talk about it more specifically. As a result, we have a widely accepted model of how communication works. Figure 7.1 illustrates a version of this model.

Communication begins when the sender of a message encodes the message. This means the sender translates his or her thoughts and feelings into words, gestures, and facial expressions. The sender then transmits the encoded message by writing, speaking, and other personal contact. If communication is working properly, the intended audience receives the message and is able to decode, or interpret, it correctly.

As you might imagine, mistakes can occur at any step in the process. Later, this chapter discusses barriers to communication and ways to avoid them. The sender of the message can be aware of communication problems by paying attention to feedback. **Feedback**, in this sense, is the way the receiver responds—or fails to respond—to the message. Feedback may take the form of words or behavior. For example, employees' behavior gave one executive feedback that they were paying attention to the information the company was giving them about its financial performance. At that company, besides running a pool to bet on football scores, employees began using the financial data they received from the company to bet on the size of their monthly profit-sharing bonus.[1] In the earlier example of Mary Yu, the engineers' lack of response to her reports of customer complaints

feedback
The way the receiver of a message responds (or fails to respond) to the message.

FIGURE 7.1

The Communication Process

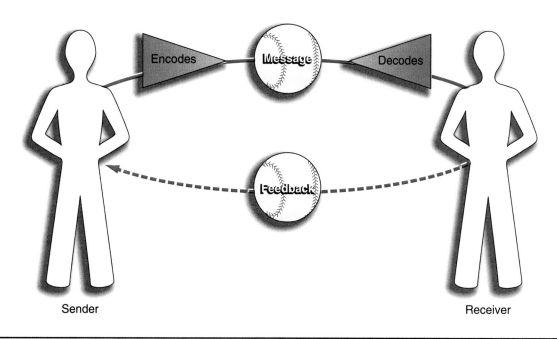

was feedback to Mary. It may mean that the engineers did not understand her message, that they did not agree with it, or that Mary does not realize how long it takes to make changes.

Hearing versus Listening

Notice in the model that the receiver must decode the message. This means that the receiver as well as the sender of the message has an active role to play in communication. If the receiver is not playing that role, then communication is not occurring.

In many cases, this means the receiver of the message must *listen* to it rather than just *hear* it. Hearing means the brain is registering sounds. Most of us have at some point heard a parent nagging at us to clean our room or a co-worker complaining about working conditions. When Mary Yu told the engineers at her company about customers' complaints, they probably heard her talking, too.

Listening, in contrast, means paying attention to what is being said and trying to understand the full message. This is the meaning of "decoding" a message. When parents nag a lot or when co-workers complain a lot, we often choose not to listen to them. Similarly, the engineers at Mary's company have not indicated to her that they have listened to her message.

Thus, as the model of the communication process shows, when we want communication to work, we need to make sure that people are listening to messages as well as sending them. Because communication is an essential part of the supervisor's job, the supervisor must practice good listening skills, as well as good writing and speaking skills. The next section discusses listening in greater detail.

Communicating Effectively

Supervisors need to understand the requests that cross their desks and the questions that employees raise. They need to know when the boss is angry or impressed. They need to know that employees understand their instructions. When supervisors are succeeding at such responsibilities, they are communicating effectively. As summarized in Figure 7.2, effective communication is most likely to occur when the parties communicate from the receiver's viewpoint, learn from feedback, use strategies for effective listening, and overcome barriers to communication.

Communicate from the Receiver's Viewpoint

As obvious as it is that other people do not share all our experiences, views, priorities, and interests, it is easy to forget this when we are communicating. But these differences make the intended audience more likely to ignore or misunderstand the messages we send. For example, a business owner may find it fascinating and noteworthy that his company has been in the family for four generations. But skilled sales personnel know that customers would rather hear about how the company's services will benefit them. The salespeople therefore communicate with the audience's viewpoint in mind; they focus on what the company can offer customers.

This sales principle applies to all kinds of communication. Simply put, if you want the receiver's attention, interest, and understanding, you must communicate from his or her viewpoint. Applying this principle includes such tactics as using vocabulary that the receiver will understand, referring to experiences shared with the receiver, and addressing the receiver's interests. Thus, in explaining to employees that the department will be reorganized, a supervisor would focus on topics like job security and job design rather than on how the changes will make the company more profitable or more like its nearest competitor. After all, it is only natural for employees to be most concerned with their own jobs. William V. Haney proposes some questions to ask when focusing on the other party(ies) to a communication:[2]

- This is what the message means to me, but what does it mean to them?
- What would I mean if I were in another's shoes?
- Does my interpretation of their words coincide with their viewpoint (as I see it)?

Learn from Feedback

Feedback can help the supervisor communicate effectively. When the supervisor sends a message, he or she generally expects a certain kind of response. For example, suppose a supervisor explains a policy requiring that all employees take their lunch break at some time between 11:00 A.M. and 1:00 P.M. One type of feedback would be the expressions on employees' faces—do they seem to understand, or do they look confused? Or employees might respond with words; one employee might

FIGURE 7.2
Techniques for Effective Communication

Communicate from the receiver's viewpoint.

Learn from feedback.

Use strategies for effective listening.

Overcome barriers to communication.

ask whether this means they are to take a two-hour lunch break. Another type of response comes from the employees' behavior later on. If the employees understood the message, no one will be away at lunch after 1:00 P.M. By evaluating the words, facial expressions, and behavior of the people who received the message, the supervisor can determine whether the receivers understood the message or need more information.

Likewise, the supervisor can use feedback when he or she is receiving a message. In particular, when the supervisor is uncertain about the meaning of a message, he or she can ask the sender to clarify it. Asking questions is usually a smarter tactic than taking a guess.

Use Strategies for Effective Listening

"Things just aren't done like they used to be," grumbled Tom Wiggins to Allen Pincham, his supervisor at the construction site. "Oh, boy," thought Allen, "here we go again with the complaining." Allen began studying some blueprints, ignoring Tom until he blew off some steam and returned to work. Later that week, the general contractor confronted Allen with a report he had received from Tom that some work was not being done according to code. Tom had complained that he had tried to inform Allen but that his attempts had been ignored.

Better listening could have saved the construction project much expense, and could have saved Allen Pincham much embarrassment. As described earlier, listening is a key part of communication. However, most supervisors could be better

Nonverbal clues may be as important as verbal ones. By evaluating facial expressions, a supervisor can determine whether employees understand a message.

Source: © 1992 Comstock, Inc.

listeners. (Test your own listening skills by taking the Self-Quiz.) Table 7.1 lists 10 rules for being a good listener.

Effective listening begins with the commitment to listen carefully. The supervisor should avoid assuming that a message is going to be boring or irrelevant and should instead decide to listen carefully, trying to identify important information. For example, when an employee complains often about seemingly petty matters, the complaints may hide a broader concern that the employee is not stating directly. If the supervisor does not have time to listen when someone wants to talk, he or she should schedule another time to continue the conversation.

The supervisor also should concentrate on the message. He or she should tune out distractions. A major type of distraction is planning one's own responses; another is assuming that the listener has nothing interesting to say. When it is hard to tune out distractions, it sometimes helps to take brief notes of what the person is saying, focusing on the key points.

If the speaker uses words or phrases that stir up an emotional reaction, the supervisor should try to control those emotions so that they do not interfere with understanding. One way to respond is to consider whether the speaker is merely trying to vent emotions. In that case, the best response is to listen and acknowledge the emotions without agreeing or disagreeing. Wait until the employee is calm before trying to solve a problem. When the employee is calm enough, it is

SELF-QUIZ *Are You an Effective Listener?*

For each statement, check Yes if the statement is true about you or No if the statement does not describe you. Mark your answers as truthfully as you can in light of your behavior in the last few meetings or gatherings you have attended.

		Yes	No
1.	I frequently attempt to listen to several conversations at the same time.	☐	☐
2.	I like people to give me only the facts and then let me make my own interpretation.	☐	☐
3.	I sometimes pretend to pay attention to people.	☐	☐
4.	I consider myself a good judge of nonverbal communications.	☐	☐
5.	I usually know what another person is going to say before he or she says it.	☐	☐
6.	I usually end conversations that do not interest me by diverting my attention from the speaker.	☐	☐
7.	I frequently nod, frown, or whatever to let the speaker know how I feel about what he or she is saying.	☐	☐
8.	I usually respond immediately when someone has finished talking.	☐	☐
9.	I evaluate what is being said while it is being said.	☐	☐
10.	I usually formulate a response while the other person is talking.	☐	☐
11.	The speaker's "delivery" style frequently keeps me from listening to content.	☐	☐
12.	I usually ask people to clarify what they have said rather than guess at the meaning.	☐	☐
13.	I make a concerted effort to understand other people's point of view.	☐	☐
14.	I frequently hear what I expect to hear, rather than what is said.	☐	☐
15.	Most people feel that I have understood their point of view when we disagree.	☐	☐

According to communication theory, you are a good listener if you answered No to questions 1, 2, 3, 5, 6, 7, 8, 9, 10, 11, and 14 and Yes to questions 4, 12, 13, and 15. If you missed only one or two questions, you strongly approve of your own listening habits, and you are on the right track to becoming an effective listener. If you missed three or four questions, you have uncovered some doubts about your listening effectiveness, and your knowledge of how to listen has some gaps. If you missed five or more questions, you probably are not satisfied with the way you listen, and your friends and co-workers may not feel you are a good listener either. Work on improving your listening skills.

Source: Reprinted by permission of the publisher, from *Supervisory Management*, January 1989, © 1989, pp. 12–15. American Management Association, New York, N. Y. All rights reserved.

TABLE 7.1 **Ten Rules for Good Listening**	1. Remove distractions, and give the speaker your full attention. 2. Look at the speaker most of the time. 3. When the speaker hesitates, give a sign of encouragement such as a smile or nod. 4. Try to hear the main point and supporting points. 5. Distinguish between opinions and facts. 6. Control your emotions. 7. Be patient; do not interrupt. 8. Take notes. 9. At appropriate times, ask questions to clarify your understanding. 10. Restate what you think the speaker's point is, and ask if you heard correctly.

often useful to ask questions such as the following that look for facts underlying an emotional statement: "Stan, you say you are treated unfairly. Would you give me some examples?"

active listening
Hearing what the speaker is saying, seeking to understand the facts and feelings the speaker is trying to convey, and stating what you understand that message to be.

In many situations, the supervisor can benefit from using a technique called active listening, pioneered by psychologist Carl R. Rogers. **Active listening** involves not only hearing what the speaker is saying but also seeking to understand the facts and feelings the speaker is trying to convey and then stating what you understand the message to be. The sample dialogues in Table 7.2 illustrate two types of listening. In Example 1, the supervisor is simply hearing the employee's words; in Example 2, the supervisor is using active listening. According to Rogers, active listening is a way supervisors can help employees understand their situation, take responsibility, and cooperate. However, to use it effectively, the supervisor must do so with genuine respect for employees and belief in their ability to direct their own activities.[3]

Barriers to Communication

The model of the communication process suggests where barriers to communication can arise. In general, the sender may fail to encode the message clearly, the message may be lost in transmission, or the receiver may misinterpret the message. In practice, these categories of problems often overlap. Figure 7.3 summarizes some common barriers to communication.

Information Overload

Today's world is often called the "information age." People are bombarded with information daily. On the way to work, radio ads and billboards proclaim which brand of automobile or soft drink to buy. At the workplace, memos, magazines, and managers report on trends, policies, and responsibilities. During the course of a day, many employees get information from colleagues, computer screens, printed

TABLE 7.2

Hearing versus Active Listening

Example 1: Hearing	**Word-Processing Operator:** Hey, Wanda, is Finchburg kidding? He wants the whole report ready by the end of the day? That's impossible!
	Supervisor: But that's the job. You'll have to work as fast as you can. We're under tremendous pressure this week.
	Operator: Doesn't he realize we're behind schedule already because of the quarterly reports?
	Supervisor: Look, Don, I don't decide what the managers want. I just have to see that the work gets done, and that's what I'm trying to do.
	Operator: How can I tell my wife I'll be working late *again?*
	Supervisor: You'll have to handle that with her, not me.
Example 2: Active Listening	**Word-Processing Operator:** Hey, Wanda, is Finchburg kidding? He wants the whole report ready by the end of the day? That's impossible!
	Supervisor: Sounds like you're pretty upset about it, Phyllis.
	Operator: I sure am. I was just about caught up after doing all these quarterly reports. And now this!
	Supervisor: As if you didn't have enough work to do, huh?
	Operator: Yeah. I don't know how I'm gonna meet this deadline.
	Supervisor: Hate to work late again, is that it?
	Operator: That's for sure. I made other plans two weeks ago. Seems like everything we do around here is a big rush.
	Supervisor: I guess you feel like your work cuts into your personal time.
	Operator: Well, yeah. I know Finchburg needs this report to land a big customer. I guess that means that this job really *is* important. Maybe if Joel will help me by doing the tables, I can get out of here at a reasonable hour.

Source: Based on "Active Listening" by Carl R. Rogers and Richard E. Farson.

pages, and phone calls. In the evening, family members and the television recount the day's news. In response, it is only natural that people cope by tuning out a lot of what they see and hear.

How can the supervisor respond to this barrier to communication? An important way is to give employees only information that will be useful to them. For example, when employees need instructions, the supervisor should think them through carefully, so that he or she does not have to provide new instructions later. Also, the supervisor should be sure that employees are paying attention. The way to do this is to observe the people receiving the information and to look for feedback. The supervisor can say to an employee, "Do you understand what I want you to do? Try putting it in your own words." To his or her boss, the supervisor might say, "Do you think this idea supports your goals for the department?"

FIGURE 7.3

Barriers to Communication

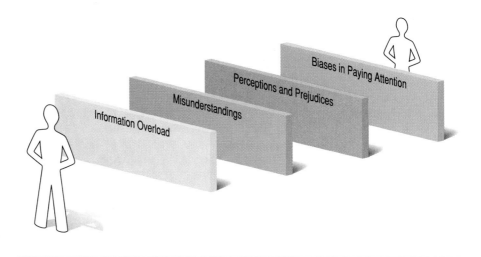

Misunderstandings

In decoding a message, the receiver of a message may make errors that lead to misunderstandings. This barrier can arise when a message is needlessly complicated. For example, imagine a supervisor who writes in a memo, "The deterioration of maintenance practices will inevitably lead to conditions that will be injurious to our heretofore admirable safety record." The person who receives this memo is likely to misunderstand it because it may be too hard to figure out what the words mean. Instead, the supervisor could write, "Because the maintenance workers are no longer tuning up the machines each month, the machines are going to wear out and cause injuries." Thus, one way to avoid misunderstandings is to keep messages simple. When the supervisor has time to prepare the message in advance, as in the case of a letter or speech, it is helpful to ask a third person such as a friend to read or listen to the message to make sure it is not likely to confuse or offend the receiver.

A related solution is for supervisors to make sure they understand what they are going to say before they create the message. This may sound obvious, but many people are guilty of speaking before they think.

When the supervisor is the receiver of a message, he or she needs to be careful to understand the true meaning of that message. The supervisor should not hesitate to ask questions about unclear points. It is also helpful to check on the meaning with such responses as "So you'd like me to…" or "Are you saying that…?"

The supervisor must keep in mind that sometimes the sender of a message prefers that the receiver *not* understand him or her. William V. Haney recounts the story of a congressman running for reelection who responded to questions following a speech. One of his constituents asked the congressman for his views on Social Security. The congressman replied with a wink, a smile, and the words "Don't worry about that subject, my friend—I'm all right on that one!" In this way, the politician pleased all of the audience members even though they were evenly divided on the issue.[4] Because of situations like this, the supervisor needs to recognize occasions when people would have a reason to be intentionally vague or misleading. On those occasions, the supervisor should interpret messages with particular care.

Word Choices To avoid misunderstandings, the supervisor should be careful to make appropriate word choices when encoding the message. Besides choosing simple words, this means avoiding words that could be ambiguous. If an employee asks, "Should I use the solvent in the bottle on the left?" the supervisor should not simply say, "Right."

It is also smart to avoid using words that attribute characteristics to another person. Saying, "You're so irresponsible!" just leads an employee to tune out a message. Instead, the supervisor could describe specific behaviors and his or her own feelings: "That's the second time this week you've made that mistake. I get annoyed when I have to explain the same procedure more than once or twice." This approach is called using "I statements" instead of "you statements." Table 7.3 gives examples of the difference between the two types of statements.

Choosing words carefully is especially important when addressing others. The careful supervisor uses a co-worker's or customer's name rather than "dear" or "honey," unless the supervisor is certain beyond a shadow of a doubt that the receiver of the message likes being called by such endearments in a business setting. New Orleans lawyer Harry McCall, Jr., learned the hard way about the importance of how people are addressed. While representing the state of Louisiana in a prison rights case being tried before the U.S. Supreme Court, McCall said, "I would like to remind you gentlemen" of a legal point. When he finished, Justice Sandra Day O'Connor asked, "Would you like to remind me, too?" Amid nervous laughter, McCall apologized profusely. Only moments later, McCall referred to the court as "Justice O'Connor and gentlemen." Justice Byron White broke in, "Just 'Justices' would be fine."[5]

Cultural Differences Another concern involves misunderstandings that result from cultural differences. The supervisor must be familiar with the communication styles of the various cultures of people with whom he or she works. For example, in Japanese society, harmony is a key value. Consistent with the high value of harmony, Japanese people often say yes (*hai* in Japanese) during a conversation as a way of signaling that they hear what the speaker is saying. Americans, in contrast, generally say yes to mean they agree with the speaker. An American talking to a Japanese might assume that they have reached an agreement when the Japanese person is just listening, not necessarily agreeing. The "Dealing with Diversity" box on page 165 provides more tips for communicating cross-culturally.

When interpreting communication styles, it can be useful to recognize American women as a different cultural group from American men. In other words, because we have different expectations for women and men, the two sexes tend to behave differently. For example, assertiveness in women is often viewed as pushiness or aggressiveness, so women tend to use a less assertive style of communication than men do. Studies show that in mixed groups, women tend to speak less and to make more use of phrases such as "Don't you think?" and "Isn't it?" than men do. At one academic conference, for example, men took an average of 53 seconds to ask questions, whereas women took only 23 seconds. And although half the audience was female, only one-quarter of the questions came from women.[6] For supervisors, this means that if they want to fully benefit from the ideas of their female employees, they must take an active role in seeing that the women have a full chance to contribute.

TABLE 7.3

Two Ways to Address Comments to Others

	You Statements	I Statements
Examples	"You're so irresponsible!"	"I'm upset that you've missed the deadline for the third time. When someone in the department misses a deadline, the whole department looks bad. What can we do?"
	"At the next department meeting, you'd better be prepared and be on time, or you're going to be sorry when we review your salary."	"I was not pleased that you were late to the meeting and unprepared. I expect a higher standard of performance."
	"You're bugging the women with those dirty jokes, so just knock it off before we get in trouble."	"I have received complaints from two of the employees in the department that you are embarrassing them by telling dirty jokes. Our company policy and the law both forbid that type of behavior."
Likely Response	Defensiveness, ignoring speaker.	Listening, collaborating on a solution.

inference
A conclusion drawn from the facts available.

Inferences versus Facts   Misunderstandings can also arise when the listener confuses inferences with facts. An **inference** is a conclusion drawn from the facts available. A supervisor may observe that an employee is not meeting performance standards. That would be a fact. If the supervisor says, "You're lazy!" he or she is making an inference based on the fact of the below-par performance. That inference may or may not be true.

Statements using the words *never* and *always* are inferences. The supervisor may claim, "You're always late." The supervisor knows that the employee has been late to work for six days straight, but the supervisor cannot know what the employee *always* does.

To overcome mistakes caused by treating inferences as facts, the supervisor should be aware of them. When sending a message, the supervisor should avoid statements that phrase inferences as facts. When listening to a message, the supervisor should be explicit about the inferences he or she is making. For example, a supervisor in a bakery could say, "When you tell me the test of the recipe was a failure, I assume you mean the quality of the bread is poor. Is that correct?"

Perceptions and Prejudices

perceptions
The ways people see and interpret reality.

Based on their experiences and values, the sender and receiver of a message make assumptions about each other. The ways people see and interpret reality are known as **perceptions**. When you look at the picture in Figure 7.4 (page 166), what do you see? You may perceive either an old woman or a young woman.

When perceptions about others are false, messages can get distorted. For example, imagine that supervisor Al Trejo has decided his employees would appreciate his paying more attention to their day-to-day problems and successes. So Al

DEALING WITH DIVERSITY

Communicating across Cultures

More often than in the past, supervisors must direct employees or serve customers who are from other cultures. In such situations, ignorance on both sides can muddy the message. The following suggestions may help supervisors meet the challenge.

Stick to simple, basic words. Every culture has its own slang and idioms, such as "over the hill." These terms sound friendly to people who understand them, but people from other cultures usually do not know what they mean. Also avoid using the jargon of your industry. Another mistake is using very formal language, such as "utilizing resources." Keep it simple.

When speaking, make sure your listener understands. Talk slowly (not loudly), and pronounce words carefully. Seek feedback by asking your listener what he or she has heard. But do not ask simply, "Do you understand?" Many people are too embarrassed to say they do not understand the message. You can also look for the following clues, which may indicate a lack of understanding:

- Nodding and smiling in a way that is not directly connected to what you are saying
- A complete lack of interruptions
- Efforts to change the subject
- A complete lack of questions
- Inappropriate laughter

Give your listener plenty of time to come up with questions. If you still are not sure that an employee has understood instructions, check on the progress of his or her work in plenty of time to make any needed corrections or clarify what you meant.

Make sure you understand what the other person is saying. Ask for clarification when you need it. Help the speaker to relax, and invite him or her to speak more slowly. If you are having trouble understanding a word pronounced by a nonnative speaker of English, try asking him or her to spell it. Most important, assume you can understand, and then *try.*

Learn about the communication styles of different cultures, and try to match the different style of another person when appropriate. For example, some cultures, like those of the Far East, consider it extremely rude to interrupt someone during a conversation, whereas people from Arabic cultures tend to tolerate interruptions as a sign of enthusiasm. Likewise, Asians are likely to view loudness as rude, while a Middle Easterner is more often comfortable with louder talking. In any case, the wise supervisor will avoid jumping to conclusions about an individual's character on the basis of cultural preferences.

Help your employees communicate. Stress the importance of keeping communication simple. Share what you learn about communication styles. Compliment employees as they make progress in cross-cultural communication.

Sources: Rose Knotts and Sandra J. Hartman, "Communication Skills in Cross-Cultural Situations," *Supervisory Management,* March 1991, p. 12; and Sondra Thiederman, *Bridging Cultural Barriers for Corporate Success: How to Manage the Multicultural Work Force* (New York: Lexington Books, 1991).

---

stops by the desk of one of his employees, Kim Coleman, and asks, "What are you doing?" Based on her experiences, Kim believes that supervisors are quick to criticize, so she perceives that Al's question is intended to determine whether she is goofing off. Feeling defensive, Kim snaps, "My work, of course." Al then perceives that Kim does not want to discuss her work with him.

prejudices
Broad generalizations about a category of people.

Broad generalizations about a category of people are known as **prejudices**. In our culture, it is common to attribute certain characteristics to women, African-Americans, Asians, blue-collar workers, and many other groups. For example, women are said to be emotional, and Asians are said to be intellectual. Of course, these characteristics often do not apply to a particular person. Imagine that a manager assumes women are irrational and highly emotional, and that a female

FIGURE 7.4

**A Drawing That
May Be Perceived in
More than One Way**

Source: Edwin G. Boring, "A New Ambiguous Figure," *American Journal of Psychology*, July 1930, p. 444. Also see Robert Leeper, "A Study of a Neglected Portion of the Field of Learning—the Development of Sensory Organization," *Journal of Genetic Psychology*, March 1935, p. 62. Originally drawn by cartoonist W. E. Hill and published in *Puck*, November 8, 1915.

supervisor who reports to him discusses her desire for a raise. Even if she outlines a series of logical points supporting her request, he may perceive her request as irrational and respond by telling her just to "Take it easy, things will work out OK." If such poor communication continues, the supervisor might eventually quit in frustration.

The way to overcome communication barriers resulting from perceptions and prejudices is to be aware of the assumptions we make. Are we responding to what a person is saying or to what he or she is wearing? Are we responding to the message or to the speaker's accent? To the words or to our beliefs about the person's race? This awareness can enable the sender as well as the receiver of a message to focus on understanding rather than assuming.

Biases in Paying Attention

Not only do people have biases about the sender or receiver of a message, they also have biases related to the content of the message itself. People tend to pay more attention to a message that seems to serve their own self-interest. They also are more apt to hear messages that fit their existing viewpoints and to discount messages that contradict those viewpoints. For example, imagine that an employee suggests a new procedure, and the supervisor says, "Your idea will never work." The employee is more likely to think the supervisor is opposed to change than that the idea was unworkable.

The supervisor can combat these biases by phrasing messages carefully to appeal to the receiver. In the case of the new idea from an employee, the supervisor might say, "Thank you for your suggestion. I estimate that it will save us about $50 a month. Can you think of a way we can modify it so that implementing it will cost less than $1,500?" This response shows the supervisor was paying attention to the suggestion and recognized at least some of its merit.

Types of Messages

When Sandy walked into her cubicle at the insurance company where she worked, there was a note on her desk. "See me," it said, and it was signed by her supervisor. "Uh-oh," thought Sandy nervously, "what did I do?"

Sandy walked into her supervisor's office and saw that he was smiling. "Congratulations," he said, "you got the raise we requested."

verbal message
A message that consists of words.

In this example, Sandy's supervisor communicated with her through a note, a facial expression, and spoken words. As you can see, two of the messages were **verbal messages**; that is, they consisted of words. The third—the smiling face—was a **nonverbal message**, that is, one conveyed without words.

nonverbal message
A message conveyed without using words.

Nonverbal Messages

How can anyone get a point across without using words? While the idea of non-verbal messages might seem surprising or unimportant at first, we continuously send and receive messages through our facial expressions, posture, and other non-verbal cues. In the example of Sandy and her supervisor, the message conveyed by the supervisor's facial expression was as important as the verbal message "See me." The smile, unlike the note, conveyed to Sandy that her supervisor had good news.

Major types of nonverbal messages are gestures, posture, tone of voice, facial expression, and even silences. We learn the meaning of many such messages just by participating in our culture. From experience, we can recognize a surprised face, a friendly handshake, or a cool silence in response to something we say. Our culture also teaches us the "proper" distance to stand from the person with whom we are talking (part of a concept known as personal space—see Figure 7.5). To think of how readily we interpret nonverbal messages, imagine that a supervisor is discussing with an employee a problem with her work, and she drops her eyes, looking away from the supervisor. Based on the usual assumptions in American culture, the supervisor is apt to conclude that the employee is dishonest, uninterested, or guilty of something.

Of course, we learn the meaning of these nonverbal messages from our culture, and people from other cultures have a different nonverbal vocabulary. Thus, in the previous example, if the employee is a Cambodian woman, she may be trying to communicate respect; looking her supervisor in the eye, according to Cambodian

FIGURE 7.5

The Etiquette of Proper Distance: Some Cross-Cultural Examples

- Americans, on average, stand 2 feet apart when conducting business.
- Middle Eastern males typically stand up to 18 inches apart.
- Asians and many African cultures leave a space of 3 feet or more.

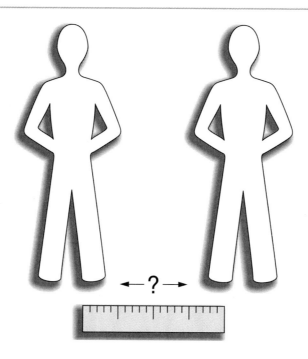

Source: Based on Sondra Thiederman, *Bridging Cultural Barriers for Corporate Success: How to Manage the Multicultural Work Force* (New York: Lexington Books, 1991), p. 132.

culture, would be rude.[7] The meanings of nonverbal cues vary even among different groups of people born in the United States. For example, Anglo-Americans tend to maintain eye contact when listening but allow their eyes to wander somewhat when they are speaking, while African-Americans are more apt to follow the opposite pattern, maintaining steadier eye contact when they are speaking.[8]

Failing to recognize such different interpretations of nonverbal signals can be misleading, as in the case of an Anglo-American who concludes, on the basis of eye contact, that an African-American listener is not interested in what he or she is saying. Not observing cultural differences can even be embarrassing. President George Bush learned on a 1992 trip to Australia that the two raised fingers that signal V for victory in the United States are considered an obscene gesture by Australians when the back of the hand is turned outward, as Bush's was.[9]

A supervisor needs to send the kinds of nonverbal signals that communicate he or she is businesslike and professional.[10] Some ways supervisors can send these

The verbal message "May I help you?" is written on the uniform of this Rose's Stores sales associate. As important is the non-verbal message—a smile.

Source: Courtesy of David Sciabarasi, photographer.

signals are to sit or stand straight, use open hand gestures, and sit with their hands resting comfortably in their lap. Dressing conservatively signals that the supervisor commands respect and has self-control. Smiling when appropriate and readily shaking hands indicate enthusiasm and interest. Finally, a pleasing, moderate tone of voice gets respect from others. The supervisor can develop such a voice by practicing with a tape recorder or friend.

When a person is sending nonverbal messages as well as communicating through words, the nonverbal message may have more influence on the receiver. Thus, a *Chicago Tribune* reporter found that it was common at City Hall to send memos stating that needed repairs were emergencies, but the word *emergency* carried less weight than whether the memo was hand-delivered or sent through the office mail system.[11] Figure 7.6 shows the weight that different components of a message may carry. If the relative importance of nonverbal communication seems surprising, imagine that someone is saying, "You're in trouble!" in an angry tone of voice. Now imagine the same person saying that while laughing. Are the messages identical?

Verbal Messages

Most nonverbal communication supplements verbal messages. People send verbal messages by speaking (oral communication) or writing (written communication). In the example at the beginning of this chapter, Loretta Flanagan effectively combined the two types of verbal communication. She talked with staff members in order to develop procedures, then put the procedures in writing.

FIGURE 7.6

Relative Contributions of Several Factors to Total Impact of a Message

When a message is both verbal and nonverbal, the nonverbal message may have more impact on the receiver than the words themselves. Psychologist Albert Mehrabian has found that the relative impact of words, vocal tones (tone of voice), and facial expressions is as shown in this pie chart.

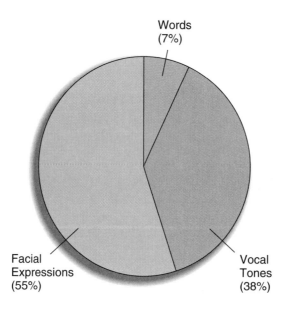

Source: Data from Albert Mehrabian, "Communication without Words," *Psychology Today,* September 1968, pp. 53–55.

Oral Communication   To communicate with employees, supervisors usually depend on oral communication. Every day supervisors talk to employees to explain work duties, answer questions, assign tasks, check progress, and solve problems. This type of communication gives the supervisor an opportunity to send and receive many nonverbal cues along with the verbal ones. Thus, a supervisor can benefit from applying nonverbal communication skills when talking to employees. For example, the supervisor should use a well-moderated tone of voice and allow plenty of time for questions.

Most oral communication occurs face-to-face. It also takes place on the telephone, in meetings, and at formal presentations. (Meetings are discussed in Chapter 17.) At many organizations today, phone callers can leave a message using voice mail. The caller dials the employee's extension number. If the employee doesn't answer, the caller states his or her message, and it is recorded for the employee to hear later.

Speaking before a group is a type of oral communication that makes many supervisors nervous.[12] The nervousness can be positive if it inspires supervisors to be well prepared. Following these steps can help the supervisor prepare:

1. The supervisor should start by learning about the audience. What are the listeners' values and interests, and what do they already know about the topic?
2. Next, the supervisor should spell out the main point of the presentation and the three or four supporting points. For example, the main point might be that the department needs a full-time secretary, and the supporting points would describe the benefits. Or the main point might be that employees can benefit from managing their time better, and the supporting points would be some ideas for doing so.
3. When the supervisor has a clear plan for what to say, he or she should write notes on index cards. It is important to speak naturally, and doing so usually requires speaking from notes rather than reading a script.
4. Finally, the supervisor should practice the speech until it is easy to deliver. For useful feedback, the supervisor can practice with a video camera, a tape recorder, or a friend.

If the supervisor wants more formal, in-depth help with speaking before a group, the organization may be willing to send him or her to one of the many training seminars available or to a speech class at a community college.

Written Communication   It often is important to have a record of what people tell one another. Therefore, much of the verbal communication that occurs in organizations is in writing. Some general guidelines for effective written communication appear in the "Tips from the Firing Line" box on the next page. Common forms of written communication include memos, letters, reports, bulletin board notices, posters, and electronic messages.

Memos (short for *memoranda*) are an informal way to send a written message. At the top of the page, the sender types the date, receiver's name, sender's name, and subject matter. Because of their informality, memos lend themselves to communication within an organization.

People writing to someone outside the organization usually send a letter. A letter is considered more formal than a memo but has basically the same advantages and disadvantages. Specifically, both provide a written document for the receiver to review, and both take a relatively long time to prepare and deliver.

Analysis of how to meet a need or solve a problem takes the form of a report. A report describes the need or problem, then proposes a solution. Many reports contain charts and graphs to make the message simpler to understand. Another helpful technique for a report longer than a page or two is to start off with a paragraph that summarizes the contents of the report. Busy managers can review what the report is about, even if they cannot sit down right away and read every word.

Written messages can also be sent electronically. A facsimile (fax) machine duplicates the sender's document at the receiver's location. Many businesses allow people to send electronic mail (E-mail) by typing a message into a computer, saving it, then having the computer notify the receiver that he or she has a message. Whenever the receiver is using a computer on the same system, the receiver can look at the message. Modern E-mail software makes communication easier in many ways. For example, a program called *BeyondMail* allows the user to set rules for how the system will sort and forward mail, signals the user when an urgent message has been received, and routes messages to someone else if the user is away from the workplace.[13]

Writing Effectively

A lot of people get to be supervisors even though they write poorly. However, if you want to stand out in a positive way, clear writing will impress many people. Here are some tips to polish your writing skills:

- Know what you want to say. This may sound obvious, but fuzzy communication often occurs when the sender of a message has not really thought through the message. Ask yourself what your main point is.

- Organize your thoughts. Usually this means creating an outline. Put your main point near the beginning of your message.

- Write the way you talk. Most of us can get our point across when we are talking. We use simple, direct sentences. But when we are writing, it can be tempting to try to sound formal and fancy. The result is usually that we muddy up the message. Here are some pitfalls to avoid:

  –Noun phrases (nouns describing nouns). For example, it takes work to figure out these phrases: health care coordination mechanisms, machine control automation device.

  –Redundant expressions (two or more words that mean the same thing). Common examples are *first and foremost*, *various and sundry*, and *past history*.

  –Pompous words. For example, *endeavor* is a fancy way to say *try*, *ascertain* just means *find out*, and

facilitate means *help*. Using pompous words is more likely to annoy than to impress someone.

- Review what you have written. If you do your work on a computer, a lot of software programs are available to help you with this. Most word-processing programs contain a spelling checker. If you have difficulty with grammar, you also might want to try using one of the many programs that review a document and point out grammatical problems. But beware: computers cannot understand what you are writing, so they can make or miss mistakes. A computer review is no substitute for your own eyes. You also might want to have a friend or co-worker review some of your writing.

- Practice writing. Take advantage of opportunities to write at work. You can supplement these efforts with writing classes and other writing on your personal time. For example, you can write letters to relatives or your senator, keep a journal, or send a note to the editor of your local newspaper. The more you write, the easier it will get.

- Expose yourself to good writing. That means you should read. Unfortunately, textbooks and professional journals are not always the best places to find good writing. Try reading national newsmagazines, or ask your librarian to suggest some well-written books.

To communicate a single message to many people, the organization may use bulletin board notices and posters. These are efficient but impersonal ways to send messages, so they usually supplement more personal types of communication. For example, if a factory's managers want to promote quality, they can use posters that say "Quality First." But for the message to be effective, management, including supervisors, should also praise individuals for doing quality work, discuss quality when evaluating performance, and set an example in the quality of their own work.

Technology and Message Types

Developments in technology have provided more ways to deliver messages than our parents could have selected or even imagined. Electronic mail and fax machines make it possible to deliver a written message as quickly as a spoken one.

A video conferencing system, supported by Indiana Bell, enables Eli Lilly and Company employees at their world headquarters to see, hear, and interact with other employees in offices around the globe.

Source: Mark Joseph, photographer.

Thanks to teleconferencing, a group of widely scattered people can participate in a meeting without traveling farther than their usual commute to work. When they do travel, people can use cellular phones and portable computers to send and receive messages while en route or when they reach their destination.

Developments such as these provide exciting options. They also make it more difficult to select which way to send any given message. Furthermore, the ability to send and receive information not only in the workplace but also in one's home, car, and plane seat can contribute to the information overload described earlier in the chapter.

Choosing the Most Effective Method of Sending Messages

With so many ways to send a message, which is the best for a supervisor to use? While face-to-face communication conveys the most information (words plus tone of voice plus body language plus immediate feedback), the most effective method for a message depends on the situation. Therefore, when deciding whether to call, meet with, or write to someone, the supervisor should consider time limits, the complexity and sensitivity of the issue, the need for a record of the communication, the need for feedback, and cases of illiteracy.

Time Limits When the supervisor needs to reach someone in a hurry, a letter or memo may be too time-consuming. An employee might be easy to find at his or her desk or on the shop floor. However, the fastest way to reach someone in the organization often is to make a phone call. For contacting people who spend much of their day away from the phone or taking other calls, a fax message, electronic mail, or voice mail allows the supervisor to leave a message and then move on to something else.

The fastest way to reach someone in the organization is to make a phone call. This Motorola portable cellular telephone, being used in Hong Kong Harbor, can be especially valuable to supervisors in the field such as sales managers.

Source: Motorola, Inc.

Complexity and Sensitivity of the Issue   A complex message is clearer if written. For example, the results of a survey or the analysis of a work group's performance would be easiest to understand in a written report. To present such information in a meeting, it makes sense to supplement the oral report with written handouts, slides, posters, or overhead transparencies. When speed is critical in communicating complex information to someone outside the organization, it may be worth the cost to use a fax machine or a computer modem to send the information electronically.

When a message is sensitive, there is no substitute for communicating face-to-face. Holding a one-on-one or group meeting allows the person communicating to defuse anger and dispel misconceptions. It gives the receivers of a message a chance to air their feelings and ask questions. For example, a supervisor who needs to discipline an employee must make sure the employee understands the problem and has a chance to present his or her point of view. Similarly, an announcement of layoffs or restructuring also should be made in person.

Need for Record   As you will learn in Chapter 16, a disciplinary action calls for a written record as well as a face-to-face meeting. A supervisor in such a case would need to combine a written message with oral communication. Other actions that call for written records include placing an order and establishing goals for an employee or department.

Need for Feedback   The easiest way to get feedback is to send an oral message. The listeners at the meeting or on the telephone can respond immediately with comments and questions. If feedback is critical, face-to-face communication is more effective than a telephone conversation because the person delivering the message can watch facial expressions as well as hear reactions. Do people look confused, excited, angry, satisfied? If a supervisor explaining a new procedure says, "Do you understand?" and the employee responds with a doubtful "I guess so," the supervisor knows he or she needs to try giving an example or some other clarification.

Illiteracy In many settings, some employees lack reading skills. If the supervisor believes that one or more employees cannot read the message, the supervisor will need to find ways to deliver it through the spoken word, pictures, gestures, or some other means of communication. This situation arises when an employee cannot read at all or reads too poorly to understand a particular message. Some employees may read well in other languages but not in English; in such a case, the supervisor may want to make written messages available in other languages.

The issue of illiteracy is a sensitive one. Supervisors therefore must be tactful and look carefully for signs that employees have trouble reading. Employees with reading difficulties are typically embarrassed about this problem and try to hide it.

Communicating in Organizations

In business, government, and other organizations, communication tends to follow certain patterns. Understanding these patterns can help the supervisor make the best use of them.

Direction of Communication

downward communication
Organizational communication that involves sending a message to someone at a lower level.

Do you remember the organization charts in Chapter 3? When someone sends a message to a person at a lower level, **downward communication** is occurring. The supervisor is receiving a downward communication when he or she receives instructions or an evaluation from the boss, or when he or she receives a memo from top management describing a new company policy. The supervisor is sending a downward communication when he or she discusses a problem with an employee or tells an employee how to perform a task. Employees expect to receive enough downward communication so that they will understand how to do their jobs, and they typically like to know enough to feel they understand what is going on.

upward communication
Organizational communication that involves sending a message to someone at a higher level.

When someone sends a message to a person at a higher level, **upward communication** is occurring. The supervisor is receiving an upward communication when an employee asks a question or reports a problem. The supervisor is sending an upward communication when he or she tells the boss how work is progressing or asks for a raise. Bosses especially want to receive upward communications about matters that are controversial or may affect the boss's own performance.

To be well informed and to benefit from employees' creativity, the supervisor should encourage upward communication. One way to do this is to listen well, applying the strategies for effective listening described earlier in this chapter. The supervisor should respond to employees so they know their spoken and written messages have been received. Another means of encouraging upward communication is to establish a formal way for employees to provide comments and suggestions, as with a suggestion box. Boeing Commercial Airplanes encourages upward communication by having its supervisors act as "enablers" when employees make suggestions. For example, if a production worker has thought of a better way to produce a part, the employee tells his or her supervisor, who can invite someone from the engineering department to come to the shop floor and discuss the idea.[14] Through such efforts, communication becomes an important part of improving quality at Boeing.

lateral communication
Organizational communication that involves sending a message to a person at the same level.

When someone sends a message to a person at the same level, **lateral communication** is occurring. Supervisors send and receive lateral communications when they discuss their needs with co-workers in other departments, coordinate their group's work with that of other supervisors, and socialize with their peers at the company.

Why should a supervisor know about the directions of communication? One way to use this information is for the supervisor to be sure that he or she is participating in communication in all directions. The supervisor should be participating in enough downward communication that employees know what is expected of them and the supervisor understands what is happening in the organization. The supervisor should be participating in enough upward communication that his or her boss is aware of the supervisor's accomplishments and employees feel encouraged to offer ideas. Finally, the supervisor should be participating in enough lateral communication that the work of his or her department is well coordinated with the work of other departments.

Formal and Informal Communication

formal communication
Organizational communication that is work-related and follows the lines of the organization chart.

In an organization, the communication that follows the lines of the organization chart, as in most of the examples just used, is known as **formal communication**. Formal communication is directed toward accomplishing the goals of the organization. For example, when a supervisor discusses an employee's performance with that employee, the supervisor is helping the employee do high-quality work. When a supervisor gives the boss a report of the department's activities for the week, the supervisor is helping the boss perform his or her responsibilities for controlling.

However, much of the communication that occurs in an organization is directed toward meeting people's individual needs. For example, managers and employees alike may spend time discussing the performance of their favorite sports teams, the behavior of their children or boss, and good places to eat lunch. Such communication is called **informal communication**.

informal communication
Organizational communication that is directed toward individuals' needs and interests and does not necessarily follow formal lines of communication.

Gossip and Rumors   Much informal communication takes the form of gossip and rumors. According to Allan J. Kimmel, a psychology professor at Fitchburg State College, gossip is small talk about people.[15] People use gossip as a way to indicate what behavior is acceptable. Thus, if an employee participated in gossip implying that her boss was gay, it is not surprising that the remarks were interpreted as a value judgment—as a slur, in fact.[16] By gossiping, this employee was in effect commenting on whether the boss's perceived behavior was acceptable. Similarly, employees gossiping about who got promoted or who is dating the new employee in Payroll are typically airing and refining their views about promotion policies and love affairs between co-workers.

In contrast, Kimmel says, "Rumors are what people say among themselves to try to make sense out of what's going on around them." For example, if a factory gets a visit from the company's board of directors, employees at the factory may spread rumors that the factory is to be sold or the operations moved to South Korea. When people are afraid, they spread rumors to soothe themselves by trying to get at the facts. Thus, rumors tend to circulate most during crises and conflicts. Unfortunately, rumors are often false.

Although rumors and gossip are a fact of life in the workplace, it does not look good for a supervisor to participate in spreading either one of these. As a member of management, the supervisor is expected to know and report the facts about company business. And when a supervisor spreads information, it is safe to assume that word will eventually get around that he or she is the person behind the message. Here are some guidelines for keeping rumors and gossip under control:[17]

- Do not share any personal information about other employees, including your desire or intention to criticize or discipline an employee. Discuss the matters with others only when they truly need to know, as when you must discuss a personnel matter with your boss or someone in the human resources department.
- When you hear company information, such as plans for expansion or cutbacks, keep it to yourself until the organization makes an official announcement. Otherwise, if the information is inaccurate or the plans fall through, you could embarrass yourself and upset your boss or employees.
- If you hear a rumor, investigate it and find out the truth and the cause. The rumor may be a tipoff that employees are worried or angry about something, and it is the supervisor's job to address those concerns.

grapevine
The path along which informal communication travels.

The Grapevine The path along which informal communication travels is known as the **grapevine.** The grapevine is important to supervisors because employees use it as a source of information. Thus, the supervisor must expect that employees sometimes have information before the supervisor has delivered it. Supervisors also must realize that employees may be getting incorrect information this way, especially in times of crisis or conflict.

The grapevine springs up on its own, and managers are generally unable to control it. However, knowing about the grapevine can help the supervisor seek out and correct misinformation. The supervisor can also take some steps to see that at least some of the messages in the grapevine are positive and in line with the organization's objectives:[18]

- Regularly use the tools of formal communication to inform employees of the organization's version of events.
- Be open to discussion, becoming someone employees will turn to when they want a rumor confirmed or denied.
- Use performance appraisal interviews as a way to listen to employees as well as give them information.
- Have a trusted employee act as a source of information about the messages traveling the grapevine.
- When necessary, issue a formal response to a rumor in order to clear the air.

Summary

7.1   Describe the process of communication.
The communication process occurs when people send and receive information. It begins when someone encodes a message by putting it into words or nonverbal cues. The sender of the message transmits it in some way, such as by speaking or writing. Then the receiver of the message decodes, or interprets, it. Usually the receiver gives the sender feedback.

7.2   Distinguish between hearing and listening.
Hearing occurs when the brain registers sounds. Listening occurs when the person who hears sounds also pays attention and tries to understand.

7.3   Describe techniques for communicating effectively.
Effective communication is most likely to occur when the parties communicate from the receiver's viewpoint, learn from feedback, use strategies for effective listening, and overcome barriers to communication. To listen effectively, the listener should make a commitment to listen, set aside time for listening, and then concentrate on the message. The listener also should try to control his or her emotions, not letting an emotional reaction interfere with understanding.

7.4   Identify barriers to communication, and suggest ways to avoid them.
Barriers to communication include information overload, misunderstandings, perceptions and prejudices, and biases in paying attention to messages. Ways to avoid these barriers include encoding messages carefully and simply, observing feedback, avoiding name-calling, being aware of inferences and prejudices, and phrasing messages to appeal to the receiver.

7.5   Distinguish between verbal and nonverbal messages, and name types of verbal messages.
Verbal messages consist of words. Nonverbal messages are messages encoded in some other way, such as facial expressions, gestures, or tone of voice. Types of verbal messages include face-to-face discussions, phone calls, memos, letters, reports, and electronic-mail messages.

7.6   Identify the directions in which communication can flow in an organization.
Organizational communication may be upward, downward, or lateral. Upward communication travels to the sender's superior. Downward communication travels from boss to subordinates. Lateral communication occurs between people at the same level.

7.7   Distinguish between formal and informal communication in an organization.
Formal communication travels along the lines of the organizational chart and is related to accomplishing the goals of the organization. Informal communication may travel in any direction between any members of the organization. It tends to be aimed at achieving personal, rather than organizational, objectives.

7.8   Describe the role of the grapevine in organizations.
The grapevine is the path of much of the organization's informal communications. Much of the information that travels through the grapevine is gossip and rumors. The supervisor generally cannot control this flow of information but should be aware that it exists and that he or she may have to correct misinformation. In addition, by encouraging communication with employees, the supervisor may be able to ensure that some of the messages in the grapevine are positive.

Key Terms

communication	prejudices	lateral communication
feedback	verbal messages	formal communication
active listening	nonverbal messages	informal communication
inference	downward communication	grapevine
perceptions	upward communication	

Review and Discussion Questions

1. Phyllis Priestley, a supervisor, wants to tell her boss what she plans to accomplish at a leadership seminar she will be attending next week. She decides to do so in the form of a memo. Briefly describe how this communication will follow the model shown in Figure 7.1.

2. Can a person be hearing well but not listening well? Can a person be listening well but not hearing well? Explain.

3. Every Monday morning, Ron Yamamoto, a supervisor, must attend a divisional meeting to discuss progress and make plans. Ron finds that most people at the meetings are long-winded and that the meetings as a whole are boring. However, he needs to know what is going on in the division. What are some ways Ron can listen effectively, even though he is bored?

4. Name three barriers to communication, and suggest a way to overcome each.

5. The following examples describe some ways to send messages. Indicate whether each is verbal or nonverbal. For each verbal message, indicate whether it is oral or written.
   a. a long silence accompanied by an icy stare
   b. a letter delivered by fax machine
   c. voice mail
   d. laughter

6. As the supervisor of the mail room, you need to report to your boss that a sack of mail has been misplaced (you are not sure how it happened). Would you want to send this message through written or oral communication? Would you want to deliver it face-to-face? Describe the form of communication you would choose and why you would choose it.

7. Face-to-face communication conveys the most information, because the people communicating can learn from each other's body language and tone of voice, as well as from the words themselves. However, why shouldn't a supervisor always choose face-to-face communication over other ways to communicate?

8. A supervisor believes that employees are not providing enough information about what they are doing. How can the supervisor encourage more upward communication from the employees?

9. Which of the following organizational communications are formal, and which are informal?
   a. a memo providing information about the company picnic
   b. a meeting at which employees discuss the department's goals for the month
   c. a rumor about a new vacation policy
   d. a discussion between a supervisor and an employee about who will win the World Series

10. Should a supervisor participate in informal communication? If so, when? If not, why not?

A SECOND LOOK

This chapter described various categories of communication: verbal and nonverbal, oral and written, formal and informal. Which kinds of communication can you identify in the opening example, of Loretta Flanagan?

Class Exercise

Before class, or when your instructor sets aside time in class, read the following memo. The writer was an employee of the U.S. Department of Transportation:

The purpose of this PPM [Policy and Procedure Memorandum] is to ensure, to the maximum extent practicable, that highway locations and designs reflect and are consistent with Federal, State and local goals and objectives. The rules, policies and procedures established by this PPM are intended to afford full opportunity for effective public participation in the consideration of highway location and design proposals by highway departments before submission to the Federal Highway Administration for approval. They provide a medium for free and open discussion and are designed to encourage early and amicable resolution of controversial issues that may arise.*

1. Did you find this memo easy to understand? If not, why not? Did the author succeed in communicating?

2. As a class, try to rewrite this paragraph so that it is easier to understand. If you are not sure where to begin, consider the sentences one by one. Review the writing tips in the box on page 172, and try answering these questions:

    a. Are there any long sentences that you can divide into two or more?

    b. *Who* is doing *what* in each sentence? Try to rephrase each sentence so that it is easy to define these items.

    c. Where did the writer use two or more words when one word would mean the same thing?

    d. Do these sentences sound natural, as if the writer were talking to you? Using a dictio-nary if you need to, figure out what each sentence means, then think about how you would say it if you were talking to someone.

3. Compare the class's rewritten paragraph with the following (you may have found better solutions):

    This PPM is intended to ensure that the design and location of highways meet the goals of the Federal, State and local governments. It tries to let the public participate fully when highway departments consider proposals to send to the Federal Highway Administration for approval. The policies and procedures in this memorandum provide a basis for open discussion. As a result, the people involved should be able to resolve any conflicts early on.

4. As a supervisor, how can you put into practice the techniques that worked in this class exercise?

CASE

Getting Employees to Communicate Ideas

During his career as a maintenance supervisor, John Morgan (who recently retired) wanted to learn from employees' suggestions and ideas. However, he found that employees were often slow to come forward. Morgan concluded that many companies' systems for employee suggestions actually discouraged ideas by making the process too complicated and costly for employees to bother with simple ideas.

Morgan never had the authority to change a company's suggestion policy, but he was able to try some other approaches within his department. He installed a bulletin board in the maintenance department. Then he told his employees that they should post *all* maintenance suggestions on the bulletin board, no matter what their dollar value. So as not to conflict with the company's policies, he also encouraged employees to submit big-ticket ideas through the corporate suggestion system.

Every suggestion posted on the bulletin board remained there for at least five working days. Employees were encouraged to read the suggestions often. If anyone saw a problem with an idea, that employee was to remove it from the bulletin board and bring it to the weekly employee meeting.

At the weekly meetings, employees discussed any idea that was brought in. First the person who came up with the idea would explain it, then the person who removed the idea from the bulletin board would describe his or her concerns. The group would solve any problems or make other adjustments, then vote on whether to try the suggestion.

If no one removed a suggestion from the bulletin board after five working days, the employee who posted the idea was to put it into effect. At the weekly employee meetings, those who submitted such ideas explained them and announced when

*Reprinted in Kenneth W. Houp and Thomas E. Pearsall, *Reporting Technical Information* (New York: Macmillan, 1984), p. 187.

they would go into effect. No debate was allowed, because no one had objected to the idea.

After a suggestion had been acted on for a month, the employees could discuss it at their weekly meeting and vote on whether to reverse the change. However, Morgan's policy was that no one would criticize the suggester for having tried the idea. As a result, Morgan saw that employees did not suffer unpleasant consequences for making suggestions, and they were likely to come up with more ideas in the future. Morgan also posted a sign to give employees recognition for being innovative. The sign showed the total number of suggestions made for the year to date, the number of suggestions implemented, and the average number of suggestions made per employee.

Upper management at Morgan's company asked him to give a presentation to them on his suggestion system. Instead, Morgan had his employees give the presentation. He did so to show the importance of employees' participation.

Afterward, the number and frequency of suggestions in Morgan's department increased even more.

1. Besides the suggestions themselves, what messages are described in this case? Consider that the messages may be nonverbal as well as verbal.
2. When his employees made suggestions, how did supervisor John Morgan give them feedback? How did the feedback affect the employees?
3. How do you think Morgan's efforts to encourage upward communication affected the quality of his department's work? Do you think this system would work as well in other situations, such as with servers in a restaurant or salesclerks in a store? Why or why not?

Source: "Suggestions: The Hidden Resource," *Maintenance Supervisor's Bulletin* (Bureau of Business Practice), February 10, 1992, pp. 1–4.

8

In every affair consider what precedes and what follows, and then undertake it.
—**Epictetus**

Problem Solving and Decision Making

LEARNING OBJECTIVES

8.1   Identify the steps in the rational model of decision making.

8.2   Discuss ways people make compromises in following the decision-making model.

8.3   Describe guidelines for making decisions.

8.4   Explain how probability theory, decision trees, and computer software can help in making decisions.

8.5   Discuss advantages and disadvantages of making decisions in groups.

8.6   Describe guidelines for group decision making.

8.7   Describe guidelines for thinking creatively.

8.8   Discuss how supervisors can establish and maintain a creative work climate.

8.9   Identify ways to overcome barriers to creativity.

THE SATISFACTION OF SOLVING PROBLEMS

Marilyn Bowie is a nurse manager for obstetrical care at St. Joseph's Hospital and Medical Center in Phoenix, Arizona. She supervises 80 employees, including nurses, nursing assistants, student assistants, and unit secretaries. When Bowie became a supervisor, she had to switch to solving different kinds of problems than she had as a nurse. As a nurse, she made "life-and-death decisions" pertaining to individual patients. In her current position, Bowie solves problems involving the support of the people who now make those life-and-death decisions. She considers problem solving to be the most satisfying part of her job.

One problem that Bowie solved concerned staffing her unit. An employee of Bowie's had been in school for a while and eventually received her degree. At that time, the employee wanted a new job. Bowie and her director valued the employee's strengths, such as courtesy and willingness to work, so Bowie was able to persuade her director to let her create a new position for the employee. The employee now handles secretarial duties and also teaches the nurses and managers how to use the hospital's computers. Bowie says creating the job for this employee "has been paid back tenfold," thanks to the employee's talents.

Another problem tackled by Bowie involved the entire structure of her unit. She observed that new mothers at the hospital were not being educated as well as they might have been and that mothers and babies were sometimes not being discharged properly. Bowie met with her staff to discuss these symptoms, and the group concluded that the problem lay with having separate nurses for the mothers and their new babies. The group developed the idea of "couplet nursing" at St. Joseph's, that is, a system in which each mother and her baby are cared for by the same nurse. Bowie formed a task force of staff members that meets regularly to continue discussing ideas to make the new system work better. According to Bowie, "group consensus was very important" in making the new system work.

No matter how carefully a supervisor plans, no matter how effectively a supervisor leads, he or she is bound to encounter problems. Human imperfections, new challenges from the environment in which the department operates, and the desire to achieve higher quality are only three sources of problems for the supervisor to solve. Therefore, in the words of management consultant Clark Wigley, "Success does not equal no problems (as in 'If I were a good manager, I would have no problems'). Success is having and solving the right problems."[1] Wigley means that the best managers (including supervisors) are those who know what issues to focus on and who respond to problems in a positive way. By solving the right problems—the ones that can improve the quality of work—effective supervisors improve their department's activities and the service they deliver to their customers.

decision
A choice from among available alternatives.

A **decision** is a choice from among available alternatives. Solving problems involves making a series of decisions: deciding that something is wrong, deciding what the problem is, deciding how to solve it. The "Dealing with Diversity" box describes how these decisions apply to the problem of sexual harassment. (Training employees to avoid sexual harassment is covered in Chapter 14.) Successful problem solving depends on good decisions. This chapter describes how supervisors make decisions and offers some guidelines for doing so effectively. The chapter includes a discussion of decision making in groups and suggestions for thinking creatively.

The Process of Decision Making

Much of the supervisor's job is making decisions, which cover all the functions of management. What should the supervisor or the department accomplish today or this week? Who should handle a particular project or machine? What should the supervisor tell the boss about the customer who complained yesterday? Do employees need better training or just more inspiration? How can the supervisor end the ongoing dispute between two staff members? These are just a few of the problems a typical supervisor has to act on.

In many cases, supervisors make decisions like these without giving any thought to the process of deciding. A supervisor automatically does something because it feels right or because the supervisor has always handled that problem that way. When the decision seems more complex, the supervisor is more likely to give thought to the decision-making process. For example, in deciding whether to purchase an expensive piece of machinery or whether to fire an employee, the supervisor might make a careful list of pluses and minuses, trying to include all the relevant concerns, be they economic, practical, or ethical. (Making ethical decisions is discussed in Chapter 19). But even though many decisions seem to be automatic, supervisors can improve the way they make decisions by understanding how the decision-making process works in theory and in practice.

Solving the Problem of Sexual Harassment

In days of testimony before the Senate Judiciary Committee in October 1991, law professor Anita Hill accused her former boss, Judge Clarence Thomas, of sexual harassment, and Thomas refuted her charges. While neither of them ever fully proved his or her case, the controversy dramatically highlighted the issue of sexual harassment. As defined by the federal Equal Employment Opportunity Commission (EEOC), sexual harassment is "unwelcome sexual advances, requests for sexual favors, and other verbal and physical conduct of a sexual nature" that "has the purpose or effect of unreasonably interfering with an individual's work performance or creating an intimidating, hostile, or offensive work environment."

In the wake of the Hill-Thomas hearings, the number of sexual harassment charges filed with the EEOC increased dramatically. For example, the number of claims of sexual harassment filed in the fourth quarter of 1991 was 71 percent higher than a year earlier—1,244 compared with 728 in 1990. These numbers suggest that the problem is not going to go away and that it affects not only national figures but supervisors nationwide.

A charge of sexual harassment is a serious one. Court decisions have held employers liable for the misdeeds of their employees unless the organization actively tries to prevent the misbehavior and responds effectively when it does occur. Therefore, when an employee charges a member of the organization with sexual harassment, the supervisor has no choice but to conclude there is a problem.

To decide what the nature of the problem is, the supervisor must see that the complaint is investigated properly. Generally, the investigation would involve a third party, such as a personnel official, interviewing everyone involved. The supervisor must carefully avoid expressing an opinion or imposing his or her interpretation on the situation.

Whether harassment occurs depends on how the behavior affects the recipient, not on the intent of the person performing the behavior. Thus, if lewd jokes and pornographic pictures create a climate that feels hostile and intimidating to an employee, it does not matter that the person who told the jokes and hung up the pictures thought they were just funny. It is not surprising that perceptions vary from one person to another, and differences tend to be especially great between the sexes. For example, in a 1981 study of people in Los Angeles County, 67 percent of the men said they would feel flattered to be propositioned by a co-worker of the opposite sex, but 63 percent of women said they would feel offended.

Finally, with the support of higher-level management, the supervisor must decide how to solve the problem. One approach that does *not* work is ignoring the offensive behavior in the hope it will go away. The victim telling the offender to stop is effective more than half the time. Especially since men and women tend to interpret actions differently, it may be helpful to describe to the offender the kind of behavior that would be acceptable.

Of course, the supervisor cannot afford to let an employee handle the problem alone. Working with the human resources department, the supervisor needs to identify a prompt and firm response to charges that are proven. The response might be to move the employee to another department or shift, or even to fire him or her.

Sources: Alan Deutschman, "Dealing with Sexual Harassment," *Fortune,* November 4, 1991, pp. 145, 148; Robert T. Gray, "How to Deal with Sexual Harassment," *Nation's Business,* December 1991, pp. 28, 30–31; Carol Kleiman, "Sex Harassment Complaints on the Rise," *Chicago Tribune,* March 7, 1992, sec. 1, pp. 1, 12; Janice Murphy, "Sexual Harassment at Work," *Healthcare Trends & Transition,* January 1992, pp. 45–48; and Charlene Marmer Solomon, "Sexual Harassment after the Thomas Hearings," *Personnel Journal,* December 1991, pp. 32–37.

A basketball coach, such as Jim Calhoun from the University of Connecticut shown here, is a supervisor who must make instant decisions.

Source: Courtesy of Manny Millan/*Sports Illustrated.*

The Rational Model

If you could know everything, you could make perfect decisions. How would an all-knowing person go about making a decision? He or she would probably follow the rational model of decision making, illustrated in Figure 8.1.

Identify the Problem   According to this model, the decision maker first identifies the problem. Recall from Chapter 5 that it is important to distinguish the symptoms of a problem from the problem itself. Usually what the supervisor notices first are the symptoms, so he or she has to look for the underlying problem. For example, Dave Frantz finds that he has to work 60 hours a week in order to do his job as supervisor of a group of workers for a janitorial service. Dave works hard and spends little time socializing, so his effort is not the problem. He observes that he spends approximately half his time doing paperwork required by higher-level management. He decides that the major problem is that he spends too much time on paperwork. (Along the way, Dave may find and resolve minor problems as well.)

Identify Alternative Solutions   The next step is to identify the alternative solutions. In the example, Dave thinks of several possibilities. He might delegate the paperwork to other employees, hire a secretary, buy a personal computer and software that will automate some of the work, or get relieved of some of the paperwork.

FIGURE 8.1

The Rational Model of Decision Making

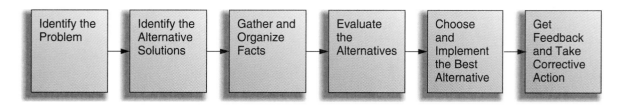

Gather and Organize Facts   Next the decision maker gathers and organizes facts. Dave asks his boss if he really has to do all the paperwork; the boss says yes. From the human resources office, Dave gets information on the pay scale for secretaries. He evaluates whether any of his work can be delegated, and he collects ads for and magazine articles about various personal computers and software.

Evaluate Alternatives   With the information gathered, the supervisor evaluates the alternatives. Dave determines that he cannot eliminate or delegate the paperwork. He calculates that a personal computer would cost much less than a secretary, though a secretary would save more of his time. He predicts that his boss will be more open to his buying a computer than to his hiring a secretary.

Choose and Implement the Best Alternative   The supervisor next chooses and implements the best alternative. In the example, Dave decides to buy a personal computer. He prepares a report showing the costs and benefits of doing so. He emphasizes how the company will benefit when he is more efficient and can devote more time to leading and controlling employees. He selects the brand and model of computer that he thinks will best meet his needs at a reasonable cost.

When evaluating and selecting alternatives, how can the supervisor decide which is best? Sometimes the choice is obvious, but other times the supervisor needs formal criteria for deciding, such as these:

- The alternative chosen should actually solve the problem. In the example, ignoring the paperwork might enable Dave to leave on time, but it would not solve the problem of how to get the job done.
- An acceptable alternative must be feasible. In other words, the supervisor should be able to implement it. For example, Dave learned that requesting less paperwork was not a feasible solution.
- The cost of the alternative should be reasonable in light of the benefits it will deliver. Dave's employer might consider a personal computer to be a reasonable expense, but the cost of a full-time secretary is large compared with the benefits of making Dave's job easier.

Get Feedback   The last step is to get feedback and take corrective action. In the example, Dave takes his proposal to his boss, who suggests some additions and changes. Dave orders the computer. When it arrives, he automates some of his work, using his experiences to improve upon his original ideas.

When a decision will affect the course of someone's career or the expenditure of a lot of money, the supervisor will want to make the best decision possible. One way of doing so is to try to complete each of the steps in the rational model. In general, then, supervisors can benefit from using this model when they are making complex, formal decisions or when the consequences of a decision are great.

Human Compromises

The example of the rational model of decision making may sound far removed from the daily experiences of most supervisors. Often supervisors have neither the time nor the desire to follow all these steps to a decision. Even when supervisors try to follow these steps, they often have trouble thinking of all the alternatives or gathering all the facts they need. Sometimes it is not clear which alternative is the best.

Given these human and organizational limitations, supervisors—and all decision makers—tend to make compromises most of the time. These are summarized in Figure 8.2. The result may be a less than perfect decision, but it is typically one the decision maker is willing to live with. If a supervisor is aware of the kinds of compromises people make, the supervisor is more apt to be aware of when he or she is using them. In addition, the supervisor may find that although some kinds of compromises are useful in some situations, others are to be avoided as much as possible.

Simplicity   Although we often think we have approached a problem with a fresh perspective and analyzed all the options, most people really take a simpler approach. Usually what we are doing is just thinking over our experiences and considering ways we have handled similar problems in the past. If we consider a few possibilities, we conclude that we have covered them all. People tend to select an alternative that they have tried before and that has delivered acceptable results. The downside of this approach is that it tends to bypass new and innovative solutions, even though they sometimes deliver the best results.

satisficing
Choosing an alternative that meets minimum standards of acceptability.

Satisficing   When time, cost, or other limitations such as the tendency to simplify make it impossible or unreasonable to find the best alternative, decision makers settle for one they consider good enough. Choosing an alternative that meets minimum standards of acceptability is known as **satisficing**. The process of satisficing is also known as bounded rationality (that is, the decision maker places limits, or *bounds*, on the *rational* model of decision making). Figure 8.3 shows how bounded rationality works. The decision maker considers alternatives only until he or she finds one that meets his or her minimum criteria for acceptability.

For example, a supervisor who is fed up with tardiness might first be inclined to fire everyone who was late this week. But she knows that will be demoralizing, will create a sudden and large need for hiring and training, and will probably not impress her boss. She rejects that alternative. Then she remembers she had tried giving "timeliness awards" last year, but that did not work, so she rejects that alternative. Finally, she remembers reading an article that recommends spelling out the consequences of the undesirable behavior, then letting the employee experience those consequences. She decides to try that approach. There probably are other ways to solve the problem (maybe even better ways), but the supervisor does not spend any more time trying to think of them.

FIGURE 8.2

Human
Compromises in
Decision Making

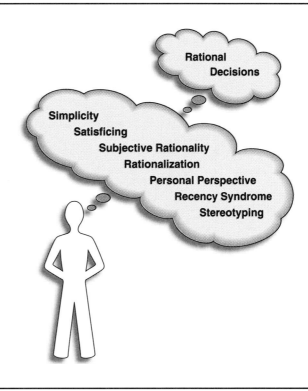

FIGURE 8.3

The Process of
Satisficing

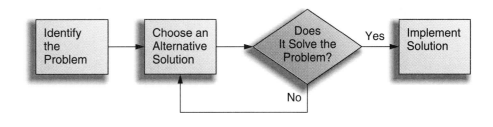

Subjective Rationality   When people analyze alternatives, they tend to rely on their intuition and gut instincts rather than on collecting impartial data. For example, a sales supervisor might estimate, "I think orders will be up next year, but just slightly, say, 2 percent." The sales supervisor did not arrive at that figure through marketing research or an analysis of industry data but relied on his experience with the trends that demand for the product has followed. Thus, even when the process for arriving at the decision is otherwise rational, the numbers used in the process may be subjective. As a result, they may be less than completely accurate.

Rationalization   People tend to favor solutions that they believe they can justify to others. For example, production supervisor Renata King knows that her boss focuses on containing costs. When Renata is considering alternative ways to approach a problem, she tends to favor the low-cost alternative. Another alternative might be more successful, but Renata feels that whatever the outcome, her boss is likely to appreciate her effort to keep costs down.

Personal Perspective   In supervising computer programmers, Abraham Wassad has to review their documentation and the instructions they write for using their programs. Abraham pointed out to one programmer that some portions of his instructions needed clarification. "It's OK the way it is," insisted the programmer. "*I* understand it."

People often make this programmer's mistake: assuming everyone sees things the way he does. If instructions are clear to the programmer, he thinks they must be clear to any (reasonable) person. Such assumptions can lead to incorrect decisions in many areas, including how much information to convey, what working conditions are most important to employees, or what product characteristics customers want. To avoid this problem, decision makers must find out what other people are thinking, and then take those views into account.

Recency Syndrome   People more readily remember events that have occurred recently. This tendency is known as the **recency syndrome**. For example, a supervisor might remember that the last time she gave a negative performance appraisal the employee became hostile but not that a similar situation two years before led an employee to improve his performance. Clearly, in most situations, an event should not carry more weight just because it is more recent. This is one reason decision makers need to be careful to consider the alternatives as fully as is reasonable.

Stereotyping   Chapter 7 described stereotyping as a barrier to communication. Stereotyping also interferes with rational decision making because it limits the decision maker's understanding of the people involved.[2] Rigid opinions about categories of people distort the truth that people offer a rich variety of individual strengths and viewpoints. For example, the stereotype that black people are athletic may seem flattering on its face, but it is insulting as well as misleading when applied to a particular black employee whose particular strengths are reliability and a gift for public speaking. No doubt, this employee would rather be recognized for her own unique talents than for some stereotypical ones, and a supervisor who can do that will be best able to lead her.

The cure for stereotyping is *not* to assume that everyone is alike. Not only does this assumption oversimplify the situation, it is in effect an insult to other people. It ignores the strengths and values people receive from their culture, some of which may be precious to them. Rather, the supervisor should make a conscious, ongoing effort to learn about the various groups of people represented in the workplace. The purpose is to acquire information that serves as a starting point for understanding others while recognizing that the individuals within any group are unique. In addition, the supervisor needs to be aware of his or her stereotypes about people and situations. In making a decision, the supervisor should consider whether those stereotypes truly describe the situation at hand.

recency syndrome
The tendency to more easily remember events that have occurred recently.

Guidelines for Decision Making

Should the supervisor always avoid human compromises in making decisions? Not necessarily. In some situations, seeking to match the rational model would just be too costly and time-consuming. However, as described in the "Tips from the Firing Line" box on the next page, there are a variety of ways the supervisor can make many decisions more rationally. Also, the following paragraphs provide further guidelines for making decisions in the workplace.

Consider the Consequences

The supervisor should be aware of the possible consequences of the decision. For example, hiring and firing decisions can have great consequences for the performance of the department. Purchases of inexpensive items are less critical than purchases of major equipment and computer systems. Some decisions affect the safety of workers, whereas others make just a slight difference in their comfort.

When the consequences of a decision are great, the supervisor should spend more time on the decision. He or she should try to follow the rational model of decision making, seeking to include as many alternatives as possible. When the consequences of the decision are slight, the supervisor should limit the time and money spent in identifying and evaluating alternatives. This may mean the supervisor must accept some of the human compromises described earlier.

Respond Quickly in a Crisis

When a nuclear reactor is overheating, there is no time for the supervisor to weigh each employee's qualifications and to select the best employee for each task in handling the crisis. When a store's customer is shouting about poor service, there is no time to list all the possible responses. In both cases, the supervisor needs to take action fast.

In a crisis, the supervisor should quickly select the course of action that seems best. This is an application of satisficing. Rather than waiting to evaluate other alternatives, the supervisor should begin implementing the solution, interpreting feedback to see whether the solution is working.

Inform the Boss

The supervisor's boss does not want to hear about every single minor decision the supervisor makes each day. However, the boss does need to know what is happening in the department. The supervisor should inform the boss about major decisions. These would include decisions that affect the department's meeting its objectives and the supervisor's responses to a crisis, as well as any decision that might be controversial.

Ways to Make Decisions More Rational

Many decision makers like to rely on their intuition, and they are often satisfied with the results. However, according to Stanford professor James L. Adams, an expert on decision making, the best results come from backing up the intuitive process with a variety of analytical tools, from statistics to computer software. Analyzing a problem formally can improve the quality of the decisions that result. Here are some techniques for putting that advice into practice:

- Make a checklist of the factors that may influence the decision.
- Collect data by conducting research instead of relying on existing information. (Caution: This tactic can generate greatly relevant information, but it can be costly, so be sure the problem warrants the expense.)
- Get advice from people with various backgrounds—co-workers in other departments, colleagues at other organizations, consultants, and your employees.
- Hold an informal brainstorming session. As described later in the chapter, this is a meeting at which participants offer all the ideas that come to mind, no matter how outrageous.
- Try approaching the problem from a fresh angle. Use different words to describe it, and make sure you are looking at the problem, not just the symptoms.
- Inject a little humor when you need to take a fresh look at the problem or break a deadlock. Relax and fantasize a little about the solution.

Source: Pam Miller Withers, "The Smarter Way to Make Decisions," *Working Woman*, March 1990, pp. 31–32.

When the boss needs to know about a decision, it is usually smart for the supervisor to discuss the problem before reaching and announcing the decision. The boss may see an aspect of the problem that has escaped the supervisor or may have different priorities that will lead him or her to veto or modify the supervisor's solution. For example, in the story that opened this chapter, when Marilyn Bowie wanted to create a new position for a valued employee, her director gave approval on the condition that Bowie not increase her total budget. Knowing and adjusting for such information while weighing the alternatives is less embarrassing to the supervisor and avoids annoying the boss. Of course, in a crisis, the supervisor may not have time to consult with his or her boss and has to settle for discussing the decision as soon as possible afterward.

Be Decisive but Not Inflexible

Sometimes it is difficult to say which alternative solution is most likely to succeed or will bring the best results. Two alternatives may look about equally good, or perhaps none of the choices look good enough. In cases such as these, the supervisor may find it hard to move beyond studying the alternatives to selecting and implementing one of them. However, avoiding a decision is just another way to decide to do nothing—and in many cases doing nothing is clearly not the best choice. Furthermore, employees and peers find it frustrating to work for someone who never seems to make up his or her mind or get back to them with answers to their questions. Therefore, supervisors need to be decisive.

To train firefighting supervisors and their employees to make quick and accurate decisions in a crisis, AAI/MICROFLITE Simulation International has developed the AAI's FireTrainer™.

Source: Courtesy of Michael Melford © 1992.

Being decisive means reaching a decision within a reasonable amount of time. What is reasonable depends on the nature of the decision. A supervisor should not spend hours deciding what assignments to give technicians each morning. In contrast, selecting a candidate to fill a job opening will probably take days. The latter decision requires more time because it is more complex and its consequences are greater. Within whatever time frame is appropriate for the decision, the supervisor should pick the alternative that looks best (or at least acceptable), then focus on implementing it.

Certain kinds of behavior are typical of a supervisor who is decisive.[3] A decisive supervisor quickly clears his or her desk of routine matters. When such matters arise, the supervisor promptly refers questions or problems to the proper people, delegates appropriately, and keeps work moving. A decisive supervisor assumes complete responsibility for getting the facts needed when he or she must solve a problem. Finally, a decisive supervisor keeps his or her employees informed of what they are expected to do and how they are progressing relative to their objectives.

Being decisive does not mean the supervisor is blind to signs that he or she has made a mistake. When implementing a solution, the supervisor needs to seek feedback that indicates whether the solution is working. If the first attempt at solving a problem fails, the supervisor must be flexible and try another approach.

A decisive supervisor assumes responsibility for getting the facts to solve a problem. Data stored in computer networks is very helpful to today's supervisor, who may need instant access to information.

Source: © 1992, Comstock, Inc.

Avoid Decision-Making Traps

Some supervisors seem to delight in emergency deadlines and crisis situations. These supervisors act as though each decision they make is a life-or-death issue. But good planning can avert many crises, and life-or-death issues are not the usual stuff of the supervisor's job. Making a major issue out of each decision does not make the supervisor more important; it just interferes with clear thinking. The supervisor must be able to put each issue into perspective so that he or she can calmly evaluate the alternatives and devote an appropriate amount of time to finding a solution.

Another trap for decision makers is responding inappropriately to failure. When a supervisor makes a wrong decision, the supervisor will look best if he or she acknowledges the mistake. Finding someone to blame just makes the supervisor seem irresponsible. At the same time, supervisors need not dwell on their mistakes and agonize over them. It is more important to learn whatever lesson the mistake can teach and then to move on.

In an effort to save time or work independently, some supervisors fail to draw on easily available information. One important source of information is precedent. Have some of the alternatives been tried before? If so, what was the outcome? Answering these questions can help the supervisor evaluate alternatives more realistically. Similarly, by consulting with other members of the organization or with outside experts, the supervisor often can find readily available data that will improve his or her decision.

Sometimes supervisors are tempted to promise too much. This mistake traps many supervisors because the promises keep people happy, at least until the promises are broken. For example, a supervisor may promise an angry employee a raise before being sure the budget can handle it. This may seem to solve the problem of the employee's anger, but the promise will backfire if the supervisor cannot deliver on it. Similarly, a supervisor may tell her boss that she can continue meeting existing deadlines even while a new computer system is being installed. She is not sure of this, but making the promise is a way of avoiding a confrontation with her boss (until the department does miss a deadline). Ultimately, everyone will be more pleased if supervisors make realistic promises. Then it is possible to arrive at solutions that will work as expected.

Tools for Decision Making

In preparing a budget for next year, LaTanya Jones, manager of a store's appliance department, needed to determine how many sales associates should work each day of the week. At a factory that produces air conditioners, production supervisor Pete Yakimoto was trying to determine why the rate of defects had recently been rising and what to do to correct the problem. Pete's employees complained that they were making mistakes because they had to work too fast, and Pete wondered if hiring more workers could be justified economically.

Problems such as these are difficult to solve mentally. Usually the supervisor facing such complex decisions needs tools and techniques for analyzing the alternatives. Some widely used tools are probability theory, decision trees, and computer software.

Probability Theory

Sometimes a supervisor needs to choose which course of action will have the greatest benefit (or least cost), but the supervisor cannot completely control the outcome. Therefore, the supervisor cannot be 100 percent sure what the outcome will be. For example, a sales supervisor can tell salespeople whom to call on but cannot control the behavior of the customers. And Pete Yakimoto in the previous example can recommend that new workers be hired, but he has only limited control over how the workers will perform. In statistical terms, these situations with uncertain outcomes are said to involve risk.

probability theory
A body of techniques for comparing the consequences of possible decisions in a risk situation.

To make decisions about risk situations, the supervisor can compare the consequences of various decisions by using **probability theory**. To use this theory, the supervisor needs to know or be able to estimate the value of each possible outcome and the likelihood (probability) that this outcome will occur. For example, a production supervisor is comparing two stamping presses. The supervisor wants to use a press to produce $1 million in parts per year. Press A costs $900,000, and Press B costs $800,000. Based on the suppliers' claims and track record, the supervisor believes there is a 90 percent chance that Press A will last 10 years (thus producing $10 million in parts) and only a 10 percent chance that it will fail after 5 years (thus producing $5 million in parts). The supervisor believes there is a 30 percent chance that Press B will fail after 5 years.

To use probability theory to make decisions about risk situations, the supervisor can start by putting the possible outcomes into table format. Table 8.1 shows the possible outcomes for the stamping presses in the example. In this case the supervisor subtracted the cost of the press from the value of what the press could

TABLE 8.1
Possible Outcomes for a Risk Situation

	Five Years of Production	Ten Years of Production
Press A	$5 million – $900,000 = $4.1 million	$10 million – $900,000 = $9.1 million
Press B	$5 million – $800,000 = $4.2 million	$10 million – $800,000 = $9.2 million

Note: Outcomes are computed as value of production minus cost of press.

TABLE 8.2
Expected Value of Possibilities

	Five Years of Production	Ten Years of Production
Press A	$4.1 million × .10 = $410,000	$9.1 million × .90 = $8.2 million
Press B	$4.2 million × .30 = $1.3 million	$9.2 million × .70 = $6.4 million

Note: Values are computed as possible outcome (from Table 8.1) times probability of outcome.

produce in 5 or 10 years. Notice that because Press B is cheaper, the possible outcomes for that press are greater. Remember, however, that Press B is also more likely to fail after 5 years. To find the *expected* value (EV) of each possible outcome, multiply the possible outcome (O) by the probability of that outcome (P). Stated as a formula, $EV = O \times P$. Table 8.2 shows the results of this computation. The supervisor should select the press with the highest expected value—in this case, Press A.

Decision Trees

In the real world, most decisions involving probability are at least as complex as the previous example about purchasing machinery. Sorting out the relative value of the choices can be easier with a graph to refer to. Thus, for making decisions in risk situations, the supervisor may find it helpful to use a decision tree. A **decision tree** is a graph that helps in decision making by showing the expected values of decisions under varying circumstances.

As depicted in Figure 8.4, a decision tree shows the available alternatives, which stem from decision points. For each alternative, one of several chance events may occur. As before, the decision maker estimates the probability of each chance event occurring. To find the expected value of each outcome, the decision maker multiplies the probability by the value of the outcome ($EV = O \times P$). The decision maker should select the alternative for which the expected value is greatest.

For example, in Figure 8.4, a sales supervisor is trying to decide whether to hire a new salesperson at a salary of $40,000. The supervisor estimates that with the new salesperson on board, there is a 60 percent chance that the department's sales will increase from $200,000 to $250,000. Without the new salesperson, the chance for the sales increase is just 50 percent. The supervisor assumes that, at worst, the department will hold steady in either case. The dollar value of each

decision tree
A graph that helps decision makers use probability theory by showing the expected values of decisions under varying circumstances.

FIGURE 8.4
A Simple Decision Tree

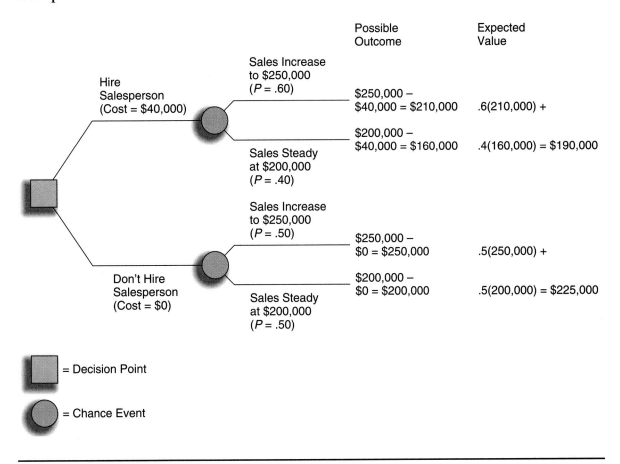

= Decision Point

= Chance Event

possible outcome is the amount of sales minus the cost of the choice (hiring or not hiring). To find the expected value of each choice, the supervisor multiplies the probability of each outcome by the value of that outcome. Assuming there is a 60 percent chance of sales increasing if the supervisor hires that salesperson (and a 40 percent chance of sales remaining steady), the expected value of hiring is .60($210,000) + .40($160,000), or $190,000. The expected value of not hiring is $225,000. Based on the greater expected value for not hiring, the supervisor would decide that it makes more economic sense not to hire a salesperson at this time.

decision-making software
A computer program that leads the user through the steps of the formal decision-making process.

Computer Software

Some computer programs have been developed to help people make decisions. This **decision-making software** leads the user through the steps of the formal decision-making process, illustrated in Figure 8.1. Besides having the user identify alternatives, the programs ask the user about his or her values and priorities.

For help in sorting out information, a supervisor might also use spreadsheet or data base management software. Spreadsheet software, such as *Lotus 1-2-3*, *Excel*, and *SuperCalc*, helps the user organize numbers into rows and columns and can automatically perform computations such as adding a column of numbers. A data base management program, such as *dBASE*, *R:base*, and *DataPerfect*, systematically stores large amounts of data and makes it easy for the user to request and retrieve specific categories of data. A computerized index of periodicals at your library is an example of such software. In addition, software companies are continually developing new ways to help users find and manipulate information. For example, a program called *MailBag* lets users retrieve electronic-mail messages containing a specified word, phrase, or number.[4]

These kinds of computer software do not make decisions for supervisors. However, they can make it easier for supervisors to organize their thoughts and gather information. It is up to the supervisor to creatively identify alternatives and use his or her judgment in selecting the best solution.

Group Decision Making

Some organizations allow or expect supervisors to work with others in arriving at a decision. For example, to decide how to meet production targets, a supervisor might seek input from his or her employees. The supervisor might encourage them to come up with a solution themselves. The supervisor also might call on peers in other departments to share their expertise. As described at the beginning of this chapter, Marilyn Bowie has effectively used her staff's input for deciding to use a couplet unit at the hospital and for improving the quality of care.

Advantages and Disadvantages

Group decision making has some advantages over going it alone. Group members can contribute more ideas for alternatives than an individual could think of alone. Since people tend to draw on their own experiences when generating and evaluating alternatives, a group will look at a problem from a broader perspective. This is important because, in the words of Clark Wigley, problems are like beach balls: there is no one place you can stand on the ball and see the whole ball. Likewise, he explains,

> no matter where you stand in an organization, regardless of how much you get paid, how many degrees you have, or how many years of experience, there is no place where you can stand and see the whole problem.[5]

Also, people who are involved in coming up with a solution are more likely to support the implementation of that solution. They will better understand why the solution was selected and how it is supposed to work, and they will tend to think of it as their solution. (Chapter 17 elaborates on ways organizations are enjoying these benefits by giving employees responsibility for making many kinds of decisions, with supervisors focusing on enabling the employees to carry out that responsibility.)

A group looks at a problem from a broader perspective. At General Electric Company, global teams, such as this one with members from Japan, India, and the United States, discuss global "Work-out" strategies.

Source: Photo by Brownie Harris/Courtesy of GE.

Of course, there are also disadvantages of group decision making. An individual usually can settle on a decision faster than a group can. Figure 8.5 humorously illustrates this disadvantage. Also, there is a cost to the organization when employees spend their time in meetings rather than producing or selling. A third drawback is that the group can reach an inferior decision by letting one person or a small subgroup dominate the process. Finally, groups sometimes fall victim to **groupthink**, or the failure to think independently and realistically that results when group members prefer to enjoy consensus and closeness.[6] Here are some symptoms of groupthink:

groupthink
The failure to think independently and realistically as a group because of the desire to enjoy consensus and closeness.

- An illusion of being invulnerable
- Defending the group's position against any objections
- A view that the group is clearly moral, "the good guys"
- Stereotyped views of opponents
- Pressure against group members who disagree
- Self-censorship, that is, not allowing oneself to disagree
- An illusion that everyone agrees (because no one states an opposing view)
- Self-appointed "mindguards"—people who urge other group members to go along with the group

For example, during the making of the movie *The Bonfire of the Vanities*, many of the people involved had doubts about casting decisions and changes in the story line, but they did not tell the director, Brian DePalma. DePalma wondered about the wisdom of some of the decisions, but since no one objected, he convinced himself that his decisions were correct. Perhaps that is why the $50 million movie was a flop at the box office.[7]

A Potential Drawback of Group Decision Making

Source: © 1992 DILBERT reprinted by permission of UFS, Inc.

When the supervisor notices that his or her group is showing the symptoms of groupthink, it may be time to question whether the group is really looking for solutions. If the supervisor is the group leader, he or she should be sure to encourage a variety of viewpoints by inviting suggestions and encouraging group members to listen with an open mind. Another way to overcome groupthink is to appoint one group member to act as devil's advocate, challenging the position of the majority. When the group has reached a decision, the leader can also suggest that everyone sleep on it and then settle on a final decision at a follow-up meeting.

Using Group Decision Making

Given the advantages and disadvantages of group decision making, the supervisor would be wise to involve employees in some but not all decisions. When a decision must be made quickly, as in an emergency, the supervisor should make it alone. Individual decisions also are appropriate when the potential benefit of a decision is so small that the cost of working as a group is not justified. But when the supervisor needs to build support for a solution, such as measures to cut costs or improve productivity, the group process is useful. Group decision making can also be beneficial when the consequences of a poor decision are great. In such situations, the benefits of the group's collective wisdom are worth the time and expense of gathering the input.

The supervisor can have the group actually make the decision, or the group may simply provide input, leaving the supervisor more decision-making responsibility. For example, the supervisor might ask a group just to generate alternatives. If the group is to make the decision, the supervisor may let group members select any alternative, or the supervisor may give the group a few alternatives from which to choose. Whenever supervisors ask for input, they should be sure they intend to use the information. Employees are quickly wise to—and offended by—a supervisor who only pretends to be interested in their ideas.

Encouraging Participation   Since a main benefit of making decisions as a group is the variety of opinions and expertise available, a supervisor leading a decision-making meeting should be sure that everyone is participating. One basic way of encouraging participation is for the supervisor to avoid monopolizing the discussion. The supervisor should focus on hearing participants' opinions rather than stating his or her own. Also, some group members will find it easier than others to speak up. The supervisor should notice which participants are quiet and should ask their opinions about specific topics being discussed. Finally, the supervisor can encourage participation by reacting positively when people contribute ideas. A barrage of criticism or ridicule will quickly discourage group members from speaking.

Andrew S. Grove, the chief executive of Intel Corporation, recommends an interesting approach to group decision making.[8] First, the supervisor assembles the group and spends plenty of time describing the problem to be solved. The supervisor should not assume that employees understand the problem as well as he or she does, but should allow enough time for employees to ask questions. Then the supervisor divides the employees into groups—if possible, with a variety of levels and specialties represented in each group. The supervisor assigns each group a task and a deadline and asks the groups to report on their progress at the next meeting. In this way, the supervisor stimulates the employees by delegating responsibility and giving them all a chance to excel in front of their peers.

brainstorming
An idea-generating process in which group members state their ideas, a member of the group records them, and no one may comment on the ideas until the process is complete.

Brainstorming   Another way to generate ideas in a group is to use brainstorming. **Brainstorming** (illustrated in Figure 8.6) is an idea-generating process in which group members state their ideas, no matter how far-fetched these may seem. A member of the group records all the ideas, and no one may criticize or even comment on an idea until the end of the process. To enforce this rule, the supervisor might try the tactic used by Armstrong International's David M. Armstrong. At a meeting he called to generate new-product ideas, Armstrong handed each employee an M&M's candy and said, "You are allowed one negative comment during the meeting. Once you make that comment, you must eat your M&M's. If you don't have an M&M's in front of you, you can't say anything negative." As a result, the group members willingly collaborated on an idea.[9]

Hearing other people's ideas often stimulates group members' thinking. The supervisor can further open people's thought processes through such mind-expanding tactics as meeting in the work area rather than the usual conference room, asking people outside the group to identify problems, or asking employees to prepare for the meeting by individually listing problems to name at the meeting.[10] Whatever techniques are used, once all the ideas are listed, the group can evaluate which ones hold the most promise.

FIGURE 8.6

The Brainstorming Process

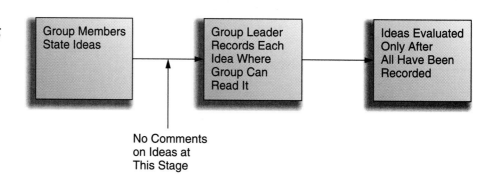

Group Members State Ideas → Group Leader Records Each Idea Where Group Can Read It → Ideas Evaluated Only After All Have Been Recorded

No Comments on Ideas at This Stage

Creativity

When Rebecca Liss, a branch operations manager with Kemper Securities, hired a new employee, Gail, Liss had to be creative. With Gail on board, Liss's group was larger than it ever had been, but she had no additional office space or computer terminals. That meant two employees would somehow have to share a terminal. Working with her staff, Liss developed the idea to arrange the desks into an island formation with a computer terminal between the two employees who were to share it.

creativity
The ability to bring about something imaginative or new.

As in this example, creative thinking can lead to excellent solutions. **Creativity** is the ability to bring about something imaginative or new. In the case of decision making, it means being able to generate alternatives that are innovative or different from what has been used in the past. When a problem seems unsolvable, the supervisor is especially in need of creativity to find a fresh approach.

A common notion is that some people are creative, whereas the rest of us are stuck with following routine and ordinary courses of action. Taking the Self-Quiz will provide you with a measure of the state of your own creative skills. If you do not score as high as you would like, take heart—it appears that people can develop their ability to be creative.

Thinking More Creatively

A fundamental way to become more creative is to be open to your own ideas. When trying to solve a problem, think of as many alternatives as you can. Jot them all down without rejecting any; evaluate them only when you are done. This is like the group process of brainstorming, described earlier in the chapter. In fact, when you can, brainstorming with a group can help stimulate the creativity of the other participants as well as your own. Whether you are alone or in a group, practice should help your ideas flow more easily.

Years ago, advertising executive James Webb Young described a five-step technique for generating creative ideas:[11]

SELF-QUIZ   *How Creative Is Your Thinking?*

Circle a number next to each statement to indicate whether that statement is true of you always, often, seldom, or never.

		Always	Often	Seldom	Never
1.	You are stimulated by complex problems and situations that tax your thinking.	4	3	2	1
2.	You dislike the sort of rigid problem solving that attacks every single problem with a similar, mechanical approach.	4	3	2	1
3.	You encourage open discussion and disagreement among your people.	4	3	2	1
4.	You read voraciously to expand your experience.	4	3	2	1
5.	You entertain new ideas with enthusiasm rather than skepticism.	4	3	2	1
6.	You ask numerous questions, never worrying about whether they reveal your ignorance.	4	3	2	1
7.	You look at things from a variety of viewpoints before making a decision.	4	3	2	1
8.	You surround yourself with people who promote distinctly different points of view.	4	3	2	1
9.	You make decisions that others call "innovative."	4	3	2	1
10.	You search for new and better ways of approaching work within your organizations.	4	3	2	1

The higher your score, the higher your creative abilities.

Source: Craig R. Hickman and Michael A. Silva, "What's Your Creativity Quotient?" *Working Woman*, September 1985, p. 30.

1. Gather the raw materials by learning about the problem and by developing your general knowledge. Young says, "Constantly expanding your experience, both personally and vicariously, [matters] tremendously in an idea-producing job."[12]
2. Work over those materials in your mind. As you think of partial ideas, jot them down so you can refer to them later.
3. Incubate; let your unconscious mind do the work. Instead of thinking about the problem, do whatever stimulates your imagination and emotions, such as listening to music.

4. Identify an idea. It will probably pop into your head unexpectedly.
5. Shape and develop the idea to make it practical. Seek out constructive criticism.

Decades after Young developed this technique, it still remains practical.

Notice from Young's guidelines that creative thinking is not always a conscious process. Sometimes creative ideas come from dreaming or daydreaming, or they just seem to pop into your head while you are doing something else. If you are stuck on a problem, try leaving it for a while. Walk the dog, take a shower, work on a different kind of task. Above all, do not neglect time for resting and daydreaming. If you are trying to solve the problem as a group, and the discussion does not seem to be going anywhere, consider adjourning or at least taking a break, then continue the discussion at a later meeting.

Some people find it worthwhile to call in an expert who can provide training in thinking more creatively. According to one recent count, more than half of the *Fortune* 500 companies had provided employees with training programs in creativity.[13] Other experts provide consulting services. Consultant William J. J. Gordon once advised a small company that was trying to tackle the problem that potato chips take up too much shelf space but packing them more tightly causes them to crumble. Gordon asked, "What in nature reminds you of potato chips?" Someone compared chips to dried leaves; both crumble when pressed together. That thought led someone else to observe that *wet* leaves will pack together without crumbling. With that inspiration, the group came up with the idea of shaping potato slices before they dry—a process the group later sold to Procter & Gamble for use in making Pringles potato chips.[14] The creative tactic this group used—looking for analogies—is one that any group could use for creative problem solving.

Establishing and Maintaining a Creative Work Climate

The supervisor can benefit from the entire work group's creativity by establishing a work climate that encourages creative thinking. The most important step a supervisor can take in this regard is to show that he or she values creativity. When employees offer suggestions, the supervisor should listen attentively and look for the positive aspects of the suggestions. The supervisor should attempt to implement employees' ideas and should give them credit.

When ideas fail, the supervisor should acknowledge that failure is a sign that people are trying. The supervisor should help employees see what can be learned from the failure. The aim is to avoid discouraging employees from making more suggestions in the future.

Overcoming Barriers to Creativity

Often supervisors and employees have difficulty being creative because they are afraid their ideas will fail. The supervisor can overcome this barrier to creativity in employees by accepting that failures occur, as described in the previous section. Overcoming your own fear of failure is more challenging; in fact, the organization may not always reward creativity. The best the supervisor can do is to keep in mind that a lack of creativity will probably prevent big successes as well as big failures. If an idea does fail, the supervisor should acknowledge the problem and not try to pass the blame on to someone else. The emphasis should be on finding a solution, not on placing blame. Most bosses admire supervisors who try ideas after careful thought and who focus on learning from mistakes rather than passing blame. If the supervisor prepares contingency plans (see Chapter 2) and is prepared to focus on solutions, the supervisor's approach is likely to impress his or her superiors, even when the specific idea does not work out as hoped.

Another barrier to creativity is being overly busy. As described earlier, creative thinking requires time for quiet and rest. If the supervisor cannot get these at the workplace, he or she needs to allow time for thinking elsewhere—at home, while walking in the woods, while driving. For example, the supervisor can try turning off the television for a while each evening. Besides reflection, a good substitute for TV watching is reading. (The imagination required to read a book actually helps people develop their ability to think, but the average American adult reads only 24 minutes a day.[15])

Isolation also interferes with creativity. Supervisors need to talk to co-workers in other departments of the organization. They need to talk—and listen—to their employees. Colleagues in other organizations can be a good source of ideas, and so can friends and family members. However, the supervisor must be careful about spending a lot of time with the same few people. They are less likely to be sources of fresh ideas than are new or less familiar acquaintances.

Summary

8.1 Identify the steps in the rational model of decision making.

According to the rational model, the decision maker first identifies the problem and then identifies the alternative solutions. Next he or she gathers and organizes facts. The decision maker evaluates the alternatives and then chooses and implements the best alternative. Finally, he or she gets feedback and takes corrective action.

8.2 Discuss ways people make compromises in following the decision-making model.

People usually take a simpler approach to decision making, considering only the alternatives that come readily to mind. The result may be a satisficing solution—one that meets minimum standards of acceptability. People tend to analyze alternatives subjectively, relying on intuition and instinct, and they tend to favor solutions they can justify. People's analysis also tends to be clouded by adoption of a personal perspective, the tendency to remember recent events best, and the use of stereotypes.

8.3 Describe guidelines for making decisions.

Supervisors should be aware of the possible consequences of their decisions. In a crisis, a supervisor should respond quickly. With regard to crises and other situations that influence the department's performance, supervisors should inform their boss about the decision—if possible, before making it. Supervisors should be decisive but flexible. They should avoid decision-making traps such as treating all problems as crises, responding inappropriately to failure, failing to draw on available information, and promising too much.

8.4 Explain how probability theory, decision trees, and computer software can help in making decisions.

Probability theory defines the expected value of an outcome in a risk situation as the value of the possible outcome times the probability of that outcome. The decision maker using this theory selects the outcome with the greatest expected value. A decision tree is a graph that shows the expected values of decisions under varying circumstances. Thus, it helps the decision maker use probability theory. Decision-making software leads the user through the rational decision-making process, and spreadsheet and data base management software helps users organize their information. The software does not make the decision but helps the user think through the problem more logically.

8.5 Discuss advantages and disadvantages of making decisions in groups.

One advantage of group decision making is that group members will bring more viewpoints and information to bear on a problem. Also, people who are involved in coming up with a solution are more likely to support the implementation of the solution. Disadvantages are that groups make decisions more slowly than individuals, the process is more costly, and groups may fall victim to groupthink, suppressing different viewpoints.

8.6 Describe guidelines for group decision making.

The supervisor can benefit from group decision making when time permits and when the consequences of a poor decision justify the cost of group decision making. Group decision making is also useful when the supervisor needs to build support for the alternative selected. The group may actually make the decision, or it may provide input such as suggested alternatives, letting the supervisor make the final decision. A supervisor leading a decision-making meeting should make sure that everyone is participating. One technique that is useful for generating ideas is brainstorming.

8.7 Describe guidelines for thinking creatively.

A fundamental way to become more creative is to be open to your own ideas. Creative thinkers develop a broad store of information related to the problem and to a variety of other interests, and they let their unconscious mind work while they do activities that stimulate their imagination. Thus, the supervisor should set aside time for dreaming and daydreaming. Taking a break can be helpful when ideas do not seem to be flowing.

8.8 Discuss how supervisors can establish and maintain a creative work climate.

Supervisors should show that they value creativity. They should listen to and encourage suggestions. When ideas fail, supervisors should acknowledge that failure is a sign that people are trying. Instead of focusing on blaming, the supervisor should see what lessons can be learned from the failure.

8.9 Identify ways to overcome barriers to creativity.

Some barriers to creativity are fear of failure, excessive busyness, and isolation. To overcome these barriers, supervisors need to remember that failing inevitably accompanies trying; to set aside time for thinking and resting; and to communicate with co-workers and peers in other organizations.

Key Terms

decision	probability theory	groupthink
satisficing	decision tree	brainstorming
recency syndrome	decision-making software	creativity

Review and Discussion Questions

1. What are the steps in the rational model of decision making? Do you think supervisors usually follow all these steps as described? Defend your answer.

2. What is satisficing? Can this approach to decision making be more appropriate than the rational model? If so, when? If not, why not?

3. Franklin Jones, a supervisor in the buying department for a store such as J. C. Penney, says, "I think these men's jackets are going to be hot this fall. Let's place a big order." What kind of compromises to rational decision making is he using in making his decision? What would be a more rational approach, according to the decision-making model?

4. In each of the following situations, what is interfering with the supervisor's ability to make the best decision? Suggest how the supervisors can improve their decision making in these situations.
   a. "I think this new answering machine model should be blue," said the design supervisor. "I *like* blue."
   b. "Let's conduct training at three o'clock on Fridays," said the customer service supervisor. "After all, it's been slow the last couple of Friday afternoons."
   c. "I'll bet we could boost sales by attracting more women," said the sales manager at an auto dealership. "To generate some traffic, we could hold a little fashion show or a makeup demonstration or something like that every week or so."

5. The chapter presents several guidelines for decision making (consider the consequences, respond quickly in a crisis, inform the boss, be decisive but not inflexible, and avoid decision-making traps). How would such guidelines influence the way a nursing supervisor handles the following two situations?
   a. The supervisor is scheduling nurses for the next month.
   b. One of the nurses calls on Friday afternoon to say her father just died, so she will be out next week.

6. What are some decision-making traps? How can a supervisor avoid these?

7. Rita McCormick is the supervisor of the state office that processes sales tax payments. She has noticed that workers are falling behind and wants to get authorization either to hire two more employees or to schedule overtime until the work gets caught up. Rita estimates that there is an 80 percent chance the work load will continue to be this high and a 20 percent chance that work will fall back to previous levels, which the current employees can handle during regular working hours. (She assumes there is no chance of less work in the future.) Because she will have to pay time and a half for overtime, she assumes that the cost of paying overtime for a year will be $150,000, whereas a work force with two more employees will cost only $140,000.
   a. Construct a decision tree for this problem.
   b. Which alternative should the supervisor choose?

8. What are some advantages of making decisions as a group? What are some disadvantages?

9. Under what conditions is it beneficial to use group decision making?

10. Roberto Gonzalez wants to make his solutions more creative. When he has a problem to solve, he sits down at his desk and tries to generate as many alternative solutions as he can. Unfortunately, he usually gets frustrated before he comes up with an alternative that satisfies him, so he just picks an acceptable solution and tries to implement it. How can Roberto modify his decision-making process to come up with more creative ideas?

11. How can supervisors foster creativity in their department or work group?

A SECOND LOOK

The story at the beginning of this chapter describes how Marilyn Bowie solved two problems in her job as nurse manager. How did Bowie apply principles of group decision making to solve these problems?

Class Exercise

The class divides into groups of five or six people. Each group will brainstorm solutions for the following problem: The head librarian for an art museum's library has been directed to cut expenses by 15 percent. The library currently operates during the same hours as the museum (10:00 to 5:00 every day except Wednesday, when the museum is open until 9:00 in the evening). Half of the library's budget goes for salaries—the head librarian plus two reference librarians and a clerk. One-quarter of the budget goes to purchase books and periodicals, and another one-quarter goes to operating expenses such as the library's share of heat and lighting. Given this information, how can the library cut expenses with a minimal impact on the quality of its service?

1. Each group picks a facilitator to record its ideas.
2. Group members suggest ideas, and the facilitator writes them down where everyone can see them. No one is to comment on the ideas at this point.
3. When group members feel they are out of ideas, the group discusses the ideas listed and picks the most promising one(s). The facilitator should try to make sure that all group members contribute to this discussion.
4. As a class, discuss the following questions:
   a. Did hearing other people's ideas help you come up with more ideas?
   b. How did it feel to hear ideas without commenting on them? How did it feel to express ideas, knowing that no one was to criticize them?
   c. How well did your group carry out this assignment? What could it have done better? Was it difficult to get everyone to participate?
   d. Is brainstorming an appropriate technique for solving a problem such as this one? Why or why not?

CASE

Problem Solving: A New Product Idea

Kathleen Fernee, a manager of technical consumer research at Colgate-Palmolive, has received training in techniques for thinking creatively. Thus, when company executives asked her to lead the development of a new tennis shoe, she set about trying to inspire some creative thinking. Says Fernee, "We wanted a totally new shoe, not just an improved one."

To solve the problem, she assembled a team for a "creativity session." The team members included representatives from advertising, manufacturing, and marketing, as well as a physician and a tennis coach. The group tried various mental exercises to stimulate brainstorming.

Then the group began talking about the problem in terms of the word *light*. Explains Fernee, "We completely got away from the idea of shoes and started thinking about the foot. How little could we wear on the foot and still have it function optimally?" To answer that question, the group did more than just talk about playing tennis. As the meeting wore on, the participants wound up playing tennis barefoot at midnight.

From their barefoot tennis experience, the group members found that the ball and heel of the foot work independently. Furthermore, people who play tennis off the heel are more likely to hurt their ankles than those who play off the ball of the foot. From these insights the group eventually came up with a design in which the tennis shoe has two loosely attached pieces of light material, one piece for the ball of the foot and one for the heel. This shoe was marketed by Etonic under the brand name Catalyst.

1. What was the problem to be solved by the people in this case? What types of decisions would the group have to make in order to solve this problem?

2. Based on the information given, do you think the group reached a solution that was creative? Explain.

3. Was this an appropriate type of problem for group decision making? Explain.

Source: Magaly Olivero, "Some Wacko Ideas That Worked," *Working Woman*, September 1990, pp. 147, 222.

9

Forget [people's] mistakes and zero in on one small thing they do right. Praise them and they'll do more things right and discover talents and abilities they never realized they had.

—**Mary Kay Ash, founder of Mary Kay Cosmetics, quoted in** *Bits & Pieces*

Motivating Employees

LEARNING OBJECTIVES

9.1 Identify the relationship between motivation and performance.

9.2 Describe content theories of motivation.

9.3 Describe process theories of motivation.

9.4 Explain when financial incentives are likely to motivate employees.

9.5 Describe pay plans using financial incentives.

9.6 Discuss the pros and cons of keeping pay information secret.

9.7 Identify ways supervisors can motivate their employees.

MOTIVATING THROUGH TEAM SPIRIT

James Huskisson is regional sales manager for Liquid Carbonic Cylinder Gas Products, a company originally founded to sell carbon dioxide for fountain drinks. He helps the sales representatives in his region develop new business and resolve problems with existing customers. An important part of his job is motivating—that is, giving the salespeople various kinds of incentives to work hard and deliver high-quality service.

According to Huskisson, the most important way he motivates is by building team spirit. He holds sales meetings at which the sales reps can meet one another and share leads for new business. Says Huskisson, "It is critical that the reps have respect for each other and be able to work as a team."

Huskisson also runs sales contests. At Liquid Carbonic, salespeople can win awards for most new business signed, most renewal business, most improved sales rep, highest profit, and overall best sales rep. The monetary rewards are important, explains Huskisson, but the employees also are motivated by the recognition for a job well done.

In addition, he finds it helpful to give a humorous award to the lowest-performing sales rep as a way to motivate him or her to do better next time.

The sales representatives at Liquid Carbonic are paid a base salary plus a bonus. The bonus is paid each quarter based on how much the rep's sales grew during that time. If Huskisson were able to set up the company's pay system, however, he would rather pay a yearly bonus based on how well the sales rep meets performance criteria established at the beginning of the year. He believes that such an arrangement would enable the supervisor to measure performance more fairly and to promote teamwork more effectively.

motivation
Giving people
incentives that cause
them to act in desired
ways.

Giving people incentives that cause them to act in desired ways is known as **motivation**. Supervisors must motivate their employees to do good work, to complete assignments on time, and to have good attendance, among other things. At Liquid Carbonic, the sales contests and bonuses are intended to motivate the sales representatives. When employees are motivated and also have the ability—the necessary skills, equipment, supplies, and time—they are able to perform well (see Figure 9.1). Thus, the objective of motivating employees is to lead them to perform in ways that meet the goals of the department and the organization. Because supervisors are evaluated largely on the basis of how well their group as a whole performs, motivation is an important skill for supervisors to acquire.

This chapter discusses how the supervisor can make good use of the link between employees' objectives and their performance. It describes theories of what motivates employees, and it provides practical suggestions for ways supervisors can motivate.

How Does Motivation Work?

"What's wrong with these people?" exclaimed Martha Wong about the salesclerks she supervises in the shoe department. "We pay them good wages, but when we hit a busy season like this, nobody's willing to put forth the extra effort we need—giving up a break once in a while or even just moving a little faster." Martha needs to figure out what to do to make the employees *want* to work harder. Perhaps they expect more money, or perhaps they want something else, such as a feeling of being part of a team.

Imagine that supervisors like Martha could know just what motivates employees. For example, imagine that all salespeople are motivated solely by the money they earn and that social scientists have devised an accurate formula to determine how much money the company must pay to get a given amount of selling. Suppose that all secretaries are motivated by flexible work hours and all production workers are motivated by recognition from the plant manager. A company that knew this would be in a position to devise the kinds of rewards that employees want. The supervisor could hand out the rewards and would know that if employees had the necessary skills, they would do good work.

Of course, there is no such simple knowledge about motivation. Instead, supervisors have to rely on a variety of theories that social scientists have developed. None of the theories are perfect, proven explanations of how to get employees to behave in a certain way, but they all give supervisors some guidance. Being familiar with the better-known theories can help supervisors think of ways to motivate that may apply in their workplaces.

Content Theories

Some theories of motivation have focused on what things motivate workers. These are called content theories because they focus on the content of the motivators. Although money is the motivator that comes most readily to mind, some people

FIGURE 9.1

The Effect of Motivation on Performance

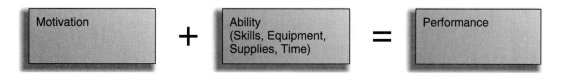

respond more to other sources of satisfaction. To help you think about what motivates *you*, try the Self-Quiz on the next page.

Three researchers whose content theories of motivation are widely used are Abraham Maslow, David McClelland, and Frederick Herzberg.

Maslow's Hierarchy of Needs Psychologist Abraham Maslow assumed that what motivates people is unmet needs. When a person's need for something is not met, the person feels driven, or motivated, to meet that need. To give a basic example, a person who needs food feels hungry and therefore eats something.

According to Maslow's theory, the needs that motivate people fall into five basic categories: physiological needs, security needs, social needs, esteem needs, and self-actualization needs. Physiological needs are the ones required for survival—needs such as food, water, sex, and shelter. Security needs involve keeping yourself free from harm. In modern society, these might include insurance, medical checkups, and a home in a safe neighborhood. Social needs include the desire for love, friendship, and companionship. People seek to satisfy these needs through the time they spend with family, friends, and co-workers. Esteem needs are the needs for self-esteem and the respect of others. Two ways these needs are met are through acceptance and praise. Finally, self-actualization needs describe the desire to live up to your full potential. Someone on the path to meeting these needs will not only be doing his or her best at work and at home but will also be developing mentally, spiritually, and physically.

Maslow's theory is that these needs are organized into a hierarchy (levels of importance) such as the one shown in Figure 9.2. The needs at the bottom of the hierarchy are the most basic needs, the ones people try to satisfy first. The needs at the top are the ones people try to satisfy only when most of their other needs are met. Thus, people first try to satisfy their need for food and shelter, then their need for safety, and so on until they seek to satisfy their need for self-actualization. However, people may be seeking to meet more than one category of needs at a time.

Based on this view, people tend to rely on their jobs to meet most of their physiological and safety needs through paychecks and benefits such as health insurance. Needs higher on the hierarchy can be satisfied in many places. For example, people satisfy some of their social needs through their relationships with family and friends outside of work, and they may seek to meet their self-actualization needs through volunteer work or participation in the life of a church, mosque, or synagogue. Nevertheless, work can also be a place where

SELF-QUIZ   *What Motivates You?*

What makes a job appealing to you? Rank the following job factors from 1 to 12. Assign 1 to the factor you consider most important and 12 to the factor you consider least important.

_1_	1.	Work that is interesting and meaningful
_1_	2.	Good wages or salary
_2_	3.	Authority to make important decisions
_2_	4.	Comfortable work environment, such as a clean, modern laboratory, fancy store, or attractive office
_1_	5.	Likable co-workers
_1_	6.	Good relationship with supervisor
_2_	7.	Clear understanding of the department's and company's goals and performance
_1_	8.	Appreciation and recognition for doing a good job
_1_	9.	Opportunities to learn new skills
_0_	10.	Prestigious title or occupation
_1_	11.	Chance for advancement
_1_	12.	Job security

FIGURE 9.2

Maslow's Hierarchy of Needs

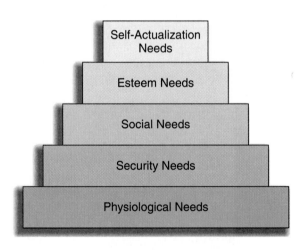

people satisfy higher-level needs. An employee who is applauded for solving a difficult problem or who takes pride in skillfully performing a craft such as carpentry is meeting some higher-level needs at work.

According to Maslow's hierarchy, social needs are the desire for love, friendship, and companionship.

Source: Courtesy of The Stock Market, Ed Bock, 1989.

Maslow's hierarchy is a widely cited view of motivation, but it does have shortcomings. Critics (including Maslow himself) have noted that the theory is based on clinical work with neurotic patients and was not tested much for relevance to the work setting.[1] Are the needs identified by Maslow really all-inclusive? Do they describe people of many cultures, or just the majority of Americans? The lack of studies investigating the hierarchy of needs makes it impossible to answer such questions with certainty. However, the popularity of this theory implies that it can be helpful in offering suggestions about what motivates people.

Applied to a work situation, Maslow's theory means the supervisor must be aware of the needs that particular employees are currently trying to meet. During a serious recession, a factory supervisor may find that many employees are highly motivated just to be able to get and keep a job so they can pay their bills. In contrast, employees who are less worried about keeping a job may respond well to spontaneous dinners such as the ones hosted by the Richard Michael Group, a Chicago placement firm. Staff members are invited to bring their spouse or a friend, and the company credits the resulting friendships with keeping employees on the payroll much longer than the industry average.[2] At Quill Corporation, a mail-order office supply business in Lincolnshire, Illinois, motivation is based on building the self-esteem of employees. For example, the company offers tuition reimbursement to help employees develop skills, and management views the company's attractive landscaping and its dress code as ways to create an appealing and professional atmosphere that will help employees feel good about themselves.[3] The "Dealing with Diversity" box describes another area in which companies are broadening their recognition of employee needs.

DEALING WITH DIVERSITY

Meeting the Needs of Working Parents

When most working parents were men married to full-time homemakers, employers could easily motivate the majority of employees with a basic package of benefits such as health insurance and vacation time. But most families do not fit that pattern today; there are now more single parents and more two-income families. As a result, employees' needs include help with juggling the often-conflicting demands of home and work. Some organizations have responded with "family-friendly" policies—benefits tailored to the needs of working parents.

One typical dimension of a family-friendly policy is flexible work hours. Flexible hours may mean allowing employees some leeway in choosing which eight hours a day to work, an arrangement that is often called flextime. Another possibility is that organizations may allow employees to arrange part-time work. For example, Pam Burns was on the verge of quitting her job with GE Medical Systems in Milwaukee when she became pregnant with her second child. But her division allowed her to work three days a week and still get full health benefits, so Burns stayed on. "My new work schedule is the best thing that's come along," says Burns, who plans to continue the part-time schedule until her younger child is in kindergarten. Other employees in the division pitch in to make up for Burns's short work week, so the part-time schedule does not cost the company any money.

The organization can enable part-time employees to handle the work load by allowing two employees to share the duties of a single position. Such an arrangement is called job sharing. For example, Northeast Utilities encourages employees interested in job sharing to find a partner; if they cannot identify someone, the company will do the necessary recruiting.

Quaker Oats Company seeks to be a leader in family-friendly policies. Besides having offered unpaid family leave before it was required by law, the company provides some creative benefits. Quaker will match 25 cents for every dollar an employee sets aside to pay for child care. For breast-feeding mothers returning to work, the company provides a "Mother's Room" containing breast pumps, a refrigerator, and lactation counseling. Parents of school-age children can use a telephone counseling service at which former teachers help parents with school-related concerns.

The view among many human resources experts is that family-friendly policies are an important way to get and keep the best workers. According to Robert Montgomery, vice-president of human resources at Quaker Oats, "There was a time when companies expected employees to not let their families interfere with work. Today that can't be done." In fact, considering employees' family needs may actually be beneficial to the employer. Aetna Life & Casualty Company reports that its family leave policy saved the company $2 million in 1991. Says U S West's chief executive, Richard D. McCormick, "Employees are so eager for flexibility, they'll make the program work."

How motivated are employees to make these policies work? Consider the case of two job-sharing legal secretaries of a San Francisco law firm. They planned their pregnancies so that each could cover for the other during their maternity leaves.

Source: "Employees Take Pains to Make Flextime Work," *The Wall Street Journal*, August 18, 1992, p. B1; Carol Kleiman, "'Family-Friendly' Policies Can Be Financially Friendly to Firms," *Chicago Tribune*, September 7, 1992, sec. 4, p. 2; Cindy Lampner, "Part-Time Goes Professional," *Resources*, 2d quarter 1992, p. 2; and Eileen Ogintz, "Quaker Takes Hand in Helping Families," *Chicago Tribune*, September 23, 1992, sec. 3, pp. 1, 4.

With this model, the supervisor cannot assume that all employees want the same thing all the time. Thus, supervisors need to use a variety of rewards that meet a variety of needs. For example, in a contest that seeks ideas to improve quality, a supervisor might offer a cash bonus, a ceremony recognizing the contributions of

Motivation can come from developing team spirit. Ronnie Taylor, a supervisor on the day shift at Tyson Foods in Shelbyville, Tennessee, is shown enjoying the annual softball tournament, which helps develop good relationships among employees.

Source: Courtesy of Kelly/Mooney.

the winners, and a poster showing how the suggested improvements are helping everyone look better. Some employees may respond to the money, others to the praise, and still others to the team spirit.

McClelland's Achievement-Power-Affiliation Theory   In the 1960s, David McClelland developed a theory of motivation based on the assumption that through their life experiences, people develop various needs. His theory focuses on three such needs:

1. *The need for achievement*—the desire to do something better than it has been done before
2. *The need for power*—the desire to control, influence, or be responsible for other people
3. *The need for affiliation*—the desire to maintain close and friendly personal relationships

According to McClelland, people have all of these needs to some extent. However, the intensity of the needs varies from one individual to the next. The nature of a person's early life experiences may cause one of these needs to be particularly strong.

The relative strength of the needs influences what will motivate a person. A person with a strong need for achievement is more motivated by success than by money. This person tends to set challenging but achievable goals and to assess risk carefully. Someone with a strong need for power tries to influence others and seeks out advancement and responsibility. A person with a strong need for affiliation gives his or her ambitions a back seat to the desire for approval and acceptance.

McClelland's theory differs from Maslow's in that it assumes different people have different patterns of needs, whereas Maslow's theory assumes the same pattern of needs for all people. Thus, McClelland takes into account individual differences. Both theories, however, imply that supervisors need to remember there are a variety of possibilities for what will motivate employees.

Herzberg's Two-Factor Theory Frederick Herzberg's research led him to conclude that employees' satisfaction and their dissatisfaction stem from different sources. According to the two-factor theory, dissatisfaction results from the absence of what Herzberg calls *hygiene factors*, which include salary and relationships with others. For example, someone whose pay is poor—say, a physical therapist earning $5,000 less than the average for her position and experience—is going to be dissatisfied with the job. In contrast, satisfaction results from the presence of what Herzberg terms *motivating factors*, which include opportunities offered by the job. Thus, an employee who sees a chance to be promoted is likely to be more satisfied with the current job than one who does not. Table 9.1 lists the items that make up each category of factors.

Herzberg found that employees are most productive when the organization provides a combination of desirable hygiene factors and motivating factors. Based on this theory, an organization cannot ensure that its employees will be satisfied and productive just by giving them a big raise every year. Employees will also need such motivating factors as being able to learn new skills and assume responsibility. As with the other content theories, Herzberg's tells supervisors that they need to consider a variety of ways to motivate employees.

Process Theories

Another way to explain how motivation works is to look at the process rather than the specific motivators. Theories that pertain to the process of motivation are known as process theories. Two major such theories are expectancy-valence theory and reinforcement theory.

Vroom's Expectancy-Valence Theory Assuming that people act as they do in order to satisfy the needs they feel, Victor Vroom set out to explain what determines the intensity of people's motivation. He decided that the degree to which people are motivated to act in a certain way depends on two things:

1. *Valence*—the value a person places on the outcome of a particular behavior. For example, a person may highly value the prestige and the bonus that result from submitting a winning suggestion in a contest to collect ideas for improving quality.
2. *Expectancy*—the perceived probability that the behavior will lead to the outcome. The person in the example may believe that her idea has a 50-50 chance of winning in the quality improvement contest.

As shown in Figure 9.3, Vroom's expectancy-valence theory says that the strength of motivation equals the perceived value of the outcome times the perceived probability of the behavior resulting in the outcome. In other words, people are most motivated to seek results they value highly and think they can achieve.

This theory is based on employees' *perceptions* of rewards and whether they are able to achieve those rewards. The employees may place different values on

TABLE 9.1	*Hygiene Factors*	*Motivating Factors*
Two-Factor Theory: Hygiene Factors and Motivating Factors	Company policy and administration	Opportunity for achievement
	Supervision	Opportunity for recognition
	Relationship with supervisor	Work itself
	Relationship with peers	Responsibility
	Working conditions	Advancement
	Salary and benefits	Personal growth
	Relationship with subordinates	

FIGURE 9.3

Vroom's Expectancy-Valence Theory

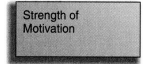

rewards than the supervisor does, and they may have different opinions about their abilities. If the supervisor believes he or she has in place a good system of rewards, yet employees do not seem to be motivated, the supervisor might investigate whether employees think they are expected to do the impossible. To learn this, supervisors must be able to communicate well, as described in Chapter 7.

Skinner's Reinforcement Theory From the field of psychology comes reinforcement theory, pioneered by B. F. Skinner. This theory says that people behave as they do because of the kind of consequences they experience as a result of their behavior. Broadly speaking, people keep doing things that lead to consequences they like, and people avoid doing things that have undesirable consequences. For example, praise feels good to receive, so people tend to do things for which they receive praise.

This theory implies that supervisors can encourage or discourage a particular kind of behavior by the way they respond to the behavior. They can administer **reinforcement**, which can involve either giving a desired consequence or ending a negative consequence in response to behavior the supervisor wants. Or the supervisor can administer **punishment**, which is an unpleasant consequence of the behavior the supervisor wants to end. For example, as described in the story at the beginning of this chapter, when salespeople at Liquid Carbonic perform well, they can earn bonuses or win contests (a form of reinforcement). And the lowest-performing sales rep receives the undesirable attention of winning a "prize" for

reinforcement
A desired consequence or the ending of a negative consequence, either of which is given in response to a desirable behavior.

punishment
An unpleasant consequence given in response to undesirable behavior.

behavior modification
The use of reinforcement theory to motivate people to behave in a certain way.

rating at the bottom (a form of punishment). Using reinforcement theory to motivate people to behave in a certain way is known as **behavior modification**. In everyday language, we call it "using the carrot and the stick."

For long-term results, reinforcement is more effective than punishment. In fact, psychologists have found that repeated punishment (or failure) can lead to an unhappy consequence called "learned helplessness."[4] This means that if an employee is punished over and over for failing in some aspect of his or her work, the employee will eventually believe that he or she simply is unable to succeed at the job. Such an employee begins to approach the job passively, based on the belief that he or she will fail, no matter what.

Motivation Theories and the Law

One element that most of these motivation theories have in common is that supervisors must consider individual differences in designing rewards. In other words, what motivates one person may not motivate another, so supervisors need to offer a variety of rewards to motivate most effectively. However, the types of rewards the supervisor may use are not entirely under his or her control. Not only does the supervisor have to follow the organization's policies, but a variety of laws require that employers provide certain types of benefits. For example, federal laws set requirements for overtime pay, rest breaks, health insurance for retirees, and many other areas. The details of these laws are beyond the scope of this book, but most organizations have a human resources professional or department that is responsible for helping the organization comply with laws related to benefits.

The requirements of the Family and Medical Leave Act of 1993 are worth noting, however, because they affect the supervisor's role in scheduling work and staffing the department. Under this federal law, organizations with 50 or more employees within a 75-mile radius must give employees up to 12 weeks of unpaid leave to care for a newborn, adopted child, or foster child within one year of the child's arrival. These employers must also offer this time off if employees need to care for a seriously ill child, parent, or spouse or if they themselves have medical conditions that prevent them from doing their job. During the time off, the employer must continue to pay the employee's health insurance premiums. The employer also must guarantee that the employee will be able to return to his or her job or an equivalent one. If the need for the leave is foreseeable, the employee must give the organization 30 days' notice.

Money as a Motivator

Some supervisors and other managers assume that the main thing employees want out of a job is money. Most people do work in order to earn at least enough to get by. Therefore, though money is only one of the available ways to motivate employees, it is an important one.

When Money Motivates

Based on the content theories of motivation, it makes sense that money motivates people when it meets their needs. The opportunity to earn more can be very important to a college student, considering the high cost of college tuition and the potentially great impact of a college degree on the student's future life-style. (Of course, there are individual differences. Some students prefer to lead a simple life-style and would rather have enough time to study than spend time earning a lot of money.) A retired person or a married person whose spouse earns a comfortable income might work primarily for nonfinancial rewards such as a sense of accomplishment or the satisfaction that comes from performing a needed service.

For money to work as a motivator, employees must believe they are able to achieve the financial rewards the organization offers. Thus, if a theater company offers its staff a bonus for selling a given number of season-ticket subscriptions over the telephone, the bonus will motivate the employees only if they believe they can sell that many tickets. Or if an organization pays a bonus for employee suggestions that improve quality, the bonus will motivate employees only if they believe they are capable of coming up with ideas management will consider worthwhile.

Pay Plans Using Financial Incentives

The way a pay plan is structured can influence the degree to which employees are motivated to perform well. Some pay plans offer bonuses, commissions, or other kinds of pay for meeting or exceeding objectives. For example, a growing number of organizations tie raises and bonuses to success in retaining existing customers and meeting established quality goals.[5] Others, such as the Quaker Oats pet food plant in Topeka, Kansas, pay employees a higher rate for learning additional skills, including how to operate lift trucks and computer-controlled machinery.[6] Such pay plans are said to use **financial incentives**.

financial incentives
Payments for meeting or exceeding objectives.

Supervisors rarely have much say in the type of pay plan an organization uses. However, it helps to understand the kinds of pay plans that offer a financial incentive. Knowing whether the organization's pay system is designed to motivate gives the supervisor clues about employees' needs for nonfinancial incentives. If the organization's pay plan includes financial incentives yet the employees seem not to be motivated, the supervisor might look for other kinds of motivators. On the other hand, if the organization's pay plan contains no financial incentives, the supervisor might seek permission to include money for bonuses in the department's budget.

piecework system
Payment according to the amount produced.

Piecework System The **piecework system** pays people according to how much they produce. This method is often used to pay independent contractors, that is, people who are self-employed and perform work for the organization. For example, a magazine might pay a writer a fixed rate for each word, or a clothing manufacturer might pay for each shirt sewed. Farmworkers may be paid according to how much they harvest. However, few employees are paid by this system.

Production Bonus System   Employees in a production department may receive a basic wage or salary plus a bonus that consists of a payment for each unit produced. For example, an employee might earn $8.50 an hour plus 20 cents for each unit produced. This is called a production bonus system. If employees do not seem motivated by a production bonus system, one possible problem is that the bonus is not large enough to be worth the extra effort.

Employees who work faster earn more money under such a system, but the pay system does not necessarily encourage *quality* work. One production bonus system that does account for quality, as well as several other factors employees can control, is the one in use at Natural Decorations, an Evergreen, Alabama, maker of dried-flower and artificial-flower arrangements.[7] This system is summarized in Table 9.2. Employees start with 50 points, then each month the company uses various factors to calculate the bonus points each employee earns for the month. (Employees are not charged for a negative score.) The bonus points were worth $1 each in 1991, and the company had hoped to increase their value to $2 by 1993.

commissions
Payment linked to the amount of sales completed.

Commissions   In a sales department, employees may earn **commissions**, or payment linked to the amount of sales completed. For example, upon the sale of a house that a real estate agent listed for her brokerage, the agent might receive a commission of 2 percent of the sale price. The selling agent and the brokerage also would get commissions.

Most organizations that pay commissions also pay a basic wage or salary. Otherwise, the financial uncertainty can worry employees so much that it interferes with motivation. There are, however, some people who like the unlimited earnings potential of a commission-only job.

It is possible to use commissions with employees other than salespeople. De Mar Plumbing, Heating and Air-conditioning of Clovis, California, pays its "service advisers" (plumbers and installers) entirely on commission. Depending on the type of work they handle, the employees earn a 15- to 20-percent base commission on parts sold and labor billed. They earn additional commissions for calling on first-time customers and receiving compliments from customers. Some advisers find they cannot live with this system, and they quit; but for those who stay, the potential earnings are unlimited. In 1991 the top service adviser earned $60,000—about twice the industry average. And management is happy, because revenues are rising faster than the payroll.[8]

Payments for Suggestions   In an effort to build employee participation and communication, many companies pay employees for making suggestions on how to cut costs or improve quality. Typically, for the employee to receive payment, the suggestion must be adopted or save some minimum amount of money. The size of the payment may be linked to the size of the benefit to the organization. In other words, an idea with a bigger impact results in a bigger payment.

group incentive plan
A financial incentive plan that rewards a team of workers for meeting or exceeding an objective.

Group Incentive Plans   Organizations today are increasingly focusing on ways to get employees and their supervisors to work together as teams. A financial incentive to get people to work this way is the **group incentive plan**. This type of plan pays a bonus when the group as a whole exceeds some objective. An organization measures the performance of a work unit against its objectives, then pays a bonus if the group exceeds the objectives. For example, Cabletron Systems, a computer

	Factor	Formula	Number of Points
TABLE 9.2 **Production Bonus System at Natural Decorations**	Starting points		50
	Tardiness	−5 × number of days =	_____
	Time off	−10 × number of days =	_____
	Absenteeism	−15 × number of days =	_____
	Reworks	−5 × number of times =	_____
	Violations of safety, maintenance, and procedural rules	−5 × number of times =	_____
	Production time above average	+2 × number of days =	_____
	Production time below average	−2 × number of days =	_____
	Total Bonus Points =		_____

Source: Reprinted with permission, *Inc.* Magazine, February 1992. Copyright 1992 by Goldhirsh Group, Inc., 38 Commercial Wharf, Boston, Mass. 02110.

cable maker based in Rochester, New Hampshire, wants its telephone salespeople to cooperate with its outside sales force, rather than compete for leads and other information. So the company pays employees quarterly bonuses, half of which are based on how well their region meets sales goals and half on how well the entire company meets its sales goals.[9]

profit-sharing plan A group incentive plan under which the company sets aside a share of its profits and divides it among employees.

A frequently used type of group incentive is the **profit-sharing plan**. Under such a plan, the company sets aside a share of its profits earned during a given period, such as a year, and divides these profits among the employees. The assumption is that the better the work done, the more the company will earn and, therefore, the bigger the bonuses. In the past, profit sharing was mostly limited to executives, but more and more companies today are sharing profits among all employees. For example, steelmaker Nucor Corporation contributes a minimum of 10 percent of pretax earnings to its profit-sharing plan. Once a year, about 20 percent of that money is paid to the company's employees; individuals receive the remainder of their share when they leave the company.[10] In 1990 the average hourly employee earned $36,000, which is considered good pay in the areas where Nucor's plants are located.[11]

gainsharing A group incentive plan in which the organization encourages employees to participate in making suggestions and decisions, then rewards the group with a share of improved earnings.

Taking this approach one step further, an increasing number of companies are adopting **gainsharing**. Under a gainsharing program, the company encourages employees to participate in making suggestions and decisions on how to improve the way the company or work group operates. Then, as performance improves, employees receive a share of the greater earnings. Thus, gainsharing seeks to motivate not only by giving financial rewards but also by making employees feel they have an important role as part of a team. The case at the end of this chapter describes the use of gainsharing at B. F. Goodrich.

Secrecy of Wage and Salary Information

In our society, money is considered a private matter, and most people do not like to talk about what they earn. Thus, in private (nongovernment) organizations, employees, including managers, generally do not know one another's earnings (although supervisors do know what their subordinates earn). In contrast, because taxpayers ultimately pay the wages and salaries of government employees, these employees' earnings are public information, often published in local papers.

Does secrecy help or hurt the usefulness of money as a motivator? Certainly, it does not make sense to disclose information if it will just embarrass employees. However, surveys that ask employees to estimate their co-workers' earnings indicate that most employees overestimate what others earn.[12] The result can be dissatisfaction, because employees believe they are underpaid in comparison.

To motivate employees with the possibility of a raise and a belief that pay rates are fair, the organization must let them know what they can hope to earn. A typical compromise between maintaining privacy and sharing information is for the organization to publish pay ranges. These show the lowest and highest wage or salary the organization will pay an employee in a particular position. Employees do not know how much specific people earn, but by looking at the ranges they can see what they can hope to earn if they get a raise, promotion, or transfer to another position.

How Supervisors Can Motivate

Most of the discussion in this chapter has been about the theories of motivating. These theories suggest some practical ways supervisors can motivate. Several possibilities are summarized in Figure 9.4.

Making Work Interesting

When employees find their work interesting, they are more likely to give it their full attention and enthusiasm. In general, work is interesting when it has variety and allows employees some control over what they do. Some ways to make work more interesting are job rotation, job enlargement, and job enrichment.

job rotation
Moving employees from job to job to give them more variety.

Job rotation involves moving employees from job to job to give them more variety. For example, the employees in a production department may take turns operating all the machines in the factory. Job rotation requires that employees have relatively broad skills. As a result, the supervisor or company must provide for **cross-training**, or training in the skills required to perform more than one job. The opportunity to learn new skills through cross-training can in itself motivate employees. The management of Highland Park Hospital in Highland Park, Illinois, developed a plan for cross-training with the initial goal of cutting costs for nursing personnel. However, nurses' responses to the program were so positive that management realized the nurses saw cross-training as a way to make their work more interesting.[13]

cross-training
Training in the skills required to perform more than one job.

job enlargement
An effort to make a job more interesting by adding more duties to it.

Job enlargement is an effort to make a job more interesting by adding more duties to it. Thus, a machine operator might be responsible not only for running a particular machine but also for performing maintenance on the machine and

FIGURE 9.4

**Some Ways
Supervisors Can
Motivate Employees**

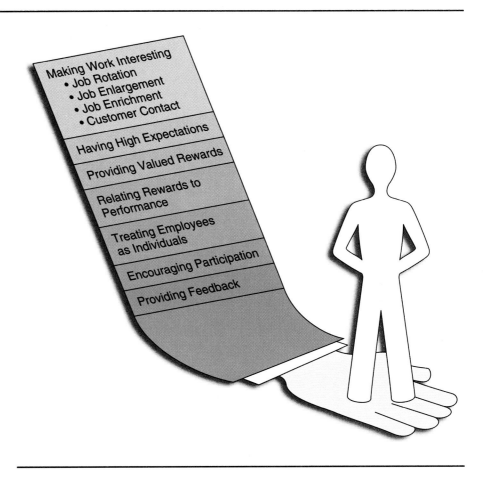

job enrichment
The incorporation of
motivating factors into
a job—in particular,
giving the employee
more responsibility and
recognition.

inspecting the quality of the parts produced with the machine. As with job rotation, this approach assumes that variety in a job makes it more satisfying, with the result that employees are more motivated.

Job enrichment is the incorporation of motivating factors into a job. The kinds of factors that are considered to enrich a job are the ones Herzberg called motivators (see Table 9.1). Generally, a job that has been enriched gives employees more responsibility to make decisions and more recognition for good performance. Thus, enriched jobs are more challenging but, presumably, also more rewarding. For example, instead of requiring salespeople in a department store to call a supervisor whenever a customer comes to them with a complaint, the store might authorize them to handle complaints as they see fit. They would have to call the supervisor only if solving the problem would cost the store more than some set amount, say, $500.

When modifying jobs to make them more interesting, it is important for the organization and supervisor to remember that not all employees are motivated by the same things at the same time. Thus, while some employees may eagerly accept the new variety in their jobs, others are likely to be less enthusiastic. Some workers may think that jobs are being redesigned simply to get more work out of people for

Learning new skills can make work more interesting. At the Direct Response Group of Capital Holding, a DRG Lifetime Learning Center was established in 1991 to help employees gain cross-functional skills. The videotaped role play pictured here allows employees to simulate real-life situations in a team-oriented environment.

Source: Courtesy of Alen MacWeeny, photographer.

the same amount of money. The supervisor must be careful to emphasize the advantages of the new arrangement and to listen to employees' reactions.

Another way to make work meaningful is to give employees some contact with the people who receive and use their products or services. Nurses and salespeople are routinely in contact with the people they serve; however, production workers and accounting personnel have less customer contact. Sometimes the supervisor can arrange to have workers visit the users of the products or services. For example, a group of production workers might be able to visit a customer who is having trouble operating a machine the company manufactures. The workers would not only be able to help the customer, they might also get some ideas on how to make the machine better. Accounting personnel might visit the people in the company who use their reports, meeting with these employees to make sure they understand and are satisfied with the reports.

Having High Expectations

Effective motivation can lead to performance beyond employees' own expectations of themselves. When someone expects a lot of us, we often find that we can do a lot. When little is expected, we tend to live up to those limiting expectations. In either case, we call the expectations a self-fulfilling prophecy.

The direct relationship between expectations and performance is known as the **Pygmalion effect**. The name comes from the Greek myth of Pygmalion, a king of Cyprus who carved a statue of a beautiful maiden and then fell in love with her. He so wished she were real that she became real.

Pygmalion effect
The direct relationship between expectations and performance; high expectations lead to high performance.

According to the Pygmalion effect, a supervisor who says, "You're so dense, you never get the procedures right," will not motivate effectively. Rather, the employee will decide that understanding procedures is beyond his or her capacity. So a supervisor who wishes employees to set high standards for themselves must

Job enrichment is the incorporation of motivating factors into a job. Kim Delaney, a resource manager at Amoco Productions' South Permian Basin Business Unit, has been recognized for encouraging risk taking and ingenuity among members of a multidisciplinary work group.

Source: Courtesy of Amoco Corporation.

think and speak with the assumption that the employees are capable of meeting high standards. For example, the supervisor might say, "These procedures are complicated, but I'm sure that if you study them regularly and ask questions, you can learn to follow them."

General H. Norman Schwarzkopf, who came to prominence during the Persian Gulf war, has described how he put the Pygmalion effect to work earlier in his career when he was in charge of helicopter maintenance. He asked how much of the helicopter fleet could fly on any given day, and the answer was 75 percent. Recalled Schwarzkopf, "People didn't come in at 74 or 76, but always at 75, because that was the standard that had been set for them. I said, 'I don't know anything about helicopter maintenance, but I'm establishing a new standard: 85 percent.'" Before long, 85 percent of the fleet could fly each day.[14]

Providing Rewards That Are Valued

The content theories of motivation indicate that a variety of rewards may motivate and that not all employees will value the same rewards at the same time. The supervisor's challenge is to determine what rewards will work for particular employees at particular times. This involves appreciating the needs people are trying to meet and the variety of ways a supervisor can provide rewards.

Of course, there are some limits on a supervisor's discretion in giving rewards. For example, company policy or a union contract may dictate the size of raises employees get and the degree to which raises are linked to performance as opposed to seniority or some other measure. However, supervisors can use the theories of motivation, coupled with their own experience, to identify the kinds of rewards over which they have some control. For example, a supervisor has great freedom in administering such rewards as praise and recognition. Job assignments are another area in which many supervisors have some discretion. Employees who have a high need for achievement (McClelland's theory) or are trying to meet esteem or self-actualization needs (Maslow's theory) may appreciate opportunities for additional training. Employees who have a high need for affiliation or who are seeking to meet social needs may appreciate being assigned to jobs that involve working with other people.

Relating Rewards to Performance

Whatever rewards the supervisor uses, they should be linked to employees' performance. Unfortunately, according to a recent survey of about 5,000 employees, less than half saw a clear link between good job performance and higher pay.[15] If there is a connection, employees should be aware of it and understand it. Linking rewards to the achievement of realistic objectives is a way to help employees believe they can attain desired rewards. As Vroom's expectancy-valence theory described, rewards are most likely to motivate employees when the employees see them as achievable.

A basic way to link rewards to performance is with the use of objectives, as described in Chapter 2. For example, the management by objectives (MBO) system provides rewards when employees meet or exceed the objectives they have helped set for themselves. Thus, if a museum's cafeteria workers are supposed to leave their work areas spotless at the end of each shift, they know whether they have done what is necessary to receive their rewards, such as regular pay raises or extra time off.

Using clear objectives to help motivate employees is an important way to make sure that when employees try hard, they are trying to do the right things. Consultant and trainer Will Kaydos writes, "You only have to imagine a basketball court without baskets to realize that motivating someone without clear goals and measures is practically impossible."[16] Just think of the players earnestly shooting the ball in any direction; of course, the coach wants their efforts to be more focused. (For information on how to communicate goals and other information to employees, see Chapter 7.)

Treating Employees as Individuals

Most of the theories of motivation emphasize that different things motivate individuals to different degrees. If a supervisor is to succeed at motivating, he or she has to remember that employees will respond in varying ways. The supervisor cannot expect that everyone will be equally excited about cross-training or overtime pay. Some employees might prefer an easy job or short hours so that they have time and energy for outside activities. Figure 9.5 shows how American workers rated various job characteristics in a recent poll.

As much as possible, the supervisor should respond to individual differences. As described in "Tips from the Firing Line" (page 230), this may include special sensitivity to the needs of senior employees or those who have reached the end of their career path. When a particular type of motivation does not seem to work with an employee, the supervisor should try some other motivator to see if it better matches the employee's needs.

FIGURE 9.5

Job Characteristics Rated Important by American Workers

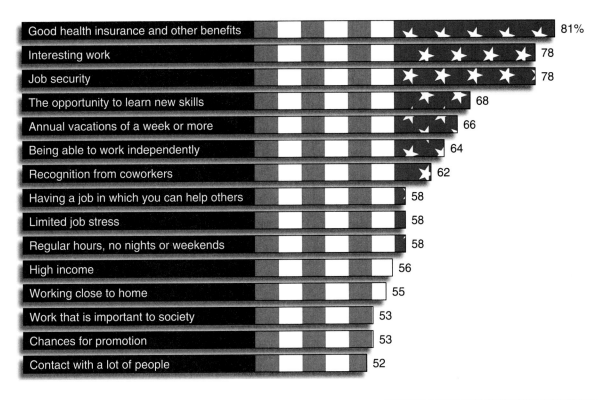

Good health insurance and other benefits	81%
Interesting work	78
Job security	78
The opportunity to learn new skills	68
Annual vacations of a week or more	66
Being able to work independently	64
Recognition from coworkers	62
Having a job in which you can help others	58
Limited job stress	58
Regular hours, no nights or weekends	58
High income	56
Working close to home	55
Work that is important to society	53
Chances for promotion	53
Contact with a lot of people	52

Source: Data from 1991 Gallup poll cited in Patricia Braus, "What Workers Want," *American Demographics*, August 1992, pp. 30–31ff.

Encouraging Employee Participation

One way to learn about employees' needs as well as to benefit from their ideas is to encourage employees to participate in planning and decision making. As discussed in Chapter 8, employees tend to feel more committed when they can contribute to decisions and solutions. They also are likely to cooperate better when they feel like part of a team. (Chapter 17 provides more ideas on working as a team.)

Providing Feedback

People want and need to know how well they are doing. Part of the supervisor's job is to give employees feedback about their performance. When the supervisor tells an employee that he or she is meeting or exceeding objectives, the employee knows that he or she is doing something right. When the supervisor tells an employee

TIPS FROM THE FIRING LINE

Motivating Experienced Employees

When an employee has held a position for a number of years, that employee has probably neared or reached the top of the pay range for the position. In addition, it is no longer a challenge to learn the job, and the employee is probably looking for other job-related sources of satisfaction. The supervisor can't motivate such an employee through the promise of a raise for good performance, but here are some other ideas that may work:

- *Give extra responsibility*—This may be as simple as saying, "You know the job" rather than giving instructions for carrying out a routine familiar to the experienced employee. Or the supervisor may assign one-time tasks such as acting as the leader for a project, writing a report, or helping to set up at a sales meeting.
- *Make the employee a source of ideas*—The supervisor may ask the experienced employee for suggestions. In that case, it's important either to use the suggestion or to give the employee a reason for not doing so. Most likely, the other employees will see that the supervisor respects the wisdom of the experienced employee, and they also will seek out that employee's advice. This not only boosts the self-esteem of the experienced employee, it enables him or her to impart the company's traditions and practices to newer employees.
- *Use prestige symbols*—The supervisor can find ways other than money to recognize the special accomplishments of the experienced employee. For example, a production employee might be assigned to represent the department on a safety or quality committee. If higher-level management agrees it would be consistent with personnel policy, the experienced employee might receive a new job title, such as senior sales specialist or senior engineer. If the budget permits, a sales supervisor might consider giving the experienced salesperson a fancier company car than the other salespeople get.
- *Consider a lateral transfer*—The supervisor can let his or her peers in other departments know about the experienced employee's skills. If another department asks the employee to transfer there, it shows the employee that the organization values his or her abilities. Having an experienced employee move to another department is a loss to the supervisor, but it may prevent the employee from leaving the organization. Also, as a result of the broader experience, the employee may ultimately become more valuable than ever.

Sources: Jack Falvey, "Managing 'Senior Citizens,'" *Sales & Marketing Management*, February 1992, pp. 11, 14; and Bureau of Business Practice, *The Front Line Supervisor's Standard Manual* (Waterford, Conn.: Prentice-Hall, 1989).

that he or she is falling short of objectives, the employee knows that he or she needs to improve. Most people will try to improve when given a chance to do so.

An important kind of feedback is praise. People want to know that their efforts are appreciated, and they will try harder for people who appreciate them. In monitoring employees, the supervisor should look for ways they are performing well. The supervisor should let the employees know, in specific terms, that he or she appreciates the good work and that it benefits the organization.

There are many ways to deliver praise. For example, a nursing supervisor might write a memo to a nurse, stating that the supervisor has noticed his courteous manner with patients and that it gives patients a good impression of the hospital. Or a supervisor on a police force might tell one of the officers that he appreciates it that the officer's paperwork is always complete and legible. At Adams

& Adams Building Services of Enfield, Connecticut, managers carry cards bearing a message of congratulations. Whenever a manager sees an employee doing a high-quality job, the manager gives the employee a card. Twice a year, the employees enter their cards in a drawing for various prizes.[17] Whatever approach the supervisor uses for praising, the behaviors that he or she praises do not have to be dramatic. Praise is so easy to give and its potential rewards are so great that the supervisor can and should use it routinely, as long as it is sincere.

Summary

9.1   Identify the relationship between motivation and performance.
To perform well, employees must be motivated. But motivation leads to good performance only when accompanied by ability, including enough skills, equipment, supplies, and time.

9.2   Describe content theories of motivation.
Content theories of motivation attempt to identify what motivates people. According to Maslow's hierarchy of needs, people have five major categories of needs—physiological, security, social, esteem, and self-actualization—arranged in a hierarchy. People attempt to satisfy lower-level needs before they focus on higher-level needs. According to McClelland, people have achievement, power, and affiliation needs. The intensity of each kind of need varies from person to person. Herzberg's two-factor theory says that employees are dissatisfied when hygiene factors are absent, and they are satisfied when motivating factors are present.

9.3   Describe process theories of motivation.
Process theories attempt to explain how motivation works. According to Vroom's expectancy-valence theory, the intensity of a person's motivation depends on the value the person places on the outcome of a behavior multiplied by the perceived probability that the behavior will actually lead to the outcome. Thus, for a person to be motivated highly, the person must not only value the results of his or her efforts but also believe he or she can achieve the results. Reinforcement theory, pioneered by B. F. Skinner, says that people behave as they do because of the kind of consequences they experience as a result of their behavior. The supervisor can therefore influence behavior by administering the consequences (in the form of reinforcement or punishment).

9.4   Explain when financial incentives are likely to motivate employees.
Money motivates people when it meets their needs. The employees must believe they are able to achieve the financial rewards the organization offers.

9.5   Describe pay plans using financial incentives.
Under a piecework system, employees are paid according to how much they produce. A production bonus system pays a basic wage or salary plus a bonus based on performance (for example, an amount per unit assembled). Commissions are payments tied to the amount of sales completed. Some organizations pay employees for making useful suggestions on how to cut costs or improve quality. Group incentive plans pay a bonus when the group as a whole exceeds an objective. Profit-sharing and gainsharing plans are types of group incentives.

9.6   Discuss the pros and cons of keeping pay information secret.
Keeping employees' pay secret respects their desire for privacy. However, for employees to be motivated by the possibility of greater earnings and a sense that pay rates are fair, they must know what they can hope to earn. Typically, an organization balances these needs by publishing pay ranges that show the least and most the organization will pay an employee in a particular job.

9.7   Identify ways supervisors can motivate their employees.
Supervisors can motivate employees by making work interesting through such means as job rotation,

job enlargement, job enrichment, and contact with users of the product or service. Other ways to motivate include having high expectations of employees, providing rewards that are valued, relating rewards to performance, treating employees as individuals, encouraging employee participation, and providing feedback, including praise.

Key Terms

motivation

reinforcement

punishment

behavior modification

financial incentives

piecework system

commissions

group incentive plan

profit-sharing plan

gainsharing

job rotation

cross-training

job enlargement

job enrichment

Pygmalion effect

Review and Discussion Questions

1. Describe the categories of needs that Maslow identified in his hierarchy. Does this hierarchy seem complete to you, or can you think of any other categories of needs that people try to meet?

2. What are the three categories of needs that McClelland identified in his theory? Which category of needs do you think is strongest for you?

3. What are the hygiene factors and motivating factors described by Herzberg? Consider your current job or the one you held most recently. Which of these factors are (were) present at that job? How would you say they affect(ed) your level of satisfaction? Your level of motivation?

4. How can the content theories of motivation guide supervisors in motivating employees?

5. John Lightfoot believes he has a 75 percent chance of earning a bonus of $100. Mary Yu believes she has a 75 percent chance of qualifying for a raise of $1,000 a year. According to Vroom's expectancy-valence theory, would it be correct to conclude that Mary will be more intensely motivated by her potential reward than John will be by his? Explain.

6. Andre Jones supervises computer programmers. He expects each programmer to turn in a progress report by quitting time each Friday.

   a. Name at least one way Andre can use reinforcement to motivate employees to turn in their reports on time.

   b. Name at least one way Andre can use punishment to motivate employees to turn in their reports on time.

   c. Which of these approaches do you think would be most successful? Why?

7. In which of the following situations do you think money will be an effective motivator? Explain.

   a. The economy is slow, and even though the salespeople think they are doing their best, sales are down. Sales supervisor Rita Blount tells the sales force that anyone whose weekly sales are up by 10 percent next week will receive a $5,000 bonus.

   b. A retailer such as Radio Shack announces that the top performer in the store will be a prime candidate for a management job in a store the company is opening in another state. Whoever takes the job will receive a raise of at least 9 percent.

   c. A respiratory therapist who is the parent of two high-school-age children can earn an extra $500 this month by accepting a schedule that involves working on weekends.

8. Describe the following pay plans.

   a. Production bonus system

b. Commissions
c. Group incentive plans
9. Antonio Delgado supervises the police officers of the fourth precinct. What are some ways in which he can make their work more interesting?
10. What is the Pygmalion effect? How can a supervisor use it to motivate employees?
11. What is wrong with each of the following attempts at motivation?
   a. A sales supervisor for an insurance company believes that employees appreciate an opportunity to broaden their experience, so she rewards the top performer each year with an all-expenses-paid leadership seminar. The seminar lasts a week and is conducted at a hotel in a city 200 miles away.
   b. The supervisor of a hospital cafeteria awards one employee a $50 bonus each month. To give everyone an equal chance at receiving the bonus, the supervisor draws from a jar names written on slips of paper.
   c. A maintenance supervisor in a pickle factory believes that if employees are qualified, they should be able to tell whether they are doing a good job. Therefore, the supervisor focuses his motivation efforts on thinking up clever rewards to give out each year to the best performers.

A SECOND LOOK

Given the information about motivating Liquid Carbonic's sales force in the story at the beginning of this chapter, how well would you expect the company's incentives to motivate its sales representatives? Explain. What, if any, additions or improvements would you suggest to the way Huskisson motivates the sales reps?

Class Exercise

If you have not already done so, answer the Self-Quiz questions on page 214. Then, by a show of hands, determine how many class members selected each response as being most important and how many selected each response as least important. The instructor might tally the responses on the chalkboard or overhead projector or fill in the following table:

	Number of Students Rating the Item	
Self-Quiz Item	Most Important	Least Important
1.	_____	
2.	_____	
3.	_____	
4.	_____	
5.	_____	
6.	_____	
7.	_____	

	Number of Students Rating the Item	
Self-Quiz Item	Most Important	Least Important
8.	_____	
9.	_____	
10.	_____	
11.	_____	
12.	_____	

Discuss the following questions:
- Which response(s) did most class members choose as most important?
- Which response(s) did most class members choose as least important?
- Do you think these choices are typical of most employees today? Why or why not?
- How could a supervisor use this information to motivate employees?

CASE

Gainsharing at B. F. Goodrich

The 62 hourly and professional employees at B. F. Goodrich's Terre Haute, Indiana, plant manufacture vinyl resins used in a number of applications. To improve performance, the plant's management decided to institute a gainsharing plan. The management committee that recommended the use of gainsharing initially thought that the most important incentive of the plan would be the potential bonuses. However, the task force of employees who set up the system ranked the bonus last among the eight goals for the plan. Most important, thought the employees, was improved plantwide communication.

To involve employees, the task force set up a plantwide group called the Error Cause Removal (ECR) team. This team consists of managers and nonmanagement employees from all areas of the plant. The ECR team solicits and investigates ideas from employees. At least once a month, the team meets and decides whether to implement any of the ideas. The team has the authority to spend up to $500 to implement an idea; more expensive ideas must be approved by management. The individuals who submit the ideas do not receive a bonus for suggesting them; rather, they share in whatever benefits the whole plant gets from using the ideas.

In addition, ECR team representatives and supervisors hold regular shift and department meetings to discuss problems and brainstorm possible solutions. The groups submit the best ideas to the ECR team.

To determine financial rewards, the company set a base level of quality, productivity, cost, and customer service. When the plant saves money through improved quality and productivity or through reduced costs, employees receive 10 to 50 percent of the gain, depending on how important it is. Half of the bonus is paid to the employees in their regular paycheck, and the other half is placed in a reserve account. If performance falls below the base levels, the amount in the reserve accounts is reduced. At the end of the year, the employees receive the money remaining in the reserve account. (A negative balance at the end of the year would be absorbed by the company, not charged to the employees.)

The gainsharing plan rewards employees in other ways, too. It provides information on a bulletin board displaying news about performance, ideas, and goals. Special celebrations recognize employees. To keep connected with customers, employees conduct plant tours and visit vendors and suppliers.

Since the program started, employees have suggested hundreds of ideas. At the same time, the role of supervisors has changed. Rather than focusing on overseeing the work of others, they now spend their time coordinating, planning, and teaching. In addition, quality and productivity have improved at the plant, and costs and complaints have fallen. Since then, gainsharing has been adopted at B. F. Goodrich's Deer Park, Texas, facility. This chemical operation with almost 100 employees has experienced similar success with the program.

1. As described in this case, what kind(s) of motivation does B. F. Goodrich use?
2. Based on the information given, what needs do the employees have? Which of these needs does the motivation program help meet?
3. As a supervisor, would you prefer a motivation system such as the one at B. F. Goodrich, or one that rewards your performance as an individual? Why?

Sources: Robert L. Masternak, "Gainsharing: A Bonus Plan or Employee Involvement?" *Compensation & Benefits Review*, January–February 1992, pp. 46–54; and Robert L. Masternak, "Gainsharing at B. F. Goodrich: Succeeding Together Achieves Rewards," *Tapping the Network Journal*, Fall–Winter 1991, pp. 13–16.

10

A company cannot increase its productivity. People can.
—Robert Half

Improving Productivity

LEARNING OBJECTIVES

10.1   Define *productivity*.

10.2   Identify constraints on productivity.

10.3   Describe how productivity and productivity improvements
       are measured.

10.4   Identify the two basic ways in which productivity may
       be improved.

10.5   Describe cost-control strategies available to supervisors.

10.6   Explain why employees have fears about productivity
       improvement, and tell how supervisors can address
       those fears.

PRODUCTIVITY PAYS

As the founder and president of Classic Kitchen and Baths in Mercer Island, Washington, Jinny Bray supervises three employees, two full-time and one part-time. The full-time employees are a foreman and a carpenter's helper, and the part-time employee is a designer who draws the designs for the construction projects handled by the company. In addition, Bray oversees the work of suppliers and subcontractors.

To stay in business, Bray must be concerned with the quantity and quality of results she gets from her employees and subcontractors. She needs to be sure that when she is paying them to work, they are actually working. Thus, she takes note of which workers are the most likely to engage in personal talk on the job. When the chatting interferes with work, she tries to schedule some of the talkative workers to come in on different days from others. She does not want to dampen the cooperative spirit among the workers, so she tries to be subtle in discouraging the personal talk.

Another challenge for Bray is satisfying all the requirements of government building codes. When Bray believes the government inspectors are being unrealistic, she must discuss and resolve the matter with them. However, because Bray's company adheres to the building codes on all projects, this problem remains a minor one.

productivity
The amount of results (output) an organization gets for a given amount of inputs.

When Jinny Bray is addressing issues such as how much work subcontractors are doing or the way government regulations add to the cost and time needed for completing a project, she is concerned with productivity. **Productivity** is the amount of results (output) an organization gets for a given amount of inputs. This relationship can be summarized in an equation like the one shown in Figure 10.1. Thus, productivity can refer to the amount of acceptable work employees do for each dollar they earn or the number of acceptable products manufactured with a given amount of resources.

This chapter takes a deeper look at the meaning of productivity and how it is measured. It describes the two basic ways to increase productivity—controlling quality and controlling costs. The chapter suggests ways that supervisors can participate in efforts to improve productivity.

The Productivity Challenge

Stiff competition from around the world is forcing U.S. businesses to pay attention to productivity. In addition, widespread opposition to paying higher taxes is forcing governments to see whether they can make their operations more productive. For supervisors to help improve productivity, they must understand why it is important and what limits an organization's productivity.

Trends in Productivity in the United States

When the productivity of organizations in a country is improving, people benefit in a number of ways. They can get goods and services at lower prices or with lower taxes than they otherwise could. Employers tend to pay higher wages and salaries to workers who are more productive. People also have access to more and better goods and services. Because of such benefits, statisticians keep track of productivity trends in various countries.

Overall, the performance of U.S. businesses is mixed.[1] The amount of goods and services produced by the average U.S. worker is higher than that for any other industrialized nation. In 1990 the average U.S. worker produced $45,100 worth of goods and services, compared with $34,500 produced by the average Japanese worker. However, U.S. productivity is growing more slowly than before the 1970s and more slowly than in other industrialized nations, such as Germany and Japan, and this is a cause for concern.

The slower growth does not necessarily mean employees are reluctant to work better and faster. Rather, organizations sometimes hesitate to invest in the equipment and training needed to enable employees to work more efficiently. Organizations also can make more use of such improvement practices as total quality management (described in Chapter 6) and teamwork (described in Chapter 17). The need for improvement is especially great in the service (nonmanufacturing) sector of the economy. Four-fifths of the work force hold service jobs, but productivity gains have been slowest in the nonmanufacturing sector.

FIGURE 10.1

The Productivity Formula

American workers face stiff competition from around the world. These engineers at Hewlett-Packard's computer plants in Guadalajara are an example of the world-wide challenge to the productivity of the American worker.

Source: Courtesy of Alan Levenson, photographer.

Constraints on Productivity

When you read about the ways to improve productivity, keep in mind that several constraints limit the impact of a supervisor or even of a higher-level manager. Supervisors and other managers should be aware of these constraints so that they can either plan ways to overcome them or set realistic goals within them. Some of the most important constraints on productivity are management limitations, employee attitudes and skills, government regulations, and union rules.

Management Limitations   For operative employees to contribute to improving productivity, they must believe that management is truly committed to this objective. But all too often employees believe that management is more interested in the next quarter's profits than in producing high-quality goods or services as efficiently as possible. They become frustrated especially when managers do not seem to listen to their ideas for improvements.

The most important way supervisors can overcome this constraint is to set a good example. Supervisors should demonstrate by their actions as well as their words that they are interested in the department's productivity. This behavior includes seeing that the job is done right the first time, as well as using resources wisely. On a personal level, wise use of resources includes being well organized. To test your own level of personal productivity, take the Self-Quiz.

Supervisors also must communicate instructions clearly and plan carefully so that employees are able to live up to managers' expectations. Furthermore, the supervisor should listen to employees' concerns and ideas about improving productivity. If the organization has a formal program for submitting ideas, the supervisor can offer to help employees write down or explain their suggestions.

Employee Attitudes and Skills   Improving productivity involves making changes. As will be discussed in Chapter 12, people have a natural tendency to resist change, as it is challenging and often frightening. When employees have a negative attitude toward productivity improvements, they will not be motivated to make the changes work. As described in the "Dealing with Diversity" box, attitudes may seem to be a problem when employees or the supervisor are experiencing "culture shock." Part of the supervisor's job is to identify employee attitudes and, when necessary, to help employees take a more positive view. (The last section of this chapter addresses this issue in greater detail.)

The skills of employees also influence how effective productivity-building efforts will be. When the organization wants each member to contribute more to the goods or services it produces, each member must either work faster or do the job differently. Some employees are able to do new tasks or do their job in a new way with little or no training. Other employees understand only one way of working. When employees are willing to learn, the way to overcome this constraint may simply be to provide more training. When employees are either unwilling or unable to learn, this constraint is more difficult to overcome.

Government Regulations   Businesses and other organizations in the United States are regulated in many areas. Laws determine the payment of overtime wages, provisions that must be made for disabled persons, limits on polluting the environment, minimum safety standards for goods produced, the use of child labor, and many other aspects of operating an organization. As mentioned in the story of Jinny Bray at the beginning of this chapter, construction companies also must contend with extensive building codes.

SELF-QUIZ *Test Your Personal Productivity*

Answer each of the following questions by circling Y for yes or N for no.

Y N   1. Does it often take you more than 10 minutes to unearth a particular letter, bill, report, or other paper from your files (or from piles of paper on your desk)?

Y N   2. Do things amass in corners of closets or on the floor because you cannot decide where to put them?

Y N   3. Are there papers on your desk, other than reference materials, that you have not looked through for a week or more?

Y N   4. Has your electricity or another utility ever been turned off because you forgot to pay the bill?

Y N   5. Within the last two months, have you forgotten any scheduled appointment, anniversary, or specific date you wanted to acknowledge?

Y N   6. Do your magazines and newspapers pile up unread?

Y N   7. Do you frequently procrastinate so long on a work assignment that it becomes an emergency or panic situation?

Y N   8. Has anything ever been misplaced in your home or office for longer than two months?

Y N   9. Do you often misplace keys, glasses, gloves, handbags, briefcases, or other such items?

Y N   10. Does your definition of "working in organized space" mean fitting as many objects as you can into a limited area?

Y N   11. Do you feel that your storage problems would be solved if you had more space?

Y N   12. Do you want to get organized but everything is in such a mess that you do not know where to start?

Y N   13. Do you regularly receive letters, comments, or calls that begin: "You haven't gotten back to me yet, so…"?

Y N   14. Are you harassed by frequent interruptions—whether phone calls or visitors—that affect your ability to concentrate?

Y N   15. Are you so busy with details that you are ignoring opportunities for new business or promotional activities?

Y N   16. When you get up in the morning, do you know what your two or three primary tasks are?

Y N   17. By the end of an average day, have you accomplished at least the most important tasks you set for yourself?

For questions 1 to 15, give yourself one point for each Y you circled. For questions 16 and 17, give yourself one point for each N you circled. Here is how to interpret your total:

4 or less	Systems are under control!
5–8	Disorganization is troublesome.
9–11	Life must be very difficult.
12 or more	You are disorganized to the point of chaos.

Source: Adapted by Corinne Livesay from Stephanie Winston, *Getting Organized: The Easy Way to Put Your Life in Order* (New York: Warner Books, 1978), and Stephanie Winston, *The Organized Executive: New Ways to Manage Time, Paper, and People* (New York: W. W. Norton & Co., 1983).

Following these orders costs money, but the laws and regulations reflect values considered important by the majority in our society. For example, it might be cheaper to hire children to assemble electronic components, but few people want to return to the days of children laboring long hours within factory walls. Likewise, scrubbers on smokestacks cost money, but clean air to breathe is essential. Even when government regulations seem illogical or unreasonable, the organization can face serious penalties for ignoring or disobeying them. Thus, with regard to government regulations, the proper role of supervisors and other managers is to know these regulations and seek ways of improving productivity without violating the law.

Union Rules   Union contracts typically specify rules for what tasks particular employees may do, what hours they may work, and how organizations may use employees. Sometimes an organization's managers see a way to improve productivity that violates one of these rules. For example, it might be more efficient to have two employees learn each other's jobs so they can get the work done even when one of them is away or busy. However, the union contract might contain a rule against this.

Sometimes it is possible to overcome such constraints, although that usually takes time. If the organization explains how everyone will benefit from the changes, the union may agree to revise the contract. For example, if the alternative is for the company to lay off employees, the union management may prefer to change work rules. Of course, while the supervisor can propose changes, overcoming these constraints is not part of the job of a supervisor. Supervisors have to do their best to get work done as efficiently as possible under the existing work rules.

Measurement of Productivity

Basically, productivity is measured with the equation in Figure 10.1. This equation says that productivity is the amount of output produced with the inputs used. Table 10.1 provides examples of inputs and outputs for several types of organizations. The productivity equation can compare the output and input for an individual, a department, an organization, or even an entire country's paid work force. Supervisors are concerned most directly with the productivity of their department and their individual employees, so the remaining discussion focuses on those areas.

By applying basic arithmetic to the formula for productivity, the supervisor can see what has to change for productivity to increase. The right side of the equation

Coping with Culture Shock

According to Sondra Thiederman, president of Cross-Cultural Communications, a San Diego-based training firm, culture shock is "a state of mind that occurs when people find themselves immersed in a strange culture." People in a strange culture find that others do not respond to their behaviors in expected ways, that they no longer know how they are expected to behave, and that they no longer receive the credit they expect for their achievements, skills, and ideas. As a result of these experiences, a person undergoing culture shock may have such responses as depression, loneliness, aggression, short attention span, frustration, passivity, and quickness to fatigue.

We tend to think about culture shock as affecting only immigrant employees. However, others are at risk as well. U.S. employees from other than the dominant culture—such as blacks in a predominately white workplace or women in a primarily male workplace—also may experience culture shock. So may managers who have been trained in managing according to the rules and principles that apply to white mainstream U.S. workers but find themselves supervising employees from many backgrounds. For example, it may be frustrating to get employees to participate in decision making if many of them are from a background that expects leaders to be authoritarian.

From the organization's viewpoint, an important consequence of culture shock is that the people experiencing it are less productive. For example, an employee experiencing loneliness may gravitate toward others of the same cultural background. Besides limiting that employee's own contacts, this behavior may cause other employees to become resentful of those who stick together. Aggression displayed by an employee experiencing culture shock may lead to many disputes and a generally disruptive atmosphere.

The supervisor who is experiencing culture shock or coping with it in others may conclude that the solution is to avoid hiring diverse employees. The supervisor thinks that if he or she can just get a group of employees who are alike, then the problem will go away. However, the more that people are exposed to diversity and the more they learn about it, the more comfortable they will be.

Therefore, two important first steps toward healing culture shock involve exposure to a variety of groups and education about them. Supervisors may find that they and their employees can benefit from formal training in this area. It is also helpful to be open and honest about the problem. Discussing feelings helps to defuse them and leads people to a better understanding of one another.

Source: Sondra Thiederman, *Bridging Cultural Barriers for Corporate Success: How to Manage the Multicultural Work Force* (New York: Lexington Books, 1991), pp. 5–10.

is a fraction. Remember that when the top (numerator) of a fraction gets bigger, the number becomes greater. When the bottom (denominator) of a fraction gets bigger, the number becomes smaller. For example, $\frac{3}{2}$ is greater than $\frac{1}{2}$, and $\frac{1}{5}$ is less than $\frac{1}{3}$. So to increase productivity, the supervisor needs to increase outputs, reduce inputs, or both.

Consider an example. An employee at the secretary of state's office processes 96 driver's license applications in the course of an eight-hour day. As shown in Figure 10.2, one way to measure this employee's productivity is $\frac{96}{8}$, or 12 applications per hour. The supervisor might note that a more experienced employee can process 20 applications per hour, so by this measure, the first employee is less experienced than desirable. He or she might need more training or motivation or just more experience.

TABLE 10.1	Organization	Inputs	Outputs
Examples of Inputs and Outputs	Bus line	Buses; gas, oil, and other supplies; terminals; drivers; ticket sellers; managers; tickets; schedules; funds; data	Transportation services to passengers
	Manufacturing firm	Trucks; plants; oil, rags, and other supplies; raw materials; purchased parts; production workers; supervisors; engineers; storekeepers; bills of material; inventory records; production schedules; time records; funds; data	Products for use by customers
	Hospital	Ambulances; hospital rooms; beds, wheelchairs, X rays; receptionists; administrators; nurses; doctors; medicines, drugs, splints, bandages, food, and other supplies; medical charts; funds; data	Health care service to patients
	Police force	Cars and vans; offices; police officers; forms; handcuffs, radios, guns, office supplies, and other supplies; office furniture; equipment for forensic research; uniforms; funds; data	Protection of public safety

Source: Adapted from Samuel C. Certo, *Modern Management*, 5th ed. (Boston: Allyn and Bacon, 1992), p. 550.

FIGURE 10.2
Productivity Measurements

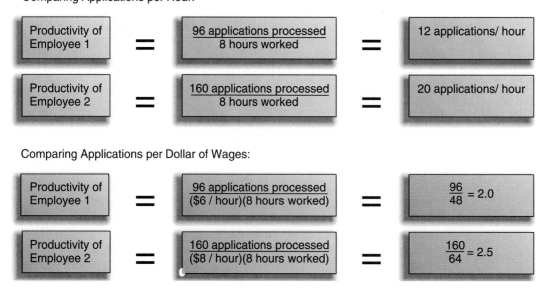

Comparing Applications per Hour:

$$\text{Productivity of Employee 1} = \frac{96 \text{ applications processed}}{8 \text{ hours worked}} = 12 \text{ applications/ hour}$$

$$\text{Productivity of Employee 2} = \frac{160 \text{ applications processed}}{8 \text{ hours worked}} = 20 \text{ applications/ hour}$$

Comparing Applications per Dollar of Wages:

$$\text{Productivity of Employee 1} = \frac{96 \text{ applications processed}}{(\$6 / \text{hour})(8 \text{ hours worked})} = \frac{96}{48} = 2.0$$

$$\text{Productivity of Employee 2} = \frac{160 \text{ applications processed}}{(\$8 / \text{hour})(8 \text{ hours worked})} = \frac{160}{64} = 2.5$$

Productivity is enhanced by increasing employee skills. At Flowers' "new-generation" bakery in Jamestown, North Carolina, bread techni-cian Leon McIntyre (right), learns the fine points of an automated batch control system from trainer Steve Brinkley (left).

Source: Coutesy of Ovak Arslanian.

But the organization is also interested in the *cost* of the employee. So the supervisor might measure the input as the employee's cost per day (hourly wage times number of hours). If the employee earned $6 per hour, the productivity measure would be 96/($6 × 8), or 2 (see Figure 10.2). If the employee who can process 20 applications per hour earns $8 per hour, that employee's productivity would be 160/($8 × 8), or 2.5. Thus, the more experienced employee is more productive, even taking into account his or her higher wages.

Bear in mind that the "output" measured in the productivity formula is only goods and services of acceptable quality. A rude salesclerk and a production worker making defective components are not really productive. In these cases, the produc-tivity formula would include only the number of correctly made components or the amount of sales made courteously and accurately. The production worker illus-trated in Figure 10.3 has evidently missed this point.

The following anecdote illustrates the importance of quality in determining productivity. A professor of sociology specializing in management was hospitalized at Yale–New Haven Hospital. He requested a meeting with the hospital's vice-president of patient services, and he asked her what the hospital was doing to study the effectiveness of its nurses. The vice-president explained that the hospital evalu-ated nurses' work in terms of the time they spent on particular tasks. "No, don't count that," replied the professor. "It's not important. What you have to document is the impact of problem solving on a patient's outcome." He explained that his nurse had solved two of his own problems—uncomfortable surgical dressing and constipation—by getting the right employees involved. She had done this in just a few minutes, but the professor valued that effort more than if she had spent hours in his room talking with him. Thus, he believed that the proper measure of the nurse's productivity was her success in solving his problems.[2]

FIGURE 10.3

Quantity without Quality Does Not Boost Productivity

"I don't get it! I turn out a record 370 units, and I don't even get a lousy 'thank you!'"

Source: Copyrighted material reprinted with permission of *Front Line Supervisor's Bulletin*, July 10, 1992, p. 4., and the Bureau of Business Practice, 24 Rope Ferry Road, Waterford, Conn. 06386.

Improving Productivity by Controlling Quality

The 10-page report came back to the word-processing department so full of corrections that the department's supervisor, Molly O'Donnell, concluded that it would have to be entirely retyped. When she showed it to the operator responsible, Molly said, "What happened? This isn't the first time." "It's not my fault!" exclaimed the operator. "Finkelstein's handwriting is impossible to read."

When problems like this occur, a department has to have enough employees to fix mistakes as well as do the initial work. That cuts into productivity. Quality analysts say that 20 to 40 percent of costs are for waste and the correction of defects.[3] Part of the supervisor's job, therefore, is to think of and implement ways to get the job done right the first time. In Molly's case, she might look for ways to help word-processing operators who are having trouble reading the handwriting on the documents they prepare. Or she might investigate other ways for people in the organization to submit their work; for example, people could tape-record their documents for the word-processing operators to transcribe. (Chapter 6 discusses ways supervisors can maintain and improve quality. Other ways to control quality are to follow principles of controlling [Chapter 5] and problem solving [Chapter 8].)

An example of an organization that boosted productivity by improving quality is IBM's Austin, Texas, manufacturing facility for electronic circuit cards—the "engines" that run computers. The company had tried saving money through automation but found that the robots it installed were not flexible enough. So the company turned its attention to ways of making the production process more efficient. The work force was divided into six "focus factories," each of which has the machines needed to make a few different products, rather than the entire factory making all the products. Employees receive training in the entire production process and in how to maintain the machines they operate. With this broad knowledge, the employees understand what is going on in their area and can help spot and correct problems. Thus, when an assembly line was loaded with the wrong parts one day, employees noticed the mistake, stopped the line, and corrected the problem after only four bad parts had been made. Automated inspection equipment would have missed such a problem, and the company would have had to remake thousands of panels instead of just four.[4]

Improving Productivity by Controlling Costs

When supervisors and other managers look for ways to boost productivity, they often start by looking at their costs per unit of output. Productivity improves when the department or organization can do as much work at a lower cost. It also improves when output rises without a cost increase.

Determining Costs

It is not surprising that before the supervisor can make intelligent decisions about how to trim costs, he or she has to know where the money is going. The most important source of such information is budget reports, described in Chapter 5. By reviewing budget reports regularly, the supervisor can see which categories of expenses are largest and identify the areas in which the department is spending more than planned. Those are the first areas in which the supervisor should investigate possibilities for improvement. In addition, the supervisor should spend time with workers, observing how they use the department's resources, including their time. The process of gathering information about costs and identifying needed improvements is part of the supervisor's control function.

Cost-Control Strategies

To lower costs, supervisors can use a number of strategies. Some basic alternatives are summarized in Figure 10.4. These strategies are not mutually exclusive. Supervisors can get the greatest productivity by using as many of these strategies as will work. In deciding which strategies to use, the supervisor should consider which will appeal to higher-level management, which will be acceptable to employees, and which involve areas within the supervisor's control.

An important part of many of these strategies is encouraging and using employees' ideas for saving money. Operating the machines, preparing the reports, and serving the clients or customers gives employees a close-up view of how things are done. This enables them to see the shortcomings of the way the organization does things.

Cost-Control Strategies

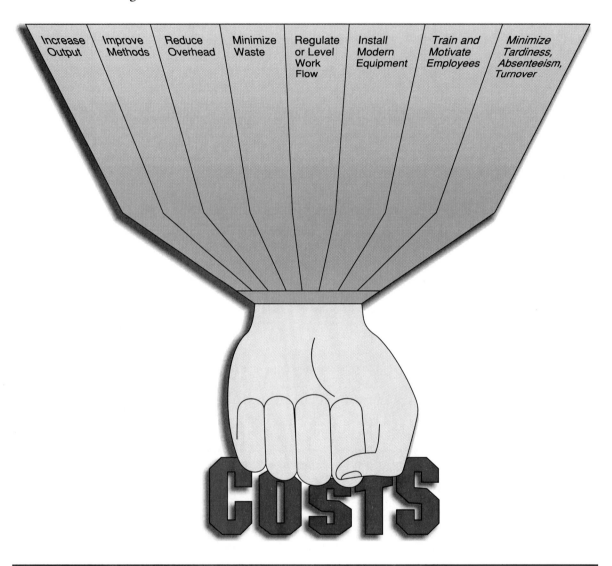

Examples abound. American Airlines has a program called "IdeAAs in Action" that asks for and evaluates suggestions, then rewards the employees and supervisors who provide them. The company estimates that cost-cutting ideas from employees saved $58 million in 1991 alone.[5] A contest held by Advance Transformer Company generated several hundred cost-saving ideas. One came from Ward Huege, an employee in the company's data-processing department, who arranged for the company to switch to environmentally safe paper that will cost several thousand dollars less than the paper that was previously used.[6] At

Employees often have great ideas to save their companies money. This task force consists of representatives from Best Foods' marketing, purchasing, packaging technology, engineering, manufacturing, and logistics management departments. They redesigned the *Mazola* corn oil bottle, which reduced packaging by 32 percent.

Source: Courtesy of Kelly-Mooney photography.

United Electric Controls Company, based in Watertown, Massachusetts, assembler Vinny Petrillo responded to a call for suggestions by asking why the company was ordering a type of switch with three unnecessary terminals. Petrillo was spending up to two hours a day removing the terminals. The company investigated and learned that switches without the terminals were available for less money but that the buyer had never known to ask.[7]

Increase Output Remember that the numerator in the productivity equation (Figure 10.1) represents what the department or organization is producing. The greater the output at a given cost, the greater the productivity. Thus, a logical way to increase productivity is to increase output without boosting costs.

In practical terms, what does this mean? Sometimes, by applying themselves, people can work faster or harder. Servers in a restaurant may find they can cover more tables than before, and production workers in a factory may find they can assemble more components than before. Of course, it is not always possible to increase output without sacrificing quality.

Needless to say, this way to improve productivity is the method that most often makes employees unhappy. A supervisor who wants to boost productivity by increasing output must first make sure that the new goals for output are reasonable—perhaps by including the employees in the decision-making process. The supervisor must also communicate the new goals carefully, emphasizing any positive aspects of the change. For example, the supervisor might note that if employees are more productive, the organization has a chance to remain competitive without layoffs.

Improve Methods A less stressful way to do more with a given amount of resources is to improve methods. In many cases, there is a better, more efficient way to get something done. According to consultant Mary Crabtree Tonges, there are only limited ways of doing the same thing better or faster. The major improvements in productivity result from taking a fresh look at what needs to get done. Tonges uses as an example a nursing staff that is constantly running errands to other departments in order to collect specimens, supplies, and equipment. The nurses can work somewhat more efficiently if someone sets priorities for errand running and improves the forms used for getting supplies. But bigger gains can come from finding better ways to move specimens and supplies around than having nurses act as messengers.[8]

A potentially powerful approach to improving methods is to apply the principles of job enlargement and job enrichment, described in Chapter 9. Enlarging and enriching jobs makes them more interesting. This should motivate employees to deliver higher quality as well as work harder.

Like managers at all levels, supervisors should constantly be looking for ways to improve methods. Some ideas will come from supervisors themselves. (Chapter 8 provides some suggestions for creative thinking.) Also, because employees see the problems and pitfalls of their jobs, they often have excellent ideas for doing the work better. Supervisors therefore should keep communication channels open and actively ask for ideas.

overhead
Expenses not related directly to producing goods and services; examples are rent, utilities, and staff support.

Reduce Overhead   Many departments spend more than is necessary for **overhead**. This covers rent, utilities, staff support, company cafeteria, janitorial services, and other expenses not related directly to producing goods and services. Typically, an organization allocates a share of the total overhead to each department based on the department's size. This means the supervisor has limited control over the department's overhead expenses. However, supervisors can periodically look for sources of needless expenses, such as lights left on in unoccupied areas or messy work areas that mean extra work for janitorial staff. By reducing these costs to the company, the supervisor ultimately reduces the amount of overhead charged to the department.

Staff departments in particular can be guilty of contributing too much to the cost of overhead by generating unnecessary paperwork. Supervisors and their employees who produce or handle reports and forms should evaluate this paperwork to make sure it is needed. Keith Snidtker, facility services manager for GAF Corporation of Wayne, New Jersey, tells of a company that had a full-time employee who spent the entire day filling out reports that no one used.[9] Another company described by Snidtker eliminated copies of documents and reports being sent to employees who had been transferred or had retired or died—and reduced the number of documents generated per year by 22,000. Another way to reduce the amount of paper is to make sure that when a procedure calls for a form with several parts, all the parts are actually used.

Minimize Waste   Waste occurs in all kinds of operations. A medical office may order too many supplies and wind up throwing some away or taking up unnecessary storage space. A factory may handle materials in a way that produces a lot of scrap. A sales office may make unnecessary photocopies of needlessly long proposals, contributing more to landfills than to the company's profits.

down time or idle time
Time during which employees or machines are not producing goods or services.

A costly form of waste is **down time** or **idle time**—time during which employees or machines are not producing goods or services. This term is used most often in manufacturing operations, but it applies to other situations as well. In a factory, idle time occurs while a machine is shut down for repairs or while workers are waiting for parts. In an office, idle time occurs when employees are waiting for instructions, supplies, or a response to a question they asked the supervisor.

detour behavior
Tactics for postponing or avoiding work.

Another form of wasted time results from **detour behavior**, or tactics for postponing or avoiding work. Employees and their supervisors use a wide variety of detour behavior. Perhaps a supervisor takes time to enjoy a cup of coffee and the newspaper before turning to the day's responsibilities. Or an employee may stop by a friend's desk to chat on the way back from a meeting. Detour behavior may be especially tempting when a person's energy is low or when a person is facing a particularly challenging or unpleasant assignment. (The opposite of detour behavior is effective time management, discussed in Chapter 11.)

Wasted time may be a more important measure of lost productivity than wasted costs are. Management consultants at the Boston Consulting Group compared their U.S. clients' performance with that of their Japanese competitors and found that the Japanese companies were producing goods in half the time with fewer workers in smaller factories.[10] The difference was that the Japanese companies actively sought ways to manufacture products efficiently. In contrast, a U.S. manufacturer of heavy vehicles spent 45 days to prepare an order for assembly and just 16 *hours* actually assembling the product. The Boston Consulting Group concluded that companies should emphasize cutting time, rather than dollar costs, from operations.

Supervisors should be on the alert for wasted time and other resources in their department. They can set a good example for effective time management and can make detecting waste part of the control process (see Chapter 5). Often, employees are good sources of information in this area. They may be eager to suggest ways to minimize waste. The supervisor might consider holding a contest to find the best ideas.

Regulate or Level the Work Flow   An uneven flow of work can be costly, as illustrated in Figure 10.5. When work levels are low, the result is idle time. When the department faces a surge in demand for its work, employees have to work extra hours to keep up. The result may be that the department has to pay workers overtime rates—one and a half or two times normal wages—during peak periods. In addition, people are rarely as efficient during overtime hours as they are during a normal workday; they just get tired. If the supervisor can arrange to have a more even flow of work, the department can be staffed appropriately to get the job done during normal working hours, rather than overtime hours, without a lot of employees being idle during slow periods.

There are several steps a supervisor can take to regulate the work flow in his or her department:

1. The supervisor should first make sure that he or she is doing an adequate job of planning for the work that is required. (Chapter 2 provides guidelines for planning.)
2. The supervisor may also find it helpful to work with his or her boss and peers in other departments or to form teams of employees to examine and solve the problems with work flow. By cooperating, they can help make the work flow more even or at least more predictable. For example, a boss who travels extensively may assign a lot of work upon her return, not realizing that she is clustering deadlines together rather than spreading them out for an even work flow. Or the sales department may be submitting orders to the production department in batches rather than as soon as they are received.

FIGURE 10.5

The Costs of Uneven Work Flow

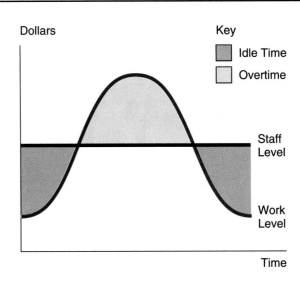

3. If the work flow must remain uneven, the supervisor may find it best to use temporary employees during peak periods. This approach can work if the temporary employees have enough training in the needed skills.

Install Modern Equipment   Work may be slowed because employees are using worn or outdated equipment. If that is the case, the supervisor may find it worthwhile to replace it with modern equipment. According to Brian Papke, president of the U.S. division of Japanese toolmaker Yamazaki Mazak, modern computer-controlled tools are so superior to the machinery they were designed to replace that an organization will be most successful if it tears out its old equipment and actually gives it away to competitors.[11] Although the strategy of installing modern equipment is most obvious for manufacturing departments, many workplaces can benefit from using modern equipment, including up-to-date computer technology.

Ingersoll Milling Machine Company, which makes customized machines for heavy industries, has a rule that any machine that is 10 years old will be replaced unless someone on the staff can show why the company should keep it. Explains Ingersoll's president, Fred S. Wilson, "Some machines you're justified in keeping because technology hasn't changed much, but in most 10-year periods, you'll see a better idea coming along." With this strategy, the company reduced the number of machines it used from 154 to 81, yet it produced twice the output and made nine times the sales volume.[12]

payback period
The length of time it will take for the benefits generated by an investment (such as cost savings from machinery) to offset the cost of the investment.

In deciding to buy new equipment, or in recommending its purchase, the supervisor needs to determine whether the expense will be worthwhile. One way to do this is to figure out how much money per year the new equipment will save—for example, in terms of lower repair costs, less down time, and more goods produced. Then the supervisor computes the number of years it will take before the savings will offset the cost of buying the equipment. This time is known as the **payback period**. The way to compute a payback period is with the first formula

FIGURE 10.6

Basic Formulas for Evaluating an Investment

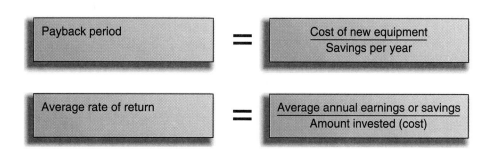

$$\text{Payback period} = \frac{\text{Cost of new equipment}}{\text{Savings per year}}$$

$$\text{Average rate of return} = \frac{\text{Average annual earnings or savings}}{\text{Amount invested (cost)}}$$

shown in Figure 10.6. Thus, if a computer system will cost $120,000 and is expected to save the office $40,000 per year, the payback period is three years ($120,000/$40,000 per year). Higher-level management or the finance department usually has an opinion on what payback period is acceptable for the organization.

Another way to evaluate whether an investment is worthwhile is to find the **average rate of return (ARR)** for that investment. ARR is a percentage that represents the organization's average annual earnings for each dollar of a given investment. For example, an ARR of 15 percent means that each dollar invested yields income (or savings) of 15 cents a year. A basic formula for ARR is the second equation in Figure 10.6. For the computer system in the previous example, the ARR would be the $40,000 annual savings divided by the $120,000 cost, or .33— a 33 percent return. To see whether this return is acceptable, the supervisor compares it with what the money spent could earn if it were invested in other ways. Again, higher-level management or the finance department usually has established standards for this measure.

Payback period and ARR as described here are just two of the simplest ways to evaluate investments. Other, more complex, methods take into account such factors as the timing of payments and earnings. For the supervisor with access to a computer, software is available to compute payback period, average rate of return, and other analyses of whether an investment is financially worthwhile. Warsaw, Indiana–based Azure Software sells a program called *Project Analysis for Capital Equipment Expenditures (PACEE)*, which defines the needed information, makes suggestions, calculates a variety of statistics, and then summarizes the results with graphs and numbers. *PACEE* takes into consideration such user-defined variables as the benefits of quality and the value of greater market share.[13]

Train and Motivate Employees   For employees to work efficiently, they need a good understanding of how to do their jobs. Thus, a basic way to improve productivity is to train employees. For example, Hector Ruiz, the general manager of Motorola's Boynton Beach, Florida, plant, says that training has allowed the plant to produce three times as many pagers with only 22 percent more manufacturing employees.[14] (Chapter 14 discusses types of training and the supervisor's role in providing training.)

As you learned in Chapter 9, training alone does not lead to superior performance; employees also must be motivated to do good work. In other words,

average rate of return (ARR)
A percentage that represents the average annual earnings for each dollar of a given investment.

Technology can streamline complex tasks. Earleen Hanson, finishing room supervisor at a Minnesota mill of Potlatch Corporation, oversees the automated storage and retrieval system, which keeps track of inventory and automatically moves huge paper rolls in and out of the vertical storage racks.

Source: Photography by Tom Tracy. Reprinted by permission of Potlatch Corporation.

employees must want to do a good job. (For ideas on how to motivate employees, see Chapter 9.)

Minimize Tardiness, Absenteeism, and Turnover   Lack of motivation is often the problem underlying time lost to tardiness and absenteeism. When employees dislike their jobs or find them boring, they tend to use excuses to arrive late or not at all. This lost time is costly. In most cases, the organization is paying for someone who is not actually working. Furthermore, other employees may be unable to work efficiently without the support of the missing person. As a result, minimizing absenteeism and tardiness is an important part of the supervisor's job. (Chapter 16 provides some guidelines for this task.)

Absenteeism may be the first step to leaving the company. The employee misses more and more days, and then finally quits altogether. The rate at which employees leave an organization is known as **turnover**. High turnover is expensive, because the organization must spend a lot of money to recruit and train new employees. For example, according to a recent estimate, it costs $2,500 to replace a hotel worker.[15] Therefore, an important part of controlling costs is to keep good employees with the organization.

Fel-Pro, which manufactures gaskets in the Chicago suburb of Skokie, is known nationwide for retaining employees by offering family-oriented benefits. For example, the company provides tuition benefits to employees and their chil-

turnover
The rate at which employees leave an organization.

dren, has an on-site day-care center, gives employees a $1,000 bond at the birth of a child, and makes summer jobs available for employees' children. Turnover and absenteeism rates at Fel-Pro are lower than at comparable companies, and over one-third of its employees have been with the company for 10 years or more.[16]

Supervisors can minimize turnover by applying the principles of motivation, described in Chapter 9. In general, supervisors should identify what employees want from their job and meet those needs when possible. At Pittsburgh-based G.S.I. Transcomm Data Systems, this means letting employees switch jobs within the company. For example, receptionist Kelly Gezo moved into a sales job and eventually became the company's top salesperson.[17]

Employees' Fears About Productivity Improvement

A highly productive organization is in an ideal position to thrive and grow. Thus, employees can benefit from productivity improvements. This is true especially when efforts to boost productivity focus on improving the quality of processes rather than simply cutting payroll costs. Even so, many employees react with fear when managers start talking about improving productivity.

Employees may have good reason to be fearful. Many have experienced and most have heard of cost reductions that have led to less overtime pay, more difficult work, and even layoffs. For example, AT&T's plan to have a computerized voice-recognition system handle information calls meant the elimination of as many as 6,000 jobs for long-distance operators.[18] When layoffs occur, the people who are left behind often have to struggle to keep up with the work that still has to be done.

Supervisors must respond to these fears. The "Tips from the Firing Line" box provides some suggestions. Most important is to be prepared with information. If a supervisor does not understand the types of changes to be made and the reasons for the changes, the supervisor should discuss the matter with his or her boss as soon as possible. After obtaining a clear view of the organization's plans and goals, the supervisor should present this information to the employees. In doing so, the supervisor should emphasize what the benefits will be and avoid dwelling on the negatives. At AT&T, for example, supervisor Corliss Kyles doubted that customers would like the voice-recognition systems, but she decided not to share her views, for fear of further hurting morale.[19]

Sometimes it is hard to see how individual employees will benefit, but at other times the benefits are clear. At Ingersoll, the manufacturer that updates its equipment every 10 years, the move toward automation has never been intended to reduce the work force. In fact, the number of employees has remained at around 2,000, and their work has become more interesting. For example, machine operators now learn to do maintenance on their machines. As a result, says machinist Terry Coleman, "I understand better how the machine works, and that really helps me do my job. We keep a running list of problems that we could have with the machine and anticipate those problems with our scheduled maintenance."[20]

When the supervisor gives information about productivity improvement, the employees should have an opportunity to ask questions. If the supervisor cannot answer some of the questions, he or she should promise to get answers—and then do so. Although information alone will not make employees enthusiastic about a productivity program, uninformed employees will almost certainly suffer from low morale.

TIPS FROM THE FIRING LINE

Cutting Costs without Hurting Morale

When employees hear about cost cutting, they often think of layoffs and extra work. Not surprisingly, then, cost-cutting efforts can cut into morale. But if supervisors handle the job right, they can minimize the damage. Here are some ideas:

- Explain why cuts are necessary. According to Don Olson, chief executive officer of Virginia Mason Hospital in Seattle, "[Employees] have to see how the budget cuts fit into the overall picture, and they have to sense that they're helping the overall good."
- Watch out for rumors. In many organizations, word of budget cuts leaks out before managers can make official announcements. Once the rumors start flying, employees start getting wrong information. Let employees know you are aware of rumors, give correct information, and invite them to tell you what they are hearing so you can clear up any confusion or mistakes.
- Tell employees how they can benefit. Explain how greater success for the organization can translate into greater benefits for individual employees. Sometimes the primary benefit is simply job security.
- Ask for ideas. When employees participate in decision making, they feel more in control and understand better the limits of what can be

done. In addition, the organization benefits from the creativity of many people.
- Ask for feedback. When you have a plan, tell employees about it and listen to their reactions. You may be able to improve the plan.
- Be a role model. If you enjoy special privileges because you are a supervisor, see if you can lead the way by making sacrifices yourself.
- Focus on the future. When you see problems or mistakes, emphasize how to do better, not who is to blame.
- Be honest. For example, do not say that things will get better in six months unless you really know they will.
- Be patient. It takes a while to feel the benefits of cost cutting.
- Keep employees informed. As costs come down, tell employees about the department's progress. Use specific numbers when you can.
- Show your concern. Talk with and listen to employees about their fears and frustrations related to the cost-cutting efforts. Says Olson, "If your staff knows that you care, you'll get results."

Source: "How to Cut Costs without Cutting Employee Morale," *Employee Relations and Human Resources Bulletin*, October 7, 1991, pp. 6–8.

Summary

10.1   Define *productivity*
Productivity is the amount of results (output) an organization gets for a given amount of inputs such as labor and machinery. Typically, it refers to the amount of acceptable work employees do for each dollar they earn or the number of acceptable products manufactured with a given amount of resources.

10.2   Identify constraints on productivity.
Management limits productivity when it does not seem truly committed to improving it. Employee attitudes and skills limit productivity when employees are unable or unwilling to meet standards for performance. Government regulations impose responsibilities on organizations that limit their productivity to achieve other objectives. At a unionized organization, the union contract may contain work rules that limit productivity.

10.3   Describe how productivity and productivity improvements are measured.
To measure productivity, divide the amount of outputs by the amount of inputs. Outputs are the amount of work done or goods and services pro-

duced, assuming that these are of acceptable quality. Inputs may be measured as dollars, hours, or both. Productivity increases when output increases, input decreases, or both.

10.4   Identify the two basic ways productivity may be improved.
Two ways to improve productivity are to improve quality and to control costs. Controlling costs involves producing the same amount of goods or services at a lower cost or producing more at the same cost.

10.5   Describe cost-control strategies available to supervisors.
The supervisor may increase output by having people or machines work faster or harder. A more effective approach may be to improve methods—that is, to get things done more efficiently. The supervisor may identify ways to reduce overhead and minimize waste, including idle time as well as wasted physical resources. Regulating or leveling the work flow can make staffing more efficient. Installing modern equipment reduces costs when the new equipment is more efficient. To cut costs related to personnel, the supervisor should take steps to minimize tardiness, absenteeism, and turnover.

10.6   Explain why employees have fears about productivity improvement, and tell how supervisors can address those fears.
Many employees are fearful of productivity improvements because many organizations make such changes through layoffs and extra work for the remaining employees. Supervisors can respond by keeping employees informed about the organization's plans, emphasizing the benefits, and listening to employees.

Key Terms

productivity	detour behavior	average rate of return (ARR)
overhead	payback period	turnover
down time (or idle time)		

Review and Discussion Questions

1. What is productivity? Why is it important? Should all organizations, or only for-profit companies, be concerned about productivity? Explain.
2. How can the following groups limit productivity? How can supervisors respond to those constraints?
   a. managers
   b. employees
   c. governments
   d. unions
3. At the claims-processing office for All-Folks Insurance, 25 employees process 2,500 claims a day. The claims-processing office for Purple Cross Insurance uses a state-of-the-art computer system, and its 15 employees process 3,000 claims a day.
   a. Which office is more productive?
   b. At which office would you expect employees to be paid more? Why?
4. In question 3, suppose that half the claims processed by the employees at Purple Cross contain errors and all of the claims processed at All-Folks are done correctly. Which office would you say is more productive? Why?
5. Where can supervisors get information to help them determine costs?
6. How would you expect employees to respond to each of these efforts to cut costs?
   a. a plan to increase output by scheduling fewer rest breaks
   b. a plan to increase output by hiring someone to bring supplies to laboratory workers, rather than having them go after their own supplies
7. What are overhead expenses? Can supervisors control them? Explain.
8. At a telemarketing office, 36 employees make phone calls to people's homes, trying to sell services for the company's clients. When the

employees arrive at work, the supervisor hands each of them a list of the homes that employee is to call. However, the supervisor is sometimes tied up in a meeting or on the phone, so the employees have to wait to get their lists. They use the time to discuss their family or social lives and to carry on a long-running Trivial Pursuit tournament.

What productivity problem is occurring in this office? Suggest at least one way the supervisor can address this problem.

9. How can an even flow of work help productivity?

10. A maintenance supervisor learned that installing a type of high-efficiency light bulb in the building can save the organization $1,000 a year. Replacing the current system with the new one would cost about $2,500.

    a. What is the payback period for this system?

    b. What is the average rate of return?

c. Do you think this is a worthwhile investment? Why or why not?

11. How does high turnover hurt productivity? What can a supervisor do to minimize turnover?

12. Why do employees sometimes resist productivity improvements? How can supervisors prepare for and respond to employees' attitudes?

A SECOND LOOK

In the story of Jinny Bray at the beginning of this chapter, building codes are considered a constraint on the productivity of her construction company. In what ways, if any, might Bray be able to overcome this constraint?

Class Exercise

This class exercise requires supplies: jigsaw puzzles, one for each five or six students in the class. Puzzles with no more than 500 pieces would probably work best.

Divide the class into groups of six to eight students. Each group works on its puzzle for a length of time agreed on for the whole class, such as 15 minutes.

When time is up, the class discusses the following questions:

1. Compare the productivity of the groups. How will you measure productivity? When the whole class agrees on a proper measure, each group computes its own productivity.

2. Which group was most productive? Why? Did it use methods that could have helped the other groups?

3. How could you have improved the productivity of your group?

CASE

Productivity Improvements at Harley-Davidson

For decades Harley-Davidson made motorcycles according to the old standards of mass production. Setting up big milling machines took hours or even days, so the company tried to reduce idle time by making as many of a single type of part as it could before moving on to another. Typically, the company kept about three months' worth of parts on hand waiting to be used when other components had been made. During the wait, some of the parts would rust, and minor flaws that kept parts from fitting together might go undetected. In addition, management expected that some parts would contain defects, so Harley hired inspectors to spot errors and workers to correct them.

This approach seemed to work just fine, until Harley lost a big share of its market to competition from Japan. The competitors produced better-quality motorcycles at a lower cost. Harley's managers took a careful look at how the Japanese competitors were operating. They learned that there were fresh ways to improve the manufacturing process. According to Vaughn Beals, the company's chairman, "We discovered that the key reason for our lack of competitiveness was poor management....We were being wiped out by the Japanese because they were better managers...who understood their business and paid attention to detail."

First, the company learned that setup times for machines were not fixed, as management had thought. Harley determined how employees could change over production machines quickly and easily. This meant that the company could produce smaller lots of parts to be immediately assembled. As a result, problems could be detected faster, and the company did not have to pay for a lot of storage space.

The company also rethought the way work was done. Machines were grouped into cells containing everything needed to make a particular part. Each cell is overseen by one operator. This means that parts no longer need to be hauled around the factory to get to the machines that do each type of process. Instead, certain employees are responsible for delivering finished parts to assembly-line workers.

Management sought employees' advice on solving production problems. Line workers also can stop production of parts that are not meeting specifications and make the necessary adjustments without checking with their supervisor.

With its manufacturing changes, Harley has been able to cut its costs and improve its quality. For example, the time it takes the company to build a motorcycle frame has fallen from 30 days to 2 days. The company has regained some of its lost market share. Employees are happy, too. Says production worker Jerome Szczepanski, "I like this better than the old way. There's more to do."

1. What cost- and quality-control strategies can you identify in this case?
2. Imagine that you were a supervisor at Harley-Davidson at the time the company began making changes in how it manufactures motorcycles. How would you present the changes to your employees? What would you tell them or not tell them?
3. The case does not describe specifically the job of supervisors at Harley, but read between the lines. How do you think supervisors' jobs changed as a result of the productivity improvements? For example, what kinds of problems do you think supervisors handled before and after? Do supervisors have more or less control? More or less interesting jobs?

Sources: Christopher Boehme, "Harley-Davidson's Long Marriage of Mechanics and Art," *Northwest Airlines Magazine*, November 1991, pp. 22–28; Jon Van, "Mass Production Is Out; Quality, Skills Are In," *Chicago Tribune*, November 3, 1991, sec. 1, pp. 1, 12–13; and Jon Van, "Leaks No Longer Stain Harley-Davidson Name," *Chicago Tribune*, November 4, 1991, sec. 1, p. 6.

11

Every moment spent in planning saves three or four in execution.
—Crawford Greenwalt

Managing Time and Stress

LEARNING OBJECTIVES

11.1 Describe how supervisors can evaluate their use of time.

11.2 Describe ways to plan the use of time.

11.3 Identify some time wasters and how to control them.

11.4 Describe sources and consequences of stress.

11.5 Identify factors that cause stress in employees.

11.6 Explain how supervisors can personally manage stress.

11.7 Identify ways organizations help their employees manage stress.

PRIORITIZING GETS AN A

Alfred E. Clark is principal of Cregier Vocational High School in Chicago, where he supervises 110 employees, including 47 teachers and 23 nursing instructors, as well as assistant principals, counselors, and other support staff. Many Cregier students perform six to eight grades below their grade level, and a number of the students have been identified as having learning or behavior disorders. Besides the standard high school education, the school offers a program to train high schoolers and adults to become licensed practical nurses.

Juggling the complex and diverse needs of this group of employees and students would overwhelm many people, but Clark keeps on top of his responsibilities. He emphasizes planning as the way to do so. Clark sets priorities and schedules his activities according to what is most important; the top priority, says Clark, is to "stay focused on the children." In addition, previous training in the military taught Clark to expect the unexpected and be ready for crises.

Clark's organized approach to the way he uses time allows him not only to fulfill his role as principal but also to spend time with his family and to coach semipro football. That well-rounded approach to life also helps him cope with the stresses of his job. Clark tries to leave the tensions of the workplace behind when he leaves each day, and he works off stress through physical activity such as swimming and power walking.

On a bad day, it feels as though everything is out of control. Instead of working on what he or she wanted to, the supervisor attempts to solve unexpected problems and soothe upset employees and customers. While workdays like this affect employees and managers at all levels, they are a particular problem for supervisors, because the supervisor's people-oriented job means there are many needs and conflicts. To minimize and cope with these difficult times, supervisors must manage time and stress.

This chapter describes basic techniques of time management and stress management. It identifies ways supervisors can control how they use time. Then it discusses what stress is and how supervisors can cope with it themselves and help employees cope with it.

Time Management

Sean Mulligan's typical day is hectic. Just when he gets on the phone, someone is at the door with a problem, and he almost never finds the time to sit down and ponder the problem. By the end of the day, Sean is exhausted, but he would be hard-pressed to say what he accomplished. Lisa Ng's days are also busy, but when someone interrupts her, Lisa pulls out her calendar and makes an appointment for later. She starts out each day knowing what tasks are essential, and she always manages to complete them.

Which kind of supervisor would you rather have working for you? Which kind would you rather be? Time is the only resource we all have in equal shares: everyone gets 24-hour days. To evaluate your own responses to time pressures, take the Self-Quiz.

Supervisors who are in control of the way they use their time find that their jobs are easier and that they can get more done. Needless to say, getting a lot done is a good way to impress higher-level management. The practice of controlling the way you use time is known as **time management**.

time management
The practice of controlling the way you use time.

Time management techniques can be as simple as putting things away as soon as you are done with them, using an appointment calendar to keep track of your schedule, and getting all the information you need *before* you start on a project.[1] This chapter provides broad guidelines for time management; the details, of course, are up to each supervisor. Lisa Kanarek, a Dallas-based professional organizer who gives seminars and individual advice on getting organized, says, "There's not just one way to get organized…because no two people can work the same way."[2]

Understanding How You Use Time

Before you can take control over the way you use time, you have to understand what you are already doing. A practical way to learn about your use of time is to keep a **time log**. This is a record of what activities you are doing hour by hour throughout the workday. Figure 11.1 on page 265, provides an example. Each half-hour during the day, write down what you did during the previous half-hour. Do not wait until the end of the day; this level of detail is too difficult to remember.

time log
A record of what activities a person is doing hour by hour throughout the day.

SELF-QUIZ *How Does Time Pressure Affect You?*

To assess the degree to which time pressure influences your life, answer all questions by circling the number of the best alternative, even if no single answer seems exactly right.

1. In a typical week, how often do you wear a watch?
    (1) regularly   (2) part of the time   (3) occasionally   (4) almost never

2. How many hours do you sleep in an average week night?
    (1) 5 or less   (2) 6   (3) 7   (4) 8 or more

3. When driving, how often do you speed?
    (1) regularly   (2) often   (3) seldom   (4) almost never

4. While driving, as you approach a green traffic signal that is turning to yellow, you are most likely to:
    (1) speed up to get through before it turns to red
    (4) slow down and wait for it to turn green

5. (1) When I have a train or plane to catch, I like to arrive as close as possible to the departure time so I won't have to waste time sitting around.
    (4) I always try to leave extra time to get to an airport or train station so I won't have to worry about missing a flight or train.

6. (1) At a restaurant, I like my food served as soon as possible after I've ordered.   (4) I don't mind waiting a few minutes for the food I've ordered.

7. (1) I like microwave ovens because they cut down on meal preparation time.
    (4) I'd rather spend extra time preparing meals than use a microwave oven regularly.

8. (1) I often use a remote-control device to scan a lot of television channels to see what's on.   (4) To me, a remote-control is a convenient tool for turning the TV on or off from a distance, adjusting the volume, or occasionally changing channels.

9. (1) With so many other demands on my time, I find it hard to keep up friendships.   (4) I try to make time to see my friends regularly.

10. Compared with your life 10 years ago, would you say you have more or less leisure time?
    (1) less   (2) about the same   (3) a bit more   (4) a lot more

11. How would you compare the amount of time you spend running errands today with the amount you spent 10 years ago?
    (1) more   (2) about the same   (3) somewhat less   (4) a lot less

12. During the past year, how many books have you read for pleasure from beginning to end?
    (1) 0–2   (2) 3–5   (3) 6–10   (4) 11 or more

13. How good are you at glancing at your watch or a clock without anyone noticing?
    (1) very good   (2) good   (3) fair   (4) not good at all

14. How would you rate your ability to conduct a conversation and appear to be paying attention while thinking about something else at the same time?
    (1) excellent   (2) good   (3) fair   (4) poor

15. How often do you find yourself interrupting the person with whom you're talking?
    (1) regularly (2) often (3) occasionally (4) rarely

16. When talking on the telephone, do you:
    (1) do paperwork, wash dishes or do some other chore? (2) straighten up the surrounding area? (3) do small personal tasks (e.g., file nails, reset watch)? (4) do nothing else?

17. In an average week, how many evening or weekend hours do you spend working overtime or on work you've brought home?
    (1) 16 or more (2) 11–15 (3) 6–10 (4) 0–5

18. On a typical weekend, do you engage primarily in:
    (1) work for income? (2) errands, household chores, and child care? (3) leisure activities? (4) catching up on sleep and relaxation?

19. In a typical year, how many weeks of paid vacation do you take?
    (1) 1 or less (2) 2 (3) 3 (4) 4 or more

20. On the whole, how do you find vacations?
    (1) frustrating (2) tedious (3) relaxing (4) rejuvenating

21. How often do you find yourself wishing you had more time to spend with family and friends?
    (1) constantly (2) often (3) occasionally (4) almost never

22. During a typical day, how often do you feel rushed?
    (1) constantly (2) often (3) occasionally (4) almost never

23. Which statement best describes your usual daily schedule?
    (1) There aren't enough hours in the day to do everything I have to do.
    (2) On the whole I have enough time to do what I have to do. (3) I can usually do the things I have to do with time left over. (4) The day seems to have more hours than I'm able to fill.

24. During the past year, how would you say your life has grown?
    (1) busier (2) about the same (3) somewhat less busy (4) a lot less busy

Add the total of all numbers circled. A score of 25–40 indicates you are *timelocked*; 41–55, *pressed for time*; 56–71, *in balance*; 72–86, *time on hands*.

Source: "How Does Time Pressure Affect You?" from TIMELOCK by Ralph Keyes. Copyright © 1991 by Ralph Keyes. Reprinted by permission of HarperCollins Publishers, Inc.

After you have kept a time log for at least one typical week, review your log. Ask yourself the following questions:

- How much time did I spend on important activities?
- How much time did I spend on activities that did not need to get done?
- How much time did I spend on activities that someone else could have done (perhaps with some training)?
- What important jobs did I not get around to finishing?

FIGURE 11.1

Format for a Time Log

Date: _____

Time	Activity	Others Involved	Location
7:30–8:00			
8:00–8:30			
8:30–9:00			
9:00–9:30			
9:30–10:00			
10:00–10:30			
10:30–11:00			
11:00–11:30			
11:30–12:00			
12:00–12:30			
12:30–1:00			
1:00–1:30			
1:30–2:00			
2:00–2:30			
2:30–3:00			
3:00–3:30			
3:30–4:00			
4:00–4:30			
4:30–5:00			
5:00–5:30			

From your review, you may see some patterns. Do you have a certain time of day for phone calls or meetings? Do you frequently interrupt what you are doing to solve a problem or move on to something more interesting? Do you tackle the most important jobs first or the easiest ones? Answers to questions such as these will help you see the areas in which you need to change. After you have tried applying the principles in this chapter for a while, you might want to try keeping a time log again in order to see how you have improved.

Keeping a time log is also helpful for people who feel out of control of their personal time. For example, if you are frustrated at not spending enough time with loved ones or cannot seem to find the time for charitable work, you can keep a log of how you use your hours outside of work. You may find that you are spending a lot of time on an unimportant activity that you can let go of to free time for something else.

Planning Your Use of Time

Based on what you learned from keeping a time log, you can plan how to better use your time. Although few of us would want to achieve the level of time management portrayed in Figure 11.2, you need to make sure that the most important things get done each day before you move on to less important activities. To do so, you need to set priorities. Thus, your planning consists of deciding what you need to do and which activities are most important. This is the practice recommended by principal Alfred E. Clark in the description at the beginning of this chapter.

Planning your use of time begins with the planning process described in Chapter 2. If you follow the guidelines in that chapter, you will routinely establish objectives for the year, specifying when each must be completed. With these yearly

FIGURE 11.2

A Superhuman Level of Time Management

Source: © 1992 by Nicole Hollander. Reprinted with permission.

Take Up the Slack

Slack periods at work are unproductive. Here are a few ideas to turn those wasted hours into productive time:

- *Prepare a list of fill-in tasks in advance*, so you will be ready when someone has run out of work.
- *Conduct training sessions on certain jobs* or on the use of certain tools or machinery.

- *Make sure necessary supplies are in proper order* for all workers in the department.
- *Teach employees the job skills of others*, when people are absent, others can step in for them.
- *Clean up and organize your work area.*

Source: "Take Up the Slack," *Front Line Supervisor's Bulletin*, May 25, 1992, p. 3.

objectives in mind, you can figure out what you need to accomplish in shorter time periods—each quarter, month, and week. Review your objectives regularly, and use them to plan what you will need to accomplish each week and day.

Making a "To Do" List Many people find it helpful to spend a few minutes at the end of each week writing a "to do" list of what they must accomplish during the next week. When you have made a list of things to do, write an *A* next to all the activities that must be completed that week; these are your top priorities. Then write a *B* next to all the activities that are important but can be postponed if necessary. Label everything else *C*; these are your lowest priorities for the week. Schedule times for doing your A-level and B-level activities. If you have more time, you will work on your C-level activities. The "Tips from the Firing Line" box provides some ideas of activities to do when you or your employees have extra time to fill. As you complete each activity on the "to do" list, check it off.

How do you know when is the best time to do the activities on your list? Here are some guidelines to follow for creating weekly and daily schedules:

- First record all the activities that must take place at a set time. For example, you do not have any choice about when to schedule your regular Monday morning staff meeting or the appointment you made with your boss for three o'clock on Thursday.
- Next, find times for your remaining A-level activities. Try to avoid scheduling them at the end of the day (on a daily plan) or week (on a weekly plan). If a crisis comes up, you will need another chance to finish these activities. Schedule your B-level activities next.
- Schedule the most challenging and most important activities for the times of day when you are at your best. If you are sleepy after lunch or get off to a slow start in the morning, schedule top-priority activities for times when you are more alert. Consultant Tom Peters reports that when writing a recent book, he worked from 4:00 A.M. to 7:30 A.M., napped for an hour, and then returned to work. He thus benefited from his most creative time, between 4:00 A.M. and 11:00 A.M.[3]
- Schedule time for thinking, not just for doing. Remember from Chapter 8 that the creative process requires time for reflection.

- Do not fill up every hour of the day and week. Leave some time free to handle unexpected problems and questions from your employees and others. If problems do not occur, so much the better. You will have time for the C-level activities.

Planning with a Computer   A supervisor who has access to a computer will be able to benefit from time management software. For example, PowerCore's *Network Scheduler 3* allows users of a computer network (personal computers linked together to share information) to plan their own time and to coordinate their time with others on the network. Among its many features, the program lets each user fill in information on calendars and "to do" lists and review it later, as well as look at multiple calendars to see when everyone is available for a meeting or other group activity. (A security feature enables individual users to keep their peers from reading private information.) The user can look at a calendar for a month, a week, or a single day and can have the computer emit an alarm when it is time for a specified appointment.

Other kinds of software also can help the supervisor with time management. A type of program known as a desktop organizer can dial the phone and keep records of calls made, let the supervisor take notes and print them out later, and perform a number of calendaring functions similar to those described for *Network Scheduler 3*. Some desktop organizer programs are *Sidekick*, *Agenda*, and *WordPerfect Library/Office*. In addition, the Windows operating system includes some desktop organizer features.

Controlling Time Wasters

Many supervisors find that certain activities and attitudes are what most often leads them to waste time. As illustrated in Figure 11.3, the most common time wasters are meetings, phone calls, paperwork, unscheduled visitors, procrastination, perfectionism, failure to delegate, and inability to say no. Notice that some of the activities are necessary; the problem is that the supervisor does not always handle them wisely. To manage time well, the supervisor needs to get control over these potential time wasters.

Meetings   The main reason many supervisors hate meetings is that meetings often waste time. People slowly drift into the room, then devote time to chatting while waiting for latecomers or catching up on yesterday's sporting events or social life. When the formal meeting finally gets under way, the discussion may drift off onto tangents, and perhaps the group never even completes the task that it gathered to carry out. Meetings like these are understandably a source of frustration.

When you attend a meeting chaired by someone else, it is hard to control wasted time. You can encourage careful use of time by being prompt. If meetings tend to start late, you might bring along some reading material or other work to do while you wait. If the discussion at the meeting seems irrelevant, you might try tactfully asking the speaker to explain how the current discussion will help in accomplishing the goal of the meeting.

When you call a meeting, you can use time wisely by starting promptly. If the discussion veers off course, politely remind participants about the subject at hand.

FIGURE 11.3

Common Time
Wasters

Meetings   Procrastination

Phone Calls   Perfectionism

Paperwork   Failure to Delegate

Unscheduled Visitors   Inability to Say No

It is also smart to set an ending time for the meeting. If you cannot solve the problem in the time allotted, schedule a follow-up meeting. (Chapter 17 provides more ideas for holding effective meetings.)

Phone Calls   Usually when other people call you, they have no way of knowing whether the time is convenient. Consequently, most of us get phone calls when we are busy with something else. Because they often interrupt the flow of work, telephone calls can be time wasters.

One way to take control of your time is to remember that you are not a slave to the telephone. If someone such as a secretary is available to screen your calls, have that person answer your phone when you are working on top-priority jobs. If you answer the phone while you are in a meeting or involved in something important, explain to the caller that you cannot give the call the attention it deserves at that time, and schedule a time to call back when it will be convenient for both of you. Of course, you have to use this approach carefully. If the person calling is your boss or a customer, the phone call may be your top priority.

When you are placing calls yourself, think ahead. Schedule time for making calls each day, keeping in mind different time zones if you are calling long-distance. Before you call someone, make sure you have the information you will need close at hand. It does not make sense to call a client and then place that person on hold while you run to get the file containing the answers he or she wanted. Not only does that waste time, it annoys the person who has to wait. If the person you are calling is not available, ask when you can reach him or her, rather than simply leaving a message. That way, you have control over when the call will be made.

The phone can be a time saver as well as a time waster. When you have a meeting or appointment on your calendar, call to confirm it. If you need to meet with someone away from the workplace, call to get directions rather than waste time by driving around and looking for the meeting place.[4]

To avoid distractions at the office and to reduce commuting time and expense, increasing numbers of employees are working at home. Illinois Bell Telephone Company has initiated a Work-at-Home Planning Center.

Source: Courtesy of Mark Joseph, photographer.

Paperwork and Reading Material   Supervisors spend a lot of time reading and writing. They receive mail, reports, and magazines to read, and they must prepare reports, letters, and memos to send to others. Reading and writing are not necessarily a waste of time, of course. But many supervisors do these activities inefficiently, so they become time wasters.

Most advice on how to manage paperwork is based on the principle of handling each item only once. Set aside time just to read all the papers that cross your desk. At that time, decide whether each item is something you need to act on. If not, throw it away immediately. If you must act, then decide on the most efficient response. An efficient way to respond to a memo is to write a brief response across the top and return the memo to the sender. If you have a secretary, you can keep a tape recorder by your side and dictate responses to letters as you read them. Or consider whether you can respond to a letter with a phone call. If you learn that you must set time aside to do research or prepare a report, then schedule that time immediately.

With regard to reading material, most supervisors have a multitude of magazines, newsletters, and newspapers to choose from. Each supervisor will find that some of these are very helpful, others somewhat helpful, and still others not relevant to his or her work. To cut time spent wading through the unhelpful publications, the supervisor should decide which ones are useful and cancel subscriptions to the rest. With the publications that are somewhat helpful, it is wise to look at the table of contents for relevant information rather than turn every page. If the supervisor finds that an internal report he or she receives is not providing useful information, the supervisor might do several people in the organization a favor by asking to be taken off the distribution list.

Unscheduled Visitors   Supervisors are interrupted at times by unscheduled visitors. These may be customers, peers, employees, salespeople, or anyone else who turns up without an appointment. Because seeing these people is an unplanned use of time, the interruptions can interfere with getting the job done. Figure 11.4 shows some broad guidelines for handling this potential problem.

When the supervisor regularly spends time with unscheduled visitors on unimportant matters, a lot of time gets wasted. As with other potential time wasters, the key is to know which interruptions are important. For example, if an angry customer demanding to see the manager interrupts a supervisor in a store, an important part of the supervisor's job is to make that customer happy. If a supervisor's boss occasionally drops in to discuss an idea, the supervisor will probably have to work around the boss's schedule. But when a co-worker in another department stops in to report on his vacation or a salesperson shows up unannounced, the interruption is not such a high priority.

With low-priority interruptions, the supervisor needs to diplomatically take control over his or her time. In the case of the co-worker back from vacation, the supervisor might say, "It's great to hear you had fun last week. Why don't we have lunch together so you can tell me all about it?" When salespeople call without an appointment, the supervisor can ask them simply to leave some literature. Another response to unscheduled visitors is to set a time limit. For example, the supervisor might say, "I've got five minutes. What's on your mind?" If the problem seems to deserve more time, the supervisor can arrange to meet the visitor later.

A similar tactic applies to the related problem that occurs when people stop at the supervisor's desk and ask, "Can you spare a minute?" The request sounds so small, but soon the minute has grown to an hour as the supervisor listens to the person and tries to help with the problem. The supervisor's defense can be to take the request literally. Say, "Sure, I can spare a minute," then look at your watch. When a minute is up, say, "I'm sorry, but I really can't spend more than a minute on this right now. Let's schedule another time to talk." Then do so.[5]

Standing is a useful signal. If you see an unwanted visitor heading toward your office, stand and meet the visitor at your door, then talk to him or her there. This sends a message that you expect the conversation to be brief. Meeting with someone else at his or her desk or a conference room allows you to get up and leave when you have completed your business. If you meet with someone in your office, standing up when you finish sends a signal that the meeting is over.

Interruptions from employees can be tricky to handle. Part of the supervisor's job is to listen to employees and help them with work-related problems. At the same time, a constant stream of interruptions may mean that employees have too little training or authority to handle their work. If an employee interrupts with problems, one approach is to listen and then ask, "What do you suggest we do about that?" This shows the employee that the supervisor expects him or her to participate in finding solutions. With practice, the employee may learn to handle problems more independently. If the problem is not urgent—for example, if it is not holding up the employee's work—the supervisor may want to schedule a later time when supervisor and employee can meet to work on the problem. At that time, of course, the supervisor should give priority to the meeting with the employee and discourage inter-

FIGURE 11.4

Handling Unscheduled Visitors

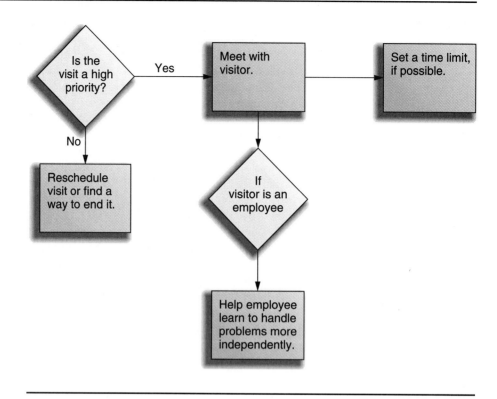

ruptions from others. Employees will learn that the supervisor will listen and work with them, though not necessarily on a moment's notice.

Procrastination Sometimes it is hard to get around to starting an activity. Maybe you have to write a proposal to buy a new computer system. You are not quite sure how to write that kind of proposal, so you are grateful when the telephone rings. You chat on the phone for a while, and that conversation reminds you that you need to follow up on an order with one of your suppliers. So you make another phone call. You get up to stretch your legs and decide it is a good time to check on how your employees are doing. Bit by bit, in this way, you manage to get through the entire day without doing any work on the proposal. This process of putting off what needs to be done is called **procrastination**.

Procrastination is a time waster because it leads people to spend their time on low-priority activities while they avoid the higher priorities. The best cure for procrastination is to force yourself to jump in. To do that, focus on one step at a time. Decide what the first step is, and then do that step. Then do the next step. You will find that you are building momentum and that the big job no longer feels so overwhelming. If you need more incentive to get started, set deadlines for completing each step, and give yourself a reward for completing each step. For example, you might decide that as soon as you complete the first step, you will go for a walk in the sunshine, call a customer who loves your product, or take a break to open your

procrastination
Putting off what needs to be done.

Standing is a useful signal to keep conversations short.

Source: © 1993 Comstock, Inc.

mail. If the project seems thoroughly unpleasant, you can concentrate on the rewards. Of course, the ultimate reward will be finishing the job.

Perfectionism   One reason people put off doing necessary work is that they are afraid what they do will not live up to their standards. Although high standards can inspire high performance, perfectionism can make people afraid to try at all. **Perfectionism** is the attempt to do things perfectly. It may sound like a noble goal, but human beings are imperfect. Expecting to be perfect therefore dooms a person to failure.

perfectionism
The attempt to do things perfectly.

Instead of being a slave to perfectionism, determine the highest standard you can realistically achieve. You may be able to meet a higher standard by drawing on the expertise of employees and peers. When you find yourself avoiding a difficult task, remind yourself that your goals are realistic, and then give the job your best try.

Failure to Delegate   Perfectionism often underlies the failure to delegate work. Even when someone else can do a job more efficiently in terms of that person's cost and availability, a supervisor may resist delegating because the supervisor believes he or she is the only one who can really do the job right. This attitude stands in the way of appropriate delegating. The result in terms of time management is that the supervisor has too much to do. Instead, the supervisor should delegate effectively, as described in Chapter 3.

Rebecca Liss, a branch operations manager for Kemper Securities, uses delegation as one of her major strategies for time management. Liss's office must cope with a rush of business at the end of each trading day. Offers to buy and sell stock must be placed immediately, before the prices change, but many customers call in their orders during the last 5 or 10 minutes before the stock market closes. To manage under the pressure, Liss delegates, realizing also that if her employees make mistakes, that is a way for them to learn. "If you can't manage your time," says Liss, "you can't get the job done."

Inability to Say No To control your use of time, you must be able to say no when appropriate. However, it is easy to let other people and their demands control how we use our time, so we end up overextending ourselves by taking on more tasks than we can possibly do well. How do you react when someone asks you to chair a committee, manage a new project, or take an active role in a local charity? Most people are uncomfortable saying no when the opportunity is for a worthwhile project or they do not want to hurt somebody's feelings. But when we take on too many things, we cannot do our best at any of them.

If someone comes to you with an opportunity that will require a significant commitment of time, learn to tell the person politely that you will consider the offer and will reply at some specific time, say, by the end of the week. Then assess what you are already committed to and what your priorities are. Decide whether you should agree to take on this new task. In some cases you will decide you have time for it. In other instances you will decide you do not have enough time to do justice to the new task, and you will have to decline. If your life is already busy but the opportunity seems important, it can be useful to ask, "What activity am I willing to give up in order to make time for this new one?"

Whatever you decide, this thoughtful approach does both yourself and the other person a favor. If you do not have the time to complete a task well and on time, it is better to give the other person a chance to find somebody else to take on the task. None of us like to find out that the person we have been counting on is overcommitted and just does not have enough time to get the job done right. It is generally easier to look for someone else in the first place.

Stress Management

Failure to manage time wisely is one reason supervisors find their jobs difficult. It is frustrating to leave the workplace knowing that you did not accomplish anything you really wanted to that day. Supervisors also find it difficult to hear a lot of complaints, to work in a dangerous environment, and to try living up to unrealistic expectations. To cope in such situations, supervisors can use the techniques of stress management.

Stress

stress
The body's response to coping with environmental demands.

Conditions such as a dangerous workplace, high expectations, and frequent complaints can lead to stress. In this sense, **stress** refers to the body's response to coping with environmental demands. People experiencing stress typically undergo such physiological changes as faster heartbeat, higher blood pressure, and muscle tension. Such responses are adapted to the kinds of challenges faced by early peoples, who would need to run from or physically fight many kinds of danger, such as wild animals.

Certain occupations, such as air traffic controlling, can generate high levels of stress. Technological advances such as this Hughes-built common controller work station for the Canadian Automated Air Traffic System are being designed to relieve stress in such occupations.

Source: Courtesy of Hughes Aircraft of Canada, Ltd.

In general, people experience stress when they must cope with such environmental demands as change, frustration, uncertainty, danger, or discomfort. Usually when we think of stress, we think of the response to problems—for example, arguments, cold, or long hours of work. But stress also results from the challenges that stimulate us and from the happy changes in our lives. Thus, buying a car is stressful, and so is getting married or promoted.

Consequences of Stress Stress is a fact of life. Indeed, life would be boring without some sources of stress, and most people seek out some degree of stress. For example, some people are attracted to jobs billed as challenging or exciting—the ones likely to be most stressful. In fact, as Figure 11.5 shows, employees tend to perform best when they are experiencing a moderate degree of stress. Challenging goals or exciting work leads people to do their best.

But too much stress brings problems, especially when the sources of stress are negative (for example, a critical boss or unsafe working conditions). As Figure 11.5 shows, performance falls when the amount of stress moves from moderate to high. In a highly stressful environment, people are more apt to come down with heart disease, high blood pressure, ulcers, and possibly other diseases. Because of illness and unhappiness, they take more time off from work. When employees are at work, the sources of stress may be distractions that keep them from doing their best and may make them prone to having accidents.

Besides hurting the organization through poor performance and attendance, excess stress can hurt employees as individuals. People experiencing stress tend to feel anxious, aggressive, frustrated, tense, and moody. They may be overly sensitive to criticism and have trouble making decisions. Such people may be more likely to

FIGURE 11.5

Stress Levels and Performance

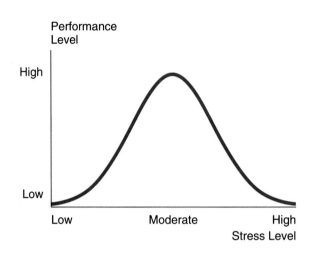

have trouble maintaining mutually satisfying relationships with loved ones, including spouses and children. They may be unable to get enough sleep. People under stress are also at risk for abusing drugs and alcohol.

Because of all these potential negative consequences of stress, it is important for supervisors to notice when employees seem to be experiencing more stress than they can handle effectively. Table 11.1 lists some signs that indicate when employees may be experiencing excess stress. If some of these signs exist, the supervisor should try reducing the stress employees are experiencing and might recommend some coping techniques. (Some approaches to stress management are described later in the chapter.)

burnout
The inability to function effectively as a result of ongoing stress.

Burnout When a person cannot cope with stress over an extended period of time, the person may experience burnout. **Burnout** is the inability to function effectively as a result of ongoing stress. Employees who are burned out feel drained and have lost interest in doing their job. Typically, burnout occurs in three stages:

1. The employee feels emotionally exhausted.
2. The employee's perceptions of others become calloused.
3. The employee views his or her effectiveness negatively.

Being burned out is worse than just needing to take a vacation. Therefore, it is important to cope with stress before it leads to burnout.

Some signs of excess stress that may indicate burnout are listed in Table 11.1. When a supervisor observes these signs, the supervisor should not only seek to reduce stress, as described earlier, but should also be sure that employees are being rewarded for their efforts. Burnout is especially likely to occur when people feel they are giving of themselves all the time, with little or no returns. It is thus especially common among employees in the helping professions such as health care and teaching.

TABLE 11.1

Possible Signs of Excess Stress

Decline in work performance

Increase in use of sick days

Increase in number of errors and accidents

Moodiness and irritability

Fatigue

Loss of enthusiasm

Aggressive behavior

Difficulty making decisions

Family problems

Apparent loss of concern for others and their feelings*

Feeling that it's impossible to help other people*

Feeling of inability to get your job done fully or well*

*Possible signs of burnout

Causes of Stress   Why do some people suffer more from stress than others? The obvious possible reasons are that some people have characteristics that make them more prone to stress and that some people live or work in conditions that produce more stress. That is, some people can tolerate more stress than others, and some jobs cause more stress than others. The "Dealing with Diversity" box describes a way in which some women, for example, are particularly vulnerable to stress.

Some medical researchers have observed that the people who are more likely to have heart disease (presumably a sign of stress) tend to have a similar kind of personality. The researchers named this the Type-A personality. A **Type-A personality** refers to someone who is constantly trying to get a lot done in a hurry. The traits associated with this personality type are listed in Table 11.2. Research suggests that some Type-A people seem to thrive on their approach to life, whereas others—the ones prone to heart disease—have an excess amount of hostility. To help those at risk develop new patterns of behavior, physicians often recommend adopting contrasting traits, known as a Type-B personality. Type-B traits also are listed in Table 11.2.

Besides personal characteristics, some job factors have been linked to stress. These include the factors shown in Figure 11.6. Stress-causing job factors involve the organization's policies, structures, physical conditions, and processes (the way work gets done). Which of the factors would you expect a supervisor to be able to control?

Type-A personality
A description of someone who is constantly trying to get a lot done in a hurry.

Personal Stress Management

Pat Shahrrava supervises the nurses in a hospital's intensive care unit, and Felipe Munoz supervises a crew of fire fighters. Both of these jobs are highly stressful by nature; the organizations cannot take the stress out of fighting fires or providing intensive care in a hospital. Therefore, both supervisors must find personal ways to

DEALING WITH DIVERSITY

Stress from Work–Home Conflicts

A survey of 311 female nurses aged 50 to 70 found that women who feel tension between demands from work and demands from home are at higher risk than other women of having serious heart disease. The risk was not associated with what the women achieved or how hard they worked, but with the degree to which they felt a conflict between career and family. At greatest risk were the women who believed that having a family interfered with advancement in their career.

These results are consistent with other studies that have found that people are more likely to have heart attacks if they hold high-demand, low-control jobs. In other words, these people work under demanding conditions, but they have relatively little control over those conditions. Nursing and caring for a family are both high-demand jobs. If people find that one of those jobs hurts their advancement in the other, they could be said to have low control in juggling the two.

Fortunately, there are some ways employees, male as well as female, can balance work and family responsibilities. A good start is to set priorities. For example, different people will have different views about whether it is worth moving or working weekends to get a promotion. Then set aside time for the things you consider important, including scheduling time for family members as well as meetings. When another request conflicts with family time, a good response is simply, "I have other commitments at that time." Finally, it is less frustrating to be realistic than to expect yourself to handle everything. Rather than criticizing yourself for what you do not do, make an effort to give yourself a pat on the back for all the times you strike a balance between home and work commitments.

Sources: Marilyn Elias, "Women's Job, Home Conflicts Raise Heart Risk," *USA Today*, March 3, 1992, p. 1D; and Daniel D. Shade, "Balancing Work and Family: Suggestions from a Tightrope Walker," *Healthcare Trends & Transition*, January 1992, p. 55.

TABLE 11.2 **Behavior Patterns Associated with Type-A and Type-B Personalities**	Type A	Type B
	Moving, walking, eating rapidly	Having varied interests
	Feeling impatient with people who move slower than you	Taking a relaxed but active approach to life
	Feeling impatient when others talk about something that is not of interest to you	
	Doing two or three things at the same time	
	Feeling unable to relax or to stop working	
	Trying to get more and more done in less and less time	

Source: Adapted from Meyer Friedman and Ray H. Rosenman, *Type A Behavior and Your Heart* (New York: Fawcett Crest, 1974), pp. 100–101, summarized in Jane Whitney Gibson, *The Supervisory Challenge: Principles and Practices* (Columbus, Ohio: Merrill Publishing, 1990), p. 309.

manage the stress in their lives. A variety of techniques are available for personal stress management. These include time management (discussed in the first part of this chapter), exercise, biofeedback, meditation, and well-rounded life activities.

FIGURE 11.6

Job Factors Linked to Stress

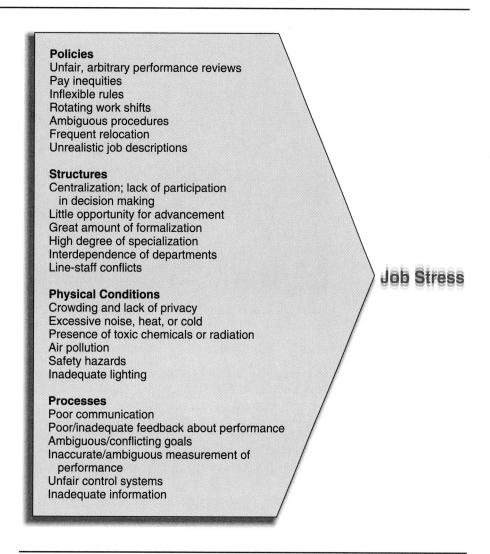

Policies
Unfair, arbitrary performance reviews
Pay inequities
Inflexible rules
Rotating work shifts
Ambiguous procedures
Frequent relocation
Unrealistic job descriptions

Structures
Centralization; lack of participation
    in decision making
Little opportunity for advancement
Great amount of formalization
High degree of specialization
Interdependence of departments
Line-staff conflicts

Physical Conditions
Crowding and lack of privacy
Excessive noise, heat, or cold
Presence of toxic chemicals or radiation
Air pollution
Safety hazards
Inadequate lighting

Processes
Poor communication
Poor/inadequate feedback about performance
Ambiguous/conflicting goals
Inaccurate/ambiguous measurement of
    performance
Unfair control systems
Inadequate information

Job Stress

Source: Samuel C. Certo, *Modern Management: Quality, Ethics, and the Global Environment.* Copyright © 1992 by Allyn and Bacon. Reprinted with permission.

Exercise Experts on stress believe that the human body developed a stress response to help people handle dangerous situations. For early peoples, such situations might have included storms or attacks by wild animals. The two basic responses available are to either fight the danger or run away. For this reason, the physical changes in response to stress are known as a "fight-or-flight syndrome." Specifically, the body responds to stress with an increased heart rate, faster breathing, greater perspiration, increased blood pressure, greater muscle strength, and decreased gastric (stomach) functioning, among other changes.

Because the body's response to stress is to get ready for physical action, it makes sense that one way to respond to workplace stress is to look for an outlet

To manage stress, some workers find it helpful to participate in sports before or after work.

Source: Courtesy of Chuck Kuhn/The Image Bank.

through physical activity. Although it is rarely if ever appropriate to punch your boss when he or she criticizes you or to run away when clients complain, other forms of exercise can provide a similar release without the negative social consequences. Some people find it helpful to run, walk, or ride a bike before or after work—or as a way to actually get to work. Others prefer to get a workout at a health club, to participate in sports, or to dance. Besides letting off steam, exercising strengthens the organs so that they can better withstand stress.

Biofeedback   People who have devoted time to developing their awareness of such automatically controlled bodily functions as pulse rate, blood pressure, body temperature, and muscle tension have learned to control these functions. Developing an awareness of bodily functions to control them is known as **biofeedback**. People use biofeedback to will their body into a more relaxed state.

biofeedback
Developing an awareness of bodily functions to control them.

Meditation   While meditation has religious overtones for many people, in its general form it is simply a practice of focusing your thoughts on something other than day-to-day concerns. The person meditating focuses on his or her breathing, on a symbol, or on a word or phrase. People who practice regular meditation find that it relaxes them and that the benefits carry beyond the time spent meditating.

Well-Rounded Life Activities   For someone who gets all of his or her satisfaction and rewards from working, job-related stress is more likely to be overwhelming. No job is going to be rewarding all the time, so it helps to have other areas in life where you get rewards. For example, if your boss is impatient and fails to praise you for completing an important project, it helps to enjoy the love of friends and family members or to hear the cheers of your softball teammates when you make a good play.

In other words, people who lead a well-rounded life are more likely to experience satisfaction in some area of life at any given time. This satisfaction can make stress a lot easier to cope with. Leading a well-rounded life means not only advancing your career but also devoting time to social, family, intellectual, spiritual, and physical pursuits. For example, one person might choose to read biographies, join a volleyball team, and volunteer in a soup kitchen. Another person might take bicycle trips with the kids on weekends and be active at his or her church, mosque, or temple and a professional organization. These varied pursuits not only help people manage stress, they also make life more interesting and enjoyable.

Organizational Stress Management

Some organizations recognize that too much stress hurts performance, and they have made efforts to help employees manage stress. Organizational forms of stress management include job redesign, environmental changes, and wellness programs. Although the supervisor can rarely set up such measures single-handedly, he or she may be in a position to recommend them to higher-level managers. Also, when the organization offers these aids to stress management, knowing about them puts the supervisor in a better position to take advantage of them and to recommend them to employees.

Changes in the Job   Recall from Figure 11.6 that many characteristics of a job can be sources of stress. Just a few of the job factors linked to stress are unfair policies, ambiguous procedures, lack of opportunities for advancement, and poor communication. Many of these factors involve matters over which the supervisor has at least some control. For example, supervisors can improve their ability to be fair and to communicate instructions clearly and precisely. Thus, an important part of stress management involves identifying job factors that may be linked to stress and then modifying those factors when possible. When the supervisor cannot act alone to make such a change—for example, if he or she is not powerful enough to resolve conflicts with another department—the supervisor should be sure that higher-level management knows about the stress-related job factors and how they are affecting employees.

When the sources of stress include boring or overly difficult jobs, the organization may be able to change the job requirements to make them less stressful. As described in Chapter 9, the organization may make a routine job more interesting through job enlargement or job enrichment. In the case of jobs that are overly difficult, employees may need further training, or perhaps some responsibilities must be reassigned so that the work is divided more realistically.

Environmental Changes   As shown in Figure 11.6, some characteristics of the job environment can add to employees' stress. For example, it is a strain on employees to cope with noise, poor lighting, uncomfortable chairs, and extremes of heat and cold. When possible, the organization should reduce stress by fixing some of these problems. Often the supervisor is in an excellent position to identify needed environmental changes and to report on them to the managers who are able to make the changes. For example, employees may complain to the supervisor about uncomfortable chairs or dark work areas. (Chapter 18 discusses some changes that can improve the physical work environment.)

wellness program
Organizational activities designed to help employees adopt healthy practices.

Wellness Programs   Most organizations provide their employees with health insurance to cover their expenses if they get sick. In addition, many organizations are also actively interested in helping their employees stay well. The usual way to do this is to provide a **wellness program**, or organizational activities designed to help employees adopt healthy practices. These activities might include exercise classes, stop-smoking clinics, nutrition counseling, and health screening such as cholesterol and blood-pressure tests. Some organizations have even constructed exercise facilities for employees.

A Word About Personality

The guidelines in this chapter for managing time and stress are techniques that have worked for many people. However, the degree to which any person will succeed at using any particular technique for time or stress management depends in part on that person's personality. Though this text does not explore psychological theory, a brief look at one approach to understanding personality types may be helpful. The Myers-Briggs Type Indicator is a test that classifies people into 16 personality types based on the work of psychiatrist Carl Jung.[6] These 16 personality types describe the traits a person has along the four dimensions shown in Figure 11.7. For example, one person might be an Extrovert, an Intuitive, a Feeler, and a Perceiver. Another person will have a different combination of four traits. These traits are not considered good or bad; each has its own strengths and weaknesses.

Knowing your personality type suggests suitable techniques for managing your own time and stress. For example, an Introvert might readily find that meditating is a pleasant way to relieve stress, whereas an Extrovert may find meditating impossible but dancing with friends refreshing. Judgers are the ones who find it easy to apply such time management aids as "to do" lists. Perceivers also make those lists, but they lose them and cannot seem to make time to find them. To manage their time, these people need heroic amounts of self-discipline—or maybe a job that requires flexibility more than structure.

As this last example illustrates, when you find that a particular way of behaving does not fit your personality type, you have a choice. You can make the effort to develop the other trait, as in the case of a Feeler who lists logical criteria for making a decision that must be objective. Or you can avoid situations that require you to behave in ways that do not suit your personality.

In addition, recognizing different personality types can help you understand the behavior of others. For example, if you think your boss's head is always in the clouds, perhaps she is an Intuitive and you are a Sensor. Such insights alone can ease a great deal of stress.

FIGURE 11.7

A Basis for Categorizing Personality Types

According to the Myers-Briggs Type Indicator, a person's personality traits fall somewhere along each of these four dimensions.

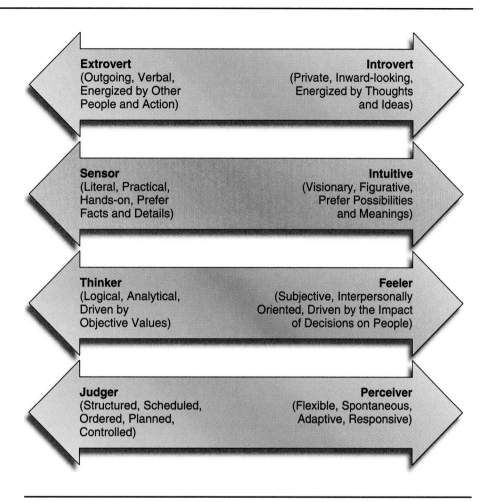

Extrovert
(Outgoing, Verbal, Energized by Other People and Action)

Introvert
(Private, Inward-looking, Energized by Thoughts and Ideas)

Sensor
(Literal, Practical, Hands-on, Prefer Facts and Details)

Intuitive
(Visionary, Figurative, Prefer Possibilities and Meanings)

Thinker
(Logical, Analytical, Driven by Objective Values)

Feeler
(Subjective, Interpersonally Oriented, Driven by the Impact of Decisions on People)

Judger
(Structured, Scheduled, Ordered, Planned, Controlled)

Perceiver
(Flexible, Spontaneous, Adaptive, Responsive)

Source: Adapted from Otto Kroeger and Janet M. Thuesen, "It Takes All Types," *Newsweek,* Management Digest advertising section, September 7, 1992, pp. 8–10.

Summary

11.1   Describe how supervisors can evaluate their use of time.
A practical way to evaluate time use is to keep a time log. The supervisor enters his or her activities for half-hour periods throughout the workday. After a week or two of keeping the time log, the supervisor reviews the information to see whether he or she is using time efficiently.

11.2   Describe ways to plan the use of time.
The supervisor can plan his or her use of time by making a list of things to do for the day or week. Then the supervisor rates each item on the list as A (things that must be done), B (things that are important but can be postponed if necessary), or C (everything else). The supervisor then schedules specific times for completing the A- and B-

level activities. When time permits, the supervisor works on the C-level activities. Also, the supervisor can plan his or her time with the help of a variety of computer software programs. Besides software designed specifically for time management, the supervisor can use programs called desktop organizers.

11.3   Identify some time wasters and how to control them.

Many meetings waste time. When the supervisor calls a meeting, he or she can start the meeting on time, keep discussion on track, and end on time. To keep control of phone calls, the supervisor can have someone screen them if possible, return calls at the same time, prepare for the calls to be made, and schedule calls rather than leave messages. To handle paperwork and reading material, the supervisor needs to handle each item only once, decide which items are essential, dictate responses or make phone calls when possible, and designate a time for reading. With unscheduled visitors, the supervisor can schedule a later meeting, stand to signal that a meeting is ending or will be short, or specify a time limit for the discussion.

The best way to handle procrastination is to tackle the project one step at a time, giving yourself rewards along the way. To combat perfectionism, the supervisor should set high but reasonable standards. Perfectionism is a cause of failure to delegate; the supervisor instead must delegate work effectively. Finally, supervisors sometimes find themselves taking on too many projects. The solution is to say no to projects they do not have time for.

11.4   Describe sources and consequences of stress.

Stress is the body's response to coping with environmental demands. These demands can come from change, frustration, uncertainty, danger, and discomfort. Stress can be stimulating, but an excessive amount of stress leads to illness and lowered performance. People under stress feel anxious, aggressive, frustrated, tense, and moody, and they may overreact to criticism. They are also at risk for abusing drugs and alcohol. When a person cannot cope with stress over an extended period of time, the person may experience burnout.

11.5   Identify factors that cause stress in employees.

People may be more likely to feel the effects of stress if they have a Type-A personality. In addition, certain job factors have been linked to stress. These involve the organization's policies, structures, physical conditions, and processes. Notably, when employees feel out of control and if the workplace is unsafe or unpredictable, employees will suffer more from the effects of stress.

11.6   Explain how supervisors can personally manage stress.

Supervisors and others can manage stress by getting exercise, using biofeedback, meditating, and leading a well-rounded life. These actions do not reduce the amount of stress the person is under, but they do make a person better able to handle the stress.

11.7   Identify ways organizations help their employees manage stress.

Supervisors and other managers can seek to eliminate or minimize the job factors linked to stress. Through such practices as job enlargement and job enrichment, the organization may make work more interesting and give employees more control. Training helps to make sure employees understand their jobs. Management may also introduce environmental changes that make the workplace safer and more comfortable. Finally, some organizations have set up wellness programs to help employees adopt healthy practices such as exercising and eating healthfully.

Key Terms

time management	perfectionism	Type-A personality
time log	stress	biofeedback
procrastination	burnout	wellness program

Review and Discussion Questions

1. Read the sample time log in Figure 11.8 (page 286). What advice can you give this supervisor about managing his time more effectively?

2. For one week keep a time log of your activities at work or at school. Follow the format of Figure 11.1. What does it tell you about your own time management habits?

3. Demetrius Jones prepared the following list of things to do:

Performance appraisal for Angela	A
Clean out files	C
Finish report due Wednesday	A
Prepare a plan for training employees	B
Find out why Kevin has been making more errors lately	B
Read professional journals	C

   a. Which activities does Demetrius consider most important? Least important?

   b. Which activities should Demetrius schedule for times when he is at his best?

   c. If Demetrius fits all these activities onto his weekly schedule and finds he has time left over, what should he do about the "free" time?

4. Assume you are the supervisor of social workers at a hospital. One of your co-workers, a nursing supervisor, asks you to meet with him in his office to discuss a mutual problem. When you arrive at the agreed-upon time, he says, "I'll be right back as soon as I deliver these instructions to one of the nurses and grab a cup of coffee." After you get started ten minutes later, the supervisor takes several phone calls, interrupting the meeting for five minutes at a time. "Sorry," he says after each call, "but that call was important." An hour into the meeting, you have not made much progress toward solving your problem.

   a. How would you feel in a situation like this? How does your co-worker's behavior affect your performance? How does it affect his performance?

   b. How could you react in this situation to improve your use of time?

5. How can supervisors cope with unscheduled visitors?

6. a. What is procrastination?

   b. How can a supervisor keep from procrastinating?

   c. How does perfectionism contribute to procrastination?

7. Which of the following is a source of stress? Explain.

   a. having a boss who gives vague and confusing instructions and then criticizes your results

   b. buying a house

   c. working at a boring job

   d. getting a promotion to a supervisory position you have been wanting for a year

8. Sales supervisor Anita Feinstein does not understand all the fuss about stress. She feels stimulated by a job that is exciting and contains many challenges. Does her attitude show that stress is not harmful? Explain.

9. Name five job factors that have been linked to stress and that you think a supervisor could have some control over.

10. How do the following responses help a person cope with stress?

    a. exercising

    b. using biofeedback

    c. meditating

    d. participating in a wellness program

A SECOND LOOK

Of the job factors linked to stress that are identified in Figure 11.6, which do you think Alfred E. Clark would encounter on his job as principal of Cregier Vocational High School? (Refer to the story at the beginning of this chapter.) Of the factors you have identified, which do you think Clark might have some control over?

FIGURE 11.8
Sample Time Log

Date: _____

Time	Activity	Others Involved	Location
7:30–8:00	—	—	—
8:00–8:30	Get coffee; check to see that everyone is on time and knows what to do.	Staff	Employee lounge; department
8:30–9:00	Look for memo containing instructions for budget proposal due tomorrow.	—	desk
9:00–9:30	Read memo; learn that ledger paper will be needed. Get ledger paper from supply room. Get more coffee.	—	desk; supply room; employee lounge
9:30–10:00	Answer questions from employee (Sue).	Sue	desk
10:00–10:30	Call dentist and make an appointment. Reread budgeting memo, highlighting key points.	—	desk
10:30–11:00	Take phone call from customer. Visit Sue's work area to see if her problem is solved.	Sue	desk; department
11:00–11:30	Call John; arrange to have lunch. Open mail.	John	desk
11:30–12:00	Take phone call from boss; discuss how to complete budget porposal.	boss	desk
12:00–12:30	Lunch	John	cafeteria

Class Exercise*

Each student, in turn, tells the class ways he or she wastes time. The instructor lists these on the blackboard or overhead projector. Then the class discusses the list.

- Which time wasters are most common?
- Are they really just time wasters, or are they also stress reducers?

*The idea for this exercise was provided by Sylvia Ong, Scottsdale Community College, Scottsdale, Arizona.

CASE

Too Much to Do?

Management consultant Ken Blanchard has made the following comments on the way people in our society use time:

> Do you find your days getting busier and busier with seemingly less and less getting done? Do you find that the busier you get, the less fulfilling your life seems to be? I know sometimes I do.
>
> Instead of saving us time, today's technology of car phones, fax machines, voice mail, E-mail, pagers, answering machines and the like seems to squeeze us of every spare minute we have. As a result, we are left with almost no time for ourselves to reflect and rejuvenate.
>
> The more we are *able* to do, the more we feel *compelled* to do and the more we *do*. This is all happening at an increasing rate, so that although we might think and dream about slowing down or taking time off, in practice, we are moving away from that dream.
>
> Working hours in the United States have increased substantially over the past 20 years. Since the end of the 1960s, Americans have increased the time they spend at work by about 160 hours per year, which represents another full month of work. In addition, the level of productivity of U.S. workers has more than doubled since 1948 due in large part to advances in technology and increased worker skills. We're getting more done, but instead of taking less time to do it, we are spending more time to do even more.
>
> In our parents' time, exhaustion came from physical work. I can remember when I used to help a farmer friend with his daily routine. We'd work like there was no tomorrow from 5 A.M. to 8 A.M., then have the most tremendous breakfast from about 8 A.M. to 9:30 A.M., followed by a full day of demanding, physical work. On those days I'd be sound asleep by 9 P.M.—and a deep, blissful sleep at that. Now we are as likely to burn out from inner exhaustion.
>
> Even vacations have lost their restful appeal for many Americans. Rather than relax, most of us simply redirect our achievement mode while on vacation so that now we spend time trying to do and see everything at the place we are visiting. We somehow don't feel that the vacation was complete and satisfying unless we've exhausted it of its potential to experience new and different things. We often come back from a vacation more tired than when we left...
>
> Rest is not an option, however, nor is it a luxury. Rest is an essential part of our regenerative powers and crucial to our understanding, enjoyment, productivity and fulfillment in life. In today's world, you have to make an effort to plan and structure downtime if you want to be sure it happens...
>
> A few years ago our company took a tour of Sea World and learned how they trained and worked with Shamu, the killer whale. I remember the trainers saying that they designed Shamu's day into five different time periods for maximum effectiveness: work time, play time, free time, rest time and learning time. I wonder how many people systematically try to cover the same priorities every day. If you don't already do it, you need to start planning reflective time on a daily basis through such activities as reading, walking, running, meditating or praying.

1. According to Blanchard, how has technology affected our use of time?
2. If a supervisor does not take much time for resting and relaxing, how do you think this affects the supervisor? How do you think it affects his or her employer?
3. How can a supervisor apply principles of time management and stress management to resolve the problems described by Blanchard in this case?

Source: Excerpted from Ken Blanchard, "In America, Rest Doesn't Come Easy," *Quality Digest*, August 1992, pp. 15, 62. Courtesy of the Blanchard Management Report.

12

The easiest, the most tempting, and the least creative response to conflict within an organization is to pretend it does not exist.
—Lyle E. Schaller

Managing Conflict and Change

LEARNING OBJECTIVES

12.1   Describe positive and negative aspects of conflict.

12.2   Identify types of conflict.

12.3   Describe strategies for managing conflict.

12.4   Explain how supervisors can initiate conflict resolution, respond to a conflict, and mediate conflict resolution.

12.5   Describe the supervisor's role during a union organization drive and collective bargaining.

12.6   Provide guidelines for working with a union steward and handling grievances.

12.7   Explain the supervisor's role in preventing strikes and operating during a strike.

12.8   Describe sources of change, and explain why employees and supervisors resist it.

12.9   Discuss how supervisors can overcome resistance and implement change.

A RECIPE FOR CHANGE

Marnie Duff operates The 1811 House, an inn located in Manchester, Vermont. The inn provides guests with lodging and breakfast. As manager of the inn, Duff supervises four employees, including a cook.

The cook at The 1811 House had worked for the previous owner and was used to preparing pancakes using a mix. Duff preferred that he make them from scratch, but the cook resisted the change. However, one day the mix ran out, and Duff gave the cook a recipe for pancakes.

The cook tried the pancake recipe, but, according to Duff, the first trial was "awful." The cook had added far too much liquid and used the turner to pat down the pancakes on the griddle. The pancakes were thin, flat, and unattractive. The guests did not complain, but it was the only breakfast for which they did not visit the kitchen with compliments.

Clearly, the cook needed more help with this change in procedure. Duff gave an on-the-spot lesson in pancake making. She showed him how to fold in the dry ingredients and made sure he did not beat the batter too much. The cook's initial reaction was to feel somewhat hurt and to doubt that Duff knew a better way. But he followed her instructions, and the next pancakes he made were much lighter and fluffier than the others.

Guests started going to the kitchen to compliment the cook on his pancakes. He would take a bow, with a salute of recognition to Duff. Thanks to the positive response, it was easy to make sure the cook followed this new procedure. He now makes all his pancakes from scratch.

In any organization, conflicts and changes are bound to occur. Whether these are constructive or destructive forces depends significantly on the supervisor's skills in managing them. This chapter addresses conflict management by examining the nature of conflict, including the conflicting views involved in labor relations, and ways to respond to conflict constructively. The chapter also discusses the role of change in the workplace and ways supervisors can implement change.

Conflict

conflict
The struggle that results from incompatible or opposing needs, feelings, thoughts, or demands within a person or between two or more people.

In the context presented in this book, **conflict** refers to the struggle that results from incompatible or opposing needs, feelings, thoughts, or demands within a person or between two or more people. If supervisor Janet Speers sees that an employee she likes is taking home office supplies, her feelings for the employee come into conflict with her belief that stealing is wrong. If her feelings and belief are both strong, she will have difficulty resolving the issue. Likewise, if two employees disagree over how to fill out time sheets for sick days, there is a conflict between the employees. In this case, the organization should have a clear procedure that will make the conflict easy to resolve.

Positive and Negative Aspects of Conflict

Sometimes conflict is a positive force. It can bring about necessary changes. For example, imagine that a business that develops computerized information systems has just hired a new systems analyst, Jordan Walsh, the first African-American in the company. The new employee gets all the boring and routine jobs—filing, running errands, proofreading the documentation. If Jordan is cheerful about his situation, the other employees will assume there is no conflict (although he may feel one internally). Of course, this situation is not good for Jordan; he is not getting the experience he needs to develop his career, he is bored every day, and he feels insulted. This arrangement is also bad for the employer. The company is paying for a systems analyst but not benefiting from his talents. Furthermore, Jordan may quit, and the company will have to bear the expense of repeating the hiring process. If, instead, Jordan complains to his supervisor about his limited role, the conflict will surface, and the resolution could leave everyone, including Jordan, better off. Thus, when conflict serves as a signal that a problem exists, it can stimulate creative response.

Nevertheless, ongoing conflict has negative consequences. People who are engaged in disputes are under stress, which, as Chapter 11 describes, takes a physical toll. In addition, people who are busy arguing and trying to persuade others to take their side are not involved in more productive activities. Finally, depending on the source of the conflict, the people involved may be angry at management or the organization, so they may vent their anger in ways that are destructive to the organization, such as taking extra time off or sabotaging machinery.

Leo Toralballa won kudos from his supervisors at American Express Company's personal-card division, but due to corporate upheaval he resigned in May 1992. A big part of supervisors' jobs involves managing and reducing conflict.

Source: Courtesy of Doug Knutson, photographer, 1807 Elliot Ave., S., Minneapolis, Minn., 55404.

Types of Conflict

Before the supervisor can respond effectively to a conflict, he or she needs to understand the real nature of that conflict. Who is involved? What is the source of the conflict? The supervisor will probably respond differently to a conflict that results from a clash of opinions than to one stemming from someone's frustration over limited resources.

As mentioned earlier, conflict may arise within an individual (intrapersonal) or between individuals or groups. The basic types of conflict involving more than one person are called interpersonal, structural, and strategic. These types of conflict are summarized in Figure 12.1.

Intrapersonal   An intrapersonal conflict arises when a person has trouble selecting from among goals. Choosing one of two possible goals is easy if one is good and the other bad. For example, would you rather earn $1 a year as a drug dealer or $1 million a year as the microbiologist who discovered a cure for cancer? Of course, we rarely if ever are faced with such obvious choices. Most choices, as illustrated in Figure 12.2, fall into these three categories:

1. A choice between two good possibilities (for example, having a child versus taking an exciting job that requires travel year-round)
2. A choice between two mixed possibilities (accepting a promotion that involves moving away from your family versus keeping your current, rather dull job to be near your family)
3. A choice between two bad possibilities (laying off two employees versus laying off yourself)

Because these choices are not obvious, they result in conflict.

FIGURE 12.1

Types of Conflict

In many cases, a supervisor lacks the expertise to resolve an intrapersonal conflict. When supervisors notice that they or one of their employees is struggling with an intrapersonal conflict, they should consider who might be able to help. People with skills in handling various types of intrapersonal conflicts include psychologists, religious advisers, and career counselors.

Interpersonal   Conflict between individuals is called interpersonal conflict. Supervisors may be involved in interpersonal conflicts with their boss, an employee, a peer, or even a customer. In addition, they may have to manage conflicts among two or more of their employees. Interpersonal conflicts may arise from differing opinions, from misunderstandings about a situation, or from differences in values or beliefs. Sometimes two people just seem to rub each other the wrong way.

According to Andrew S. Grove, chief executive of Intel Corporation, when employees are engaged in constant interpersonal conflict such as bickering and complaining about one another, it is a symptom that their supervisor is not exercising enough leadership.[1] Grove says that the supervisor might be listening to complaints too sympathetically, for example, or watching disruptive conduct too passively. Instead, the supervisor should establish and communicate guidelines for acceptable behavior. The supervisor should enforce these guidelines and live up to them him- or herself. (Chapter 4 provides a more in-depth discussion of leading employees, and a later section of this chapter describes some approaches to managing interpersonal conflict.)

FIGURE 12.2

Choices Producing Intrapersonal Conflict

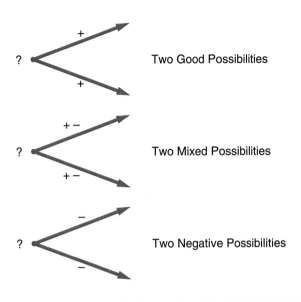

Two Good Possibilities

Two Mixed Possibilities

Two Negative Possibilities

Structural   Conflict that results from the way the organization is structured is called structural conflict. As you learned in Chapter 3, for example, conflict often arises between line and staff personnel. Likewise, production and marketing departments are often at odds. Stated broadly, marketing wants to give customers whatever they ask for, and production wants to make what it can easily and well. Conflict also arises when various groups in the organization share resources, such as a word-processing or maintenance department. Each group wants its jobs handled first, but the support department obviously cannot help everyone first. According to Xerox vice-president Richard Palermo, persistent long-term problems are generally the result of structural conflict.[2]

Because supervisors do not decide on the organization's structure, they are rarely able to reduce the amount of structural conflict. However, they do need to be aware that it can occur and be able to recognize it. First, knowing that a conflict is structural helps prevent the supervisor from taking the issue personally. Then the supervisor may be able to minimize the costs of structural conflict by proceeding cautiously and diplomatically in conflict areas. Awareness of the conflict may also lead the supervisor to try to understand the other party's point of view and communicate it to employees.

Strategic   Most of the conflicts described so far arise unintentionally as a result of people and groups trying to work together. However, sometimes management or an individual will intentionally bring about a conflict in order to achieve an objective. Such conflicts are referred to as strategic. For example, a franchise oil-change organization might hold a contest to see which franchise can do the fastest and best oil change. Or a manager might tell two employees that they are both in the running for the supervisor's job when she retires next year. In both examples, the intention is to use competition to motivate employees to do exceptional work.

Managing Interpersonal Conflict

As restaurant manager, Phyllis Jensen schedules which hours each server will work during the upcoming week. She noticed that one of the servers, Rich Yakima, has been scowling when he gets his assignments and for hours afterward. Phyllis asked Rich about it, and he replied, "You know just what the problem is. You know I've been wanting an evening off every weekend so I can go out with my girlfriend, but every week you have me working Friday and Saturday nights. And I've noticed that Rita and Pat always get the hours they want." Responding to problems such as this one is known as **conflict management**.

conflict management
Responding to problems stemming from conflict.

Strategies

How can Phyllis manage the conflict involving Rich? She can begin by recognizing the various strategies available for conflict management: compromise, avoidance and smoothing, forcing a solution, and confrontation or problem solving. These are summarized in Figure 12.3. Based on her understanding of these strategies, Phyllis can choose the most appropriate one for the circumstances. To see which conflict management strategy you tend to select most often, take the Self-Quiz.

compromise
Settling on a solution that gives each person part of what he or she wanted; no one gets everything, and no one loses completely.

Compromise   One conflict management strategy is to reach a **compromise**. This means that the parties to the conflict settle on a solution that gives each of them part of what he or she wanted. No one gets exactly what he or she wanted, but no one loses entirely either.

When people choose to compromise, they are assuming they cannot reach a solution that is completely acceptable to everyone, but they would rather not force someone to accept a choice that is completely disagreeable. In that sense, compromise does not really solve the underlying problem. Therefore, it is most useful when the problem is relatively minor and time is limited.

Avoidance and Smoothing   Conflict is unpleasant. Hardly anyone enjoys arguments and disagreement; most of us prefer being around people who agree with us. A strategy that arises from the natural dislike of conflict is to manage conflict by avoiding it. For example, if sales supervisor Jeanette Delacroix finds the people in the human resources department stuffy and inflexible, she can avoid dealing with that department. When it is absolutely necessary to have contact with human resources, she can delegate the responsibility to a member of the sales force. A related strategy is **smoothing**, or pretending that no conflict exists.

smoothing
Managing a conflict by pretending it does not exist.

These strategies make sense if you assume that all conflict is bad. If you successfully avoid or smooth over all conflicts, life looks serene on the surface. However, people do disagree, and sometimes people with opposing viewpoints have important ideas to share. Avoiding those conflicts does not make them go away, and it does not make opposing points of view any less valid or significant. Therefore, it is important to be selective in avoiding or smoothing over conflicts. These strategies are most useful for conflicts that are not serious and for which a solution would be more difficult than the problem justifies.

FIGURE 12.3
Strategies for Conflict Management

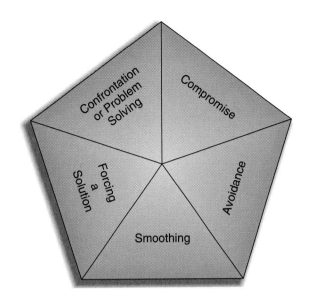

 S E L F - Q U I Z   *What Is Your Conflict-Handling Style?*

Everyone has a basic style for handling conflicts. To identify the strategies you rely upon most, indicate how often each of the following statements applies to you. Next to each statement, write *5* if the statement applies often, *3* if the statement applies sometimes, and *1* if the statement applies never.

When I differ with someone…

___3___   1.   I explore our differences, not backing down, but not imposing my view either.

___1___   2.   I disagree openly, then invite more discussion about our differences.

___5___   3.   I look for a mutually satisfactory solution.

___5___   4.   Rather than let the other person make a decision without my input, I make sure I am heard and also that I hear the other out.

___3___   5.   I agree to a middle ground rather than look for a completely satisfying solution.

___3___   6.   I admit I am half wrong rather than explore our differences.

___5___   7.   I have a reputation for meeting a person halfway.

___1___   8.   I expect to get out about half of what I really want to say.

___3___   9.   I give in totally rather than try to change another's opinion.

___3___   10.   I put aside any controversial aspects of an issue.

___5___   11.   I agree early on, rather than argue about a point.

_3_   12. I give in as soon as the other party gets emotional about an issue.

_3_   13. I try to win the other person over.

_3_   14. I work to come out victorious, no matter what.

_3_   15. I never back away from a good argument.

_1_   16. I would rather win than end up compromising.

To score your responses, add your total score for each of the following sets of statements:

Set A: statements 1–4 _14_   Set C: statements 9–12 _14_

Set B: statements 5–8 _12_   Set D: statements 13–16 _10_

A score of 17 or more on any set is considered high. Scores of 12 to 16 are moderately high. Scores of 8 to 11 are moderately low. Scores of 7 or less are considered low.

Each set represents a different strategy for conflict management:

- Set A = Collaboration (I win, you win.)

- Set B = Compromise (Both win some, both lose some.)

- Set C = Accommodation (I lose, you win.)

- Set D = Forcing/domination (I win, you lose.)

Source: Adapted from Stephen P. Robbins, *Training in Interpersonal Skills* (Englewood Cliffs, N.J.: Prentice Hall, 1989), pp. 214–216.

This point is especially important with regard to today's diverse work force. A person's point of view often seems puzzling, irritating, or downright incorrect to someone of another race, age, or sex. It takes extra work to try to understand people who are different from us and to take their views into account. However, it is important for the supervisor to make sure that all employees' views are heard, not just the views of the employees the supervisor understands best. Pretending that everyone is looking at a situation the same way does not make it so and can foster a belief among some employees that the supervisor is discriminating against them. The "Dealing with Diversity" box describes ways employees, supervisors, and other managers are learning to manage culturally based conflicts.

A related issue is that people in many non-Western cultures believe it is best to avoid conflicts.[3] In these cultures, people place a higher value on harmony than on "telling it like it is." People with these values are less likely than employees from the dominant U.S. culture to complain to their supervisor or to deliver bad news. Thus, the supervisor may not realize there is a problem such as a dispute between employees or the possibility a task will be completed late. A supervisor must tactfully ensure that his or her employees recognize that the supervisor wants to be aware of any problems so that he or she can help resolve them.

Coping with Culturally Based Conflicts

A manager from the dominant U.S. culture saw two Arab-American employees arguing. He decided to let them work it out. Instead, the incident exploded. The manager did not realize that the two employees expected a third party to intervene. Whereas the dominant U.S. culture emphasizes individual action and privacy, Arab culture places more value on achieving a win-win result, often with the aid of mediation.

Which cultural view was right in the situation, the manager's or the employees'? The answer, of course, is that it does not matter, but if the manager wants to resolve conflicts, he or she must understand the ways that different cultures operate. A common assumption today is that we are all human, all the same at the core, but this assumption can lead people to ignore important differences. In effect, it boils down to avoiding or smoothing over areas of conflict rather than understanding and resolving conflicting points of view.

People can learn to appreciate cultural differences in a variety of ways. Some consultants specialize in coaching employees, supervisors, and other managers in how to identify and talk about differences. Cornell University's Theatre Outreach group has developed a program designed to teach about such issues by acting out scenes showing conflicts related to diversity. During a typical half-day session, the group presents four scenes, along with audience participation and group discussion of what went wrong and how to solve the problem.

Some organizations adopt a more in-depth approach, having consultants train a group of employees to serve as "consulting pairs." Consulting pairs are pairs of employees who spend 10-15 percent of their time resolving disputes stemming from racism and sexism. For example, Chuck Mays served as part of a consulting pair at Miller Brewing Company. He says, "Managers can be doing things they have done for years. They don't have any idea that they're turning an employee off."

Diversity training and the use of consulting pairs are designed to help people see problems and conflicts more accurately. For example, when consultant Bob Abramms conducted diversity training at a large oil company, he mailed participants orientation packages containing an article titled "Black Managers: The Dream Deferred." Many of the managers who received the packet sent the article to the group's only black manager, thinking he would be interested. When the group met, Abramms said to his mostly white audience, "You're the ones that need to read [the article]. Tom *knows* what it's like."

Sources: Dan Fost, "Education to Back Up Affirmative Action," *American Demographics*, April 1992, pp. 17–18; Stephenie Overman, "Conflict? Act Out a Solution," *Executive Female*, September–October 1991, pp. 14–15; and Jolie Solomon, "As Cultural Diversity of Workers Grows, Experts Urge Appreciation of Differences," *The Wall Street Journal*, September 12, 1990, pp. B1, B8.

Forcing a Solution   Because ignoring or avoiding a problem does not make it go away, the supervisor may want to try a more direct approach to ending a conflict. One possibility is to force a solution. This means that a person with power single-handedly decides on what the outcome will be. For example, if machinist Pete Desai complains to his supervisor that he never gets overtime assignments, the supervisor can respond, "I make the assignments, and your job is to do what you're told. This weekend it's going to be Sue and Chuck, so make the best of it." Or if two supervisors present conflicting proposals for allocating space among their departments, a committee of higher-level managers could select one proposal, allowing no room for discussion. Forcing a solution is a relatively fast way to man-

At Grand Metropolitan, an international company which specializes in consumer businesses, open communications among its diverse employees are encouraged. This Strategic Technology Development group in the food sector consists of 14 men and 12 women, from six countries.

Source: Courtesy of Grand Metropolitan PLC 1992—John Engstrom, photographer.

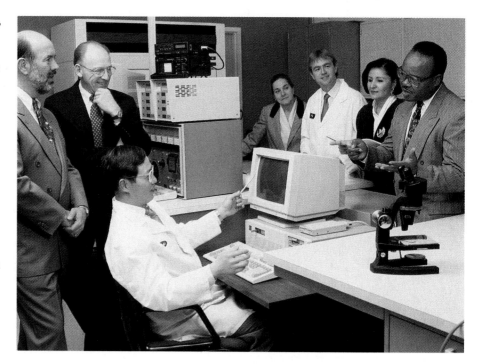

age a conflict, and it can therefore be the best approach in an emergency. However, it can leave bad feelings, which may lead to future conflict.

conflict resolution
Managing a conflict by confronting the problem and solving it.

Confrontation or Problem Solving   The most direct—and sometimes the most difficult—way to manage conflict is to confront the problem and solve it. This is the conflict management strategy called **conflict resolution**. Confronting the problem requires listening to both sides and attempting to understand rather than place blame. Next the parties should identify the areas in which they agree and the ways they can both benefit from possible solutions. Both parties should examine their own feelings and take their time at reaching a solution. The "Tips from the Firing Line" box suggests specific ways to resolve conflicts. (Chapter 8 provides further guidelines for problem solving.)

Confronting and solving a problem makes a different assumption about the conflict than do other strategies for conflict management. The other strategies tend to assume that the parties have a *win-lose conflict*. In other words, the outcome of the conflict will be that one person wins (gets an outcome that he or she wants), and the other person must therefore lose. In contrast, the conflict resolution strategy assumes that many conflicts are *win-win conflicts*. The resolution to such a conflict can leave both parties better off. Both sides can feel like winners.

Initiating Conflict Resolution

When the supervisor has a conflict with another person, he or she needs to take action to resolve that conflict constructively. Otherwise, as described earlier, the conflict is unlikely to go away on its own. When initiating conflict resolution, the

Creative Conflict Resolution

For conflict among employees to be a positive force for change, the supervisor needs to create the conditions for group problem solving. Here are some ideas for doing so:

- Hold a meeting to discuss the problem. The atmosphere should be one of trust.
- Include everyone who is involved in the conflict. Let participants know this is a chance for them to give their side of the story.
- Allow everyone to present his or her position. Rather than allow the meeting to become an argument, simply note each viewpoint.
- Be suspicious about easy agreements. If the group seems to be arriving at a quick decision, it

may mean people are uncomfortable with conflict and therefore are avoiding the problem.
- Do not allow the person with the most rank to control the process. One person's desires should not determine the outcome.
- Break the issue into parts. Determine what the major and minor concerns are. The solution should address the significant points you uncover.

Source: "Maintenance Mainstream: Getting the Best Out of Conflict," *Maintenance Supervisor's Bulletin*, November 10, 1991, p. 3.

supervisor should act as soon as he or she is aware of the problem. As the problem continues, the supervisor is likely to get increasingly emotional about it, which only makes resolution more difficult.

To initiate conflict resolution, prepare by understanding what the conflict is. Focus on behavior (which people can change), not on personalities (which they cannot change). What is the action that is causing the problem, and how does that action affect you and others? For example, you might tell a supervisor in another department, "I haven't been getting the weekly sales figures until late Friday afternoon. That means I have to give up precious family time to review them over the weekend, or else I embarrass myself by being unprepared at the Monday morning staff meetings." When used politely, this type of approach even works with a boss. For example, you could say, "I haven't heard from you concerning the suggestions I made last week and three weeks ago. That worries me, because I think maybe I'm giving you too many ideas or not the right kind."

After you have stated the problem, listen to how the other person responds. If the other person does not acknowledge that there is a problem, restate your concern until the other person understands or until it is clear that you cannot make any progress on your own. Often you will find that a conflict exists simply because the other person had not realized your point of view or your situation. When you have begun communicating about the problem, the two of you can work together at finding a solution. Restate your solution to be sure that both of you agree on what you are going to do. Figure 12.4 summarizes this approach.

Responding to a Conflict

Sometimes the supervisor is party to a conflict that is bothering someone else. When the other person makes the supervisor aware of the conflict, it is up to the supervisor to respond in a way that makes it possible to reach a solution. If an

FIGURE 12.4

Initiating Conflict Resolution

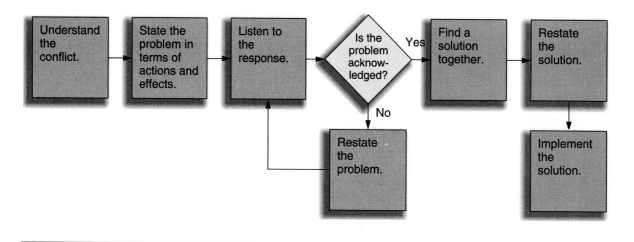

employee says, "You always give me the dirty assignments," it is not helpful to get angry or defensive.

Understand the Problem The constructive way to respond to a conflict is to first listen to the other person and try to understand what the problem is really about. If the other person is emotional, it is a good idea to let that person vent his or her feelings first, then get down to discussing the problem. Try to interpret the problem in the kinds of terms you would use to express the problem yourself. This means that you need to avoid statements of blame and find out what specific actions the other person is referring to. For example, when the employee says, "You always give me the dirty assignments," the supervisor can ask the employee to give specific examples and then to describe how he or she feels about the behavior.

Understanding the problem can be complicated if one of the people involved has a "hidden agenda." A hidden agenda is a central concern that is left unstated. Typically, the person with a hidden agenda is angry or upset about something but directs those feelings toward some other issue. For example, a colleague in another department explodes, "What's wrong with you? The numbers in your report are off by a mile!" But your colleague is not really angry because you made a mistake; he is nervous because he has to make a presentation to the board of directors and wonders if the incorrect numbers are your way to mislead him so that he looks uninformed and you can get the promotion he wants. Or maybe your colleague has simply had a frustrating day, and your mistake is the last straw.

If another person's feelings seem to be out of proportion to the problem he or she is describing, it is probably worthwhile to look for a hidden agenda. Finding one can save you from trying to resolve the wrong conflict. In addition, when you are upset about something yourself, it is usually more constructive to describe the problem directly than to leave others guessing at your hidden agenda.

Work on a Solution   When you understand the problem, build an environment of working together on a solution. To do this, agree with some aspect of what the other person has said. In the example, you might say, "You've really disliked your last three assignments." Then you and the other person should be ready to begin identifying possible solutions. The final step is to agree on what the solution will be and how you will carry it out. Figure 12.5 summarizes this approach.

Mediating Conflict Resolution

Sometimes the supervisor is not personally involved in a conflict, but the parties ask the supervisor for help in resolving their conflict. If the parties to the conflict are peers of the supervisor, getting involved can be risky, and the supervisor might be wiser to refer his or her peers to a higher-level manager—tactfully, of course. If the parties to the conflict are the supervisor's employees, then mediating the conflict is part of the supervisor's job and an important way to keep the department functioning as it should.

To mediate a conflict, the supervisor should follow these steps:

1. Begin by establishing a constructive environment. If the employees are calling each other names, for example, have them focus on the issue rather than on such destructive behavior.
2. Ask each person to explain what the problem is. Get each person to be specific and to respond to others' charges.
3. When everyone seems to understand what the problem is, have each employee state what he or she wants to accomplish or what will satisfy him or her.
4. Restate in your own words what each person's position is. Ask the employees if you have understood them correctly.
5. Have all participants suggest as many solutions as they can. Begin to focus on the future.
6. Encourage the employees to select a solution that benefits all of them. They may want to combine or modify some of the ideas suggested.

FIGURE 12.5

Responding to a Conflict

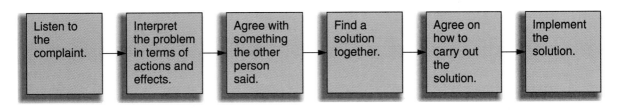

7. Summarize what has been discussed and agreed on. Make sure all participants know what they are supposed to do in carrying out the solution, and ask for their cooperation.

Labor Relations: The Supervisor's Role

labor relations
Management's role in working constructively with unions that represent the organization's employees.

Many of the conflicts in the workplace arise between management and operative employees. For example, it is common for an employee to wish to be paid more than the organization is willing to pay. To give themselves more power in managing conflicts such as those over pay, working conditions, and job security, employees have formed unions. Management's role in working constructively with unions is called **labor relations**. Thus, effective labor relations is an important part of managing conflict in unionized organizations.

Unions

Unions as we know them began forming in the United States during the late 1800s. Employees, who then worked as long as 12 hours each day, banded together to persuade employers to shorten work hours, pay higher wages, and improve safety. Today unions continue to negotiate with organizations over similar issues.

Union membership has fallen from over 22 percent of the work force in the mid-1970s to slightly over 16 percent in 1992.[4] This drop accompanies a decline in the industrial sector of the economy, where membership was traditionally strongest. The power of unions is thought to have declined along with the numbers. For example, during the 1980s, many unions made major concessions in negotiations with employers. Wage increases to union members were less than the Consumer Price Index in all but one year between 1983 and 1990.[5]

Unions represent an organization's operative employees, and managers represent the owners, so it is not surprising that unions and management often have conflicting views. Although both parties benefit from the employer being healthy, they differ on the details of how to achieve organizational well-being. For example, keeping costs such as wages and benefits low increases the company's profits (or requires less taxes for a government organization), at least in the short run. But high wages and generous benefits are to the employees' advantage, at least in the short run. In the long run, of course, the success of the organization requires that it be generous enough to attract good employees yet spend conservatively enough to produce goods or services efficiently (making a profit, in the case of a business).

The Organization Drive

Inherent conflicts come to the surface during union organization drives, for example. An organization drive is the union's attempt to be elected to represent an organization's workers. Management typically resists such efforts, based on the belief that a union will interfere with managers' ability to make decisions in the best interests of the company. Managers also fear that the union will convert employees' loyalty to the company into loyalty to the union. The union, in turn, tries to persuade employees that management has never had their interests at heart and that they will be better off if they can bargain collectively with management.

The process of organizing begins when a few employees decide they want to be represented by a union or when union leaders target an organization as a likely candidate. Union representatives then go to the company to organize. If at least 30 percent of the employees sign an authorization card stating they want the union to represent them, the union may request an election. The employees vote by secret ballot. If a majority of the employees who vote favor the union, the union becomes the representative of all the employees in the bargaining unit.

Although managers generally want to keep unions from organizing their employees, federal law says supervisors and other managers may not restrain employees from forming or joining a union. Supervisors are allowed to state their views about unions. However, they may not threaten employees with punishment for forming or joining a union, and they may not promise rewards for working against the union. A supervisor who is unsure about what specific kinds of comments are permitted should consult with the organization's human resources department. It is also unlawful for a union to try to pressure employees into joining. If the supervisor thinks the union is violating this law, he or she should inform the human resources department.

Collective Bargaining

collective bargaining
The process of seeking to reach a contract spelling out the rights and duties of unionized workers and their employer.

Conflicts tend to surface also when management and the union are engaged in collective bargaining. **Collective bargaining** is the process of seeking to reach a contract spelling out the rights and duties of unionized workers and their employer. Typically, bargaining begins with the union and management setting forth their demands. Since the two parties usually differ on what is acceptable, they then discuss how to resolve the major areas of conflict. If they need help in resolving the conflict, they may call in a **mediator** or **conciliator**, a neutral person who helps the two sides reach agreement.

mediator or conciliator
A neutral person who helps opposing parties reach agreement.

A supervisor seldom has a direct role in collective bargaining. However, management may ask the supervisor to provide information that will help during the bargaining process. This is another reason for the supervisor to keep careful records concerning employees.

The Labor Contract

A typical labor contract contains such provisions as guidelines for union membership; procedures for handling grievances (described later in this chapter); policies about regular and overtime pay, benefits (including vacations and holidays), and work hours; and agreements concerning safety and health. The supervisor must abide by the terms of this contract, so he or she must be familiar with it. A supervisor who is unfamiliar with the labor contract may unintentionally cause a problem by, for example, asking an employee to do something that is forbidden by the contract or using a procedure for discipline that is prohibited. Ignoring a provision in the contract, such as the length of rest periods, may be interpreted as an agreement to change the contract. The supervisor can also minimize conflict by treating all employees fairly and consistently. Not only is this good practice whether or not there is a union, but federal law prohibits supervisors and other managers from discriminating against union members.

Working with the Union Steward Part of the supervisor's job under a labor contract is to maintain a good relationship with the union steward. A **union steward** is an employee who is the union's representative in a particular work unit. Employees go to the union steward with their contract-related questions and complaints.

To minimize conflict and to resolve problems that do arise, the supervisor needs to cooperate with the union steward. The supervisor should treat the union steward with respect and tell him or her about problems and upcoming changes. If the supervisor and union steward have a cooperative relationship, they often can resolve problems themselves rather than subject the organization and its employees to the cost and stress of an ongoing dispute.

Grievances Employees who believe they have been treated unfairly under the terms of the labor contract may bring a formal complaint, or **grievance**. Typically, when an employee brings a grievance, he or she first meets with the supervisor and union steward to look for a solution. Most of the time, the three of them are able to resolve the problem. If not, higher-level managers and union representatives meet to look for a solution. If they cannot reach an agreement, the parties might agree to bring in an outside arbitrator. An **arbitrator** is a neutral person who reaches a decision on how to resolve a conflict. Both parties must adhere to the terms set by the arbitrator.

To avoid this costly and time-consuming process, supervisors should make sure that employees have a chance to be heard. In many cases, using the principles discussed earlier in this chapter, the supervisor can resolve conflicts before the employee even files a grievance. When a grievance is filed, the supervisor should take it seriously. This means gathering complete information and trying to resolve the problem as quickly as possible. Conflicts that are allowed to continue are likely to seem more significant to both parties.

According to arbitrator Arthur J. Hedges, the supervisor's role is particularly important in arbitration cases involving employees who were discharged because their job performance was declining.[6] Often the supervisor put up with the employee as long as he or she could. Then the employee had a particularly bad day, and the supervisor fired him or her. The union filed a grievance claiming that the employee was discharged without just cause and that the employer failed to give corrective discipline and warning notices so the employee could correct the problem. Says Hedges, "First-line supervisors are key to winning such cases," which is because the supervisor is the person responsible for making sure the employee is aware of any performance problems and the consequences of failing to improve. (Chapter 16 provides more detail on how to handle problems with employee behavior.)

Strikes

Occasionally, the parties are unable to reach an agreement during collective bargaining, and the employees vote to go on strike. During a **strike**, the employees leave their jobs and refuse to come back until there is a contract. The use of strikes

---

union steward
An employee who is the union's representative in a particular work unit.

grievance
A formal complaint that the terms of a labor contract have been violated.

arbitrator
A neutral person who reaches a decision on how to resolve a conflict; both parties must adhere to the decision.

strike
Refusal by employees to work until there is a contract.

During collective bargaining, employees and management are sometimes unable to reach an agreement, and the employees vote to go on strike. In 1992, the United Auto Workers union members went on strike against management at Caterpillar Inc.'s giant bulldozer plant in East Peoria, Illinois.

Source: Courtesy of Al Harkrader/photographer.

has been declining in recent decades. According to the U.S. Department of Labor, there were 381 major strikes in 1970, 187 in 1980, and only 40 in 1991.[7] In general, striking during the term of a contract—a **wildcat strike**—is illegal.

wildcat strike
Refusal by employees to work during the term of a labor contract.

The Supervisor's Role in Preventing Strikes Although the supervisor has little control over whether union and management representatives reach an agreement during collective bargaining, the supervisor does have a role in minimizing the likelihood of a strike. Treating employees fairly and reasonably fosters good relations between employees and management. In such a climate, employees are less likely to desire a strike. Good communication practices also enable employees to understand management's point of view and give them a chance to vent their frustrations while staying on the job.

The Supervisor's Role during a Strike   Once the employees have voted to strike, there is little the supervisor can do to resolve the conflict. If the circumstances of the strike do not involve unfair labor practices by the employer, the employer may hire replacement workers. In such a case, the supervisor must tackle the challenge of training and getting to know a new work force. The supervisor will have to adjust goals and expectations to allow for the new employees' inexperience.

In the case of a wildcat strike, the supervisor should follow the practices listed in Table 12.1. Notably, the supervisor should carefully observe what is occurring and encourage employees to abide by the contract and return to work. The supervisor should not make agreements or even discuss the problem that led to the wildcat strike.

Change in the Workplace

During the last decade, almost half of all U.S. companies were restructured, over 80,000 were acquired or merged with other companies, and hundreds of thousands were "downsized," that is, management reduced the total number of employees.[8] These are some of the most dramatic changes organizations can make, but by no means are they the only ones. For organizations to succeed—that is, for businesses to make a profit and for nonprofit and government organizations to carry out their mission efficiently—they must adapt to changes in their environment. For example, the organization must respond when a new competitor enters the marketplace or a new law limits how it may operate. Organizations adapt to the environment by changing with it.

Because change is a fact of organizational life, supervisors do not decide *whether* organizations should change but *how* to make the changes work. They must learn to live with and implement change. To do this, it helps to recognize the various factors that can affect the success of a change:

- *The change agent (person trying to bring about the change)*—This person should have skills in bringing about change and solving the related problems, as well as expertise in the area affected.
- *Determination of what to change*—Any changes should make the organization more effective in delivering high quality.
- *The kind of change to be made*—The change can involve process and equipment; policies, procedures, and job structure; and such people-related variables as attitudes and communication skills.
- *Individuals affected by the change*—Some people are more open to change than others. Also, people will see some changes as beneficial to them but others as harmful.
- *Evaluation of change*—An evaluation can indicate whether it is necessary to modify the change process or make further changes.

Supervisors are the organization's primary link to operative employees, so they must understand how employees are likely to respond to changes. They must be

TABLE 12.1	Stay on the job.
Guidelines for Supervising during a Wildcat Strike	Notify higher management by telephone or messenger.
	Carefully record the events as they happen.
	Pay strict attention to who the leaders are, and record their behavior.
	Record any lack of action by union officials.
	Report all information as fully and as soon as possible to higher management.
	Encourage employees to go back to work.
	Ask union officials to instruct employees to go back to work.
	Do not discuss the cause of the strike.
	Do not make any agreements or say anything that might imply permission to leave work.
	Make it clear that management will discuss the issue when all employees are back at work.

Source: Leslie W. Rue and Lloyd L. Byars, *Supervision: Key Link to Productivity,* 4th ed. (Homewood, Ill.: Richard D. Irwin, 1993), p. 325.

able to communicate information about the changes to employees, and they must help employees respond positively. A good way to begin is by understanding what may cause management to see a need for change.

Sources of Change

As summarized in Figure 12.6, changes can originate with management, employees, or external forces. Organizations change when management sees an opportunity or a need to do things better. A need may arise because performance is not adequate, as in the case of the flat pancakes at The 1811 House (see the story at the beginning of this chapter). Examples of an opportunity are a new computer system that is more efficient or a new procedure that can lead to higher-quality service.

Even an organization's employees may bring about changes. Forming a union could lead to changes in how management reaches agreements with employees, as well as in what the conditions are under which the employees work. Many organizations actively respond to suggestions from employees on how to improve quality and cut costs.

As the U.S. work force becomes increasingly diverse in terms of age, race, and sex, it seems likely that the forces for change from employees are likely to strengthen. People of diverse backgrounds are likely to offer a greater variety of creative solutions. In addition, the challenge of working harmoniously with different kinds of people can itself lead to a push for changes, such as provisions for different religious holidays or guidelines on how to treat people fairly.

Some changes are imposed from outside. New laws and regulations often lead to changes within organizations. A local government organization might have to make changes in response to voters' refusal to approve a tax increase. A series of lawsuits might cause an organization to reexamine how it makes a product. The size and composition of the work force may affect who the organization

FIGURE 12.6

Sources of Change

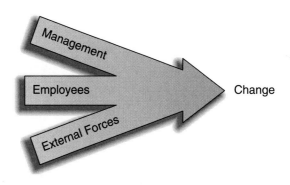

hires and how much training it provides. Economic trends are also important. For example, businesses usually are able to seek growth more aggressively when the economy is expanding.

Resistance to Change

With regard to changes designed to improve productivity, Chapter 10 mentioned that employees are likely to be fearful about change. In fact, any kind of change is uncomfortable to some degree. Management consultant Ken Blanchard writes, "If you don't feel awkward when you're trying something new, you're probably not really doing anything differently."[9] It is just human nature to recognize that a change requires work, be it adoption of a new way to do things or completion of a major training program. Change also carries the risk that the person will be worse off than before, as in the case of the staffers laid off by the politician illustrated in Figure 12.7.

Not only operative employees, but supervisors themselves may have misgivings about some of the changes they must introduce. As with employees, their fears are sometimes well founded. For example, Eastman Kodak Company eliminated 30 percent of the managers of its apparatus division, doing away with four levels of management. As a result, first-line supervisors, who in the past had simply carried out orders, had to begin setting goals and making strategies. According to Frank Zaffino, who heads the division, some of the supervisors could not handle the new responsibility. Said Zaffino, "They were used to being star technicians, not communicators or leaders."[10]

People resist change most when they are not sure what to expect or why the change is necessary. In such situations, change stirs up fear of the unknown, another normal human response. Furthermore, when people do not understand the reasons for change, the effort to change does not seem worthwhile. Thus, before the cook at The 1811 House could appreciate the benefits of no longer using a mix, Marnie Duff had to help him discover the superior quality of pancakes made from scratch.

FIGURE 12.7

A Change That Leaves Employees Worse Off

Source: Reprinted by permission: Tribune Media Services.

Implementing Change

To implement change, the supervisor must overcome resistance, see that the change is made, and ensure that the change endures. Noted behavioral scientist Kurt Lewin has set forth a model for this process.[11] As shown in Figure 12.8, Lewin's model says that to make a change, people must go through three phases:

1. Unfreezing, which occurs when people recognize a need for change
2. Changing, which occurs when people begin trying to behave differently
3. Refreezing, which involves making the new behavior part of oneself or part of the organization's regular processes.

This model shows that before a change can occur, the supervisor must ensure that employees recognize the need for it and that after employees begin changing he or she must follow up to make sure the change becomes established practice.

Unfreezing In the unfreezing phase, the supervisor or other person responsible for implementing the change must make it clear why a change is needed. For example, an employee might need to know how a new tool will make her job easier, or a department's employees might need to know that greater profits will result from a restructuring. Because people tend to resist change, as described earlier, they may not be eager to hear such information. Thus, the major part of unfreezing may involve overcoming resistance to change.

According to Ken Blanchard, a primary reason for the failure of many efforts to make changes is that management does not consider the employees' point of view.[12] However, the organization can overcome resistance by addressing employees' concerns. Because supervisors are management's link to operative employees,

FIGURE 12.8

Lewin's Model of Change

the organization relies heavily on supervisors to do this. In general, employees want to know what is happening and how it will benefit them. They also appreciate any assurance the supervisor can give that the organization will support them so they are capable of making the change.

Key to overcoming resistance is good communication (see Chapter 7). The supervisor should tell employees about a change as soon as he or she learns about it. In describing the change, the supervisor should first make sure the employees understand it, then explain how the change is likely to affect them. The supervisor should be as positive about the change as possible, citing any benefits to the employees. For example, will a change mean that jobs will be more interesting? Are bonuses likely to increase as a result of greater profits? In addition, the supervisor should communicate how the organization will help employees cope. Will there be training in how to follow new procedures? Will the organization provide counseling or other assistance to employees being laid off?

Of course, the supervisor should not try to hide bad news, such as the possibility that some employees will lose their jobs. Oakland, California–based consultant Ben Harrison provides the following advice for communicating about organizational change:

> Stick to the truth. Acknowledge fears and possibilities. Celebrate small wins, but be open about bad times. And don't overrepresent the company's point of view. People need emotional support during these periods, so now isn't the time to spout the usual management jargon.[13]

The supervisor should give the employees plenty of opportunity to express their concerns and to ask questions. It is better for the supervisor to hear concerns and questions than for such thoughts merely to circulate in the rumor mill, where employees can give one another misleading or incorrect information. The supervisor should answer as many questions as he or she can and get the answers to the rest as soon as possible.

When employees are upset about a change, the supervisor will probably have to listen to expressions of sadness and anger as well as questions. The supervisor need not dwell on these feelings but should accept and acknowledge them without argument. It is unfair and unwise to tell employees they are overreacting. "People 'overreact' to a change when they're reacting more than we are," says change expert William Bridges. He explains that people experience change subjectively, and one subjective experience is as valid as another. Furthermore, he says, discounting people's feelings shuts off further communication.[14]

In listening to and answering questions, the supervisor should bear in mind that some employees will think of questions only after some time has passed. Thus, the supervisor should provide opportunities for employees to ask questions on an ongoing basis, not just at the time of the announcement.

Change can bring positive results. Two years ago when the organizational structure of Kodak's black-and-white film manufacturing was changed from a vertical/departmental form to a horizontal/self-directed team form, these "zebras" saw dramatic results. Productivity, profitability, and morale soared.

Source: Courtesy of John Abbot, photographer.

Changing When employees appreciate the need for a change and have received any necessary training, they are ready to begin altering their behavior. The key to implementing change is to build on successes. The supervisor should determine what aspects of the change he or she has control over, then seek to carry out those aspects of the change successfully. The supervisor should point out each success the group achieves along the way. As employees see the change achieving desirable results, they are more likely to go along with it and even embrace it.

The supervisor might have control over scheduling the change. In such a case, the supervisor should make sure that the deadlines on the schedule are reasonable. As employees meet each deadline, the supervisor can point out their on-time achievements. For example, imagine that an accounting department is installing a new computer system. Instead of simply focusing on whether everyone is using the system properly, the supervisor can establish dates for setting up various pieces of equipment and learning to operate different parts of the system. Then the supervisor can note that the terminals arrived on time, that everyone learned how to log on and enter their password in a single training session, and so on.

The supervisor might also have control over which people are directly involved in the change or the order in which people get involved. In the case of the accounting department, the supervisor might recognize that some employees are already enthusiastic about the new system or are at least flexible and open to change. These people should learn the system first, then such key employees can spread their enthusiasm around and help the other employees when it is their turn to learn. Similarly, when there is a group of employees who work together well and enjoy each other's company, it makes sense to try to keep these employees together. For example, if the company is adding another shift, it might be a good idea to keep the group of employees together in one shift. When a change involves bringing together two groups of employees from different organizations, locations, or shifts, the supervisor might try teaming up employees from each group to build cooperation.[15]

Refreezing   For the change process to be complete, employees must make the changed behavior part of their routine. However, because new procedures are less comfortable than the old and familiar ones, employees may revert to their old practices when the initial pressure for change eases.[16] That is just a natural response, but it can become a problem unless the supervisor acts to get everyone back on track. The supervisor should remind employees about what they have achieved so far and what is expected of them in the future. The supervisor can apply the principles of motivation described in Chapter 9. An important part of refreezing is for employees to be rewarded for behavior that shows they have made the desired change.

Proposing Change

In many situations, a supervisor wants to make a change but needs to ask higher-level management for authority to implement it. A supervisor also is wise to ask his or her boss about changes when they may be controversial, difficult to implement, or of major importance. These situations call for a proposal to higher-level management.

To propose a change effectively, the supervisor should begin by analyzing the change he or she has in mind. How will it help the organization better achieve its goals? Will it improve quality or productivity? What steps are required to carry out the change? How much will the change cost? Who will carry out the change? What training will be required? Only when the answers to these questions confirm that the change is beneficial and feasible is the supervisor in a valid position to continue with the proposal.

Recall that the change process begins with convincing others of the need for a change (unfreezing, in Lewin's model). Some organizations actively cultivate suggestions for improvement; in such an organization it may be relatively easy to sell a change. In other organizations management may view change more cautiously. Thus, it is often important for the supervisor to begin by helping management see the situation giving rise to the need for a change. The supervisor may have to do this before even mentioning that he or she has an idea for changing something.

Once management is ready for the proposal, the supervisor should have one ready to submit. Except in the case of simple changes, the supervisor should make his or her proposal in writing. At the beginning of the proposal should be a brief summary of what the change is and why it should be made. Then the supervisor can provide details about the procedure for change and the costs and benefits involved. (For more suggestions about upward communication and reports, see Chapter 7; for guidelines about maintaining good relations with your boss, see Chapter 17.)

Summary

12.1 Describe positive and negative aspects of conflict.

Conflict is a positive force when it leads to necessary changes by signaling that a problem exists. However, ongoing conflict puts people under stress and takes up time that can be spent more productively. When conflict involves anger at management or the organization, it may lead to destructive behavior.

12.2 Identify types of conflict.

Conflict may be intrapersonal, or within a person. Conflict between individuals is called interpersonal. Structural conflict results from the way the organization is structured. Strategic conflict is brought about intentionally to achieve some goal, such as motivating employees.

12.3 Describe strategies for managing conflict.

One strategy is to compromise, or agree to a solution that meets each party's demands only partially. Another approach is to avoid the conflict or to pretend it does not exist (smoothing). Forcing a solution occurs when a person with power selects and imposes the outcome. None of these strategies tries to solve the underlying problem. Confronting and solving the problem is often called conflict resolution.

12.4 Explain how supervisors can initiate conflict resolution, respond to a conflict, and mediate conflict resolution.

To initiate conflict resolution, a supervisor can interpret the conflict in terms of the action causing the problem and the effects of that action. The supervisor then states the problem in those terms and listens to the response; when the parties are communicating, they can find a solution and agree on what each person will do.

To respond to a conflict, a supervisor can hear the other person's complaint and interpret it in terms of the action causing the problem and the effects of that action. Then the supervisor can build cooperation by agreeing with part of the statement and working with the other person to reach a solution.

To mediate conflict resolution, the supervisor begins by establishing a constructive environment, then asks each person to explain what the problem is and state what he or she wants. Next the supervisor restates each position, asks for suggested solutions, and encourages the parties to select a mutually beneficial solution. Finally, the supervisor summarizes what has been agreed.

12.5 Describe the supervisor's role during a union organization drive and collective bargaining.

During an organization drive, the supervisor may state his or her views about the union. However, the supervisor may not threaten employees about forming or joining a union and may not promise rewards for working against the union. If the union tries to coerce employees into supporting the union, the supervisor should report those activities. During collective bargaining, the supervisor provides management with information that will help it bargain.

12.6 Provide guidelines for working with a union steward and handling grievances.

The supervisor should cooperate with the union steward and treat that person with respect. He or she should tell the steward about problems and upcoming changes and should try to resolve problems with the steward rather than let them escalate. Supervisors should try to avoid grievances by giving employees a chance to be heard and trying to resolve conflicts. When a grievance is filed, the supervisor should take it seriously, gathering information and trying to resolve the problem as quickly as possible.

12.7 Explain the supervisor's role in preventing strikes and operating during a strike.

The supervisor should foster good relations with employees by treating them fairly and communicating effectively. This minimizes the chance employees will want to strike. During a strike, the supervisor may have to train and oversee replacement workers. During a wildcat strike, the supervisor should carefully observe what is occurring and encourage employees to go back to work. The supervisor should not make agreements or even discuss the problem that led to the wildcat strike.

12.8 Describe sources of change, and explain why employees and supervisors resist it.

Change can come from management in response to an opportunity or need to do things better. It can come from employees in the form of unionizing or making suggestions. Change can be imposed by external forces such as the government. Employees and supervisors resist change because it typically requires extra effort and sometimes leaves people worse off. Other reasons for resisting change are fear of the unknown and worry that one is incapable of making the change.

12.9 Discuss how supervisors can overcome resistance and implement change.

To overcome resistance to change, supervisors can recognize and respond to employees' feelings. They can also keep employees informed about the change, being realistic but emphasizing any benefits. The supervisor should give employees opportunities to ask questions about the change. To implement change, the supervisor should build on successes. This includes communicating successes as they occur, setting reasonable deadlines for the steps that must be taken, and involving first the people who are most likely to be enthusiastic.

Key Terms

conflict	labor relations	grievance
conflict management	collective bargaining	arbitrator
compromise	mediator	strike
smoothing	conciliator	wildcat strike
conflict resolution	union steward	

Review and Discussion Questions

1. What is conflict? Can a conflict be beneficial? Explain.
2. Imagine you are a production supervisor at a hand-tool manufacturer such as Snap-On Tools. Your boss says, "I know you were looking forward to your trip to Hawaii next month, but we will be stepping up production, and three new employees will be joining your group. I wish you would consider staying to make sure everything goes smoothly."
   a. What is the nature of the conflict in this situation? In other words, what two goals is it impossible for you to achieve at the same time?
   b. What are some possible ways to resolve this conflict? List as many solutions as you can think of.
   c. Which solution do you prefer? How could you present it to your boss?
3. Identify each of the following conflicts as interpersonal, structural, or strategic.
   a. The production department's goal is to make parts faster, and the quality-control department wants slower production to reduce the rate of defects.
   b. A salesperson does not take telephone messages for her co-workers because she believes she has a better chance of being

the department's top performer when her co-workers do not return their calls.

c. One of the cashiers at a supermarket is much older than the others, and he does not spend much time talking to them. The other cashiers criticize him for not being a team player.

4. What are the drawbacks of managing conflict by compromising? Is it ever a good idea to compromise? Explain.

5. Rachel Gonzalez supervises servers at a restaurant. She knows that many of them have been upset about the hours she has scheduled for them, but she believes that people should not argue. So she avoids discussing the subject, and she posts the following week's schedule just before leaving for the day. What is wrong with Rachel's approach to conflict management? What would be a better way to manage this conflict?

6. Ron Herbst is a supervisor in a clinical laboratory. He has noticed that one of his employees regularly comes to work in a surly mood. The employee is getting his work done on time, but his attitude seems to be affecting the other employees.

a. How can Ron initiate conflict resolution with this employee? How should he describe the problem?

b. If the employee responds to Ron's statement of the problem by saying, "I'm fine. Don't worry about me," what should the supervisor do and say?

7. What takes place during a union organization drive? What restrictions is the supervisor under during this time?

8. What is the difference between a mediator and an arbitrator?

9. During the term of a labor contract, a group of employees becomes angry about a new policy they believe is unfair, and they leave their work areas to walk off the job. In an effort to keep them working, their supervisor calls out, "Hey, not so fast! Why don't you tell me what the problem is, and we'll work out a solution." Is this an acceptable way for the supervisor to handle the situation? Explain.

10. The managers of a soft-drink bottling company decide that production workers will each learn several jobs and rotate among those jobs. They have read that this technique improves productivity, and they believe that workers will be happier because their jobs will be more interesting. However, many of the employees and their supervisors are reluctant to make the change. What could explain their resistance?

11. How can a supervisor overcome resistance to change?

12. In what ways can a supervisor build on successes to ensure that a change is implemented successfully?

A SECOND LOOK

Recall the story at the beginning of this chapter. Why do you think the cook resisted changing the way he made pancakes? How did his supervisor, Marnie Duff, overcome that resistance?

Class Exercise

This exercise is based on role playing. One class member takes the role of the supervisor, and two class members act as the employees. The supervisor leaves the room for five minutes as the employees act out the following scenario:

Pat and Chris work in a word-processing department, preparing reports and letters on computer terminals.

Pat trips on the cord to Chris's computer, shutting it off and erasing the project Chris was working on. Chris is upset. If Chris does not finish the job by the end of the day, this failure to meet a deadline will show up on Chris's performance records and hurt Chris's chances for getting a raise. In addition, the manager who requested the work will be upset, because this is an important project.

This is just a basic scenario; the employees should be creative in adding details. For example, they can address the following questions:

- Did Pat erase the files on purpose?
- Has Pat ever done something like this before?
- Do these employees otherwise get along?
- Are communications in general and this conflict in particular complicated by some difference between the employees (age, sex, race, etc.)?

After the two class members have acted out the scene, the supervisor returns to the room, and the role playing continues as the employees bring their conflict to the supervisor. The supervisor should try to manage the conflict.

When the supervisor is satisfied with how the conflict has been handled (or when 10 minutes have elapsed), the class discusses the following questions:

1. Did the supervisor understand the real problem? If not, what was the real problem?
2. Did the supervisor and employees solve the problem? Was the solution a good one?
3. In what ways was the supervisor effective in resolving the conflict? How could the supervisor improve his or her approach?
4. What other possible solutions might the supervisor and employees have considered?

CASE

A Conflict over Job Discrimination

Lauri Schwefel is a sergeant with the Milwaukee Police Department. A career in law enforcement was a longtime dream of Schwefel's. However, her path to that position was a rocky one.

Following her graduation from high school, Schwefel moved to Milwaukee, where she enrolled in college and eventually joined Milwaukee's police force. Continuing her studies part-time, Schwefel earned a bachelor's degree in criminology and law, then began to pursue a master's in labor relations.

During this time, Schwefel began to record experiences that she believed indicated the police department was treating her unfairly because she was a woman. Her major complaints were that she was assigned to foot patrol rather than squad-car duty more often than her male peers, that the locker and rest room facilities for the half dozen women in the precinct were inadequate, and that she was not permitted to attend several training seminars that her male colleagues went to.

Schwefel took her concerns to the chief of police. A few months later, she received a three-day suspension for violating a rule against holding an off-duty job without permission. Schwefel explains she was tending bar without pay for friends and believes the suspension was in retaliation for complaining.

At about this time, Schwefel took the sergeant's exam, receiving the second highest score out of the 456 officers taking the exam. She was among the first five women to be promoted to sergeant. Then, three months later, Schwefel filed a sex discrimination complaint with Wisconsin's Equal Rights Division.

During the following months, the police department launched several investigations into Schwefel's conduct. Most troubling for Schwefel was a charge that she had broken a departmental rule forbidding officers from "bad-mouthing" one another. The department found her guilty of calling male police officers "drunks and druggies" in a conversation overheard in a restaurant, and she was demoted to patrol officer. Schwefel contends she had merely been quoting and criticizing a newspaper article. She appealed the demotion and added it to her complaints of sex discrimination. The government ordered the police force to reinstate her on the grounds there was no evidence to support the complaint of bad-mouthing officers.

After a four-year battle, Schwefel settled the lawsuit for $72,000 (of which she kept $25,000 after paying fees and debts). According to a co-worker, officer Kathleen Gorlewski, the effort was worthwhile: "Her suit helped make Milwaukee a better place for women officers to work." However, although Schwefel agrees that the attitude toward women on the force has improved, she says, "I had been blacklisted. Some of my fellow officers wouldn't talk to me. I had risked my career and put my personal life on hold for four years. I would never do it again."

1. What conflicts are described in this case?

2. Based on the information given, what strategies did Schwefel use for managing each of these conflicts?

3. Do you think these were the best strategies she could have used? Explain.

Source: Suzanne Seixas, "She Blew the Whistle on Sexual Bias," *Money*, December 1991, pp. 102–105ff.

Part Two
Application Exercises

Exercise 1. Communicating Effectively

You learned many principles in Chapter 7 ("Communicating") to help you improve your communication skills. This exercise reviews six of those principles and gives you a chance to see how you can use them to improve supervisory communications.

Instructions

1. Review the list of communication principles in the following chart:

Communication Principles

a. Use feedback to verify your message has been received accurately

b. Practice active listening

c. Select appropriate method for sending your message

d. Be tuned in to nonverbal messages

e. Be well prepared when speaking before a group

f. Understand the important role of informal communication in the workplace— particularly rumors, gossip, and the grapevine

2. Read the scenarios and determine which of the communication principles the supervisor violated in each. The principle you choose should indicate the one that the supervisor could have used to achieve a more positive outcome. (Hint: Each principle will be used only once; there is one *most* correct answer for each.)

Application Exercises were prepared by Corinne Livesay, Liberty University, Lynchburg, Virginia.

Scenario   **Principle**

On Tuesday afternoon the plant manager gave each of the twelve supervisors throughout the plant a five-   1. _____
page document that spelled out some changes in the employee handbook that would be effective the
following month. The plant manager instructed the supervisors to call departmental meetings sometime
within the next three days to present the changes to their own staff. Jeff sent out a notice to his
employees to be at a forty-five-minute meeting on Thursday afternoon. Several unexpected events
occurred that demanded most of Jeff's time during the next two days. Jeff did manage to make it to the
meeting; however, he had only a few minutes beforehand to skim the document. He ended up mostly
reading aloud from the document at the meeting.

Pete went to talk to his supervisor about a personal problem. He left the meeting feeling as though he   2. _____
hadn't gotten through to his boss because his boss seemed preoccupied and distracted throughout their
entire conversation.

Sid was on his way out the door to meet a customer for a business lunch at a local restaurant. He stopped   3. _____
long enough to give about ninety seconds of hurried instructions on a task he needed one of his
employees to do for a 3 P.M. deadline that same day. Sid finished his instructions by glancing at his
watch and saying, "I'm going to be late for my luncheon appointment. You got everything OK, didn't
you?" The employee mumbled, "Yeah, I guess so," and Sid was out the door.

Krista overheard one of the employees in her department telling someone on the phone that he had   4. _____
heard from a reliable source that the company was going to pink-slip 10 percent of the employees on
Friday. Krista shook her head in disgust and thought to herself, "Another ridiculous rumor. With all the
rumors floating around this place, I could spend all my time dispelling rumors. I'll let this one die a
natural death on Friday; I don't have time to deal with it right now."

Shannon had a long "to do" list for the day and decided to dispense with as many items as she could first 5. _____
thing in the morning using the E-mail system. She had gotten rid of six rather routine tasks by sending
messages to the appropriate people. She composed and sent a seventh message that contained
considerable confidential information about one of her employees. The next day Shannon's boss spoke
with her about a negative situation that had arisen as a result of her seventh message being accessed by
some people who should not have seen it. Her boss told her to consider more carefully the messages she
chose to send via E-mail.

Michael had decided to delegate a major portion of an important project to Susan, his most capable   6. _____
employee. He called Susan to go over some of the specifics of the project—one that he saw as a great
opportunity for her to show higher management what she was capable of doing. Susan, however, did not
share Michael's enthusiasm about her new work assignment. Michael appeared to ignore her
expressionless face. He chose instead to respond to her verbal responses when, for example, he asked her
if she agreed this was an exciting project; she had responded after a few seconds of silence with a
mere "Yes."

Exercise 2. Using Innovative Thinking to Solve Problems

As you learned in Chapter 8 ("Problem Solving and Decision Making"), a major challenge in the problem-solving process is generating creative solutions. As supervisors work to get their teams involved in this process, it helps to understand the various working styles that each member prefers. Wilson Learning Corporation, a worldwide training firm, has developed a comprehensive training program entitled "The Innovation Series" that examines strategic innovation management and its role in quality improvement and employee empowerment.[1]

The four *Innovation Styles* (trademark of Wilson Learning Corporation) that Wilson identifies are as follows:

Style	Approach	Contribution to Team
Modifying	"Modifiers" are stimulated by facts and make decisions based on them. They prefer to move forward one step at a time, building on what is known and proven.	Modifiers add stability and thoroughness to a team's creative process.
Exploring	"Explorers" are stimulated by insights and use them to gather more information. They thrive on the unknown and the unpredictable and are comfortable challenging assumptions and using analogies to approach problems from new angles.	Explorers contribute to teams by questioning basic assumptions and models.
Visioning	"Visioners" are stimulated by insights and make decisions based on those insights. They focus on ideal results and let those images guide them.	Visioners provide teams with long-term direction and momentum.
Experimenting	"Experimenters" are stimulated by facts and use them to gather more information. They generate new ideas by combining established processes.	Experimenters contribute to teams by combining input from everyone to ensure workable, consensus-based solutions.

Wilson Learning Corporation has developed a quick quiz* to help you determine your style.

---

*This quick quiz is an adaptation of a fully validated instrument and has no research compiled as to its validity. For information on the fully validated instrument which is adapted here, please call the number below.

1. Permission granted by Wilson Learning Corporation, Eden Prarie, Minn. (800–328–7937), to provide this brief introduction to The Innovation Series.

Instructions

1. For each of the following eight statements, divide a total of five points between the two possible responses. Assign the most points to the statement that you identify with the most. If you give five points to one option, give zero points to the other. If you give four points to one option, give one point to the other, and so on.

2. As you consider each statement, keep this question in mind: "How do I handle challenges most successfully in my current job?" If you are a full-time student not currently employed, ask yourself, "How do I handle most successfully the challenges I face as I pursue my education?"

1. I like solving problems best when
   _____ a. there are some standard ways to go about solving them.
   _____ b. there needs to be a new way to go about solving them.

2. One of my strengths is
   _____ c. seeing how different ideas and viewpoints can be related.
   _____ d. being highly committed to making things work.

3. I can help innovation by making sure there is
   _____ a. steadiness and thoroughness when developing new ideas.
   _____ b. open-mindedness to a wide range of assumptions and ideas.

4. Sometimes, I might hinder constructive change by
   _____ c. "leaving others behind" when I focus on future goals.
   _____ d. getting lost in the details of implementation and forgetting the goal.

5. I am best at solving problems that
   _____ a. are specific and have a single, best answer.
   _____ b. need many perspectives and alternatives to be considered.

6. I am most successful when I deal with
   _____ c. insights and connections among ideas.
   _____ d. detailed, factual information.

7. I like to find solutions by
   _____ a. applying expert ideas in new ways.
   _____ b. using metaphors and analogies for new insights.

8. I like to find solutions by
   _____ c. imagining the best possible outcome for everyone.
   _____ d. combining the most practical ideas of many people.

Source: Adapted from Craig Steinburg, "Computing Your Innovation Style," *Training & Development*, December 1992, p. 11.

3. Transfer your points to the following chart:

Statement	a	b	c	d
1				
2				
3				
4				
5				
6				
7				
8				
Total points				
Style	Modifying	Exploring	Visioning	Experimenting

You probably use a combination of the four Innovation Styles; however, your highest score identifies your preferred style. Supervisors must learn to appreciate and encourage the use of all four styles in the problem-solving process.

Exercise 3. Developing Motivational Methods

Chapter 9 ("Motivating Employees") deals with one of the most challenging areas for supervisors. This exercise will help you develop a comprehensive list of motivating methods upon which you can draw when faced with employees whom you feel are not performing to their full potential.

Instructions

1. Listed here are five suggested categories of motivational methods. Drawing upon what you have learned about motivation in this class and elsewhere, create a list of methods, techniques, and strategies that can serve you as a source of ideas on how to motivate people.

2. For purposes of this exercise, do not be concerned about the economic impact of your ideas or a plan for carrying them out. For example, if you suggest a bonus to reward your employees for good performance, there is no need to provide a formula for computing the bonus. At the same time, however, do not make ridiculous suggestions that would not make good business sense, such as suggesting that you reward all employees and their families with a two-week, all-expenses-paid vacation to Bermuda.

3. First develop your list alone. Then the class could share ideas and you could add others' ideas to your personal list. Or you may prefer to get into groups and develop a group list that when completed you can copy for each group member. There will undoubtedly be many days in your management career when you will be able to use this list to help you generate some ideas on how to motivate an unmotivated employee. Also, the list can be improved over time as you develop greater expertise in being a motivational leader.

Things I can do to be a motivational leader	Characteristics of a motivating work environment	Ways to reward my employees for good performance	Strategies I can use to improve the way work is done	Organizational policies or benefits
Help employees set challenging yet achievable goals	Products and services employees believe in	Publish achievements in company newsletter	Communicate clear performance standards	Flexible work schedules to accommodate personal and family needs

Things I can do to be a motivational leader	Characteristics of a motivating work environment	Ways to reward my employees for good performance	Strategies I can use to improve the way work is done	Organizational policies or benefits

PART THREE

Supervision and Human Resources

13

A great deal of the agony of separation could be eliminated by working at…the selection process. Making sure not only that the candidates can *do the job,…but that they* will *do the job.*

—Donald H. Sweet

Selecting Employees

LEARNING OBJECTIVES

13.1 Explain how supervisors use job descriptions and job specifications to work with the human resources department in selecting employees.

13.2 Describe possible sources of employees.

13.3 Identify the steps in the selection process.

13.4 Discuss how supervisors should go about interviewing candidates for a job.

13.5 Identify types of employment tests.

13.6 Describe the requirements of antidiscrimination laws.

13.7 Explain how hiring decisions are affected by the Americans with Disabilities Act (ADA).

13.8 Describe the requirements of the Immigration Reform and Control Act (IRCA) of 1986.

HARD WORKERS WANTED

As communications supervisor in the office of a pediatric dentist in Tempe, Arizona, Jill Strode supervises four employees—a secretary, an insurance coordinator, and two business assistants. Under her direction, these employees handle the business end of running a dental practice. Their tasks include doing insurance paperwork and communicating information to patients and their parents.

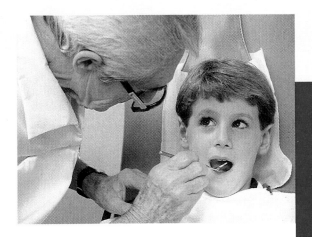

When there is a job opening among these positions, Strode is responsible for all aspects of hiring a replacement. To find qualified candidates, she places an ad in the newspaper or talks to her colleagues in the field. When she has identified people who might be suitable for the job, she interviews them. She selects the candidate who seems best qualified, obtains the approval of her boss, Dr. Longfellow, and then makes an offer.

Interviewing job candidates is one of Strode's favorite tasks. She views the interview as a meeting between equals, not an occasion to test the candidate. Says Strode, "If you use too much control, you don't get the best information." Rather, Strode tries to put the candidate at ease and to create an environment where the interviewer and candidate can talk about "the good and the bad."

Once, frustrated by "a string of bad hires," Strode interviewed a young woman she had previously talked to but not hired. She showed the woman a statement she had prepared that spelled out the qualifications she was looking for. The statement focused on attitude and the employee's conduct with patients and coworkers. The candidate reacted to the statement by saying, "That's the *least* you should expect from an employee!" Strode hired that candidate, who proved to be a hard worker and a loyal employee.

An organization's employees can make or break the quality of its goods or services and, in the case of a business, determine the size of its profits. Enthusiastic, well-qualified people are more likely to deliver high quality than indifferent, unqualified people. This is especially true in today's leaner organizations; when fewer employees are getting the work done, each employee has a greater impact on the organization's overall performance. Thus, it is in the supervisor's best interests to do a good job in helping to select employees.

This chapter addresses the supervisor's role in working with the organization's human resources (or personnel) department to select employees. It describes how organizations can recruit candidates and decide whom to hire. Finally, it addresses some legal issues that supervisors and others in the organization must be aware of when hiring. These issues include compliance with laws that forbid discrimination, require employers to make the workplace accessible, and give employers a role in curbing illegal immigration.

Working with the Human Resources Department

The supervisor's role in the selection process can vary greatly from one organization to another. Especially in small organizations, such as the dental practice Jill Strode works for, the supervisor may have great latitude in selecting employees to fill vacant positions. Other organizations have formal procedures that require the human resources department to do most of the work, with the supervisor simply approving the candidates recommended. In most cases, the supervisor works to some extent with the human resources department. In this way, the supervisor benefits from that department's skills in screening and interviewing candidates, as well as from its familiarity with laws regarding hiring practices.

To select the right employees, the supervisor and the human resources department have to be clear about what jobs need to be filled and what kind of people can best fill those jobs. The supervisor provides this information by preparing job descriptions and job specifications, consulting with the human resources department as needed. A **job description** is a listing of the characteristics of the job, including the title, duties involved, and working conditions. A **job specification** is a listing of the characteristics desirable in the person performing the job; these include educational and work background, physical characteristics, and personal strengths. Table 13.1 details some of the kinds of information to include in job descriptions and job specifications. Figures 13.1 and 13.2 show a sample job description and a sample job specification for a systems analyst.

Experience is only one possible way to measure whether people are qualified. Personal characteristics such as willingness to work as part of a team might be at least as important. When Honda opened a manufacturing plant in the United States, it recruited workers without experience in the auto industry. To explain this approach, Al Kinzer, a vice-president for Honda America Manufacturing, said, "We didn't want people with bad habits. Birth is easier than resurrection."[1]

The supervisor should provide the information that applies to the particular job. If a job description and job specification already exist for a position, the supervisor should review them to make sure they reflect current needs. Preparing and using these materials helps the supervisor base hiring decisions on objective criteria—how

job description
A listing of the characteristics of a job, including the job title, duties involved, and working conditions.

job specification
A listing of the characteristics desirable in the person performing a given job, including educational and work background, physical characteristics, and personal strengths.

TABLE 13.1

Contents of the Job Description and Job Specification

Job Description	Job Specification
Job title	Education
Location	Experience
Job summary	Availability to work overtime
Duties, including backup functions during peak periods	Skills—technical, physical, communication, and interpersonal
Productivity and quality standards	Training
Machines, tools, and equipment	Judgment and initiative
Materials and forms used	Emotional characteristics
Relationships—supervision and teams, if any	Physical effort
Working conditions	Responsibilities
Hazards	Unusual sensory demands (sight, smell, hearing, etc.)

Sources: Samuel C. Certo, *Modern Management*, 5th ed. (Boston: Allyn and Bacon, 1992), p. 316; and J. E. Osborne, "Job Descriptions Do More than Describe Duties," *Supervisory Management*, February 1992, p. 8.

FIGURE 13.1

Sample Job Description: Systems Analyst

> **Job Title**
> Systems Analyst
> **Department**
> Programming and Systems Analysis
> **General Description**
> Responsible for systems analysis and design, programming specifications and development, and systems implementation and documentation.
> **Duties and Responsibilities**
> 1. Prepare complete studies of assigned systems including:
>   a. review of work assignments.
>   b. analysis of work flow.
>   c. study of work load pattern.
>   d. study of backlogs and overload points.
> 2. Prepare feasibility studies.
> 3. Prepare programming specifications for the necessary programs for the system(s).
> 4. Prepare complete systems documentation for assigned systems.
> 5. Work with the programming staff to make certain that programming specifications are completed in an efficient manner.
> 6. Maintain appropriate files in a professional fashion.

Source: Stephen E. Catt and Donald S. Miller, *Supervision: Working with People*, 2nd ed. (Homewood, Ill.: Irwin, 1991), p. 343.

FIGURE 13.2

**Sample Job
Specification:
Systems Analyst**

Job Title
Systems Analyst
Qualifications
Education: Minimum of baccalaureate degree in a field such as business,
              accounting, or management information systems.
Experience: At least 2 years as a systems analyst. Programming experience in
              widely used computer languages.
Skills: Technical writing ability required.
              Ability to identify alternative courses of action and make timely
              decisions based on factual information and logical assumptions.
              Ability to retain perspective while working on detail.
              Demonstrate creativity and initiative in completing work assignments.
              Develop and maintain good working relations with system users.

Source: Stephen E. Catt and Donald S. Miller, *Supervision: Working with People*, 2nd ed. (Homewood, Ill.: Irwin, 1991), p. 344.

sor should review them to make sure they reflect current needs. Preparing and using these materials helps the supervisor base hiring decisions on objective criteria—how well each candidate matches the requirements of the job. Without them, the supervisor risks hiring people just because he or she likes them better than others. In the words of Bruce Male, president of TravCorps, a temporary-nursing service, "Most often we make the mistake of hiring in our own image."[2]

Recruitment

recruitment
Identifying people interested in holding a particular job or working for the organization.

To select employees, the supervisor and human resources department need candidates for the job. Identifying people interested in holding a particular job or working for the organization is known as **recruitment**. Recruitment involves looking for candidates from both inside and outside the organization.

Looking inside the Organization

Many employees are eager to accept a promotion. Less commonly, employees welcome the variety of working in a new department or at a different task even when the transfer does not involve more money or prestige. As mentioned in Chapter 9, such changes can be a source of motivation for employees. Motivation of employees is only one way the organization benefits from promotions and transfers. In addition, the promoted or transferred employees start the new job already familiar with the organization's policies and practices. It may be easier to train new people for entry-level jobs than to hire outsiders to fill more complex positions.

To find employees who are interested in and qualified for a vacant position, the supervisor or human resources department recruits within the organization. The

Job descriptions can vary widely, even within the same company. Sergio Bardaji (left) is a manager with the Metro–New York territory for food services, and Emmanuel Geerinckx (right) is a Jacobs Suchard coffee buyer, shown here in Choisy Le Roi, France. Both work for Philip Morris Companies, Inc.

Source: Courtesy of Greg Beechler, photographer.

two basic ways of conducting such internal recruitment are through job postings and employee referrals. A job posting is a list of the positions that are vacant in the organization. Typically, the job posting gives the title of the job, the department, and the salary range. In addition, the supervisor's employees may be able to recommend someone for the job. In many cases they recommend friends or relatives who do not currently work for the organization, or they may meet qualified candidates at meetings of trade or professional groups. Some organizations pay employees a bonus for referrals if the candidate is hired.

Looking outside the Organization

Especially if an organization is growing, it will need to find at least some of its employees by looking outside the organization. New-hires are less familiar with the organization, but they bring fresh ideas and skills that the organization currently lacks. The basic ways to identify qualified candidates outside the organization are through advertising, employment agencies, and schools.

Help-wanted advertisements, such as the ones shown in Chapter 1, are a popular way to recruit candidates for a job. Most people at some time or another read the want ads in their local paper to see what jobs are available. Besides advertising in newspapers, organizations can advertise in journals and magazines directed toward a specialized audience. For example, a research laboratory looking for a writer might advertise in *Technical Communications*, and a manufacturer looking for an engineer to develop new products might advertise in *Design News*. Advertising in these kinds of specialized publications limits the recruiting to candidates with a background (or at least an interest) in the relevant field.

Employment agencies seek to match people looking for a job with organizations looking for employees. These agencies may be government run, in which case they do not charge for their services. Other employment agencies are private. Many private agencies charge the employer for locating an employee; some charge the person looking for a job. In either case, the agency collects a fee only when someone is hired. Using an agency makes sense when the organization lacks the time or expertise to carry out an effective recruiting effort. Agencies also help screen candidates, a step in the selection process described in the next section of this chapter.

Depending on the requirements of the job, the supervisor might want employees who have recently graduated from high school, a community college, a trade school, a prestigious university, or some other type of school. In such cases, the organization might seek job candidates through schools that are appropriate. Large organizations that expect to hire many recent graduates sometimes send recruiters to talk to students at the targeted schools. Many schools also arrange various kinds of listings of employers who are interested in hiring. Recruiting through schools is a way to limit candidates to those with the desired educational background.

The Selection Process

In recent years, organizations typically have had many more candidates than they have needed to fill their vacant positions. Thus, once an organization has identified candidates for a job, it begins the major work: the selection process. Through this process, the supervisor and human resources department seek to find the person who is best qualified to fill a particular job. Figure 13.3 shows how the various steps in the selection process narrow the field of candidates. Usually the human resources department does the initial screening, and the supervisor makes the final decision.

Screening from Employment Applications and Résumés

Candidates for a job respond to recruitment by filling out an employment application or sending in a résumé. Figure 13.4 shows a sample employment application. (Résumés are discussed in the Reference Guide.) The first stage of the selection process is to review the applications or résumés to screen out candidates who are unqualified or who are less qualified than others. The objective of screening is to narrow the pool of applicants to the number that the supervisor or human resources department wants to interview for the job.

Usually someone in the human resources department takes care of the screening process. This person compares the applications or résumés with the job descrip-

FIGURE 13.3

The Selection Process

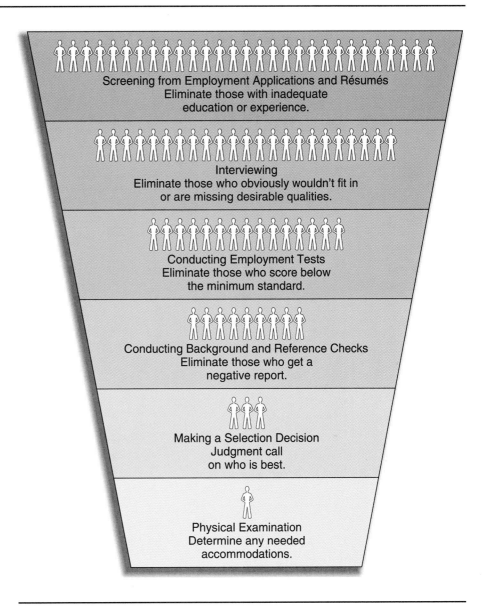

Screening from Employment Applications and Résumés
Eliminate those with inadequate
education or experience.

Interviewing
Eliminate those who obviously wouldn't fit in
or are missing desirable qualities.

Conducting Employment Tests
Eliminate those who score below
the minimum standard.

Conducting Background and Reference Checks
Eliminate those who get a
negative report.

Making a Selection Decision
Judgment call
on who is best.

Physical Examination
Determine any needed
accommodations.

tion prepared by the supervisor. As noted in Figure 13.3, candidates who obviously do not meet the qualifications called for in the job description are eliminated.

While the supervisor seldom participates actively in this process, he or she sometimes knows of a candidate he or she would like to consider. In such cases, the supervisor can send the human resources department the name of this person, asking that the person be included in the selection process. It would be unusual for the human resources department to screen out a person that the supervisor wants included.

FIGURE 13.4

Sample Employment Application

APPLICATION FOR EMPLOYMENT
(PRE-EMPLOYMENT QUESTIONNAIRE) (AN EQUAL OPPORTUNITY EMPLOYER)

PERSONAL INFORMATION

DATE

NAME (LAST, FIRST, MIDDLE) SOCIAL SECURITY NUMBER

PRESENT ADDRESS (STREET, CITY, STATE, ZIP)

PERMANENT ADDRESS (STREET, CITY, STATE, ZIP)

PHONE NO. ARE YOU 18 YEARS OR OLDER? Yes ☐ No ☐

ARE YOU EITHER A U.S. CITIZEN OR AN ALIEN AUTHORIZED TO WORK IN THE UNITED STATES? Yes ☐ No ☐

EMPLOYMENT DESIRED

POSITION DATE YOU CAN START SALARY DESIRED

ARE YOU EMPLOYED NOW? IF SO MAY WE INQUIRE OF YOUR PRESENT EMPLOYER?

EVER APPLIED TO THIS COMPANY BEFORE? WHERE? WHEN?

REFERRED BY

EDUCATION	NAME AND LOCATION OF SCHOOL	*NO OF YEARS ATTENDED	*DID YOU GRADUATE?	SUBJECTS STUDIED
GRAMMAR SCHOOL				
HIGH SCHOOL				
COLLEGE				
TRADE, BUSINESS OR CORRESPONDENCE SCHOOL				

LAST FIRST MIDDLE

GENERAL
SUBJECTS OF SPECIAL STUDY OR RESEARCH WORK

SPECIAL SKILLS

ACTIVITIES: (CIVIC, ATHLETIC, ETC.)
EXCLUDE ORGANIZATIONS, THE NAME OF WHICH INDICATES THE RACE, CREED, SEX, AGE, MARITAL STATUS, COLOR OR NATION OF ORIGIN OF ITS MEMBERS.

U.S. MILITARY OR NAVAL SERVICE RANK PRESENT MEMBERSHIP IN NATIONAL GUARD OR RESERVES

*The Age Discrimination in Employment Act of 1987 prohibits discrimination on the basis of age with respect to individuals who are at least 40 years of age.

TOPS FORM 3285 (89-8) (CONTINUED ON OTHER SIDE) LITHO IN U.S.A.

FORMER EMPLOYERS (LIST BELOW LAST THREE EMPLOYERS, STARTING WITH LAST ONE FIRST).

DATE MONTH AND YEAR	NAME AND ADDRESS OF EMPLOYER	SALARY	POSITION	REASON FOR LEAVING
FROM				
TO				
FROM				
TO				
FROM				
TO				
FROM				
TO				

WHICH OF THESE JOBS DID YOU LIKE BEST?

WHAT DID YOU LIKE MOST ABOUT THIS JOB?

REFERENCES: GIVE THE NAMES OF THREE PERSONS NOT RELATED TO YOU, WHOM YOU HAVE KNOWN AT LEAST ONE YEAR.

NAME	ADDRESS	BUSINESS	YEARS ACQUAINTED
1			
2			
3			

THE FOLLOWING STATEMENT APPLIES IN: MARYLAND & MASSACHUSETTS. (Fill in name of state)
IT IS UNLAWFUL IN THE STATE OF ______________ TO REQUIRE OR ADMINISTER A LIE DETECTOR TEST AS A CONDITION OF EMPLOYMENT OR CONTINUED EMPLOYMENT. AN EMPLOYER WHO VIOLATES THIS LAW SHALL BE SUBJECT TO CRIMINAL PENALTIES AND CIVIL LIABILITY.

Signature of Applicant

IN CASE OF EMERGENCY NOTIFY (NAME, ADDRESS, PHONE NO.)

"I CERTIFY THAT THE FACTS CONTAINED IN THIS APPLICATION ARE TRUE AND COMPLETE TO THE BEST OF MY KNOWLEDGE AND UNDERSTAND THAT, IF EMPLOYED, FALSIFIED STATEMENTS ON THIS APPLICATION SHALL BE GROUNDS FOR DISMISSAL.

I AUTHORIZE INVESTIGATION OF ALL STATEMENTS CONTAINED HEREIN AND THE REFERENCES LISTED ABOVE TO GIVE YOU ANY AND ALL INFORMATION CONCERNING MY PREVIOUS EMPLOYMENT AND ANY PERTINENT INFORMATION THEY MAY HAVE, AND RELEASE ALL PARTIES FROM ALL LIABILITY FOR ANY DAMAGE THAT MAY RESULT FROM FURNISHING SAME TO YOU.

I UNDERSTAND AND AGREE THAT, IF HIRED, MY EMPLOYMENT IS FOR NO DEFINITE PERIOD AND MAY, REGARDLESS OF THE DATE OF PAYMENT OF MY WAGES AND SALARY, BE TERMINATED AT ANY TIME WITHOUT PRIOR NOTICE AND WITHOUT CAUSE."

DATE SIGNATURE

DO NOT WRITE BELOW THIS LINE

INTERVIEWED BY DATE

REMARKS:

NEATNESS ABILITY

HIRED: ☐ Yes ☐ No POSITION DEPT.

SALARY/WAGE DATE REPORTING TO WORK

APPROVED: 1. EMPLOYMENT MANAGER 2. DEPT. HEAD 3. GENERAL MANAGER

This form has been designed to strictly comply with State and Federal fair employment practice laws prohibiting employment discrimination. This Application for Employment Form is sold for general use throughout the United States. TOPS assumes no responsibility for the inclusion in said form of any questions which, when asked by the Employer of the Job Applicant, may violate State and/or Federal Law.

Interviewing Candidates

When the human resources department has narrowed down the list of candidates to a few people, the next step is to interview them. Objectives of interviewing include narrowing the search for an employee by assessing each candidate's interpersonal and communication skills, seeing whether the supervisor and employee are comfortable with one another, and learning details about information on the application or résumé. In addition, the candidates have an opportunity to learn about the organization, which helps them decide whether to accept a job offer.

Depending on the policies and practices of a particular organization, the supervisor may participate in interviewing. For example, the candidates may meet first with someone in the human resources department and then with the supervisor. For this reason, supervisors can benefit from understanding how to interview effectively. The "Tips from the Firing Line" box provides some ideas for effective interviewing.

Learning and carrying out effective interviewing practices may seem like a lot of trouble at times. When tempted to look for shortcuts, the supervisor should

A Logical Approach to Interviewing

According to consultant William Swan, most managers do not know how to interview effectively. Swan says studies show that most interviewers decide whether to hire within the first six to eight minutes of the interview. They base their decision on such unreliable indicators as a firm handshake, pleasant smile, or resemblance to a successful employee. As an alternative approach, Swan recommends using these more logical techniques:

- *Know the job requirements.* Be specific about what skills and general traits are required, as well as the specific demands posed by the job and company.
- *Make the interview friendly and relaxed.* All you can learn from a stressful, high-pressure interview is how the candidate responds to stress in an interview. Furthermore, candidates are likely to be less open and frank when they feel under fire.
- *Ask candidates to describe their work history, beginning with their earliest experiences.* People think in chronological order; that is, they start with the earliest events, then move on to more recent events. Because this is a more natural thought pattern, people who describe their work history in this order are more apt to be spontaneous.

- *Listen first.* Use the first part of the interview to listen to the candidate describe his or her interests and experiences. Then you will know what aspects of the job to stress in the final portion of the interview. And if you decide you are not interested in the candidate, you can save time by keeping the description of the job brief.
- *Ask open-ended questions and follow-up questions.* Use questions that lead to explanations, not just one-word answers. Such questions often start with the words *what*, *tell me*, *explain*, and *describe*. After the candidate provides an answer, pause before you continue. Sometimes the silence will encourage the candidate to provide more information.
- *Take notes.* According to research, when interviewers do not take notes, they are most influenced by what happened at the beginning and end of the interview—an approach that can neglect key data. Taking notes does not have to be hard. Just jot down key words and phrases on a sheet of paper attached to a clipboard.

Source: William Swan, "The Art of the Interview," *Working Woman*, May 1990, pp. 96–97.

bear in mind the significance of selection interviews. For any new employee, the organization will spend tens, maybe hundreds, of thousands of dollars on salary, benefits, and training. Thus, it is at least as important to collect the information needed for making the right hiring decision as it is to do the research for making other investments of comparable size. Viewed in this light, carefully preparing for and conducting a selection interview is well worth the time and effort.

Preparation for the Interview To prepare for the interview, the interviewer should review the job description and develop a realistic way to describe the job to candidates. The interviewer also should review the applicant's résumé or job application. The interviewer should consider whether the information given there suggests some specific questions to ask. For example, the interviewer might want to know why a candidate chose a particular major in school or switched fields—perhaps, for example, a candidate left a job as a salesperson to become a mechanic. The interviewer will also want to inquire about any time gaps between jobs. Finally, the interviewer should arrange for an interview location that meets the conditions described in the next section.

Interviewing can be stressful. Some interviewers create a less formal setting by eliminating the desk between themselves and the candidate.

Source: Courtesy of Four by Five, Inc.

Interview Conditions Most job candidates feel at least a little bit nervous. This can make it hard for the interviewer to tell what the person would be like on the job. Therefore, it is important for the interviewer to conduct the interview under conditions that put the candidate at ease. Good interview conditions include privacy and freedom from interruptions. Seating should be comfortable. Some interviewers sit next to the candidate at a small table, rather than behind a desk, to create a less formal, more equal setting. Other ways to put candidates at ease include offering a cup of coffee and taking a minute or two for comments on a general, noncontroversial topic such as the weather.

Privacy is sometimes difficult for a supervisor to arrange. Many supervisors do not have an office with a door to close. If possible, the supervisor should arrange to use a conference room or someone else's office. At the very least, a supervisor interviewing in a cubicle should hang a Do Not Disturb sign outside.

Content of the Interview After making the candidate comfortable, the interviewer should begin by asking general questions about the candidate's background and qualifications. The interviewer should also ask candidates about their goals and their expectations for the job. The following questions are among those most commonly asked:[3]

- Why do you want to work for our organization?
- What kind of career do you have planned?
- What have you learned in school to prepare for a career?
- What are some of the things you are looking for in an organization?
- How has your previous job experience prepared you for a career?
- What are your strengths? weaknesses?
- Why did you choose the school you attended?

FIGURE 13.5

The Interviewing Process

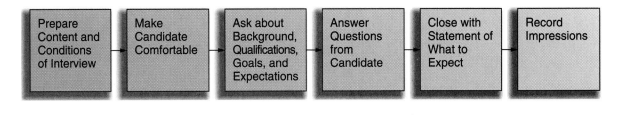

- What do you consider to be a worthwhile achievement of yours?
- Are you a leader? Explain.
- How do you plan to continue developing yourself?
- Why did you select your major?
- What would you like to know about my organization?

When the interviewer has asked enough questions to gauge the candidate's suitability for the position, he or she should give the candidate a chance to ask questions. This not only can help the candidate learn more, but it can give the interviewer insight into the candidate's understanding and areas of concern.

The interviewer should close by telling the candidate what to expect regarding the job, such as a phone call in a week or a letter by the end of the month. As soon as the candidate has left, the interviewer should jot down notes of his or her impressions. Memories fade fast, especially when the interviewer has many candidates to meet with. Figure 13.5 summarizes the steps in the interviewing process.

The questions the interviewer asks must be relevant to performance of the job. This means the interviewer may not ask questions having to do with the candidate's age, sex, race, marital status, children, religion, and arrest (as opposed to conviction) record. For example, the interviewer may not ask, "So, are you planning to have any children?" or, "What nationality is that name?" Such questions violate antidiscrimination laws, described later in this chapter. Table 13.2 identifies many permissible and impermissible questions. If the supervisor is in doubt about whether a particular question is allowable, he or she should check with the human resources department before asking it.

structured interview
An interview based on questions the interviewer has prepared in advance.

unstructured interview
An interview in which the interviewer has no list of questions prepared in advance but thinks of questions based on the applicant's responses.

Interviewing Techniques   The person who conducts the interview may choose to make it structured, unstructured, or a combination of the two. A **structured interview** is one based on questions the interviewer has prepared in advance. By referring to the list of questions, the interviewer covers the same material with each candidate. In an **unstructured interview**, the interviewer has no list of questions prepared in advance but thinks of questions based on the applicant's responses. An unstructured interview gives the interviewer more flexibility but makes it harder to be sure that each interview covers the same material.

A practical way to combine these two approaches is to prepare a list of questions that must be covered with each candidate. Then, if the interviewer wants the

TABLE 13.2

Permissible and Impermissible Questions for Selection Interviews

Category	Interviewer May Ask	Interviewer May Not Ask
Name	Current legal name; whether candidate has ever worked under another name	Maiden name; whether candidate has ever changed his or her name; preferred courtesy title (e.g., Ms., Miss, Mrs.)
Address	Current residence; length of residence	Whether candidate owns or rents home, unless it is a bona fide occupational qualification (BFOQ) for the job; name and relationship of person with whom applicant resides
Age	Whether the candidate meets a minimum age requirement set by law (such as being 21 to serve alcoholic beverages)	Candidate's age; to see a birth certificate; how much longer candidate plans to work before retiring; dates of attending elementary or high school; how applicant feels about working for a younger (or older) boss
Sex	Candidate's sex if it is a BFOQ (as in the case of a model or rest room attendant)	Candidate's sex if it is not a BFOQ
Marital and family status	Whether the candidate can comply with the work schedule (must be asked of both sexes if at all)	Candidate's marital status; whether the candidate has or plans to have children; other family matters; information about child-care arrangements; questions about who handles household responsibilities; whether candidate is seeking work just to supplement the household income
National origin, citizenship, race, color	Whether the candidate is legally eligible to work in the United States; whether the candidate can prove this, if hired	Candidate's national origin, citizenship, race, or color (or that of relatives); how candidate feels about working with or for people of other races
Language	List of languages the candidate speaks or writes fluently; whether the candidate speaks or writes a specific language if it is a BFOQ	Language the candidate speaks off the job; how the candidate learned a language

Sources: Richard D. Irwin, Inc., Management Guidelines, Appendix 2, December 1, 1991; Robert N. Lussier, *Supervision: A Skill-Building Approach* (Homewood, Ill.: Irwin, 1989), pp. 254–255; and Janine S. Pouliot, "Topics to Avoid with Applicants," *Nation's Business*, July 1992, pp. 57–58.

open-ended question
A question that gives the person responding broad control over the response.

closed-ended question
A question that requires a simple answer, such as yes or no.

candidate to clarify a response to a particular question, the interviewer asks a follow-up question. For example, he or she might say, "Please tell me about your reasons for handling the problem that way." It is not necessary to ask the questions in the order written, so long as all of them are covered eventually. A candidate's comments may lead the interviewer to want to move to a question further down on the list. Even though the format varies somewhat from candidate to candidate, this approach ensures that the interviewer does not omit important topics from some interviews.

Within either a structured or an unstructured interview, the interviewer may ask questions that are open-ended or closed-ended. An **open-ended question** is one that gives the person responding broad control over the response. A **closed-ended question** is one that requires a simple answer, such as yes or no. An example

Category	Interviewer May Ask	Interviewer May Not Ask
Arrests and convictions	Whether the candidate has been convicted of a felony; other information if the felony is job related	Whether the candidate has ever been arrested; information about a conviction that is not job related
Height and weight	No questions	Candidate's height or weight
Health history and disabilities	Whether the candidate is able to perform the essential functions of the job; how (with or without accommodation) the candidate can perform essential job functions	Whether the candidate is disabled or handicapped; how candidate became disabled; health history; whether the candidate smokes; whether the candidate has AIDS or is HIV positive
Religion	Whether the candidate is a member of a specific religious group when it is a BFOQ; whether the candidate can comply with the work schedules	Religious preference, affiliations, or denomination; name of applicant's priest, pastor, rabbi, or other religious leader
Personal finances	Credit rating if it is a BFOQ	Candidate's credit rating; other information about personal finances, including assets, charge accounts; whether candidate owns a car
Education and work experience	Job-related education and experience	Education and experience that are not job related
References	Names of people willing to provide references; names of people who suggested that the candidate apply for the job	Reference from a religious leader
Military service	Information about job-related education and experience; whether candidate was dishonorably discharged	Dates and conditions of discharge; eligibility for military service; experience in foreign armed services
Organizations	List of memberships in job-related organizations such as unions or professional or trade associations	Memberships in any organizations that are not job related and would indicate race, religion, or other protected group; candidate's political affiliation

of an open-ended question is "What experiences in your past job will help you carry out this one?" Examples of closed-ended questions are "Did you drive a forklift on your last job?" and "Which shift do you prefer to work?"

Open-ended questions tend to be more useful in interviewing, because they lead candidates to provide more information. For example, to learn how thoroughly a candidate has researched the job (an indication of how serious he or she is about the position), the interviewer might ask, "What would you look for if you were hiring a person for this position?"[4] Loretta M. Flanagan, who directs Westside Future, an organization dedicated to reducing infant mortality, uses open-ended questions to learn about job candidates' human relations and problem-solving skills. For example, she might pose this question to a candidate for a case worker position:

A high, drug-using pregnant woman comes into the office, wanting immediate help. She has missed two previously scheduled appointments. The case manager is busy with another client and has a second client arriving in 20 minutes. How do you handle such competing demands?

Of course, there is no single correct answer. Flanagan looks for candidates who show an ability to set priorities and to justify the course of action selected.

Because the candidate decides how to answer an open-ended question, the answer sometimes is not clear enough or specific enough. In such a case, the interviewer will want to probe for more details. He or she might say, "Can you give me an example of that?" or, "What do you mean when you say your last job was 'too stressful'?"

Problems to Avoid   When conducting an interview, the supervisor needs to avoid some common errors in judgment. One of these is making decisions based on personal biases. For example, the supervisor may dislike earrings on men or the dreadlocks hairstyle worn particularly by some African-Americans. However, these characteristics seldom, if ever, would determine how well a candidate would carry out a job. Likewise, being a friend or relative of the supervisor is not a good predictor of job performance. Making a hiring decision based on these and other biases can lead the interviewer to exclude the person who is best qualified.

halo effect
The practice of forming an overall opinion on the basis of one outstanding characteristic.

Another source of errors is the **halo effect**, which means forming an overall opinion on the basis of one outstanding characteristic. For example, many people will evaluate someone's personality on the basis of the person's handshake. "She has a firm grasp," an interviewer might think with regard to a candidate. "I can tell that she's energetic, decisive, and gets along well with people." In fact, the candidate may or may not have all those desirable traits. The interviewer needs to look for evidence of each trait, not just lump them all together.

In the example of making judgments based on a handshake, the interviewer is drawing conclusions about personality based on the candidate's body language. A study by Robert Gifford of the University of Victoria suggests that this is a risky approach.[5] Gifford asked 18 experienced interviewers to watch videotapes of selection interviews and to rate the candidates on several traits. Gifford compared the experts' ratings with the results of written tests measuring the same traits. The experts were not always on target. For example, they considered an applicant to be highly motivated if he or she smiled, gestured, and talked a lot. However, the written tests did not support an association between this kind of behavior and motivation.

The supervisor also needs to avoid giving candidates a misleading picture of the organization. If a candidate seems desirable, it can be tempting to describe the organization in glowing terms so that the candidate will want to work there. But if the reality is not so wonderful, the new employee is bound to be disappointed and angry. He or she may even quit. On the other hand, within the bounds of being realistic, the supervisor should give a good impression of the organization and its people. Even if the candidate is not the best person for the job, he or she may someday be a customer or be in a position to influence other people's views about the organization.

Administering Employment Tests

From a résumé or employment application, it is relatively easy to see where a candidate worked and went to school, but how can you tell whether a candidate really has the skills to do the job? Just because Pete Wong works for the marketing division at a candy company does not mean he knows how to sell candy (maybe that is why he wants to leave). Just because Ruth Petersen got a college degree in engineering does not mean she can apply her knowledge to working with others to prepare the layout of an actual plant.

One way to see whether employees have the necessary skills is to administer an employment test. A variety of employment tests are available:

aptitude test
A test that measures a person's ability to learn skills related to the job.

- Tests that measure an applicant's ability to learn skills related to the job are known as **aptitude tests**.
- The applicant may take a **proficiency test** to see whether he or she has the skills needed to perform a job. An example is a typing test for a secretarial position.

proficiency test
A test that measures whether the person has the skills needed to perform a job.

- For jobs such as assembling that require physical skills, applicants may take a **psychomotor test**, which measures a person's strength, dexterity, and coordination.
- Sometimes organizations also use personality tests, which identify various personality traits. One application of these tests would be in filling sales positions; an organization might use a test that compares the applicant's personality with the overall personality of people who have been successful at selling in the past. A logical use of personality tests is to test qualified applicants to find out whether they are a good fit for a particular job.[6] For example, someone who focuses on the big picture rather than on details might be a good worker but probably is not suited to keeping track of a large inventory. Likewise, someone who enjoys working with people might be well suited for a job that requires employees to perform as part of a team.

psychomotor test
A test that measures a person's strength, dexterity, and coordination.

- Finally, some organizations test for drug use, especially when the use of drugs by employees poses a serious safety risk, as in the case of machine operators or pilots. Such tests are controversial, but they are legal in most states.[7]

Usually the human resources department handles the testing of applicants.

Some tests contain language or other biases that make them easier for employees of one ethnic group than another. Using these tests could violate antidiscrimination laws, described later in this chapter. If a supervisor wants to use employment tests, the supervisor should have the tests reviewed by the human resources department to make sure that they are not discriminatory.

Despite these restrictions, employers can be creative in devising employment tests. At Advanced Network Design of La Mirada, California, Dave Wiegand, the company's president, interviews and hires salespeople. As his interview with a candidate nears an end, Wiegand leaves the conference room for his office, asking the candidate to call him there and pretend to be a salesperson trying to set up an appointment with a potential customer. Wiegand and two colleagues listen to the candidate's approach over Wiegand's speakerphone. Next, Wiegand gives the candidate specifications for two products and asks the candidate to sell him one product over the other.[8] These two tests weed out candidates with poor selling skills, and they allow Wiegand to give fair consideration to people who do not interview well but would make good salespeople.

Conducting Background and Reference Checks

According to Carl King, president of Team Building Systems of Houston, Texas, 30 percent of all résumés contain false information.[9] A basic way to verify that the information on a job application or résumé is correct is to check references. Not only can checking an employee's background save the organization from hiring an unqualified person, it can protect the organization from lawsuits. The courts have held employers responsible for crimes committed by employees when the organization did not reasonably investigate an applicant's background and hired someone with a history of misdeeds for a position where he or she could do harm.[10]

The supervisor or a member of the human resources department may call or write to schools and former employers, or the organization may pay an employee-screening company to do a background check. The $100 or so per candidate that it costs to use one of these companies can be well worthwhile in an organization that is too small for a human resources staff.[11]

Applicants may give several kinds of references:

- Personal references (people who will vouch for the applicant's character)
- Academic references (teachers or professors who can describe the applicant's performance in school)
- Employment references (former employers who can verify the applicant's work history)

Most people can think of a friend or teacher who can say something nice about them, so the main use of personal and academic references is to screen out the few cases of people who cannot do so.

Previous employers are in the best position to discuss how an applicant has performed in the past. However, to avoid lawsuits from former employees, many organizations have a policy of not giving out much information about past employees. Often a background check will yield only that the applicant did in fact hold the stated position during the dates indicated. Some employers may be willing to discuss the applicant's performance, salary, promotions, and demotions. Because previous employers are cautious about what they disclose, a phone call to a former supervisor can be more fruitful than a written request for information. People are often willing to make statements over the phone that they will not commit to writing.

Making the Selection Decision

The final decision of whom to hire is usually up to the supervisor. Typically, more than one person will survive all the preceding steps of the screening process. As a result, the final decision is usually a judgment call. Jill Strode, described at the beginning of this chapter, once resolved such a dilemma by paying each of two candidates to work for one day (on separate days). Observing them on the job made the selection easier. A supervisor can improve his or her selections by applying the principles of effective decision making covered in Chapter 8.

Martha Mendoza, executive director of HIMRI, a community organization that is part of the Chicago Healthy Start Initiative, is responsible for hiring or supervising 52 employees. When selecting new employees, Mendoza checks their references.

When the supervisor has selected the candidate to hire, the human resources department or supervisor offers the job to the candidate. The person who offers the job is responsible for negotiating pay and fringe benefits and for settling on a starting date. If none of the candidates a supervisor has identified seem satisfactory, the supervisor need not pick one but can repeat the recruiting process, perhaps looking in new places or trying to attract better candidates by offering more money.

Requesting a Physical Examination

In the past, many organizations have required that job candidates pass a physical examination. But since Congress passed the Americans with Disabilities Act (described later in the chapter), experts have advised that employers request a physical exam only after a job offer is made.[12] A physical examination after the job offer helps the organization determine whether the person is physically able to fulfill job requirements, yet the timing of the exam reduces the risk that someone will sue the company for refusing to hire him or her because of a disability. Another use of the physical exam is to determine whether the person is eligible for any life, health, and disability insurance that the company offers as benefits.

An illness, disability, or pregnancy may not be used as the basis for denying a person a job unless it makes the person unable to perform the job. If a physical examination suggests a condition that may interfere with the person's ability to perform the essential functions of a job, the company—most likely someone in the human resources department—should ask how it can adapt the equipment or job to accommodate that person. Because of these limitations on the use of information from physical examinations, most organizations will want the human resources department to handle these exams and the issue of how to accommodate employees with disabilities. The supervisor can then focus on the candidates' experience and talents.

Legal Issues

Congress has passed laws that restrict employment decisions. Most of these laws are designed to give people fair and equal access to jobs based on their skills, rather than on such personal traits as race or physical disabilities. Whatever the supervisor's role in selecting employees, he or she must be aware of the laws affecting hiring so that he or she can help to ensure that the organization's actions are legal.

Antidiscrimination Laws

Certain federal laws prohibit various types of employment discrimination:

- Under Title VII of the Civil Rights Act of 1964 (commonly known as Title VII), employers may not discriminate on the basis of race, color, religion, sex, or national origin in recruiting, hiring, paying, firing, or laying off employees, or in any other employment practices. The government agency charged with enforcing this law is the **Equal Employment Opportunity Commission**.

Equal Employment Opportunity Commission
The federal government agency charged with enforcing the Civil Rights Act.

- The Age Discrimination in Employment Act of 1967, as amended in 1978 and 1986, prohibits employers from discriminating on the basis of age against people over 40 years old.
- The Rehabilitation Act of 1973 makes it illegal to refuse a job to a disabled person because of the disability if the disability does not interfere with the person's ability to do the job.
- The Pregnancy Discrimination Act of 1978 makes it unlawful to discriminate on the basis of pregnancy, childbirth, or related medical conditions; a pregnancy-related disability must be treated as any other disability.
- Disabled veterans and veterans of the Vietnam War receive protection under the Vietnam Era Veterans Readjustment Act of 1974, which requires federal contractors to make special efforts to recruit these people. (This is a type of affirmative action, described in the next paragraph.) In deciding whether a veteran is qualified, the employer may consider the military record only to the extent it is directly related to the specific qualifications of the job.

Figure 13.6 summarizes the categories of workers protected by the antidiscrimination laws. Although some people criticize these laws as a burden on employers, keep in mind that it is to the organization's benefit to make employment decisions on the basis of people's skills rather than their personal traits.

To move beyond simply obeying antidiscrimination laws by avoiding unfair practices, many organizations have established affirmative action programs. **Affirmative action** refers to plans designed to increase opportunities for groups that have traditionally been discriminated against. In effect, these plans are an active attempt to promote diversity in the organization, not just to treat everyone the same way.

affirmative action
Plans designed to increase opportunities for groups that have traditionally been discriminated against.

For example, the management of Corning concluded the company would eventually face staffing problems if it knew how to hire, manage, and promote only white males. As a result, the company now compensates some managers in part on how well they hire and retain women and minorities. In addition, the company has sought to make its location in upstate New York more attractive to minority

FIGURE 13.6

Categories of Workers Protected by Antidiscrimination Laws

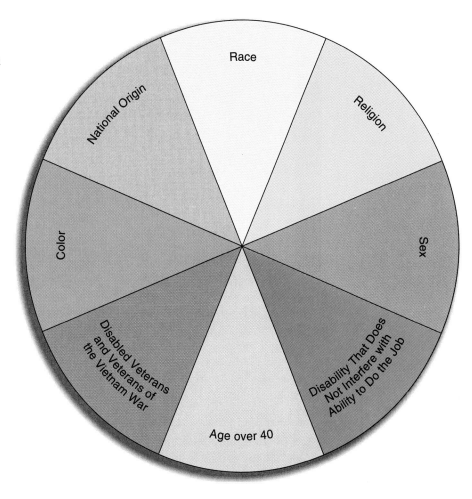

employees. For example, Corning has worked with local stores to increase minority employment, persuaded the local cable TV company to offer the Black Entertainment Television channel, and made plans to sponsor a program for training local teachers in sensitivity to racial and ethnic differences.[13]

Taking another approach, Kansas City Power & Light (KCPL) and Penn Valley Community College have developed a program designed to give women and minorities a chance to learn the lineworker's trade. The program includes academic classes in relevant technologies, coupled with hands-on experience, including climbing 45-foot utility poles. KCPL has committed to hiring 14 of the program's graduates each year; the other graduates are well qualified for jobs at other utilities. KCPL benefits from having a pool of well-qualified potential employees, while women and minorities gain access to well-paying jobs.[14]

Some people mistakenly think that affirmative action involves setting up artificial quotas that favor some groups at the expense of others. However, as the preceding examples show, organizations can use other ways to increase opportunities. Another example is that some companies make a point of doing some of their recruiting at schools with many students who are members of racial minorities.

People who favor affirmative action policies argue that since there are often several candidates with the qualifications to fill any given job, it makes sense to intentionally give some jobs to people from disadvantaged groups. This not only helps to correct past injustices but also benefits the organization by building a diverse work force. Whatever your opinion of affirmative action, it is important to note that—except for employers that have federal contracts or subcontracts—the law does not require organizations to set up these programs. Rather, affirmative action programs are one possible response to laws against discrimination.

Workplace Accessibility

Some organizations believe that hiring people with disabilities is too costly, because it may require the company to provide special facilities. The "Dealing with Diversity" box describes some of the thinking that has led employers to resist hiring disabled workers. But in 1990, Congress passed the Americans with Disabilities Act (ADA), which prohibits employers from discriminating on the basis of mental or physical disability in hiring and promotion. Organizations also must avoid discrimination in public accommodations, transportation, government services, and telecommunications.

Accommodations for Employees with Disabilities   Employers must make accommodations for employees with disabilities if the necessary accommodations are "readily achievable"—that is, easy to carry out and possible to accomplish without much difficulty or expense. Table 13.3 shows the timetable under which the specific provisions of the ADA go into effect. Businesses may receive a tax credit of up to $15,000 to help offset the cost of making their establishments accessible.

This law extends beyond wheelchair accessibility to require accommodations for any disabled employee who can perform the essential functions of a job. This means accommodating a variety of disabilities, including impaired sight and hearing. Among people outside of institutions, the four most common disabilities are arthritis, high blood pressure, hearing impairment, and heart disease.[15]

A number of ways to accommodate disabled workers draw on computer technology. For example, Julie Wilkinson, a computer analyst with American National Bank, is blind. Using a computer that has a Braille display and allows her to give voice commands, Wilkinson can read her mail and print out documents. She can take notes on a portable Braille unit that can later enter the information into the computer. Other computer systems have been designed for a Colorado accountant who can only move one eyebrow, for an Allstate computer worker who has no use of his hands or legs, and for a meteorologist who has cerebral palsy and operates the system with his toe.[16]

One benefit to organizations that comply with the ADA is that it encourages employers to take advantage of a large pool of potential workers whose talents are often ignored. Larry Gorski, director of the City of Chicago Office for People with Disabilities, estimates that 67 percent of the nation's 43 million disabled people are unemployed.[17] Hiring a disabled person has proved worthwhile for Dow Corning, which more than 25 years ago hired George Gant, who has multiple sclerosis. To

DEALING WITH DIVERSITY

Myths about Physical Disabilities

Under federal law, employers may not discriminate against disabled people who are capable of performing the essentials of a job. If, as expected, this means that more people with disabilities will be joining the work force, supervisors and others in the organization must understand these people and what they can offer. One place to start is with abandoning some common myths:

- *Myth #1: People with disabilities can perform only menial or entry-level jobs.* In fact, disabled people already are working at almost all professional levels in almost every field.
- *Myth #2: A disability is an ongoing tragedy; disabled people are therefore brave and heroic.* When disabilities are treated as simply inconveniences, they need only be inconveniences. In other words, disabilities are not tragic when people have access to the accommodations they need.
- *Myth #3: People with disabilities do not really want to work.* Like everyone else, disabled people

want material belongings and the satisfaction of a job well done.
- *Myth #4: People with disabilities are more likely to have on-the-job accidents.* In fact, disabled people overall have a lower rate of accidents than the nondisabled work force.
- *Myth #5: When an organization hires employees with disabilities, insurance rates go up.* Some health rates may rise, but for the most part, insurance rates are based on the hazards of the work and the employer's accident record.
- *Myth #6: Employees with disabilities are often absent from work.* In the experience of most companies, the attendance records of disabled employees are at least as good as those of nondisabled employees.

Source: Hugh H. McDonough, "Hiring People with Disabilities," *Supervisory Management*, February 1992, pp. 11–12.

TABLE 13.3 **Americans with Disabilities Act: Deadlines for Compliance**	**Date**	**Requirements**
	August 26, 1990	Newly purchased or leased mass-transit vehicles must be accessible to persons with disabilities.
	January 26, 1992	Most existing public accommodations and mass transit must be accessible when modifications are "reasonably achievable."
	July 26, 1992	Businesses with 25 or more workers may not discriminate in the employment of persons with disabilities.
	January 26, 1993	New public accommodations intended for occupancy after this date must be accessible.
	July 26, 1994	Businesses with 15–24 workers may not discriminate in the employment of persons with disabilities.

Source: Adapted from Wilma Randle, "Opening Opportunities for Disabled: Confusion, Debate Still Trail New Law," *Chicago Tribune*, December 1, 1991, sec. 7, p. 1.

enable him to work at Dow, the company installed ramps, made bathrooms accessible, and provided parking. Gant, in turn, has blessed the company by developing many chemical patents, training other employees, and establishing processes to improve the commercialization of Dow's products and services.[18]

At the Ottertail Power Company in Minnesota, Duane Rose helped enlarge the lobby to include this handicapped-accessible elevator.

Source: Courtesy of Ottertail Power Co.

What Supervisors Can Do Supervisors can take several steps to comply with the ADA. One is to review and revise job descriptions.[19] Since the organization may not discriminate against those who can perform the essential functions of the job, each job description should indicate what is essential. It should focus on the results the employee must achieve, rather than the process for achieving those results. For example, a job description for a telephone lineworker might say "Repair telephone lines located at the top of a pole" but not "Climb telephone poles."[20] In addition, supervisors should make sure that production standards are reasonable; current employees should meet those standards.

When interviewing candidates, the supervisor should be careful not to ask whether they have a physical or mental condition that would prevent them from performing the job. Rather, after making a job offer, the organization will seek to accommodate any impairments the person may have. Similarly, the supervisor should not ask for candidates' health history, including any on-the-job injuries that candidates have suffered.

Immigration Reform and Control Act

By passing the Immigration Reform and Control Act (IRCA) of 1986, Congress gave employers responsibility for helping to discourage illegal immigration. The IRCA forbids employers from hiring illegal immigrants and requires employers to screen candidates to make sure that they are authorized to work in the United States. At the same time, however, employers may not use these requirements as a rationale for discriminating against candidates because they look or sound "foreign."

This means that the employer must verify the identity and work authorization of *every* new employee. To do this, the employer can ask each new employee to show such documentation as a valid U.S. passport, unexpired Immigration Authorization Service document, unexpired work permit, birth certificate, driver's license, or social security card.[21] In large organizations, this law primarily affects the human resources department, giving it an extra task in the hiring process. In small organizations, however, the supervisor may be responsible for verifying that all his or her new employees are authorized to work in the United States.

Summary

13.1 Explain how supervisors use job descriptions and job specifications to work with the human resources department in selecting employees.

The supervisor prepares job descriptions to specify the characteristics of each job in his or her department or work group. The supervisor prepares job specifications to indicate the desirable characteristics of the person performing each job. The supervisor and the staff of the human resources department use this information to make objective decisions about which people can best perform each job.

13.2 Describe possible sources of employees.

The organization may recruit inside and outside the organization. Current employees may be promoted or transferred to fill job openings, or they may recommend people for jobs at the organization. Outside the organization, employees can be recruited through help-wanted advertisements, employment agencies, and schools.

13.3 Identify the steps in the selection process.

Based on employment applications or résumés, the staff of the human resources department screens out unqualified candidates. Next the human resources department and/or the supervisor interview candidates. The organization may administer employment tests. For candidates the organization is still interested in, background and reference checks are conducted. The supervisor makes a selection decision, after which the candidate may be asked to take a physical examination.

13.4 Discuss how supervisors should go about interviewing candidates for a job.

First, the supervisor should prepare for the interview by reviewing the job description and the applicant's résumé or job application, planning questions, and arranging for a place to interview that offers privacy and freedom from interruptions. When the candidate arrives, the supervisor should make him or her comfortable and then ask about the candidate's goals and expectations for the job. The questions must be relevant to performance of the job and should include open-ended questions. Then the candidate should have a chance to ask questions. The supervisor should close the interview by telling the candidate what to expect. As soon as the candidate leaves, the supervisor should make notes of his or her impressions.

13.5 Identify types of employment tests.

Aptitude tests measure a person's ability to learn job-related skills. Proficiency tests measure whether a person has the skills needed to perform a job. Psychomotor tests measure a person's strength, dexterity, and coordination. Personality tests identify a person's personality traits. Some organizations also test for drug use.

13.6 Describe the requirements of antidiscrimination laws.

The organization, including the supervisor, must avoid actions that discriminate on the basis of race, color, religion, sex, national origin, age over 40 years, or physical or mental disability, including pregnancy-related disabilities. These laws apply to recruiting, hiring, paying, firing, and laying off employees and to any other employment practice. In addition, federal contractors and subcontractors must use affirmative action to encourage the employment of minorities and veterans of the Vietnam War. When evaluating the qualifications of veterans, the employer may use only the portions of the military record that are related to job requirements.

13.7   Explain how hiring decisions are affected by the Americans with Disabilities Act (ADA).
The ADA prohibits discrimination on the basis of mental or physical disability against people who can perform the essential functions of a job. Instead, employers must make accommodations for employees with disabilities if the necessary accommodations are readily achievable. To comply with

the law, supervisors should review and revise job descriptions to make sure they indicate what functions of the job are essential. When interviewing candidates, the supervisor should avoid asking about disabilities and the candidate's health history.

13.8   Describe the requirements of the Immigration Reform and Control Act (IRCA) of 1986.
Under the IRCA, employers are responsible for helping to discourage illegal immigration. They may not hire people who are not authorized to work in the United States, yet they may not discriminate against people who simply appear to be foreigners. Thus, employers must verify the identity and work authorization of every new employee.

Key Terms

job description

job specification

recruitment

structured interview

unstructured interview

open-ended question

closed-ended question

halo effect

aptitude test

proficiency test

psychomotor test

Equal Employment Opportunity Commission

affirmative action

Review and Discussion Questions

1. What information is contained in a job description and a job specification? How do the supervisor and human resources department use these materials?
2. This chapter quotes a business executive as saying people tend to "make the mistake of hiring in [their] own image." What does this mean? How does this tendency make it more difficult for organizations to build a diverse work force?
3. In recruiting for each of the following positions, what source(s) of candidates would you recommend using? Explain your choices.
    a. a receptionist for a city government office
    b. a printing press operator
    c. a graphic artist for an advertising agency
    d. a nurse for an adult day-care facility
4. Describe what happens during the screening process. What does the human resources department look for when reading employment applications and résumés?

5. Supervisor Lisa Kitzinger is interviewing candidates for a computer operator job. Lisa works in a cubicle, and she has a secretary who could help out. What can Lisa do to put candidates at ease?
6. Which of the following questions is (are) appropriate for a job interview? Explain your answers.
    a. "Do you attend church regularly?"
    b. "What computer languages have you used?"
    c. "What would you like to be doing five years from now?"
    d. "Are you married?"
    e. "What are your hobbies?"
7. How can an interviewer combine the techniques of the structured and unstructured interview?
8. What errors of judgment do interviewers commonly make? How can they avoid these problems?

9. An airline like Delta has a policy that all its employees must receive a physical examination before they start working for the company. At what point in the selection process should the company request the examination? How may the airline use this information?

10. Which of the following actions would be considered discriminatory under federal laws? Explain your answers.
    a. A company creates a policy that all employees must retire by age 65.
    b. A supervisor gives the biggest raises to men, because they have families to support.
    c. A company that recruits at colleges and universities has a practice of making at least 20 percent of its visits to schools that are historically black.
    d. In a department where employees must do a lot of overtime work on Saturdays, the supervisor avoids hiring Jews because Saturday is their day of rest.

11. Joel Trueheart supervises customer service representatives for a toy company. The employees handle complaints and questions from customers calling the company's toll-free telephone number. To fill a vacancy in the department, Joel has reviewed many résumés and is in the process of interviewing a few candidates. One of the most impressive résumés is that of Sophia Ahmad, but when Joel meets her, he is startled to observe that she seems to be blind. What should Joel do to make sure he is complying with the Americans with Disabilities Act?

A SECOND LOOK

Earlier it was mentioned that Jill Strode, whose story began the chapter, made a final employee selection after observing two candidates work in the office for a day. What kinds of information could she gather from this observation? Can you suggest any ways of gathering the same or similar kinds of information during a selection interview?

Class Exercise

This exercise simulates an abbreviated version of the selection process. Imagine that the manager of a family-style restaurant such as Denny's needs to hire a server. Working together, with the instructor recording notes on the blackboard or overhead projector, the class develops a job description and job specification. When in doubt about the details, class members should use their imaginations. The objective is for the class to agree that these two lists are reasonable and complete.

When the job description and job specification are complete, the class develops a list of a few interview questions that would indicate whether a candidate is appropriate for this job. Besides creating questions to ask, the class might also consider other ways to determine this information during an interview (for example, observing some aspects of the candidates' behavior).

Next, four class members take on the following parts for a role play:

1. The restaurant manager
2. Candidate #1: a college student with eagerness but no restaurant experience
3. Candidate #2: a woman who appears to be at least 60 years old and who was a server for eight years during the 1950s
4. Candidate #3: a man with four years' experience as a server in five different restaurants

The class members taking these roles should feel free to add details to these descriptions of "themselves." The person acting as the supervisor interviews each candidate for no more than about five minutes each. (A real interview would probably last much longer.)

Finally, the class discusses one or both of these topics:

- *Selecting a candidate:* By a show of hands, the class votes for which candidate they would recommend hiring. What are your reasons for choosing a particular candidate?
- *Interviewing techniques:* Did the manager interview objectively, based on the criteria deter-

mined at the beginning of the exercise? Did the interview cover all the important points? Did the manager use open-ended or closed-ended questions? How did the manager's style of questioning help or hurt the information-gathering process? Did the candidates have a chance to ask questions? Did the manager obey the antidiscrimination laws? How did the interviewing experience feel to the candidates? to the manager?

The role-playing interviews could be videotaped and then played back during the discussion.

CASE

In Search of Skilled Laborers

With all the talk of recession and unemployment in recent years, it might seem amazing that manufacturing companies have been having trouble finding skilled workers to fill entry-level jobs. True, the number of such jobs has not exactly skyrocketed, but the demand to hold such jobs has fallen. The sons and daughters of today's laborers and craftspeople are no longer interested in holding jobs like their parents held.

For example, Ingersoll Milling Machine Company's personnel director, Brian Howard, thought it would be easy to fill blue-collar jobs with candidates near the company's location in Rockford, Illinois. But he was disappointed with the kinds of candidates who applied. Recalls Howard, "We had people…that I thought were dyslexic or something because they were printing their letters backwards." In desperation, Howard traveled all the way to northern Wisconsin to find qualified candidates at a two-year technical school in Chippewa Falls.

Part of the difficulty is that today's manufacturing jobs often require more skills than in the past. Formerly, a blue-collar worker would punch the clock and then operate a single machine all day long. But today workers might be expected to participate in problem-solving meetings, to suggest improvements, and to handle a variety of tasks as part of a team. Consequently, according to Don Rice, vice-president of human resources for Torrington Company, a manufacturer of bearings, "We hire people for their heads as well as their hands and arms."

Other companies are broadening the search. Some are establishing apprenticeships to train people in machining, welding, and other trades. Some are visiting high schools and even grade schools to talk about the advantages of a career in manufacturing. These recruiting efforts sometimes prove disappointing. Ron Bullock, the president of Bison Gear & Engineering Corporation, visited a career night for manufacturers at a high school in Downers Grove, Illinois. The total turnout of students was two boys.

1. What sources of job candidates are mentioned in this case? What other sources might these companies use?
2. In the past, when manufacturing jobs were relatively simple and routine, what kinds of characteristics would you look for in a job candidate if you were a supervisor?
3. How would your requirements be different today at a company such as Torrington, which expects employees to participate in decision making?

Source: Michael Arndt, "Wanted: Skilled Labor; Will Educate," *Chicago Tribune*, April 26, 1992, sec. 7, pp. 1, 5.

14

We now believe that learning and knowledge are our only sustainable competitive advantage.

—**W. G. High, Manager, Human Resource Development, Saturn Corporation**

Training Employees

LEARNING OBJECTIVES

14.1 Discuss reasons for conducting an orientation for new employees.

14.2 Describe how the supervisor and human resources department can work together to conduct an orientation.

14.3 Identify methods for conducting an orientation.

14.4 Describe the training cycle.

14.5 Explain how supervisors can decide when employees need training.

14.6 Identify types of training.

14.7 Describe how supervisors can use coaching to support training.

14.8 Discuss how supervisors can evaluate the effectiveness of training.

BACK TO THE BASICS

In Raleigh, North Carolina, Charles Weathersby supervises 34 maintenance workers at North Carolina State University (NCSU). His challenges include responding to situations that involve workers' not being able to read well enough to do their jobs. This inability is costly and risky because employees who cannot read are more likely to make mistakes or cause injuries. For Weathersby, the solution is to train employees in the reading skills they lack.

The first step is identifying which employees need help. This can be challenging because people who lack basic skills are often ashamed and try to hide their illiteracy. "There've been times I haven't realized an employee couldn't read or write," says Weathersby. "Then when I hand an individual a work order and see his or her face go blank, I get the message." Besides staring blankly at written instructions, another indication of reading problems is making mistakes in following written orders. For example, Weathersby says, "We use special chemical-resistant epoxys in the veterinary school and in laboratories. Workers have applied them in the wrong place, and we've spent two days scraping off the coating."

Then comes what Weathersby considers the hardest part of training employees who need help in basic skills: getting employees to participate in training. NCSU offers employees a literacy training program through Wake Technical Community College. To persuade employees to enroll in this program, Weathersby points out to them what they are missing by not being able to read well enough. He also explains that more education can lead to promotions.

After employees decide to participate in the training program, Weathersby's job turns to helping them succeed. "Scheduling poses problems," explains Weathersby, "because we have to make transportation arrangements. I'm running my own school bus shuttle here because our maintenance facilities are so spread out." Class sessions run from 11:00 A.M. to 1:30 P.M. (paid time), and the workday ends two hours later. To fill the two-hour time slot at the end of the day, Weathersby assigns employees in training to tasks near the classes. Besides being flexible with employees, Weathersby helps by informally tutoring them when they come to him with questions about their coursework. And when co-workers make fun of the employees in the program, Weathersby's job includes stopping this destructive behavior.

Weathersby believes that the literacy training is well worth the time and effort required. "I end up with better employees," he explains. "If nothing else, the time loss is more than made up by cutting down on the extra supervisory time that's needed by nonreaders."

Source: "In-House Schoolhouse: Build Reading Skills on the Job," *Maintenance Supervisor's Bulletin*, June 10, 1992, pp. 1–4. Photo courtesy of Lucy Coulbourn, NCSU Information Services.

training
Increasing the skills that will enable employees to better meet the organization's goals.

Supervisors are responsible for making sure that their employees know what to do and how to do it. Good selection practices ensure that employees are capable of learning their jobs and perhaps already know how to carry out many of the tasks they were hired to perform. However, even the best employees need some degree of training. In this context, **training** refers to increasing the skills that will enable employees to better meet the organization's goals.

Businesses in the United States spend $210 billion a year on employer-based training.[1] They do so because it meets important needs. New employees need a chance to learn the specific ways things are done in the organization. In addition, employees are best equipped to contribute in a changing workplace when they have an opportunity to learn new skills and improve existing ones through a variety of training programs. Well-trained employees can deliver higher quality than poorly trained people. Training can improve productivity by holding down a variety of costs, from overtime pay for employees unfamiliar with their jobs, to workers' compensation and lost time of employees injured when they fail to follow safe practices, to lawsuits arising from misconduct such as sexual harassment (see the "Dealing with Diversity" box). Finally, well-trained employees are likely to be more satisfied because they know what they are doing and how it contributes to achieving the organization's goals. Figure 14.1 on page 360 shows areas in which recently surveyed U.S. companies were conducting training.

This chapter describes types of training and how supervisors can participate in training their employees. It begins by discussing employees' first learning experience: orientation. Next it discusses types of training available once employees are on board and describes how supervisors can help assess when training is needed. The chapter also addresses the topics of coaching employees and evaluating the success of training efforts.

Orientation of New Employees

orientation
The process of giving new employees the information they need to do their work comfortably, effectively, and efficiently.

Do you remember your first day at your current or most recent job? When you arrived, you might not have known where you would be working or where the rest rooms were. You probably did not know your co-workers or how they spent their lunch hour (eating and playing cards in a nearby cafeteria? working out at a local gym?). You might not have known the details of how to carry out your job, including where and how to get the supplies or materials you would need.

The uncertainty you felt because of this lack of information is common to new employees in all kinds of organizations. To help employees over this hurdle, organizations provide formal or informal orientation programs. **Orientation** refers to the process of giving new employees the information they need to do their work comfortably, effectively, and efficiently.

Why Orient New Employees

An employee who spends the day hunting for the photocopier, trying to figure out how to operate a cash register, or looking for someone to explain how to fill out a purchase order is not working efficiently. The primary reason organizations have orientation programs is that the sooner employees know basic information related to doing their job, the sooner they can become productive. They can work faster

Training Employees to Prevent Sexual Harassment

The problem of sexual harassment was introduced in Chapter 8. An employee who sexually harasses another employee hurts the organization in several ways. First, the person who is being harassed is upset and unable to work as effectively as possible. If that person complains, disciplining the harasser may involve transferring or dismissing him or her, resulting in the loss of an otherwise qualified employee. And if the harassed person sues, the company faces the embarrassment and expense of defending itself in court. Clearly it is in the organization's best interests to prevent harassment.

According to George Stillman of Rockville, Maryland–based BNA Communications, most instances of sexual harassment result from ignorance. In other words, people of the opposite sex tend to interpret words and actions differently. For example, whereas men often view a proposition as flattering, women are more apt to react negatively. Likewise, when women behave in a way they view as simply friendly, men are likely to interpret their behavior as a come-on. Such differences in perception also occur among people of different cultures. So to make sure employees know how to avoid harassment, an increasing number of organizations are providing training in this area.

David P. Tulin, president and lead trainer of Tulin DiversiTeam Associates, based in Philadelphia, offers the following lessons in avoiding sexual harassment:

- When in doubt, do not say or do it.
- When in doubt, ask if it is all right.
- If the behavior is unwanted, stop the behavior.
- Do not assume that friendliness equals sexual interest.

Tulin emphasizes that sexual harassment is not defined by the intent of the actor but by the effect of his or her behavior on the person being harassed.

Source: Peggy Stuart, "Prevent Sexual Harassment in Your Work Force," *Personnel Journal*, December 1991, p. 34.

and with fewer errors, and their co-workers and supervisor can spend less time helping them.

Not only does orientation give new employees the knowledge they need to carry out their work, it also reduces their nervousness and uncertainty. This frees new employees to focus on their jobs rather than their worries, thereby boosting employee efficiency. It also leads employees to be more satisfied and less likely to quit.

Another reason for conducting orientation is to develop a positive attitude in employees. The time spent conducting an orientation session shows that the organization values the new employees. This will almost certainly add to their feelings of satisfaction and desire to cooperate as part of the organization's team. It can make new employees feel more confident that joining the organization was a good idea. In addition, work is more satisfying when we know how to do it well. Therefore, by preparing employees, orientation can boost job satisfaction. The organization, in turn, benefits because employees with positive attitudes are more likely to do good work.

Who Conducts the Orientation

In a small organization, supervisors often are responsible for orienting their employees. It may even be up to each supervisor to figure out how to conduct the orientation. Large organizations more often have a formal orientation program

FIGURE 14.1

Areas in Which Surveyed Companies Provided Training

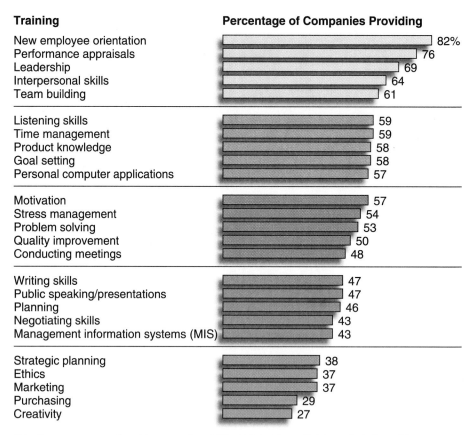

Training	Percentage of Companies Providing
New employee orientation	82%
Performance appraisals	76
Leadership	69
Interpersonal skills	64
Team building	61
Listening skills	59
Time management	59
Product knowledge	58
Goal setting	58
Personal computer applications	57
Motivation	57
Stress management	54
Problem solving	53
Quality improvement	50
Conducting meetings	48
Writing skills	47
Public speaking/presentations	47
Planning	46
Negotiating skills	43
Management information systems (MIS)	43
Strategic planning	38
Ethics	37
Marketing	37
Purchasing	29
Creativity	27

Note: Responses were gathered from a number of different industries and job types, including training, human resources, sales and marketing, and customer service.

conducted by the human resources department. But even in such cases, the supervisor has a role in orientation. While the formal orientation program focuses on information pertaining to the organization as a whole, the supervisor still has information to convey about the specifics of holding a particular job in a particular department.

What to Cover in the Orientation

When the human resources department and supervisor share responsibility for conducting an orientation, the human resources department typically covers topics related to the organization's policies and procedures. These include hours of work (including breaks), location of company facilities such as the lunchroom and exercise facilities, procedure for filling out timesheets, and policies regarding perfor-

At W. W. Grainger, Inc., new branch employees attend the "College of Customer Contact" program. Graduates of the one-week program are estimated to gain the equivalent of three to six months of work experience.

Source: Courtesy of W. W. Grainger, Inc.

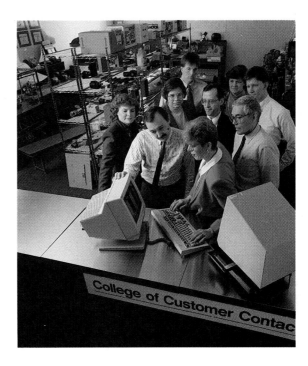

mance appraisals, pay increases, and time off. The human resources department also handles the task of having new employees fill out the necessary paperwork such as enrollment forms for insurance policies and withholding forms for tax purposes. The person conducting the orientation should explain each of these forms to the new employees.

The supervisor is responsible for orientation topics related to performing a particular job in a particular department. The supervisor explains to the employee what the department does and how these activities contribute to the goals of the organization. If the supervisor covered this information in the selection interview, he or she should repeat it during the orientation process. As described later, the supervisor's orientation should include pointing out the locations of facilities the employee will need to use. If the department has any policies and procedures of its own, the supervisor should explain these as well.

The supervisor's orientation should also provide instructions on how to perform the job. For simple jobs, the supervisor may be able to explain the whole job at once, checking back a few times to make sure the new employee understands what to do. Most jobs are more complex than this, requiring the supervisor to give an overview of the job's responsibilities and then, over the course of days or weeks, show the employee how to do different aspects of the job. To build morale while training, the supervisor can also explain why the employee's job is important—that is, how it contributes to meeting department and organizational objectives.

The supervisor should prepare and follow a checklist of the topics to cover during orientation of new employees. Figure 14.2 is adapted from a checklist distributed to supervisors at Swift and Company that is printed on a 2" × 3" card so that supervisors can easily refer to it. In preparing a checklist, the supervisor should include items that fit his or her particular situation.

FIGURE 14.2

Sample Checklist for Orientation

> **Supervisors' Checklist:**
> **The Right Start for New Hourly Paid Employees**
>
> A. Explain (before employee starts the job):
>   1. Rate of pay, including overtime.
>   2. Pay day.
>   3. Initial job or assignment.
>   4. Hours—call out—holiday pay— no tardiness.
>   5. Starting and quitting time.
>   6. Lunch period—relief periods.
>   7. Whom to call if unable to come to work (give name and phone number on card).
>   8. Work clothes arrangement— laundry.
>   9. No smoking areas.
>   10. Safety rules—no running—mesh gloves—reporting all accidents, etc.
>   11. Sanitation—this is a food factory.
>   12. Name benefits (will explain later).
>   13. Possible job difficulties—sore muscles, hands, dizziness, nausea, etc. (encourage to stick it out).
>   14. Buying of company products.
>   15. Nothing from plant without order.
>   16. Importance of quality product.
>
> B. Show:
>   1. Locker—rest rooms.
>   2. Lunch room.
>   3. Where employee will work—introduce to supervisor and immediate co-workers
>   4. Explain the job—use J.I.T.
>
> C. Talk to new employee (to encourage):
>   1. Twice first day.
>   2. Once each day the next four days.
>
> D. After one week, explain:
>   1. Vacation.
>   2. S & A.
>   3. Hospitalization.
>   4. EBA—Group.
>   5. Pension.
>   6. Suggestion plan.
>   7. Union contract, if organized plant (probationary period).

Source: Adapted from a Swift and Company document.

What Methods to Use

The methods the supervisor uses will depend on the organization's policies and resources. For example, a large organization with a human resources department may provide a handbook of information for new employees and spell out orientation procedures to follow. In a small organization, it may be up to the individual supervisor to develop and use the orientation methods. Some common methods include using an employee handbook, conducting a tour of the facilities, and encouraging the involvement of co-workers.

employee handbook
A document that describes an organization's conditions of employment, policies regarding employees, administrative procedures, and related matters.

Employee Handbook   If the organization publishes an employee handbook, the employee should be introduced to this document during the orientation. An **employee handbook** describes an organization's conditions of employment (e.g., attendance, behavior on the job, performance of duties), policies regarding employees (e.g., time off, hours of work, benefits), administrative procedures (e.g., filling out timesheets and travel expense reports), and related matters. The supervisor should show the employee what topics are covered in the handbook and describe how to use it to find answers to questions. For example, an employee might use the handbook to learn when it is possible to change health insurance plans or how long he or she must work in order to qualify for three weeks' vacation.

Tour of Facilities   Another important orientation method is to give the employee a tour. The tour might start with the employee's own work area, which should already be prepared with the supplies, tools, or equipment the employee will need. The supervisor then shows the employee the locations of physical facilities he or she will need to know about, including rest rooms, water fountain, coffee station, and photocopier, and where to get supplies, parts, or other materials needed to do the job.

During the tour, the supervisor should introduce the new employee to the people he or she will be working with. Friendly, positive words during introductions can help make the new employee part of the team. For example, in introducing a new nurse to her colleagues in the hospital, a supervisor might say, "This is Janet Strahn. She's one of the top graduates from Northern, and I know we're all going to appreciate her help." Or in introducing a new maintenance mechanic to a machine operator in the department, a supervisor might say, "Pedro is the guy you'll need if your machine goes down." In both examples, the supervisor is emphasizing the importance of the new employee to the department.

Involvement of Co-Workers   The new employee's co-workers have an important role to play in orientation. Their behavior toward the new employee goes a long way toward making him or her feel either welcome or like an outsider. Therefore, the supervisor should ask all employees to help welcome newcomers. If the organization tries to build team spirit through such activities as clubs and sports teams, the supervisor should see that these are well publicized so that new employees can easily participate. The supervisor may encourage co-workers to invite a new employee to join them on breaks and at lunch. On the employee's first day, the supervisor can help the new employee feel welcome by inviting him or her to lunch.

Follow-Up   Besides the initial giving of information, orientation should involve follow-up. The supervisor should check with new employees at the end of their first day and their first week to make sure they understand what they are supposed to be doing and know where to get what they need. During the initial orientation and each follow-up, the supervisor should encourage employees to ask questions.

Of course, the supervisor should not stop following up after one week. Regularly checking on employees' performance and progress is part of the supervisor's control responsibilities.

Training

As mentioned earlier, employees need continued training even after they have worked for the organization for years. Training shows employees how to do the basics of their jobs and then helps them improve their skills. It also helps employees adapt to changes in the workplace. Because change occurs in every organization (see Chapter 12), the need for training continues.

One organization that appreciates the importance of training is Xerox Corporation, which spends $250 million to $300 million (about 4 percent of its payroll cost) each year on training its 110,000 employees. The training covers a variety of areas, including sales, service, and technical courses.[2] Another company that places heavy emphasis on training is Federal Express. To support the company's concern for quality and its reliance on technology, Federal Express trains customer service people for five to six weeks before they begin work. Couriers train for three to four weeks before beginning to make deliveries.[3]

The Training Cycle

The process of providing training takes place in a cycle of steps, shown in Figure 14.3. The first step is to identify a need for training. As described in the next section of this chapter, identifying training needs is part of the supervisor's job. In addition, higher-level management or the human resources department may identify a need for various kinds of training.

Next, the supervisor or other person proposing the training sets objectives for the training. These objectives are based on a comparison of the current level and the desired level of performance and skills. The training objectives should meet the criteria for effective objectives, as described in Chapter 2. Thus, they should be written, measurable, clear, specific, and challenging but achievable.

Also as part of planning the training, the supervisor decides who will participate in the training program. For example, training how to prevent and avoid sexual harassment applies to all employees, so the whole department would be involved. But training how to operate a new piece of equipment would include only those who would use that equipment. This decision may take into account the interests and motivation levels of employees, as well as their skills. For example, an employee who is eager to advance in the organization will want to participate in many training activities to develop a variety of skills. An employee who is interested primarily in job security will probably want just enough training to keep up-to-date on how to do the job.

The last step in planning training is to choose the training method. Some training methods are described later in this chapter. If selecting a training method is part of the supervisor's role, he or she may wish to consult with the human resources department or a training expert to learn which techniques will best meet the objectives of the training.

Once the training has been planned, someone conducts it. In some cases, the trainer may be the supervisor or even one of the department's employees. In other cases, a professional trainer is more appropriate. The choice depends on the supervisor's or employee's expertise, the content and type of training, and the time available for training. The "Tips from the Firing Line" box on page 366 provides some guidelines for conducting training.

After the training is over, the supervisor evaluates the results of the training. Did it meet the objectives? The last section of this chapter discusses the evaluation of training in greater detail. Evaluation completes the training cycle by helping the supervisor identify needs for additional training.

FIGURE 14.3
The Training Cycle

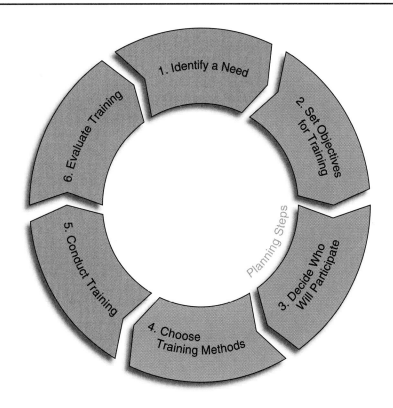

The Training Cycle:
1. Identify a Need
2. Set Objectives for Training
3. Decide Who Will Participate
4. Choose Training Methods
5. Conduct Training
6. Evaluate Training

Planning Steps

The Training Time Frame

Although the supervisor does not always conduct training for employees, part of his or her job includes recognizing when employees need further training. Besides pinpointing when individual employees have particular needs, the supervisor should decide on the most convenient time to meet those needs with a training program. The supervisor makes such decisions because it is he or she who observes employees in action.[4]

The supervisor has several ways to identify training needs. First, the supervisor can observe problems in the department that suggest a need for training. For example, if a restaurant's customers are complaining about the quality of service, the manager might conclude that some or all of the staff needs training in how to satisfy customers. Or if the same defect keeps occurring in the bushings produced at a factory, the production supervisor should investigate whether the people making the part know how to operate their machinery.

Another way to obtain information about training needs is to ask employees. Often, employees have opinions about what they must learn to do a better job. A good time to discuss training needs is during performance appraisals, covered in the next chapter. In addition, the supervisor should encourage employees to communicate their needs as they arise.

Guidelines for Conducting Training

Supervisors and their employees sometimes conduct training in areas where they have expertise. When supervisors conduct training, they should familiarize themselves with the following tips. When an employee conducts training, the supervisor should first spend time going over these training guidelines with the employee-trainer.

- *Prepare thoroughly.* Know what you are going to teach, and prepare notes on the material you will cover. Check any equipment you will use. Also think about who you will be teaching. How much do they know already? How familiar are they with the terms you use?
- *Teach just enough and no more.* Learners can get overwhelmed with information. The training should focus first on the fundamentals of the task. When the trainees are ready to move on, introduce more involved aspects of the job.
- *Phrase information in positive terms.* Another way to simplify learning is to use positive statements. Tell people the right way to do things rather than focus on what to avoid. For example, say, "Turn off the printer before you start to change the ribbon," rather than, "Don't leave the printer on when you're changing a ribbon."
- *Provide opportunities for hands-on experience.* People learn more when they can try out the concepts they hear about. And by watching trainees try out techniques, the trainer can show them what they are doing right or wrong.

- *Be supportive.* Do not be critical of learners who make mistakes. Instead, focus on what they need to change to do the job correctly. Compliment learners on their successes, however small they may seem.
- *Provide a positive role model.* The person conducting training must exhibit the kind of behavior that the training is designed to develop. For example, trainers should be cooperative, efficient, and productive.
- *Know when to stop.* At some point, every learner needs a chance to try the job on his or her own. When the learner has demonstrated understanding of a task, pull back and see if he or she can do it without close supervision. At the same time, remain available to answer questions.

By following these tips—especially by keeping the message clear and simple and by praising learners—the trainer makes the training easier and more enjoyable. This is important because learning is a voluntary activity. The supervisor can require that an employee attend a training session, but it is up to the employee to pay attention and learn the material.

Sources: Bureau of Business Practice, *The Front Line Supervisor's Standard Manual* (Simon & Schuster, 1989); and correspondence from Debbie Jansky, Milwaukee Area Tech Institute, Milwaukee, Wisc.

Finally, the supervisor can identify training needs when carrying out the planning function. Changes expected to occur in the future often require that affected employees receive training in new skills or procedures. For example, if a department or organization will be introducing a new phone system, employees will need to learn how to use it.

Of course, it is not always up to the supervisor to decide when training is required. Government regulations, union work rules, or company policy may dictate training in certain circumstances. If the state mandates some number of continuing education classes for teachers, if the union requires an apprenticeship of so many months for pipefitters, or if the company's top managers decide that everyone needs to take a class in total quality management, the supervisor's job is to make sure that his or her employees are getting the required training.

FIGURE 14.4
Types of Training

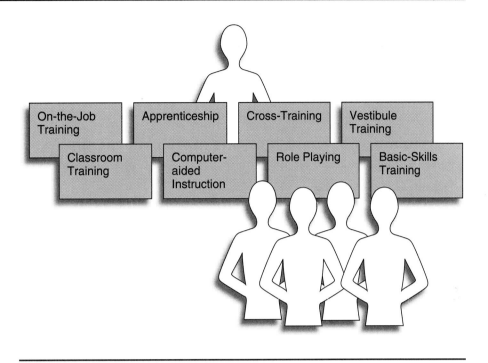

Types of Training

A variety of types of training is available for employees; Figure 14.4 summarizes the major types. In selecting or recommending a type of training, the supervisor should consider the expense relative to the benefits of the training, the resources available, and trainees' needs for practice and individualized attention. The supervisor should consider that, according to educators, people retain only these percentages of what is taught:[5]

- 10 percent of what they read
- 20 percent of what they hear
- 30 percent of what they see
- 50 percent of what they see and hear
- 70 percent of what they see and describe
- 90 percent of what they describe while doing

No matter what type of training is used, the supervisor should be sure that the trainer understands the objectives of the training and how to carry it out. The supervisor should also see that the employees receiving the training are praised when they show progress.

on-the-job training
Teaching a job while trainer and trainee do the job at the work site.

On-the-Job Training   In many cases, the easiest way to learn how to perform a job is to try it. Teaching a job while trainer and trainee do the job at the work site is called **on-the-job training**. The trainer—typically a co-worker or the supervisor—shows the employee how to do the job, and then the employee tries it.

On-the-job training is often the best way to learn a task. At an AT&T factory on Batam Island, Indonesia, a trainer from Singapore shows a new employee how to make a telephone.

Source: Courtesy of Munghi Ahmed, photographer.

An employee who learns in this way benefits from actually being able to try out the skills and techniques being taught. From the results being produced, the employee and trainer can immediately see whether the employee understands what the trainer is trying to teach. However, on-the-job training carries the risk that an inexperienced employee will make costly and even dangerous mistakes. Thus, this training is most suited for learning tasks that are relatively simple or when the costs of an error are not too high. For more complex or risky tasks, it may be wiser to use other forms of training before or instead of on-the-job training.

apprenticeship
Training that involves working alongside an experienced person, who shows the apprentice how to do the various tasks involved in a job or trade.

Apprenticeship   Many tradespeople learn their trade through an **apprenticeship**. This involves working alongside an experienced person, who shows the apprentice how to do the various tasks involved in the trade. Thus, apprenticeship is a long-term form of on-the-job training. (Many apprenticeship programs also require that apprentices complete classroom training.) Most apprenticeships are in the building trades, such as carpentry and pipefitting. However, Fuchs Copy Systems of West Allis, Wisconsin, uses an apprenticeship program to attract and retain enough qualified service technicians for the copiers it sells. Fuchs hires high school and college students to work during the summer or part-time during the school year doing actual repairs—specifically, rebuilding the developer units of the copiers.[6]

According to recent estimates, only 2 percent of U.S. high school graduates complete apprenticeships.[7] Reasons for this low rate include union work rules and the American emphasis on college education (as opposed to learning a trade). An apprenticeship program is more complicated to set up than simple on-the-job training for individual tasks. However, it can help the supervisor organize his or her plans to meet training needs that require months or years of learning.

Cross-Training   As you learned in Chapter 9, an increasing number of organizations are using job rotation, meaning that employees take turns performing various jobs. Job rotation requires that employees learn to perform more than one job. Teaching employees another job so that they can fill in as needed is known as cross-training. Employees who have completed cross-training can enjoy more variety in their work, and their supervisor has more flexibility in making assignments.

Cross-training does not apply only to operating various machines in a factory. Sterling, Virginia–based Global Mail Ltd., which delivers international mail, uses cross-training with its newly hired salespeople. Before they begin sales training, they spend one to three days apiece working in the areas of customer service, accounting, operations, and telephone sales. Handling the paperwork and customer complaints shows the salespeople the consequences of a salesperson writing up an order incorrectly or promising a customer too much.[8]

In planning cross-training, the supervisor should make sure that employees spend enough time practicing each job to learn it well. Some jobs are more complex than others and will require more training time. Also, some employees will learn a given job faster than others will.

vestibule training
Training that takes place on equipment set up in a special area off the job site.

Vestibule Training   While on-the-job training is effective, it is not appropriate as initial training for jobs in which the costs of an error are great, such as piloting or nursing. In those cases, people learn principles or techniques before doing the actual job. A type of training that allows employees to practice using equipment off the job is **vestibule training**. The employees undergoing vestibule training use procedures and equipment set up in a special area called a vestibule. For example, a large retail store might set up a training room containing cash registers, or an airline might use a simulated cabin for training flight attendants.

Vestibule training is appropriate when the organization hires people who do not already know how to use its equipment. It lets employees learn to operate the equipment without the pressure of accidents occurring, customers getting impatient, or other employees depending on a minimum amount of output. Note that while employees are participating in vestibule training or other off-the-job training, they are not producing goods or services for the organization. This adds to the expense of such training. However, if the organization hired only people who already had all the necessary skills, it would probably have to pay a higher wage or salary and might have a difficult time finding enough qualified candidates.

Classroom Training   Other than vestibule training, most off-the-job training involves some form of classroom instruction. Such training takes place in a class or seminar where one or more speakers lecture on the topic to be covered. Seminars are available from a variety of sources on many topics, so the supervisor who is considering attending or sending employees to a seminar should first make sure that the topic to be covered will be relevant to job performance. Classroom training can also occur at the workplace, even if the organization lacks the time or facilities for formal classes. For example, during the monthly staff meetings at Phelps County Bank in Rolla, Missouri, each department took turns giving a one-hour presentation about its functions and products.[9]

The main advantage of classroom training is that the person conducting it can deliver a large quantity of information to more than one person in a relatively short span of time. Depending on the format and trainer, it can be a relatively inexpensive way to convey information. A disadvantage is that most of the communication travels in one direction—from the lecturer to the audience. One-way communication is less engaging and memorable. In addition, classroom training rarely allows the learners to practice what they are learning. Classroom training can be more effective when it includes computer-aided instruction and role playing.

Computer-aided Instruction   Rather than listening to someone lecture, employees can receive instruction via a computer terminal. In some computer-aided instruction programs, the computer displays information and then generates and scores test questions, keeps track of the trainee's performance, and tells the trainee what activities to do next. Other programs may perform only some of these training functions. This is a common way of learning to use a new computer program; the software comes with a series of lessons that give the user a chance to try using it.

To train 45,000 customer-contact employees, couriers, and ground operations personnel around the world, Federal Express makes extensive use of computers. The company trains and tests through an interactive video network; that is, the training system and the trainees are able to send each other messages, which trainees can read on their video screens. The trainees work at their own pace, and the system adapts the program to meet each trainee's needs. After an employee takes a test measuring his or her knowledge, the system tells the employee what he or she still needs to learn. In addition, the company offers college courses and degree programs on personal computers, delivered by an electronic university network.[10]

Some computer-aided training takes the form of simulations. The computer displays conditions that an employee might have to face. For example, a flight simulator would show pilot trainees the cockpit and the view from the window. Another simulation might be of dials and other readouts monitoring the performance of machinery. The trainee uses the computer's keyboard or some other device to respond to the situation displayed by the computer, and the simulator responds by showing the consequences of the trainee's actions. This enables the trainee to practice responding to conditions without suffering the real consequences of a mistake, such as a plane crashing or a boiler exploding.

Training through computer-aided instruction has a significant cost advantage when there are many trainees. The organization may not have to pay a person to act as trainer. In addition, trainees can work at their own pace, which prevents the frustration that arises from a class moving too fast for them to understand material or too slow to maintain their interest. However, some people are nervous about using a computer. In such cases, the supervisor or other trainer must serve as a source of encouragement and help. Also, computer-aided instruction has the disadvantage that employees have no chance to work as a team, ask questions, or exchange ideas.

role playing
A training method that involves assigning roles to participants, who then act out the way they would handle a specified situation.

Role Playing   To teach skills in working with other people, the organization may use **role playing**. This method involves assigning roles to participants, who then act out the way they would handle a specified situation. Some of the class exercises in this book use role playing. A technique that enhances the usefulness of role play-

High-technology training teaches people complex tasks. Here, a pilot uses a dual touch-sensitive video screen inside a Saab 340A/B simulator at Flight-Safety International in New York.

Source: Courtesy of Flight-Safety International.

ing is to videotape the session and then play it back so participants can see how they looked and sounded.

This method of training gives people a chance to practice the way they react to others. Thus, it is especially useful for training in human relations skills such as communicating, resolving conflicts, and working with people of other races or cultures. People who have acted out a particular role—say, the role of supervisor—generally have more understanding and sympathy for that person's point of view. The major potential drawback of role playing is that, to be most useful, it requires a trainer with expertise in conducting it.

A variation on the standard type of role playing is the use of board games that have been developed to teach by showing the consequences of various decisions under different conditions. For example, the Society of Manufacturing Engineers markets a game called the Competitive Manufacturing Game, which teaches modern techniques for improving quality and productivity. Players make decisions related to running a manufacturing operation, such as laying out equipment and investing in improvements, to see who can come up with the most profitable strategy. Or an organization can use a customized game, such as those created by Union City, California–based Corporate Games. The company's games, based on client-supplied information, include indoor and outdoor team competitions, game-show activities, adventure hunts, and murder mysteries.[11]

Basic-Skills Training An often-heard complaint among employers today is that it is increasingly difficult to find enough employees with the basic skills necessary to perform modern jobs. Robert Fowler, president of Hampden Papers in

Holyoke, Massachusetts, says, "There used to be a time when we had plenty of jobs for people who were functionally illiterate, but today our machines are very complex."[12] Despite the need for sophisticated employees, many employers cannot even assume that employees are able to read and do basic arithmetic. Indications that employees cannot read or perform other basic tasks include recurrent accidents and mistakes.

More and more employers are responding to this problem by conducting their own training in basic skills. One such employer is North Carolina State University, as described in the story at the beginning of this chapter. The Armenian Nursing Home in Jamaica Plains, Massachusetts, offers its 75 employees classes in English as a second language; classes in basic reading, writing, and arithmetic; a program leading to a high school diploma; and a course leading to a practical-nursing certificate.[13] In 1991 alone, White Storage and Retrieval Systems, based in Kenilworth, New Jersey, offered 7,000 hours of training in subjects ranging from English as a second language to the use of small tools.[14]

Organizations that offer such programs not only improve the skills of their workers but also attract and keep employees who are highly motivated. At White Storage and Retrieval Systems, for example, employee turnover fell from 25 percent before the company began its training program to only 10 percent a few years afterward.[15] However, basic-skills education offers some challenges to the employer. One is that employees may resist attending because they are embarrassed or afraid the organization will punish them if it finds out they do not have basic skills. To address this challenge, the organization should name the program carefully, calling it something like "workplace education" or "skills enhancement." Supervisors and other managers should reassure employees that participating in the program does not place their jobs in danger. In addition, experts recommend rewarding employees for participating in a basic-skills program. For example, at Loxcreen Company, a South Carolina manufacturer of screen doors, employees are paid at half of their basic wage rate for their time in class.[16]

Coaching to Support Training

coaching
Guidance and instruction in how to do a job so that it satisfies goals for performance.

After employees have received training, the supervisor needs to help them maintain and use the skills they have acquired. To do so, the supervisor takes on the role of coach. **Coaching** is guidance and instruction in how to do a job so that it satisfies goals for performance. Much coaching is done informally to support the more formal training process. Basically, the supervisor observes employees and works with them to solve problems he or she identifies. For coaching to be effective, the supervisor should work on only one problem at a time.

In this role, the supervisor observes employees' performance daily and provides feedback. When employees are properly using their skills, the supervisor should praise them. When employees make a mistake, the supervisor should point it out, describing the behavior rather than calling the employee names. For example, the supervisor might say to a salesclerk, "I saw you snap at a customer. That doesn't fit our standards for customer relations." Then the supervisor and employee should decide how to correct the problem. Sometimes this part of coaching uncovers the need for training. Later, the supervisor again observes the

FIGURE 14.5

The Coaching Process

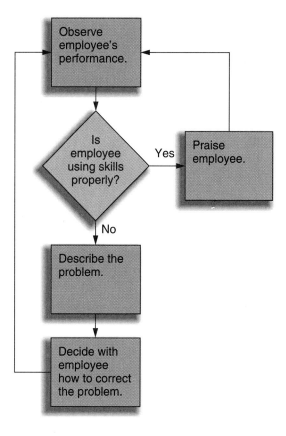

employee's performance to make sure the employee understood what to do and is doing it. Figure 14.5 summarizes the process of coaching.

Notice that the process of coaching is different from simply telling employees what to do. Instead, using techniques from Chapter 8, the supervisor and employee work together to solve performance problems. Acting as a coach therefore is especially important for supervisors in organizations that encourage employees to participate in decision making and teamwork.

Evaluation of Training

The supervisor is often the person in the best position to determine whether training is working. The most basic way to evaluate training is to measure whether the problem addressed by the training is being solved. Are new employees learning their job? Is the defect rate falling? Do employees use the new computer system properly? Are customers now praising the service instead of complaining about it?

Evaluating training is a critical step for supervisors. Watching a previously taped session at The Print & Copy Factory are Allen Hom, Bryan Ho, Sean Skipper, and Joe Balderas.

Source: Courtesy of Robert Holmgren, photographer.

Looking for answers to such questions is central to the control process, described in Chapter 5.

Other people can provide information to help the supervisor evaluate training. The employees who have participated in the training might fill out a questionnaire, such as the one shown in Figure 14.6. Or the organization might set up a team of people to evaluate the organization's training methods and content. This approach has been used at Kansas Gas and Electric Company (KG&E) of Wichita, Kansas.[17] KG&E's power generation department set up a task team—consisting of one plant operator, two mechanics, one electrician, one technician, and the training supervisor—to meet on an as-needed basis and review the department's apprenticeship program. The team surveyed the department's supervisors and trade workers to learn what skills were necessary. Based on the results of that survey, the team modified the information covered in the apprenticeship program so that it includes all the skills actually used by employees.

As in the case of KG&E, if the evaluation suggests that training is not meeting its objectives, the training may have to be modified or expanded. The type of training may not be appropriate for the training needs. For example, new employees who are having difficulty learning job skills may not have enough opportunity to practice what they are being taught. To identify what kinds of changes to make, the supervisor can ask questions such as the following:

FIGURE 14.6

Questionnaire for Evaluating Training

Title of Program _____

Date _____ Job Title _____

Directions: Please indicate your response to each question and return this questionnaire to the program leader. Your responses are confidential. DO NOT SIGN YOUR NAME ON THIS EVALUATION INSTRUMENT.

1. In my opinion, this program was: (check one)
   ____ Excellent   ____Very good   ____Good   ____ Fair   ____Poor

2. Did the program meet the objectives stated in the outline given to you? (check one)
   ____ Yes   ____ No

3. Did the program meet *your* expectations? (Check one)
   ____ Yes   ____ No   If you checked no, please explain _____
   _____

4. Were the training facilities adequate? (Check one)
   ____ Yes   ____ No   If you checked no, please explain _____
   _____

5. In my opinion, the instructor was: (check one)
   ____ Excellent   ____Very good   ____Good   ____ Fair   ____Poor

6. How important was each of these training elements?
   (check one for each element)
   Videotapes   ____Very important ____Worthwhile ____Not important
   Role playing   ____Very important ____Worthwhile ____Not important
   Lecture   ____Very important ____Worthwhile ____Not important
   Handouts   ____Very important ____Worthwhile ____Not important
   Group discusssion   ____Very important ____Worthwhile ____Not important

7. To what extent did you participate in the program? (check one)
   ____ A lot   ____Just enough   ____Somewhat   ____ Not at all

8. How much will the content of this program help you to perform your job responsibilities? (check one)
   ____ A lot   ____Just enough   ____Somewhat   ____ Not at all

9. What other types of training programs are of interest to you? Indicate your preferences. _____
   _____

10. How can this program be improved? Indicate your suggestions._____
    _____

11. Other comments and suggestions. Please indicate any other comments/ suggestions that you feel will be useful in planning future training programs.
    _____
    _____
    _____
    _____
    _____

Source: Donald S. Miller and Stephen E. Catt, *Human Relations: A Contemporary Approach* (Homewood, Ill.: Richard D. Irwin, 1989), p. 330. Used by permission of Donald S. Miller.

- Was the trainer well prepared?
- Did he or she communicate the information clearly and in an interesting way?
- Did the training include visual demonstrations, not just verbal descriptions, of how to do the task?

- Were the employees well enough prepared for the training program?
- Did the employees understand how they would benefit from the training?
- Did employees have a chance to ask questions?
- Did the employees receive plenty of praise for their progress?

Whatever the outcome, training represents a cost to the organization. Consequently, it is worth conducting only when it leads to improved performance, as measured by increased quantity, quality, or both. Training that does not produce results should be changed or discontinued.

Summary

14.1   Discuss reasons for conducting an orientation for new employees.
The primary reason is that the sooner employees know basic information related to their job, the sooner they can become productive. Orientation also reduces the nervousness and uncertainty of new employees, and it develops a positive attitude in them by boosting job satisfaction.

14.2   Describe how the supervisor and human resources department can work together to conduct an orientation.
In a small organization, the supervisor may conduct most or all of the orientation. In a large organization, the human resources department may handle most of the task. In either case, it is up to the supervisor to convey information about the specifics of holding a particular job in a particular department. This includes explaining what the department does and what the new employee's job entails. Typically, the human resources department covers topics related to the organization's policies and procedures.

14.3   Identify methods for conducting an orientation.
During the orientation, the new employee should be introduced to the organization's employee handbook. The supervisor (or someone else) should give the employee a tour of the workplace, pointing out facilities the employee will need to use. During the tour, the employee should be introduced to the people he or she will be working with. The supervisor should instruct the other employees in their role of welcoming the new employee. At the end of the first day and the first week, the supervisor should follow up with the new employee to make sure he or she understands the new job.

14.4   Describe the training cycle.
First, the supervisor (or someone else) identifies a need for training. The next steps involve planning the training: setting objectives, deciding who will participate, and choosing the training method. Then someone conducts the training. The last step is to evaluate the success of the training. Evaluation sometimes suggests needs for additional training.

14.5   Explain how supervisors can decide when employees need training.
The supervisor may observe problems in the department that indicate a need for training. The supervisor may ask employees about what kinds of training they need. Planning for expected changes also uncovers training needs.

14.6   Identify types of training.
The organization may use on-the-job training, which involves learning while performing a job. Related training methods are apprenticeship and cross-training (training employees in more than one job). The training may also take place off the job, through vestibule training or in a classroom. Classroom training can be more effective when it includes computer-aided instruction and role playing. Some computer-aided instruction involves simulations. Finally, in an organization where employees lack basic skills such as the ability to

read directions or work with numbers, the organization may offer basic-skills training.

14.7 Describe how supervisors can use coaching to support training.

To help employees maintain and use the skills they have acquired, the supervisor takes on the role of coach. He or she guides and instructs employees in how to do a job so that it satisfies goals for performance. The supervisor observes employees' performance and provides feedback—either praise or the description of a mistake. When there is a problem, the supervisor and employee work together to devise a solution. Finally, the supervisor reviews the employee's performance to make sure the employee understood what to do and is doing it.

14.8 Discuss how supervisors can evaluate the effectiveness of training.

To evaluate training, the supervisor measures whether the problem addressed by the training is being solved. In addition, participants in the training may fill out a questionnaire in which they evaluate their experience. When training is not producing the desired results, the supervisor should attempt to find out why and then correct the problem.

Key Terms

training	on-the-job training	role playing
orientation	apprenticeship	coaching
employee handbook	vestibule training	

Review and Discussion Questions

1. What is training? What needs of the organization can it meet?
2. What is orientation? What are some benefits of providing orientation to new employees?
3. When Al DeAngelis started his new job as a computer programmer, he arrived in his department at 9:30 A.M., after having spent time in the human resources department filling out forms. Marcia Eizenstadt, Al's supervisor, shook his hand and said, "Al, I'm so glad you're starting with us today. We need your talents tremendously." Then, explaining that she would be tied up all day in important planning meetings, Marcia showed Al to his desk and gave him an employee handbook to look at. "Read this carefully," said Marcia. "It'll tell you everything you need to know about working here. Hopefully by tomorrow or the next day we'll have a chance to sit down and go over your first assignment." Al spent the rest of the day reading the manual, wishing for a cup of coffee, and trying to smile pleasantly in response to the quizzical looks he was getting from other employees passing in the hall and glancing into his cubicle.
   a. What aspects of Al's orientation were helpful?
   b. How could it have been improved?
4. What are the steps of the training cycle?
5. Who determines when training is needed? What are some indications of a need for training?
6. Phil Petrakis supervises the housekeepers at a big-city hotel. Phil has found that the easiest and fastest way to train his staff is to give them a memo describing whatever new policy or procedure he wants to teach. When the employees have read the memo, the training is complete—it is as simple as that. What is wrong with this approach?
7. Which type(s) of training would you recommend in each of the following situations? Explain your choices.
   a. teaching air-traffic controllers how to help pilots land planes safely

b. improving the decision-making skills of production workers so they can better participate in the company's employee involvement program

c. teaching a plumber how to replace sewer lines

d. teaching a receptionist how to operate the company's new telephone system

8. At a department meeting, production supervisor Lenore Gibbs announced, "Starting next month the company will be offering a class for any of you who can't read. It will take place after work in the cafeteria."

How do you think employees with reading difficulties would react to Lenore's announcement? How can she phrase the news so that employees will be more likely to attend the class?

9. What is involved in coaching employees? Why is coaching especially appropriate in organizations that encourage employee involvement and teamwork?

10. How can a supervisor evaluate the success of a training program?

A SECOND LOOK

The story at the beginning of this chapter describes basic-skills training for employees of North Carolina State University. The training itself is provided by the local community college. As described in the story, what activities in the training cycle does supervisor Charles Weathersby carry out?

Class Exercise

In this exercise, one or more students volunteer to teach the class a skill. If possible, the volunteers should have some time to prepare their "training session" before the class in which this exercise takes place. Perhaps a few "trainers" would like to work as a team. Here are some suggestions for skills to teach; use your creativity to add to the list:

• Folding paper hats
• Doing a card trick
• Communicating a message in sign language
• Making punch for a party
• Setting the clock on a VCR

After the training session(s), the class discusses the following questions:

1. How can you evaluate whether this training was successful? If possible, try conducting an evaluation of what the class learned. What do the results of this evaluation indicate?

2. What training techniques were used? Would additional or alternative techniques have made the skill easier to learn? What changes would have helped?

CASE

Orientation at Web Industries

Web Industries is a small company known as a converter. It cuts materials into smaller sizes for use by manufacturers. Until recently, Web's new employees got the same training as do new employees at many small companies: next to nothing. A new employee's supervisor would show him or her how to operate machines, and someone would describe the company's benefits package. Then it was up to the employee to sink or swim.

That changed as the company's managers began to recognize that although they thought they were too busy to train employees, they were spending just as much time fixing problems caused by lack of training. Charles Edmunson, Web's vice-president

TABLE 14.1	Week	Topics
Topics Covered in Web Industries Orientation	1	Welcome; Your Job; The Work Order; Record Keeping; Your Benefits
	2	Our Business; Teamwork; Math for Converting; Packaging Standards; Maintenance Awareness
	3	Growing Our Company; Safety; Work Order Review; Record Keeping Review; How We Compete for Customers
	4	Your Future at Web; Constant Improvement; Math Review; Packaging Review; The ESOP (employee stock ownership plan)

Source: Adapted from Leslie Brokaw, "The Enlightened Employee Handbook," *Inc.*, October 1991, pp. 50-51.

of manufacturing, gathered a cross-section of employees to brainstorm about the company's training needs and then outlined a plan for orientation. Edmunson's plan calls for 20 hour-long sessions, which take place daily for four weeks.

The trainers are Web employees, including general managers, plant managers, customer service representatives, machine operators, maintenance workers, and office workers. Each trainer of a new employee covers an aspect of the orientation with which he or she is familiar. Trainers follow an outline prepared by Edmunson. They may add examples, but they may not skip any section of the outline. Involving employees in the training builds a sense of commitment to the company and responsibility for the success of new employees. This approach is consistent with the company's overall emphasis on teamwork and employee involvement.

The orientation program covers the topics shown in Table 14.1. According to Edmunson, some of the most important material is the information about the company, its goals, and employees' future with Web. Edmunson believes that this kind of information is easy to forget about if it is not part of a formal orientation program. In fact, to make sure that all existing employees are familiar with the information, some of Web's plants started having all their employees—not just newly hired ones—participate in the training.

Other topics covered in the orientation show employees how to help the company meet its goals. For example, making employees aware of the value of parts enables them to treat the parts with the care necessary to keep costs under control. Explains Edmunson, "We've got spacers for the machines that are an eighth of an inch wide and precision-ground, and they might be worth 25 or 30 bucks. They just look like little washer tubes. A new guy, if he's not aware that this is an expensive piece, may end up tossing it in the trash dumpster." Similarly, by explaining that the company competes for business by providing customized service, the trainers let new employees know the importance of catering to customers' demands.

When employees have completed the four weeks of orientation, they evaluate the program. In their evaluation, they indicate areas that need improvement. As a result, the orientation program has been updated once so far, and additional improvements are being considered.

1. Based on the information in Table 14.1, does it appear that Web's orientation program covers all the relevant topics? If not, what is missing?
2. What aspects of orientation do you think Web's supervisors should handle? Consider that supervisors can both supplement and repeat what is covered during the formal orientation.
3. If you were a production supervisor at Web, how would you feel about having one of your machine operators taking an hour or two each month to conduct training for new employees? Explain.

Source: Leslie Brokaw, "The Enlightened Employee Handbook," *Inc.*, October 1991, pp. 49–51.

15

Evaluation is a time for accounting; for comparing actions with consequences; for detecting flaws and making improvements; for planting the seeds of future challenge.
—Don Koberg and Jim Bagnall

Appraising Performance

LEARNING OBJECTIVES

15.1 Describe benefits of conducting performance appraisals.

15.2 Identify the steps in appraising performance systematically.

15.3 Discuss guidelines for avoiding discrimination in performance appraisals.

15.4 Identify types of appraisals.

15.5 Describe sources of bias in appraising performance.

15.6 Explain the purpose of conducting performance appraisal interviews.

15.7 Tell how supervisors should prepare for a performance appraisal interview.

15.8 Describe guidelines for conducting the interview.

HOW EMPLOYEES RATE

Nancy Maria Acedo is a supervisor with the Fleet Management Program for the State of Colorado. The Fleet Management Program purchases and leases to state agencies pickups, trucks, station wagons, vans, and sedans. The program is also responsible for maintaining the vehicles and providing replacement when necessary. The program's customers are the state employees who lease its cars and trucks.

Once a year Acedo must conduct a formal performance appraisal on each of the five employees she supervises. Using an appraisal form provided by the state, she rates employees in specified areas such as customer service and job performance. The possible ratings are *outstanding, commendable, good, needs improvement,* and *unacceptable.* Acedo gives the employee a progress review at least once during the appraisal year to let the employee know if there is an area in which he or she needs improvement. She gives specific examples of how to perform in that area.

One of Acedo's employees was doing a poor job of completing work on time and keeping good records. Besides pointing out this problem, Acedo helped in developing the solution. She prepared a log sheet for the employee to use. On the log sheet, the employee would record who called, when the call was made, and other information such as whether the employee mailed to a customer the maintenance card used to pay for maintenance on certain vehicles. The additional information on the log sheet turned out to be helpful. Customers had sometimes complained about not receiving a customer card, and the log sheets provided useful information for resolving such problems.

performance appraisal
Formal feedback on
how well an employee
is performing his or
her job.

Formal feedback on how well an employee is performing his or her job is known as a **performance appraisal** (or a performance review or performance evaluation). Like the State of Colorado, most organizations require that supervisors conduct a performance appraisal on each of their employees regularly, typically once a year. Therefore, it is important for supervisors to know how to appraise performance fairly.

This chapter discusses reasons for conducting performance appraisals and describes a process for appraising performance systematically. It describes various types of appraisals used by organizations today. It tells how to avoid biases and how to conduct an appraisal interview.

Purposes of Performance Appraisal

Performance appraisals provide information necessary for employees to improve the quality of their work. To improve, employees need to hear how they are doing. As described in Chapters 5 and 7, the supervisor should provide frequent feedback. Performance appraisals supplement this informal information with a more thought-out, formal evaluation. (If employees are getting enough informal feedback, they probably will not be surprised by the results of the appraisal.) A formal performance appraisal ensures that feedback to an employee covers all important aspects of the employee's performance. Based on this information, the employee and supervisor can plan how to improve weak areas. In this way, performance appraisals support the practice of coaching, described in Chapter 14. One company that actively uses this benefit of performance appraisals is Datatec Industries of Fairfield, New Jersey, which installs computer systems in stores. At Datatec, all employees rate each other's performance monthly or quarterly. The frequency of these appraisals helps employees to see problem areas early, when they are easier to resolve.[1]

An appraisal also can help motivate employees. Most people appreciate it when their supervisor spends time discussing their work and praises them for good performance. And because employees like to know what is going on, just hearing the supervisor's viewpoint can be motivating. Employees also tend to put forth the most effort in the areas that get appraised. Therefore, by rating employees on the kinds of behavior it considers important, the organization encourages the employee to try hard in those areas. For example, Com-Corp Industries, a Cleveland metal stamper that makes light bulb shields for General Motors, wants its employees to participate in making suggestions and to develop skills that will improve the company's competitiveness. Therefore, the company's performance appraisals include a section in which employees are rated on "making the company a better place to work" through such activities as suggesting improvements or actually making improvements in their work area.[2]

Finally, performance appraisals provide important records for the organization. They are a useful source of information when deciding on raises, promotions, and discipline, and they provide evidence that these were administered fairly. In the case of employees whose behavior or performance is a problem, an appraisal documents the problem. (The next chapter discusses such employees in greater detail.)

Awards are a highly visible part of performance appraisal when performance meets or exceeds standards. Barbara Breisch and Paul Soldridge received Air Products' Quality Pulse Awards in 1991 for significantly improving service.

Source: Courtesy of Air Products and Chemicals, Inc.

A Systematic Approach to Appraising Performance

For appraisals to deliver their potential benefits, they must be as fair and accurate as possible. Supervisors therefore should be systematic in appraising performance. They should follow a thorough process, use objective measures when possible, and avoid discrimination.

The Appraisal Process

As illustrated in Figure 15.1, the appraisal process takes place in four steps. The supervisor establishes and communicates expectations for performance, establishes and communicates standards for measuring performance, and observes individual performance, measuring it against the standards. Based on this information, the supervisor reinforces performance or provides remedies.

Establish and Communicate Expectations for Performance During the planning process, the supervisor determines what he or she wants the department or work group to accomplish (see Chapter 2). Through action plans, the supervisor spells out who is to do what to accomplish those objectives. From this information, it is relatively easy to specify what each employee must do to help the department or work group meet its objectives. One approach is to list the three to five major responsibilities of each position; the appraisal then focuses on these responsibilities.[3]

FIGURE 15.1

The Process of Performance Appraisal

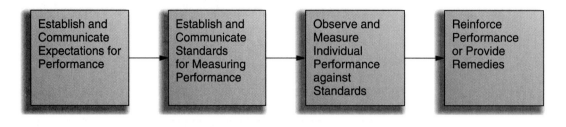

For example, suppose Francine Bloch supervises the delivery personnel for a chain of appliance stores in Dallas. Each driver is to deliver every appliance on his or her truck without damaging anything. In addition, the department expects that each driver will operate the vehicle safely. Finally, all personnel are expected to be polite to customers.

As described in Chapter 5, the supervisor must make sure employees know and understand what is expected of them. To do this, the supervisor should make sure that objectives for the employees are clear and should communicate them effectively (see Chapter 7). Employees are most likely to understand and be committed to objectives when they have a say in developing them. At Eastman Chemical Company, supervisors meet with each employee to establish mutually acceptable performance goals and expectations.[4]

Establish and Communicate Standards for Measuring Performance   The expectations for performance are a type of objective. Therefore, according to the standards for objectives described in Chapter 2, each expectation should be measurable. In appraising performance, the supervisor's task includes deciding how to measure employees' performance and then making sure employees know what will be measured. In the case of Francine's employees, the standards would include delivering all appliances without damage, having zero accidents or traffic tickets, and receiving no complaints from customers about their service.

Observe and Measure Individual Performance against Standards   Through the control process (see Chapter 5), the supervisor should continuously gather information about each employee's performance. This is an ongoing activity, not something the supervisor saves to do when filling out appraisal forms. When preparing a performance appraisal, the supervisor compares this information with the standards for the employee being appraised. In the case of Francine, she would keep records of uncompleted deliveries, damage, accidents, traffic tickets, and customer complaints (and compliments). When appraising a particular employee's performance, she can see how often those problems arose with the employee.

Reinforce Performance or Provide Remedies   To keep employees motivated and informed, the supervisor needs to tell them when they are doing something right, not just when they are making a mistake. Thus, the final step of the appraisal process includes reinforcement for good performance. This can be as simple as pointing out to employees the areas in which their performance is good. For example, Francine might compliment one of the drivers on receiving a letter of praise from a customer or on having caused no damage to appliances during the year. The supervisor might want to comment that this information will be in the employee's permanent record with the organization.

In areas where the employee falls short of the standards, the employee needs to know how to improve. The supervisor may state a remedy, but it is often more effective to ask the employee to help in solving the problem. In the case of a driver who has received two traffic tickets for illegal left turns, Francine might point out this situation and ask the driver for an explanation. Assume the driver replies that he was confused because he was lost. With that information, Francine and the driver can work together on determining how to get the driver better acquainted with finding his way around the Dallas area.

Because Francine and the driver are treating the underlying problem, rather than Francine just telling the driver to stop getting tickets (the symptom), the driver's performance in this area can improve in the future. In general, to move beyond discussing symptoms to uncover the underlying problems, the supervisor can ask which of the following kinds of causes led to the poor performance:

- *Inadequate skills*—If the problem is that the employee lacks certain skills, the supervisor should see that he or she gets the necessary training, as described in the previous chapter.
- *Lack of effort*—If the problem is a lack of effort on the employee's part, the supervisor may need to apply the principles of motivation discussed in Chapter 9.
- *External conditions*—If the problem is something beyond the control of supervisor and employee, such as a poor economy, lack of cooperation from another department, or a strike by suppliers, the appraisal standards and ratings should be adjusted so that they are fair to the employee.
- *Personal problems*—If performance is suffering because the employee has personal problems, the supervisor should handle the situation as described in the next chapter.

In investigating the underlying problem, it may be helpful for the supervisor to ask what he or she can do to help the employee reach goals.[5] Before the appraisal is over, the employee should have a clear plan for making necessary changes.

What to Measure in the Appraisal

Waitress Kelly O'Hara was furious as she walked out of her performance appraisal interview. "Irresponsible!" she muttered to herself, "Lazy! Who does he think he is, calling me those things? He doesn't know what he's talking about." As you can see from Kelly's reaction, labeling people with certain characteristics is not a constructive approach to conducting an appraisal. Labels tend to put people on the defensive, and they are difficult, if not impossible, to prove.

Instead, the performance appraisal should focus on *behavior* and *results*. Focusing on behavior means the appraisal should describe specific actions or patterns of behaving. Focusing on results means describing the extent to which the employee has satisfied the objectives for which he or she is responsible. In Kelly's case, if her supervisor had noted that he had received several complaints about slow service, he and Kelly could have worked on a plan to minimize such complaints. That approach would be more constructive than simply evaluating her as "lazy," because it tells the employee exactly what is expected. Focusing on the achievement of objectives is also more fair, assuming that the employee helped to set the objectives.

In many cases, the supervisor uses an appraisal form that requires him or her to draw conclusions about the employee's personal characteristics. For example, the supervisor might need to rate the employee's dependability or attitude. Although such ratings are necessarily subjective, the supervisor can try to base them on observations about behavior and results. One approach is to record at least one specific example for each category rated. A rating on a personal characteristic seems more reasonable when the supervisor can show the facts that support his or her conclusion.

EEOC Guidelines

As described in Chapter 13, the Equal Employment Opportunity Commission (EEOC) is the government agency charged with enforcing federal laws against discrimination. The EEOC has published the Uniform Guidelines on Employee Selection Procedures, which include guidelines for designing and implementing performance appraisals. In general, the behaviors or characteristics measured by a performance appraisal should be related to the job and to succeeding on the job. For example, if the appraisal measures "grooming," then good grooming should be important for success in the job. Because of this requirement, the supervisor and others responsible for the content of performance appraisals should make sure that what they measure is still relevant to a particular job.

Just as hiring should be done on the basis of candidates' ability to perform the essential tasks of a particular job, so appraisals should be based on whether the employee succeeds in carrying out those essential tasks. The ratings in a performance appraisal should not be discriminatory. That is, they should not be based on the employee's race, sex, or other protected category but on whether the employee meets standards of performance. Furthermore, the employee should know ahead of time what those standards are, and the organization should have in place a system for employees to ask questions about their rating.

Performance Appraisals and Pay Reviews

Many organizations review the employee's wage or salary level at the time of the performance appraisal. This reinforces the link the company makes between performance and pay increases. An employee with an excellent rating would be eligible to receive the largest allowable increase, whereas someone rated as a poor worker might not get any raise or only a cost-of-living increase.

There is a drawback to reviewing wages and salaries at the same time that performance is reviewed. Employees tend to focus on the issue of money, so it is harder for the supervisor to use the performance evaluation as an opportunity for motivating and coaching. Thus, many experts recommend conducting the two types of reviews at separate times. The supervisor, of course, has little choice in this matter. If the supervisor must review pay rates at the same time as performance, he or she must keep in mind the need for extra effort in emphasizing performance, and it is especially important to provide feedback about performance throughout the year.

Types of Appraisals

Many techniques have been developed for appraising performance. Usually the human resources department or higher-level management dictates which type(s) the supervisor will use. By having all supervisors use the same approach, the organization makes it easier to keep records showing performance over time, especially when an employee reports to more than one supervisor during his or her employment. Although the supervisor has to use the appraisal format selected for the whole organization, he or she may be able to supplement it with other information if it seems helpful. The supervisor can use the "Comments" section of a preprinted form or attach additional information to it, as Nancy Acedo does when appraising the employees of Colorado's Fleet Management Program.

Graphic Rating Scales

graphic rating scale
A performance appraisal that rates the degree to which the employee has achieved various characteristics.

The most commonly used type of appraisal is the **graphic rating scale**. This appraisal rates the degree to which the employee has achieved various characteristics, such as job knowledge or punctuality. The rating is often given in terms of a score, such as 1 to 5, with 5 representing excellent performance and 1 representing poor performance. Some appraisal forms include space for comments so the supervisor can provide support for his or her ratings. Figure 15.2 is a sample appraisal form using a graphic rating scale.

The main advantage of a graphic rating scale is that it is relatively easy to use. In addition, the scores make it easy to see whether an employee has improved in various areas. However, the ratings themselves are subjective. What one supervisor considers "excellent" may seem just "average" to someone else. Also, many supervisors tend to rate everyone as being at least a little bit above average. Some appraisal forms attempt to overcome these problems by containing descriptions of excellent or poor behavior in each area.

paired-comparison approach
A performance appraisal that measures the relative performance of employees in a group.

Paired-Comparison Approach

The **paired-comparison approach** measures the relative performance of employees in a group. The supervisor lists the employees in the group and then ranks them. One method is to compare the performance of the first two employees on

FIGURE 15.2

Sample Graphic Rating Scale

NAME _____ DEPT. _____ DATE _____					
		Outstanding	Good	Satisfactory	Fair	Unsatisfactory

		Outstanding	Good	Satisfactory	Fair	Unsatisfactory
Quantity of work	Volume of acceptable work under normal conditions	☐	☐	☐	☐	☐
	Comments:					
Quality of work	Thoroughness, neatness, and accuracy of work	☐	☐	☐	☐	☐
	Comments:					
Knowledge of job	Clear understanding of the facts or factors pertinent to the job	☐	☐	☐	☐	☐
	Comments:					
Personal qualities	Personality, appearance, sociability, leadership, integrity	☐	☐	☐	☐	☐
	Comments:					
Cooperation	Ability and willingness to work with associates, supervisors, and subordinates toward common goals	☐	☐	☐	☐	☐
	Comments:					
Dependability	Conscientious, thorough, accurate, reliable with respect to attendance, lunch periods, reliefs, etc.	☐	☐	☐	☐	☐
	Comments:					
Initiative	Earnestness in seeking increased responsibilities. Self-starting, unafraid to proceed alone	☐	☐	☐	☐	☐
	Comments:					

Source: John M. Ivancevich, *Human Resource Management: Foundations of Personnel*, 5th ed. (Homewood, Ill.: Irwin, 1992), p. 307.

the list. The supervisor places a checkmark next to the name of the employee whose performance is better. The supervisor repeats the process, comparing the first employee's performance with that of the other employees. Then the supervisor compares the second employee on the list with all the others, and so on until each pair of employees has been compared. The employee with the most checkmarks is considered most valuable.

The supervisor can also compare the employees in terms of several criteria, such as work quantity and quality. For each criterion, the supervisor ranks the employees from best to worst, assigning a 1 to the lowest-ranked employee and the highest score to the best employee in that category. Then the supervisor adds up all the scores for each employee to see who has the highest total score.

The paired-comparison approach is appropriate when the supervisor needs to find one outstanding employee in a group. The supervisor can use it to identify the best candidate for a promotion or special assignment. Paired comparison makes some employees look good at the expense of others, however, which makes this technique less useful as a means of providing feedback to individual employees.

Forced-Choice Approach

forced-choice approach
A performance appraisal that presents the appraiser with sets of statements describing employee behavior; the appraiser must choose which statement is most characteristic of the employee and which is least characteristic.

In the **forced-choice approach**, the appraisal form gives the supervisor sets of statements describing employee behavior. For each set of statements, the supervisor must choose which one is most characteristic of the employee and then which one is least characteristic of the employee. Figure 15.3 illustrates part of an appraisal form using the forced-choice approach.

These questionnaires tend to be set up in a way that prevents the supervisor from saying only positive things about employees. Thus, the forced-choice approach is used when an organization finds that supervisors have been rating an unbelievably high proportion of employees as above average.

FIGURE 15.3

Sample Forced-Choice Appraisal

Instructions:	Rank from 1 to 4 the following sets of statements according to how they describe the manner in which _____ performs

(name of employee)

the job. A rank of *1* should be used for the most descriptive statement, and a rank of *4* should be given for the least descriptive. No ties are allowed.

1. _____ Does not anticipate difficulties

   _____ Grasps explanations quickly

   _____ Rarely wastes time

   _____ Easy to talk to

2. _____ A leader in group activities

   _____ Wastes time on unimportant things

   _____ Cool and calm at all times

   _____ Hard worker

Source: John M. Ivancevich, *Human Resource Management: Foundations of Personnel*, 5th ed. (Homewood, Ill.: Irwin, 1992), p. 310.

FIGURE 15.4

Sample Behaviorally Anchored Rating Scale (BARS)

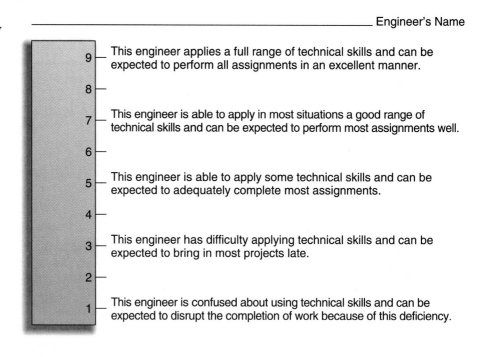

_____ Engineer's Name

9 — This engineer applies a full range of technical skills and can be expected to perform all assignments in an excellent manner.

8 —

7 — This engineer is able to apply in most situations a good range of technical skills and can be expected to perform most assignments well.

6 —

5 — This engineer is able to apply some technical skills and can be expected to adequately complete most assignments.

4 —

3 — This engineer has difficulty applying technical skills and can be expected to bring in most projects late.

2 —

1 — This engineer is confused about using technical skills and can be expected to disrupt the completion of work because of this deficiency.

Source: John M. Ivancevich, _Human Resource Management: Foundations of Personnel_, 5th ed. (Homewood, Ill.: Irwin, 1992), p. 312.

Essay Appraisal

Sometimes the supervisor must write a description of the employee's performance. The supervisor might be expected to answer questions such as, "What are the major strengths of this employee?" or, "In what areas does this employee need improvement?" These essay appraisals are often used along with other types of appraisals—notably, graphic rating scales. They provide an opportunity for supervisors to describe aspects of performance that are not thoroughly covered by an appraisal questionnaire. The main drawback of essay appraisals is that their quality depends on the supervisor's writing skills.

Behaviorally Anchored Rating Scales (BARS)

behaviorally anchored rating scales
A performance appraisal in which the employee is rated on scales containing statements describing performance in several areas.

Some organizations pay behavioral scientists or organizational psychologists to create **behaviorally anchored rating scales** (BARS). These scales rate employee performance in several areas, such as work quantity and quality, using a series of statements that describe effective and ineffective performance in each area. Thus, in each area, the supervisor selects the statement that best describes how the employee performs. The statements in the rating scales are different for each job title in the organization. Figure 15.4 shows a behaviorally anchored rating scale measuring the performance area of engineering competence.

FIGURE 15.5

Sample Checklist Appraisal

	Yes	No
1. Does the employee willingly cooperate with others in completing work assignments?	_____	_____
2. Does the employee have adequate job knowledge to perform duties in a satisfactory manner?	_____	_____
3. In terms of quality, is the employee's work acceptable?	_____	_____
4. Does the employee meet deadlines for the completion of work assignments?	_____	_____
5. Does the employee's record indicate unexcused absences?	_____	_____
6. Does the employee follow safety rules and regulations?	_____	_____

Source: Stephen E. Catt and Donald S. Miller, *Supervision: Working with People*, 2nd ed. (Homewood, Ill.: Irwin, 1991), p. 374.

The major advantage of using BARS is that this technique is tailored to the organization's objectives for employees. Also, because it uses statements describing behavior, BARS is less subjective than some other approaches. However, developing the scales is time-consuming and therefore relatively expensive.

Checklist Appraisal

A checklist appraisal contains a series of questions about the employee's performance. Figure 15.5 shows the format of such an appraisal. The supervisor answers yes or no to the questions. Thus, the checklist is merely a record of performance, not an evaluation by the supervisor. The human resources department has a key for scoring the items on the checklist; the score results in a rating of the employee's performance.

This type of appraisal is easy to complete. However, it has several disadvantages. The checklist can be difficult to prepare, and each job category will probably require a different set of questions. Also, the supervisor has no way to adjust the answers for any special circumstances that affect performance.

critical-incident appraisal
A performance appraisal in which the supervisor keeps a written record of incidents that show positive and negative ways the employee has acted; the supervisor uses this record to assess the employee's performance.

Critical-Incident Appraisal

To conduct a **critical-incident appraisal**, the supervisor keeps a written record of incidents that show positive and negative ways the employee has acted. The record should include dates, people involved, actions taken, and any other details that are relevant. At the time of the appraisal, the supervisor reviews the record to reach an overall evaluation of the employee's behavior. During the appraisal interview, the supervisor should give the employee a chance to offer his or her views of each incident recorded.

For occupations such as medicine, critical incident appraisals are very valuable.

Source: Courtesy of © 1993 Comstock, Inc.

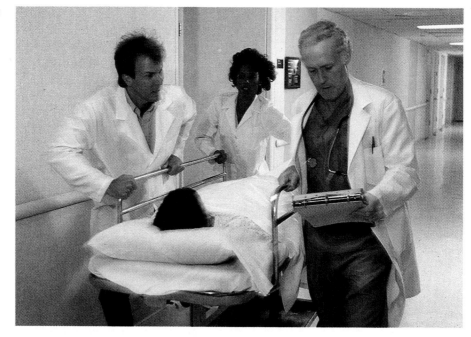

This technique has the advantage of focusing on actual behaviors. However, keeping records of critical incidents can be time-consuming, and even if the supervisor is diligent, he or she will probably miss some important incidents. Also, supervisors tend to record negative events more than positive ones. As a result, the appraisal may be overly harsh.

Work Standards Approach

work standards approach
A performance appraisal in which the appraiser compares the employee's performance with objective measures of what an employee should do.

To use the **work standards approach**, the supervisor tries to establish objective measures of performance. A typical work standard would be the quantity produced by an assembly-line worker. This amount should reflect what a person could normally produce. The supervisor then compares the employee's actual performance with the standards. This approach to evaluating performance applies best to production workers.

Management by Objectives (MBO)

Chapter 2 introduced management by objectives (MBO) as a planning tool. In an organization that uses MBO, the supervisor will also use this approach for appraising performance. The supervisor compares the employee's accomplishments with the objectives for that employee. If the employee has met or exceeded his or her objectives, the appraisal will be favorable. The main advantages of this system are that the employee knows what is expected and the supervisor focuses on results rather than more subjective criteria.

Assessments by Someone Other than the Supervisor

A supervisor cannot know how an employee behaves at all times or in all situations. Nor can the supervisor always appreciate the full impact of the employee's behavior on people inside and outside the organization. To supplement what the supervisor cannot know, other people can offer insights into an employee's behavior. For this reason, supervisors may combine their appraisals with self-assessments by the employee or with appraisals by peers and subordinates.

The supervisor can ask the employee to complete a self-assessment before the appraisal interview. Then the supervisor and employee can compare the employee's evaluation of his or her own behavior with the supervisor's evaluation. This can stimulate discussion and insights in areas where the two are in disagreement.

Peer appraisals are less common. As noted earlier in this chapter, one company that does use them is Datatec Industries. And at Eastman Chemical, employees who work in teams appraise the performance of their team members. The teams do this in meetings, where they discuss each team member's strengths and areas needing improvement.[6] It seems reasonable to expect that employees will react most positively to peer appraisals if all employees are able to participate in appraising on an equal basis (as opposed to using peer appraisals once in a while for selected employees).

At an increasing number of major corporations, including Amoco, Cigna, and Du Pont, subordinates rate how well their bosses manage.[7] Typically, the ratings are anonymous, to protect the workers. The purpose of these subordinate appraisals is to give managers information they can use to supervise more effectively and make their organization more competitive. The appraisals also support the trend toward giving operative employees a greater voice in how an organization is run. The "Tips from the Firing Line" box on page 394 provides some ideas for having employees appraise the supervisor.

An unusual twist to subordinate appraisals is used at Cleveland-based Com-Corp Industries. Three times a year, each Com-Corp employee reviews the company's performance. These reviews are a source of ideas for improving efficiency and quality. For example, one employee pointed out that bad welds were costing the company $500 a week in unacceptable parts; in response, the company found ways to reduce the defect rate from 1 percent to 0.2 percent.[8]

Sources of Bias

Ideally, supervisors should be completely objective in their appraisals of employees. Each appraisal should directly reflect the employee's performance, not any biases of the supervisor. Of course, this is impossible to do perfectly. Just as we all make human compromises in our decision-making strategies (see Chapter 8), we have biases in evaluating what other people do. Supervisors need to be aware of these biases so they can limit or eliminate the effect of the biases on the appraisals they make. Figure 15.6 (page 395) summarizes sources of bias that commonly influence performance appraisals.

TIPS FROM THE FIRING LINE

Getting Employees to Appraise Your Performance

Appraisals by subordinates can be a useful source of information for supervisors. Employees rarely feel they are in a position to tell the boss how his or her behavior affects them, so asking for an appraisal can open up the lines of communication. However, the supervisor should bear in mind that many employees will be reluctant to answer frankly a question such as, "What do you think of me?" Rather, the supervisor should ask questions that do not require the employee to comment directly on the supervisor's abilities.

A relatively simple way to set up this type of appraisal is to hold a staff meeting. Discuss your need to hear an honest appraisal of your skills. Then ask employees to respond anonymously to a questionnaire you distribute.

Here are the kinds of questions that can get employees to open up:

- How can I help you do your job better?
- What do you wish I did differently?
- Are my directions usually clear, or do you depend on your co-workers to help you figure out what your tasks usually are?

- Do I often change my mind and alter your assignments after you have already begun them?
- Do I usually edit your work without improving it?
- Am I usually open to new ideas and innovative plans?
- Do you think that I am disappointed in your work?
- Do I provide constructive criticism?
- Do you trust me?
- Do I help develop your skills?
- Am I available to you when you need more help?
- Do I create or operate in a crisis mode too often?

At first, hearing the responses to such questions may be uncomfortable. You probably will not enjoy receiving criticism from employees. However, if you allow time for the responses to sink in so that you can learn from them, these comments can help you to be an excellent supervisor.

Source: Adele Scheele, "Are You a Bad Boss?" *Working Woman*, April 1992, pp. 32, 35.

---

harshness bias
Rating employees more severely than their performance merits.

leniency bias
Rating employees more favorably than their performance merits.

central tendency
The tendency to select employee ratings in the middle of a scale.

Some supervisors are prone to a **harshness bias**. In other words, they rate employees more severely than their performance merits. New supervisors are especially susceptible to this error, because they may feel a need to prove that they should be taken seriously. Unfortunately, the harshness bias also tends to frustrate and discourage workers, who resent the unfair assessments of their performance.

At the other extreme is the **leniency bias**. Supervisors with this bias rate their employees more favorably than their performance merits. A recent study suggests that the leniency bias is widespread. In 70 percent of the appraisals prepared by the managers studied, the managers had inflated their ratings of employees.[9] A supervisor who does this may want credit for developing a department full of "excellent" workers. Or the supervisor may simply be uncomfortable confronting employees with their shortcomings. The leniency bias may feel like an advantage to the employees who receive the favorable ratings, but it cheats the employees and department of the benefits of truly developing and coaching employees.

A bias that characterizes the responses to many types of questionnaires is **central tendency**. This is the tendency to select ratings in the middle of the scale. People seem more comfortable on middle ground than taking a strong stand at either extreme. This bias causes the supervisor to miss important opportunities to praise or correct employees.

FIGURE 15.6

Sources of Bias in Performance Appraisals

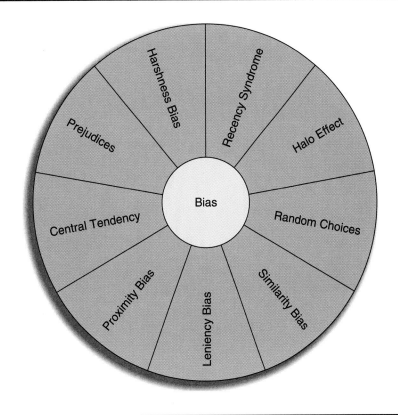

proximity bias
The tendency to assign similar scores to items that are near each other on a questionnaire.

Proximity means nearness. The **proximity bias** refers to the tendency to assign similar scores to items that are near each other on a questionnaire. Obviously, this can result in misleading appraisals.

When using a type of appraisal that requires answers to specific questions, the supervisor might succumb to making *random choices*. The supervisor might do this when uncertain how to answer or when the overall scoring on the test looks undesirable. For example, if a supervisor thinks an appraisal is scoring the employee too low, the supervisor might throw in some favorable ratings in areas he or she does not feel strongly about. Supervisors who catch themselves making random choices should slow down and try to apply objective criteria.

similarity bias
The tendency to judge others more positively when they are like yourself.

The **similarity bias** refers to the tendency to judge others more positively when they are like ourselves. Thus, we tend to look more favorably on people who share our interests, tastes, background, or other characteristics. For example, in appraising performance, a supervisor risks viewing a person's performance in a favorable light because the employee shares his flair for dressing in the latest fashions. Or a supervisor might interpret negatively the performance of an employee who is much shyer than the supervisor.

As described in Chapter 8, the *recency syndrome* refers to the human tendency to place the most weight on the events that have occurred most recently. In the case of a performance appraisal, the supervisor might give particular weight to a

The Circle of Excellence award is a part of the appraisal process at Fleetwood Enterprises. Fleetwood produces recreational vehicles and manufactured housing. It presents the award to the retailer that best achieves outstanding levels of customer satisfaction.

Source: Courtesy of Fleetwood Enterprises, Inc.

problem the employee caused last week or an award the employee just won. However, the supervisor should be careful to consider events and behaviors that occurred throughout the entire period covered by the review. The most accurate way to do this is to keep records throughout the year, as described earlier with regard to conducting a critical-incident appraisal.

The *halo effect* was introduced in Chapter 13. It refers to the tendency to generalize one positive or negative aspect of a person to the person's entire performance. Thus, if supervisor Ken Olson thinks that a pleasant telephone manner is what makes a good customer service representative, he is apt to give high marks to a representative with a pleasant voice, regardless of what she actually says to the customers or how reliable her performance is.

Finally, the supervisor's *prejudices* about various types of people can unfairly influence a performance appraisal. The supervisor needs to remember that each employee is an individual, not merely a representative of a group. Say, for example, that a supervisor believes African-Americans generally have poor skills in using Standard English. The supervisor needs to recognize that this is a prejudice about a group, not a fact to apply to actual employees. Thus, before recommending that a black salesperson needs to improve her speaking skills, the supervisor must consider whether the salesperson really needs improvement in that area or whether the supervisor's prejudices are interfering with an accurate assessment of the employee. This is especially important in light of the EEOC guidelines discussed earlier in the chapter.

The Performance Appraisal Interview

The last stage of the appraisal process—the stage at which the supervisor reinforces performance or provides remedies—occurs in an interview between supervisor and employee. At this time, the supervisor describes what he or she has observed and discusses this appraisal with the employee. Together they agree on areas for improvement and development. The Self-Quiz (page 398) lets you test your own interviewing skills. If you have never yet been a supervisor, apply the questions to the way your current or most recent supervisor has appraised your performance.

Supervisors often dread conducting appraisal interviews. Pointing out another person's shortcomings can be unpleasant at best. To overcome these feelings, it helps to focus on the benefits of appraising employees. The supervisor can cultivate a positive attitude by viewing the appraisal interview as an opportunity to coach and develop employees.

Purpose of the Interview

Quite simply, the purpose of holding an appraisal interview is to communicate information about the employee's performance. Once the supervisor has evaluated the employee's performance, the supervisor needs to convey his or her thoughts to the employee. An interview is an appropriate setting for doing so, because it sets aside time to focus on and discuss the appraisal in private. The interview is also an opportunity for upward communication from the employee. By contributing his or her viewpoint and ideas, the employee can work with the supervisor on devising ways to improve performance. (Chapter 7 provides guidelines for communicating effectively.)

Preparing for the Interview

Before the appraisal interview, the supervisor should allow plenty of time for completing the appraisal form. The supervisor should complete the form carefully and thoughtfully, not in a rush during the hour before the interview. Besides filling out the form, the supervisor should think about how the employee is likely to react to the appraisal and should plan how to handle the employee's reactions. The supervisor should also be ready with some ideas for how to correct problems noted in the appraisal.

The supervisor should notify the employee about the appraisal interview ahead of time. Giving the employee a few days' or a week's notice allows the employee to think about his or her performance. Then the employee can contribute ideas during the interview.

In addition, the supervisor should prepare an appropriate meeting place. The interview should take place in an office or other room where supervisor and employee will have privacy. The supervisor should arrange to prevent interruptions such as phone calls.

SELF-QUIZ *Your Appraisal Interview Technique*

This scale is designed to help you improve your performance appraisal interviews and discussion with employees. Circle the number that best reflects where you currently fall on the scale. When you have finished, total the numbers circled in the space.

		Agree Strongly					Disagree Strongly			
1.	I let the employee do most of the talking.	10	9	8	7	6	5	4	3	2	1
2.	I make an intense effort to listen to the employee's ideas.	10	9	8	7	6	5	4	3	2	1
3.	I am prepared to suggest solutions to problems and development needs but let the employee contribute first.	10	9	8	7	6	5	4	3	2	1
4.	My statements about performance are descriptive and specific, not judgmental.	10	9	8	7	6	5	4	3	2	1
5.	I reinforce the positives in performance as well as seek ways to improve below-standard performance.	10	9	8	7	6	5	4	3	2	1
6.	I try to encourage the employee's ideas about expanding performance.	10	9	8	7	6	5	4	3	2	1
7.	I invite alternatives rather than assume there is only one way to approach an issue.	10	9	8	7	6	5	4	3	2	1
8.	I use open-ended, reflective, and directive questions to stimulate discussion.	10	9	8	7	6	5	4	3	2	1
9.	I am specific and descriptive when I express a concern about performance.	10	9	8	7	6	5	4	3	2	1
10.	My employees know I want them to succeed.	10	9	8	7	6	5	4	3	2	1

Total _____

A score between 90 and 100 indicates you should be leading successful discussions. A score between 70 and 89 indicates significant strengths plus a few improvement needs. A score between 50 and 69 reflects some strengths, but a significant number of problem areas as well. A score below 50 calls for a serious effort to improve in several categories. Make a special effort to grow in any area where you scored 6 or less, regardless of your total score.

Source: Reprinted with the permission of Macmillan Publishing Company from SUPERVISOR'S SURVIVAL KIT, Sixth Edition by Elwood N. Chapman. Copyright © 1993 by Macmillan Publishing Company.

Conducting the Interview

At the beginning of the interview, the supervisor should attempt to put the employee at ease. Employees are often uncomfortable at the prospect of discussing their performance. An offer of coffee and a little small talk may help to break the ice.

If the employee completed a self-appraisal, the supervisor can begin by reviewing this with the employee, asking him or her to give reasons for the various ratings. Then the supervisor describes his or her rating of the employee and the way the supervisor arrived at the rating. The supervisor can start by describing his or her overall impressions and then move into an explanation of the contents of the appraisal form. The supervisor should explain the basis for the ratings, using specific examples of the employee's behavior and results. Most employees are waiting for the "bad news," so it is probably most effective to describe areas for improvement first. Then the supervisor should focus on the employee's strengths. People need to know what they are doing well so that they will continue and so that they know their efforts are appreciated.

After describing his or her evaluation of the employee's performance, the supervisor should give the employee time to offer feedback. The employee should be able to agree or disagree with the supervisor's conclusions, as well as to ask questions. This is an important time for the supervisor to keep an open mind and apply the listening skills discussed in Chapter 7. Hearing the employee's reactions is the first step toward resolving any problems described in the appraisal.

When the supervisor and employee understand each other's point of view, they should reach a decision on how to solve problems described in the appraisal. Together they come up with as many alternatives as they can think of and then select the solutions that seem most promising. The best solution may be one in which the supervisor also must make changes, such as keeping the employee better informed or improving working conditions. (Chapter 8 provides further guidelines for decision making and problem solving.)

At the end of the interview, the supervisor and employee are usually required to sign the appraisal form. By doing so, they acknowledge that the interview has been conducted and that the employee has read and understood the form. (If the employee refuses to sign, the supervisor can try explaining that this is all the employee's signature means. If that explanation does not persuade the employee to sign, the supervisor can note on the appraisal form that the employee refused to sign and can check with the human resources department regarding other procedures to follow.) The employee should receive a copy of the appraisal form. The supervisor should close the interview on a positive note, with a comment such as, "You've been doing a great job," or, "I think that with the plans we've made, your work will soon be up to standards." Figure 15.7 summarizes the interviewing process.

Even after the interview is over, the supervisor continues appraising performance. He or she needs to follow up on any actions planned during the interview. Is the employee making the promised changes? Is the supervisor providing the resources, such as training, that are necessary for improvements to occur? This follow-up should be an ongoing process, not an activity left for the next year's performance appraisal.

FIGURE 15.7

The Process of Conducting a Performance Appraisal Interview

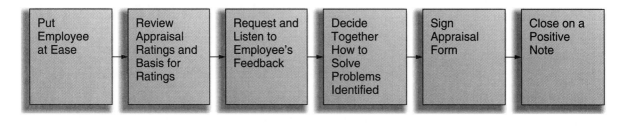

Summary

15.1 Describe benefits of conducting performance appraisals.

Performance appraisals provide information necessary for improved performance. Appraisals can motivate employees by demonstrating the supervisor's and organization's interest in them, keeping them informed, and indicating what areas of performance are important. Performance appraisals also provide important records for the company. Managers use this information for decisions on raises, promotions, and discipline.

15.2 Identify the steps in appraising performance systematically.

First, the supervisor establishes and communicates expectations for performance; then he or she establishes and communicates standards for performance. The supervisor observes each employee's performance, measuring it against the standards. Finally, the supervisor provides reinforcement for acceptable or excellent performance and works with the employee to develop remedies for inadequate performance.

15.3 Discuss guidelines for avoiding discrimination in performance appraisals.

As much as possible, the appraisal should focus on objective measures of behavior and results—specifically, how well the employee carries out the essential tasks of his or her job. The behaviors and

employee characteristics measured should be related to the job and to succeeding on the job.

15.4 Identify types of appraisals.

Graphic rating scales rate the degree to which an employee has achieved various characteristics, such as job knowledge and punctuality. The paired-comparison approach measures the relative performance of employees in a group. The forced-choice approach presents the supervisor with sets of statements describing employee behavior, and the supervisor chooses which statement is most characteristic of the employee and which is least characteristic. An essay appraisal includes one or more paragraphs describing the employee's performance. Behaviorally anchored rating scales (BARS) rate employee performance in several areas by using a series of statements that describe effective and ineffective performance in each area. A checklist appraisal consists of a series of yes-or-no questions about the employee's performance. A critical-incident appraisal is based on an ongoing record of incidents in which the employee has behaved positively or negatively. The work standards approach is based on establishing objective measures of performance, against which the employee's performance is compared. Management by objectives is a system of developing goals with employees and comparing their performance to those goals. In addition, the supervisor may have employees prepare self-assessments, peer assessments, or appraisals of the supervisor (usually anonymous).

15.5 Describe sources of bias in appraising performance.

Supervisors who want to prove they are tough may succumb to the harshness bias, rating employees too severely; supervisors who hate to deliver bad news may succumb to the leniency bias, rating employees too favorably. The central tendency leads some supervisors to give their employees rankings in the middle of the scale rather than take a strong position. The proximity bias refers to the tendency to assign similar scores to items that are near each other on a questionnaire. Random choices sometimes are made when the appraiser is uncertain about answers or uncomfortable with the overall rating. The similarity bias is the tendency to judge others more positively when they are like oneself. The recency syndrome may lead the supervisor to give too much weight to events that have occurred recently. The halo effect leads people to use one positive or negative trait to describe a person's entire performance. Finally, people are influenced by their prejudices about groups.

15.6 Explain the purpose of conducting performance appraisal interviews.

The purpose of conducting an interview is to communicate to the employee the supervisor's impressions of the employee's performance. In addition, it is an opportunity for the employee to present his or her viewpoint and ideas so that supervisor and employee can work together on improving performance.

15.7 Tell how supervisors should prepare for a performance appraisal interview.

The supervisor should take as much time as is necessary to complete the appraisal form thoughtfully. The supervisor should also think about how the employee is likely to react and should plan how to handle his or her reactions. The supervisor should come up with ideas for resolving problems noted in the appraisal. The supervisor should notify the employee about the interview ahead of time and should prepare an appropriate place to meet without interruptions.

15.8 Describe guidelines for conducting the interview.

First, the supervisor should attempt to put the employee at ease. Then the supervisor and employee should go over the self-appraisal, if any, and the supervisor's appraisal of the employee. The supervisor should focus first on areas for improvement and then on areas of strength. The employee should have time to give feedback; then the supervisor and employee should work together to develop solutions to any problems identified. The supervisor and employee sign the appraisal form, and then the supervisor closes with a positive comment. After the interview, the supervisor needs to follow up to make sure that planned actions are taken.

Key Terms

performance appraisal

graphic rating scale

paired-comparison approach

forced-choice approach

behaviorally anchored rating scales

critical-incident appraisal

work standards approach

harshness bias

leniency bias

central tendency

proximity bias

similarity bias

Review and Discussion Questions

1. What is a performance appraisal? How do organizations benefit from using performance appraisals?

2. June Pearson was just promoted to a job as supervisor of the bookkeeping department at an insurance company. Based on the company's

schedule for appraising performance, she needs to conduct an appraisal of Ron Yamamoto, one of the employees, only a month after she started the job. June cannot find any records of goals established for Ron, so she asks his peers and others with whom he has contact to describe Ron's performance. Based on this information, June completes an appraisal form and conducts an interview.

   a. Which steps of the systematic approach to appraising performance has June omitted?

   b. How do you think Ron will react to this interview?

   c. Can you think of anything else June could have done to improve this particular appraisal? Explain.

3. How can a supervisor avoid illegal discrimination in performance appraisals?

4. At a manufacturing company in the south suburbs of Chicago, one policy stated that each manager and employee must be appraised at one-year intervals. At the same time, the company conducts a review of the person's wages or salary, usually giving at least a small raise. In recent years, like many manufacturers, this company has become very concerned about reducing costs. The policy about conducting performance appraisals has been modified: managers' appraisals now must be conducted *at least* a year after the manager's salary was last reviewed. One supervisor was reviewed in December of one year, then in February (14 months later), and then in May of the third year.

   a. What reasons do you think the supervisor's boss had for delaying the performance appraisals so that they were more than a year apart?

   b. What effects do you think the delays had on the supervisor?

5. What type of performance appraisal is used most often? What are advantages and disadvantages of this approach?

6. At a company that sells X-ray equipment, an important new sales territory is opening up.

Patrick O'Day, the supervisor of the company's sales force, wants to assign the territory to the best-qualified salesperson. How can Patrick compare the performance of the members of the sales force to select the best candidate for the job?

7. Give an advantage and a disadvantage of using each of the following types of appraisals:

   a. essay appraisal

   b. behaviorally anchored rating scales (BARS)

   c. checklist

   d. critical-incident appraisal

8. Consider again the situation described in question 2. What sources of bias do you think are most likely to be a problem in this situation? Explain.

9. What should a supervisor do to prepare for a performance appraisal interview?

10. Reginald DeBeers hates conducting appraisal interviews, so he has the process down to a science. Fifteen minutes before the end of the workday, he meets with the employee who is to be appraised. He gets right down to business, explaining what the employee's ratings are and how he arrived at each number. Then the employee and supervisor sign the form. By then, it is quitting time, and Reginald rises to shake hands with the employee, saying either, "Keep up the good work," or, "I'm sure you'll do better next time."

     What parts of the interviewing process does Reginald omit? What are the consequences of leaving out these steps?

A SECOND LOOK

Based on the information given in the story at the beginning of this chapter, what type(s) of appraisal does Nancy Acedo use?

Class Exercise

For this exercise, the class will conduct either a self-appraisal of performance in the course or an appraisal of the instructor's performance. Either the instructor or the class may decide which type of appraisal to conduct.

The class discusses the design and content of the appraisal. What type(s) of appraisal would be most useful? What areas of performance should be appraised?

Once the appraisal form has been developed, class members complete their appraisal on an individual basis. If the appraisal is of the instructor, a class member or the instructor may collect all the appraisals and prepare a report of their contents for the class to discuss with the instructor. If self-appraisals are used, students may pair up to discuss their results. How can you make this discussion as constructive as possible?

CASE

Appraising Employees in a Dental Office

The story at the beginning of Chapter 13 introduced Jill Strode, who supervises office staff in a dental office. One of Strode's accomplishments was to develop a system for appraising the performance of the employees she supervises.

For each employee, Strode spells out the specific areas of responsibility that will be evaluated. The areas she evaluates match the responsibilities stated in the employee's job description. Thus, for the check-out receptionist, she indicates that she will evaluate how that person handles five areas of responsibility, including check-out procedures and telephone communications. In evaluating how the employee handles each area, Strode looks for specific traits, such as knowledge, initiative, innovation, and courtesy. The following excerpts from an appraisal of the check-out receptionist illustrate the format of the appraisals:

JOB RESPONSIBILITY: Check-Out Procedures and Folder Routing ...

Accuracy: Very good overall. Attention to details is superb in all areas. Seldom forgets any part of the 'check-out' procedure.
Example: Ability to pick up on errors made in charting, double-checking folders for missed steps (insurance, scheduling, etc.), thoroughness.
Innovation: Below average. This area has remained unchanged since we installed the system. Procedural changes have been suggested by Supervisor and implemented by check-out receptionist. Needs improvement.
Example: Complaints with folder errors and patient flow have been verbalized; however, suggestions for changes or improvement in procedures have not been offered. Space limitations in check-out area still a concern...suggestions for improvements?

To review the performance appraisal with the employee, Strode sets up a formal appraisal meeting. She has developed the following agenda, or list of topics to cover during the meeting:

1. Review specific areas of responsibility that will be evaluated. Make any changes or additions if needed.
2. Appraisal for each specific area
   a. Set goals for improvement and change (at least two improvements/changes for each)
   b. Set training dates (if needed)
   c. Get feedback from staff on appraisal from Supervisor
3. Overall appraisal of traits as exemplified in daily activities and actions.
4. Review goals and training dates.
5. Questions and answers from list.
6. Open forum for discussion: Employee to Supervisor

Strode then follows up to make sure that the employee and supervisor carry through on the goals and plans they established during this interview.

1. Based on the information given, what type of performance appraisal has Strode developed?
2. Would you consider this a useful type of appraisal for clerical employees in a dental practice? Can you suggest any additions or improvements?
3. Based on the agenda Strode uses for appraisal interviews, what principles of effective appraisals does she follow?

Source: Jill Strode.

16

If it becomes necessary to discipline employees, they should be told "why" and be given every chance to be heard.

—Johnson & Johnson Company

Supervising "Problem" Employees

LEARNING OBJECTIVES

16.1 **Identify common types of problem behavior among employees.**

16.2 **Tell why and when supervisors should counsel employees.**

16.3 **Describe counseling techniques.**

16.4 **Discuss effective ways of administering discipline.**

16.5 **Describe the principles of positive discipline and self-discipline.**

16.6 **Explain how supervisors can detect and confront troubled employees.**

16.7 **Describe how supervisors can direct troubled employees in getting help and then follow up on the recovery efforts.**

16.8 **Discuss the role of the supervisor's boss and the human resources department in helping the supervisor with problem employees.**

ARRESTING PROBLEM SITUATIONS

Tommy Hunnicutt, Jr., supervises two crews for Harris Tire Company in Lynchburg, Virginia. One crew of eight men services vehicles with brake jobs, wheel alignments, and new-tire installations. The four employees in the other crew work in the company's 64,000-square-foot warehouse.

One day a man (we will call him Sam) came to Harris Tire looking for work. He followed up persistently and told Hunnicutt that he would work for a week without pay so the company could try him out risk free. After a brief reference check, the company hired Sam to work in the warehouse for $5 per hour. Sam was very dependable, and his attitude was good.

About six months later, a neighbor who lived behind Harris Tire's warehouse called the company's owner. The neighbor said that on several occasions he had witnessed somebody on the roof of the warehouse throwing tires into the empty lot behind the warehouse. Later in the evening, the neighbor would see three people arrive in a car to pick up the tires.

The owner contacted the Lynchburg Police Department. Over the next few days, police investigated the charges. They caught the people picking up the tires from the empty lot and arrested them immediately. Later that evening, the police picked up Sam. The day after Sam was released on bail, he was rearrested—this time for selling crack cocaine.

Harris Tire Company estimates that it lost 60 Bridgestone tires to this employee.

Source: Corinne R. Livesay, Liberty University, Lynchburg, Va. Photo courtesy of © 1993 Comstock, Inc.

When the supervisor has done a good job of selecting, training, motivating, and appraising, most employees will be capable and will perform well. Even so, supervisors will occasionally face the challenge of a "problem" employee—one who seems persistently unwilling or unable to follow the rules or meet performance standards. In general, problem employees fall into two categories: (1) employees *causing* problems—for example, by starting fights or leaving early—and (2) employees *with* problems, such as an employee whose money worries are a distraction from work. By handling such employees appropriately, the supervisor can help resolve the problem without hurting the morale or performance of the other employees.

This chapter provides guidelines for supervising problem employees. It describes some common problems requiring special action on the part of the supervisor and explains two basic courses of action to take: counseling and discipline. The chapter also discusses how to help the troubled employee (one who has personal problems that make him or her unable to respond to basic counseling or discipline). Finally, the chapter describes the kinds of support a supervisor can expect from superiors and the human resources department.

Problems Requiring Special Action

For the third straight Monday, Peter Dunbar had called in sick. The other employees were grumbling about having to do extra to make up for his absences, and rumors were flying about the nature of Peter's problem. Peter's supervisor knew she would have to take action, beginning with some investigation into what the problem was.

When supervisors observe poor performance, they tend to blame the employee for lacking ability or effort. But when supervisors or employees need to explain their own poor performance, they tend to blame the organization or another person for not providing enough support.[1] This inconsistency suggests that it takes some digging to uncover the true source of a performance problem. For example, the supervisor might consider the following questions:

- Has the employee performed better in the past?
- Has the employee received proper training?
- Does the employee know and understand the objectives he or she is to accomplish?
- Is the supervisor providing enough feedback and support?
- Has the supervisor encouraged and rewarded high performance?
- Are other employees with similar abilities performing well? Or are they experiencing similar difficulties?

Although persistent failure to perform up to standards results from many problems, the problems that supervisors most commonly encounter are absenteeism and tardiness, insubordination and uncooperativeness, alcohol and drug abuse, and employee theft.

Absenteeism and Tardiness

An employee who misses work, even part of a day, is expensive for an employer. Often the company must pay for those unproductive hours—for example, if the employee calls in sick. In addition, the other employees are less productive when they must cover for someone who is absent or tardy.

Of course, employees who really are sick should take time off. The company provides sick days for good reasons: to allow employees to rest and recover and to prevent them from infecting the rest of the work force. The problem arises with absences that are unexcused or recur with suspicious regularity. In addition, missing work is often a sign of a deeper problem, such as a family crisis, anger about something at work, or plans to leave the organization.

Insubordination and Uncooperativeness

When poor performance results from not understanding how to do a job, the solution is relatively simple. The supervisor must make sure that instructions are communicated clearly and that the employee is receiving the proper training. But sometimes an employee performs poorly or breaks rules because he or she chooses to do so. Such an employee may simply be uncooperative, or the employee may engage in **insubordination**—that is, deliberate refusal to do what the supervisor or other superior asks.

Many kinds of negative behavior fall into these categories. An employee may have a generally poor attitude—criticizing, complaining, and showing a dislike for the supervisor and the organization. Or he or she might get into arguments over all kinds of issues. An employee may make an art form out of doing as little as possible. The employee might spend most of the day socializing, joking around, or just moving slowly. Another employee might regularly fail to follow rules—"forgetting" to wear safety equipment or to sign out at lunchtime. For example, an actual case of insubordination and uncooperativeness was reported by a supervisor who complained of an employee who would disregard the supervisor's instructions to do something, saying she would get to it later. This employee also persisted in interrupting the supervisor to ask questions, then she would walk away muttering under her breath.[2]

Kerry Connolly, a human resources manager at Wang Laboratories, points out that sarcastic, hostile, or passive behavior is actually a symptom of an underlying problem.[3] Thus, for example, an employee who never takes the initiative and does just enough to get by may have a personal problem that is distracting that employee from focusing on work. The supervisor's job, according to Connolly, is to "get to the source" through the use of coaching, described later in the chapter.

insubordination
Deliberate refusal to do what the supervisor or other superior asks.

Alcohol and Drug Abuse

Unsafe practices, sloppy work, and frequent absences may be symptoms of a deeper problem. Some employees abuse alcohol or drugs on or off the job. According to a recent estimate, one out of six workers has a serious drug problem.[4] The most abused substance is alcohol, with approximately 18 million Americans having a serious drinking problem, according to the National Council on Alcoholism and Drug Dependence.[5]

These employees are expensive to the organization. According to a widely cited estimate, drug abuse costs U.S. industry about $50 billion a year. Although the accuracy of this number has been criticized,[6] there are clearly many ways in which drug abuse by employees hurts organizations. Not only are substance-abusing employees less productive than they could be, they are more likely to

Improving skills can help eliminate the threat of poor performance. These Plumley Cos. employees, who took company-sponsored high school equivalency classes, celebrate their graduation.

Source: Courtesy of Mark Tucker, photographer.

quit, boosting costs for recruitment and training. Substance abusers are more likely to cause accidents; the National Safety Council estimates that almost half of the two million industrial accidents reported each year are related directly to alcohol or drug abuse.[7] Disabilities related to substance abuse can lead to higher use of disability and sick benefits, as well as higher insurance costs. For example, over a recent five-year period, employees with an alcohol or drug problem were absent from work 113 days more than the average employee and filed an average of $23,000 more in medical claims.[8] Finally, drug abusers may steal from the organization in order to support their habit.

In supervising a suspected substance abuser, it is important to note that federal antidiscrimination law treats substance abuse as a disability. Therefore, the supervisor should encourage the employee to get help, even if doing so requires adjusting the employee's work schedule or permitting the employee to take a disability leave in order to get treatment. In addition, actions taken with regard to the employee should focus on work performance, not on the substance abuse itself. For example, the supervisor might warn, "If I catch you picking fights with your co-workers again, I will have to suspend you." This warning addresses the employee's job-related behavior.

At the same time, the supervisor, like higher-level managers, is responsible for ensuring that the workplace is safe for employees and others.[9] This means that if an employee's suspected substance abuse is creating a hazard, the supervisor *must*

Substance abusers are more likely to cause accidents, to be less productive, and to quit, causing higher recruitment and training costs. The National Safety Council estimates that almost half of the 2 million industrial accidents reported each year are directly related to alcohol or drug abuse.

Source: Courtesy of © 1992 Comstock, Inc.

act. (The section on troubled employees later in this chapter provides guidelines that apply to handling employees who abuse drugs or alcohol.)

Employee Theft

The story of Harris Tire at the beginning of this chapter describes an employee who was stealing from his employer. The U.S. Chamber of Commerce recently estimated that employee theft of companies' inventory, supplies, and money costs U.S. employers $40 billion a year.[10] Oddly enough, an employee of the aerospace company Allied-Signal once spotted a large jet part from the company at a bar in Crown King, Arizona. Robert R. Smith, general supervisor for plant security at Allied-Signal's Fluid Systems Division, commented, "We have had some things walk out of here. Usually it's not airplane parts, because they're not worth much without the rest of the plane. More often, it's computer equipment and tools."[11] The manager of a store complains the employees "steal sandwiches, meat, potatoes, tools, equipment, and whatever else we do not nail down."[12]

Not all thefts involve money or tangible goods. Employees can also "steal time" by giving the employer less work than they are paid for. Thus, employees are guilty of stealing time when they take extra sick leave or alter their time cards. A supervisor of a Pennsylvania health care facility once told his employer that he would need weeks to recover from a totally disabling back injury. Suspicious, the organization had the supervisor investigated; the investigator spotted him lifting a set of golf clubs from his rental car at an Arizona golf course.[13]

When employee theft is viewed broadly to include the theft of time, the problem is especially great. Allied-Signal's Smith says that most studies have found that one-third of employees steal.[14] In an anonymous survey of employees at 26 supermarket chains nationwide, 46 percent of the employees said they had stolen cash or personal property from work, 49 percent said they had helped someone else steal, and 62 percent admitted to stealing work time.[15]

The widespread nature of this problem indicates that supervisors must be on their guard against employee theft. Besides following the broad guidelines in this chapter for handling employee problems, the supervisor should take measures to prevent and react to theft. Each organization has its own procedures, varying according to type of industry. In addition, supervisors should carefully check the background of anyone they plan to hire (see Chapter 13). They should make sure that employees follow all procedures for record keeping. They should take advantage of ways to build employees' morale and involvement, as described in many chapters of this book; employees who feel like a part of the organization are less likely to steal from it. Supervisors should make sure employees understand the costs and consequences of theft. Perhaps most important, supervisors should set a good example, following principles of ethical behavior as described in Chapter 19. If supervisors do suspect an employee is stealing, advises the Small Business Administration, they should not try to investigate the crime themselves. Rather, they should report their suspicions to their boss and to the police or professional security consultants.[16]

Counseling

If the supervisor responds to problem behavior immediately, he or she will sometimes be able to bring the problem to a quick end without complex proceedings. For example, in the case of an employee who constantly complains about the way things are done, the supervisor can respond to each complaint by calmly asking the employee to suggest some alternatives. Not only does this discourage complaining, but it may uncover some good, new ways of operating. In many cases, however, the supervisor must take further steps to demonstrate the seriousness of the problem behavior.

counseling
The process of learning about an individual's personal problem and helping him or her resolve it.

Often the most constructive way a supervisor can address problem behavior is through counseling. **Counseling** refers to the process of learning about an individual's personal problem and helping him or her resolve it. For a relatively simple problem, such as tardiness caused by staying up too late watching television, the employee may recognize a solution that he or she can carry out with or without the supervisor's help. For more complex problems, such as those stemming from financial difficulties or substance abuse, the solution will involve getting help from an expert. In either case, because counseling is a cooperative process, with supervisor and employee working together, employees are likely to respond more positively to counseling than to a simple order that they "shape up or ship out."

Counseling employees can lead to improved job satisfaction, motivation, and increased productivity.

Source: Courtesy of © 1992 Comstock, Inc.

Benefits of Counseling

Counseling benefits employees in several ways. It can ease their worries or help them find a way to solve their problems. Working cooperatively with the supervisor to resolve a problem gives the employee a sense that the supervisor and organization are interested in his or her welfare. This belief, in turn, can improve job satisfaction and motivation. The resulting improvements in productivity benefit the employee when performance is rewarded.

The organization benefits, too. Employees who receive needed counseling are well motivated and more likely to meet performance standards. The changes in the employee's attitudes carry over to other employees' work as well. When personal problems affect one employee's work, the others suffer consequences such as working harder to make up for the problem employee's lapses. Also, being around someone with a negative attitude tends to drag down the spirits of the others in the group. After counseling improves the problem employee's performance and attitude, the whole group tends to do better.

Appropriate Times to Counsel

The supervisor should counsel employees when they need help in determining how to resolve a problem that is affecting their work. Sometimes an employee will approach the supervisor with a problem, such as worries about his or her marriage or concern as to whether he or she is doing a good job. At other times, the supervisor may observe that an employee seems to have a problem; for example, the quality of the employee's work may be declining.

It is essential for the supervisor to remember that he or she lacks training to help with many kinds of problems. A supervisor is not in a position to save a marriage, resolve an employee's financial difficulties, or tell how to handle an alcoholic family member. The supervisor should help the employee resolve the problem only when qualified to do so. In other cases, the supervisor should simply listen, express his or her concern, and refer the employee to a professional trained to handle that type of problem. The human resources department may be able to suggest sources of help.

Counseling Techniques

Counseling involves one or more discussions between the supervisor and the employee. These sessions should take place in a location where there will be privacy and freedom from interruptions. As illustrated in Figure 16.1, the sessions may be directive or nondirective.

directive counseling
An approach to counseling in which the supervisor asks the employee questions about the specific problem; when the supervisor understands the problem, he or she suggests ways to handle it.

Directive versus Nondirective Counseling   The most focused approach to counseling is **directive counseling**. With this approach, the supervisor asks the employee questions about the specific problem. Then the supervisor listens until he or she understands the source of the problem. Then the supervisor suggests ways to handle the problem.

For example, assume that Bill Wisniewski, a computer programmer, has been absent a number of times during the past month. The supervisor might ask, "Why have you been missing so many days?" Bill replies, "Because my wife has been sick, and someone needs to look after my kids." The supervisor would follow up with questions about Bill's wife's condition (for example, to learn whether the problem is likely to continue), the ages and needs of Bill's children, and so on. Then the supervisor might suggest finding alternative sources of care, perhaps referring Bill to a company program designed to help with such problems.

nondirective counseling
An approach to counseling in which the supervisor primarily listens, encouraging the employee to look for the source of the problem and to propose possible solutions.

In most cases, the supervisor and employee will find it most beneficial to help the employee develop and change rather than to look only for solutions to a specific problem. To accomplish this, the supervisor can use **nondirective counseling**. With this approach, the supervisor primarily listens, encouraging the employee to look for the source of the problem and to propose possible solutions. In the preceding example, the supervisor would ask open-ended questions such as, "Would you tell me more about that?" Ideally, by working out his own solution, Bill would find that he has the ability to resolve many family problems without missing a lot of work.

The Counseling Interview   As summarized in Figure 16.2, the counseling interview starts with a discussion of what the problem is. It then moves to consideration of possible solutions and selection of a solution to try. The interview ends with the supervisor scheduling a follow-up meeting.

The person who requested the counseling begins by describing the problem. If the employee requested help, the employee should begin. If the supervisor set up the interview because something seemed wrong, the supervisor should begin. As when conducting performance appraisals, the supervisor should focus on behavior and performance, not on such abstract concepts as attitude. The supervisor should

FIGURE 16.1

Directive versus Nondirective Counseling

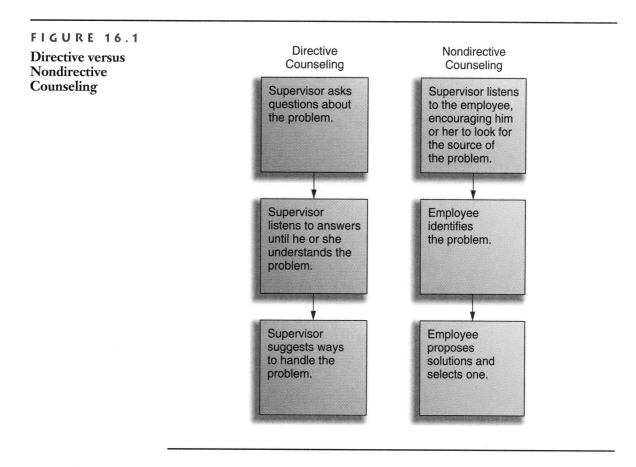

Directive Counseling

Supervisor asks questions about the problem.

Supervisor listens to answers until he or she understands the problem.

Supervisor suggests ways to handle the problem.

Nondirective Counseling

Supervisor listens to the employee, encouraging him or her to look for the source of the problem.

Employee identifies the problem.

Employee proposes solutions and selects one.

FIGURE 16.2

The Counseling Interview

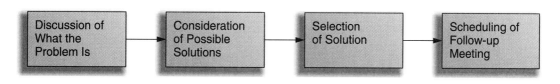

Discussion of What the Problem Is → Consideration of Possible Solutions → Selection of Solution → Scheduling of Follow-up Meeting

encourage the employee to do the same. For example, if the employee says, "The other employees are prejudiced against me," the supervisor should ask the employee to describe what actions led the employee to that conclusion. In addition, the supervisor should use the principles of active listening, described in Chapter 7.

Because counseling often takes place as a result of personal problems the employee is having, the employee may be emotional during counseling sessions.

The supervisor needs to be prepared for crying, angry outbursts, and other signs of emotion. He or she should be calm and should reassure the employee that emotions are not innately good or bad. Of course, there are appropriate and inappropriate ways to express emotions. For example, imagine that a salesperson in a hardware store has a 10-year-old son with behavior problems. It would not be appropriate for the salesperson to express his worry and frustration by snapping at customers.

Next, the supervisor and employee should consider ways to solve the problem. Rather than simply prescribing a solution, the supervisor can usually be more helpful by asking the employee questions that will help the employee come up with ideas. Employees are more likely to cooperate in a solution they helped to develop. Asking an employee to suggest solutions can be an especially effective way to end constant whining and complaining by that employee.[17] When the supervisor and employee agree on a solution to be used, the supervisor should restate it to make sure the employee understands. (Chapter 8 provides more detailed guidelines for mutual problem solving.)

Finally, the supervisor should schedule a follow-up meeting. This should take place just after the employee begins to see some results. At the follow-up meeting, employee and supervisor will review their plans and discuss whether the problem has been or is being resolved. For example, in the case of the salesperson in the hardware store, the supervisor might say, "I've noticed that we haven't received anymore customer complaints about your service. In fact, one woman told me you went out of your way to help her." Notice that the supervisor is focusing on work performance, which he is qualified to discuss, rather than on the employee's family problems. If the employee replies, "Yes, I've been so much calmer ever since I started talking to that counselor about my son," the supervisor has a good indication that the employee is resolving his problem.

Discipline

discipline
Action taken by the supervisor to prevent employees from breaking rules.

"I can't stand Marcia's surly attitude any longer!" fumed Don Koh, her supervisor. "If she doesn't cut it out, she's going to be sorry." This supervisor is eager for the employee to experience the consequences of her behavior. However, despite the anger and frustration that can be generated by supervising a problem employee, it is important for the supervisor to apply discipline in constructive ways. **Discipline** is action taken by the supervisor to prevent employees from breaking rules. In many cases, effective discipline can quickly bring about a change in an employee's behavior.

Administering Discipline

In administering discipline, the supervisor should distinguish between discipline and punishment. As described in Chapter 9, punishment is an unpleasant consequence given in response to undesirable behavior. Discipline, in contrast, is broader; it is a teaching process. The supervisor explains the significance and consequences of the employee's behavior, then, if necessary, lets the employee experience those consequences.

The specific ways in which the supervisor applies these steps may be dictated by company policies or the union contract, if any. Thus, the supervisor must be familiar with the policies and rules that apply. These should include respecting the rights of employees in the discipline process. Employees' rights include the following:[18]

- The right to know job expectations and the consequences of not fulfilling those expectations
- The right to receive consistent and predictable management action in response to violations of the rules
- The right to receive fair discipline based on facts
- The right to question management's statement of the facts and to present a defense
- The right to receive progressive discipline (described in the next section)
- The right to appeal a disciplinary action

The Discipline Process Before administering discipline in response to problem behavior, the supervisor needs to have a clear picture of the situation. The supervisor may observe the problem him- or herself, or someone may tell the supervisor about the problem. In either case, the supervisor needs to collect the facts before taking further action.

As soon as possible, the supervisor should meet with the employees involved and ask for each employee's version of what happened. For example, a supervisor believed that one of her employees was using the office phone for personal business. The employee had a girlfriend in England, and the supervisor suspected the company was paying for the employee's long-distance calls to her. The solution to this problem would come not from making hasty accusations or from issuing a general memo about company policy but from asking the employee directly and privately what his phone conversations were about.[19] In getting the employee's version of a problem, the supervisor should use good listening practices (see Chapter 7) and resist the temptation to get angry.

When the supervisor observes and understands the facts behind problem behavior, disciplining an employee takes place in as many as four steps, illustrated in Figure 16.3. These steps are warnings, suspension, demotion, and dismissal. They progress from the least to the most severe action a supervisor can take. A warning is unpleasant to hear, but it is important to inform employees of the consequences of their behavior before taking more punitive measures. Suspension, demotion, and discharge are more upsetting to an employee because they hurt the employee in the pocketbook.

A warning may be either written or oral. Some organizations have a policy that calls for an oral warning followed by a written warning if performance does not improve. Both types of warning are designed to make sure that the employee understands the problem. A warning should contain the following information:

- What the problem behavior is
- How the behavior affects the organization
- How and when the employee's behavior is expected to change
- What actions will be taken if the employee's behavior does not change

For example, a supervisor might say, "I have noticed that in the last two staff meetings, you have made hostile remarks. These not only have disrupted the meetings,

FIGURE 16.3

Possible Steps in the Discipline Process

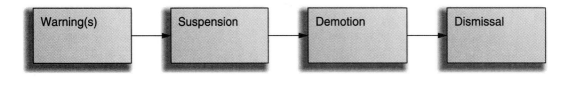

they lead your co-workers to take you less seriously. I expect that you will refrain from such remarks in future meetings, or I will have to give you a suspension." The warning should be brief and to the point. In the case of a written warning, it is wise practice to ask the employee to sign the warning, which documents that the first step in the discipline process took place. If the employee refuses to sign the warning, even with minor changes, the supervisor should note the employee's refusal or should call in someone (such as the supervisor's boss) to witness the refusal.

A **suspension** involves requiring that the employee not come to work for a set period of time; the employee is not paid for the time off. The length of the suspension might run from one day to one month, depending on the seriousness of the problem. Suspensions are useful when the employee has been accused of something serious, such as stealing, and the supervisor needs time to investigate.

A **demotion** is transferring an employee to a job involving less responsibility and, usually, lower pay. Sometimes a demotion is actually a relief for an employee. The employee may have been goofing off or performing poorly because the job was more than he or she could handle. In such a case, the employee welcomes being returned to a job where he or she is competent. More often, however, a demotion leads to negative feelings. It feels like a punishment that continues for as long as the employee holds the lower-level job.

Dismissal, also called termination or discharge, means relieving the employee of his or her job. Dismissal is not really a success for the organization, because it generates the need to recruit, hire, and train a new employee. Nevertheless, there are times when the supervisor must dismiss an employee who commits a serious offense or will not respond to other forms of discipline. Occasionally the employee or supervisor may decide that correcting a problem is impossible, or at least too difficult or expensive.[20] Besides continued failure to correct problem behavior, the types of actions that may lead a supervisor to dismiss an employee include deliberately damaging the organization's property, fighting on the job, or engaging in dangerous practices (for example, drinking on the job in the case of a railroad employee). Dismissing an employee is never easy; the "Tips from the Firing Line" box provides guidelines that may help to smooth the process. In addition, many organizations have policies requiring the supervisor to involve higher-level management before dismissing an employee. Supervisors should be familiar with any such policy and follow it.

In following the steps of the discipline process, the supervisor should keep in mind that the objective is to end the problem behavior. The supervisor takes only as

suspension
Requiring that an employee not come to work for a set period of time; the employee is not paid for the time off.

demotion
Transfer of an employee to a job involving less responsibility and, usually, lower pay.

dismissal
Relieving an employee of his or her job.

Responsible Firing

Nobody likes to terminate employees. Fortunately, a supervisor who does a good job of selecting and motivating employees will hardly ever have to fire anyone. The ultimate goal in responsible firing is to minimize the number of times you will have to use most of these guidelines:

- First, hire the right employees. This means considering whether a potential employee not only has the skills to carry out the job but also has a positive work attitude and is a good fit with co-workers.
- Communicate objectives and job standards clearly. Employees cannot do what you expect unless they know what that is.
- Keep track of performance. Do not wait for the annual performance appraisal to notice that something is wrong.
- Respond to problems as soon as you discover them. Work with the employee to develop solutions, then follow up.
- When you need to fire, do it right away. Do not waste time agonizing over the decision; that will just allow the problem to get worse. (But if the employee is a union member, be sure to follow required practices such as giving the employee prior notice of his or her right to have a union representative attend disciplinary and termination meetings.)
- Terminate the employee in your office or another location where you have privacy and can control the length of the meeting.
- Announce the termination near the end of the day, preferably not the day before the employee's birthday or a major holiday. Give a reason for the firing, answer questions, and express your regrets. The meeting should take no more than 10 or 15 minutes.

- Sit down, and have the employee sit down. This makes it easier to keep emotional reactions under control.
- Have someone witness the firing. The third person should be someone who does not work directly with the terminated employee—for example, a member of the human resources department. After you have announced the termination and answered any questions, leave the room. The third person then remains to explain the details of the termination, such as the amount of any severance pay and how long insurance benefits will last. You might also give the terminated person a list of this kind of information.
- Soon after the firing, for the sake of morale, explain to the remaining employees the reason for the termination.
- Call the employee a week or two later to conduct an exit interview. Assure the employee that what he or she says will not affect severance benefits or references. Then ask what it was like to work for the organization and how it could be a better place to work.
- Analyze what happened. What was it about the former employee that led you to terminate him or her? How could you have predicted it in the hiring process? How could you have corrected it in the supervising process? The objective of this analysis is to avoid repeating the same mistake in the future.

Sources: William J. Ransom, "The Pain of Firing: Several Ways to Reduce the Hurt," *Industrial Engineering*, January 1992, p. 12; Leah Rosch, "The Anguish of Firing: How to Handle the Task Every Boss Dreads," *Your Company*, Spring 1992, pp. 20–21; and Ellyn E. Spragins, "How to Fire," *Inc.*, May 1992, pp. 66–67, 72.

many steps as are necessary to bring about a change in behavior. The supervisor's ultimate goal is to solve the problem without dismissing the employee. Recruiting and hiring a replacement employee is time-consuming and expensive. However, in the case of some serious actions, company policy may require dismissal.

Guidelines for Effective Discipline   When an employee is causing a problem, be it tardiness, theft of company property, or an uncooperative attitude, the supervisor needs to act immediately. That is not always easy to do. Pointing out poor behavior and administering negative consequences are unpleasant tasks. However, by ignoring the situation, the supervisor signals that he or she does not consider the problem serious. As a result, the problem gets worse. The employee may increase the problem behavior, and other employees may follow his or her example, seeing that there are no consequences. In contrast, when Kathleen R. Tibbs was an in-flight supervisor with Eastern Airlines, she faced up to the unpleasant task of disciplining an employee with unacceptable attendance. Tibbs had the employee removed from the payroll for seven days, which moved the employee to address the personal problems that led to her poor attendance.

When discussing the problem with the employee involved, the supervisor should focus on learning about and resolving the issue at hand. This meeting is no time for name calling or for dredging up instances of past misbehavior. Nor is it generally useful for the supervisor to dwell on how patient or compassionate he or she has been. Instead, the supervisor should listen until he or she understands the problem and then begin discussing how to correct the problem in the future. Talking about behaviors instead of personalities makes it easier for the employee to understand what is expected.

The supervisor should keep emotions in check. Although it is appropriate to convey sincere concern about the problem, the supervisor's other feelings are largely irrelevant and can stand in the way of a constructive discussion. When an employee breaks the rules or seems unwilling to do a good job, it is only natural for a supervisor to feel angry. The supervisor should get control over this anger before confronting the employee so that the supervisor can be objective rather than hostile. Being calm and relaxed when administering discipline tells the employee that the supervisor is confident of what he or she is doing.

Discipline should be a private matter. The supervisor should not humiliate an employee by chewing the employee out in front of everyone else. Humiliation only breeds resentment and may actually increase problem behavior in the future.

The supervisor also should be consistent in administering discipline. One way to do this is to follow the four steps of the discipline process outlined earlier. Also, the supervisor should respond to all instances of misbehavior rather than, say, ignore a longstanding employee's misdeeds while punishing a newcomer.

These guidelines for effective discipline are summarized in Figure 16.4.

Documentation of Disciplinary Action   Employees who receive discipline sometimes respond by filing a grievance or suing the employer. To be able to justify his or her actions, the supervisor must have a record of the disciplinary actions taken and the basis for the discipline. These records may be needed to show that the actions were not discriminatory or against company policy. As noted earlier, one type of disciplinary record is a signed copy of any written warning. In addition, other disciplinary actions should be recorded in the employee's personnel file, as directed by the human resources department.

Supervisors often use past performance appraisals as documentation of the need for disciplinary action. However, this often backfires because so many supervisors are reluctant to give negative evaluations. For example, if an appraisal says an employee's work was average, was adequate, or met only minimal performance

FIGURE 16.4

Guidelines for Effective Discipline

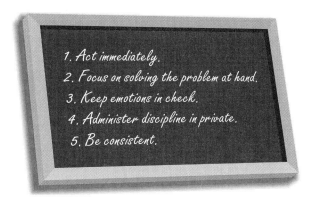

1. Act immediately.
2. Focus on solving the problem at hand.
3. Keep emotions in check.
4. Administer discipline in private.
5. Be consistent.

standards, that appraisal does not support an action to dismiss the employee. This is one reason it is essential for the supervisor to give accurate performance appraisals, as described in the previous chapter.

Documentation is especially important when the supervisor must terminate an employee. Because the experience is so emotional, some former employees respond with a lawsuit. The employee's file should show the steps the supervisor took leading up to the termination. The supervisor also should record the specific behaviors that led him or her to dismiss the employee.

Positive Discipline

positive discipline
Discipline designed to prevent problem behavior from beginning.

Ideally, discipline should not only end problem behavior, it should also prevent problems from occurring. Discipline designed to prevent problem behavior from beginning is known as **positive discipline**, or preventive discipline. An important part of positive discipline is making sure employees know and understand the rules they must follow. Along with communicating what the rules are, the supervisor should explain the consequences of violating rules. For example, a production supervisor might explain that it is company policy to dismiss any employee caught operating machinery while under the influence of drugs or alcohol.

The supervisor can also administer positive discipline by working to create the conditions under which employees are least likely to cause problems. Employees may engage in problem behavior when they feel frustrated. For example, if the organization sets a sales quota higher than salespeople think they can achieve, they may give up and goof off instead of trying their best. Or if manufacturing employees complain about unsafe working conditions but no changes are made, they may adopt a negative attitude in the face of what seems to be the company's lack of concern for their safety. This reaction is related to another source of problem behavior: feeling as if one is not an important part of the organization. This leads employees to believe that they and management are at odds with one another rather than working together. As a result, some employees may turn their energy toward seeing what they can get away with.

To combat such problems, the supervisor needs to be aware of and responsive to employees' needs and ideas. The supervisor should encourage upward communication (described in Chapter 7). As much as possible, the supervisor should also promote teamwork (see Chapter 17) and encourage employees to participate in decision making and problem solving (see Chapter 8). Good motivation techniques (described in Chapter 9) also help prevent the frustration and alienation that can lead to problem behavior.

At some companies, positive discipline includes a day off with pay for employees who fail to respond to efforts to educate them about following the rules and meeting performance standards. This suspension, known as a **decision-making leave**, is a day off during which the employee is supposed to decide whether to return to work and meet standards or to stay away for good. If the employee chooses to come back, he or she works with the supervisor to develop objectives and action plans for improvement.

Finally, the supervisor should not only punish problem behavior but should reward the kinds of behavior that are desirable. Thus, the supervisor should not just punish employees who are uncooperative but should reward employees for contributing to the department's performance. For example, the supervisor should recognize those who make suggestions for improvement or resolve sticky problems. (Chapter 9 provides more specific suggestions for rewarding employees.)

decision-making leave
A day off during which a problem employee is supposed to decide whether to return to work and meet standards or to stay away for good.

Self-Discipline

An effective program of positive discipline results in self-discipline by employees. In other words, employees voluntarily follow the rules and try to meet performance standards. Most people get satisfaction from doing a job well, so self-discipline should result when employees understand what is expected. Supervisors can help to encourage self-discipline by communicating not only the rules and performance standards, but the reasons for those rules and standards.

In addition, a supervisor who takes long lunch breaks or spends hours chatting with friends on the phone is in no position to insist the employees put in a full workday. If supervisors expect employees to follow the rules, they must set a good example by practicing self-discipline themselves.

Troubled Employees

So far, this chapter has focused on problems that can be solved by giving employees more information or helping them to change their behavior. But some employees have problems that make them unable to respond to a simple process of discipline or counseling. These troubled employees include people who are substance abusers or have psychological problems.

Detection of the Troubled Employee

The first signs that the supervisor has a troubled employee tend to be the kinds of discipline problems described earlier in this chapter. For example, the supervisor may notice that an employee is frequently late or that the quality of the employee's

TABLE 16.1

Possible Signs of Alcohol or Drug Use

Slurred speech

Clumsy movements and increased accidents

Personality changes

Decreased ability to work as part of a team

Smell of alcohol on the employee's breath

Growing carelessness toward personal appearance and the details of the job

Increase in absenteeism or tardiness along with unbelievable excuses

Daydreaming

Leaving the work area; making frequent visits to the rest room

Violence in the workplace

work has been slipping. If disciplinary action or counseling seems ineffective at resolving the problem, the supervisor may have a troubled employee.

In the case of substance abuse, the supervisor might notice signs that the employee has been using alcohol or drugs. The examples listed in Table 16.1 are among the most common. (Note that these are only hints that the employee *might* be using drugs or alcohol. There may be other explanations for these kinds of behavior.) Perhaps the supervisor will even find the employee has possession of drugs or alcohol. When an employee is suspected of drug use, some organizations have a policy of confirming the suspicion through the use of drug testing.

Because there may be another explanation for symptoms that look like the effects of using alcohol or illicit drugs (for example, taking prescription medications), the supervisor should avoid making accusations about what he or she believes is going on. For example, the supervisor should not say, "I see you've been drinking on the job." Rather, the supervisor should focus on job performance: "I see something is hurting the quality of your work this week. Let's talk about what the problem is and how to solve it."

Confrontation of the Troubled Employee

Ignoring a problem does not make it go away. Thus, hoping an alcoholic employee will seek help rarely works. It only helps the employee believe in the illusion that the substance abuse is not causing significant problems. After all, if the boss does not complain, how bad can his or her work be? Therefore, when the supervisor suspects a problem, he or she needs to confront the employee.

The first step is to document the problem. The supervisor should keep notes of instances in which an employee's performance is not acceptable. (This might be part of the critical-incident approach to appraisal described in the preceding chapter.) When collecting this information, the supervisor should be sure to keep such notes on all employees whose performance is slipping, not just on one person the supervisor is targeting.

When the supervisor has enough evidence to support his or her suspicions, the supervisor should meet with the employee and confront him or her. The supervisor should go over the employee's performance, describing the evidence of a problem. Then the supervisor should refer the employee to a source of counseling or other help. For example, the supervisor could say, "I don't know what's wrong with you, but I want you to see an employee assistance counselor."[21] Finally, the supervisor should explain the consequences of not changing. In some cases, accepting help may be a requirement for keeping the job. Thus, the supervisor might say, "There's no shame in getting help, and we'll keep it private. But you are responsible for doing your job safely and up to standards. If you don't, I'll have to follow our disciplinary procedures for unacceptable performance." Experts agree that this type of warning from a supervisor can be one of the most effective ways to motivate a substance-abusing employee to get help. Says Carol Cepress of the Hazelden treatment center in Center City, Minnesota, "The reality that your job is on the line is usually quite an eye-opener."[22]

During the confrontation, the employee may become angry or defensive. This is a common reaction in such situations, so the supervisor should not take it personally or overreact. The employee also may come up with excuses that sound particularly sad and compelling. In any case, the supervisor must continue to focus on the employee's behavior on the job and the way the employee's behavior affects the organization. No matter how outraged the employee or how impressive or creative the excuse, the employee's behavior must improve.

Aid in and Evaluation of Recovery

Most organizations have developed procedures for providing help to troubled employees. When the supervisor believes that problems are occurring because the employee is troubled, the supervisor needs to investigate what the organization's procedures are. In most cases, the place to start is with the human resources department.

The type of treatment program tends to depend on the size of the organization. Many small organizations refer troubled employees to a counseling service. Another policy is simply to tell the employee to get help or else lose his or her job. A supervisor should be careful in pursuing the latter approach. If possible, the ultimate objective should be the employee's rehabilitation, rather than his or her dismissal. Rehabilitation is not only more compassionate, it tends to be less costly than hiring and training a new employee, and it is less likely to violate antidiscrimination laws.

employee assistance program (EAP)
A company-based program for providing counseling and related help to employees whose personal problems are affecting their performance.

Other organizations, especially large ones, offer an **employee assistance program (EAP)**. An EAP is a company-based program for providing counseling and related help to employees whose personal problems are affecting their performance. It may be simply a referral service or may be fully staffed with social workers, psychologists, nurses, career counselors, financial advisers, and other professionals. These programs are voluntary (employees do not have to participate unless they want to) and confidential (participation is a private matter). The "Dealing with Diversity" box describes how EAPs have been adapting to meet the needs of a more diverse work force.

The reason for providing EAPs and other sources of counseling is to improve the employee's performance. It is up to the supervisor to see that the treatment plan is producing the desired results at the workplace. Any signs of improvement not related to performance—for example, abstinence from alcohol—are irrelevant from the supervisor's point of view.

DEALING WITH DIVERSITY

Employee Assistance Programs Adapt to a Changing Work Force

As the diversity of the U.S. work force has increased, employers have broadened their concept of the kinds of help troubled employees will need. Employee assistance programs (EAPs) have expanded their services accordingly. Originally, EAPs focused on helping employees recover from substance abuse. Some of the relatively new services being offered include financial or career counseling, referrals for child care and elder care, AIDS education and counseling, and "cultural adjustment counseling," which is directed toward helping employees work with others of a different cultural background.

Experts give several reasons for the expansion of coverage. One is that in recent decades there has been more sensitivity to the need for counseling and acceptance of people seeking it. More people are open to the idea that "well people" might want counseling and benefit from it. Another trend is that employees in recent years have been working longer hours. This gives employees less flexibility to seek help outside the organization. Furthermore, Americans tend to be less able to rely on an extended family for help than in the past. For example, working parents might not have a parent or sibling who can help them with child care. They turn to the EAP instead.

At Personal Performance Consultants, an employee assistance program based in St. Louis, one of the most common requests is for help in balancing family and work responsibilities. Consequently, an increasing number of the employers served by this EAP are offering counseling and referrals related to child care and elder care. With more people remaining healthy and active as they grow older, Personal Performance Consultants also counsels employees on leisure activities for older people.

Source: Deborah Shalowitz, "Employee Assistance Plan Trends," *Business Insurance*, June 24, 1991, pp. 24–25.

Support from Superiors and the Human Resources Department

Supervising problem employees is a delicate matter. Supervisors must be careful to motivate and correct rather than to generate hostility and resentment. At the same time, supervisors must be careful to follow organizational procedures, union requirements (if any), and laws regarding fair employment practices. Fortunately, supervisors can get support from their superiors and from the organization's human resources department.

When employees' problems do not respond to initial attempts at counseling, the supervisor should try discussing the problem with his or her boss. The boss may be able to offer insights into how to handle the problem. In addition, some steps, such as suspension or dismissal, may require that the supervisor get authorization from a higher-level manager.

It is also wise to consult with the human resources department. People in that department have information about company policies regarding discipline and how to document it. They can advise the supervisor on how to proceed without breaking laws, violating a contract with the union, and putting the organization at risk in case of a lawsuit. In addition, personnel specialists have expertise that can make them good sources of ideas on what to say or what corrective measures to propose. Sometimes just talking about a strategy helps the supervisor think of new ways to approach the problem.

Summary

16.1   Identify common types of problem behavior among employees.
The problems that supervisors most often encounter are absenteeism and tardiness, insubordination and uncooperativeness, alcohol and drug abuse, and employee theft.

16.2   Tell why and when supervisors should counsel employees.
Counseling helps employees solve their problems, which enables them to perform better at work. It therefore improves productivity as well as the attitudes and job satisfaction of employees. Supervisors should counsel employees when they need help in determining how to resolve a problem that is affecting their work. When an employee has a problem that the supervisor is unqualified to help with, the supervisor should refer the employee to a professional.

16.3   Describe counseling techniques.
Counseling consists of one or more discussions between the supervisor and the employee. These discussions may involve directive counseling, in which the supervisor asks the employee questions to identify the problem and then suggests solutions. Or the discussions may be nondirective, with the supervisor primarily listening and encouraging the employee to look for the source of the problem and identify possible solutions. At the beginning of the interview, the person who identified the problem describes it, focusing on behavior and performance. Next, the supervisor and employee consider ways to solve the problem. Finally, the supervisor schedules a follow-up meeting to review the planned solution and determine whether the problem is being resolved.

16.4   Discuss effective ways of administering discipline.
In administering discipline, the supervisor explains the significance and consequences of the employee's behavior; then, if necessary, the supervisor lets the employee experience those consequences. A typical process of discipline occurs in stages, with the supervisor administering first one or more warnings, then a suspension, then demotion, then dismissal. The supervisor takes as many of these steps as are necessary to resolve the problem behavior. The supervisor should administer discipline promptly, privately, impartially, and unemotionally. The supervisor should document all disciplinary actions.

16.5   Describe the principles of positive discipline and self-discipline.
Positive discipline focuses on preventing problem behavior from ever beginning. It can include making sure employees know and understand the rules, creating conditions under which employees are least likely to cause problems, using decision-making leaves when problems occur, and rewarding desirable behavior. Effective positive discipline results in self-discipline among employees; that is, employees voluntarily follow the rules and try to meet performance standards. Supervisors who expect self-discipline from their employees must practice it themselves.

16.6   Explain how supervisors can detect and confront troubled employees.
The supervisor can look for discipline problems and investigate whether these are symptoms of personal problems. In the case of substance abuse, the observer might notice signs that the employee is using alcohol or drugs. When the supervisor suspects that an employee is troubled, the supervisor should document the problem and then meet with the employee and describe the evidence of a problem, focusing on the employee's performance at work. The supervisor should refer the employee to a source of help and explain to the employee the consequences of not getting help. The supervisor should be careful not to overreact to an emotional response or creative excuses.

16.7   Describe how supervisors can direct troubled employees in getting help and then follow up on the recovery efforts.
Supervisors should learn their organization's procedures for helping troubled employees and then follow those procedures. This may involve referring employees to help outside the organization or to the organization's employee assistance program.

CHAPTER 16 SUPERVISING "PROBLEM" EMPLOYEES **425**

The supervisor is responsible for seeing that the employee's performance is improving, not for evaluating evidence of improvement unrelated to work.

16.8 Discuss the role of the supervisor's boss and the human resources department in helping the supervisor with problem employees.
The supervisor's boss and the human resources department can help the supervisor handle problem employees in ways that follow organizational guidelines, legal requirements, and the union contract (if any). A supervisor with a problem employee should discuss the problem with his or her boss, so that the boss can offer advice and provide necessary authorization for such steps as suspension or dismissal. The supervisor should also consult with the human resources department to get information about the organization's policies for handling problem employees, as well as suggestions for handling the specific problem.

Key Terms

insubordination	discipline	positive discipline
counseling	suspension	decision-making leave
directive counseling	demotion	employee assistance program (EAP)
nondirective counseling	dismissal	

Review and Discussion Questions

1. Sometimes problem behavior is really just a symptom of a deeper problem with the employee. For each of the following behaviors, give an example or two of the kind of problem that might lead to that behavior.
   a. A salesclerk is often late for work, especially during the summer months.
   b. An electrician does as little as he can get away with, letting his co-workers pick up the slack.
2. What is counseling? What are some benefits of counseling employees?
3. An employee explains to her supervisor that her performance has been slipping because she has been distracted and frightened by threats from her former husband.
   a. Should the supervisor counsel the employee about her job performance? Explain.
   b. Should the supervisor counsel the employee about the threats from her former husband? Explain.
4. While counseling an employee, a supervisor made the following statements. What is wrong with each statement? What would be a better alternative for each?
   a. "Your laziness is becoming a real problem."
   b. "Knock off the shouting! The way your performance has been lately, you have no right to be angry."
   c. "What you need to do is to take this job more seriously. Just focus on getting your work done, and then we won't have a problem."
5. What are the steps in the discipline process? In what kinds of situations would a supervisor take all these steps?
6. What additional type of information should be included in the following warning to an employee?

   I noticed that you returned late from lunch yesterday, as well as on three days last week. This upsets the other employees, because they get back promptly in order to give others a chance to take their breaks. Beginning tomorrow, I expect you to be back on time.

7. Describe four guidelines for disciplining employees effectively.
8. Ruth DeAngelis, supervisor of programs for a city park district, wants to apply the principles of positive discipline. What actions might she take to do so?

9. a. What are some signs that an employee has been abusing alcohol or drugs?

   b. Why should a supervisor avoid making a statement such as "You've been coming to work high lately"?

10. What steps should a supervisor take in confronting an apparently troubled employee?

11. What is an employee assistance program (EAP)? What is the purpose of such programs?

12. Tom Chandrasekhar has a problem with one of the production workers he supervises. The worker has been ignoring Tom's instructions regarding the new procedures for operating a

lathe, preferring to follow the old procedures. What kind of help can Tom get from his boss and the human resources department in handling this problem?

A SECOND LOOK

In the story of Harris Tire Company at the beginning of this chapter, what kind of problem behavior did Sam exhibit? If you were Tommy Hunnicutt, how would you have handled this situation?

Class Exercise

This is a role-playing exercise. One class member volunteers to take on the role of supervisor. Another classmate volunteers to be the problem employee. Here is the scenario:

> Chris Johnson has a been teller in the main branch of a bank for five years. Lately, Chris has been making a lot of mistakes. Chris often counts out money wrong and has had to redo many receipts that contain errors. Customers have begun complaining about the mistakes Chris makes and the detached, distracted manner in which Chris provides service. But at Chris's most recent performance appraisal, just two months ago, Chris's overall rating was excellent, leading to a generous wage increase. Chris's supervisor, Pat Smith, must decide how to respond to the decline in Chris's performance.

Before the role play begins, the class discusses what the supervisor should do. Based on the information given, should Pat use counseling, discipline, both, or neither? Once the class agrees on a general strategy, the two volunteers act it out.

Then the class discusses what happened:

- Did the supervisor do a good job of applying the techniques selected? What did the supervisor do well? What could the supervisor have done better?
- Do the employee and supervisor seem to have arrived at a workable solution? Explain.
- How can the supervisor follow up to see if the employee is improving?

CASE

Heading Off Problems with a Video Game

With drug use putting employees, customers, and others at risk, many companies have tried to eliminate the problem through random drug testing. However, that approach has been controversial; some people consider it an invasion of privacy. Critics argue that the problem is not whether employees are using drugs but whether their on-the-job performance is acceptable.

But how can you test performance before employees start working? Some companies have found a solution in *Factor 1000*, a software program marketed by Performance Factors Inc. (PFI), based in Alameda, California. *Factor 1000* is based on a program originally developed in the 1950s to help select pilots who could fly unstable aircraft. It tests hand–eye coordination by requiring the employee to use a knob to center a diamond-shaped image that sways between two posts on the screen. Succeeding requires much concentration and practice.

To use the system, an employer has each employee perform the test many times, establishing a base average performance. Then, when employees arrive at work, each employee types in his or her ID number at a small console connected to a personal computer. The employees "play" the "game," and *Factor 1000* compares their performance with their average.

Some organizations using the system include food processor Cargill, defense contractor Hercules, and a number of smaller companies. One of the smaller companies is R. F. White, a petroleum distributor based in Upland, California. After *Factor 1000* was used for one year there, accidents fell by 67 percent; errors, by 92 percent; and workers' compensation claims, by 64 percent.

PFI sells the test, but it does not tell employers how to respond to the results. If an employee flunks, what should the supervisor do? At some companies using the program, the policy is to refer an employee who flunks to the company's employee assistance program. Presumably, some situations, such as repeated failures, could lead to disciplinary action, even termination. At the very least, a supervisor can assign a worker who flunks the test to handle the least risky tasks that day.

At companies using *Factor 1000*, most failures have not seemed to involve substance abuse. Observes Marc Silverman, PFI's president and cofounder, "Severe fatigue or illness can be more dangerous than a disgusting drunk [person] because it's not visible." In many cases, employees who fail the test admit that personal problems are distracting them too much to handle a sensitive job that day. In contrast, drug testing does not seem to be effective in deterring accidents. The Federal Railroad Administration has found that only 3.2 percent of workers involved in railroad accidents tested positively for drugs.

1. Imagine that you supervise truck drivers for a delivery company that uses *Factor 1000* to test its drivers. One Monday morning, an employee flunks the test for the first time. This driver has never had an accident and has received only one traffic ticket in his 10 years with the company. How would you handle this problem?
2. After your actions in response to question 1, the employee passes the test each day for the rest of the week. The next Monday morning, he flunks again. What would you do then?
3. Do you think flunking this test would ever be a valid basis for terminating an employee? Explain.

Source: Joan O'C. Hamilton, "A Video Game That Tells If Employees Are Fit for Work," *Business Week*, June 3, 1991, p. 36.

Part Three
Application Exercises

Exercise 1. Identifying What to Look for in Job Candidates

Chapter 13 ("Selecting Employees") covers the steps involved in making sound employee selection decisions. Finding employees who have the necessary skills to meet today's workplace challenges is not an easy task. Most organizations are facing similar challenges: adapting to technological changes, improving quality, dealing with work-force diversity, reorganizing work around teams, and empowering employees at all levels to improve customer service—to name a few. This exercise focuses your attention on the skills employers are looking for in today's job candidates, and it gives you practice at developing interview questions that will help you in your evaluation of prospective employees.

Instructions:

1. Study Chart 1.
2. Match the letter of each specific skill from Chart 1 with the appropriate descriptor in Chart 2. (Each answer will be used only once. The first two have been done for you.)
3. In the space in Chart 2 after each descriptor, write an interview question you could ask job candidates to give you insight into their abilities in each area; assume you are interviewing job candidates to fill a job as bank teller. (The first two are already filled in, to give you an idea of some sample questions.)

Application Exercises were prepared by Corinne Livesay, Liberty University, Lynchburg, Virginia.

CHART 1: SIXTEEN JOB SKILLS CRUCIAL TO SUCCESS[1]

Category of Skill	Specific Skills in Each Category	Answer
Foundation	knowing how to learn	a.
Competence	reading	b.
	writing	c.
	computation	d.
Communication	listening	e.
	oral communication	f.
Adaptability	creative thinking	g.
	problem solving	h.
Personal management	self-esteem	i.
	goal setting and motivation	j.
	personal/career development	k.
Group effectiveness	interpersonal skills	l.
	negotiation	m.
	teamwork	n.
Influence	organizational effectiveness	o.
	leadership	p.

CHART 2: DESCRIPTORS OF SPECIFIC SKILLS

Answer	Descriptor and Interview Question
i.	1. Employers want employees who have pride in themselves and their potential to be successful. *Question: Can you describe a task or project you completed in your last job that you were particularly proud of?*
h.	2. Employers want employees who can think on their feet when faced with a dilemma. *Question: If you had a customer return to your teller window and claim, in a rather loud and irritated voice, that you had made a mistake, how would you handle the situation?*

[1.]Adapted from Anthony P. Carnevale, *America and the New Economy* (San Francisco: Jossey-Bass, 1991), pp. 165–182.

Answer	**Descriptor and Interview Question**
	3. Employers want employees who can assume responsibility and motivate co-workers when necessary. *Question:*
	4. Employers want employees who will hear the key points that make up a customer's concerns. *Question:*
	5. Employers want employees who can learn the particular skills of an available job. *Question:*
	6. Employers want employees who can resolve conflicts to the satisfaction of those involved. *Question:*
	7. Employers want employees who have some sense of the skills needed to perform well in their current jobs and who are working to develop skills to qualify themselves for other jobs. *Question:*
	8. Employers want employees with good math skills. *Question:*
	9. Employers want employees who can work with others to achieve a goal. *Question:*
	10. Employers want employees who can convey an adequate response when responding to a customer's concerns. *Question:*

Answer	Descriptor and Interview Question
	11. Employers want employees who have some sense of where the organization is headed and what they must do to make a contribution. *Question:*
	12. Employers want employees who can come up with innovative solutions when needed. *Question:*
	13. Employers want employees who can clearly and succinctly articulate ideas in writing. *Question:*
	14. Employers want employees who know how to get things done and have the desire to complete tasks. *Question:*
	15. Employers want employees who can get along with customers, suppliers, and co-workers. *Question:*
	16. Employers want employees to be analytical, to summarize information, and to monitor their own comprehension of the reading task. *Question:*

Exercise 2. Exploring Productivity Software for Supervisors

In Chapter 15 ("Appraising Performance"), Figure 15.1 provides an overview of how supervisors conduct performance appraisals. This exercise elaborates on that model by showing you how you can use ManagePro *(trademark of Avantos Performance Systems)—the first product of its kind in a new category of business productivity software, goal and people management (GPM)—to improve your performance management skills.*[2]

Instructions:

You are one of seventeen supervisors at Tybro, a major toy manufacturer in the Midwest. Place yourself in the scenario described below.

Scenario During a meeting with your boss, he shows you an article from *The Wall Street Journal,* "PC Program Lets Machines Help Bosses Manage People," and says to you, "I want to find out more about whether *ManagePro,* the software program reviewed in this article, could help our Tybro supervisors and managers, and I'd like you to be the one to answer that question for me. Probably the best way for you to find out is to register to attend the one-day *ManagePro* seminar, and then you can make your recommendation when you return, based upon your hands-on experience."

You attend the seminar and learn a great deal about the performance management process. Following are some of the highlights of what you learned about *ManagePro.*

Overview of **ManagePro** The seminar trainer explained that *ManagePro* is based on fundamental, proven management processes that meet the basic performance needs that your employees have:

Employees' Performance Needs	Management Process
"Tell me what we're trying to achieve, and let's agree on what is expected of me."	*Set clear, measurable goals* that support the key business objectives with specific checkpoints and due dates.
"Let's discuss how I'm doing."	*Monitor progress* on each goal at a frequency determined by the capability of the people involved.
"Help me to improve."	*Provide adequate feedback and coaching* to keep people informed and help them improve performance. Surveys consistently show that employees have very little sense of what their boss thinks of their performance. Giving regular feedback to your people and helping them through coaching are critical parts of managing.
"Reward me for my contribution."	*Evaluate, recognize, and reward people's contributions.* If people feel that performance pays off, they will work harder to achieve success.

[2] Permission granted by Avantos Performance Systems, Inc., to include the *ManagePro* information contained in this exercise. For further information on *ManagePro,* contact Avantos Performance Systems, 5900 Hollis Street, Suite C, Emeryville, Calif. 94608, or call 1-800-AVANTOS.

Throughout the day you learned how these processes are reinforced throughout *ManagePro* in (1) the way the program is structured, (2) the tools it provides, and (3) the advice available in the Management Advisor.

Program Structure   As you try out the program, you find that information is simple to enter using fill-in-the-blank forms, outlines, and spreadsheet like tables. Information is also easy to view and manipulate at multiple levels of detail. You find yourself quickly manipulating the program, using your mouse and pointing and clicking at the icons (pictures) of what you need. Everything is very intuitive and easy to follow. Changes made through any part of the program at any level are automatically reflected throughout the program. For example, if you reorganize your goals in the Goal Planner/Outliner, the changes are automatically reflected in the People Status Board.

Some of the key features of *ManagePro* include the following:

- The Goal Planner/Outliner allows you to organize your goals. Goals can be divided into layers of subgoals, given start and due dates, and delegated to a person or team. Click-and-drag movement makes it easy to organize and reorganize goals. (See Figure A on page 435.)
- The Goal Status Board gives a view of pending goals and their progress. Color-light indicators alert you to items that require action. For example, yellow means at least one subgoal is behind schedule. (See Figure B on page 436.)
- The People/Team Planner allows you to organize people, track goals associated with people, and manage information on feedback, coaching, and performance reviews.
- The People Status Board prompts you to periodically consider getting updates on goal progress and giving feedback, coaching, and recognition at a frequency determined by you for each individual or team. For example, you can have *ManagePro* remind you to give a certain employee feedback every three months. This will help you build up your people management discipline so that important activities and processes do not fall between the cracks. (See Figure C on page 436.)

Tools   Some of *ManagePro's* support tools include the following:

- The **Calendar** displays year-, month-, week-, and day-at-a-glance graphic views of events and deadlines.
- The **Action List** provides a customizable view of action items and status relating to all goals and actions in *ManagePro*, including people management actions such as progress reviews.
- The **Reports** allow you to generate a variety of standard reports on goals, planning, calendars, action lists, and people management information.

Management Advisor   One other major component of the program is accessed by selecting the Management Advisor button, which allows you to receive context-sensitive management tips and techniques compiled by experts. The Management Advisor helps new supervisors learn and apply management processes on the job; it also provides a refresher and specific diagnostic support for the experienced supervisor.

FIGURE A
Stay Organized

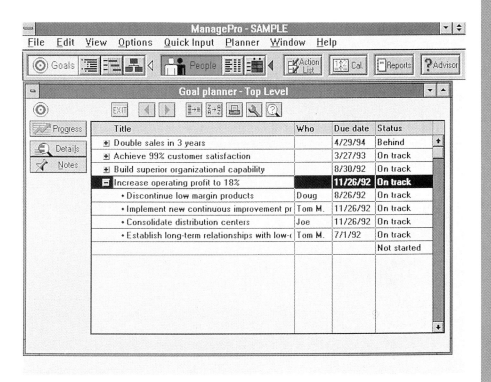

Conclusion

You return to your office the following day and sit down at your desk to prepare your recommendation to your boss on *ManagePro*. You are definitely sold on the idea that Tybro supervisors (and for that matter, all levels of management at Tybro) would greatly benefit by using this GPM software. In support of your recommendation, you will answer the following questions:

1. What management processes does *ManagePro* support?
2. What three features of *ManagePro* most impressed you as beneficial to improving your performance management and that of your company as a whole? Why?

FIGURE B

**Stay on Top of
Your Goals**

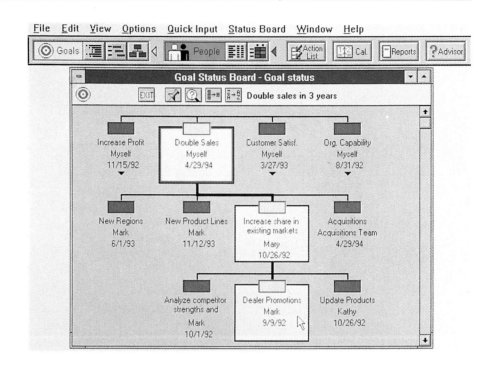

FIGURE C

**Effectively Manage
Your People**

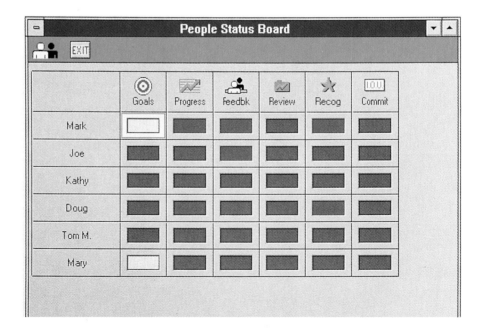

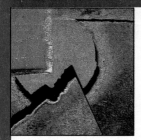

PART FOUR

Special Challenges of the Supervisor

17

None of us is as smart as all of us.
—Company slogan of Stanley Bostitch, Inc.

Groups and Teamwork

LEARNING OBJECTIVES

17.1 Explain why people join groups.

17.2 Identify types of groups that exist in the workplace.

17.3 Discuss how supervisors can get groups to cooperate with them.

17.4 Describe characteristics of groups in the workplace.

17.5 Identify the stages in the development of groups.

17.6 Explain why teamwork is important.

17.7 Describe how the supervisor can lead a team so that it is productive.

17.8 Discuss how to plan for effective meetings.

17.9 Provide guidelines for conducting effective meetings.

TEAMWORK AT BOSTITCH IS A STAPLE ACTIVITY

At its factory in West Greenwich, Rhode Island, Stanley Bostitch, Inc., makes specialty staples and nails. At one time excess coating was being applied to the staples and nails, and the excess had to be disposed of at a cost of $180 per drum. A supervisor tried to find a way to reduce the waste but failed.

Then the company had a group of employees—five coating machine operators and their foreman—try to solve the problem. The group met one hour per week for 12 weeks. Group members collected data on every machine and identified which machines experienced problems most often. Upon examining those machines, the group determined that a particular valve was causing the excess coating. The group contacted the manufacturer of the valves and had an engineer there help them redesign the valve. Finally, the group tested the redesigned valve and found that it solved the problem.

The cost of the solution was $1,085 to buy and install the new valves plus the cost of

60 worker-hours spent in meetings to solve the problem. The total savings amounts to over $380,000 per year. Bostitch's manufacturing manager, Deborah Pannullo, believes that, in general, groups outperform individuals in finding solutions to waste problems, especially when groups have been trained in techniques for improving quality or other areas of operations.

Source: "Recapture Lost Energy—Reuse Waste," *Maintenance Supervisor's Bulletin*, March 10, 1992 Supplement, pp. 1–3. Photo courtesy of © 1993 Comstock, Inc.

group
Two or more people who interact with one another, are aware of one another, and think of themselves as being a group.

Much of the work that involves supervisors takes place in groups. To define that term formally, a **group** is two or more people who interact with one another, are aware of one another, and think of themselves as being a group. The supervisor must see that groups of employees work together to accomplish objectives. And as a member of management groups and teams of employees, the supervisor helps make plans and decisions. Many of these group activities take place in meetings.

This chapter discusses how the supervisor can work effectively as a leader and member of a group. It describes some general characteristics of groups—why people join them, what kinds of groups operate in the workplace, how groups can be described, and how they develop. Then the chapter discusses efforts to build employee participation through the use of groups known as teams. Finally, the chapter provides guidelines for holding meetings.

Reasons for Joining Groups

When Felicia Watt accepted a position as math teacher at West Junior High School, she became a member of two groups—the teaching staff at the school and the teachers' union representing her district. She also decided to join a citywide organization of black education professionals to receive moral support and to participate in service projects sponsored by the organization. In addition, the principal of West Junior High asked Felicia to serve on a committee to plan an innovative math and science curriculum. And upon learning that Felicia likes to eat sushi, one of the other teachers invited her to join a group of four teachers who visit a local Japanese restaurant about once a month.

As this example shows, people belong to groups for many reasons. Sometimes group membership simply goes along with being an employee. In particular, all employees are members of the organization that employs them, most are part of a division or department, and some also join a union when they go to work for a particular company. At other times, employees join a group because their supervisor or some other manager asks them to. In such cases, an employee may join the group to advance his or her career or simply to avoid going against the boss's wishes. Finally, an employee may join a group because being a member satisfies personal needs. Some of the most common personal reasons for joining a group are the following:

- *Closeness*—Being members of the same group builds ties among people. Friendships generally result from the shared experiences that come from membership in some kind of group—for example, a class at school or a bowling team.
- *Strength in numbers*—Having ties to others gives people confidence they may not have when they are acting alone. Their sense of confidence is well founded. In an organization, a group of people tends to be more influential than one person acting alone.
- *Common goals*—When people have a goal to meet, they can get moral and practical support by working with or alongside others who have the same or a similar goal.
- *Achievement of personal objectives*—Membership in a group can help people achieve personal objectives in a variety of ways. The time spent with group

members can be enjoyable. Membership in certain groups can enhance a person's prestige. And in a related vein, group membership can satisfy people's desire to feel important.

Groups in the Workplace

As mentioned earlier, all the employees of an organization form a group. But except at very small organizations, most employees cluster into smaller groups. Some examples are departments, task forces, and groups that meet for lunch to play cards, do needlework, or talk about baseball. When this chapter refers to groups, it generally means these small groups—that is, groups small enough that all members can interact with one another.

To fully benefit from the various groups in an organization, the supervisor needs to be able to identify them. The first step is to recognize the various categories of an organization's groups. Then the supervisor can apply several principles for building cooperation on the part of the groups.

Functional and Task Groups

functional groups
Groups that fulfill ongoing needs in the organization by carrying out a particular function.

Some groups fulfill ongoing needs in the organization by carrying out a particular function, such as producing goods, selling products, or investing funds. These are called **functional groups**. For example, a hospital's accounting department has the ongoing responsibility for keeping accurate records of the flow of money into and out of the organization. In most cases, a functional group is one that appears on a company's organization chart.

task groups
Groups that are set up to carry out a specific activity and then disband when the activity is completed.

Other groups are set up to carry out a specific activity and then disband when the activity is completed. These are called **task groups**. For example, at Master Industries, Inc., of Ansonia, Ohio, a task group was responsible for buying the company's brooms and dustpans and for finding places to hang them.[1] Presumably, such a task could be completed in a matter of weeks. Another task group would be a committee formed by a supervisor to identify ways to promote safety in the workplace. This kind of task could go on for years with no definite end date, because it is unlikely the job of promoting safety would ever be finished.

Formal and Informal Groups

formal groups
Groups set up by management to meet organizational objectives.

The examples of functional and task groups are also types of **formal groups**. These are groups set up by management to meet organizational objectives. Thus, these groups result from the management function of organizing (described in Chapter 3). A customer service department is a formal group, as is a committee charged with planning the company picnic.

informal groups
Groups that result when individuals in the organization develop relationships to meet personal needs.

Other groups result when individuals in the organization develop relationships to meet personal needs. These are **informal groups**. For example, if a few employees like to jog during their lunch hour, they might find themselves jogging together and eventually building friendships around this shared activity. Most employees

A task group carries out a specific activity. This team from Air Products and Chemicals was formed to help build a Port Arthur, Texas, hydrogen supply system.

Source: Courtesy of Air Products and Chemicals, Inc.

welcome the opportunity to be part of informal groups because these groups help satisfy social needs, and the friendships can make work more enjoyable.

As occurred in the case at the end of this chapter, informal subgroups can develop among members of a formal group when the formal group fails to meet some personal needs.[2] For example, when some group members feel angry at the group's leader or uncertain about whether they really belong, they may form a subgroup. Subgroups may also form when some group members feel uncomfortable with the way they are expected to behave—for example, if they are expected not to express their feelings. In such a situation, the people who form a subgroup may feel more comfortable with the other members of the subgroup.

Getting the Group to Work with You

As described in Chapter 8 and the opening example of Bostitch, groups have a lot to offer with regard to decision making and problem solving. A group can generate a creative solution that a single person might not think of, and the group process can build support by letting people make decisions about what affects them. How can the supervisor make the most of these potential benefits of working with groups? Figure 17.1 summarizes some possible tactics.

An important step is for the supervisor to make sure all members of a formal group know what they can and should be doing. This includes setting effective group objectives, as described in Chapter 2, and clearly communicating those objectives. Group members also need to understand their authority, including the limits on what they can do. For example, a group assembled to solve a problem

This design team at SBE, Inc., is an example of a formal group. The company designs high-performance computer products for equipment manufacturers.

Source: Courtesy of SBE, Inc.

should know whether it is to implement the solution or simply to suggest solutions, letting the supervisor choose an alternative and implement it.

Besides communicating expectations, the supervisor should keep groups informed about what is happening in the organization and what changes are planned for the future. Making the effort to communicate with groups is a way of demonstrating that they are important in the organization. It also tends to create a climate in which group members will readily let the supervisor know about what is happening in the group.

The supervisor should support the group when it wants to bring legitimate concerns to higher management. For example, if some problem is keeping employees from getting their work done on time or up to standards, the supervisor should do what is possible to help get the problem corrected. However, this does not mean having an attitude toward management of "us versus them." The supervisor is a part of management and must act accordingly.

When the supervisor is responsible for setting up a group, he or she can help it function well by making good choices about whom to assign to the group. In many cases, it helps to combine people with a variety of strengths or backgrounds. At the same time, the supervisor needs to be careful about splitting up informal groups when creating a formal one; doing so could hurt morale within the formal group. In addition, as discussed later in this chapter, the number of group members can be important. Although it is sometimes important to include all employees, for many tasks the group will work best if there are between 5 and 10 members.

FIGURE 17.1
Tactics for Getting the Group to Work with You

Communicate expectations (objectives and authority).

Keep the group informed.

Support the group when it has legitimate concerns.

Choose the right members for the group.

Some of the guidelines for supervision discussed in previous chapters will also help get the group's cooperation. For example, supervisors should treat all employees fairly and impartially. They should respect the position of the group's informal leader. They should try to find ways to give rewards to the group as a whole, rather than just to individual employees. Finally, supervisors should encourage the group to participate in solving problems. As a result of following these practices, the supervisor can benefit by receiving the group's support.

Characteristics of Groups

As you can easily conclude from the discussion so far in this chapter, as well as from personal experience, working with a group is not like working alone. Social scientists have summarized a number of characteristics of groups, including ways to describe them, how effective they are, and what pressures they place on individuals. Supervisors who are aware of this theoretical information can use it to understand what is happening in a group situation. They can decide whether the group is effectively supporting the achievement of organizational objectives or whether they need to step in and make changes.

When looking at the ways in which groups are the same or different, it helps to consider some basic ways of describing groups. Some of the most useful characteristics include roles, norms, status, cohesiveness, size, homogeneity, and effectiveness. These are summarized in Figure 17.2.

Roles

roles
Patterns of behavior related to employees' positions in a group.

The character taken on by each actor in a play is the actor's role. In an organization's groups, the various group members also take on **roles**, or patterns of behavior related to their position in the group. Some common roles you may have

FIGURE 17.2

Ways to Describe Groups

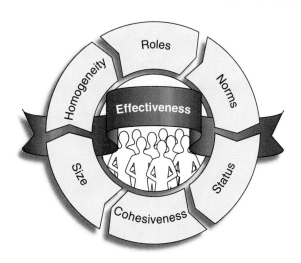

encountered—or even held—include those of the (formal or informal) leader of a group, the scapegoat, the class clown, and the person others take their problems to.

What leads a person to take on a role? Sometimes a person's formal position in an organization dictates a certain role. For example, as described in Chapter 1, certain kinds of behavior are expected of a supervisor. Another source of a person's role is a combination of the person's beliefs about how he or she ought to behave and other people's expectations about how that person will act. For example, if Anne displays empathy toward one of her colleagues who is going through a divorce, Anne may eventually find that everyone in the department wants to cry on her shoulder when a problem arises. If she continues to respond with sympathy and concern, she may take on a role in which she hears other people's troubles but is expected not to complain herself. Similarly, if Stuart makes wisecracks during a couple of meetings, group members may start expecting to hear jokes and funny remarks from him on a regular basis.

The kinds of roles people select serve different purposes. People may take on a role, such as leader or organizer, that helps the group get its work done. Or they may take on a role that holds the group together, as in the case of someone who can be counted on to smooth ruffled feathers whenever there is a conflict between group members. Finally, group members may take on roles that help them meet personal needs. Thus, in the earlier example of Stuart, he may be making jokes to cover up his own discomfort with being a group participant.

A supervisor needs to be aware of roles because recognizing them can help the supervisor encourage desirable behavior or bring about a change in undesirable behavior. For example, the supervisor would probably want to include an informal group's leader in planning how to carry out a change in policy. Or a supervisor who finds an employee's wisecracks to be a distraction during meetings needs to understand that other people may be encouraging this employee's behavior. Thus, to get the employee to stop, the supervisor will have to end the encouragement of the wisecracks as well as the wisecracks themselves.

role conflicts
Situations in which a person has two different roles that call for conflicting types of behavior.

Sometimes supervisors also have to resolve problems involving **role conflicts**. These are situations in which a person has two different roles that call for conflicting types of behavior. Suppose, for example, that several employees have been members of a volleyball team for several years. At work, one of them is promoted to be supervisor of the others, with the expectation that he will end the goofing off that has been common in the department. The supervisor's role as teammate conflicts with his role as strict supervisor. The way the supervisor resolves this conflict—which role he chooses—will influence his performance as a supervisor as well as his relationship with the employees.

Norms

norms
Group standards for appropriate or acceptable behavior.

Groups typically have standards for appropriate or acceptable behavior. These are called the group's **norms**. For example, in some work settings the employees have a norm of doing only what is expected of them and no more. They may fear that if they do an exceptional amount of work, management will expect that much from them every day. A new employee eager to develop a strong work record could anger the others if he or she violates the norm by doing "too much." Other norms may be stated, rather than implied. An example would be an organization's expectation that everyone will arrive at work on time.

When a member of the group violates a norm, the group responds by pressuring the person to conform. Formal groups have procedures for handling violations of norms that are group policies, as in the case of being on time to work. In the case of unofficial norms, a typical first step would be for someone to point out to the violator how he or she is expected to behave. If that does not work, the group may resort to shutting the person out, ridiculing the person, or even threatening him or her with physical harm.

In the example of employees with a norm of doing no more than is required, the norm hurts the organization. When a supervisor finds that a group of employees seems to be behaving in a way that works against the achievement of organizational objectives, the supervisor might investigate whether these employees are following some norm of an informal group. This might be the case, for example, when half a dozen employees in the department regularly leave work 15 minutes early. One way to change such a norm would be to look at the way the organization treats the behavior. With the employees who leave early, perhaps the organization or supervisor does not properly reward those who follow rules regarding work schedules. In trying to persuade employees to change or ignore an informal group's norm, the supervisor must remember that violating norms carries negative consequences for group members.

Status

status
A group member's position in relation to others in the group.

A group member's **status** is his or her position in relation to others in the group. Status depends on a variety of factors, which may include the person's role in the group, title, pay, education level, age, race, and sex. Thus, in one group, the person with the highest status might be a male who is the tallest and owns a cottage by a lake. The others find this person's presence impressive and hope for invitations to the cottage, so his status is great.

Status is important to supervisors because the group members with the highest status have the most effect on the development of group norms. The group members with lower status tend to pattern their behavior after that of the high-status members. If a supervisor wants to reinforce or change group norms, the supervisor will have the most success if he or she focuses on the high-status members of the group.

Cohesiveness

cohesiveness
The degree to which group members stick together.

The degree to which group members stick together is known as the group's **cohesiveness**. In other words, cohesiveness refers to the "glue" that holds the group together. A cohesive group has members who want to stay with the group even during stresses on the group. They abide by its norms even when under pressure to follow other norms.

Groups that are cohesive work harder than others and are more likely to accomplish their objectives. Thus, when a group's objectives support those of the organization, the supervisor will want the group to be cohesive. The supervisor can foster cohesiveness in several ways:

- By emphasizing to group members the ways in which they have common characteristics and goals. A supervisor of a research department might point out proudly that this is a select group of talented individuals working on an important project.
- By emphasizing areas in which the group has succeeded in achieving its goals. A history of successes—such as accomplishing a task or increasing the status of members—tends to improve cohesiveness.
- By keeping the group small enough (say, no more than eight members) that everyone feels comfortable participating. When more employees report to a supervisor, he or she might want to support the formation of more than one group.
- By encouraging competition with other groups. In contrast, cohesiveness diminishes when group members are competing with one another.
- By encouraging less active members to participate in group activities. Groups tend to be most cohesive when everyone participates to about the same extent.

Size

An organization's groups may vary widely in terms of size. As few as two people can form a group. For group members to know and communicate with one another, the group could have as many as 15 or 16 members. Beyond 10 or 12 members, however, there is a tendency for informal subgroups to form.[3]

An important reason for being aware of group size is that big groups typically operate differently from small ones. Small groups tend to reach decisions faster and to rely less on formal rules and procedures. Also, quiet group members are more likely to participate in a small group. If group processes seem overly cumbersome—for example, if the group tends to take too long in reaching decisions—the supervisor might consider dividing the group into subgroups of, say, eight or fewer members per group. A bigger group might make sense when a lot of work

Cohesive groups are more likely to accomplish their objectives. Westinghouse Broadcasting's Group W productions provides an example of a cohesive group in an upbeat, humorous variety series called "Way Cool" for 9- to 13-year-olds.

Source: Courtesy of Westinghouse Electric Corp.

needs to get done and the individual group members can work independently most of the time.

Homogeneity

homogeneity
The degree to which the members of a group are the same.

The degree to which the members of a group are the same is known as **homogeneity**. Thus, a *homogeneous* group is one in which group members have a lot in common. When group members have many differences, the group is called *heterogeneous.* Ways in which group members can be alike or different include age, sex, race, work experience, education level, social class, personality, and interests.

The members of a homogeneous group enjoy a number of benefits. Perhaps most significant is that people feel most comfortable being around others who are like themselves. This may be the reason that homogeneous groups offer better cooperation among members, greater satisfaction, and higher productivity, at least for simple tasks.

With such benefits of homogeneity, it might seem a shame that the U.S. work force is becoming more diverse. But for complex, creative tasks, a heterogeneous group can perform better than a homogeneous one. Because group members offer a variety of skills, experience, and viewpoints, the group as a whole has broader skills and knowledge, and it can examine problems from different points of view. The "Dealing with Diversity" box describes the benefits to the organization when its largest group—its employees—is not too homogeneous.

Effectiveness

The preceding characteristics of groups can affect whether a particular group is effective—that is, whether it achieves what it set out to do. For the supervisor, a group's effectiveness is one of its most important characteristics. In general, the

Better Results from Diverse Groups

Studies show that groups with diverse membership perform complex tasks better than do homogeneous groups. For example, in her book *Change Masters*, Rosabeth Moss Kanter compared the long-term financial performance of *Fortune* 500 companies using affirmative action programs with the performance of companies that lacked such practices. Kanter found significantly higher long-term profitability and growth at companies that used affirmative action. She attributed the difference to management practices that led to greater worker productivity.

More to the point, Robert Hayles, vice-president of cultural diversity for Minneapolis-based Grand Metropolitan Food Sector, uses an exercise that demonstrates the effect of diversity on how well groups perform. In workshops, he divides participants into three kinds of groups: (1) groups in which everyone is the same sex, (2) groups in which everyone is the same race, and (3) mixed groups. He asks each group to come up with a way to use $300 to benefit everyone in the workshop. Then the class evaluates each group's idea. Nine times out of ten, the mixed groups score highest on creativity.

Hayles attributes these results to the different viewpoints of various types of people. The more diverse the group's membership, the more points of view group members bring to a problem. As a result, the solution is more creative.

Source: Julia Lawlor, "Diversity Provides Rewards," *USA Today*, April 24, 1992.

organization's formal groups should be as effective as possible. The supervisor wants informal groups to be effective only to the extent that this supports organizational goals. For example, a company softball team that builds morale and improves working relations is properly effective. A clique that hurts morale among the employees who feel left out may be effective to its members but is not supporting organizational objectives.

The Development of Groups

In a sense, groups are living organisms with life stages. They grow, are subjected to stresses, and either mature or die as a result of the stresses. As illustrated in Figure 17.3, one view of group development is that groups may pass through the following stages:[4]

- *Orientation*—When a group first forms, its members tend to be highly committed to the group but do not yet have the experience and skills to work together efficiently. Group members tend to be concerned about what the group is supposed to do and how they will fit in. The supervisor's role is primarily to clarify objectives and provide direction.
- *Dissatisfaction*—If group members are able to learn their roles and the group's objectives, the group moves to the dissatisfaction stage. Although group members are more competent at working together, their initial enthusiasm has given way to disappointment with the day-to-day reality of being part of the group. While continuing to help group members develop competence, the supervisor must focus more on encouraging and motivating them.

FIGURE 17.3

**Stages of Group
Development**

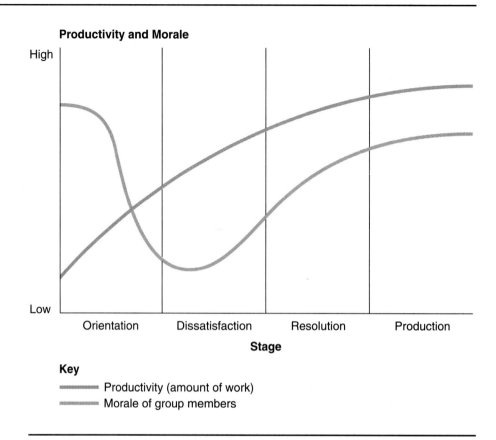

- *Resolution*—If group members are able to reconcile the differences between their initial expectations and the realities they experience, the group moves to the resolution stage. During this time, group members continue to be more productive, and their morale also improves. The supervisor should focus on helping with conflict resolution and should encourage group members to participate in planning and decision making.
- *Production*—If group members continue to resolve conflicts and develop a workable structure for the group, their output and morale will continue to increase. The group is effectively working as a team. When group structure must change or other issues arise, the group resolves them quickly. The supervisor should give group members as much autonomy as possible.
- *Termination*—At some point, many groups must come to an end. If the group had reached the production stage, group members may be sad. If the group ends before that stage, members are more likely to be relieved.

Getting a group to the resolution and production stages is challenging for most supervisors, who tend to be more comfortable at telling employees what to do than at resolving conflicts and fostering employee development.

Teamwork

team
A group of people who must collaborate to some degree to achieve common goals.

As organizations look for ways to involve employees in decision making and problem solving, they are increasingly expecting their employees to work in teams. A **team** is a group of people who must collaborate to some degree to achieve common goals.[5] In most cases, when the organization forms a team, someone is appointed to be team leader. Often the team leader is a supervisor, and the team consists of operative employees.

Being an effective team leader draws on many of the same skills as are required of an effective supervisor.[6] For example, the team leader needs excellent communication skills, patience, fairness, and good rapport with team members. In addition, because the purpose of the team is to draw on the expertise of all team members, the team leader will need to rely most on a leadership style that encourages involvement. In most cases, this means that the team leader will need to practice democratic leadership and coaching.

self-managing work teams
Groups of 5 to 15 members who work together to produce an entire product.

In the 1970s it became popular to form teams in which employees suggested ways to improve the quality of their work. More recently, organizations have expanded their use of teams by creating **self-managing work teams**. These are groups of 5 to 15 members who work together to produce an entire product. The team members rotate jobs, schedule work and vacations, and make other decisions affecting their area of responsibility. For example, at GM's Saturn plant in Spring Hill, Tennessee, over 150 work teams interview and approve new team members, decide how to run their own area, and accept budget responsibility. One Saturn team rejected some assembly equipment and turned to another supplier whose equipment seemed safer.[7]

Benefits of Teamwork

A basic benefit of using work teams is that the organization can more fully draw upon the insights and expertise of all its employees. At the beginning of this chapter, the story about Bostitch showed how a team of employees solved a problem that a supervisor was unable to solve alone. At the Brandel Care Center, a skilled-care facility in Northbrook, Illinois, staff members from a variety of disciplines discuss the needs of individual patients each quarter. A group that met to discuss the needs of an elderly patient who was disoriented but otherwise in good health included the supervising nurse, a nursing assistant, the social service director, the activity director, the chaplain, and a physical therapy/rehabilitation aide. (The patient's physician also participated by submitting a written review.) In the marketing arena, some companies are setting up sales teams combining technical and sales experts to better address the needs of their major customers. For example, the big producers of computer hardware, including IBM, Digital Equipment Corporation, and Tandem, combine experts in hardware, software, and technical support to help customers fully use the computers they buy.[8]

Teams can also serve as motivators. Employees who participate in planning and decision making are more likely to take responsibility for the quality of what they do. They also tend to be more enthusiastic about their work. Responsible, enthusiastic employees are more likely to work hard and deliver high quality. Such motivation occurred when the Tactical Electronics Division of Motorola's Government Electronics Group in Scottsdale, Arizona, began letting employees redesign production processes. As a result, says employee Doug Boone, "There was a great change around here. People were very relaxed, motivated, and happy." Joe Beard, another employee in the division, adds, "Most people, if you tell them what to do, they'll work at that pace. But if you let them decide how to do things, they'll surprise you."[9]

Ultimately, motivating employees and drawing on their strengths should enhance the performance of the organizations that use self-managing work teams. A recent survey of *Fortune* 1000 companies suggests that this is, in fact, the case. According to that study, about two-thirds of the companies that used employee involvement programs reported improvements in productivity, customer service, and the quality of their goods or services.[10] After Johnson Filtration Systems—a subsidiary of Waste Management Systems located in New Brighton, Minnesota—started using self-managing work teams, the company saw many performance measures improve. Not only did revenues and profits rise, for example, but on-time delivery jumped to 95 percent from 60 percent, and costs related to catching and fixing errors have fallen from 23 percent of sales to 7 percent.[11]

Leading the Team

Whether an organization's teams will achieve these benefits depends in part on the teams' leaders. Broadly speaking, the goal of the team leader is to develop a productive team. Experts in teamwork have linked the productivity of teams to whether the teams have the following characteristics:[12]

- *Openness and honesty*—These are signs that group members trust one another. Of course, tact and timing are important, too.
- *Leadership that does not dominate*—The leader is flexible, changing with conditions and circumstances.
- *Decisions made by consensus*—Although the leader will sometimes have to make a decision alone or reject suggestions, team members should have a voice in making many decisions. The objective is to achieve consensus. Table 17.1 distinguishes consensus from some of the alternative ways to reach a decision.
- *Acceptance of assignments*—Team members should willingly take on the tasks that must be done, then do them correctly and on time. Team members should view work as a cooperative effort, helping each other out as needed.
- *Goals that are understood and accepted*—These give the team purpose and direction. Team members should view accomplishing these goals as the team's primary purpose.
- *Assessment of progress and results*—Team members should focus on results.
- *Comfortable atmosphere*—Some conflict can stimulate desirable action and change, but there should be a basic level of cooperation.
- *Involvement and participation*—Team members should be involved in the work of the group. When a team member is reluctant to speak up at meetings, one solution is to seek his or her input during a one-on-one meeting. This shows such a person you are interested without embarrassing him or her.[13]

TABLE 17.1

Consensus and Its Alternatives

Style of Decision Making	Description
Consensus	A decision that the majority favors and that the minority, after having been heard and having enough time to persuade the majority, agrees to support and implement
Near consensus	A decision where silence is encouraged and interpreted as consent or where participants are pressured to agree
Majority vote	A decision in which the majority wins and the minority is assumed to go along willingly
Minority wins	A decision made by a powerful minority and not supported by the majority
Handshake	A decision made on the basis of a suggestion from one person to another, who gave instant support and permission to proceed
Self-authorization	A decision that a team member makes and begins to implement under the assumption that, since no one objected, the team agreed

Source: Adapted from Glassman, Edward (1991) *Creativity Handbook*, published by the LCS Press, 112 Kenan Street, Chapel Hill, NC 27516–2528.

- *Debate and discussion*—If everyone agrees all the time, it may be a sign that team members are unable or unwilling to contribute.
- *Atmosphere of listening*—Team members should listen to each other, even when they disagree.
- *Access to information*—All team members need to know what is happening.
- *Win-win approach to conflict*—Using the techniques described in Chapter 12, team members should work to resolve conflicts in ways that let everyone be a winner.
- *Relatively low turnover*—Members of a team must have a close relationship, which is impossible when the team's membership keeps changing.

An example of a team with these characteristics is a multidisciplinary team used by Westinghouse to redesign an electronic chassis (an electronically wired framework into which subassemblies can be plugged). The team's goals were to reduce the complexity and time required to manufacture the chassis. The team brainstormed new approaches to design and manufacturing. Team leader F. Suzanne Jenniches instructed the engineers on her team to look for the reasons behind the way things were done: "Their answer could not be 'Because that's the way we've always done it,'" said Jenniches. Ultimately, the team reduced the number of solder joints and wire connections in the chassis from 1,700 to 0—the new chassis could be produced using only electronic data. Assembly time shrank from six weeks to four hours.[14]

The team leader who can stimulate this high-quality performance is one who focuses on enabling team members to do their best.[15] This kind of leader coaches employees—asking them questions that help them decide how to handle a situation, rather than simply telling them what to do. The team leader encourages team members by expressing understanding and appreciation of their ideas and feelings.

The team leader knows when it is time to help the group stay on track and when he or she needs to act to get balanced participation from team members. This style of leading may seem to leave a supervisor with less power than one who gives directions and checks up on performance. However, this leadership style enables the supervisor to build on the strengths and expertise of the whole group, which should leave everyone in a stronger position.

Selection of Team Members   If the team leader is responsible for selecting the team members, this may involve selecting candidates for jobs that involve teamwork, or the supervisor may select existing employees to participate in a team devoted to a particular task. In either case, the supervisor should look for people who work well with others. If the team is to include people from several departments, the team leader should talk to other supervisors and employees to learn which employees would do best. In hiring for the new Toyota auto manufacturing plant in Georgetown, Kentucky, where the employees were to participate in self-managed work teams, the company used a test in which applicants worked together to perform tasks. Experts watched the applicants to see how well they got along with one another, how much they listened to one another, and whether they seemed concerned about others.[16]

team building
Developing the ability of team members to work together to achieve common objectives.

Team Building   Once the team leader knows who will be on the team, he or she must develop the group's ability to work together to achieve common objectives. This process is known as **team building**. Team building includes several activities: setting goals, analyzing what needs to be done and allocating work, examining how well the group is working, and examining the relationships among the team members.[17]

At some organizations, a consultant with expertise in team building carries out this process. However, especially at small organizations, hiring someone can be too expensive. Consultant Edward Glassman describes a three-step approach by which the supervisor can conduct team building:[18]

1. Set aside time at the end of team meetings to discuss the quality of the interactions during the meeting, as well as the creativity of the results. Ask what went well and what needs to be improved.
2. Ask each team member to rate, on a scale of 1 to 10, how well the meeting went in terms of (a) whether everyone participated equally, (b) whether the team member influenced the outcome, and (c) whether the outcome was creative. Prepare a written summary of the ratings, and discuss them at the next team meeting.
3. Use a questionnaire to ask team members how they see the team and team leader in terms of effectively accomplishing goals. Such questionnaires are readily available from consultants in training, management, and human resources development.

Communication Style   The way the team leader communicates with the other team members will influence the success of the team. In general, the team leader should create a climate of trust and openness. He or she should encourage team members to collaborate. The team leader also should acknowledge disagreement, not squelch it. To see whether you already have a communication style that would

Craftsmanship was important in selecting members of this sensory evaluation program at McCormick & Company. The group initiated various methods of taste testing that are now industry standards.

Source: Courtesy of McCormick & Company, Inc.

make you an effective team leader, or whether you need to make some changes to fill that role, take the Self-Quiz on the next page.

Rewards For teams to remain productive, members must be rewarded appropriately. The organization should reward the entire team for its accomplishments, rather than emphasizing individual rewards. (Chapter 9 describes group incentives.) Also, because not all team members will value the same kinds of rewards, the rewards should be varied enough that everyone will feel motivated. For example, the typical salesperson is motivated by money, whereas technical people might be more interested in recognition and promotion. Thus, for a sales team, one approach might be to use the company's basic incentive plan and also to ask the team members to reach a consensus on what additional reward they would enjoy receiving for a specific accomplishment.[19]

Labor Law and Teamwork

An important issue concerning teamwork is whether employee teams violate federal labor law. Specifically, the National Labor Relations Act of 1935 contains a provision forbidding employers from dominating or interfering with the formation

S E L F - Q U I Z   *How Do You Communicate as a Team Leader?*

In response to each item, circle the answer that reflects what you think you always do (SA), often do (A), rarely do (D), and never do (SD). Your answer should reflect your own perceptions of the way you communicate. Be honest with yourself; you are the only one who will see the results.

1.	When people talk, I listen attentively; that is, I do not think of other things (e.g., my response, a deadline, etc.) or read while someone is talking to me.	SA	A	D	SD
2.	I provide the information the group needs, even if someone else is its source.	SA	A	D	SD
3.	I get impatient when people disagree with me.	SA	A	D	SD
4.	I ask for and carefully consider advice from other people.	SA	A	D	SD
5.	I cut off other people when they are talking.	SA	A	D	SD
6.	I tell people what I want, speaking rapidly, in short, clipped sentences.	SA	A	D	SD
7.	When people disagree with me, I listen to what they have to say and do not respond immediately.	SA	A	D	SD
8.	I speak candidly and openly, identifying when I am expressing opinions or feelings rather than reporting facts.	SA	A	D	SD

of any "labor organization," defined as "any organization of any kind, or any employee representation committee which exists for the purpose of dealing with employers concerning grievances, wages, hours of employment, or conditions of work." This provision—designed to prevent employers from interfering with organizing efforts by setting up sham unions—seems to prohibit teams that address the issues identified.[20]

In practical terms, it appears that teamwork need not lead to government sanctions. First, a recent ruling by the National Labor Relations Board suggests that while this government agency will set limits, it will not seek to prohibit most teams.[21] Furthermore, unions are unlikely to challenge unionized companies in this area,

9.	I finish other people's sentences.	SA	A	D	SD
10.	I find it difficult to express my feelings, except when stresses build up and I become angry.	SA	A	D	SD
11.	I am conscious of how I express myself: facial expressions, body language, tone of voice, and gestures.	SA	A	D	SD
12.	When people disagree with me, I avoid arguments by not responding.	SA	A	D	SD
13.	During meetings, I prefer to listen rather than to talk.	SA	A	D	SD
14.	When I talk, I am concise and to the point.	SA	A	D	SD
15.	I prevent arguments during team meetings.	SA	A	D	SD

Agreeing (SA or A) with items 1, 4, 8, 11, and 14 and disagreeing (D or SD) with all the rest suggests that you encourage openness and candor; you create a climate of trust by involving the team in important decisions that affect their lives. You communicate clearly and concisely and balance task and process dynamics.

Agreeing with items 2, 3, 5, 6, and 9 suggests you tend to be task-oriented and dominate the team. You are frequently intolerant of disagreement and may squelch involvement and discussion. But disagreeing with these items does not necessarily indicate that you encourage collaboration; it could be blocked by passive communication.

Agreeing with items 7, 10, 12, 13, and 15 suggests you squelch disagreement by avoiding it and therefore undermine the team's task and process dynamics. A lack of leadership will more likely destroy a team than will tyrannical leadership. At least people know what to expect from a tyrant.

---

because most have approved of teams. However, during an organizing drive at a nonunionized company, the union could challenge the use of teams.

There are some precautions that supervisors and other managers can take to avoid violating the law. Managers who participate in team meetings can make sure they do not criticize the union at those meetings. Some legal experts recommend avoiding any discussion of topics that could be a matter for union bargaining, such as working conditions or pay, focusing instead on specific work-related projects or problems.[22] Teams also should *not* be set up to represent the company's employees, and they should have power to solve problems, rather than dealing with management to seek a resolution.[23] Perhaps most important, a supervisor or other manager who wants to form a team should get legal advice on how to form and operate it without violating the law.[24]

Making the Most of Being a Meeting Participant

Most managers and other employees spend a lot of time in meetings. In his book *In an Average Lifetime*, Tom Heymann estimates that on average an American worker spends about three years of his or her career life in meetings. Some of that time inevitably will be wasted. However, there are ways to benefit from meetings beyond helping to accomplish the meeting's objectives.

Decide what role you can play in each meeting you attend. Consider what role you are expected to play and what role you may be invited to play when it is time for questions and suggestions during the meeting. When you are new in a group, you may decide to spend a few meetings playing the role of listener and observer. When you have more experience, you will probably want a more dynamic role.

Be prepared for the meeting. Record the date and time of the meeting on your calendar. Be aware of the purpose of the meeting. Find out whether you are supposed to have ready a report or some other kind of information.

Arrive on time. If the meeting does not get under way when scheduled, there are valuable ways to use the time. You can stand near the door and greet others as they arrive; this is a kind of networking. If you are planning to make any proposals, you can test the reactions on a few people. And if you are going to make a presentation, you can use the time to review your notes.

Be selective about where you sit. Choose a spot where the action is. Management consultant Mike

Woodruff recommends the seat directly opposite the person who will be leading the meeting or the seat next to that person. Either spot will draw attention to you. Try not to sit next to a familiar peer, because you will miss the opportunity to trade remarks with someone you would like to get to know better. And if a senior manager is running the meeting, avoid the seat next to your boss. The risk is that everyone will pay attention to your boss and ignore you.

Bring a notepad and pencil. You will want to show you are prepared to record ideas or plans.

Be a good communicator. This includes listening carefully when others are speaking. When you speak, do it with authority and enthusiasm. When disagreements erupt, encourage the group to cooperate in finding a solution. If someone directs an offensive remark to you, respond by asking the person to clarify what he or she has just said, or restate the remark in your own words and ask if you heard the other person correctly.

Finally, take every meeting seriously. Even when others seem to be trivializing the situation, you should behave professionally. In this way, you show that you have high standards.

Sources: Colleen Dudgeon, "Working Smart: You Endure Lots of Meetings, So Get a Lot Out of Them," *Chicago Tribune*, June 7, 1992, sec. 6, p. 9; and Sophia C. Werning, "Meeting Savvy: Building Power and Image through Meetings," *Healthcare Trends & Transition*, January 1992, pp. 39–40ff.

Meetings

As mentioned at the beginning of this chapter, much of the work of teams and other groups takes place in meetings. When groups plan, solve problems, and reward successes, they usually do so in a meeting. Although the supervisor's role may be as participant or as leader of the meeting, this chapter emphasizes the supervisor's role as meeting leader. The principles described here apply to other situations as well, but supervisors will have less ability to make improvements when someone else is conducting the meeting. The "Tips from the Firing Line" box provides some ideas for making the most of being a meeting participant.

Reasons for Meetings

Meetings should take place when they serve a purpose. As obvious as this sounds, many supervisors and other managers hold meetings at a regularly scheduled time, whether or not they have something particular to accomplish. Thus, when the supervisor is thinking of calling a meeting, he or she should consider specifically what the meeting is intended to accomplish. If the supervisor wants to call a meeting as a way to make small matters seem important, to prove he or she is being democratic, or to rescue a lost cause (such as building a groundswell of support for an idea the boss has vetoed), the supervisor should not call the meeting.[25]

There are several valid reasons for holding a meeting. One is to convey news to a group of people. Doing this in a meeting gives the supervisor a chance to see and respond to people's reactions to the news. A meeting is also appropriate when the supervisor wants the group to participate in decision making. (Chapter 8 describes the pros and cons of decision making in a group.) Finally, the supervisor may use meetings to prepare group members for a change and to build support for the change. (Chapter 12 describes this process.)

As much as possible, a meeting should be scheduled at a time that is convenient for all participants. Times that tend to cause problems are peak working hours and the last few hours before a weekend or holiday. However, if a meeting is supposed to be brief, it makes sense to schedule the meeting for a half-hour before lunch or quitting time.

Preparing for the Meeting

To prepare for a meeting, the supervisor should decide who is to attend and where to meet. When the purpose of a meeting is to convey information to the whole department, naturally the whole department should be invited to the meeting. But in many cases, the participants are to provide or evaluate information. In these cases, the supervisor should invite only those who have the needed information or expertise.

The location of the meeting usually depends on the facilities that the organization has available. For a very small meeting, the participants might be able to meet in the supervisor's office. Larger meetings can take place in a conference room. When the whole department is to be involved, finding a big enough space can be a challenge. In general, it is more comfortable to meet casually in the work area than to squeeze a big group into a stuffy conference room.

agenda
A list of the topics to be covered at a meeting.

One of the most basic preparation tasks is to draw up an **agenda**. This is a list of the topics to be covered at the meeting. A practical approach is to put the most important topics first, to be sure they will be covered before time runs out. To keep the focus on important topics, it is helpful to recall the purpose of the meeting. Figure 17.4 is an agenda that was used by Austen Press, the publisher of this book, at a meeting the editor called to discuss progress on the book. Notice in the example that, besides the topics to be covered, the agenda states the name of the group that is meeting, as well as the location, the date, and the starting and ending times of the meeting.

The agenda should be distributed to all participants before the meeting is to take place. Participants should receive the agenda in time to review it before the meeting and make any necessary preparations. In addition, the supervisor or other person calling the meeting should make sure that participants have received any other documents they need to be prepared to contribute.

FIGURE 17.4

Sample Agenda: Austen Press

Team for *Supervision* Text

Sheraton O'Hare

June 23, 1992

8:30 a.m. – 3:00 p.m.

1. Workbook (8:30–10:00)

   a.   Components and process

   b.   Possible sources of material

   c.   Tentative schedule

2. Remaining manuscript work (10:00–12:00)

   a.   Examples in text

   b.   Opening vignettes

   c.   End-of-chapter material

   d.   Changes based upon reviewer feedback

3. Working lunch (12:00–1:00)

4. Videos (1:00–2:00)

5. Ancillaries (2:00–3:00)

   a.   Components

   b.   Process

Conducting the Meeting

Meetings should begin promptly at the scheduled starting time. This demonstrates respect for the time of others, and it encourages people to be on time. It is also helpful to announce an ending time and to end the meeting promptly. Of course, critical issues sometimes come up near the end of a meeting. In such a situation, the group can agree together on whether to extend the meeting or to continue the discussion at another time.

To make sure that meetings are as fruitful as possible, there are several ways the supervisor can help to facilitate the discussion. One is to rephrase ideas that participants express. For example, if an employee on a printing company's health and safety committee says, "We've got to do something about the fumes in the shop," the supervisor might comment, "You're recommending that we improve ventilation." This type of response helps to ensure that the supervisor and other participants understand what has been said. Of course, the supervisor has to use this technique with care; the participants can become annoyed if the supervisor sounds like their echo. Also, the supervisor should summarize key points often enough to make sure everyone is following the discussion. Times to summarize include the conclusion of each agenda item, the end of the meeting, and times people seem to be having trouble following the course of the discussion.

The supervisor should be careful not to dominate the discussion; instead, he or she should make sure that everyone has a chance to participate. Having everyone sit around a table or in a circle makes people feel more involved.[26] Some people naturally find it easier than others to speak up during a meeting. It is up to the person leading the meeting to encourage everyone to contribute. Often that is as simple as saying something like, "Mary, what do you think about the suggestions that have been proposed so far?" Quieting participants who are monopolizing a discussion can be a more delicate matter. One approach is to go around the table (not starting with a talkative person) and hearing each person's views on some topic. Also, the supervisor can have a one-on-one talk with the person who is monopolizing discussions. At this time, the supervisor can let the person know his or her contributions are important but that the lengthy discourse is unnecessary.[27]

Throughout the meeting, the supervisor should take notes on what is being decided. This helps the supervisor summarize key points for participants. In addition, it helps the supervisor recall what actions are to be taken later and by whom.

When it is time for the meeting to end, the supervisor should help bring it to a close. A direct way to do this is to summarize what has been covered, state what needs to happen next, and thank everyone for coming. For example, at the end of a meeting called to decide how to make the company's purchasing decisions more efficient, the supervisor might say, "We've selected three interesting possibilities to explore. Max will research the costs of each, then we'll meet back here in two weeks to select one." Then the supervisor's job becomes one of following up to make sure that plans are carried out. As in the example, following up may include planning another meeting.

Figure 17.5 summarizes these guidelines for conducting a meeting.

Overcoming Problems with Meetings

A frequent complaint about meetings is that they waste time because participants stray from the main topic and go off on tangents. Thus, an important job for the supervisor is to keep the discussion linked to the agenda items. When a participant begins discussing an unrelated topic, the supervisor can restate the purpose of the meeting and suggest that if the topic seems important, it could be covered in another meeting.

In steering the discussion back on course, it is important to avoid ridiculing the participants and to respect their efforts to contribute. As described in earlier chapters, the supervisor can do this by focusing on the effects of particular kinds of behavior, rather than on the personalities of the participants. For example, if a par-

FIGURE 17.5

Guidelines for Conducting a Meeting

Begin and end on time.
Restate key points.
Encourage participation by all.
Take notes.
Bring the meeting to a close.

ticipant tends to interrupt when others are speaking, the supervisor should not say, "Don't be so inconsiderate." A more helpful comment might be, "It's important that everyone in our group have a chance to state his or her ideas completely. Interruptions discourage people from participating." In addition, the supervisor can thank each participant for his or her ideas and attendance at the meeting.

Other problems arise because the leader and participants have failed to prepare for the meeting. For example, if there is no agenda, the discussion may ramble aimlessly. Or if someone does not bring necessary background information, the participants may be unable to make plans or reach decisions, so the meeting is unproductive. These kinds of problems lead to frustration and anger among participants who feel they are wasting precious time. The solution is to follow the guidelines described earlier, including creation and distribution of an agenda well before the meeting. When the supervisor is prepared to lead the meeting but others are unprepared to participate, the supervisor might consider rescheduling the meeting.

Summary

17.1 Explain why people join groups.
People may join a group because membership in that group goes along with being an employee. Employers may ask employees to join particular groups such as committees or task forces. An

employee also may join a group because doing so satisfies personal needs such as closeness, strength in numbers, common goals, and achievement of personal objectives.

17.2 Identify types of groups that exist in the workplace.

Functional groups fulfill ongoing needs in the organization by carrying out a particular function. Task groups are set up to carry out a specific activity and then disband when the activity is completed. Formal groups are set up by management to meet organizational objectives. Informal groups result when individuals in the organization develop relationships to meet personal needs.

17.3 Discuss how supervisors can get groups to cooperate with them.

The supervisor should make sure all members of a formal group know what they can and should be doing. The supervisor also should keep groups informed about what is happening in the organization and what changes are planned. The supervisor should support the group when members want to bring legitimate concerns to higher management. When the supervisor is responsible for setting up a group, he or she should combine people with a variety of strengths and backgrounds, while avoiding separation of members of informal groups. In addition, the techniques for effective supervision described in the preceding chapters apply to supervising groups as well as individuals.

17.4 Describe characteristics of groups in the workplace.

Group members have various roles, or patterns of behavior related to their position in the group. Group members are expected to follow norms, or the group's standards for appropriate or acceptable behavior. The status of each group member depends on a variety of factors, which may include his or her role in the group, title, pay, education level, age, race, and sex. Some groups are more cohesive than others; that is, the members of some groups are more likely to stick together in the face of problems. Groups may vary widely in terms of size, with subgroups likely to form in groups of more than 10 or 12 members. Homogeneity refers to the extent to which group members are the same. All of these characteristics can influence the effectiveness of a group. In general, a supervisor wants a group to be effective when its goals support the achievement of organizational goals.

17.5 Identify the stages in the development of groups.

In the orientation stage, the group first forms, and its members are highly committed to the group but lack the experience and skills to work together efficiently. Next, in the dissatisfaction stage, group members are more competent at working together but their initial enthusiasm has given way to disappointment with the group. During the resolution phase, group members continue to be more productive and their morale improves as group members begin to resolve their conflicts. By the production phase, the group is effectively working as a team with still higher morale and productivity. At some point, many groups also pass through a termination phase, during which group activity ends.

17.6 Explain why teamwork is important.

Teams bring employees together to collaborate on solving problems and making decisions. By using teams, the organization can more fully draw upon the insights and expertise of all its employees. Teams can also motivate employees by giving them a say in how things are done. As a result, organizations that use teams can benefit from improved performance, measured by higher quality and greater productivity and profits.

17.7 Describe how the supervisor can lead a team so that it is productive.

If building the team includes selecting team members, the supervisor should include people who work well with others. Then the supervisor builds the team by helping it set goals, analyze what needs to be done and allocate the work, examine how well the group is working, and examine the relationships among team members. The supervisor can increase the success of the team through effective communications that create a climate of trust and encourage collaboration. The supervisor should see that teams receive rewards valued by team members.

17.8 Discuss how to plan for effective meetings.

The supervisor should determine the purpose of the meeting and be sure that the purpose is a valid reason for holding a meeting. He or she should schedule the meeting at a convenient time and should plan who is to attend and where the meeting will take place. The supervisor should create an agenda, which lists the topics to be covered at the meeting. The agenda should be distributed to all participants far enough in advance that they can be prepared to contribute at the meeting.

17.9   Provide guidelines for conducting effective meetings.

Meetings should start and end promptly. The supervisor should facilitate the discussion through such means as rephrasing what participants say and summarizing key points. The supervisor should make sure that everyone participates in the discussion. He or she should take notes of what is being decided. The supervisor should keep the discussion on track by reminding participants of the topic under consideration. Like all the participants, the supervisor should be well prepared for the meeting.

Key Terms

group	roles	homogeneity
functional groups	role conflicts	team
task groups	norms	self-managing work teams
formal groups	status	team building
informal groups	cohesiveness	agenda

Review and Discussion Questions

1. Think of your current job or the most recent job you have held. (If you have never been employed, consider your role as a student.)
   a. What groups are you a member of? For example, what organization are you an employee of? What division or department do you work in? Are you a member of any informal groups?
   b. Why did you join each of these groups?
2. In the following examples, identify the type of group, using the choices given.
   a. a committee charged with coordinating a company's move to a new location (functional group or task group?)
   b. the personal lending department of a savings and loan institution (functional group or task group?)
   c. a task force responsible for identifying ways to reduce waste (formal or informal group?)
   d. four manufacturing engineers who regularly meet for lunch, during which time they poke fun at the design flaws in the company's products (formal or informal group?)
3. Joseph Dittrick is a supervisor in the marketing department of a toy manufacturer. He is responsible for leading a group of employees in finding ways to improve a product about which the company has received many customer complaints. In what ways can Joseph encourage the group to be as effective as possible?
4. Why do supervisors need to know about each of the following characteristics of groups?
   a. roles of group members
   b. status of group members
5. Yolanda Gibbs supervises employees in the reference department of a public library. She heads a group of employees who meet once a month to discuss ways to improve the quality of services delivered at the library. So that the group members will work hard, Yolanda wants the group to be cohesive. How can she encourage the cohesiveness of this group?
6. A supervisor observes that the members of a committee are not as enthusiastic about their work as they were when the committee got under way. How can the supervisor help the committee move into the resolution stage of group development?
7. For a work team to be productive, what characteristics should it have?
8. A manufacturer of office equipment has established teams of employees to identify ways to cut costs.
   a. In what ways do you think such teams are similar to basketball teams?
   b. How can the leaders of these teams help them to be as productive as possible?

9. How can a supervisor at an organization with self-managing work teams help the organization avoid violations of federal labor law?

10. Bonnie First supervises respiratory therapists at a large community hospital. One day her boss said, "Your department used too much overtime again last week. I want you to propose a solution to this problem, and I think you need to involve the employees in finding the solution. Get back to me in a week with your ideas." So that she would have time to prepare for the next meeting with her boss, Bonnie decided she needed to hold a department meeting the next day. She had a couple of the therapists spread the word to meet at 1:00 the next afternoon.

    At the meeting, Bonnie described the problem. To her disappointment, no one seemed to have any suggestions. So she said,

"Well, unless someone has a better idea, you're just going to have to help each other out more when someone is having trouble keeping up. And don't hesitate to ask me to pitch in, too."

    How could the supervisor have better planned this meeting?

11. What are some ways to encourage everyone at a meeting to participate?

A SECOND LOOK

In the example of the group that solved the problem of excess coating of staples and nails at Stanley Bostitch Inc., was this a functional group or a task group? A formal group or an informal group? Explain.

Class Exercise

The class divides into teams of three to five people each (preferably the same number of people on each team). Each team seeks to accomplish all three of the following tasks:

1. Compute pi (22/7) to five decimal places.
2. Draw a map of the campus.
3. Write a poem about meetings.

The instructor may allow the teams time (20–30 minutes suggested) to complete all three tasks during one class session, or 10 minutes may be set aside at the end of each of three class sessions.

    When time is up for all three tasks, each group member evaluates the performance of his or her group, using the form in Table 17.2. Then the class as a whole discusses the following questions:

- How well did each group accomplish the three tasks?
- Did each group concentrate only on completing the tasks, or did some groups take time to make plans and to evaluate how well team members were working together (i.e., team building)?
- What roles did the members of your team have?
- What norms developed for your team?
- Given the chance, would you have preferred to work on these tasks alone? Would your results have been more or less creative? More or less accurate?
- What changes might have helped your team function better?

CASE

The U Team

The assistant vice-president of a 600-bed urban hospital brought together six critical-care head nurses to form a nursing management team. Eventually three new members joined the group.

The nurses met once a week with the team leader and also began meeting informally for lunch without the leader.

TABLE 17.2

Evaluation of Group Performance

Task	Completed? (Yes or No)	Quality of Work (Poor; Fair; Excellent)	Participation (One Person; Two or More; All Group Members)	Ability of Group Members to Work Together (Poor; Fair; Excellent)
Computing pi				
Drawing map				
Writing poem				

Through these activities, the group seemed to develop a moderate level of intimacy and a high level of cohesiveness. Team members cooperated with one another, covering each other's units when needed. They supported one another personally and professionally.

Six months after the last new member joined the team, a series of memos began to circulate among the team members. The memos were written in a kind of code; the letters were reversed so that the memos could be read when held up to a mirror. The contents of the memos was basically nonsense. Each was signed "The U Team."

Some of the nurses found the memos humorous, but others expressed concern and anxiety. As a result, the team leader investigated. Three of the head nurses admitted that they had sent the memos as a prank.

Further investigation revealed that much tension had developed in the group during the previous months. The most recent new member was not accepting activities considered to be group norms. One of the original members had gone along with the group but had been uncomfortable, and that nurse aligned with the new member. In addition, some members felt jealous and resented what they saw as unfairness in the department.

Some head nurses had to lay off employees, whereas others did not. Yet none of these tensions had come to the surface during the group's formal and informal meetings.

Three weeks before the first U Team memo had circulated, the team leader appointed to a task force the three head nurses whose units were located on the hospital's ground floor. The others heard about the task force through the grapevine and felt left out. So they formed the "Up Team," or "U Team" for short, with the name referring to their location on top floors of the hospital. While they claimed the subgroup and memo were a joke, these reflected the nurses' displeasure at being left out.

1. At what stage of group development was this team when the U Team memos circulated? Explain.
2. How might the team leader move the team to the next stage of group development?
3. What, if anything, could the team leader have done to prevent these problems from arising in the first place?

Source: Dorothy Miller, "Group Dynamics: Handling Subgroups," *Nursing Management*, December 1991, pp. 33–35.

18

Health, work, and environment rank among the most important areas of social concern today, and the point where these concerns converge—the workplace—has become a microcosm of national conflict.
—Nicholas A. Ashford

Safety and Health in the Workplace

LEARNING OBJECTIVES

18.1 Describe the role of the OSHAct, the Occupational Safety and Health Administration (OSHA), and the National Institute for Occupational Safety and Health (NIOSH) in regulating safety and health in the workplace.

18.2 Describe the supervisor's responsibilities under the OSHAct.

18.3 Identify basic categories of health and safety hazards in the workplace.

18.4 Discuss common safety and health concerns and how employers are addressing them.

18.5 Identify benefits of workplace safety and health programs.

18.6 Identify characteristics of an effective safety and health program.

18.7 Describe the role of the supervisor in promoting safety and health in the workplace.

PUTTING A STOP TO HAZARDS

According to Du Pont senior development specialist Anthony Cantarella, safety has been a concern at Du Pont for almost 200 years. It had to be, because the company started out as a manufacturer of explosives. The focus on safety has continually improved through team-work and employee involvement. In the 1950s, the company assigned a group of plant man-agers to find out why some plants had a better safety record than others. The managers learned that at the most successful plants, managers spent more time observing the safety practices of their employees.

As a result of this investigation, Du Pont launched a program it calls STOP, which stands for Safety Training Observation Program. While management treats safety as a concern that each facility must address indi-vidually, the corporation does provide training that covers two levels: STOP for Supervisors and STOP for Employees.

According to a STOP brochure, STOP for Supervisors is based on the view that supervi-sors have "a primary responsibility for on-the-job safety." The program trains supervisors to take a systematic approach to observing, cor-recting, and reporting unsafe acts in the work-place and preventing them from recurring. The idea is to make supervisors better observers, not to make them catch and punish employees.

When a supervisor approaches an employee who is working, the supervisor observes the employee from head to toe, think-ing about all the ways the employee could be injured. For example, the employee might not be wearing a necessary hard hat. The supervi-sor talks to the employee about what the super-visor has observed, making sure the employee understands the job and safety procedures. This positive approach is thought to be more effective than simply punishing employees who engage in unsafe practices.

STOP training also covers how supervi-sors should handle employee reactions. For example, some employees may take safety pre-cautions when they notice the supervisor observing them. If the supervisor thinks the employee is following safety precautions sim-ply in response to being observed, the supervi-sor discusses this with the employee. Again, the objective is to be sure that employees understand the need for the safety precautions.

The Du Pont program also includes STOP for Employees, which emphasizes that safety is the responsibility of everyone. This program trains operative employees to recognize and eliminate unsafe acts and conditions from their work areas. They do this by observing their work areas and identifying ways to exchange safe acts for unsafe ones. As part of their train-ing, the employees visit a work site within their plant and look for ways to improve safety there.

STOP appears to be a success at Du Pont. In a recent year the company's 120,000 employees experienced fewer than 40 lost-time injuries.

Source: "One Company's Technique Takes Hold: Putting a STOP to Unsafe Behaviors," *OSHA Compliance Advisor*, September 23, 1991, pp. 3–6. Photo courtesy of Du Pont Company.

As Du Pont's supervisors are well aware, maintaining the safety and health of employees is a major task. According to the Labor Department's Bureau of Labor Statistics, in 1989 among the almost 79 million workers in the private sector, there were more than 6.5 million occupational injuries and illnesses.[1] Adding to the challenge, many of the problems suffered by today's workers are newly recognized—complaints such as injuries related to repetitive motion and the less-than-optimal design of workstations. It is important to note that these problems are not limited to factory settings. For example, the industry with the greatest number of job-related injuries in 1989 was restaurant work, where employees are especially at risk for sprains, falls, and burns.[2]

This chapter describes the role of the federal government in regulating safety and health in the workplace. It then discusses types of safety and health hazards, including some specific concerns common to many work settings. Finally, the chapter describes programs through which organizations attempt to promote safety and health, and it identifies the role of the supervisor in this area.

Government Regulation of Safety and Health

Many organizations recognize that safeguarding the health and well-being of employees in the workplace is not only ethical but also essential to attracting and keeping qualified personnel. Unfortunately, this view has not always prevailed. As a result, the government has stepped in to regulate the safety and health of the workplace.

Terrible accidents occurred when the Industrial Revolution brought together inexperienced workers with new and unfamiliar machinery. Beginning primarily in the early 1900s, state governments passed inspection laws and set up workers' compensation programs to provide benefits for employees injured on the job. In 1913 Congress created the Department of Labor, whose duties include the improvement of working conditions. In spite of such actions, however, public sentiment in favor of protecting workers continued to grow.

Occupational Safety and Health Act (OSHAct) of 1970
The federal law that sets up government agencies to conduct research regarding occupational health and safety, set health and safety standards, inspect workplaces, and penalize employers that do not meet standards.

Occupational Safety and Health Act (OSHAct) of 1970

The most far-reaching of the laws regulating workplace safety and health is the **Occupational Safety and Health Act (OSHAct) of 1970** . As stated in the law itself, it is intended "to assure so far as possible every working man and woman in the nation safe and healthful working conditions and to preserve our human resources." The OSHAct sets up government agencies to conduct research regarding occupational health and safety, set health and safety standards, inspect workplaces, and penalize employers that do not meet standards. Penalties can be severe, including fines of $7,000 per day for failure to correct a violation and jail terms of six months for falsifying records to deceive inspectors.

Occupational Safety and Health Administration (OSHA)
The agency of the federal government charged with setting and enforcing standards for workplace health and safety.

OSHA and NIOSH

The OSHAct established two government agencies to see that employers carry out its provisions. The **Occupational Safety and Health Administration (OSHA)**, a part of the U.S. Department of Labor, is the government agency charged with setting and enforcing standards for workplace health and safety. To see that organizations are meeting its standards, OSHA's inspectors may visit companies but must show a search warrant before conducting an inspection. In addition, OSHA operates a program of free on-site consultations through which independent consultants evaluate the organization's work practices, environmental hazards, and health and safety program. As long as the organization follows the consultant's recommendations, it bears no penalties for the shortcomings identified.[3]

OSHA's regulations have been criticized as excessively far-reaching and even petty. As a result, the agency in 1978 eliminated over 1,000 of its standards to focus on the most significant concerns. Many standards remain, and whatever the supervisor and other managers think of them, it is important that the organization comply with the standards.

The **National Institute for Occupational Safety and Health (NIOSH)** is the government agency responsible for conducting research related to workplace safety and health. It is a part of the Department of Health and Human Services. NIOSH provides OSHA with information necessary for setting standards.

National Institute for Occupational Safety and Health (NIOSH)
The agency of the federal government responsible for conducting research related to workplace safety and health.

The Supervisor's Responsibility under the OSHAct

Given the extent of OSHA regulations that exist, and the thousands of pages interpreting those regulations, a supervisor cannot be expected to be familiar with all the regulations. However, supervisors do need to understand what kinds of practices are required to preserve health and safety in their department. In addition, the OSHAct imposes some specific responsibilities that apply to supervisors.

The OSHAct requires that supervisors keep records of occupational injuries and illnesses. The supervisor must record these on OSHA forms within six working days after learning of the injury or illness. Figure 18.1 details which types of accidents and illnesses must be recorded.

The supervisor also may have to accompany OSHA officials when they conduct an inspection at the organization. Such inspections occur in response to a request by an employer, a union, or an employee or when OSHA's own schedule calls for them. (The employer may not penalize an employee who requests an investigation or reports a possible violation.) During the inspection, it is important to be polite and cooperative. This is not always as easy as it sounds, for the inspection may come at an inconvenient time, and the supervisor may be tempted to view it as unwanted interference. However, being uncooperative is no way to foster good relations with the agency and could even lead the inspectors to be tougher than they otherwise might be.

Because chemical hazards are widespread in the modern workplace, OSHA has issued a right-to-know rule requiring that employees be informed about the chemicals used where they work. Each organization must have available information about what chemical hazards exist in the workplace and how employees can protect themselves against those hazards. The information must include labels on containers of chemicals and hazardous materials, as well as Material Safety Data Sheets (MSDSs), both of which identify the chemicals, describe how to handle them, and identify the risks involved. The supervisor should make certain that this information is available for all chemicals that are brought into, used in, or produced at the workplace he or she supervises. If the supervisor finds that some information is still needed, the suppliers of the chemicals and other hazardous substances should be able to provide it.

FIGURE 18.1

Accidents and Illnesses That Must Be Recorded under OSHAct

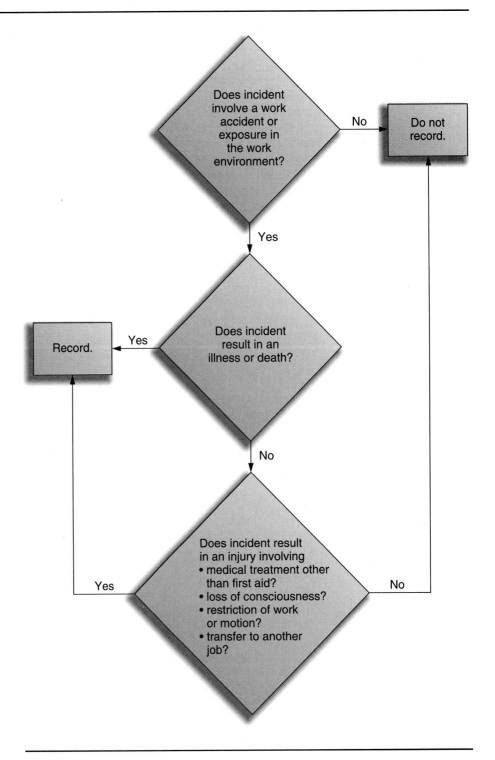

Chemicals pose serious hazards in the workplace. OSHA's right-to-know rule provides for the labeling of chemicals and hazardous materials. Material Safety Data Sheets must identify the chemicals and describe how to handle them.

Source: Courtesy of © 1992 Comstock, Inc.

Types of Safety and Health Problems

Because supervisors have an important role to play in maintaining a safe and healthy workplace, they need to be aware of some of the problems that commonly arise. These include health hazards and safety hazards.

Health Hazards

As a result of stressful working conditions, an air-traffic controller developed a stomach ulcer. A farmworker believes that working with pesticides for years is the cause of her dizzy spells. These are examples of conditions in the work environment that may gradually hurt the health of the people there. Such conditions are **health hazards**. In general, health hazards may be physical, chemical, biological, or stress-inducing. Figure 18.2 summarizes these basic categories.

Physical health hazards include noise, vibration, radiation, temperature extremes, and furniture and equipment that are not properly designed for the user's comfort. For example, operating noisy equipment can impair an employee's hearing. Exposure to radiation can make a person more vulnerable to cancer. Improperly designed furniture can contribute to muscle aches and repetitive-motion disorders (described later in this chapter).

Chemical hazards may be present in dusts, fumes, and gases. They include chemicals that are carcinogenic—that is, causes of cancer. Examples of chemical hazards are asbestos, coal dust, lead, and benzene. A recent study found that women who handled certain chemicals used in making microchips had miscarriages at a rate more than twice that of women who had no contact with those

health hazards
Conditions in the work environment that may gradually hurt the health of the people there.

FIGURE 18.2

Types of Health Hazards

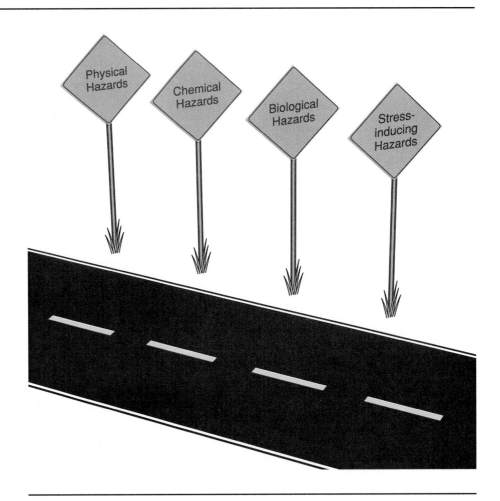

chemicals.[4] One occupational group that is at great risk for chemical hazards is firefighters, who report much higher than average rates of various cancers. Experts in occupational health attribute the problem to burning chemicals and synthetic materials, which are much more common than they were a few decades ago.[5] As a result, more fire departments today require that firefighters routinely use safety equipment and masks.

Biological hazards include bacteria, fungi, and insects associated with risks to people's health. Modern office buildings, which tend to be sealed tight against the elements, can be fertile ground for such health hazards. Thus, at a financial services company in the Northeast, employees complained of feeling sick, and the cause turned out to be microbes in the air-conditioning system.[6] Likewise, overwatering plants can encourage the growth of molds in the standing water, and those molds can circulate on air currents, making employees ill.

Stressful working conditions also may harm the health of employees. For example, employees may be more apt to suffer from stress-related illnesses if their work requires them to take risks, please an unpredictable boss, or witness a lot of suffering. (Chapter 11 describes the consequences of stress and ways to manage it.)

Safety Hazards

safety hazards
Conditions in the workplace that may lead to an injury-causing accident.

A **safety hazard** is a condition in the workplace that may lead to an injury-causing accident. Common types of injuries include cuts, broken bones, burns, and electric shocks. Safety hazards typically arise from personal behavior (that is, unsafe acts) or conditions of the physical environment. As Figure 18.3 shows, unsafe acts cause the majority of accidents.

Personal behavior as a safety hazard refers to practices by managers and employees that create an environment in which accidents may occur. This behavior may be as basic as carelessness or as obvious as drinking on the job. Sometimes employees cause a safety hazard by refusing to follow proper procedures or to use safety equipment such as goggles or gloves. Supervisors and other managers can contribute by failing to enforce safety measures or requiring employees to work such long hours that they do not get enough rest to think clearly. Requiring employees to work rotating shifts also is associated with greater accident rates.[7]

FIGURE 18.3

Causes of On-the-Job Accidents

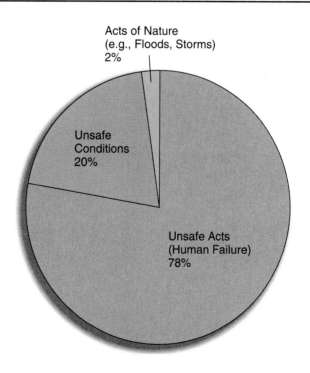

Source: Data from *The Front Line Supervisor's Standard Manual* (Bureau of Business Practice, 1989), p. 155.

Some companies provide services to deal with particularly hazardous materials. International Technology Corporation identifies and helps control radiological or chemical hazards.

Source: Courtesy of Charles Thatcher/Tony Stone Images.

Some employees are said to be "accident-prone"—that is, more likely to have accidents than other people are. These employees tend to be people who act on impulse, without careful thought, and who do not concentrate on their work. Many employees who are vulnerable to accidents have negative attitudes about their job, co-workers, or supervisor. Perhaps they find the work boring. Sometimes people who are otherwise careful are vulnerable to accidents. When people are struggling with personal problems or do not get enough sleep, they may become accident-prone. Therefore, the supervisor needs to pay attention to the behavior of all employees to recognize which of them are especially at risk for causing an accident on any given day. The supervisor may need to restrict the activities of an employee who is temporarily accident-prone or even to send that person home. If the problem continues, the supervisor may have to use the counseling and discipline procedures described in Chapter 16.

Hazardous working conditions also can lead to accidents. Problems to watch for are as varied as a messy work environment, electrical cords lying where people might trip over them, poor lighting, and a lack of protective devices on machinery. David Cooper fell and injured his knee when he slipped on a grease spot near the grill at the McDonald's restaurant where he was working. Explained Cooper, "It's not like they're unclean with the floor, but when things get busy, it gets slippery with grease and sauce."[8]

When the supervisor observes unsafe conditions, he or she should take one of the following actions, listed in order of priority:[9]

1. Remove the hazard.
2. Guard the hazard if it cannot be removed.
3. Warn of the hazard with a sign or other signal if it cannot be guarded.
4. Notify the proper authority if you cannot remove or guard the hazard on your own. Recommend a solution, then follow up to make sure that the condition has been corrected.

This is essentially the approach used at San Antonio, Texas–based Frontier Enterprises, which runs restaurant chains. The most common accidents at the restaurants were slips and falls, so employees now receive instructions to mark any spill with a cone bearing a "caution" message and then to clean up the spill immediately.[10]

With back and neck injuries accounting for one-fifth of all workplace injuries,[11] it is especially important to look for safety hazards that may cause such injuries. Ways to prevent back injuries include designing the job to minimize injuries, training employees to use lifting techniques that minimize strain on the back, reducing the size or weight of objects to be lifted, using mechanical aids, and making sure that workers assigned to do a job are strong enough to do it safely. The position that puts the most stress on the back is sitting.[12] Supervisors of office employees should therefore be sure that employees have comfortable chairs and enough opportunities to stand up and move around.

Common Concerns

Several common concerns about safety and health in the workplace are especially significant because they are widely occurring, or at least widely discussed. As summarized in Figure 18.4, these include smoking, alcoholism and drug abuse, the use of video display terminals, repetitive-motion disorders, and AIDS.

Smoking   Of all U.S. workers, an estimated 22 to 27 percent smoke cigarettes.[13] According to a report by the Surgeon General of the United States, cigarette smoking causes more death and disability among U.S. workers than does exposure to hazardous substances in the workplace. Smoking has been associated with cancer, heart disease, and lung diseases such as emphysema. A recent study found that the overall health costs for smokers are 18 percent higher than for nonsmokers.[14] In addition, people who smoke may be more vulnerable to the effects of other hazards than are people who do not smoke. Even nonsmokers can suffer some of the ill effects of smoking when they are exposed to secondhand smoke. This exposure is often called "passive smoking." Besides being a health hazard, cigarette smoking can be a safety hazard, because lit cigarettes can cause fires or explosions when handled carelessly or too near flammable substances.

Because the consequences of cigarette smoking are potentially serious, many organizations have restricted the amount of smoking allowed in the workplace. In many locations, the restrictions are also required by state or local law. According to a 1991 survey by the Society for Human Resource Management, 85 percent of companies had imposed some restrictions on smoking, with more than one-third banning it from the premises altogether.[15] Some organizations have a policy of hiring only nonsmokers. For example, Turner Broadcasting System not only restricts smoking to designated areas, it also in 1986 stopped hiring smokers.[16] Supervisors can help to minimize the effects of smoking in the workplace by enforcing the organization's restrictions and by providing encouragement and recognition to employees who are trying to quit smoking.

Alcoholism and Drug Abuse   As described in Chapter 16, alcoholism and drug abuse are serious problems in the workplace. The abuse of alcohol and other drugs can be costly to the organization. One reason is that people who are under the influence of these substances are more likely to be involved in accidents. Many organizational policies therefore call for strong action when an employee is found to be under the influence.

Part of the supervisor's role in promoting safety involves counseling and disciplining employees with these problems. (For more information on how supervisors should respond, refer to Chapter 16.)

FIGURE 18.4

Common Concerns about Safety and Health in the Workplace

- Smoking

- Alcoholism and Drug Abuse

- Use of Video Display Terminals (VDTs)

- Repetitive-Motion Disorders

- AIDS

video display terminal (VDT)

The screen on which a computer displays information.

Use of Video Display Terminals (VDTs)   A **video display terminal (VDT)** is the screen on which a computer displays information. Users of VDTs have complained that working with or near these screens causes a variety of health problems. The most common complaints have involved eyestrain, muscle soreness, and pregnancy problems.

Many VDT operators complain about eyestrain. A Louis Harris poll found that eyestrain was the most common complaint among office workers, almost half of whom named it as a serious concern.[17] Staring at the flickering lights on a screen for hours can tire the eyes. In addition, the contrast between the darkness of the typical VDT screen and the surrounding brightness of the room may cause eyestrain. Another source of strain may be glare from light sources on the screen.

Working for extended periods in front of a VDT can lead to sore muscles in the back, arms, legs, and back of the neck. This is probably because VDT operators generally sit in one position for a long time. Consider, for example, the job of typing a report. Do you remember the old-fashioned method with a manual typewriter? First the typist rolled in a sheet of paper. Then at the end of each line, the typist pressed a lever to move the paper up to the next line. At the end of a page, the typist removed one sheet of paper and inserted another. When the report was finished, the typist generally would have to walk somewhere to show it to the boss or file it. In contrast, preparing a report on a computer allows the typist to do all of these tasks—even the filing—by pressing keys on a keyboard. While this is much more efficient, it does not allow for stretching and relaxing one's eyes, arms, or legs.

Some reports have suggested that VDT use is also linked to pregnancy problems, notably miscarriages. One explanation is that the radiation emitted by the VDTs is the source of the problem. At this time, the research results do not consistently support or refute a link between VDT use and pregnancy risks. The

Health and Safety of Pregnant Workers

Until recently, some companies have sought to prevent birth defects by forbidding pregnant workers from holding hazardous jobs. However, in a 1991 ruling, the U.S. Supreme Court determined that employers may not ban women from such jobs. Doing so would violate sex discrimination laws by forcing women to choose between holding a job and having a baby. Nevertheless, the court held, women who remain in these jobs may sue the employer for damages if a child is born with injuries caused by hazardous working conditions.

In light of this court ruling, what can employers do to protect female employees of childbearing age? First, they should make sure that employees understand any dangers they face at work. The assumption is that employees will avoid pregnancy-related risks if they are informed about them.

In addition, the organization can encourage employees to ask for a reassignment to a less hazardous job if they become pregnant. The reassignment must be voluntary. The organization may not reduce the employee's pay, benefits, or seniority rights.

If the employee can not be reassigned, the organization can give the employee leave during her pregnancy, including full pay and a guarantee of getting the job back after the baby is born.

As a last resort, the organization might ask an employee who is pregnant to sign a statement that she understands the risks involved in staying at the hazardous job. This may at least give the organization some protection if the employee later sues for birth defects caused by work-related hazards.

Source: Deborah L. Jacobs, "Pregnant Workers and the Law," *Your Company*, Spring 1992, p. 15.

"Dealing with Diversity" box describes the way organizations should address this and other concerns related to the protection of pregnant employees.

Fortunately, there are ways to reduce or eliminate the problems associated with VDT use. A workstation that includes VDTs should be well designed for comfort, including such features as an adjustable screen, a wrist rest, a device to minimize glare on the screen, and an adjustable chair and worktable. Employees who use VDTs should take rest breaks. NIOSH recommends a 15-minute break after two continuous hours of VDT use—or after one hour if the use involves intense concentration. One way to provide breaks is to rotate assignments so that employees spend only part of the day working with a VDT. To minimize the possible risks of radiation, VDTs should be at least four feet from one another, and employees should sit at least two feet from the sides and back of any screen.[18] Those who are concerned about radiation may also wish to install radiation shields on their computer or to use only the low-emission VDTs now on the market.

Repetitive-Motion Disorders   Advances in machinery and electronic equipment have made it possible for workers to perform repetitive functions at an increasingly rapid pace. But repeatedly applying force to the same muscles or joints can result in injuries, known as **repetitive-motion disorders**. According to the Bureau of Labor Statistics, there were six times as many reports of repetitive-motion disorders in 1990 as in 1982. As a result, these disorders have come to account for half of all occupational illnesses in the United States.[19]

repetitive-motion disorders
Injuries that result from repeatedly applying force to the same muscles or joints.

To minimize the possible risks of radiation, VDTs should be at least four feet from one another, and employees should sit at least two feet from the sides and back of any screen.

Source: Courtesy of © 1993 Comstock, Inc.

An example of these disorders is carpal tunnel syndrome, which involves pain in the wrist and fingers. This is a common complaint among those who type at a keyboard all day or perform other tasks involving the wrist, such as making the same cut in chickens all day long at a poultry processor. Los Angeles *Times* columnist Bob Jones took time off after years of working at a computer left him in a constant state of pain that no therapy seemed able to alleviate. Said Jones, "If this disease was a matter of just enduring pain when I typed, that would be one thing. But I can't garden, cook, play sports, pick up and play with my 11-month-old son when I want."[20] Some people in the newspaper business have speculated that stiff competition for jobs in that field has led many reporters and columnists to try to cope with the pain rather than complain about it.

An organization can take several measures to prevent repetitive-motion disorders. These include designing jobs and workstations to allow for rests, using adjustable furniture, and avoiding awkward movements and bad posture. This type of response to the problem is an application of **ergonomics**, the science concerned with the human characteristics that need to be considered in designing tasks and equipment so that people will work most effectively and safely. While supervisors need not be experts in ergonomics, they can cultivate an awareness of these issues. M. Franz Schneider of Humantech proposes a straightforward way to determine whether a job or equipment is ergonomically designed: simply ask, "Would I do it that way?" According to Schneider, "If you can answer 'yes,' then [the job or equipment] passes the ergonom-

ergonomics
The science concerned with the human characteristics that need to be considered in designing tasks and equipment so that people will work most effectively and safely.

ics test. If you say, 'Thank God I'm in management,' then it doesn't."[21] Another measure is to encourage employees who are in pain to seek medical attention right away. Supervisors should never tell their employees to work through pain, as this may aggravate an existing injury.

acquired immune deficiency syndrome (AIDS)
The incurable and fatal illness that is caused by the HIV virus.

AIDS Although other illnesses are more widespread, probably the most feared is the **acquired immune deficiency syndrome (AIDS)**, caused by the HIV virus. The biggest reason for the fear is that, as of this writing, AIDS remains incurable and fatal. Fortunately, it is not highly contagious; people cannot catch it from touching a person with AIDS or sharing a drinking fountain or rest room. Instead, the HIV virus is transmitted through the exchange of bodily fluids, as can occur through sexual activity, blood transfusions, and the sharing of contaminated hypodermic needles, as well as between an infected mother and a fetus.

Of course, most of the activities involving the transmission of the HIV virus would not (or should not) be part of the work that goes on in organizations. The major exception would be health care institutions where hypodermic needles are used. These organizations should have procedures for the proper handling and disposal of the needles to prevent the spread of AIDS and other serious diseases such as hepatitis.

In most work settings, the major concern with regard to AIDS is how to treat employees who are carrying the HIV virus or who have AIDS. Fairness and federal antidiscrimination laws both dictate treating these employees in the same way as anyone else with a disability. As long as the employees can perform their job, they should be allowed to remain. At some point, the organization may have to make reasonable accommodations to allow them to continue working. These accommodations might include allowing an ill employee to complete job assignments at home.

When an employee has AIDS, the supervisor also must confront the fears that other employees are likely to have about working with that employee. With help from the human resources department, the supervisor may need to educate the other employees about AIDS and how it is transmitted. Despite these efforts, some employees may shun a co-worker with AIDS. Therefore, the supervisor and others in the organization must do their best to protect the confidentiality of such a person. If an employee with AIDS or the employee's co-workers are having trouble coping, the supervisor may wish to refer them to the organization's employee-assistance program, if one exists. (These programs are described in Chapter 16.)

Workplace Programs to Promote Safety and Health

Many employers have instituted formal programs to promote the safety and health of employees. The program may include training, safety meetings, posters, awards for safe performance, and safety and health committees. A typical committee includes operative employees and managers, perhaps with a membership that rotates among the employees. The safety committees at Frontier Enterprises' restaurants include employees from each area of the restaurant.[22] The duties of such a committee can include regularly inspecting work areas, reviewing employees' suggestions for improving health and safety, and promoting awareness about safety. The committee might also sponsor the organization's contests or awards for safe practices.

Some organizations have extended their safety and health programs to cover off-duty conduct by employees that contributes to health problems. These efforts may be part of a *wellness program*, described in Chapter 11. For example, some wellness programs seek to discourage employees from smoking altogether (not just restricting smoking at work), and others seek to teach healthy eating and exercise habits. At some organizations, employees with specified unhealthy conditions (such as being overweight or smoking) must pay more for health insurance, and at others employees are offered financial incentives to practice healthy habits.[23] For example, Control Data Corporation charges smokers more than nonsmokers for health insurance premiums, and it adds $10,000 to the death benefits paid to employees killed in auto accidents if they are wearing seat belts.[24]

The rationale for offering such programs is that they may reduce the health insurance premiums borne by employers. However, employers need to be cautious in how they extend safety and health programs to cover off-duty conduct. Over 20 states have passed laws that prohibit employers from making employment-related decisions on the basis of a person's off-duty behavior or life-style.[25] Furthermore, evidence exists that many employees ignore these efforts or, worse, resent their employer's involvement in their personal life. For example, when Security Pacific National Bank offered $120 to any employee who participated in health screening and promised to meet health guidelines, only 60 percent of executive staff and only 28 percent of low-salary workers took advantage of the offer.[26]

Benefits

By reducing the number and severity of work-related injuries and illnesses, safety and health programs can cut organizations' costs in a number of areas. These include health and workers' compensation insurance, defense of lawsuits, repair or replacement of equipment damaged in accidents, and wages paid for lost time. The savings can be significant; for every car they make, the Big Three automakers spend $900 to care for an occupational illness or injury.[27] In addition, safety and health programs can motivate employees, reduce turnover, and help prevent pain and suffering among employees and their families. Finally, an organization that is a safe and healthy place to work is more likely to enjoy good relations with the government and community and should have an easier time recruiting desirable employees.

Characteristics of an Effective Program

Basically, a safety and health program is effective when it succeeds in minimizing the likelihood that people will be injured or become ill as a result of conditions in the workplace. The program is most likely to be effective when all levels of management demonstrate a strong commitment to the program. In addition, all employees need to be trained in the importance of safety and ways to promote health and safety in the workplace. This training should give employees an ongoing awareness of the need to behave in safe ways. Employees also should believe that the organization's safety and health program is effective and worthwhile. One way to build their faith in the program is to involve them in planning and carrying out the program.[28] Finally, the organization should have a system for identifying and correcting hazards before they do damage.

Role of the Supervisor

Top management's support of safety measures is important, and the organization may have a safety director or other manager responsible for safety programs. Even so, the practical reality is that it is up to the supervisor to see that employees follow safety precautions. After all, the supervisor is the one who observes and is responsible for employees' day-to-day performance. Unfortunately, it often takes a serious injury before some supervisors appreciate why they must enforce safety rules and procedures. Supervisors who avoid enforcing these rules because they are afraid employees will react negatively are missing the point of why the rules exist. They also are failing to recognize that they have an important role in maintaining a safe and healthy workplace.

Training and Hazard Prevention   The supervisor needs to see that employees understand and follow all procedures designed to maintain safety and health. New employees must be well trained in how to do their job safely, and more experienced employees need training when they take on new responsibilities or when the organization introduces new procedures, materials, or machinery. In addition, employees need reminders about safe practices. Besides comments from the supervisor, the reminders can include posters, items in the company or department newsletter, and presentations by one employee to the others. Statistics about the department's performance, such as number of accidents during this year compared with last year, can be posted on bulletin boards or reported in the newsletter. In addition, OSHA requires that companies with more than 10 employees display the safety and health poster shown in Figure 18.5, which provides information about employees' rights and responsibilities under the OSHAct.

The supervisor of shift workers needs to provide additional guidance in safe practices.[29] Employees will be more alert and better able to concentrate if they adapt their overall life-style to working night shifts or rotating shifts. They must make an extra effort to get enough quality sleep during the day, seeking out a quiet, dark, cool place for doing so. People who are naturally alert late at night will probably sleep best if they do so right after working at night, whereas others will do better if they sleep just before going in to work at night. People who work a night shift will also be more comfortable if they eat relatively light foods during their shift, avoiding heavy, greasy items.

To help prevent accidents and work-related illnesses from occurring in the first place, the supervisor should encourage employees to participate in the promotion of safe and healthy conditions. One way to do this is to emphasize that employees share in the responsibility for creating a safe work setting. Du Pont's Anthony Cantarella uses the example of an electrical cord that an employee tripped on, injuring herself. Says Cantarella, "The cord didn't get there by itself. Somebody put it there. You might call the cord an 'unsafe condition,' but it was really someone's unsafe act that led to that condition."[30] In addition, the supervisor should be responsive to employees' complaints related to safety. The supervisor should see that the health and safety committee or the appropriate individual

FIGURE 18.5

OSHA Safety and Health Poster

JOB SAFETY & HEALTH PROTECTION

The Occupational Safety and Health Act of 1970 provides job safety and health protection for workers by promoting safe and healthful working conditions throughout the Nation. Provisions of the Act include the following:

EMPLOYERS

All employers must furnish to employees employment and a place of employment free from recognized hazards that are causing or are likely to cause death or serious harm to employees. Employers must comply with occupational safety and health standards issued under the Act.

EMPLOYEES

Employees must comply with all occupational safety and health standards, rules, regulations and orders issued under the Act that apply to their own actions and conduct on the job.

The Occupational Safety and Health Administration (OSHA) of the U.S. Department of Labor has the primary responsibility for administering the Act. OSHA issues occupational safety and health standards, and its Compliance Safety and Health Officers conduct jobsite inspections to help ensure compliance with the Act.

INSPECTION

The Act requires that a representative of the employer and a representative authorized by the employees be given an opportunity to accompany the OSHA inspector for the purpose of aiding the inspection.

Where there is no authorized employee representative, the OSHA Compliance Officer must consult with a reasonable number of employees concerning safety and health conditions in the workplace.

COMPLAINT

Employees or their representatives have the right to file a complaint with the nearest OSHA office requesting an inspection if they believe unsafe or unhealthful conditions exist in their workplace. OSHA will withhold, on request, names of employees complaining.

The Act provides that employees may not be discharged or discriminated against in any way for filing safety and health complaints or for otherwise exercising their rights under the Act.

Employees who believe they have been discriminated against may file a complaint with the nearest OSHA office within 30 days of the alleged discriminatory action.

CITATION

If upon inspection OSHA believes an employer has violated the Act, a citation alleging such violations will be issued to the employer. Each citation will specify a time period within which the alleged violation must be corrected. The OSHA citation must be prominently displayed at or near the place of alleged violation for three days, or until it is corrected, whichever is later, to warn employees of dangers that may exist there.

PROPOSED PENALTY

The Act provides for mandatory civil penalties against employers of up to $7,000 for each serious violation and for optional penalties of up to $7,000 for each nonserious violation. Penalties of up to $7,000 per day may be proposed for failure to correct violations within the proposed time period and for each day the violation continues beyond the prescribed abatement date. Also, any employer who willfully or repeatedly violates the Act may be assessed penalties of up to $70,000 for each such violation. A minimum penalty of $5,000 may be imposed for each willful violation. A violation of posting requirements can bring a penalty of up to $7,000.

There are also provisions for criminal penalties. Any willful violation resulting in the death of any employee, upon conviction, is punishable by a fine of up to $250,000 (or $500,000 if the employer is a corporation), or by imprisonment for up to six months, or both. A second conviction of an employer doubles the possible term of imprisonment. Falsifying records, reports, or applications is punishable by a fine of $10,000 or up to six months in jail or both.

VOLUNTARY ACTIVITY

While providing penalties for violations, the Act also encourages efforts by labor and management, before an OSHA inspection, to reduce workplace hazards voluntarily and to develop and improve safety and health programs in all workplaces and industries. OSHA's Voluntary Protection Programs recognize outstanding efforts of this nature.

OSHA has published Safety and Health Program Management Guidelines to assist employers in establishing or perfecting programs to prevent or control employee exposure to workplace hazards. There are many public and private organizations that can provide information and assistance in this effort, if requested. Also, your local OSHA office can provide considerable help and advice on solving safety and health problems or can refer you to other sources for help such as training.

CONSULTATION

Free assistance in identifying and correcting hazards and in improving safety and health management is available to employers, without citation or penalty, through OSHA-supported programs in each State. These programs are usually administered by the State Labor or Health department or a State university.

POSTING INSTRUCTIONS

Employers in States operating OSHA approved State Plans should obtain and post the State's equivalent poster.

Under provisions of Title 29, Code of Federal Regulations, Part 1903.2 (a) (1) employers must post this notice (or facsimile) in a conspicuous place where notices to employees are customarily posted.

More Information

Additional information and copies of the Act, specific OSHA safety and health standards, and other applicable regulations may be obtained from your employer or from the nearest OSHA Regional Office in the following locations:

To report suspected fire hazards, imminent danger, safety and health hazards in the workplace, or other job safety and health emergencies, such as toxic waste in the workplace, call OSHA's 24-hour hotline: 1-800-321-OSHA

Atlanta, GA	(404) 347-3573
Boston, MA	(617) 565-7164
Chicago, IL	(312) 353-2220
Dallas, TX	(214) 767-4731
Denver, CO	(303) 844-3061
Kansas City, MO	(816) 426-5861
New York, NY	(212) 337-2378
Philadelphia, PA	(215) 596-1201
San Francisco, CA	(415) 744-6670
Seattle, WA	(206) 442-5930

 This information will be made available to sensory impaired individuals upon request. Voice phone (202) 523-8615; TDD message referral phone: 1-800-326-2577

Washington, D.C.
1991 (Reprinted)
OSHA 2203

Lynn Martin

Lynn Martin, Secretary of Labor
U.S. Department of Labor
Occupational Safety and Health Administration

Getting Employees to Think "Safety First"

Getting employees to be safety-conscious can be a challenge. After all, the supervisor is also encouraging employees to think of other important goals such as productivity and quality. However, there are some specific actions the supervisor can take to get employees to recognize the importance of safety.

- Start each week by holding a brief safety awareness meeting. Talking about a safety topic on Monday morning can get employees to think about working safely.
- Review safety reports at staff meetings. If an accident has occurred, take time to talk about what happened and how to prevent the problem from recurring.
- Discipline workers who behave in an unsafe manner. Employees must realize there are consequences for unsafe actions.

- Recognize employees with good safety records. It is important to reward positive behavior, not just focus on problems.
- Post statistics about accidents. At one organization, the supervisor made a map of his department and posted it on the bulletin board. Whenever an accident occurred, the supervisor marked the location with a pin so employees could see where accidents were happening. This method is a striking way to show employees where hazards exist.
- Emphasize your concern that employees stay safe for their own well-being and the sake of their families. Do not just dwell on the department's statistics, but show your compassion as well.

Source: "Make Safety Job #1," *Front Line Supervisor's Bulletin* (Bureau of Business Practice), May 10, 1992, p. 4.

investigates such complaints. Any hazardous conditions should be corrected immediately. The "Tips from the Firing Line" box summarizes some guidelines for promoting a "safety first" attitude.

Prompt Responses When the supervisor observes a violation of health and safety guidelines, he or she should respond immediately and consistently. Failure to react is a signal to employees that the guidelines are not really important. First, the supervisor should try to understand why the violation occurred. Does the employee understand what the proper procedures are? If the employee understands the procedures but still resists following them, the supervisor should try to find out why. For example, if an employee complains that some safety equipment is uncomfortable to use, investigating the complaint may turn up a more effective alternative, such as a greater selection of safety glasses or a way to set up a job so that less safety equipment is required. In spite of complaints, however, the supervisor must insist that employees follow safety procedures, even when they seem inconvenient. As with other kinds of rules, the supervisor may have to take disciplinary action when safety rules are violated. (See Chapter 16 for a discussion of discipline.)

Quality of Work Life As mentioned earlier in the chapter, fatigue, boredom, and dissatisfaction can make a person accident-prone. Therefore, by combatting these problems, the supervisor can promote safety and health. These efforts may include improving the quality of work life—seeking ways to make jobs more interesting and satisfying. Although no one has actually proved that there is a link between quality of work life and employee safety and health, it seems reasonable to assume that interested, satisfied employees will tend to be healthier and more careful. (Chapter 9 offers some guidelines for expanding and enriching jobs.)

Also, in the case of shift workers, the supervisor can help minimize fatigue by encouraging the organization to place employees on a single shift or to rotate shifts so that employees go to work later and later, rather than earlier and earlier or in no steady pattern. Making sure there is bright lighting also will help employees stay alert at night.

Setting an Example   Of course, as with any other area where the supervisor wants employees to behave in a certain way, the supervisor must set a good example. The supervisor therefore must follow safe practices him- or herself. For example, a supervisor who uses tools improperly, creates a tower of soft-drink cans on a filing cabinet, or tries to troubleshoot a photocopier without first turning off the power is voiding the effect of even the most eloquent lecture on safety in the workplace.

Summary

18.1   Describe the role of the OSHAct, the Occupational Safety and Health Administration (OSHA), and the National Institute for Occupational Safety and Health (NIOSH) in regulating safety and health in the workplace.
The Occupational Safety and Health Act (OHSAct) of 1970 sets up government agencies—such as OSHA and NIOSH—to conduct research regarding occupational health and safety, set health and safety standards, inspect workplaces, and penalize employers who do not meet standards. OSHA sets and enforces the standards and conducts inspections, whereas NIOSH conducts research related to workplace safety and health.

18.2   Describe the supervisor's responsibilities under the OSHAct.
Supervisors must be familiar with the kinds of practices required to preserve health and safety in their department. They also must keep formal records of occupational injuries and illnesses. They may have to accompany OSHA officials when they inspect the workplace. They should be sure that employees have information about chemical hazards, as required by OSHA's right-to-know rule.

18.3   Identify basic categories of health and safety hazards in the workplace.
Health hazards may be physical, chemical, biological, or stress-inducing. Safety hazards include personal behavior (that is, unsafe acts) and unsafe conditions of the physical environment.

18.4   Discuss common safety and health concerns and how employers are addressing them.
Cigarette smoke can cause a variety of illnesses in smokers and the people who breathe secondhand smoke. As a result, many organizations have limited smoking in the workplace. The abuse of alcohol and other drugs can be costly, so organizations have policies for responding to employees with these problems. Extended use of video display terminals can result in eyestrain and muscle aches, and they possibly contribute to miscarriages among pregnant employees. Organizations can address these problems with rest breaks, ergonomically designed workstations, and seating that places employees a safe distance from the screen. Repetitive-motion disorders can result when employees repeatedly apply force to the same muscles or joints. Applying ergonomics to the design of jobs and workstations can minimize such problems. Many employees are afraid of working near someone with AIDS; however, the means of transmitting this disease are limited. If an employee has AIDS, the supervisor may need to provide that employee with reasonable accommodations and educate the employee's co-workers about this disease.

18.5 Identify benefits of workplace safety and health programs.

These programs can reduce the number and severity of work-related injuries and illnesses, thereby cutting costs to the organization. In addition, safety and health programs can motivate employees, reduce turnover, and avoid pain and suffering. The improved community relations that can result may make it easier to recruit desirable employees.

18.6 Identify characteristics of an effective safety and health program.

A safety and health program is effective when it minimizes the likelihood that people will be injured or become ill as a result of conditions in the workplace. This is most likely to occur when all levels of management demonstrate a strong commitment to the program and when all employees are trained in the importance of safety and ways to promote health and safety in the workplace. Employees should believe that the organization's safety and health program is effective and worthwhile. The organization should have a system for identifying and correcting hazards before damage results.

18.7 Describe the role of the supervisor in promoting safety and health in the workplace.

It is up to the supervisor to see that employees understand and follow safety precautions. The supervisor should encourage employees to participate in promoting safe and healthy conditions. To do so, the supervisor can emphasize employees' role in prevention and respond to their complaints. When an employee violates health or safety guidelines, the supervisor should respond immediately. The supervisor can improve the quality of work life, including the way that employees are assigned to shift work, so that employees are less likely to be tired or bored and, therefore, accident-prone. Finally, the supervisor should set a good example by following safe practices.

Key Terms

Occupational Safety and Health Act (OSHAct) of 1970

Occupational Safety and Health Administration (OSHA)

National Institute for Occupational Safety and Health (NIOSH)

health hazards

safety hazards

video display terminal (VDT)

repetitive-motion disorders

ergonomics

acquired immune deficiency syndrome (AIDS)

Review and Discussion Questions

1. Describe the two government agencies established by the Occupational Safety and Health Act of 1970. What is their role in promoting safety and health in the workplace?
2. Keith Navarro is a new supervisor at a supermarket. He is worried about OSHA because he heard that the agency has so many regulations that it is impossible to keep track of them all. What general guidelines can you give Keith about his responsibilities under the OSHAct?
3. What are the basic categories of health hazards? Give an example of each.
4. Betsy Lee is the supervisor of the Central Files department of a large professional association. She is concerned about the number of minor injuries that have been occurring as a result of accidents involving employees tripping, dropping stacks of files, and colliding. A couple of the employees have complained that lighting is often poor because light bulbs are not immediately replaced when they burn out. What actions should Betsy take to minimize the safety hazards in her department?
5. What can supervisors do to minimize the effects of each of the following hazards?
   a. cigarette smoking in the workplace
   b. extended use of video display terminals

6. What is the typical role of a safety and health committee? What does the committee do?

7. A clothing manufacturer wants to set up a safety and health program. What characteristics should this program have so that it will be effective?

8. How can a supervisor keep employees informed about the organization's procedures for maintaining safety and health?

9. A foreman notices that an employee is not wearing the safety goggles required for operating a piece of grinding equipment. How should the foreman respond? What actions should he take?

A SECOND LOOK

The story at the beginning of this chapter described how supervisors at Du Pont promote safety. Besides observing employees and teaching them about safe practices, how else might the supervisors promote safety?

Class Exercise*

The class divides into teams of two to four members each. At the end of the class session or between sessions, the teams will look for and list health and safety hazards on campus. The team members may choose the area of campus to visit and investigate, or the instructor assigns the teams to specific areas (for example, parking lots, recreation areas, bookstore, classrooms). Before the teams begin, it may be helpful for the class as a whole to discuss what kinds of hazards they expect to find—wet floors, dangerous intersections, unmarked fire extinguishers, uncomfortable chairs at VDTs, sources of stress, and so on.

At the next class session, the teams report their findings to the class. The instructor may invite the campus security director to sit in on this discussion.

CASE

Promoting Safety at Pacific Lumber Company

Several years ago, the management of Pacific Lumber Company (PALCO), located in Scotia, California, decided the company needed a comprehensive safety program that would go beyond its existing efforts to avoid safety violations. The company sought to improve its program not only to meet OSHA regulations but also because work-related injuries had been rising.

Part of the expanded efforts involve training supervisors in conducting safety meetings. Explains PALCO's director of accident prevention, Jeff A. Ringwald, "I've found that it's easier to *tell* a supervisor to have a safety meeting than it is to actually have them *do* it. Most of the supervisors can run their crews and keep the production end of things going, but they find it difficult to talk to their crew from a public speaking standpoint."

Training is a hands-on activity, supplemented with written materials. The company assigns an experienced worker to help each new employee until the new person is ready to do the job alone.

To help management and all employees see how their efforts are working, the company tries to provide feedback. Explains Ringwald, "The program's no good if you don't communicate after you try something." Each month, the company updates a graph of lost-time injuries and first-aid cases, so that everyone can compare the current year's per-

---

*This exercise is based on ideas submitted by Debbie Jansky, Milwaukee Area Tech Institute, Milwaukee, Wis.; James Mulvihill, Mankato Technical Institute; Mankato, Minn.; and Sylvia Ong, Scottsdale Community College, Scottsdale, Ariz.

formance with that of past years. So far the news has been good. In the first few years of the safety program, lost-time injuries have fallen by 52 percent.

The company also rewards employees for safe performance. At the end of every year, employees with both perfect attendance and no injuries are eligible to participate in a drawing for cash prizes. The grand prize is $15,000 toward the purchase of the American car of the employee's choice. Ten smaller prizes also are awarded. Furthermore, every employee who qualifies for the drawing receives a company jacket bearing the year's safety slogan. Adding to the recognition, the slogan is chosen in a contest among employees.

A separate program recognizes supervisors and their departments. Departments compete to see which will have the year's most significant decline in accidents, measured in terms of lost time compared with the previous year. Employees in the winning department, along with their guests, enjoy a group dinner at a local restaurant.

PALCO has found that several resources are available to help in the effort to improve the company's safety program. For example, the Timber Operators Council has a safety specialist, safety training consultants, and resources for training in conducting safety meetings. Every year PALCO invites one of the organization's training consultants to focus on a particular area of safety concerns. Other resources include information from the National Safety Council and a training program from the California Lumbermen's Accident Prevention Association.

1. What health hazards and safety hazards would you expect to be concerns at PALCO?
2. Review the characteristics of an effective safety and health program described in the chapter. Which of these characteristics does PALCO's safety program include?
3. Based on the information given, what safety-related duties do the supervisors have at PALCO? What else might PALCO's supervisors do to promote safety in the workplace?

Source: Gina C. Wilson, "'Safety Sense—Your Best Defense,'" *Quality Digest*, July 1992, pp. 40–46.

19

Honesty is the cornerstone of all success, without which confidence and ability to perform shall cease to exist.

—Mary Kay Ash

Ethics and Organization Politics

LEARNING OBJECTIVES

19.1 Define *ethics*, and explain why organizations should be concerned about ethical behavior.

19.2 Describe major types of ethical behavior that supervisors should practice.

19.3 Discuss how to make ethical decisions.

19.4 Provide guidelines for supervising unethical employees.

19.5 Define *whistleblowers*, and describe how the supervisor should treat such employees.

19.6 Describe the types of power supervisors can have.

19.7 Identify common strategies for organization politics.

19.8 Describe ways of building a power base and establishing a competitive edge.

19.9 Provide guidelines for socializing with others in the organization.

UNETHICAL, ILLEGAL ROAD LEADS TO JAIL

At P&H Plating Company, a Chicago industrial firm where 100 employees handle the plating of a variety of metals, owner and president Jeffrey Pytlarz directed the illegal dumping of toxic waste. The toxic material was a 4,000-gallon tank of cadmium cyanide, a solution the company had once used to plate materials for an electronics manufacturer. When that line of work ended, Pytlarz had to decide what to do with the cadmium solution. Processing it through the company's state-of-the-art pollution-control system would have generated so much heat that the system would have blown up. Having the waste treated off-site would have cost $40,000 to $100,000. Hard-pressed to handle the problem legally at a time when his company was losing money and had already invested heavily in pollution-control equipment, Pytlarz advised his wife, Cheryl Emrich, the company's environmental manager, to have the waste emptied into a drain at P&H's plant.

Pytlarz's plan, he says, was "to open the valve slightly and bleed out this solution a little at a time through our sanitary sewer." Emrich assigned a supervisor to carry out this order. The supervisor evidently misinterpreted the instructions, however, opening the tank's drain fully and dumping the 4,000 gallons of solution into the sewer in a single night. After passing through the sewer system and a water reclamation plant, the polluted water emptied into the North Branch of the Chicago River. Roughly 20,000 fish died as a result.

When he and Emrich discovered the empty tank, says Pytlarz, "we agonized over the decision." However, they did not report the violation to the authorities. Then, two days later, they learned about the fish dying. "At that point," says Pytlarz, "it was a little late to report the incident." Eventually, a tip from an undisclosed citizen led authorities to P&H.

Following his trial, Pytlarz was sentenced to 15 months in a federal prison. In addition, the former supervisor accused of actually dumping the waste was expected to plead guilty.

Sources: Matt O'Connor, "Couple Plead Guilty to Dumping Firm's Pollutants," *Chicago Tribune*, December 5, 1991, sec. 3, p. 18; and Jerry Poll, "P&H Plating: How Could That Happen?" *Products Finishing*, November 1992, pp. 72–83. Photo courtesy of © Rick Rusing/Tony Stone Images.

As discussed in the first chapter, a supervisor is expected to be loyal and to follow the boss's directions. But there are other standards of behavior to follow as well. Because he followed the boss's orders, a supervisor at P&H Plating harmed the environment and is accused of violating the law. To understand such situations and how to behave in them, supervisors need to be familiar with concepts of ethics.

This chapter discusses the role of ethics in the workplace. It distinguishes ethical from unethical behavior and tells how supervisors can behave ethically. It provides some suggestions for handling the challenge of supervising unethical employees and employees who report unethical or illegal behavior in the organization. Finally, the chapter discusses organization politics and how supervisors can use politics ethically and effectively to strengthen their careers.

Ethics in the Workplace

ethics
The principles by which people distinguish what is morally right.

In general, **ethics** refers to the principles by which people distinguish what is morally right. For example, most people would agree that cheating is wrong, or at least they would agree that it is unethical to cheat an elderly widow out of her life savings. Many decisions about ethics are more difficult. For example, is it cheating or just clever to pad an expense report or to take advantage of a supplier's mistake in totaling a bill? The Self-Quiz is a chance for you to examine your own standards of ethical behavior. To get an accurate score, be honest with yourself!

Some people say that "business ethics" is an oxymoron—that is, a contradiction in terms. Can businesspeople behave ethically, and if so, should they? One view is that profitability should be the overriding concern of business. This view makes it easy to behave ethically unless an ethical choice is also costly to the organization. Another view is that organizations and their employees have an obligation to behave ethically, even if doing so cuts into short-term economic advantages. The implication is that we are all better off if organizations and individuals consider the common good. A. Thomas Young, Martin Marietta Corporation's president and chief operating officer, describes ethical people this way: "[They] honor their word, follow the law, act honestly, respect other people's property, are loyal, and they work hard."[1] Presumably, as a supervisor, you are looking for just this kind of behavior in your employees.

Ethical issues are of particular concern in today's workplace. As in the example at the beginning of the chapter, modern technology has made the potential consequences of unethical decisions enormous. Consider an even more shocking example: When journalist Rushworth M. Kidder toured the Chernobyl nuclear power plant during the cleanup that followed its 1986 explosion, he learned that two electrical engineers had been conducting an "unauthorized experiment" on the night of the accident. To see how long a turbine would keep turning if they removed the power, the engineers shut down the reactor, overriding six computer-operated alarm systems and even padlocking valves open so they would not interrupt the experiment by shutting down automatically.[2]

In spite of these implications, the restructurings, cutbacks, and layoffs of recent years have made many employees afraid of being ethical when doing so conflicts with other goals. Fudging numbers on performance records or producing shoddy merchandise to keep costs down is tempting, given the alternatives. In the words of Kirk Hanson, president of the Business Enterprise Trust, an ethics

S E L F - Q U I Z *Your Ethical Standards*

Ethics have different degrees of importance to the career prospects of different people. To determine if ethics are likely to play an important role in your career, take the following quiz:

1. If my boss asked me to lie to cover one of his mistakes, I would:
   a. Quit.
   b. Lie.
   c. Say it made me uncomfortable.
   d. Do it this time but refuse if it became a pattern.

2. If I discovered that I had unintentionally violated an important regulation, I would:
   a. File a report acknowledging my mistake.
   b. Wait and see if it was as important a violation as it seemed.
   c. Discuss the situation with my boss.
   d. Try to straighten out the error and talk to my boss if I could not.

3. If I observed a fellow employee stealing from the company, I would:
   a. Report the employee.
   b. Keep an eye on the employee.
   c. Ask the employee why he or she did it and then decide what to do.
   d. Try to make the employee return what he or she stole.

4. If I knew my boss and a co-worker were having an affair, I would:
   a. Transfer to another department.
   b. Ignore it.
   c. Wait to see if I was affected.
   d. Talk to my boss to clear the air.

5. If a headhunter approached me with an attractive offer, I would:
   a. Talk it over with my boss before proceeding.
   b. Ask my current employer to beat the outside offer.
   c. Meet the representatives of the outside firm and talk to my boss if I was serious about leaving.
   d. Ask my employer to make his best offer and then take the highest offer.

6. If I thought one of my employees had a drug problem, I would:
   a. Exercise my right to ask the employee to take a drug test.
   b. Wait and see if the employee's performance declines.
   c. Talk it over with the employee.
   d. Seek guidance from the personnel department.

7. If a fellow employee was having trouble keeping up with his or her work because of family problems, I would:
   a. Try to help by taking up the slack.
   b. Advise him or her to talk to our boss.
   c. Help out for a short while.
   d. Try to talk to a member of the family.

8. If a fellow employee was a victim of racial discrimination, I would:
   a. Create a file documenting the problem.
   b. Tell the employee I would support him or her if he or she complained.
   c. Complain to a superior likely to be sympathetic.
   d. Advise the person that he or she might be happier elsewhere.

9. If I took a job with a competing company, I would:
   a. Never use information from my current job.
   b. Use information to support my new employer.
   c. Use only general information.
   d. Seek legal counsel before using information.

If you answered (a) most often, you have a strong sense of ethics but tend to be rigid. You will run into ethical conflicts in your career unless you find a very like-minded company.

If you answered (b) most often, you are too willing to compromise on ethics. You will run into trouble if your job requires you to exercise judgment without clear guidelines.

If you answered (c) most often, you have a strong sense of ethics balanced with flexibility. You can act ethically and succeed in most organizations but will leave those that are wholly unethical.

If you answered (d) most often, you are unwilling to deal with ethical conflicts. You will run into trouble when others sense that you avoid hard issues.

Source: Copyright Mark Pastin, 1993, P.O. Box 24838, Tempe, Ariz., 85285, (602) 831–6920.

research group, "Quite simply, the individual who isn't perceived as a top achiever is a candidate for a layoff."[3]

Fear of being laid off may also lead employees to cooperate with unethical activities sponsored by others. For example, a Japanese company operating in the United States reportedly had its employees unpack machine tools when they arrived from Japan and relabel them "Manufactured in the U.S." so that they could be sold to the U.S. military, which required domestic products. One employee had tried to object but was told that if he did not like it, he could look for another job.[4] The fear of losing one's job makes it all the more important for supervisors to consciously consider the ethics of their decisions and to actively foster a climate that encourages ethical behavior.

Benefits of Ethical Behavior

Besides being morally right, ethical behavior offers some potential advantages to the organization. Being known as an ethical individual or organization is a satisfying way of maintaining a reputation for high standards. St. Louis–based Bi-State Development Agency sent the following letter to its suppliers to help them handle the ethics of giving holiday gifts to the organization's employees:

> We have chosen to buy your product or service over the year solely because of its quality, price and service, and we confidently hope to do so in the future. Product excellence is the best gift we can receive at any time. Hence, at this time of the year, we know you will refrain from presenting seasonal gifts of a more personal nature to those of our organization you meet and work with. Actually, it's a policy based on our own feeling—which we know you share—that the best thing an organization like ours can do for the public is to deliver high quality service with the utmost efficiency and courtesy.[5]

Ethical behavior can improve the organization's relations with the community. "Doing it right" at Kerr-McGee's wholesale terminal in the New York Harbor area requires careful attention to environmental safeguards. Gregg Herzfeld, terminal operator, takes no shortcuts when loading or unloading petroleum products from barges.

Source: Courtesy of Kerr-McGee Corp.

At the same time this letter sets high ethical standards, it also spotlights the agency's commitment to quality.

When customers, clients, and suppliers see that they are treated ethically, they are more likely to want to work cooperatively with the organization and to do their best for it. For example, Curtis Rocca III, the head of Bio-Dental Technologies Corporation in Rancho Cordova, California, tells of the time a salesperson offered him big discounts in exchange for Bio-Dental sending the check to the salesperson's home. Instead of snapping up the low prices, Rocca called the supplier's president and told him about the offer. Says Rocca, "My call created so much goodwill we now receive preferential treatment and rock-bottom pricing."[6]

Ethical behavior can also improve the organization's relations with the community. As mentioned earlier, this tends to attract customers and topnotch employees. Ethical behavior also tends to reduce public pressure for government regulation—a situation that most managers would view as beneficial.

In contrast, the costs of unethical behavior can be high. Organizations whose employees are unethical may lose respect, customers, and qualified employees who are uncomfortable working in an environment that compromises their moral standards. Salomon Brothers, a brokerage firm that was recently the subject of a scandal involving the trading of Treasury securities, had to pay fines of $290 million for its unethical behavior.[7] And in the months after the news media began publishing complaints that Dow Corning was covering up evidence that its breast implants were unsafe, the price of stock in Corning, Inc. (one of Dow Corning's two parent companies), fell by about 15 percent.[8]

Unethical behavior has personal consequences as well. The owners of P&H Plating, described in the opening story, went to jail. Dorothea Niki Risenhoover, a supervisor at the U.S. House Post Office, lost her job and was charged with criminal activity for allegedly providing an employee with stamps to cover up his

Unethical behavior can have both personal and societal consequences. Charles Keating was convicted of wrongdoing in the savings and loan scandal. Final costs to taxpayers are still being counted.

Source: Courtesy of AP/Wide World.

embezzlement in exchange for the employee not revealing that Risenhoover had been using marijuana and cocaine supplied by the employee.[9] On a more mundane level, the supervisor may simply find that tolerating lapses of ethics leads employees to behave in increasingly unacceptable ways. For example, if the supervisor looks the other way when employees take home small items like pencils or screws, the employees may eventually start "borrowing" bigger items.

Ethical Behavior of Supervisors

If supervisors wish to see a high standard of ethical behavior in the workplace, they must behave ethically themselves. With regard to supervisors in particular, some important dimensions of ethical behavior include loyalty, fairness, and honesty. These are summarized in Figure 19.1.

As discussed in Chapter 4, a supervisor is expected to be loyal to the organization, to his or her boss, and to his or her subordinates. Of course, these loyalties sometimes conflict, resulting in ethical dilemmas. Furthermore, these loyalties may at times come into conflict with the supervisor's self-interests. If others in the organization see that the supervisor tends to put his or her own interests first, the supervisor will have difficulty earning the loyalty, trust, and respect of others.

Fairness is another important trait of supervisors. Employees expect to be treated evenhandedly. They resent it if the supervisor plays favorites or passes the blame for mistakes on to them. Supervisors may find it harder to be fair—or to convince others that they are fair—when they supervise their own relatives. Therefore, supervisors may find it wisest to avoid **nepotism**, the hiring of one's own relatives. A related problem can arise when supervisors accept a gift from a supplier or someone else who may wish to influence their judgment. Even if a

nepotism
The hiring of one's relatives.

FIGURE 19.1

Important
Dimensions of
Ethical Behavior by
Supervisors

FIGURE 19.1

Important
Dimensions of
Ethical Behavior by
Supervisors

supervisor is sure he or she can remain objective, accepting cash, lavish entertainment, or other gifts can raise questions in other people's minds about whether the supervisor can be fair. When supervisors place themselves in such a position, management tends to doubt their ability to exercise good judgment.

Honesty includes several types of behavior by the supervisor. First, when employees make a suggestion or accomplish impressive results, the supervisor should be sure that the employees get the credit. Pretending that other people's accomplishments are your own is a type of dishonesty. So is using the company's resources for personal matters. For example, a supervisor who spends work time chatting with friends on the phone or who takes supplies home for personal use is in effect stealing what belongs to the organization. Furthermore, the supervisor is demonstrating that such behavior will be overlooked, which encourages employees to be equally dishonest.

Making Ethical Decisions

Assuming that it is desirable to choose ethical behavior and to help employees do so, the challenge is to decide what action is ethical in a particular situation and then determine how to carry it out. There are no hard-and-fast rules for making ethical decisions. In some cases, two possibilities might seem equally ethical or unethical. Perhaps someone will get hurt no matter what the supervisor decides. Furthermore, as discussed in the "Dealing with Diversity" box on page 498, people from different cultures may have different measures of whether a given type of behavior is ethical or unethical.

DEALING WITH DIVERSITY

Different Measures of Ethical Behavior

Gift giving in the workplace is a practice that can lead to misunderstandings when the people involved are from different cultures. The reason is that the giving of gifts can have different meanings from one culture to another. In the United States, the giving of gifts is often interpreted as bribery, an attempt to buy influence. However, in many parts of the world, giving a gift is the proper way to indicate one's gratitude toward and respect for the receiver.

What can a supervisor do if refusing a gift might insult the giver? Most important, the supervisor must follow company policy, and in many cases that means turning down the gift. At the same time, however, the supervisor should carefully and politely explain the reason for not accepting the gift. If a supervisor has immigrant employees who might not understand American views about gift giving, this might be an area in which to educate all the employees before such a problem arises.

A company that prospered as a result of sticking by its ethical standards is Empire Southwest, a Phoenix-based distributor of Caterpillar equipment.

Empire was shut out of the market in Mexico for years because the company refused to make payoffs known as *mordita* (meaning "little bite"). However, potential customers—mining companies, farmers, and contractors—learned about Empire's determination to stick by its ethical standards. They were impressed and wanted to buy from the company. The potential customers lobbied the Mexican government and eventually got Empire the approvals necessary to open two dealerships in Mexico.

Empire's chief executive, Jack Whiteman, says, "There is no doubt in my mind that ethical behavior pays off at the bottom line." When all things are equal in competing for business, he explains, "customers frequently give us the benefit of a doubt."

Sources: Karen Berney, "Finding the Ethical Edge," *Nation's Business*, August 1987, pp. 18–19, 22–24; Sondra Thiederman, *Bridging Cultural Barriers for Corporate Success: How to Manage the Multicultural Work Force* (New York: Lexington Books, 1991), pp. 125–126.

When an ethical decision is hard to make, the following questions can help the supervisor think it through:[10]

- Have you defined the problem accurately?
- How would you define the problem if you stood on the other side of the fence?
- How did this situation occur in the first place?
- To whom and to what do you owe your loyalty as an individual and as a member of the organization?
- What is your intention in making this decision?
- How does your intention compare with the probable results?
- Who could your decision or action hurt?
- Can you discuss the problem with the affected parties before making your decision?
- Are you confident that your position will be as valid over the long term as it seems now?
- Could you comfortably disclose your decision or action to your boss, the head of your organization, your family, and society as a whole?
- What is the symbolic potential of your action if it is understood? If misunderstood?
- Under what conditions would you allow exceptions to the stand you have taken?

FIGURE 19.2

Steps to Take When an Employee Is Suspected of Unethical Behavior

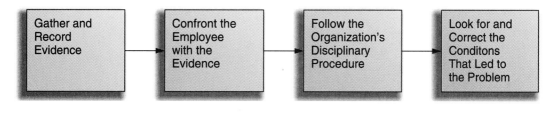

As implied by some of these questions, the supervisor can promote ethical decision making by involving others in the process. When the group discusses the issue, group members can discuss their perspective of the situation and the underlying values. Discussing the ethical implications of the decision can help the supervisor see consequences and options that he or she might not have thought of alone. (Chapter 8 provides further guidelines for group decision making.)

Deciding what behavior is ethical does not always end an ethical dilemma. As mentioned earlier, employees are sometimes afraid that doing what is morally right will cause their performance to suffer and may even cost them a job. In the words of Andrew S. Grove, president of Intel Corporation, "The nub of ethical dilemmas is not whether we understand what's right—most of us instinctively do. What we are not so sure about is whether we want to deal with the risk and hassle involved in challenging something we know is wrong."[11] Grove recommends acting only when willing to accept these risks. However, he cautions against trying to rationalize a decision not to choose an ethical act; doing so can erode your ethical standards.

Supervising Unethical Employees

It is tempting to ignore the unethical behavior of others, hoping they will change on their own. However, the problem usually gets worse, as the unethical employee sees that he or she can get away with the behavior. Consequently, when the supervisor suspects that an employee is behaving unethically, the supervisor needs to take prompt action. The steps to take are summarized in Figure 19.2.

The first step is to gather and record evidence. The supervisor needs to be sure that unethical behavior is actually occurring. For example, if the supervisor suspects that one or more employees are padding their expense accounts, the supervisor should regularly review expense reports. As soon as the supervisor sees something that looks odd, he or she should ask the employee about it.[12] After confronting the employee with the evidence, the supervisor should follow the organization's disciplinary procedure. (Discipline is discussed in Chapter 16.)

After dealing with the specific problem, the supervisor should try to understand what conditions contributed to this problem. That can help the supervisor avoid similar ethical lapses in the future. In analyzing why an employee has behaved unethically, consider whether you have created a climate for ethical behavior in the department. Have you set a good example through your own ethical behavior? Are the rewards for productivity so great that they tempt employees to cut corners with regard to ethics? Do the employees hear messages that say the organization cares only about achievements, such as, "I don't care how you get it done, just do it"? In the words of Martin Marietta's A. Thomas Young, "If you expect honesty, you get honesty. If you don't, you get what you probably deserve."[13]

Treatment of Whistleblowers

whistleblower
Someone who exposes a violation of ethics or law.

Someone who exposes a violation of ethics or law is known as a **whistleblower**. Typically, a whistleblower brings the problem first to a manager in the organization. If management seems unresponsive, he or she then contacts a government agency, the media, or a private organization. For example, as an unnamed company increased the number of personal computers it used from 2 to 200, employees often made copies of software programs rather than buying new ones. (Legally, this is somewhat like an instructor making photocopies of a textbook rather than requiring each student to buy a copy.) Someone called the toll-free hotline of the Software Publishers Association, which took the company to court. As a result, the company had to buy legitimate copies of the software and also pay a fine equal to the retail price of the additional software.[14]

The report of a whistleblower may be embarrassing as well as costly to the organization. Nevertheless, whistleblowers are protected by federal laws, the laws of several states, and some recent court decisions.[15] For example, federal laws protect employees who make complaints pertaining to violations of antidiscrimination laws, environmental laws, and occupational health and safety standards. Thus, in general, employers may not retaliate against someone for reporting a violation. Suppose an employee files a complaint of sexual harassment; the organization may not react by firing the employee who complained.

In spite of these protections, the reality is that whistleblowers often do suffer for going public with their complaints. Typically, the whistleblower's co-workers resent and reject him or her, and the whistleblower may be demoted or terminated. Even when the courts agree that the whistleblower was treated unlawfully, it can take years for that person to be compensated by the organization or even appreciated by the public. For example, engineer Thomas D. Talcott quit Dow Corning in 1976 to protest what he saw as safety problems with the company's silicone breast implants.[16] About 15 years later, that issue finally was receiving widespread publicity. Talcott at least had the credentials to start a successful consulting business when he left his job, whereas many people would have a much harder time finding work. Because of consequences such as these—and out of fairness to one's employer—a would-be whistleblower should try to resolve problems within the organization before blowing the whistle.

The supervisor's general attitude toward whistleblowing should be to discourage reports of wrongdoing when these are simply motivated by pettiness or a desire to get back at someone. But when someone does complain, the supervisor should quickly investigate the complaint and report what will be done. This lets employees know that their complaints are taken seriously and that the supervisor wants to handle them fairly and appropriately. The supervisor should bear in mind that the typical whistleblower is not merely a troublemaker but a person with high ideals and competence.[17] Keeping communication flowing and responding to problems will allow the organization to find solutions without the costs and embarrassment of public disclosure.

Organization Politics and Power

organization politics
Activities by which people seek to improve their position within the organization, generally by gaining power.

Just as some people cannot believe that ethics and business can coexist, many doubt that ethics plays a significant role in politics. We most commonly think of politics in terms of running for and holding public office. However, the term has a broader meaning. Politics refers to the tactics people use to improve their position. Thus, **organization politics** involves activities by which people seek to improve their position within the organization. Improving one's position is not in itself good or bad; therefore, politics also is not in itself good or bad. Political skills are important, however. They help the supervisor obtain the cooperation and support of others in the organization.

power
The ability to influence people to behave in a certain way.

The usual way that people use politics to improve their position is by gaining power. **Power** is the ability to influence people to behave in a certain way. For instance, one supervisor says, "I wish everyone would be at work on time," yet employees continue to come in late. Another supervisor gets employees so excited about their contribution to the company that they consistently perform above what is required of them. The second of these supervisors has more power than the first.

Sources of Power

Editorial supervisor Stan Bakker has a decade-long track record of turning manuscripts into best-sellers. When he tells one of the editors on his staff how he or she should handle a particular author or manuscript, the editor invariably follows Stan's directions. Why? Partly because Stan is the boss, and partly because the editors respect his expertise. Thus, Stan's power comes both from his position in the company and from his personal characteristics.

position power
Power that comes from a person's formal role in an organization.

Power that comes from a person's formal role in an organization is known as **position power**. Every supervisor has some position power with regard to the employees he or she supervises. Higher-level managers, in turn, have a greater degree of position power.

personal power
Power that arises from an individual's personal characteristics.

In contrast, **personal power** is power that arises from an individual's personal characteristics. Because a person does not need to be a manager in an organization to have personal power there, the supervisor may find that employees view one of their co-workers as an informal leader of their group. For example, if a supervisor announces a reorganization, one of the employees may successfully urge everyone to rally around the new plan—or may undermine morale by making fun of the changes. The informal leader in a group could be someone employees see as having expertise or being fun to work with.

A supervisor cannot eliminate personal power in subordinates, but the supervisor should be aware of it so that he or she can use it to his or her advantage. The supervisor can watch for problems that might arise when the supervisor and informal leader have conflicting goals. Perhaps more important, the supervisor can seek ways to get the informal leaders on his or her side. The supervisor might announce a decision to the informal leader first or discuss plans with that person. For example, when Marie Davis, marketing manager at IDS Financial Services, learned that she and her department would be reporting to a new vice-president, she persuaded the department's informal leaders to help make the change as easy as possible.[18]

Types of Power

Because power comes from themselves as well as from their position in the organization, supervisors can have a variety of types of power. If a supervisor has less position power than he or she would like, the supervisor might consider the following types of power to see whether there are some he or she can develop. These types are summarized in Table 19.1.

Legitimate power comes from the position a person holds. Thus, a supervisor has legitimate power to delegate tasks to employees. To exercise legitimate power effectively, the supervisor needs to be sure employees understand what they are directed to do and are able to do it.

Referent power comes from the emotions a person inspires. Some supervisors seem to light up the room when they enter; they have a winning personality that includes enthusiasm, energy, and genuine enjoyment of the job. People like working for such a supervisor and often perform beyond the call of duty because they want the supervisor to like them. A person with referent power is often called "charismatic."

Expert power arises from a person's knowledge or skills. Employees respect a supervisor who knows the employees' jobs better than they do. Their respect leads them to follow the supervisor's instructions. For example, the head of a company's research and development team might be a scientist who is well regarded in the field. The researchers would often ask for and rely on such a supervisor's advice.

Coercive power arises from fear related to the use of force. A supervisor who says, "Be on time tomorrow, or you're fired!" is using coercive power. This type of power tends to get results in the short run, but in the long run employees come to resent the supervisor and may try to get around him or her. A supervisor who often relies on coercive power should consider whether he or she is doing so at the expense of developing other, more appropriate types of power.

Reward power arises from giving people something they want. In the case of a supervisor, the reward might be a raise, recognition, or assignment to a desired shift. A supervisor who plans to rely on reward power to lead employees had better be sure that he or she is able to give out rewards consistently. Often supervisors are limited in this regard. For example, company policy may put a ceiling on the size of raises to be granted, or there may be only a few assignments that really thrill employees.

Connection power is power that stems from a person's relationship to someone powerful. For example, imagine that two supervisors are golfing buddies. One of them gets promoted to the job of manager of purchasing. The other supervisor has connection power stemming from his relationship to the new manager. Similarly, if one of the organization's employees is the daughter of a vice-president, she has connection power as a result of that family relationship. Connection power can be

TABLE 19.1
Types of Power

Power Type	Arises from
Legitimate	The position a person holds
Referent	The emotions a person inspires
Expert	A person's knowledge or skills
Coercive	Fear related to the use of force
Reward	Giving people something they want
Connection	A person's relationship to someone powerful
Information	Possession of valuable information

a problem for the organization and its managers when the people who have it place the interests of their relationship ahead of the interests of the organization. However, it is a fact of organizational life.

Information power is power that arises from possessing valuable information. Someone who knows which employees are targeted in the next round of layoffs or when the boss will be out of town has information power. The secretaries of top managers have information power as well as connection power.

Political Strategies

A person's political strategies are the methods the person uses to acquire and keep power within the organization. Depending on the particular strategies a person chooses and how he or she uses those strategies, they may be ethical or unethical. The following strategies are commonly used in organizations:[19]

- *Doing favors*—People remember favors and are generally willing to help out or say a good word in return. However, doing favors solely to create an obligation is unethical.
- *Making good impressions*—Those who are skilled at organization politics know that it is important to create a positive image of themselves. Not only do they look their best, but they make sure their accomplishments are visible.
- *Cultivating the grapevine*—The saying "Knowledge is power" applies to one's position in the organization. Therefore, it is important to be connected to the grapevines that carry information in the organization (described in Chapter 7). Ways to do this include serving on committees and developing friendships and informal contacts.
- *Supporting the boss*—The supervisor's boss can be a powerful ally. Therefore, it is important to help the boss look good.
- *Avoiding negativism*—People have more respect for those who propose solutions than for those who merely criticize.
- *Giving praise*—People like to be praised, and written compliments are especially valuable. As long as the praise is sincere, the supervisor can offer it to anyone, even the boss.

FIGURE 19.3

Approaches to Building a Power Base

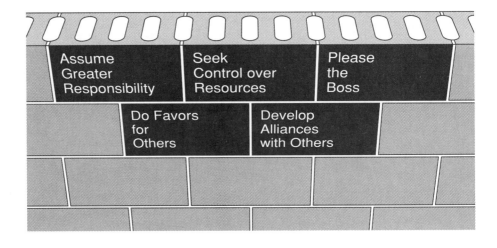

Building a Power Base

At the heart of organization politics is building a base of power. The particular approach used varies with the kinds of power an employee or manager might acquire. Figure 19.3 summarizes some possible approaches. Some people take on more and more responsibility in an effort to become needed in the organization. Others seek control over resources; the supervisor with more employees or a bigger budget is considered to be more powerful.

An important way supervisors can build their power base is to please their boss. Chapter 4 describes some tactics for doing so. Peers and subordinates who recognize that a supervisor has a close relationship with his or her boss tend to treat the supervisor carefully to avoid antagonizing the boss.

Yet another approach is for the supervisor to do favors so that others will be in his or her debt. Bribery, of course, is considered unethical. However, there are many ethical ways to do favors for others. For example, a supervisor might offer to stay late in order to help a co-worker finish a project or jump-start the co-worker's car on a cold day. Then when the supervisor needs help or a favorable word from someone, the co-worker will probably be happy to return the favor.

Doing favors can help the supervisor with one of the other techniques for building a power base: developing alliances with others in the organization. The supervisor who has many people on his or her side is able to get more done and to build a good reputation. This does not mean supervisors have to hang around with greedy, pushy, or unethical co-workers. Rather, they should identify as potential allies people they admire.[20] Ways to build alliances with these people include earning their trust, keeping them informed, and developing comfortable relationships by identifying common interests.[21]

Establishing a Competitive Edge

On the assumption that there is a limited number of promotions and other goodies to go around, organization members seek to gain a competitive edge. They try to stand out so that when raises, promotions, and choice assignments are handed out,

Getting Things Done

An important political tactic is to become known as someone who gets things accomplished around the organization. Such a person tends to receive more respect from others. Unfortunately, we all have days when it feels as though our every effort is frustrated. Management consultant Nancy K. Austin offers the following guidelines for building momentum in spite of the obstacles:

- *Demonstrate a tangible result.* Instead of getting bogged down in a big project by trying to create a perfect and complete plan, focus on a tangible result you can accomplish right away. Then build on that success with small but measurable steps toward completing the project.
- *Avoid perfectionism.* Try something. If you do not get it exactly right, make changes and try again.
- *Increase your chances to learn from failure.* Try several ideas simultaneously. Take one risk each day, such as asking your boss a difficult question or calling someone you do not really want to talk to.

- *Avoid drawing too much attention to yourself.* When you are going to try out an idea, be delicate about selling its potential until you have a success to show. Trumpeting your plan before you try it will lead you to look foolish if you make a mistake and may inspire higher-level managers to interfere with what your employees are doing.
- *Build commitment from your employees.* Involve employees in planning and making decisions about your project. Keep them informed about your plans. The resulting team spirit is likely to contribute to the project's success.
- *Ask the right questions.* Let your department be a place where people are encouraged to ask, "What's new?" and, "Why not?" and "Where do we start?" Such questions form the basis for doing something innovative.

Source: Nancy K. Austin, "Create a Pocket of Excellence," *Executive Female*, January–February 1992, pp. 42–45.

they will be the recipients. Ethical efforts to establish a competitive edge are generally based on trying to do an exceptional job. For example, a sales manager who works for a U.S. subsidiary of a Mexican conglomerate says, "Learning the language and customs [of Mexico] enabled me to impress the players in our parent company in Mexico. They now respond quickly to my requests."[22]

Some unethical approaches to establishing a competitive edge are spreading lies and rumors about peers and taking credit for the ideas and work of subordinates. Trying to look good at the expense of someone else may be effective at first. But when the truth comes into the open, the person who uses this tactic winds up the biggest loser. Other people simply learn not to trust him or her. In the long run, the most successful way to look exceptional is to produce exceptional results. The "Tips from the Firing Line" box provides some ideas for doing so.

Socializing

At many organizations, part of the game of getting ahead includes socializing with co-workers. Perhaps the people who get promoted the fastest are those who golf with the boss or go out for a drink after work on occasion. Depending on the supervisor's behavior in these situations, socializing can be helpful or can put an end to his or her career growth.

Common sense can help the supervisor handle socializing appropriately. For example, getting roaring drunk at a party is likely to lead the supervisor to behave

If handled appropriately, socializing with other employees in activities such as golf can be helpful to a supervisor's career.

Source: Courtesy of Dick Luria/Tony Stone Images.

foolishly and say things he or she will regret later. Likewise, dating a subordinate is an invitation to problems. If the relationship works out, the other employees are likely to be jealous of the subordinate and to doubt the supervisor's ability to be fair. If the relationship does not work out, the supervisor has set him- or herself up—justly or unjustly—for charges of sexual harassment by an angry subordinate.

In general, the wisest course is to be sensible but natural. For example, the supervisor should not push to be buddies with the boss or with subordinates. Nor should the supervisor use social occasions as an opportunity to make a big impression—showing off is hardly an effective way to build relationships. A more positive approach was that of a marketing coordinator who succeeded with a simple demonstration of interest in her company's president. She learned he likes rhubarb, so she made a rhubarb pie to take to an office party. "The boss had a piece [of the pie], and now he acknowledges me," reports this marketing coordinator.[23]

Summary

19.1 Define *ethics*, and explain why organizations should be concerned about ethical behavior.
Ethics refers to the principles by which people distinguish what is morally right. Organizations should be concerned about ethical behavior because modern technology has made the potential consequences of unethical behavior enormous. Treating customers, clients, and suppliers ethically enhances the organization's reputation and makes them want to work cooperatively with the organization. Ethical behavior also tends to improve community relations and to reduce public pressure for government regulation. In contrast, the costs to an organization that acts unethically can be high.

19.2 Describe major types of ethical behavior that supervisors should practice.
Supervisors should be loyal to the organization, their boss, and their subordinates. Supervisors should treat others—especially employees—fairly. Ways to dispel any doubts about one's fairness are to avoid nepotism and to decline gifts from suppliers and others seeking influence. Finally, supervisors should be honest, which includes giving subordinates credit for their accomplishments and avoiding personal use of the company's resources.

19.3 Discuss how to make ethical decisions.
The decision maker can rely on various measures of ethical behavior, such as the "golden rule" or

whether the action would result in the "greatest good for the greatest number." The supervisor can promote ethical decision making by involving others in the process. And in deciding whether to carry out the most ethical course of action, the supervisor can weigh whether doing so is too risky.

19.4 Provide guidelines for supervising unethical employees.
When the supervisor believes an employee is doing something unethical, the supervisor should take immediate action. First, the supervisor should gather and record evidence. Then the supervisor confronts the employee with the evidence and follows the organization's disciplinary procedure. After dealing with a specific problem, the supervisor should try to understand what conditions contributed to the problem and then seek to correct those conditions.

19.5 Define *whistleblowers*, and describe how the supervisor should treat such employees.
Whistleblowers are people who expose a violation of ethics or law. Organizations should not retaliate against whistleblowers. The supervisor should discourage reports of wrongdoing when they are simply motivated by pettiness or a desire for revenge. However, when someone does complain, the supervisor should quickly investigate the complaint and report what will be done.

19.6 Describe the types of power supervisors can have.
Supervisors can have legitimate power, which comes from their position in the organization; referent power, which comes from the emotions they

inspire in others; expert power, which comes from their knowledge or skills; coercive power, which comes from fear related to their use of force; reward power, which comes from giving people something they want; connection power, which comes from their relationships to people in power; and information power, which comes from the possession of valuable information.

19.7 Identify common strategies for organization politics.
Political strategies that are commonly used in organizations include doing favors, making good impressions, cultivating the grapevine, supporting the boss, avoiding negativism, and giving praise.

19.8 Describe ways of building a power base and establishing a competitive edge.
To build a power base, approaches include assuming ever greater responsibility to increase one's value to the organization, seeking control over resources, pleasing the boss, doing favors, and building alliances. Some tactics for establishing a competitive edge are doing an exceptional job, spreading rumors and lies about peers, and taking credit for the work of others. The last two approaches can backfire; when caught, the person who uses them can lose the trust of others.

19.9 Provide guidelines for socializing with others in the organization.
The supervisor should use common sense, avoiding risky behavior such as getting drunk or dating a subordinate. The supervisor should act natural, not being pushy about establishing friendships. Another type of behavior to avoid is showing off.

Key Terms

ethics	organization politics	position power
nepotism	power	personal power
whistleblower		

Review and Discussion Questions

1. In your opinion, should ethics be a major concern of a supervisor? Why or why not?
2. What kinds of ethical behavior are typically expected of supervisors? Should a supervisor

expect similar behavior from his or her employees?
3. In each of the following situations, what would have been the ethical thing for the

employees to do?* What criteria did you use to decide? What would you have done in that situation? Why?

  a. One fall, managers of Toys "R" Us sent employees to Child World stores to buy large quantities of items that had been heavily discounted. The items were then resold by Toys "R" Us.

  b. Three students at Stanford University reported that their summer employers had asked them to call up competitors, looking for information. They were to pretend that they were doing research for school.

4. Devon Price supervises a crew of maintenance workers. One day a secretary at the company took him aside and asked, "Do you know that Pete [a member of the crew] has been taking home supplies like nails and tape to work on personal projects?" What should Devon do?

5. Assume that Pete, the maintenance worker in question 4, was found to be pilfering supplies and was disciplined. Upset, he decides to act on some safety problems he has observed and complained about, and he reports them to the local office of the Occupational Safety and Health Administration. When Devon, Pete's supervisor, finds out that the department will be investigated by OSHA, he is furious. It seems as though Pete is nothing but trouble. What should Devon do?

6. Should a supervisor practice organization politics? Is it ethical to do so?

7. What are the two basic sources of power available to a supervisor? Which do you think is more important to the supervisor's effectiveness? Why?

8. Which type(s) of power is the supervisor exerting in each of the following situations?

  a. A sales supervisor promises a $50 bonus to the first salesperson to close a sale this week.

  b. One day a month, a supervisor orders out for pizza and joins her employees for lunch. The employees look forward to these gatherings—the supervisor joins them in recounting funny stories, and she usually is able to fill them in on some management plans.

  c. The supervisor in the bookkeeping department got his job thanks to a referral from his father, who regularly plays racquetball with the company's president. Since the supervisor was hired, the president has visited the bookkeeping department a couple of times to see how he is doing. The supervisor's boss is very careful to be diplomatic when he has to criticize the supervisor.

  d. When the employees in a word-processing department make many errors per page or a particularly glaring error, their supervisor posts the offending pages on the department bulletin board to shame the workers into performing better.

9. A sales supervisor believes she could be more effective if she had more cooperation from the company's credit department. If the credit of potential customers could be approved faster, her salespeople could close more sales. What political tactics would you recommend that the sales supervisor consider to get more cooperation from the credit department?

10. Many companies hold a party each December for employees and their guests. What guidelines can you offer for how to behave at such an event?

A SECOND LOOK

The story of P&H Plating at the beginning of this chapter refers to a situation in which a supervisor had to choose between obeying his boss and obeying environmental laws. What would you have advised the supervisor to do when faced with that choice?

---

*Examples are taken from Kenneth Labich, "The New Crisis in Business Ethics," *Fortune*, April 20, 1992, pp. 168, 172.

Class Exercise*

Each student completes the survey in Figure 19.4 anonymously, circling all the answers that apply. The instructor tabulates the results and distributes them for discussion at the next class session.

For each item in the survey, the class discusses the following questions:

• Which answer(s) were selected by most students?

• What is the justification for the answers selected?

• If you were the supervisor of an employee who acted in this way, how would you respond (assuming that you observed the behavior)?

• If your supervisor learned that you had acted in the way indicated by the survey response, how do you think your career would be affected?

CASE

Tempted by a Trade Secret

Several years ago, a disgruntled employee of 3M Company, Philip A. Stegora, acquired some samples of a new casting tape that 3M had developed for doctors to use in setting broken bones. He mailed the samples to four competitors of 3M— Johnson & Johnson, DePuy, Cutter Laboratories, and Zimmer. Along with the samples, Stegora enclosed an offer to explain the technology in exchange for $20,000. Under an alias, Stegora invited the companies to contact him at a Minneapolis post office box.

Stegora no doubt expected that the offer would be tempting. Johnson & Johnson, for example, once dominated the casting market with its bandage roll. But 3M's fiberglass cast was stronger and lighter; with the new improvements, it was likely to take over the market.

None of the companies contacted Stegora, however, nor did any of them notify 3M. Instead, Skip Klintworth, Jr., who was then chief executive of Carapace, Inc., a small cast maker in Tulsa, heard about the stolen samples from colleagues at DePuy and Zimmer. Klintworth reported the incident to 3M, which called the Federal Bureau of Investigation. Says Klintworth, "Nobody intended to do anything. I couldn't believe it."

The FBI traced the theft to Stegora. He was eventually convicted of mail fraud and transporting stolen property across state lines. He served 22 months in prison.

Later, while gathering evidence in another case, 3M learned that Johnson & Johnson had conducted tests on the sample the company received from Stegora. Court documents say that the sample went to a product manager, who sent them to the lab for analysis. The report from the lab went to several senior orthopedics officials, who did not forbid the company's chemists from using the findings in their research. According to a special master for the U.S. District Court in Minneapolis, Johnson & Johnson was able to use information from the tests to get a competing product to market three months before the company might otherwise have been able to. As a result, the Minneapolis court ordered Johnson & Johnson to pay 3M $116.3 million for infringing 3M's patents and taking trade secrets. Johnson & Johnson, vowing to appeal the decision, denied it had done anything wrong.

1. What unethical actions are described in this case? Were any of them justifiable?

*This exercise is based on a suggestion submitted by James Mulvihill, Mankato, Minn.

FIGURE 19.4
Survey for Class Exercise

Which of the following actions would you take?
Circle the letters of as many choices as apply to you.

1. Put false information in your résumé…
   a. If necessary in order to get a job
   b. Only about minor details
   c. If most people are doing it
   d. Never

2. Tell a competing company secrets about your employer's product or procedures…
   a. In order to land a job with the competitor
   b. In exchange for $100
   c. In exchange for $1 million
   d. Never

3. Cheat on a test used as the basis for promotions…
   a. If you have a family to support
   b. If you think the test is unfair
   c. If your co-workers are doing it
   d. Never

4. Use the office copier…
   a. To make a copy of your dentist's bill
   b. To make 6 copies of a report that is related to charitable work you do
   c. To make 50 copies of your résumé
   d. Never

5. Pad your expense account for a business trip…
   a. If you believe you are underpaid
   b. Only for small amounts that the employer won't miss
   c. Only when you are experiencing financial problems
   d. Never

6. Call in sick when you aren't sick…
   a. If you're worn out from working on a big project
   b. If your child is sick
   c. If you need to recover from the weekend
   d. Never

7. Lie about your boss's whereabouts when he or she takes a long, liquid lunch…
   a. Only if specifically instructed to do so
   b. If the boss gives you a generous raise in return
   c. Only when the person asking is your boss's superior
   d. Never

2. Who was the whistleblower in this case? What do you think motivated him to act?

3. Imagine that you, as a supervisor, received stolen new-product samples that could give you a competitive advantage.
   a. What would you do, and why? Here are some possibilities:
      • Throw them away
      • Get them analyzed
      • Notify the competitor from whom they were stolen
      • Call the FBI
   b. What if your company's product was selling poorly, and the improvements you could make based on the sample might help the company avoid laying off employees? Would that change your decision? Explain.

Source: Kevin Kelly, "When a Rival's Trade Secret Crosses Your Desk…," *Business Week*, May 20, 1991, p. 48.

Part Four
Application Exercises

Exercise 1. Understanding Benefits of Working in Groups

Chapter 17 ("Groups and Teamwork") begins with the Stanley Bostitch, Inc., company slogan "None of us is as smart as all of us." Let's see if that statement holds true for this exercise.

Instructions

1. You will perform this part of the exercise on your own. When your instructor starts the clock, you will have two minutes to fill in the U.S. state names on Chart 1. The first letter of each of the fifty states is provided. Write the state name out in full; do not use abbreviations. There should be no talking among yourselves during this first step.

2. Form into groups of three to five students to work on Chart 2. Your group should select someone to record for your group's list. Without looking back at the first chart you completed, your group will have two minutes to fill in the second chart. Speak quietly among yourselves so that other groups will not overhear your answers.

3. Your instructor will read the fifty state names so that you may check your answers. Then fill in the information about your group's performance.

Chart 1: Working alone
Number of correct answers for each group member:

_____ _____ _____ _____ _____

What is the average of these scores? _____

Chart 2: Working in groups
Number of correct answers your group completed: _____
How many in your group got the same or a better score on Chart 1 than the group got on Chart 2? _____

Application Exercises were prepared by Corinne Livesay, Liberty University, Lynchburg, Virginia.

CHART 1: WORKING ALONE

1.	A	26.	M
2.	A	27.	N
3.	A	28.	N
4.	A	29.	N
5.	C	30.	N
6.	C	31.	N
7.	C	32.	N
8.	D	33.	N
9.	F	34.	N
10.	G	35.	O
11.	H	36.	O
12.	I	37.	O
13.	I	38.	P
14.	I	39.	R
15.	I	40.	S
16.	K	41.	S
17.	K	42.	T
18.	L	43.	T
19.	M	44.	U
20.	M	45.	V
21.	M	46.	V
22.	M	47.	W
23.	M	48.	W
24.	M	49.	W
25.	M	50.	W

CHART 2: WORKING IN GROUPS

1.	A	26.	M
2.	A	27.	N
3.	A	28.	N
4.	A	29.	N
5.	C	30.	N
6.	C	31.	N
7.	C	32.	N
8.	D	33.	N
9.	F	34.	N
10.	G	35.	O
11.	H	36.	O
12.	I	37.	O
13.	I	38.	P
14.	I	39.	R
15.	I	40.	S
16.	K	41.	S
17.	K	42.	T
18.	L	43.	T
19.	M	44.	U
20.	M	45.	V
21.	M	46.	V
22.	M	47.	W
23.	M	48.	W
24.	M	49.	W
25.	M	50.	W

Questions for Discussion

1. How many individual students, working alone, did as well or better than students working in one of the groups?
2. Benefiting from the collective knowledge of a group to help solve a problem is but one advantage to working in groups. Name some other advantages of working in an effective group that normally cannot be realized when individuals work alone.

Exercise 2. Making Tough Choices in the World of Work

This exercise provides you with an opportunity to practice what you learned in Chapter 19 ("Ethics and Organization Politics").

Instructions

1. You and the rest of the class are supervisors at Martin Marietta Corporation in Orlando, Florida. You are getting ready to do the group exercise in an ethics training session. The training instructor announces you will be playing *Gray Matters: The Ethics Game. Gray Matters*, which was prepared for Martin Marietta employees, is also played at forty-one universities, including Harvard, and at sixty-five other companies. Although there are fifty-five scenarios in *Gray Matters*, you will have time during this session to complete only five scenarios.[1]

2. The training instructor asks you to form into groups of four to six supervisors and to appoint a group leader who will read the case to the group, conduct a discussion of the case, obtain a consensus answer to the case, and then report the group's answers to the training instructor. You will have five minutes to reach each decision, after which all groups will discuss their answers and the instructor will give the point values and rationale for each choice. Then you will have five minutes for the next case, until all five cases have been completed. Keep track of your group's score for each case; the group scoring the most points will be the winning team.

3. You may believe some cases lack clarity or that some of your choices are not as precise as you would have liked. Also, some cases have only one solution, whereas others have more than one solution. In still others there is no ideal solution, and you must choose the answer that is the best of those presented. Each choice is assessed points to reflect which answer is the most correct. Your group's task is to select only *one* option in each case.

Case 1. Two of your subordinates routinely provide their children with school supplies from the office. How do you handle this situation?
   a. Lock up the supplies and issue them only as needed and signed for.
   b. Tell these two subordinates that supplies are for office use only.
   c. Report the theft of supplies to the head of security.
   d. Send a notice to all employees that office supplies are for office use only and that disregard will result in disciplinary action.

[1.] Permission granted by the author of *Gray Matters* (George Sammet, Jr., Vice-President, Office of Corporate Ethics, Martin Marietta Corporation, Orlando, Florida) to use these portions of *Gray Matters: The Ethics Game* ©1992. If you would like more information about the complete game, call 1–800–3ETHICS.

Case 2. Your operation is being relocated. The personnel regulations are complex and might influence your employees' decisions about staying on the "team." Relocating with no experienced staff would be very difficult for you. What do you tell your employees about their options?

a.   State that the relocation regulations are complex; you won't go into them right now. However, you tell them that everything probably will come out OK in the end.

b.   Suggest that they relocate with you, stating that a job in hand is worth an unknown in the bush.

c.   Present them with your simplified version of the regulations and encourage them to come along.

d.   Tell them only that you'd like them to relocate with you and conserve the team, which has worked so well together.

Case 3. A friend of yours wants to transfer to your division, but he may not be the best qualified for the job. You do have an opening, and one other person, whom you do not know, has applied. What do you do?

a.   Select the friend you know and in whom you have confidence.

b.   Select the other person, who you are told is qualified.

c.   Request a qualifications comparison of the two from the human resources department.

d.   Request the human resources department to extend the search for additional candidates before making the selection.

Case 4. Your new employee is the niece of the vice-president of finance. Her performance is poor, and she has caused trouble with her co-workers. What do you do?

a.   Call her in and talk to her about her inadequacies.

b.   Ask the human resources department to counsel her and put her on a performance improvement plan.

c.   Go see her uncle.

d.   Maybe her problems are caused by the newness of the job; give her some time to come around.

Case 5. After three months you discover that a recently hired employee who appears to be very competent falsified her employment application in that she claimed she had a college degree when she did not. As her supervisor, what do you do?

a.   You are happy with the new employee, so you do nothing.

b.   Discuss the matter with the human resources department to determine company policy.

c.   Recommend that she be fired for lying.

d.   Consider her performance, length of service, and potential benefit to the organization before making any recommendation to anyone.

Reference Guide: Building a Career

Becoming a supervisor can be a first step in a rewarding career as a manager. To make the most of this step, you need to be organized and active about building your career. This reference guide describes a basic process for career development, as well as some specific career-advancement tactics.

A Process for Developing Your Career

Even in organizations with a philosophy of sharing power, the structure of the organization is somewhat like a pyramid. In other words, there are more operative employees than managers and more supervisors than top managers. This means that there will always be competition for promotions. You cannot assume that because you are a supervisor, you will automatically rise to the top of the organization. In fact, you cannot consider your position a guarantee that you will go in any particular direction.

Your chances for achieving your career goals are greatest when you follow a rational process for career development. Figure A.1 illustrates the steps of such a process.

Self-Assessment

Before you can plan a direction for your career, you need to take a look at yourself—specifically, your strengths and weaknesses, your interests, your likes and dislikes. For starters, take the Self-Quiz on page 518 to identify positive ways of describing yourself. (Then use those words whenever you are looking for a job.) Also, you might review the topics in this book. Which activities do you think you do well already? Where do you need to improve or learn more? Which aspects of supervision sound fun, and which would you prefer to avoid?

Your self-assessment will be more accurate if you also get feedback from others. Performance appraisals can be a starting point, but do not rely solely on them. Remember from Chapter 15 that appraisals are subject to many sources of error. Also get formal or informal feedback from subordinates and peers. This approach

FIGURE A.1

The Career Development Process

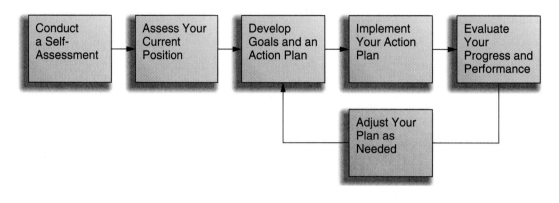

SELF-QUIZ *Evaluate Your Personality*

Mark each trait with a P (Present) to identify characteristics you presently possess or an F (Future) for those you wish to have in the future.

___ Academic	___ Cautious	___ Deliberate
___ Accurate	___ Charming	___ Determined
___ Active	___ Cheerful	___ Dignified
___ Adaptable	___ Clear-thinking	___ Discreet
___ Adventurous	___ Clever	___ Dominant
___ Affectionate	___ Competent	___ Eager
___ Aggressive	___ Competitive	___ Easygoing
___ Alert	___ Confident	___ Efficient
___ Ambitious	___ Conscientious	___ Emotional
___ Analytical	___ Conservative	___ Energetic
___ Appreciative	___ Considerate	___ Enthusiastic
___ Artistic	___ Consistent	___ Extroverted
___ Assertive	___ Cool	___ Fair-minded
___ Attractive	___ Cooperative	___ Farsighted
___ Bold	___ Courageous	___ Firm
___ Broad-minded	___ Courteous	___ Flexible
___ Businesslike	___ Creative	___ Forceful
___ Calm	___ Curious	___ Forgiving
___ Capable	___ Daring	___ Formal
___ Careful	___ Decisive	___ Frank

___ Friendly	___ Neat	___ Sensitive
___ Generous	___ Obliging	___ Serious
___ Gentle	___ Open-minded	___ Sharp-witted
___ Good-natured	___ Opportunistic	___ Sincere
___ Healthy	___ Organized	___ Sociable
___ Helpful	___ Original	___ Spontaneous
___ Honest	___ Outgoing	___ Stable
___ Hopeful	___ Painstaking	___ Steady
___ Humble	___ Patient	___ Strong
___ Humorous	___ Persevering	___ Strong-minded
___ Imaginative	___ Pleasant	___ Strong-willed
___ Independent	___ Poised	___ Supportive
___ Individualistic	___ Polite	___ Tactful
___ Industrious	___ Practical	___ Teachable
___ Informal	___ Precise	___ Tenacious
___ Intellectual	___ Progressive	___ Thorough
___ Intelligent	___ Prudent	___ Thoughtful
___ Introspective	___ Purposeful	___ Tolerant
___ Inventive	___ Quick	___ Tough
___ Kind	___ Quiet	___ Trusting
___ Leisurely	___ Rational	___ Trustworthy
___ Lighthearted	___ Realistic	___ Unaffected
___ Likable	___ Reflective	___ Unassuming
___ Logical	___ Relaxed	___ Understanding
___ Loving	___ Reliable	___ Unexcitable
___ Loyal	___ Reserved	___ Uninhibited
___ Mature	___ Resourceful	___ Verbal
___ Methodical	___ Responsible	___ Versatile
___ Meticulous	___ Retiring	___ Warm
___ Mild	___ Robust	___ Wholesome
___ Moderate	___ Secure	___ Wise
___ Modest	___ Self-confident	___ Witty
___ Motivated	___ Self-controlled	___ Zany
___ Natural	___ Sensible	

Source: G. Pasquini and C. M. Timura, *Psychology of Success: A Positive Approach to Lifelong Learning Workbook* (Homewood, Ill.: Irwin, 1990), Ch. 2.

was valuable for Michelle Milam when she was an M.B.A. candidate at Southern Methodist University. Based on self-assessment tests and reviews from former bosses, co-workers, and subordinates at Arthur Andersen, where she had worked, Milam found that she rated herself lower in most areas than her colleagues did. She concluded that she needed to build her self-confidence before starting a new job.[1]

Assessment of Current Position

Next, consider the position you currently hold and how you are performing in that position. Ask questions about your position that will help you understand your strengths. For example, what do you like about your current job? What do you dislike? What do you do well?

Also ask questions to determine whether you need to make a change. For example, does your current job give you a chance to learn new and valuable skills? Do you see realistic opportunities for advancement within your organization? You may decide that your current job does not fit your career goals at all—or at least not for much longer.

Development of Goals and Action Plan

With the information you have gathered from your self-assessment and assessment of your current position, you are ready to develop objectives for your career. Establish long-term (five years or more) as well as short-term objectives. Your short-term objectives are the intermediate steps you will need to take to reach your long-term goals.

Your objectives can include the industry you would like to work in (for example, government, entertainment, agriculture, banking), the area of work (such as sales, finance, or engineering), the size of the organization (small, medium, or large), and the location (area of the country; small-town, suburban, or urban). In making each of these choices, note which are particularly important to you and which you are willing to be flexible about. You may want to make some changes or compromises along the way. For example, you might accept a position in a big retail chain as a way to gain experience for reaching your ultimate goal of running your own hardware store ten years from now.

Do not just assume you want to climb some typical career ladder. Rather, consider the kinds of work that build on the strengths and interests you have identified in yourself. For example, if you love the noise and power of machinery, you may want to follow a career path that keeps you near the shop floor, even if that means you will never be the top executive. And if you are uncomfortable being responsible for other people and their performance, a career in management is probably not for you.

If you are not sure what path you want your career to take, many resources are available to help. Most colleges and universities have career development offices, and public libraries contain many books on the subject. Just two of the books that can help you plan a career and land a job are *What Color Is Your Parachute?* (Berkeley, Calif.: Ten Speed Press) and *Do-It-Yourself CareerKit* (Moraga, Calif.: Bridgewater Press). Ask to talk with people in the fields that interest you; most people are flattered to have a chance to share their expertise. In addition, career consultant Marilyn Moats Kennedy suggests meeting people at trade or professional groups and then asking them to let you visit them and follow them around for a day to see what their job is really like. She also suggests writing to companies and requesting biographies of managers and officers, which can show you the steps they took in their careers.[2]

When you have defined long-term and short-term objectives, determine what specific actions you need to take to reach those objectives. In other words, you devise action plans. These might include discussions with people who currently hold the kinds of jobs that interest you, as well as activities to build your skills and expertise. For example, some college students supplement their classroom work by participating in internships.

Notice that this is the same kind of planning process described in Chapter 2. That chapter's guidelines for planning apply well to the process of planning a career.

Implementation of Action Plan

Now you know what you need to do. The next step is to start doing the activities in your action plan. As obvious as that sounds, many people stall when it comes to carrying out their career plans. Perhaps the fear of failure is just too great. What if you do not get that promotion or new job when you try for it? Of course, if you do not even try, you are even less likely to get what you want.

Evaluation

As you carry out your action plans, remember to evaluate your progress and performance along the way. Are you achieving your short-term and intermediate goals? If not, do not give up. Setbacks are a part of life. Or maybe you were surprised by an opportunity to exceed your expectations. In either case, you will probably have to adjust your action plans to reflect these developments.

Kent L. Straat suggests a variety of questions to use in evaluating your performance:[3]

- What is your performance worth to your company? Have you made a measurable contribution to its performance? Is your department's budget or earnings growing? Are you solving problems, or just maintaining the status quo? Is management interested in the projects you are working on?
- Are you setting the right objectives? What does your boss think about your objectives? Do you usually achieve or exceed them? Did hard work or luck account for your successes?
- How do you compare with your peers? Does your performance stand out? How do you rank among your peers?
- Are you a leader and a motivator, or just a manager? Do you share any qualities with the leaders you know? With the people who are moving up in your company?
- What does your track record tell others about you?
- Do the people with power know what you are doing? Are you attracting promotions and job offers? Do you work at being visible (for example, by serving on committees and giving presentations)?

Straat recommends conducting this self-evaluation once a year.

Your experiences along the way not only can develop your skills but also can lead you to new interests. You may find, for example, that you are more fascinated by what is happening in a department other than your own. If so, you will want to take a fresh look at your career objectives. It may be appropriate to modify them to reflect your new strengths and interests.

Career-Advancement Tactics

Many of us would be happy with a world in which working hard and doing a good job were automatically rewarded. Of course, the world is more complicated than that. Hard work and high quality are important, but people with power have to notice, and they have to agree with the priorities you have set for where to make your efforts. To make the most of these realities, you can use a variety of tactics for career advancement. Some tactics are summarized in Figure A.2. With this approach to career development, you can benefit from appropriately using organization politics (see Chapter 19).

Develop Expertise

The people who get choice jobs are those with needed expertise. This concern is particularly relevant in today's work environment, with its many layoffs and corporate restructurings. Consultants Henry Conn and Joseph Boyett predict that the average American who begins a career in the 1990s will work in at least 10 jobs for at least five employers.[4] Thus, even the most skilled employees may find themselves hunting for a new position at various points in their career. Consequently, an important career tactic is to become an expert in valued areas. This expertise should cover a variety of skills and should not be limited to a narrow field such as cost accounting or printing press maintenance.[5] Important areas of expertise include basic supervisory and management skills, as well as knowledge of a particular trade, profession, or industry.

Expertise is not something you get once by taking a class and then retain for life. The skills you need are constantly expanding and changing. For example, there was a time when managers did not have to know how to get information on a computer or lead a team of employees. Those skills are necessary in many situations today.

As a result, part of developing expertise involves keeping up-to-date on how the needs for skills are changing and then looking for and seizing opportunities to acquire the newly important skills. This process can be especially important when you are in your fifties, when you have achieved the position you will need to hold until retirement and are too old to find another job easily.[6] Ways to acquire skills include reading informative books and magazines, attending seminars and workshops, taking classes, and participating in meetings of the professional or trade associations in your field.

You can also build your expertise by adding to your work experience. Volunteer for and accept assignments that will broaden your experience, even if they involve extra work and are not part of your job description. Also consider

FIGURE A.2

Some Tactics for Career Advancement

including lateral moves in your career path. A lateral move is a job change that does not involve a promotion, may not involve a pay increase, but does involve a new area of responsibility. A successful manager whose career path included several lateral moves is Bill Wilson, who held numerous positions with Kimberly-Clark Corporation before he left to start his own product development firm. After starting at Kimberly-Clark as an engineering trainee involved with hands-on technology, Wilson moved into research. Later he went from managing industrial products to commercial products, and then to service products. Eventually he took charge of the company's European operations and then returned to corporate headquarters, where he developed energy conservation strategies, saving the company millions of dollars. Following yet another transfer, Wilson took charge of the company's new-products division.[7]

Document Achievements

If you want your accomplishments to be appreciated, it is not enough just to have expertise or to do good work. No one can count on others to notice and appreciate everything he or she has done. Therefore, throughout your career, you must make sure that those in power know about your accomplishments. When you ask for a raise, a promotion, or a new job, you must be able to show why you are the right choice.

To do this, you will need to keep some record of what you have achieved. Whenever you get a favorable performance appraisal or a letter complimenting you for a job well done, keep a copy in your files. When your team accomplishes a goal, send a notice to the company newsletter, then keep a copy. Also save other evidence of any accomplishment you are proud of.

An important form of documentation you will need to prepare and regularly update is your **résumé**. This is a summary of your work-related skills and experience. Résumés that highlight specific accomplishments stand out from the more typical listings of colleges attended and positions held. Potential employers are most impressed by ways you have boosted revenues or cut costs. For example, it is

résumé
A summary of work-related skills and experience.

more impressive for a salesperson to have brought in a $1 million client than for him or her to have been responsible for selling to a particular territory.

It is also important to keep your résumé looking clean and professional.[8] It should be printed on good-quality white paper and look like a typewritten original. Send it—with a cover letter—in a typed envelope, and not by fax machine. (A faxed résumé not only looks tacky, it requires the recipient to pay for the paper.) When you are applying for a job, the cover letter should indicate the position you are applying for, explain how your qualifications can benefit the organization, refer to the résumé, and ask for an interview. For some sample résumés and a closer look at how to prepare a résumé, see the "Résumé Workbook" that follows this reference guide.

Find a Mentor

mentor
A higher-level manager who takes the role of showing a lower-level employee how to get along in the organization and making sure that the person gets recognized by other managers.

A higher-level manager in your organization can be an important source of guidance and other kinds of help. Therefore, you can benefit from having an ongoing relationship with such a manager. The higher-level person in this kind of relationship is often referred to as a **mentor**.

Mentors can help in a variety of ways.[9] They can improve your standing and skills in the organization by recommending you for various tasks, committees, and positions. By talking favorably about you and your achievements to others, they give you the exposure you need to get ahead. Mentors also coach, and they may stand up for you when organization politics is working against you. Finally, mentors help you develop personally by serving as role models, counseling you when you are uncertain what to do next, and encouraging you through their acceptance and friendship. These kinds of benefits are useful at every stage of a career, whether you are trying to get established, to maintain your position when your career has matured, or to plan a productive retirement.

Nevertheless, having a mentor does carry some risks. First, if your mentor becomes too dependent on you as an assistant, he or she may stifle your career by interfering with potential transfers or promotions. If your mentor loses favor in the organization, you can lose out, too, simply because you are known as an ally of that person. To avoid such risks, try to build a number of supportive relationships, rather than relying on one person to take care of you.

Who should be your mentor? An obvious choice is your own boss. However, not every boss makes a good mentor. You want someone with whom you have good rapport. To be helpful to you, the person also should have power and the respect of others in the organization.

Develop a Network of Contacts

Besides a mentor, you will need a wide range of contacts inside and outside the organization. If you have a variety of personal contacts, you will know whom to call to get a question answered or a problem solved. As shown in Figure A.3, these people are especially important when you are looking for another job. They can tell you where the good openings are (and which organizations to avoid). Like expertise, a network of contacts is especially important for older employees, who may face a greater challenge in finding a new job.[10]

FIGURE A.3

Ways People Found Their Jobs

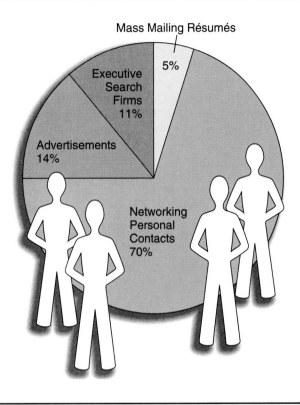

networking
The process of developing a variety of contacts inside and outside the organization.

To develop a variety of contacts—a process often called **networking**—you need to be active in the organization you work for and among your peers in your field. Volunteer to serve on committees. Join professional or trade associations, and participate in their activities. The same applies to community organizations and other causes you believe in. Look for opportunities to take on leadership roles in any of these organizations. However, be sure to select activities you actually feel committed to; if you are participating solely out of self-interest, others will catch on and will not be impressed.

When you become acquainted with people, offer them your business card. (If your company will not provide you with business cards, you can get a print shop to print cards with your name, address, and phone number for a relatively small cost.) Most people will give you their card in return. As you develop these contacts, remember that just as they may be able to help *you* out, you are making yourself available to *them*. The "Tips from the Firing Line" box provides further suggestions for networking.

Capitalize on Luck

It would be naive to pretend that good planning and expertise alone can guarantee a successful career. Some people get lucky. For example, someone might land a job with a boss who turns out to be a wonderful mentor. In any case, the people who

Networking Etiquette

If you want people to be a part of your network of contacts, you need to treat them as the important people they are for you. Leslie Smith, associate director of the National Association of Female Executives, offers the following guidelines for networking:

- *Focus on others*. Remember that successful networking is based on sharing, not on getting all you can take from others. You can lay the groundwork for a strong relationship by taking the lead in providing information or contacts.
- *Be upfront with others*. Let them know just what you want. If you are afraid to be straightforward about your needs, reevaluate your needs. Do not try to disguise an unreasonable request by being subtle.
- *Be considerate*. Respect other people's schedules. Do not call early or late on a weekend. Remember time differences if you are calling

someone in another time zone. Ask if you are calling at a good time. Identify yourself, explaining where you got the other person's name.
- *Be sensitive to changing fortunes*. Sometimes people are unemployed, so do not assume everyone you meet has a job. Instead of asking a new acquaintance, "Where do you work?" try, "What kind of work do you do?"
- *Think before joining an organization*. When you are considering involvement in an organization, ask yourself what you can contribute and how much time you can give. It is OK to limit your commitment to a set period and then move on. But remember that you are there to give as well as to receive.

Source: Leslie Smith, "Five Goals for the New Year," *Executive Female*, January–February 1992, p. 55.

are successful are those who act on the lucky breaks that come their way. Keep your eyes open to opportunities, then be ready to act when they come along.

To capitalize on luck, it helps to have the right outlook. W. Clement Stone, a pioneer in motivational thinking, advocated what he called a positive mental attitude.[11] According to Stone, the people most likely to succeed are those who expect success. To develop this expectation, Stone recommended, actively replace negative thoughts with positive ones—not unrealistic thoughts, but a positive view that is appropriate under the circumstances. For example, an insurance salesperson who thinks, "I doubt if anyone will really care about this new policy," lacks a positive mental attitude—and so does one who thinks, "I can sell this to anyone." In the latter case, the salesperson's unrealistic expectations would lead him or her to spend hours trying to persuade uninterested prospects. More in line with Stone's recommendations, the salesperson might try thinking, "The more people I present this policy to, the more sales I'll make," or, "By targeting the right people, I can sell this policy." A person with such an attitude is in the best position to be ready to make the most of the available opportunities.

Respond Positively to Setbacks

Just as we can get lucky sometimes, we also experience setbacks that we may or may not deserve. Even the best supervisor can get laid off during an economic downturn or fired when the boss is unreasonable. Or perhaps you apply for a job, knowing you are well qualified, but someone else applies who has the same qualifications as you and also went to the same college as the person who hires her.

You cannot put an end to setbacks, but you can decide how to respond to them. The key is to learn from them, then move on. When you do not achieve an objective, try to find out what went wrong. For example, if you were fired, consider the reason. Maybe you just did not fit in. Why not? What does that tell you about your strengths and weaknesses, and where would you fit in better? Perhaps it is time to adjust your goals and action plans. If you can learn something from a setback, then it was not really a failure.

Key Terms

résumé

mentor

networking

Exercise: Career Planning

Using the first three steps of the career development process described in this reference guide, develop career goals and an action plan for reaching them. Put your goals and plan in writing, being as specific as you can. If the task sounds overwhelming, remember that the goals you create are not etched in stone; you will be able to modify them based on your experiences.

In completing this exercise, consider the following questions:

- Do your goals meet the criteria for effective objectives, as discussed in Chapter 2?
- Will you expect to make lateral moves as part of your career path?
- What career-advancement tactics are included in your action plan?
- When do you plan to do your first evaluation of your progress and performance?

Résumé Workbook

Introduction

Finding a job after graduation is like climbing the rungs of a ladder. Each step is important, but you must begin with the first one. This workbook is designed to help you whether you are a stressed-out senior, a student who wishes to get a head start on your job search, or someone who is ready to make a career move.

Within these pages you will find invaluable information that will enable you to write a cover letter and a résumé which accurately portray your unique talents and personality. The effective use of this workbook will bring you one step closer to obtaining interviews for the job that you desire after graduation.

What Is a Cover Letter?

A cover letter is a one-page introduction to your résumé that briefly describes your purpose for sending the résumé. Use a cover letter to inquire about a possible job opening or to apply for a specific job. Make sure to always include a cover letter when sending a résumé. Write your cover letter to a specific person and use concise, clear sentences.

Prepared by Denise Colby. Editorial consultants: Corinne Livesay, Laurie Nutter, Shelley Siebert, and Carla Sloan. Reprinted with permission of the Liberty University Career Center © 1993, Lynchburg, VA.

Basic Cover Letter Format

Your Street Address
City, State Zip Code
Area Code and Telephone
Date

Name of Manager
Title and Department
Name of Company
Street Address
City, State Zip Code

Dear Mr./Ms. X:

State which job you are applying for and how you learned of the opening (employment agency, relative, friend, media). If you are inquiring about a possible job opening, then specify the type of job that you are seeking.

Explain why you are interested in the prospective job, company, and its services. Describe which character traits make you an ideal candidate for the job. Point out your academic background, a specific achievement, or work experience if applicable to your potential job. Try not to include the same information that is in your résumé.

Indicate you are enclosing a copy of your résumé. Conclude with a request for an appointment or personal interview at the reader's convenience. Close your letter in a manner that will encourage a speedy reply. For example, name a date on which you will call to set up your interview, ask if additional information or references are desired, or ask whether the company recruits in your area.

Sincerely,

Sign Your Name

Type Your Name

Enclosure

Cover Letter (Possible Job Opening)

35 Willow Street
Nashua, NH 03758
(000) 222–9900
March 13, 1994

Mr. William Radford
President, BestBank
118 Trenton Avenue
Nashua, NH 00099

Dear Mr. Radford:

Please consider me for any available positions you may have for an entry-level employee in your Customer Service Department.

My experience in the banking industry is varied. I have worked in the proof department, in collections, and on the teller line. This summer I had the opportunity to take on the duties of the head teller at Nation's Bank in Manchester while she was away on maternity leave.

Enclosed is a copy of my résumé. I will call your office on March 20 to see when you might be able to meet with me. I appreciate your time and consideration.

Sincerely,

Gage T. Flint

Gage T. Flint

Enclosure

Cover Letter (Specific Job Opening)

1047 Parkway Avenue
Boston, MA 09918
(000) 888-7765
April 15, 1994

Ms. Joyce Michaels, Manager
Country Dining
32 Lakeshore Drive
Boston, MA 00098

Dear Ms. Michaels:

Because your restaurant is well known for its excellent food and service, I was very excited to learn of the opportunity to assist in managing Country Dining. The position was brought to my attention by your head chef, Christopher Tyler.

As indicated on the enclosed résumé, I managed the University Snack Shop for three years while I was in college. Working with employees and interacting with customers brought me much personal satisfaction. I developed a coupon purchasing system in 1992, and it is still in use today.

I will contact your office on April 28 in order to set up a time when we can meet. I appreciate your time and consideration.

Sincerely,

Charles B. Johnson

Charles B. Johnson

Enclosure

What Is a Résumé?

A résumé is an overview of what you have to offer a prospective employer. It normally consists of sections such as caption, objective, education, experience, special categories, and references. The data can be presented in a chronological, functional, or combination format.

Types of Résumés

Chronological The chronological résumé is a list of types of experiences (education, work history, volunteer work, etc.) by date with your most recent activity presented first. Within each heading include a description of relevant information, such as the tasks you completed and your respective responsibilities. The main purpose of the chronological format is to present your résumé information in sequential order to show employers how your education, career, and abilities have progressed.

Functional The functional résumé emphasizes your skills and achievements. The basic headings, like experience, become more specific. The functional résumé may include headings such as Editing Skills, Leadership Skills, and Communication Skills. This format is not concerned with chronological order, as the chronological résumé is. The goal of the functional résumé is to communicate achievements by grouping related skills under a specific heading.

Combination The combination résumé is primarily a chronological résumé that includes some functional headings. The combination résumé may include headings such as Human Services Experience, Teaching Experience, and Business Experience. Headings are organized with the most recent experience listed first under each heading. This style capitalizes on the best aspects of the chronological and the functional formats.

Sections of a Résumé

This workbook highlights several categories that you may wish to include in your résumé. Strive to use the categories that best support your job objective. After the *caption*, order the categories based on those that present you in the most favorable way. For example, if you have a great deal of related work experience that supports your job objective, then you may choose to place *experience* before *education* on your résumé.

Caption   Place the caption at the top of your résumé and provide details where you can be contacted, if necessary. A caption should include your name, address, and telephone (Option 1). If you have a permanent and a temporary address, then include them both (Option 2). Do not use nicknames; if you are known by your middle name, then you may initial your first name (C. Todd Raymon).

Option 1

> **CHAD R. SMITH**
>
> 10 Tin Drive
> Croydon, NH 33224
> (000) 776–7765

Option 2

> **VIVIAN B. LYNN**
>
> 3 Old Street   Boston College
> Guild, NH 12112   Boston, MA 12100
> (000) 222–3333   (000) 998–0087

Objective   The purpose of a written objective in a résumé is to focus on the type of job that you would like. Writing an effective objective can be difficult, so here are a few options that are available to you.

Option 1:   Write an objective that specifically answers one or more of the following questions:

- What type of position are you seeking?
- At what type of organization or company do you want to work?
- Is there a specific geographical location where you prefer to live and work?

Examples:

- Copy editor for family magazine industry in New England.
- Research analyst for urban-based computer company.

You try Option 1:

_____

_____

_____

Option 2:   Present your objective as a skills profile. Using no more than two sentences, give an overview of the skills you want to be able to use on the job.

Examples:

- Highly motivated public speaker seeking a position that will utilize my creativity.
- Physically fit and enthusiastic individual seeking a position that will enable me to motivate children to enjoy exercise.

You try Option 2:

_____

_____

_____

Option 3:   You may wish to omit the objective section from your résumé. If you choose to do so, you should still write an objective and highlight it in your cover letter. Also, you should refer to your written objective while writing your résumé so that it maintains a clear focus. If you have selected this option, please write your objective in the following space.

Examples:

- Copy editor
- Biology teacher

You try Option 3:

_____

_____

_____

Education   Complete the following two exercises by examining the type of general educational information you might include and then listing your own.

Exercise 1:   General Education Information.

For example:

College(s) Attended	• Liberty University • University of New Hampshire
Degree(s) Earned	• Bachelor of Science
GPA	• 3.5/4.0
Major and Minor	• English, with a business minor
Graduation Date	• May 1994
Scholarships	• Chancellor's Scholarship, GPA Scholarship, Resident Assistant Scholarship

Please enter your general education information in the chart below:

College(s) Attended	• •
Degree(s) Earned	• •
GPA	• •
Major and Minor	• •
Graduation Date	• •
Scholarships	• •

Exercise 2:   List Specific Courses That Relate to Your Job Search.

For example:

• Literary Criticism	• Production Management
• Expository Writing	• Wage and Salary Administration
• Journalism	• Human Resource Management

Please list your job-related courses below:

•	•
•	•
•	•
•	•

Experience   Potential employers want to see that you have had experience. The following exercise is designed to help you remember work and volunteer experiences that support your job objective. When completing the exercise, make sure that you list *each* activity that you have completed as an employee and as a volunteer. The one experience that you overlook may be exactly what an employer is looking for, so make sure that you write all of them down. Please take note that even though you have written down all of your involvements, only the most suitable should finally be included in your résumé.

An example to guide you:

Employment	**Volunteer Work**
• Babysitter	• Prayer leader
• Waitress	• Coordinator of children's drama
• Bank teller	• Intern
• Resident assistant	• Little League coach
• Computer lab assistant	• Public speaker
• Club organizer	• Camp counselor
• House sitter	
• Construction worker	
• Research assistant	

Brainstorm and complete your own list of experience:

Employment	Volunteer Work
•	•
•	•
•	•
•	•
•	•
•	•
•	•
•	•

Now it is time to add some details to your list of experience. First, decide which experiences are most representative of your best capabilities or qualities that an employer could use to determine your qualifications for the job. Second, write down each *selected* experience, the name of your organization, the city and state where you worked or volunteered, the duration of your experience, and a brief description of your responsibilities.

For example:

- Computer Lab Assistant; Liberty University, Lynchburg, VA; 1990–1991. Oversaw the proper use of IBM '486 computers and tutored approximately fifteen students using WordPerfect and Lotus 1-2-3.
- Intern; Master Products, Lynchburg, VA; fall 1992. Worked under the management of the marketing department. Assisted in sales and layout of advertisements.
- Public Speaker; Creative Writing Workshop, Madison Heights, VA; fall 1991. Presented a weekend seminar sponsored by Writers of America, a nonprofit organization. Gave thirty seminar participants various exercises that are useful in writing clear and creative fiction.
- Club Organizer; Liberty University; fall 1991. Began a weekly literary club that discusses current trends in literature.

- Resident Assistant; Liberty University; August 1992–present. Supervised fifty female students. Exercised skills in the enforcement of rules, open communication, and proper counseling techniques. Utilized opportunities to demonstrate leadership, dedication, and reliability.
- Bank Teller; Lake Sunapee Savings Bank, Newport, NH; February 1991–August 1992. Completed customer transactions of checking and savings deposits and withdrawals. Handled large amounts of currency and balanced on a daily basis. Practiced effective communication skills to deal with the public and to represent the banking industry.
- Waitress; Schweitzer's Restaurant, Newport, NH; 1988–1991. Actively involved in food preparation, service, and cleaning responsibilities. Enjoyed the opportunity to become acquainted with various cultures and personalities. Exercised ability to effectively communicate with all types of people.

Helpful Hints   Some helpful hints are provided to assist you in completing your descriptions of your experience in a manner that will best promote your skills to your potential employer.

- Captivate your reader's attention by using clear, concise, and interesting language.
- Use consistent verb tenses and parallel grammatical constructions.
- Do not begin sentences within your description with "I." The list below will help you use phrases that start with action-oriented words.

101 Action-Oriented Words

accomplish	coordinate	exercise	maintain	reinforce
account	counsel	exhibit	manage	renovate
achieve	create	expedite	maximize	repair
acquire	delegate	facilitate	motivate	represent
administer	demonstrate	finance	negotiate	research
arbitrate	design	forecast	officiate	revise
audit	determine	formulate	organize	scrutinize
authorize	devise	gather	originate	solve
begin	direct	generate	oversee	strengthen
brief	distribute	gross	participate	supervise
budget	draft	handle	pinpoint	teach
build	edit	head	prepare	translate
calculate	educate	identify	procure	travel
catalog	eliminate	implement	program	uncover
chair	employ	improve	promote	update
command	establish	incorporate	propose	utilize
communicate	estimate	initiate	prove	verify
compose	evaluate	innovate	qualify	
conceive	examine	integrate	recognize	
confront	excel	launch	recommend	
construct	execute	lead	rehabilitate	

Now create your own activity and job description:

•
•
•
•
•
•
•
•
•
•

Special Categories If you have recently graduated from college and have little work experience, then you may wish to include an *interests* category that lists phrases which describe interests and hobbies that support your job objective. Other special categories that might support your job objective are *computer skills, special projects, certifications, professional memberships, awards, research, publications,* or *seminars.*

For example:

- Collect pictures of fossils and other extinct species
- Lived in Brazil for ten years
- Bicycled coast to coast during summer of 1989
- Oldest of seven children; often cared for siblings and managed household duties while both parents worked 50 hours per week

- Teaching certification in NH and VA
- Attended 1991 Writers Conference of America in New York
- Received Citizenship Award, Model Student Award
- Attended writing workshop that dealt with proper writing and editing processes, May 1990
- Member of Sigma Tau Delta, an English honorary society
- Enjoy researching family history of clients
- Skilled in Microsoft Word for Windows and Excel for Windows, Lotus 1-2-3, and WordPerfect
- Member of American Psychological Association
- Article featured in monthly publication of a telecommunications journal
- Attended state nursing conference and gave presentation on fertility drugs

Please enter your special category information below:

•
•
•
•
•
•
•

References   Choosing references is an important step in your job search. Following are some guidelines.

- Select three to six individuals as your references and write down their names.
- If you know someone who is well known or who has a respected position or title, then include that person in your list. Choose from faculty members, past and present employers, and personal friends.
- Contact each person and ask him or her to be your reference. If they agree to do so, then give them a copy of your résumé.

- You may choose not to include a reference statement at the bottom of your résumé. However, you should be prepared to provide each prospective employer with a typewritten list of your references' names, titles, addresses, and telephone numbers so that the references may be contacted when necessary.

For example:

Name/Title	Address/Phone	Agreed to Be Reference	Given Copy of Résumé
Dr. Tom Green Chairman	English Department Dartmouth College Hanover, NH 02117 (000) 998–9987	✓	✓
Dr. Mark Ensign President	Best Bank Newport, NH 03003 (000) 009–8876	✓	✓
Dr. Tammie Lock Professor	English Department Liberty University Lynchburg, VA 00211 (000) 323–3298	✓	✓

Please enter your reference information below:

Name/Title	Address/Phone	Agreed to Be Reference	Given Copy of Résumé

Résumé Examples

Now that you have completed all of the exercises, it is time to synthesize all of your information. The following résumés use the information you have seen as examples throughout the workbook to illustrate the three options (chronological, functional, and combination) for preparing your résumé. After looking over the sample résumés, put your own résumé together to represent your credentials most favorably and forcibly.

SUE M. CHRONOLOGICAL

RFD 2 Box 214P
Rands Pond Road
Newport, NH 03773
(000) 778–9965

Box 00000
Liberty University
Lynchburg, VA 24506
(000) 998–9909

OBJECTIVE Copy editor for family magazine industry

EDUCATION B.S., English Major; Business Minor; Liberty University, Lynchburg, VA; May 1994; GPA 3.6/4.0

EMPLOYMENT *Resident Assistant*, Liberty University. Supervised fifty female students. Exercised skills in the enforcement of rules, open communication, and proper counseling techniques. Utilized opportunities to demonstrate leadership, dedication, and reliability. August 1992–present.

Bank Teller, Lake Sunapee Savings Bank, Newport, NH. Completed customer transactions of checking and savings deposits and withdrawals. Handled large amounts of currency and balanced on a daily basis. Practiced effective communication skills to deal with the public and to represent the banking industry. February 1992–August 1992.

Computer Lab Assistant, Liberty University. Oversaw the proper use of IBM computers and tutored approximately fifteen students using WordPerfect and Lotus 1-2-3. 1990–1991.

Waitress, Schweitzer's Restaurant, Newport, NH. Actively involved in food preparation, serving, and cleaning. Enjoyed the opportunity to become acquainted with various cultures and personalities. Exercised ability to effectively communicate with all types of people. 1988–1991.

EXPERIENCE *Intern*, Chamber of Commerce, Lynchburg, VA. Worked as a research assistant and compiled data concerning assigned topics. Promoted to head researcher by the middle of the semester. Fall 1993.

Club Organizer, Word Power, Liberty University. Began a weekly club that discusses current trends in literature. Fall 1991–present.

Public Speaker, Creative Writing Workshop. Presented a weekend seminar sponsored by Writers of America, a nonprofit organization. Gave thirty Liberty students various exercises that are useful in writing clear and creative fiction. Fall 1992.

SUE P. FUNCTIONAL

27 Old Brook Road
Goshen, NH 00000
(999) 666–7765

13 Dairy Hill Drive
Lynchburg, VA 01002
(977) 667–4434

EDUCATION

Bachelor of Science, English; Liberty University, Lynchburg, VA; May 1993; GPA 3.6

University of New Hampshire, Durham, NH; Honors Program, 1989

RESEARCH SKILLS

Intern, Chamber of Commerce, Lynchburg, VA. Worked as a research assistant and compiled data concerning assigned topics. Promoted to head researcher by the middle of the semester.

LEADERSHIP SKILLS

Resident Assistant, Liberty University. Supervised fifty female students. Exercised skills in the enforcement of rules, open communication, and proper counseling techniques. Utilized opportunities to demonstrate leadership, dedication, and reliability.

Club Organizer, Word Power, Liberty University. Began a weekly literary club where members discuss current trends in literature.

COMPUTER SKILLS

Computer Lab Assistant, Liberty University. Oversaw the proper use of IBM '486 computers and tutored approximately fifteen students using WordPerfect and Lotus 1-2-3.

COMMUNICATION SKILLS

Bank Teller, Lake Sunapee Savings Bank, Newport, NH. Completed customer transactions of checking and savings deposits and withdrawals. Handled large amounts of currency and balanced on a daily basis. Exercised effective communication skills to deal with the public and to represent the banking industry.

Waitress, Schweitzer's Restaurant, Newport, NH. Actively involved in food preparation, serving, and cleaning. Enjoyed the opportunity to become acquainted with various cultures and personalities. Exercised ability to effectively communicate with all types of people.

Public Speaker, Creative Writing Workshop. Presented a weekend seminar sponsored by Writers of America, a nonprofit organization. Gave thirty seminar participants various exercises that are useful in writing clear and creative fiction.

SUE B. COMBINATION

2345 Tropical Drive
Miami, Florida 00212
(000) 776–1122

Education

Bachelor of Science, English; Liberty University, Lynchburg, VA; May 1993 GPA 3.6; worked thirty hours per week to finance education.

Editing Experience

Intern, Chamber of Commerce, Lynchburg, VA. Worked as a research assistant and compiled data concerning assigned topics. Promoted to head researcher by the middle of the semester. Fall 1992.

Leadership Experience

Resident Assistant, Liberty University. Supervised fifty female students. Exercised skills in the enforcement of rules, open communication, and proper counseling techniques. Utilized opportunities to demonstrate leadership, dedication, and reliability. Fall 1992.

Club Organizer, Word Power, Liberty University. Began a weekly club where members discuss current trends in literature. Fall 1991–present.

Communication Skills

Bank Teller, Lake Sunapee Savings Bank, Newport, NH. Completed customer transactions of checking and savings deposits and withdrawals. Handled large amounts of currency and balanced on a daily basis. Practiced effective communication skills to deal with the public and to represent the banking industry. February 1991–August 1991.

Public Speaker, Creative Writing Workshop. Presented a weekend seminar sponsored by Writers of America, a non-profit organization. Gave thirty seminar participants various exercises that are useful in writing clear and creative fiction. Fall 1991.

Computer Lab Assistant, Liberty University. Oversaw the proper use of IBM '486 computers and tutored approximately fifteen students using WordPerfect and Lotus 1 -2-3. 1990–1991.

Waitress, Schweitzer's Restaurant, Newport, NH. Actively involved in food preparation, serving, and cleaning. Enjoyed the opportunity to become better acquainted with various cultures and personalities. Exercised ability to effectively communicate with all types of people. 1988–1991.

Membership

Sigma Tau Delta, 1991–present.

Other Examples

CHARLOTTE DAVIS

12 Maple Drive
Harrisburg, PA 00110
(000) 999–0000

Objective	Human services related position dealing with children and/or adolescents
Education	B.S. Psychology; Human Services/Counseling Concentration Liberty University, Lynchburg, VA; May 1994.
Related Experience	*Camp Counselor*, Trinity Youth Camp, Keystone, FL; Summers 1990–1993. Supervised and lived in cabins with girls ages 8–12. Invested time and energy into counseling them concerning physical, social, and spiritual matters.
	Activities Coordinator and Instructor, Lynchburg Detention Center, Lynchburg, VA; Spring semester 1992. Supervised sports activities and gave seminars regarding proper exercise and nutrition. Promoted attitude of sportsmanship to a group of twenty-five junior high school students.
	Teacher's Aide, Rustburg Middle School, Rustburg, VA; September 1990–May 1991. Assisted teacher in classroom activities and recess supervision for grade 6. Gained knowledge concerning the struggles that a typical sixth grader deals with on a daily basis.
	Sunday School Teacher, White Rock Presbyterian Church, Harrisburg, PA; 1988–1990. Prepared weekly lesson, incorporating relevant crafts and visual aids, for group of 40 preschoolers.
Memberships	American Psychological Association
	Attended Virginia Psychological Association convention; gave presentation on "latch-key" children; Fall 1992
References	Available upon request

OLIVIA R. PETERS

21 Oak Drive
Atlanta, GA 00001
(000) 999–2211

Objective	Seeking entry-level position in television industry in a company located in the Southwest
Education	Bachelor of Science, Liberty University, Lynchburg, VA; May 1992 Telecommunications, Video Production concentration
Experience	*Production Manager*, WXLU-TV, Richmond, VA. Supervised the production of four biweekly shows concerning student issues. Summer 1991
	Studio Supervisor, WXLU-TV, Richmond, VA. Supervised productions, master control, editing, and quality control of student projects. Kept records of and conducted maintenance on equipment used by students. Summer 1991
	Production Technician, WTU-TV1, Roanoke, VA. Camera, chyron, audio, editing, ENG. Summer 1990
Special Project	"Peters' Part," monthly article featured in *Ready, Shoot*, a telecommunications journal that is published in the Northeast.
References	Dr. Tom Black, Chairman, Telecommunications Department, Liberty University, Lynchburg, VA 24506; (000) 244–4444
	Mr. John Wellet, President, WXLU-TV, Richmond, VA 28990; (000) 642-0000
	Mr. Gary Nichols, Vice-President, WTU-TV1, Roanoke, VA 23112; (000) 342–6753

Demo Tape Available upon Request

CHRISTOPHER J. WRIGHT

RR 1 Box 3   Box 00099
34 C Street   Ohio State University
E. Douglas, MA 00015   Columbus, OH 00006
(000) 222–7332   (000) 888–0009

OBJECTIVE   Management position in food industry

EDUCATION   Bachelor of Science; Ohio State University, Columbus, OH
                     Business Major, Concentration in Management; May 1993
                     GPA 3.85/4.0

FOOD SERVICE   **Assistant Manager,** Friendly's Restaurant, Columbus, OH; 1993–present.
EXPERIENCE   Responsible for employees' schedules, payroll, and quality customer service.
                     Currently working forty hours a week while finishing final semester of
                     college.

                     Student Manager, Marriott Food Service, Columbus, OH; 1992. Trained
                     and supervised over 75 part-time and full-time student employees.
                     Responsible for organizing meal preparation for 2,000 students per shift.

                     Caterer, The Wright Choice; summers 1988–1992. Worked as head waiter
                     for family-owned business. Able to gain working knowledge of how to
                     manage a business in the food industry.

OTHER   **Sales Clerk,** Sears, Columbus, OH; 1989–1992. Responsible for
EXPERIENCE   customer sales transactions and for taking inventory of merchandise.

ACTIVITIES   Managed a personal snack shop in dorm room of residence hall. 1991–1993.

                     Coordinator for area high school Future Business Leaders of America.
                     1990–1993.

SPECIAL   Director, summer computer project, University of Massachusetts.
PROJECT   Programming troubleshooter for new graphics package/IBM PC and
                     Macintosh versions; to be available for public use 1994.

Finishing Touches

Graphical Emphasis

- Make sure that the format of your résumé is orderly and professional.
- Design the layout so that the reader's eye will be drawn to your strongest qualities.
- CAPITALIZATION, <u>underlining</u>, **bold**, and *italic* print may be used in moderation for your name, your headings, and your strongest points.
- Make sure that you use consistent punctuation throughout your résumé.

Proofreading

- Have a competent individual with a good grasp of the English language critique your résumé concerning format, content, and mechanics.
- Make sure that your final draft is proofread by at least two individuals.
- Make sure that all errors are corrected.

Typing

- If possible, have a professional type your résumé.
- If you are typing your own résumé, then make sure that you use a typewriter that strikes a carbon (not cloth) ribbon to get the best results.
- Make sure that the correction tape works properly. Do not use correction fluid.

Word Processing

- Make sure that you save your résumé on disk so that you can revise it later, if necessary.
- Use a letter-quality printer—not a dot-matrix printer.

Paper

- Use either 100 percent cotton paper or 35 percent cotton blend.
- The color of the paper should be white, off white (ivory), light gray, or buff.
- Make sure that your cover letter, résumé, and envelope are of the same kind and color of paper.

Copies

- Make sure that the printer you select uses 100 percent cotton paper.
- Always ask for two sample copies of your résumé before ordering.
- Insist on only flawless copies.

Resources for Further Information

Allen, Jeffrey G. *The Perfect Job Reference.* New York: John Wiley & Sons, 1990.

Asher, Donald. *From College to Career.* Berkeley: Ten Speed Press, 1992.

Baxter, Rogene, and Marcelle Brashear. *Do-It-Yourself CareerKit: A Career Planning Tool.* Moraga, CA: Bridgewater Press, 1990.

Bolles, Richard Nelson. *The 1994 What Color Is Your Parachute?* Berkeley, CA: Ten Speed Press, 1994.

Corwen, Leonard. *Your Résumé: Key to a Better Job.* New York: Simon & Schuster, 1988.

Elkins, James K. *The Career Primer.* Augusta: Career Planning Services, 1990.

Furr, Thomas R. *The Street Smart Way to a Job!* Centerville, VA: Denlinger's Publishers, Ltd., 1992.

Good, Edward C. *Does Your Résumé Wear Blue Jeans?* Charlottesville: Francis L. Buck, 1985.

Hjorth, Linda Stevens. *Irwin Career Handbook.* Homewood, IL: Irwin, 1993.

Rosenburg, Arthur D., and David V. Hizer. *The Résumé Handbook.* Holbrook: Bob Adams, 1990.

Seguin, Marilyn. *The Perfect Portfolio.* Hawthorne: The Career Press, 1991.

Chapter 1

1. "A Challenge for the 1990s—Managing the Diverse Workforce," in *The Challenge of Diversity: Equal Employment Opportunity and Managing Differences in the 1990's* (Rockville, Md.: BNA Communications, n.d.).

2. Jolie Solomon, "As Cultural Diversity of Workers Grows, Experts Urge Appreciation of Differences," *The Wall Street Journal*, September 12, 1990, pp. Bl, B8.

3. Thomas G. Exter, "In and Out of Work," *American Demographics*, June 1992, p. 63.

4. Exter, "In and Out of Work."

5. See, for example, "The Spare Sex," *The Economist*, March 28, 1992, p. 20.

6. William P. Anthony, "Managing Diversity, Then and Now," *The Wall Street Journal*, July 3, 1992, p. A6.

7. "Improving Your Supervisory Skills: The Basics Plus," *Maintenance Supervisor's Bulletin* (Bureau of Business Practice), January 10, 1992, p. 2.

8. Carol Hymowitz, "When Firms Cut Out Middle Managers, Those at the Top and Bottom Often Suffer," *The Wall Street Journal*, April 5, 1990, pp. Bl, B4.

9. Story adapted from Bill Kelley, "From Salesperson to Manager: Transition and Travail," *Sales & Marketing Management*, February 1992, pp. 32–36.

10. See Connie Wallace, "Sizing Up Your New Staff," *Working Woman*, May 1990, pp. 29–31.

11. Wallace, "Sizing Up Your New Staff," p. 30.

12. Kelley, "From Salesperson to Manager," p. 34.

13. "Moving on Up: Handling Your Own Promotion," *Maintenance Supervisor's Bulletin*, December 10, 1991, pp. 1–4.

14. This paragraph is based on ideas in Roberta Maynard, "How to Be a Great Boss," *Nation's Business*, December 1991, pp. 44–45.

Chapter 2

1. *Fortune*, December 2, 1991, p. 59.

2. "Planning for Success," *Front Line Supervisor's Bulletin* (Bureau of Business Practice), February 25, 1992, pp. 1–2.

3. Henry Fersko-Weiss, "Project Managers: A New Focus on Graphics and Resource Controls," *PC Magazine*, February 11, 1992, pp. 38–39.

Chapter 3

1. "Sales Systems Help Digital Move to Account Based Selling," advertisement in *Sales & Marketing Management*, January 1992, p. 32.

2. John Grossmann, "Ken Iverson: Simply the Best," *American Way*, August 1, 1987, pp. 23–25; Richard Preston, "American Steel," *American Way*, December 15, 1991, pp. 79–82.

3. James B. Treece, "Will GM Learn from Its Own Role Models?" *Business Week*, April 9, 1990, p. 62.

4. Norma Jean Schmieding, "The Complexity of an Authority Role," *Nursing Management*, January 1992, p. 58.

5. The factors described in this paragraph are based on Harold Koontz, "Making Theory Operational: The Span of Management," *Journal of Management Studies*, October 1966, pp. 229–243; and Raymond L. Hilgert and Theo Haimann, *Supervision: Concepts and Practices of Management*, 5th ed. (Cincinnati, Ohio: South-Western Publishing Co., 1991), pp. 189–190.

6. DeAnne Rosenberg, "Delegation Is *Not* a Dirty Word," *Quality Digest*, September 1992, pp. 51–53.

7. "Getting Things Done through People," *Front Line Supervisor's Bulletin* (Bureau of Business Practice), July 10, 1992, pp. 1–2.

8. Peter F. Drucker, "Management Lessons of Irangate," *The Wall Street Journal*, March 24, 1987.

9. "Managers Who Type Too Much," *Sales & Marketing Management*, January 1992, p. 48.

Chapter 4

1. *Boardroom Reports*, August 15, 1992, p. 2, citing Paul B. Malone III, *Abuse 'Em and Lose 'Em* (Annandale, Va.: Synergy Press).

2. James M. Kouzes and Barry Z. Posner, "The Credibility Factor: What Followers Expect from Their Leaders," *Management Review*, January 1990, pp. 29–33.

3. Roger Ailes, "Lighten Up! Stuffed Shirts Have Short Careers," *Newsweek*, Management Digest special advertising section, May 18, 1992, p. 10.

4. Peter L. Thigpen, "Creating the Covenant," *Quality Digest*, August 1992, pp. 63–64.

5. Sondra Thiederman, *Bridging Cultural Barriers for Corporate Success: How to Manage the Multicultural Work Force* (Lexington, Mass.: Lexington Books, 1991), p. 80.

6. Bradford McKee, "A Business in Crisis Has No Time for Democracy," *Nation's Business*, July 1992, pp. 8, 17.

7. Walter Kiechel III, "The Boss as Coach," *Fortune*, November 4, 1991, pp. 201, 204.

8. Joseph Lipsey, personal correspondence.

9. Elwood N. Chapman, *Your Attitude Is Showing: A Primer of Human Relations*, 6th ed. (New York: Macmillan, 1991), p. 5.

10. Kouzes and Posner, "The Credibility Factor," p. 30.

11. Jim Kouzes, "The 10 Commitments of Leadership," *Quality Digest*, July 1992, pp. 47–49.

Chapter 5

1. "Privileged Information," *Boardroom Reports*, September 1, 1992, p. 2, citing T. Scott Gross, *Positively Outrageous Service: New and Easy Ways to Win Customers for Life* (New York: MasterMedia Ltd.).

Chapter 6

1. Ulf Dreber, John Condon, Bjorn Thunqvist, and Darlene Meskell, "Cost of Quality: Sweden Post Increases Customer Service *and* Saves Millions," *Quality Digest*, May 1992, pp. 45–51.

2. Taken from "Critical Quality," *Total Quality Newsletter*, January 1992, p. 8.

3. Ronald E. Yates, "Managing Quality: Certainty Not Part of the Equation," *Chicago Tribune*, January 27, 1992, sec. 4, pp. 1–2.

4. See John A. Byrne, "The Prophet of Quality," *Business Week*, January 28, 1991, p. 14.

5. Aaron Berstein, "Quality Is Becoming Job One in the Office, Too," *Business Week*, April 29, 1992, pp. 52–53, 56.

6. Definition based on Frank Voehl, "Getting Started with Total Quality," *Quality Digest*, May 1992, p. 17.

7. John Hillkirk, "New Award Cites Teams with Dreams," *USA Today*, April 10–12, 1992, pp. 1A–2A.

8. Steve Mitra, "Hospitals Try Treating Their Patients Like Customers," *Chicago Tribune*, August 2, 1992, sec. 7, p. 2.

9. Jaclyn H. Park, "Quality on Tap," *GSB Chicago* (University of Chicago Graduate School of Business), Spring 1992, pp. 20–25.

10. Park, "Quality on Tap."

11. Joshua Hyatt, "Surviving on Chaos," *Inc.*, May 1990, pp. 60–62ff.

12. "TQM and the Bottom Line," *Supervisory Management*, July 1992, p. 12.

13. "TQM 101: The Basics of Total Quality Management," *Commitment Plus* (Quality and Productivity Management Association), November 1991, pp. 1–4.

14. Mitra, "Hospitals Try Treating Their Patients Like Customers."

15. "TQM 101."

16. "The 'Heart' of TQM," *Commitment Plus* (Quality & Productivity Management Association), October 1991, pp. 1, 4.

17. Bernstein, "Quality Is Becoming Job One," p. 53.

18. "Making the Quality Connection," *Front Line Supervisor's Bulletin*, April 25, 1992, pp. 1–2.

19. Marion Harmon, "Internal Award Programs: Benchmarking the Baldrige to Improve Corporate Quality," *Quality Digest*, May 1992, pp. 20–24ff.

20. Jeremy Main, "Is the Baldrige Overblown?" *Fortune*, July 1, 1991, pp. 62–65.

21. Main, "Is the Baldrige Overblown?" p. 64.

22. This paragraph is based on information in Eugene Sprow, "Insights into ISO 9000," *Manufacturing Engineering*, September 1992, pp. 73–77.

23. Nancy K. Austin, "Hot Topics: Benchmarking," *Working Woman*, March 1992, p. 45.

24. Jerry G. Bowles, "Quality '92: Leading the World-Class Company," *Fortune*, September 21, 1992, special advertising section, p. 63.

25. Keith H. Hammonds, "Corning's Class Act," *Business Week*, May 13, 1991, p. 70.

26. "Making the Quality Connection."

27. James L. Heskett, W. Earl Sasser, Jr., and Leonard A. Schlesinger, "How to Improve Service to Improve Profits," *Boardroom Reports*, September 1, 1992, p. 8.

28. Tom Salemme, "Lessons Learned from Employees about Quality Improvement Efforts," *Tapping the Network Journal*, Fall–Winter 1991, pp. 2–6.

29. Hyatt, "Surviving on Chaos."

30. Ibid.

31. Dennis Sowards, "TQM Is a Journey: So Where Do We Begin?" *Industrial Engineering*, January 1992, pp. 24–28.

32. "Quality Improvement Requires Continuing Employee Participation," *NIBA News Bulletin* (Northern Illinois Business Association), March 1992, p. 10.

33. Ronald E. Yates, "For Motorola, Quality an Olympian Effort," *Chicago Tribune*, January 27, 1992, sec. 4, pp. 1–2.

Chapter 7

1. George Gendron, "FYI," *Inc.*, February 1992, p. 11.

2. William V. Haney, *Communication and Interpersonal Relations: Text and Cases*, 6th ed. (Homewood, Ill.: Richard D. Irwin, 1992), p. 290.

3. Carl R. Rogers and Richard E. Farson, "Active Listening," reprinted in William V. Haney, *Communication and Interpersonal Relations: Text and Cases*, 6th ed. (Homewood, Ill.: Richard D. Irwin, 1992), pp. 158–159.

4. Haney, *Communication and Interpersonal Relations*, p. 286.

5. Tony Mauro, "Justice's Gentle Reminder: She's Not a He," *USA Today*, November 14, 1991, p. 3A.

6. "The Spare Sex," *The Economist*, March 28, 1992, pp. 17–18, 20.

7. This example is taken from Sondra Thiederman, *Bridging Cultural Barriers for Corporate Success: How to Manage the Multicultural Work Force* (New York: Lexington Books, 1991), p. 24.

8. Thiederman, *Bridging Cultural Barriers*, p. 136.

9. Brett Pauly, "Off Hand: Some Well-Intentioned Gestures Don't Always Mean All's Well," *Chicago Tribune*, February 10, 1992, sec. 5, pp. 1, 3.

10. The ideas in this paragraph are based on Catherine R. Benson and Arlene M. Sperhac, "Image Building: Putting Your Best Foot Forward," *Healthcare Trends & Transition*, January 1992, pp. 26–29ff.

11. David Jackson, "Memos an Art Form at City Hall," *Chicago Tribune*, April 26, 1992, sec. 1, pp. 1, 16.

12. The ideas in this paragraph are drawn from Mary Rowland, "Shedding the Fear of Speaking," *New York Times*, May 17, 1992, p. F5; and Bristol Voss, "Speak for Yourself," *Sales & Marketing Management*, January 1992, pp. 77–82.

13. Ripley Hotch, "How to Stay in Touch over the Network," *Nation's Business*, July 1992, p. 60.

14. *Profiles in Quality: Blueprints for Action from 50 Leading Companies* (Boston: Allyn and Bacon, 1991), p. 46.

15. Patti Doten, "Flying Rumors May Mean a Crash Landing," *Chicago Tribune*, January 14, 1992, sec. 5, pp. 1, 7.

16. Lindsey Novak and Lauren Spier, "Workplace Solutions: When Gossip Gets Back to the Boss," *Chicago Tribune*, February 16, 1992, sec. 8, p. 1.

17. Based on *The Front Line Supervisor's Standard Manual* (Waterford, Conn.: Bureau of Business Practice, 1989), pp. 42–43.

18. Based on Mortimer R. Feinberg, "How to Get the Grapevine on Your Side," *Working Woman*, May 1990, p. 23.

Chapter 8

1. Clark Wigley, "Working Smart on Tough Business Problems," *Supervisory Management*, February 1992, p. 1.

2. This section is based largely on the excellent discussion of stereotypes in Sondra Thiederman, *Bridging Cultural Barriers for Corporate Success: How to Manage the Multicultural Work Force* (New York: Lexington Books, 1991), pp. 11–22.

3. This paragraph is based on *The Front Line Supervisor's Standard Manual* (Waterford, Conn.: Bureau of Business Practice, 1989), p. 55.

4. Lee Thé, "Organize Your E-MailBag," *Datamation*, March 1, 1992, p. 74.

5. Wigley, "Working Smart," p. 1.

6. See Irving L. Janis, *Groupthink: Psychological Studies of Policy Decisions and Fiascoes*, 2d ed. (Boston: Houghton Mifflin, 1982).

7. Aimee L. Stern, "Why Good Managers Approve Bad Ideas," *Working Woman*, May 1992, pp. 75, 104.

8. Andrew S. Grove, "In Search of Big Ideas," *Working Woman*, June 1992, pp. 22, 24.

9. David M. Armstrong, "Management by Storytelling," *Executive Female*, May–June 1992, pp. 38–41ff.

10. Joseph Alan Redman, "Nine Creative Brainstorming Techniques," *Quality Digest*, August 1992, pp. 50–51.

11. James Webb Young, *A Technique for Producing Ideas* (Chicago: Crain Communications, 1975).

12. Young, *A Technique for Producing Ideas*, pp. 59–60.

13. Magaly Olivero, "Get Crazy! How to Have a Breakthrough Idea," *Working Woman*, September 1990, pp. 145–147ff.

14. Magaly Olivero, "Some Wacko Ideas That Worked," *Working Woman*, September 1990, pp. 147, 222.

15. Stratford P. Sherman, "America Won't Win Till It Reads More," *Fortune*, November 18, 1991, pp. 201–204.

Chapter 9

1 See, for example, Abraham Maslow, *Eupsychian Management* (Homewood, Ill.: Richard D. Irwin, 1965); and C. P. Alderfer, "An Empirical Test of a New Theory of Human Needs," *Organization Behavior and Human Performance* 4 (1969), pp. 142–175.

2. Micheal P. Cronin, "Piquing Employee Interest," *Inc.*, August 1992, p. 83.

3. Sharon Nelton, "Motivating for Success," *Nation's Business*, March 1988, pp. 18–19ff.

4. John R. Schermerhorn, Jr., William N. Gardner, and Thomas N. Martin, "The Trouble with Bob: A Drama in Managerial Life," *Executive Female*, September–October 1991, pp. 42–47.

5. "Study: More Companies Link Compensation to Quality," *Total Quality*, April 1992, p. 6.

6. Andrea Gabor, "After the Pay Revolution, Job Titles Won't Matter," *New York Times*, May 17, 1992, p. F5.

7. Ellyn E. Spragins, "The All-Purpose Incentive System," *Inc.*, February 1992, pp. 103–104.

8. Susan Greco, "Great Pay for Great Service," *Inc.*, September 1992, p. 27.

9. Susan Greco and Phaedra Hise, "How to Unite Field and Phone Sales," *Inc.*, July 1992, p. 115.

10. Nucor Corporation brochure.

11. Aldo J. Massaferro, Jr., J. Clarence Morrison, and John C. Tumazos, "Lessons from Nucor," *Boardroom Reports*, December 1, 1991, pp. 7–8.

12. John A. Parnell, "Five Reasons Why Pay Must Be Based on Performance," *Supervision*, February 1991, pp. 6–8.

13. Rosemary F. Lyons, "Cross-Training: A Richer Staff for Leaner Budgets," *Nursing Management*, January 1992, pp. 43–44.

14. George Gendron, "FYI: Schwarzkopf on Leadership," *Inc.*, January 1992, p. 11.

15. Gabor, "After the Pay Revolution."

16. Will Kaydos, "Motivating by Measuring Performance," *Quality Digest*, May 1992, pp. 53–54, 75.

17. George Gendron, "FYI: The First Annual *301 Great Management Ideas* Sweepstakes," *Inc.*, September 1992, p. 11.

Chapter 10

1. See Myron Magnet, "The Truth About the American Worker," *Fortune*, May 4, 1992, pp. 48–51ff; Thomas A. Stewart, "U.S. Productivity: First but Fading," *Fortune*, October 19, 1992, pp. 54–57; and "Today's U.S. Worker," *Fortune*, May 4, 1992, pp. 60–61.

2. Marie Manthey, "Staffing and Productivity," *Nursing Management*, December 1991, pp. 20–21.

3. Frank Voehl, "Avoid Business Suicide," *Quality Digest*, September 1992, pp. 20, 78.

4. Jon Van, "Involved at IBM: Errors Drop after Workers Get Big Picture," *Chicago Tribune*, July 26, 1992, sec. 7, pp. 1–2.

5. "Frugality in the Air at American," *Chicago Tribune*, January 19, 1992, sec. 7, p. 5.

6. "Winners Announced in Cost Reduction Contest," *Advance Digest* (Advance Transformer Company), Fall 1991, pp. 1, 6.

7. Joshua Hyatt, "Ideas at Work," *Inc.*, May 1991, pp. 59–60ff.

8. Mary Crabtree Tonges, "Work Designs: Sociotechnical Systems for Patient Care Delivery," *Nursing Management*, January 1992, pp. 27–31.

9. "Cutting Down on Unnecessary Paperwork," *Maintenance Supervisor's Bulletin* (Bureau of Business Practice), July 25, 1992, pp. 1–4.

10. Jon Van, "Old Manufacturing Ideas Crippling U.S.," *Chicago Tribune*, November 3, 1991, sec. 1, pp. 1, 12–13.

11. Stewart, "U.S. Productivity," p. 55.

12. Jon Van, "At Ingersoll, Flexibility, Change Are a Way of Life," *Chicago Tribune*, November 5, 1991, sec. 1, p. 12.

13. Robert F. Huber, "Can You Afford Not to Buy This Justification Software?" *Production*, 1992.

14. Stewart, "U.S. Productivity," p. 57.

15. Kenneth B. Hamlet, "Slowing the Service Sector's Revolving Door," *The Wall Street Journal*, August 14, 1989, p. A8.

16. Eileen Ogintz, "The Bottom Line Is Benefits," *Chicago Tribune*, March 7, 1990, sec. 5, pp. 1, 3.

17. Bruce G. Posner, "Role Changes," *Inc.*, February 1990, pp. 95, 98.

18. Stephen Franklin, "Technology Puts AT&T Jobs on Hold," *Chicago Tribune*, March 23, 1992, sec. 4, pp. 1–2.

19. Franklin, "AT&T Jobs on Hold."

20. Van, "Ingersoll," p. 12.

Chapter 11

1. "How Jim Howard Gets So Much Done," *Boardroom Reports*, September 1, 1992, pp. 13–14.

2. Michael Barrier, "How a Dallas Consultant Helps Managers Attack the Paper Piled on Their Desks," *Nation's Business*, January 1992.

3. Tom Peters, "You, Too, Can Manage without a Time Manager," *Chicago Tribune*, August 3, 1992, sec. 4, p. 5.

4. "How Jim Howard Gets So Much Done," p. 14.

5. "Foil the Time Grabbers," *Executive Female*, July–August 1992, pp. 9–10.

6. This discussion of the Myers-Briggs Type Indicator is based largely on Otto Kroeger and Janet M. Thuesen, "It Takes All Types," *Newsweek*, Management Digest advertising section, September 7, 1992, pp. 8–10.

Chapter 12

1. Andrew S. Grove, "How to Manage Office Friction," *Working Woman*, August 1990, pp. 24, 26.

2. Thomas A. Stewart, "The Search for the Organization of Tomorrow," *Fortune*, May 18, 1992, pp. 92–98.

3. The ideas in this paragraph are from Sondra Thiederman, *Bridging Cultural Barriers for Corporate Success: How to Manage the Multicultural Work Force* (New York: Lexington Books, 1991), pp. 83–88.

4. Dana Milbank, "Unions' Woes Suggest How the Labor Force in U.S. Is Shifting," *The Wall Street Journal*, May 5, 1992, pp. A1, A14.

5. Aaron Bernstein, "Been Down So Long…," *Business Week*, January 14, 1991, pp. 30–31.

6. Arthur J. Hedges, "Reflections of an Arbitrator," *Discipline and Grievances* (Bureau of Business Practice), 1986, p. 9.

7. Robert L. Rose, "Caterpillar's Success in Ending Strike May Curtail Unions' Use of Walkouts," *The Wall Street Journal*, April 20, 1992, p. A3.

8. Price Pritchett and Ron Pound, *The Employee Handbook for Organizational Change* (Dallas: Pritchett & Associates, 1990), p. 2.

9. Ken Blanchard, "The Seven Dynamics of Change," *Quality Digest*, May 1992, pp. 18, 78.

10. Carol Hymowitz, "When Firms Cut Out Middle Managers, Those at Top and Bottom Often Suffer," *The Wall Street Journal*, April 5, 1990, pp. B1, B4.

11. Kurt Lewin, "Frontiers in Group Dynamics: Concept, Method, and Reality of Social Sciences—Social Equilibrium and Social Change," *Human Relations*, June 1947, pp. 5–14.

12. Ken Blanchard, "Six Concerns in the Change Process," *Quality Digest*, June 1992, pp. 14, 62.

13. Elaine Gregg, "How to Be a Great Boss in Bad Times," *Black Enterprise*, April 1991, p. 72.

14. Betsy Wiesendanger, "Bad News Meetings," *Sales & Marketing Management*, November 1992, pp. 66–68ff.

15. See Gregg, "How to Be a Great Boss," p. 72.

16. Blanchard, "The Seven Dynamics of Change," p. 78.

Chapter 13

1. *Total Quality Newsletter* (Lakewood Publications) 3(1), January 1992, p. 7, quoting *Honda, An American Success Story.*

2. Ellyn E. Spragins, "Hiring without the Guesswork," *Inc.*, February 1992, p. 83.

3. John M. Ivancevich, *Human Resource Management: Foundations of Personnel*, 5th ed. (Homewood, Ill: Irwin, 1992), p. A20.

4. "Brainstorming…on Personnel," *Boardroom Reports*, September 1, 1992, p. 15.

5. Martin Everett and Betsy Wiesendanger, "What Does Body Language *Really* Say?" *Sales & Marketing Management*, April 1992, p. 40.

6. Spragins, "Hiring without the Guesswork," p. 86.

7. Melissa Wahl, "Navigating the Maze of Employee Rights," *Executive Female*, September–October 1992, pp. 103–104.

8. Ellyn E. Spragins, "Test-Driving Job Applicants," *Inc.*, May 1992, p. 148.

9. Ellyn E. Spragins, "Screening New Hires," *Inc.*, August 1992, p. 82.

10. "Workers' Crimes Become Companies' Concerns," *Nation's Business*, March 1990, p. 8.

11. Spragins, "Screening New Hires."

12. See Ivancevich, *Human Resource Management*, p. 274; Bob McDonald, "Better Take the Americans with Disabilities Act Very Seriously," *Boardroom Reports*, August 15, 1992, pp. 3–4; and Ellyn E. Spragins, "Preparing for the Americans with Disabilities Act," *Inc.*, January 1992, pp. 99–100.

13. Keith H. Hammonds, "Corning's Class Act," *Business Week*, May 15, 1991, pp. 68–72, 76.

14. John Dralus and Jan Sokoloff Harness, "Working Together," *Training & Development*, December 1991, p. 16.

15. Ellyn E. Spragins, "Tapping Workers with Disabilities," *Inc.*, November 1992, p. 33.

16. Eileen Ogintz, "Technology Sees Beyond Disabilities," *Chicago Tribune*, March 8, 1992, sec. 7, p. 3.

17. Wilma Randle, "Opening Opportunities for Disabled: Confusion, Debate Still Trail New Law," *Chicago Tribune*, December 1, 1991, sec. 7, pp. 1, 4.

18. Hugh H. McDonough, "Hiring People with Disabilities," *Supervisory Management*, February 1992, p. 11.

19. These guidelines are taken from Spragins, "Preparing for the Americans with Disabilities Act."

20. McDonald, "Better Take the ADA Very Seriously," p. 4.

21. Ivancevich, *Human Resource Management*, p. 215.

Chapter 14

1. Carol Kleiman, "Employer-Based Training Is a Growing Job Source," *Chicago Tribune*, January 12, 1992, sec. 8, p. 1.

2. Kleiman, "Employer-Based Training."

3. Patricia A. Galagan, "Training Delivers Results to Federal Express," *Training and Development*, December 1991, pp. 27–33.

4. See George Piskurich, "Training: The Line Starts Here," *Training and Development*, December 1991, pp. 35–37.

5. David L. Goetsch, *Industrial Supervision in the Age of High Technology* (New York: Merrill, 1992), p. 407.

6. Ellyn E. Spragins, "Lowering Turnover by Using Apprentices," *Inc.*, May 1992, p. 145.

7. Janet Novack, "Earning and Learning," *Forbes*, May 11, 1992, pp. 150, 154.

8. Susan Greco, "A 'Finishing School' for Sales Reps," *Inc.*, October 1992, p. 30.

9. Ellyn E. Spragins, "Turning Education into a Game," *Inc.*, September 1992, p. 34.

10. Galagan, "Training Delivers Results."

11. Alessandra Bianchi, "New Businesses: Corporate Games," *Inc.*, July 1992, p. 20.

12. Ellyn E. Spragins, "Employee Illiteracy," *Inc.*, August 1992, p. 81.

13. Joan C. Szabo, "Boosting Workers' Basic Skills," *Nation's Business*, January 1992, pp. 38–40.

14. "What It Takes," *Inc.*, November 1992, pp. 105–107ff.

15. "What It Takes," p. 110.

16. Szabo, "Boosting Workers' Basic Skills."

17. "Apprenticeship Training: Time for an Update!" *Maintenance Supervisor's Bulletin*, June 25, 1992, pp. 1–4.

Chapter 15

1. Ellyn E. Spragins, "How to Fire," *Inc.*, May 1992, pp. 66–68, 72.

2. Susan Greco, "The Interactive Employee Review," *Inc.*, November 1991, pp. 73–75.

3. "Performance Reviews: Take a Positive Approach," *Front Line Supervisor's Bulletin* (Bureau of Business Practice), June 10, 1992, pp. 1–2.

4. Nancy K. Austin, "Updating the Performance Review," *Working Woman*, November 1992, pp. 32, 34–35.

5. Patricia Buhler, "Evaluating an Employee's Performance," *Supervision*, April 1991, pp. 17–19.

6. Austin, "Updating the Performance Review," p. 34.

7. Antony J. Michels, "More Employees Evaluate the Boss," *Fortune*, July 29, 1991, p. 13.

8. Greco, "The Interactive Employee Review."

9. Claire McIntosh and Laurel Touby, "Appraisals: Are You Giving A's to 'B' Employees?" *Working Woman*, May 1990, pp. 23–23.

Chapter 16

1. John R. Schermerhorn, Jr., William N. Gardner, and Thomas N. Martin, "The Trouble with Bob: A Drama in Managerial Life," *Executive Female*, September–October 1991, pp. 42–47.

2. Lindsey Novak and Lauren Spier, "Workplace Solutions: Raves Not Always a Basis for Raise," *Chicago Tribune*, sec. 8, p. 1.

3. Jim Braham, "Difficult Employees," *Industry Week*, June 19, 1989, pp. 30–35.

4. Michael Karol, "The Lows of Being High," *Graphic Arts Monthly*, September 1990, pp. 101–107.

5. William C. Symonds, "Is Business Bungling Its Battle with Booze?" *Business Week*, March 25, 1991, pp. 76–78.

6. John Horgan, "Your Analysis Is Faulty," *The New Republic*, April 2, 1990, pp. 22–24.

7. Karol, "The Lows of Being High."

8. Symonds, "Is Business Bungling Its Battle with Booze?" p. 77.

9. "Substance Abuse on the Job," *Maintenance Supervisor's Bulletin*, January 10, 1992, pp. 3–4.

10. "Preventing Crime on the Job," *Nation's Business*, July 1990, pp. 36–37.

11. Phyllis Gillespie, "Stolen Trust: Employee Theft Costs $320 Billion," *Arizona Republic*, May 4, 1992, pp. E1, E8.

12. Gerald Graham, "Reducing Staff Theft Possible: U.S. Losses Total $40 Billion a Year," *Arizona Republic*, March 19, 1989, p. E6.

13. Gillespie, "Stolen Trust," p. E8.

14. Ibid., p. E1.

15. Ibid.

16. "Curbing Crime in the Workplace," *Nation's Business*, July 1990, p. 37.

17. Joseph T. Straub, "Dealing with Complainers, Whiners, and General Malcontents," *Supervisory Management*, July 1992, pp. 1–2.

18. List of rights provided by Corinne R. Livesay, Liberty University, Lynchburg, Va.

19. Andrew S. Grove, "Personal Problems in the Office," *Working Woman*, April 1992, pp. 36, 38.

20. Donald H. Weiss, "How to Deal with Unpleasant People Problems," *Supervisory Management*, March 1992, pp. 1–2.

21. William C. Symonds, "How to Confront—and Help—an Alcoholic Employee," *Business Week*, March 25, 1991, p. 78.

22. Symonds, "How to Confront." See also Sara J. Harty, "Training Required to Spot Addicts," *Business Insurance*, June 24, 1991, pp. 12–13.

Chapter 17

1. Bradford McKee, "Turn Your Workers into a Team," *Nation's Business*, July 1992, pp. 36–38.

2. Dorothy Miller, "Group Dynamics: Handling Subgroups," *Nursing Management*, December 1991, pp. 33–35.

3. Samuel C. Certo, *Modern Management* (Boston: Allyn and Bacon, 1992), p. 497.

4. R. B. Lacoursiere, *The Life Cycle of Groups: Group Development Stage Theory* (New York: Human Service Press, 1980).

5. William G. Dyer, *Team Building: Issues and Alternatives*, 2nd ed. (Reading, Mass.: Addison-Wesley, 1987), p. 24.

6. George Milite, "The Supervisor's Role in a Project Team," *Supervisory Management*, May 1992, pp. 10–11.

7. S. C. Gwynne, "The Right Stuff," *Time*, October 29, 1990, pp. 74–84.

8. Cathy Hyatt Hills, "Making the Team," *Sales & Marketing Management*, February 1992, pp. 54, 56–57.

9. Jon Van, "Mass Production Is Out; Quality, Skills Are In," *Chicago Tribune*, November 3, 1991, sec. 1, pp. 1, 12.

10. Edward E. Lawler III, Susan Albers Mohrman, and Gerald E. Ledford, Jr., "Study Shows Strong Evidence That Participatory Management Pays Off," *Total Quality*, September 1992, pp. 1–4.

11. Marc Hequet, "Quality Concerns Come Through Unfiltered at Johnson Filtration," *The Quality Imperative*, September 1992, pp. 36–38ff.

12. Edward Glassman, "Self-Directed Team Building without a Consultant," *Supervisory Management*, March 1992, p. 6; and Louis V. Imundo, "Blueprint for a Successful Team," *Supervisory Management*, May 1992, pp. 2–3.

13. George Milite, "Communicating One-on-One with Members," *Supervisory Management*, May 1992, p. 11.

14. "F. Suzanne Jenniches: Sharp Isn't Strong Enough to Describe Her," *Industry Week*, March 2, 1992, pp. 32–33, 36.

15. The ideas in this paragraph are adapted from Jill George, "Loosening the Reins: The Transition from Supervisor to Team Leader," *Total Quality*, July 1992, p. 7.

16. Alfredo S. Lanier, "Alex Warren: Bridging the Gap between Cultures and Technologies," *GSB Chicago* (University of Chicago Graduate School of Business), Winter 1991, pp. 9–13.

17. Dyer, *Team Building*, p. 23.

18. Glassman, "Self-Directed Team Building,"

19. Hills, "Making the Team."

20. Aaron Bernstein, "Putting a Damper on That Old Team Spirit," *Business Week*, May 4, 1992, p. 60.

21. Michael P. Cronin, "Team Penalty," *Inc.*, May 1993, p. 29.

22. David F. Girard-diCarlo, Michael J. Hanlon, and Caren E. I. Naidoff, "Legal Traps in Employee Committees," *Management Review*, November 1992, pp. 27–29.

23. Cronin, "Team Penalty."

24. "Avoid Labor Law Violations in Employee Involvement Programs," *NIBA News Bulletin* (Northern Illinois Business Association), March 1992, p. 11; Dernstein, "Putting a Damper on That Old Team Spirit."

25. Roderick Wilkinson, "Forget That Meeting!" *Nursing Management*, December 1991, p. 42.

26. "Holding Meetings That Motivate," *Supervisory Management*, July 1991, p. 9 (quoting "Meetings That Motivate," *Supervisor Sense*, February 1990).

27. Milite, "Communicating One-on-One."

Chapter 18

1. David Warner, "Ways to Make Safety Work," *Nation's Business*, December 1991, pp. 25–27.

2. Merrill Goozner, "Expanding Fast-Food Industry Growing More Accident-Prone," *Chicago Tribune*, July 15, 1991, sec. 4, pp. 1–2.

3. Warner, "Ways to Make Safety Work," p. 25.

4. "Chemical Caution," *Time*, October 26, 1992, p. 27.

5. Ed Pope, "Cancer Linked to Deadly Diet of 'Smoke Eaters,'" *Chicago Tribune*, January 5, 1992, sec. 5, p. 3.

6. Doreen Mangan, "Avoid 'Sick Building' Syndrome," *Your Company*, Spring 1992, p. 7.

7. See Ron Kotulak and Jon Van, "Rotating Shifts Raise Chances of Accidents," *Chicago Tribune*, July 12, 1992, sec. 5, p. 6; and "Shiftwork: Staying Alert and Vigilant around the Clock," *Maintenance Supervisor's Bulletin*, September 10, 1992, pp. 1–4.

8. Goozner, "Expanding Fast-Food Industry," p. 1.

9. *The Front Line Supervisor's Standard Manual* (Bureau of Business Practice, 1989), p. 155.

10. Ellyn E. Spragins, "Take Charge," *Inc.*, December 1992, pp. 122–125ff.

11. "OSHA Cites Back Injuries as Top Workplace Safety Problem," *NIBA Bulletin* (Northern Illinois Business Association), March 1992, p. 13.

12. Robert A. Mamis, "Oh, That Aching Back," *Inc.*, October 1992, p. 53.

13. Christine Woolsey, "Linking Wellness to Health Care Costs," *Business Insurance*, February 17, 1992, p. 12.

14. Christine Woolsey, "Employers Monitor Lifestyles," *Business Insurance*, February 17, 1992, pp. 4–6.

15. Doreen Mangan, "When It's Time to Ban Smoking," *Your Company*, Spring 1992, p. 6.

16. Christine Woolsey, "Off-Duty Conduct: None of Employer's Business?" *Business Insurance*, February 17, 1992, pp. 10–11.

17. Christopher Conte, "Labor Letter," *The Wall Street Journal*, November 19, 1991, p. A1.

18. Patricia Fernberg, "Is Your Terminal Ill?" *Health*, March 1991, pp. 36, 38.

19. Jon Van, "Carpal Syndrome Reports Rise Sharply," *Chicago Tribune*, February 12, 1992, sec. 3, p. 3.

20. James Warren, "Typing Trauma: Computer-Related Injury Forces L.A. Times Columnist to the Sidelines," *Chicago Tribune*, April 5, 1992, sec. 5, p. 2.

21. Louise Kertesz, "Human 'Machines' Need Good Workplace Design," *Business Insurance*, April 13, 1992, p. 30.

22. Spragins, "Take Charge."

23. Woolsey, "Employers Monitor Lifestyles," pp. 4–5.

24. Laurie Cohen, "Wanted: Healthier Workers," *Chicago Tribune*, January 6, 1992, sec. 4, pp. 1–2.

25. Woolsey, "Off-Duty Conduct: None of Employer's Business?" As of 1992, the states that had banned such decisions were Arizona, Colorado, Connecticut, Illinois, Indiana, Kentucky, Louisiana, Maine, Mississippi, Nevada, New Hampshire, New Jersey, New Mexico, North Dakota, Oklahoma, Oregon, Rhode Island, South Carolina, South Dakota, Tennessee, and Virginia.

26. Shari Caudron, "Are Health Incentives Disincentives?" *Personnel Journal*, August 1992, pp. 35–38.

27. Kertesz, "Human 'Machines' Need Good Workplace Design."

28. See, for example, Woolsey, "Linking Wellness to Health Care Costs."

29. The suggestions in this paragraph are adapted from "Shiftwork: Staying Alert and Vigilant around the Clock."

30. "One Company's Technique Takes Hold: Putting a STOP to Unsafe Behaviors," *OSHA Compliance Advisor*, September 23, 1991, pp. 3–6.

Chapter 19

1. Pat Widder, "More Corporations Learning That Ethics Are Bottom-Line Issue," *Chicago Tribune*, June 7, 1992, sec. 7, pp. 1, 6.

2. Rushworth M. Kidder, "Ethics: A Matter of Survival," *The Futurist*, March–April, 1992, pp. 10–12.

3. Kenneth Labich, "The New Crisis in Business Ethics," *Fortune*, April 20, 1992, pp. 167–168ff.

4. Reported on "60 Minutes," October 4, 1992.

5. Quoted in "The Holiday Spirit," *Total Quality Newsletter*, December 1992, p. 8.

6. Robert McGarvey, "Do the Right Thing," *Entrepreneur*, October 1992, pp. 138–143.

7. Widder, "More Corporations Learning," p. 6.

8. Labich, "The New Crisis in Business Ethics," pp. 167–168.

9. "Former House Worker Accused of Conspiracy," *Chicago Tribune*, April 18, 1992, sec. 1, p. 13.

10. Adapted from Laura Nash, "Ethics without the Sermon," *Harvard Business Review*, November–December 1981, p. 81.

11. Andrew S. Grove, "What's the Right Thing? Everyday Ethical Dilemmas," *Working Woman*, June 1990, pp. 16–18.

12. Example from Grove, "What's the Right Thing?" p. 18.

13. Widder, "More Corporations Learning," p. 6.

14. Robert A. Mamis, "Don't Copy That Floppy," *Inc.*, June 1992, p. 127.

15. Cynthia Berryman-Fink, *The Manager's Desk Reference* (New York: American Management Association, 1989), pp. 342–343.

16. Tim Smart, "This Man Sounded the Silicone Alarm—in 1976," *Business Week*, January 27, 1992, p. 34.

17. Berryman-Fink, *The Manager's Desk Reference*, p. 343.

18. Connie Wallace, "Sizing Up Your New Staff," *Working Woman*, May 1990, pp. 29–30ff.

19. Donald S. Miller and Stephen E. Catt, *Human Relations: A Contemporary Approach* (Homewood, Ill.: Richard D. Irwin, 1989), pp. 200–202.

20. George Milite, "Office Politics: It's Still Out There," *Supervisory Management*, July 1992, pp. 6–7.

21. Elizabeth Leech, "Working Smart: Take Care to Build Alliances If You're Headed for the Top," *Chicago Tribune*, September 20, 1992, sec. 6, p. 9.

22. Bristol Voss, "Office Politics: A Player's Guide," *Sales & Marketing Management*, October 1992, pp. 47–52.

23. Voss, "Office Politics," p. 49.

Reference Guide: Building a Career

1. Kenneth Labich, "Take Control of Your Career," *Fortune*, November 18, 1991, pp. 87–88ff.

2. Mary Beth Sammons, "Employees Now Masters of Their Own Destinies," *Chicago Tribune*, March 29, 1992, sec. 19, p. 3.

3. Adapted from Kent L. Straat with Nellie Sabin, "'How Am I Doing?'" *Working Woman*, August 1990, pp. 55–57ff.

4. Bruce Nussbaum, "I'm Worried about My Job!" *Business Week*, October 7, 1991, pp. 94–97.

5. See Labich, "Take Control of Your Career," pp. 87–88ff; and Bruce Nussbaum, "A Career Survival Kit," *Business Week*, October 7, 1991, pp. 98–99ff.

6. Labich, "Take Control of Your Career," pp. 95–96.

7. Paula Bernstein, "Approaching a Better Job Sideways," *New Choices*, December 1989, pp. 48–50.

8. See Colleen Dudgeon, "Working Smart: Best Time for Résumé Makeover Is Now," *Chicago Tribune*, March 29, 1992, sec. 6, p. 9.

9. The ideas in this paragraph are based on Kathy E. Kram, *Mentoring at Work* (Glenview, Ill.: Scott, Foresman, 1985).

10. Labich, "Take Control of Your Career," p. 96.

11. The ideas in this paragraph are taken from Samuel A. Cypert, "W. Clement Stone's 17 Principles of Success," *Bottom Line/Personal*, March 30, 1992, pp. 1–3.

accountability The practice of imposing penalties for failing to adequately carry out responsibilities and of providing rewards for meeting responsibilities. 13

acquired immune deficiency syndrome (AIDS) The incurable and fatal illness that is caused by the HIV virus. 481

action plan The plan for how to achieve an objective. 37

active listening Hearing what the speaker is saying, seeking to understand the facts and feelings the speaker is trying to convey, and stating what you understand that message to be. 160

affirmative action Plans designed to increase opportunities for groups that have traditionally been discriminated against. 346

agenda A list of the topics to be covered at a meeting. 459

apprenticeship Training that involves working alongside an experienced person, who shows the apprentice how to do the various tasks involved in a job or trade. 368

aptitude test A test that measures a person's ability to learn skills related to the job. 343

arbitrator A neutral person who reaches a decision on how to resolve a conflict; both parties must adhere to the decision. 304

authoritarian leadership A leadership style in which the leader retains a great deal of authority. 77

authority The right to perform a task or give orders to someone else. 53

average rate of return (ARR) A percentage that represents the average annual earnings for each dollar of a given investment. 253

behavior modification The use of reinforcement theory to motivate people to behave in a certain way. 220

behaviorally anchored rating scales A performance appraisal in which the employee is rated on scales containing statements describing performance in several areas. 390

benchmarking Identifying the top performer of a process, then learning and carrying out the top performer's practices. 137

biofeedback Developing an awareness of bodily functions to control them. 280

brainstorming An idea-generating process in which group members state their ideas, a member of the group records them, and no one may comment on the ideas until the process is complete. 201

budget A plan for spending money. 31

burnout The inability to function effectively as a result of ongoing stress. 276

central tendency The tendency to select employee ratings in the middle of a scale. 394

chain of command The flow of authority in an organization from one level of management to the next. 58

closed-ended question A question that requires a simple answer, such as yes or no. 340

coaching Guidance and instruction in how to do a job so that it satisfies goals for performance. 372

cohesiveness The degree to which group members stick together. 447

collective bargaining The process of seeking to reach a contract spelling out the rights and duties of unionized workers and their employer. 303

commissions Payment linked to the amount of sales completed. 222

communication The process by which people send and receive information. 154

compromise Settling on a solution that gives each person part of what he or she wanted; no one gets everything, and no one loses completely. 294

conceptual skills The ability to see the relation of the parts to the whole and to one another. 5

conciliator A neutral person who helps opposing parties reach agreement. 303

concurrent control Control that occurs while the work takes place. 108

conflict The struggle that results from incompatible or opposing needs, feelings, thoughts, or demands within a person or between two or more people. 290

conflict management Responding to problems stemming from conflict. 294

conflict resolution Managing a conflict by confronting the problem and solving it. 298

contingency planning Planning what to do if the original plans don't work out. 38

controlling Monitoring performance and making needed corrections. 11

controlling The management function of making sure that work goes according to plan. 100

counseling The process of learning about an individual's personal problem and helping him or her resolve it. 410

creativity The ability to bring about something imaginative or new. 202

critical-incident appraisal A performance appraisal in which the supervisor keeps a written record of incidents that show positive and negative ways the employee has acted; the supervisor uses this record to assess the employee's performance. 391

cross-training Training in the skills required to perform more than one job. 224

decision A choice from among available alternatives. 184

decision tree A graph that helps decision makers use probability theory by showing the expected values of decisions under varying circumstances. 196

decision-making leave A day off during which a problem employee is supposed to decide whether to return

to work and meet standards or to stay away for good. 420

decision-making skills The ability to analyze information and reach good decisions. 5

decision-making software A computer program that leads the user through the steps of the formal decision-making process. 197

delegating Giving another person the authority and responsibility to carry out a task. 60

democratic leadership A leadership style in which the leader allows subordinates to participate in decision making and problem solving. 77

demotion Transfer of an employee to a job involving less responsibility and, usually, lower pay. 416

department A unique group of resources that management has assigned to carry out a particular task. 50

departmentalization Setting up departments in an organization. 50

detour behavior Tactics for postponing or avoiding work. 251

directive counseling An approach to counseling in which the supervisor asks the employee questions about the specific problem; when the supervisor understands the problem, he or she suggests ways to handle it. 412

discipline Action taken by the supervisor to prevent employees from breaking rules. 414

dismissal Relieving an employee of his or her job. 416

down time Time during which employees or machines are not producing goods or services. 250

downward communication Organizational communication that involves sending a message to someone at a lower level. 175

employee assistance program (EAP) A company-based program for providing counseling and related help to employees whose personal problems are affecting their performance. 422

employee handbook A document that describes an organization's conditions of employment, policies regarding employees, administrative procedures, and related matters. 362

employee involvement teams Teams of employees who plan ways to improve quality in their area of the organization. 127

Equal Employment Opportunity Commission The federal government agency charged with enforcing the Civil Rights Act. 346

ergonomics The science concerned with the human characteristics that need to be considered in designing tasks and equipment so that people will work most effectively and safely. 480

ethics The principles by which people distinguish what is morally right. 492

exception principle The control principle stating that a supervisor should take action only when a variance is meaningful. 105

feedback The way the receiver of a message responds (or fails to respond) to the message. 154

feedback control Control that focuses on past performance. 108

financial incentives Payments for meeting or exceeding objectives. 221

forced-choice approach A performance appraisal that presents the appraiser with sets of statements describing employee behavior; the appraiser must choose which statement is most characteristic of the employee and which is least characteristic. 389

formal communication Organizational communication that is work-related and follows the lines of the organization chart. 176

formal groups Groups set up by management to meet organizational objectives. 441

functional authority The right given by higher management to specific staff personnel to give orders concerning an area in which the staff personnel have expertise. 54

functional groups Groups that fulfill ongoing needs in the organization by carrying out a particular function. 441

gainsharing A group incentive plan in which the organization encourages employees to participate in making suggestions and decisions, then rewards the group with a share of improved earnings. 223

Gantt chart Scheduling tool that lists the activities to be completed and uses horizontal bars to graph how long each activity will take, including its starting and ending dates. 33

goals Objectives, often those with a broad focus. 27

grapevine The path along which informal communication travels. 177

graphic rating scale A performance appraisal that rates the degree to which the employee has achieved various characteristics. 387

grievance A formal complaint that the terms of a labor contract have been violated. 304

group Two or more people who interact with one another, are aware of one another, and think of themselves as being a group. 440

group incentive plan A financial incentive plan that rewards a team of workers for meeting or exceeding an objective. 222

groupthink The failure to think independently and realistically as a group because of the desire to enjoy consensus and closeness. 199

halo effect The practice of forming an overall opinion on the basis of one outstanding characteristic. 342

harshness bias Rating employees more severely than their performance merits. 394

health hazards Conditions in the work environment that may gradually hurt the health of the people there. 473

homogeneity The degree to which the members of a group are the same. 448

human relations skills The ability to work effectively with other people. 4

idle time Time during which employees or machines are not producing goods or services. 250

inference A conclusion drawn from the facts available. 164

informal communication Organizational communication that is directed toward individuals' needs and interests and does not necessarily follow formal lines of communication. 176

informal groups Groups that result when individuals in the organization develop relationships to meet personal needs. 441

insubordination Deliberate refusal to do what the supervisor or other superior asks. 407

internal locus of control The belief that you are the primary cause of what happens to yourself. 74

ISO 9000 A series of standards adopted by the International Organization of Standardization to spell out acceptable criteria for quality systems. 137

job description A listing of the characteristics of a job, including the job title, duties involved, and working conditions. 330

job enlargement An effort to make a job more interesting by adding more duties to it. 224

job enrichment The incorporation of motivating factors into a job—in particular, giving the employee more responsibility and recognition. 225

job rotation Moving employees from job to job to give them more variety. 224

job specification A listing of the characteristics desirable in the person performing a given job, including educational and work background, physical characteristics, and personal strengths. 330

labor relations Management's role in working constructively with unions

that represent the organization's employees. 302

laissez-faire leadership A leadership style in which the leader is uninvolved and lets subordinates direct themselves. 77

lateral communication Organizational communication that involves sending a message to a person at the same level. 176

leading Influencing people to act (or not act) in a certain way. 11

leading The management function of influencing people to act or not act in a certain way. 74

leniency bias Rating employees more favorably than their performance merits. 394

line authority The right to carry out tasks and give orders related to the organization's primary purpose. 54

Malcolm Baldrige National Quality Award An annual award administered by the U.S. Department of Commerce and given to the company that shows the highest-quality performance in seven categories. 135

management by objectives (MBO) A formal system for planning in which managers and employees at all levels set objectives for what they are to accomplish, after which their performance is measured against those objectives. 39

mediator A neutral person who helps opposing parties reach agreement. 303

mentor A higher-level manager who takes the role of showing a lower-level employee how to get along in the organization and making sure that the person gets recognized by other managers. 524

motivation Giving people incentives that cause them to act in desired ways. 212

National Institute for Occupational Safety and Health (NIOSH) The agency of the federal government responsible for conducting research related to workplace safety and health. 471

nepotism The hiring of one's relatives. 496

networking The process of developing a variety of contacts inside and outside the organization. 525

nondirective counseling An approach to counseling in which the supervisor primarily listens, encouraging the employee to look for the source of the problem and to propose possible solutions. 412

nonverbal message A message conveyed without using words. 167

norms Group standards for appropriate or acceptable behavior. 446

objectives The desired accomplishments of the organization as a whole or of part of the organization. 27

Occupational Safety and Health Act (OSHAct) of 1970 The federal law that sets up government agencies to conduct research regarding occupational health and safety, set health and safety standards, inspect workplaces, and penalize employers that do not meet standards. 470

Occupational Safety and Health Administration (OSHA) The agency of the federal government charged with setting and enforcing standards for workplace health and safety. 470

on-the-job training Teaching a job while trainer and trainee do the job at the work site. 367

open-ended question A question that gives the person responding broad control over the response. 340

operational planning The development of objectives that specify how divisions, departments, and work groups will support organizational goals. 27

organization politics Activities by which people seek to improve their position within the organization, generally by gaining power. 501

organizing Setting up the group, allocating resources, and assigning work to achieve goals. 10

organizing The management function of setting up the group, allocating resources, and assigning work to achieve goals. 48

orientation The process of giving new employees the information they need to do their work comfortably, effectively, and efficiently. 358

overhead Expenses not related directly to producing goods and services; examples are rent, utilities, and staff support. 250

paired-comparison approach A performance appraisal that measures the relative performance of employees in a group. 387

parity principle The principle that personnel who are given responsibility must also be given enough authority to carry out that responsibility. 57

payback period The length of time it will take for the benefits generated by an investment (such as cost savings from machinery) to offset the cost of the investment. 252

perceptions The ways people see and interpret reality. 164

perfectionism The attempt to do things perfectly. 273

performance appraisal Formal feedback on how well an employee is performing his or her job. 382

performance report A summary of performance and comparison with performance standards. 110

personal power Power that arises from an individual's personal characteristics. 501

piecework system Payment according to the amount produced. 221

planning Setting goals and determining how to meet them. 9

planning The management function of setting goals and determining how to meet them. 26

policies Broad guidelines for how to act. 29

position power Power that comes from a person's formal role in an organization. 501

positive discipline Discipline designed to prevent problem behavior from beginning. 419

power The ability to get others to act in a certain way. 56

power The ability to influence people to behave in a certain way. 501

precontrol Efforts aimed at preventing behavior that may lead to undesirable results. 109

prejudices Broad generalizations about a category of people. 165

probability theory A body of techniques for comparing the consequences of possible decisions in a risk situation. 195

problem A factor in the organization that is a barrier to improvement. 106

procedures The steps that must be completed to achieve a specific purpose. 29

process control Quality control that emphasizes how to do things in a way that leads to better quality. 123

procrastination Putting off what needs to be done. 272

product quality control Quality control that focuses on ways in which the product itself can be improved. 123

productivity The amount of results (output) an organization gets for a given amount of inputs. 238

proficiency test A test that measures whether the person has the skills needed to perform a job. 343

profit-sharing plan A group incentive plan under which the company sets aside a share of its profits and divides it among employees. 223

program evaluation and review technique (PERT) Scheduling tool that identifies the relationships among tasks as well as the amount of time each task will take. 33

proximity bias The tendency to assign similar scores to items that are near each other on a questionnaire. 395

psychomotor test A test that measures a person's strength, dexterity, and coordination. 343

punishment An unpleasant consequence given in response to undesirable behavior. 219

Pygmalion effect The direct relationship between expectations and performance; high expectations lead to high performance. 226

quality control An organization's efforts to prevent or correct defects in its goods or services or to improve them in some way. 121

recency syndrome The tendency to more easily remember events that have occurred recently. 190

recruitment Identifying people interested in holding a particular job or working for the organization. 332

reinforcement A desired consequence or the ending of a negative consequence, either of which is given in response to a desirable behavior. 219

reinforcement Encouragement of a behavior by associating it with a reward. 106

repetitive-motion disorders Injuries that result from repeatedly applying force to the same muscles or joints. 479

responsibility The obligation to perform assigned activities. 56

résumé A summary of work-related skills and experience. 523

role conflicts Situations in which a person has two different roles that call for conflicting types of behavior. 446

role playing A training method that involves assigning roles to participants, who then act out the way they would handle a specified situation. 370

roles Patterns of behavior related to employees' positions in a group. 444

rules Statements of specifically what to do or not do in a given situation. 30

safety hazards Conditions in the workplace that may lead to an injury-causing accident. 475

satisficing Choosing an alternative that meets minimum standards of acceptability. 188

scheduling Setting a precise timetable for the work to be done. 33

self-concept The image a person has of him- or herself. 89

self-managing work teams Groups of 5 to 15 members who work together to produce an entire product. 451

similarity bias The tendency to judge others more positively when they are like yourself. 395

smoothing Managing a conflict by pretending it does not exist. 294

span of control The number of people a manager supervises. 59

staff authority The right to advise or assist those with line authority. 54

staffing Identifying, hiring, and developing the necessary number and quality of employees. 10

standards Measures of what is expected. 101

statistical process control A statistical quality-control technique in which the operator of a process uses statistics to monitor production quality on an ongoing basis, making corrections whenever the results show the process is out of control. 125

statistical quality control Looking for defects in parts or finished goods selected through a sampling technique. 125

status A group member's position in relation to others in the group. 446

strategic planning The creation of long-term goals for the organization as a whole. 27

stress The body's response to coping with environmental demands. 274

strike Refusal by employees to work until there is a contract. 304

structured interview An interview based on questions the interviewer has prepared in advance. 339

supervisor A manager at the first level of management. 4

suspension Requiring that an employee not come to work for a set period of time; the employee is not paid for the time off. 416

symptom An indication of an underlying problem. 107

task groups Groups that are set up to carry out a specific activity and then disband when the activity is completed. 441

team A group of people who must collaborate to some degree to achieve common goals. 451

team building Developing the ability of team members to work together to achieve common objectives. 454

technical skills The specialized knowledge and expertise used to carry out particular techniques or procedures. 4

Theory X A set of management attitudes based on the view that people dislike work and must be coerced to perform. 80

Theory Y A set of management attitudes based on the view that work is a natural activity and that people will work hard and creatively to achieve objectives they are committed to. 80

Theory Z A set of management attitudes that emphasize employee participation in all aspects of decision making. 81

time log A record of what activities a person is doing hour by hour throughout the day. 262

time management The practice of controlling the way you use time. 262

total quality management (TQM) An organizationwide focus on satisfying customers by continuously improving every business process involved in delivering goods or services. 130

training Increasing the skills that will enable employees to better meet the organization's goals. 358

turnover The rate at which employees leave an organization. 254

Type-A personality A description of someone who is constantly trying to get a lot done in a hurry. 277

union steward An employee who is the union's representative in a particular work unit. 304

unity of command The principle that each employee should have only one supervisor. 58

unstructured interview An interview in which the interviewer has no list of questions prepared in advance but thinks of questions based on the applicant's responses. 339

upward communication Organizational communication that involves sending a message to someone at a higher level. 175

variance The size of the difference between actual performance and a performance standard. 103

verbal message A message that consists of words. 167

vestibule training Training that takes place on equipment set up in a special area off the job site. 369

video display terminal (VDT) The screen on which a computer displays information. 478

wellness program Organizational activities designed to help employees adopt healthy practices. 282

whistleblower Someone who exposes a violation of ethics or law. 500

wildcat strike Refusal by employees to work during the term of a labor contract. 305

work standards approach A performance appraisal in which the appraiser compares the employee's performance with objective measures of what an employee should do. 392

zero-defects approach A quality-control technique based on the view that everyone in the organization should work toward the goal of delivering such high quality that all aspects of the organization's products and services are free of problems. 127